COMMENTARIES

ON

THE PROPHET JEREMIAH

AND

THE LAMENTATIONS

VOL. V

THE CALVIN TRANSLATION SOCIETY,

INSTITUTED IN MAY M.DCCC.XLIII.

FOR THE PUBLICATION OF TRANSLATIONS OF THE WORKS OF JOHN CALVIN.

COMMENTARIES

ON THE

BOOK OF THE PROPHET JEREMIAH

AND

THE LAMENTATIONS

BY JOHN CALVIN

TRANSLATED FROM THE LATIN, AND EDITED

BY THE REV. JOHN OWEN,

VICAR OF THRUSSINGTON, AND RURAL DEAN, LEICESTERSHIRE

VOLUME FIFTH

Wipf and Stock Publishers
199 W 8th Ave, Suite 3
Eugene, OR 97401

Commentaries on the Book of the Prophet Jeremiah and the Lamentation,
Volume 5
By Calvin, John and Owen, John
Softcover ISBN-13: 979-8-3852-1681-9
Hardcover ISBN-13: 979-8-3852-1682-6
eBook ISBN-13: 979-8-3852-1683-3
Publication date 2/15/2024
Previously published by Baker Book House, 2005

This edition is a scanned facsimile of the original edition published in 2005.

COMMENTARIES

ON

THE PROPHET JEREMIAH.

Lecture One Hundred and Sixty-ninth.

CHAPTER XLVIII.

1. Against Moab thus saith the Lord of hosts, the God of Israel, Woe unto Nebo! for it is spoiled; Kiriathaim is confounded *and* taken: Misgab is confounded and dismayed.

1. Contra Moab, sic dicit Jehova exercituum, Deus Israel, Væ super Nebo, quia in vastitatem redacta est (vastata est;) destructa est Kiriathaim; pudefacta est Misgab et expavit (*vel*, anima fracta est.)

This prophecy is against the Moabites, who, though they derived their origin from Lot, and were of the same blood with the Israelites, had yet been inimical to them. This prophecy would be uninteresting, were we not to remember the history on which the application and use of what is said depends. We have said that the Moabites, as the father of their nation was Lot, were connected by blood with the Israelites; they ought then to have retained the recollection of their brotherhood, and to have dealt kindly with them; for God had spared them when the people of Israel entered into the land of Canaan. The Israelites, we know, passed through the borders of Moab without doing any harm to them, because it was God's purpose, from a regard to Lot, to preserve them for a time. But this people never ceased to contrive all manner of plots against God's people; and, as we shall hereafter see, when the state of that people became embarrassed, they cruelly exulted over them, and became more insolent than avowed enemies. Hence God prophesied against them, that the Israelites might know, as we reminded you yesterday, that their miserable condition was not overlooked by God, and that though he chastised them, yet some hope of mercy remained, as he undertook their cause and would be their defender. It was then no small comfort which this prophecy brought to the faithful; for they thus knew that God was still their father, though apparently he seemed to be severe to them. We now perceive the design of what is here said.

The case of the Moabites was different from that of the Egyptians, for the Egyptians were wholly aliens to the chosen people; but the Moabites, as we have said, were related to them. They were therefore wilful, and as it were intestine enemies; and nature itself ought to have taught them to acknowledge the Israelites as their brethren, and to cultivate mutual kindness. This cruelty and ingratitude were so hateful to God, that at length he punished them most severely. But as the Moabites remained in quietness when Judea was laid waste, and the city Jerusalem destroyed, after the overthrow of the kingdom of Israel, and the banishment of the ten tribes to distant countries, it behoved the faithful to exercise patience, which could not have been done without hope. It was this then that Jeremiah had in view, even to sustain the minds of the godly with the expectation of God's judgment, which he here denounces on the Moabites.

He says, *Against Moab;*[1] and then it follows, *Thus saith Jehovah of hosts, the God of Israel.* By the first term he designates the immense power of God, and reminds them that God is the judge of the whole world, and that his kingdom extends over all nations; but by the second expression he bears testimony to the love with which he had embraced the children of Abraham, because he had been pleased to choose them as his peculiar inheritance. *Woe,* he says, *on Nebo;*[2] which was a city in the land of Moab; *because laid waste, ashamed, taken is Kiriathaim.* He names here, as we

[1] All the versions, except the *Syriac*, which *Calvin* has followed, have "to Moab," and connect the words with the following, that is, "Jehovah says thus to Moab." The best version is, as given by *Blayney* and *Henderson*, "concerning Moab, thus saith," &c.—*Ed.*

[2] Some give this rendering, "Alas! no Nebo;" it had ceased to exist, and the reason is given, "for it is laid waste."—*Ed.*

see, some cities, and he will name more as he proceeds. *Ashamed* then and *taken is Kiriathaim; and Misgab*[1] *is ashamed and torn*, or broken in mind. It follows,—

2. *There shall be* no more praise of Moab; in Heshbon they have devised evil against it; come, and let us cut it off from *being* a nation: also thou shalt be cut down, O Madmen; the sword shall pursue thee.

2. Nulla amplius gloriatio Moab in Chesbon; cogitaverunt super eam malum, Venite et excidamus eam, ne sit gens; etiam Madmen, (*alloquitur urbem ipsam,*) excisa es (*ad verbum,* in solitudinem redacta, *sed metaphorice accipitur pro interitu,* interiit *ergo* Madmen;) post te proficiscetur gladius.

The Prophet, as before, does not speak in an ordinary way, but declares in lofty terms what God had committed to him, in order that he might terrify the Moabites; not indeed that they heard his threatenings, but it was necessary that he should denounce vengeance in this vehement manner, that the Jews might know that the cruelty and pride of the Moabites, hereafter mentioned, would not go unpunished.

Hence he says, *No more shall be the praise* or the boasting *of Moab over Heshbon.* We may learn from this place and from others, that Heshbon had been taken from the Moabites; for it was occupied by God's people, because the Moabites had lost it, as Moses relates in Num. xxi. 30, and in Deut. ii. 26, &c. But (as things change) when the Moabites became strong, they took away this city from the Israelites. Hence the Prophet says, that there would be no more boasting that they possessed that city; for he adds, *They have thought,* or devised, &c. There is here a striking allusion, for חשבון, *chesbon,* is derived from חשב, *chesheb,* to devise or to consult, as though it were a place of consultation or devisings. The Prophet then says, that as to Heshbon they *consulted against it,* חשבו עליה, *cheshbu olie.* He uses the root from which the name of the city is derived. Heshbon, then, hitherto called the place of consultation, was to have and find other counsellors, even those who would contrive ruin for it. *Come ye;* the Prophet refers here to the counsel taken by the Chaldeans, *Come ye, and let us cut her off from*

[1] Neither the *Vulg.* nor the *Syr.* gives this as a proper name, nor is there any such place found elsewhere. *Blayney* renders it "the high fortress," agreeably with the *Vulg.*, *Syr.*, and the *Targ.—Ed.*

being a nation. He then joins another city, *And thou, Madmen,*[1] *shalt be cut off, for a sword shall go after thee,* or pursue thee, as though the city itself was fleeing from the sword; not that cities move from one place to another; but when the citizens deliberate how they may drive away their enemies and resist their attacks,—when they seek aid here and there,—when they set up their own remedies, they are said to flee. But the Prophet says, "Thou shalt gain nothing by fleeing, for the sword shall pursue thee." It follows,—

3. A voice of crying *shall be* from Horonaim, spoiling and great destruction.	3. Vox clamoris (*id est,* sonora) e Choronaim, vastitas et contritio magna.

By naming many cities, he shews that the whole land was doomed to ruin, so that no corner of it would be exempt from destruction. For the Moabites might have suffered some loss without much injury had they been moderately chastised; but the Prophet shews that they would be so reduced by the power of Nebuchadnezzar, that ruin would extend to every part of the land. We now then see why this catalogue of the cities is given.

By the *voice of crying* he means howling, a loud lamentation, heard far and wide. He says that the *voice of crying* would *go forth from Horonaim,* which some think was so called, because the city consisted of two parts, a higher and a lower part. He then adds, *desolation and great destruction.* He thus explains himself, for the citizens of Horonaim would in vain cry out, because desolation and breaking or destruction would constrain them, that is, make them cry out so as to howl for the bitterness of their grief. It follows,—

4. Moab is destroyed; her little ones have caused a cry to be heard.	4. Afflicta est Moab; audire fecerunt clamorem parvuli ejus.

[1] None of the versions renders this a proper name, but as a participle from the verb which follows, and no such place is mentioned elsewhere. They must have read מדמה instead of מדמן. Then the version would be,

Even silenced thou shalt be silenced,
After thee shall go the sword.

To be silenced, in the language of the prophets, is to be subdued. See Isaiah xv. 1, when the same thing is said of Moab. The word silence forms a contrast with the boasting of Moab mentioned at the beginning of the verse. After being subdued and removed elsewhere, still the sword would follow Moab.—*Ed.*

The Prophet speaks again generally of the whole country. It is said that the land of Moab was afflicted; not that it was so then; but to make certain the prophecy, he speaks of the event as having already taken place; for the prophets, as it is well known, speaking in the person of God, relate things as yet hidden, as though they had been completed. He says that the *little ones* of Moab so cried as to be heard.[1] This is much more emphatic than if he had said that men and women cried out; for children do not soon perceive what is going on, for their understanding is not great. Men and women howl when threatenings only are announced; but little children are not moved but by present evils, and except they are actually beaten, they are not affected; and then they hardly distinguish between some slight evil and death. Hence, when the Prophet says that the little ones of Moab were heard in their crying, he means that the grievousness of its calamity would be extreme, as that little children, as though wise before their time, would perceive the atrocious cruelty of their enemies. It follows,—

5. For in the going up of Luhith continual weeping shall go up; for in the going down of Horonaim the enemies have heard a cry of destruction.

6. Flee, save your lives, and be like the heath in the wilderness.

5. Quoniam in ascensu Luhith cum fletu ascendet fletus, quia in descensu Choronaim hostes clamorem contritionis audierunt (*conjungi debet proximus versus,*)

6. Fugite, eripite animas vestras; et eritis quasi Aroer (*vel,* myrica) in deserto.

Here Jeremiah uses another figure, that the weeping would be everywhere heard in the ascent to Luhith. It is probable, and it appears from the Prophet's words, that this city was situated on a high place. He then says, that men would go up with weeping *in the ascent to Luhith;* literally, *In* (or with) *weeping shall weeping ascend.* But some read as though it were written בכה, *beke,* weeping; nor is there a doubt

[1] Here all the versions and the *Targum* differ. The *Vulg.* only has "little ones;" the *Syr.* has "her poor;" the *Sept.* take "Zoar" to be intended, according to Isaiah xv. 5, the word צוערה instead of צעוריה. The passage in Isaiah confirms this reading, though not found in any copies. Then the verse would read thus,—

Broken is Moab,
They made the cry heard at Zoar.

This is substantially the version of *Venema.*—*Ed.*

but that the verb יעלה, *iole,* refers to a person. But Jeremiah seems to have mentioned weeping twice in order to shew that men would not only weep in one place, but during the long course of their ascent, as though he had said, "They who shall be near the city shall weep, and they in the middle of their course, and those at the foot of the mountain;" that is, there shall be weeping in every place. We now then perceive the meaning of the Prophet.

He afterwards says, *In the descent to Horonaim.* It hence appears that this city was situated in a low place or on a plain; and therefore I know not why they say that one part of it was higher than the other. It might indeed be that it had a hill in it; but the place was in a level country, and had mountains around it, as we learn from the Prophet's words, *In the descent to Horonaim the enemies shall hear a cry of distress.* By saying that enemies would hear a cry,[1] he means that the citizens of Horonaim and their neighbours would become frantic through grief. For fear restrains weeping, and when any one sees an enemy near, the very sight of him checks him, so that he dares not openly to shew his grief; and then shame also restrains tears as well as sighings, for an enemy would deride our weepings in our misery. There is no doubt then, but that the Prophet here amplifies the grievousness of their sorrow, when he says, that though the citizens of Horonaim had enemies before their eyes, they would yet break forth with weeping and loud crying, and that the reproach and derision of enemies would not restrain them.

Then he adds, *Flee, save:* this is the crying of distress; for miserable men, as the case is in extreme evils, mutually exhort one another, *Flee, save your lives.* He then compares them to a tamarisk. The word ערוער, *oruor,* designates a

[1] The word *enemies* is given only by the *Vulg.;* the other versions render it "distress." The literal rendering of the verse is,—

For *in* the ascent to Luhith,
With weeping ascends weeping;
For in the descent to Horonaim,
The distress of the cry of ruin have they heard.

This version materially corresponds with Isaiah xv. 5. Weeping ascending with weeping, shews that all wept as they ascended. "The distress of the cry" is a Hebraism for distressing cry.—*Ed.*

country, as it is probable, and there were also two cities of this name. However, ערער, *oror*, is a tamarisk, as we have already seen in chap. xvii. 6. Some render it, "a tower;" and the words of Isaiah in chap. xvii. 2, are perverted by some to maintain another meaning; for they think that ערוער, *oruor*, means the cot of shepherds in the desert; but I prefer the opinion of those who render it "tamarisk," or juniper, though the Prophet seems to me to allude to the city Aroer, or to a region of that name, but I rather think to the city. He then says, *And ye shall be as a tamarisk in the desert:* and it is known from other places that Aroer was in the land of Moab.

We now then perceive what the Prophet means: that Moab would be like a juniper in the desert, that is, a barren tree, which never grows to any size; and then it is dry, because it is not cherished by any rain, nor fed by any moisture from the ground. It is in this sense, as we have stated, that our Prophet took the similitude in chap. xvii. 5-8: "Blessed," he says, "is the man who trusts in Jehovah, for he shall be like a tree planted near waters: cursed is the man who trusts in man, and who makes flesh his arm, and withdraws his heart from Jehovah; for he shall be as the tamarisk of the desert;" that is, he shall be barren and dry, without any moisture or support. It now follows:—

7. For because thou hast trusted in thy works, and in thy treasures, thou shalt also be taken; and Chemosh shall go forth into captivity *with* his priests and his princes together.

7. Propterea quod fiducia tua fuit in operibus tuis (*ad verbum*) et in thesauris tuis, etiam tu capieris; et egredietur Chamos in captivitatem, sacerdotes ejus et principes ejus simul.

Jeremiah assigns here the reason why God would take vengeance on the Moabites; but we shall hereafter see other reasons why God had been so much displeased with them. Let us then know that we are not here taught avowedly why God determined to lay waste and destroy the land of Moab; for there is here but one reason given, while there were others and greater ones, even because they had wantonly exulted over the miseries of the Jews, because they had conspired against them, because they had betrayed them, and lastly, because they had as it were carried on war with their God.

But here Jeremiah briefly shews, that were there no other reasons, the Moabites deserved that God should pour forth his wrath on them even for this, because they trusted in their own works and treasures. By works some understand herds and flocks; and in this sense they are sometimes taken, and it is an exposition that may be admitted. We may however understand by "works" fortifications, especially as "treasures" are added. He then says, that the Moabites were such that it was just that God should be roused against them, because they were inebriated with false confidence in their own power, and because they had many treasures: they hence thought that they were impregnable.

The Prophet in the meantime intimates, that the Moabites greatly deceived themselves in thinking that they were safe against God's hand, because they were strongly fortified, and because they had immense treasures laid up. Hence he says that all these things would avail nothing, for God would destroy the whole land.

Even thou,. he says, *shalt be taken.* There is no small emphasis in the particle גם, *gam*, even or also; for the Prophet expresses what would now take place; for the Moabites in vain trusted in their treasures and power, because God would notwithstanding destroy them, and his hand would penetrate into their fortresses. "God then shall find thee out equally the same, as though thou wert exposed to all dangers." They who abound in warlike preparations, furnished with all kinds of defences, think themselves exempted from the common lot of men: hence he says, *Even thou*, equally the same with any village exposed to the will of enemies, *even thou shalt be taken; and go forth shall Chemosh.* This was the tutelar God of the land, as it appears from the book of Judges and other places, and even from what Moses says, (Judges xi. 24; 1 Kings xi. 7, 33; Num. xxi. 29.) As, then, the Moabites worshipped this idol, they thought themselves safe whatever evil might be at hand. The Prophet then derides this confidence. We have said before, that the ungodly in part set up their own earthly power in opposition to God, and in part imagined that they were aided by their idols. Hence the prophets exposed these two evils, as it appears also from the present passage: the Prophet had said, "Because thou trustest in thy fortresses and treasures, even thou shalt be taken;" and now he says, "Because thou thinkest Chemosh to be a sure and invincible defence, it shall be driven into exile and be kept captive." This he said in reproach to the idol. He adds, *its priests and its princes,* even those princes, who seem to lie down safely under its shadow, they also shall be driven into exile.

8. And the spoiler shall come upon every city, and no city shall escape: the valley also shall perish, and the plain shall be destroyed, as the Lord hath spoken.

8. Et veniet vastator ad omnem urbem, neque urbs eripietur; et peribit vallis, et perdetur planities, quod (*id est,* quemadmodum) locutus est Jehova.

He confirms the previous verse; nor ought he to be deemed too wordy, for this prophecy was not announced, that it might cherish the hope and patience of the faithful only for a few days; but it was necessary for them to rest dependent for a long time on this promise, which God had given them many years before. This, then, is the reason why the Prophet confirms at large a truth in itself sufficiently clear. *Come,* he says, *shall a waster to all the cities.* It now appears more clearly why he mentioned some of the cities, though, as we shall see, they were many, even that the Israelites might know that all the land of Moab was to be given up to desolation: *Nor shall a city escape, for destroyed shall be the valley and the plain, as Jehovah has spoken.* It follows,—

9. Give wings unto Moab, that it may flee and get away: for the cities thereof shall be desolate, without any to dwell therein.

9. Date alam ipsi Moab, quia volando volabit; et urbes ejus in vastationem erunt, ut non sit qui habitet in illis.

Here is a bitter derision; for it was necessary not only to goad the Moabites, but also to pierce them through, because they were inflated with so much pride, and also because they cruelly raged against God's people, as we shall more fully see hereafter. When the Israelites were conquered, these ungodly men cast forth their taunts, and also betrayed them to their enemies. Hence the Prophet now says, *Give wings to Moab.* Though the word ציץ, *tsits,* properly means a flower, yet it means here a wing, put for wings ; as though he had said, that the Moabites could not escape destruction except by flying. In short, as they had not only so proudly despised, but had also persecuted their miserable brethren, the Prophet says, "Come shall the time when feet for running or for flight shall not be sufficient for you, your enemies being so eager in pursuit ; but you will desire to have wings." But, as we shall see, he will presently tell us, that Moab had been quiet and settling on its dregs.

He then adds, that its *cities would be a waste, so as to have no inhabitant.* He mentions the reason why Moab would need wings, even because there would be no refuge for them, for wherever it would betake itself, it would be thence driven away ; for the enemy would take all the cities, so that the whole people would be under the necessity of removing elsewhere ; he intimates, in short, that there would be no hope for life to the Moabites, except by flight, and that the swiftest. At length he adds,—

10. Cursed *be* he that doeth the work of the Lord deceitfully, and cursed *be* he that keepeth back his sword from blood.

10. Maledictus qui facit opus Jehovæ fraudulenter (*hoc est,* non bona fide,) et maledictus qui prohibet gladium suum a sanguine.

The Prophet here encourages the Chaldeans to severity, so as to make no end until they destroyed that nation. We have said that the prophets assumed different characters, so that what they said might be more impressive. The Chaldeans were not indeed the disciples of Jeremiah ; nor was this exhortation intended for them, but that the Israelites might know that what they heard from the mouth of Jeremiah was certain. He then turns to address the Chaldeans ; as he before spoke to any who might be present, "Give wings to Moab ;" so now another apostrophe follows, *Cursed,* &c.,—to whom does he speak ? to the Chaldeans ; and yet the Prophet did not address them as though he could effect anything ; but, as I have said, he had a regard to the Jews.

This passage has been very absurdly explained, and it is commonly quoted as though the Prophet had said, that special care ought to be taken by us, not to omit anything of what God commands. But they thus misrepresent the meaning. We ought therefore to bear in mind what I have already said, that these words are addressed to the Chaldeans, as though he had said, "Spare not, but shed blood, and let no humanity move you, for it is the work of God; God has armed you, that ye might fully execute his judgment and spare no blood: ye shall then be accursed, except ye execute his vengeance." It is not indeed a common mode of speaking; but as to the subject and the meaning there is no ambiguity. It is the same thing as though he had said, "Go on courageously, and boldly execute God's vengeance, inasmuch as punishment has been denounced on them." As when soldiers idly delay, the leader when present not only exhorts them but also urges them on with reproofs and threatenings, in order to rouse their alacrity; so the Prophet here shews that God, as though present with the Chaldeans, would chide their sloth, "Why do ye give over? cursed is every one who will not shed blood, and who will not destroy them from the least to the greatest."

But the whole import of the passage is found in the expression, that the destruction of that ungodly nation was *the work of Jehovah;* as if he had said, "Though the Chaldeans shall lay waste the land of Moab, and shall do this, not in order to obey God, but from avarice and ambition, yet it will be the work of God; for God has hired the Chaldeans for this end, that they might destroy the Moabites, though they may think of no such thing." It follows,—

11. Moab hath been at ease from his youth, and he hath settled on his lees, and hath not been emptied from vessel to vessel, neither hath he gone into captivity: therefore his taste remained in him, and his scent is not changed.

11. Tranquillus fuit Moab a pueritia sua (*vel,* quietus fuit Moab,) et resedit ipse super fæces suas, et non mutatus fuit a vase in vas, et in captivitatem non profectus (*aut,* non migravit;) propterea stetit sapor ejus in eo, et odor ejus non mutatus est.

Here he expresses more clearly what we have before seen, that Moab in vain promised to himself perpetual impunity, because he had for a long time been prosperous. Then the Prophet says that he would be suddenly destroyed, when God ascended his tribunal to execute his judgment.

He first says, that he had been *quiet from his childhood,*

because when the Israelites had been often harassed, that nation remained untouched, and never felt any disadvantage, as though fortified on all sides by their own defences; for they dwelt in part amidst mountains, but had a level country, as it is well known, beyond Jordan. It was a land in a moderate degree fertile, so that as they enjoyed continual peace, they collected great wealth. But it was very hard for the Israelites, when God afflicted them with various calamities, to see the Moabites secure and safe from all trouble and all losses. As, then, this thought might have grievously wounded the minds of the faithful, the Prophet here exhorts them not to envy the happiness of the Moabites, because God would at length stretch forth his hand against them, according to what was done by David, who also exhorted the faithful patiently to wait for the day of the Lord, when they saw the ungodly enjoying all kinds of pleasure, and meeting with success according to their wishes. (Ps. xxxvii. 1, 7, 8.) We now then understand the object of the Prophet.

He compares Moab to an old man, who had passed his whole life in security, without any losses, without any grief or sorrow. *Quiet*, then, *has Moab* been, or quiet *from his childhood*, even from the time he became a nation. For what was the childhood of Moab? even from the time they expelled the giants and other inhabitants and dwelt in their land. Then success ever attended them; and hence he says, that they *settled on their dregs*, so that they underwent no change. Here is another metaphor: as wine which remains in its own vessel, and is never changed into another, retains its taste, its strength, and its savour; so also the Prophet says that Moab had always been in the enjoyment of perpetual felicity, like wine which remains on its own dregs. For the dregs preserve the wine, as it is well known; for the wine, being taken off from its dregs, loses in part its own strength, and at length becomes vapid; but wine, being not changed, continues in its own strength.

We hence see how apt is the comparison, when the Prophet says, that *Moab had not been changed from vessel to vessel, but had settled on his dregs.* And he explains himself without a figure when he adds, that he had *not gone*, or removed, *into captivity.* He yet intimates that this perpetual peace would avail the Moabites nothing, because as the Lord had resolved to destroy them, he would cause the strength of Moab to fail and all his wealth to be reduced to nothing.

PRAYER.

Grant, Almighty God, that since we are so disposed to indulge sloth, and so devoted to earthly things, that we easily forget our holy calling except thou dost continually stimulate us,—O grant that the afflictions by which thou triest us, may effectually rouse us, so that leaving the world we may strive to come to thee, and devote ourselves wholly to thy service; and that we may so carry on the warfare under the various afflictions of the present life, that our minds and all our thoughts may always be fixed on the hope of that eternal and blessed rest which thine only-begotten Son our Lord has promised as having been prepared for us in heaven.—Amen.

Lecture One Hundred and Seventieth.

12. Therefore, behold, the days come, saith the Lord, that I will send unto him wanderers, that shall cause him to wander, and shall empty his vessels, and break their bottles.

12. Propterea ecce dies veniunt, dicit Jehova, et mittam ei abactores qui abigant eum, et vasa ejus evacuent, et lagenas eorum dispergant.

The Prophet said in the last lecture that the Moabites, as long as they lived prosperously, were very hardened, as impunity becomes an incentive to sin; for the ungodly, while God spares them, think that they shall never be called to an account. He now adds, that the *days* would *come*, in which God would suddenly execute vengeance on them. But he pursues the comparison which he had used; for he had said, that the Moabites were like wine which had not been poured from one vessel into another; and hence they retained their own odour, that is, they were inebriated with their own pleasures, because God had granted them peace and quietness for a long time.

Now, the Prophet, on the other hand, says that God would send to them *drivers*,[1] *to drive them away*, and who

[1] "Incliners" is the *Sept.;* "strewers," the *Vulg.;* "plunderers," the *Syr.* and *Targ.* The verb means to spread, to strew. They were those who turned the wine vessels in order to empty them. *Henderson* has

would *empty their vessels and scatter their bottles,*—the containing for the contained; though I do not disapprove of another rendering, "and destroy their bottles;" for the verb is sometimes taken in this sense. Properly it means to scatter, to dissipate; but the verb נפץ, *nuphets,* sometimes expresses a stronger idea, even to scatter or to cast forth with violence, so as to break what is thus cast forth. As to the real meaning there is not much difference: for we perceive what was God's purpose, that he would send to the Moabites enemies to drive them into exile, and thus to deprive them of those pleasures in which they had so long indulged. But this was not said for the sake of the Moabites, but that the Jews might know, that though that land had been in a quiet state, yet it would not escape the hand of God; for its long continued felicity could not render void that decree of God of which the Prophet had spoken. It now follows—

13. And Moab shall be ashamed of Chemosh, as the house of Israel was ashamed of Beth-el their confidence.	13. Et pudefiet Moab a Chamos, sicuti pudefacti sunt domus Israel a Bethel, sua fiducia.

We may see more clearly from this verse, that the Prophet does not so much address the Moabites as his own people; for he was not a teacher to the Moabites to promote their safety; on the contrary, he intended his doctrine for the benefit of the Jews, as in the present instance.

Ashamed, he says, *shall Moab be of his idol:* for we have said that Chemosh was the god of the Moabites, as every nation had its own peculiar god, even its own invention. Now, the comparison made here shews that the Prophet wished to exhort the people, to whom he was appointed a teacher, to repentance; for he set before them the example of the ten tribes. And we know that at the time Jeremiah announced this prophecy, the kingdom of Israel was destroyed. All the Israelites, then, had been driven into exile except the tribe of Judah and the half tribe of Benjamin. Now, the ten tribes, as it is well known, had, under Jeroboam, departed from the pure worship of God, and had built for themselves an altar in Bethel. Hence, then, the Prophet now says, *As ashamed were* the Israelites of their supersti-

"overturners;" but *Blayney* has the best word, "tilters," who should tilt him.—*Ed.*

tions, which they had devised for themselves, so a similar vengeance of God awaited the people of Moab; and thus he shews to the Jews what it is to trust in the only true God. The Jews were not, indeed, involved in so gross a superstition as to worship idols, at least publicly; but Ezekiel shews that they also were contaminated with this kind of pollution, and that the very sanctuary was defiled with idols; and at the same time the worship of God, according to the Law, continued to be celebrated. But the Jews had nothing but the external form: they had, indeed, the temple and the altar, they professed to worship the true God, but in the meantime impiety and contempt of true religion prevailed among them, and they had begun to involve themselves in many ungodly superstitions, as we have before seen.

What, then, does Jeremiah now do? He sets before their eyes the ten tribes whom God had destroyed, though the Israelites, as well as the Jews, had descended from the same father, even Abraham. As, then, God had inflicted so heavy a punishment on the kingdom of Israel, he now shews to the Jews, that the punishment of the Moabites was not less probable; and why? because they have, he says, their idol. God shews that this was a most atrocious wickedness, by which the Moabites had provoked his anger; for there is nothing less intolerable than for men to transfer the glory of God to their own inventions, to statues, to logs of wood, to stones, or to idols of gold and silver. We now, then, understand the object of the Prophet. It follows—

14. How say ye, We *are* mighty and strong men for the war?

14. Quomodo dicitis, Viri (fortes) nos, et viri robusti ad prælium?

15. Moab is spoiled, and gone up *out of* her cities, and his chosen young men are gone down to the slaughter, saith the King, whose name *is* The Lord of hosts.

15. Vastatus est Moab, civitates ejus excidit (*alii vertunt,* civitates ejus evanuerunt, *ut sit mutatio numeri; alii,* incola ascendit, *vel,* discessit ab urbibus ejus,) et electio juvenum descendit (*hoc est,* electi juvenes; *et est allusio ad nomen* בחריו, *nam* בחורים *dicuntur apud Hebræos adolescentes, qui sunt in flore ætatis, sed nomen hoc deducitur a* בחר, *quod est eligere, unde est etiam nomen hoc quo utitur Propheta;* electio *igitur* juvenum, *vel,* electi juvenes, descenderunt) ad mactationem, dicit Rex, nomen ejus Jehova exercituum (*id est,* cujus nomen est Jehova exercituum.)

The Prophet here reproves the pride of the Moabites, because they trusted in their own strength, and derided God and what the Prophets announced. We indeed know that ungodly men, when all things prosper with them, are moved by no fear, divest themselves of every feeling, and become so sunk in indifference, that they not only disdainfully disregard the true God, but also what is connected with moral obligation. Such, then, was the confidence which prevailed among the Moabites. Hence the Prophet here checks this foolish boasting.

How say ye, We are strong, we are warlike men? as though he had said, "These boastings, while God is seriously contending with you, are all empty, and will avail you nothing: ye think yourselves beyond the reach of danger, because ye possess great power, and are surrounded with strong defences; but God will reduce to nothing whatever you regard as your protection." *Wasted,* then, *is Moab.* He sets up this threatening in opposition to their arrogance. He indeed foretells what was to come, but speaks of it as a thing already fulfilled. *Wasted,* he says, *is Moab, and the enemy has cut off his cities.* The verb עלה, *ole,* is to be taken in a transitive sense; it is indeed a neuter verb, but the other meaning is more suitable to this place, that the enemy would cut off the cities of the Moabites. I yet allow that it may be explained otherwise, that the inhabitants would ascend or depart from his cities; for עלה, *ole,* metaphorically, indeed, signifies to ascend, and to flow off, or to go away, as they say, in smoke; and if an anomaly as to number, common in Hebrew, be approved, the sense will be, "and from his cities they have vanished."[1] And this explanation agrees

[1] There is no agreement in the Versions and *Targ.*, as to these words, nor among critics. The easiest construction is presented by *Blayney,*—

A spoiler of Moab and of her cities is gone up.

The next clause is not so well rendered by *Blayney.* He applies it to the Chaldeans. "Moab" is spoken of in this chapter, both in the feminine and in the masculine gender. In our language the neuter would be the most suitable, it and its. I render the verse thus,—

15. The waster of Moab and of its cities *is* going up,
And the choice of its youth shall descend to the slaughter,
Saith the King, Jehovah of hosts is his name.

"Going up" as ascribed to the conqueror, and "descending" to the conquered.—*Ed.*

well with what follows, *and his young men have descended to the slaughter;* that is, they who seem the strongest among them shall be drawn to destruction, or shall descend to the slaughter. But as the event seemed difficult to be believed, God is again introduced. Then the Prophet says, that he did not speak from his own mind, but announced what God had committed to him. And he adds his title, that the Jews might be more attentive to the consideration of God's power. God, he says, is he who speaks, *the King, whose name is Jehovah of hosts.* He sets up God's name in opposition to the warlike preparations, of which the Moabites, as we have seen, boasted; as though he had said, that if the Moabites had to do with mortals, they might indeed have justly gloried; but as they had a contest with the living God, all their power would vanish away, since God was prepared to execute vengeance. It follows—

16. The calamity of Moab *is* near to come, and his affliction hasteth fast.	16. Propinqua est calamitas Moab (איד, *significat infortunium et calamitatem, significat etiam interitum, ideo vertunt quidam* propinquus est interitus) ad veniendum (ut veniat,) et malum ejus (*id est,* calamitas) festinat valde.

Here the Prophet expresses something more, that the vengeance of which he spoke was near and hastening. It served to alleviate the sorrow of the faithful, when they understood that the Moabites would shortly be punished; for it was a grievous and bitter trial, when God severely chastened his own children, to see that the wicked were in the meantime spared. As, then, he deferred his judgments as to the wicked, that delay tended to drive the faithful to despair, at least they could not bear with sufficient patience the scourges of God.

This is the reason why the Prophet now says, *Near is the destruction* of the Moabites, *and their calamity hastens.* And though God did for some time yet bear with the Moabites, so that they remained in a quiet state, and revelled in their pleasures, yet this prophecy was true; for we are to bear in mind that truth, which ought ever to be remembered as to promises and threatenings, that a thousand years are as one day with the Lord: and hence is that exhortation given by the Prophet Habakkuk, "If the prophecy delays, wait for it;

for coming it will come, and will not delay." (Hab. ii. 3.) And this mode of speaking occurs often in the prophets. When, therefore, God denounces punishment on the wicked and the despisers of his Law, he says, "Behold, your day hastens," and he says this, that they might be awakened and begin to fear in due time.

But here, as I have reminded you, Jeremiah had a regard to his own people. For the faithful might have objected, and said, "What can this be? how long will God defer the punishment which he threatens to our enemies?" Hence he says, "Strengthen your minds for a little while, for God will presently stretch forth his hand and shew that he is a defender who cares for you and your safety; for he will set himself against the Moabites, because they have been unfaithful and vexatious to you." It is, then, for this reason that he says, *Near is their destruction*, and *their vengeance hastens.*

We may hence learn this useful doctrine, that whenever God promises anything, we ought to receive it as a present thing, though yet hidden and even remote. There is no distance which ought to impede our faith; but we ought to regard as certain whatever God promises, and as though it were before our eyes and in our hand. And the same ought to be the case as to threatenings; whenever God denounces anything hard and grievous, it ought to touch and move us the same as though we saw his hand armed with a sword, and as though the very execution of his vengeance was exhibited before our eyes. For we know what the Scripture teaches us elsewhere, "When the wicked shall say, Peace and security, destruction comes suddenly on them, as the pain of childbearing, which seizes a woman when she thinks nothing of it." (1 Thess. v. 3.) Let us then learn to set God's favour ever as present, and also all punishments, so that we may really fear them. It follows—

17. All ye that are about him, bemoan him; and all ye that know his name, say, How is the strong staff broken, *and* the beautiful rod!

17. Commovemini illi (*id est*, super Moab) quicunque estis in circuitu ejus, et quicunque cognoscitis nomen ejus, dicite, Quomodo fractus est baculus fortis? virga pulchritudinis (*vel*, excellentiæ, *nam* תפארת *significat decorum pulchritudine.*)

The Prophet seems indeed to exhort all neighbours to

sympathy; but we have stated for what purpose he did this; for it was not his object to shew that the Moabites deserved pity, so that their neighbours ought to have condoled with them in their calamities: but by this figurative mode of speaking he exaggerated the grievousness of the evils which were soon to happen to the Moabites; as though he had said, "This judgment of God will be so dreadful as to make all their neighbours to tremble; all who had previously known the state of the people of Moab, will be smitten with such terror as will make them to groan and mourn with them." In short, the Prophet had nothing else in view than to shew that God's vengeance on the Moabites would not be less severe and dreadful than it had been on the ten tribes, and what it would be on the tribe of Judah.

Say ye, he says, *how is the staff broken?* He introduces here all their neighbours as astonished with wonder; for the same purpose are other things mentioned, even to shew that the calamity of Moab would be deemed a prodigy, for the people thought them unassailable, and no one had ever dared to attempt anything against their land. This, then, was the reason why the Prophet here asks as one astonished, even in the person of all nations, How has it happened *that the staff is broken? and the beautiful rod?*[1] These are metaphorical words, which refer to the royal dignity and the condition of the whole people. It follows—

18. Thou daughter that dost inhabit Dibon, come down from *thy* glory, and sit in thirst; for the spoiler of Moab shall come upon thee, *and* he shall destroy thy strong holds.

18. Descende e gloria, sede in siti habitatrix filia Dibon; quia vastator Moab ascendit contra te, destructor munitionum tuarum (*vel*, quia vastatus est Moab, et supra te ascendet, &c.)

Here the Prophet turns to address the city Dibon, which was renowned among that people. The mode of speaking is well known; he calls the people of the city the *daughter of Dibon;* and he calls the daughter an *inhabitant*, because

[1] The literal rendering is,—

How has the rod of strength been broken,
The staff of honour?

"How" is by what means, or how much: the first seems to be the meaning here. The rod and the staff are the same—the sceptre an ensign of power and of honour or glory.—*Ed.*

the Moabites, as it has been said, ever rested in safety and quietness in their own habitations, for no one disturbed them. It is, then, the same as though he had said, "Ye who have hitherto been in a quiet state, *descend* now *from your glory, and dwell in thirst*."[1] By thirst he means the want of all things. Thirst is set in opposition to glory; but it is more than if the Prophet had mentioned disgrace or poverty; for there are many who are otherwise oppressed by want, and yet find fountains or streams; but when there is no drop of water to quench thirst, it is an extreme misery.

We hence see that the Prophet exaggerates the punishment of the Moabites, when he says that the citizens of Dibon would *sit in thirst, because*, he says, *ascended against thee has the waster*,[2] *and the destroyer of thy fortresses.* We may hence conclude that the city was on all sides fortified, so that it thought its defences sufficient to keep off enemies. But the Prophet derides this presumption, because the Chaldeans would come to pull down and destroy all these strongholds. It follows—

19. O inhabitant of Aroer, stand by the way, and espy; ask him that fleeth, and her that escapeth, *and* say, What is done?	19. Super viam consiste et speculare habitatrix Aroer; interroga fugientem et eam quæ elapsa fuerit, dic, Quid factum est (quid accidit?)

We have stated elsewhere why the prophets in describing calamities spoke in so elevated a style; for their object was not to seek fame or the praise of eloquence. They are not these rhetorical ornaments which the prophets used; but they necessarily spoke in a lofty style of the punishments which awaited the ungodly, because such was the hardness of their hearts that they hesitated not to despise God's threatenings, or to regard them as fables. That God's threatenings then might penetrate into the hearts of men,

[1] The verb "dwell" favours the idea adopted by some, that צמא means here a dry or thirsty land.—*Ed.*

[2] עלה, here, as in ver. 15, is a participle, and so the verb which follows. The "waster" is represented as then on his way,—

For the waster of Moab is ascending against thee,
The destroyer of thy fortresses.—*Ed.*

it was necessary to exaggerate them by means of various comparisons, as it is done here and in many places. We ought at the same time to bear in mind what I have said, that the Prophet had a regard to his own people. As the Moabites were like a hid treasure, the Jews could never have thought it possible, that the Chaldeans would at length make an inroad there; but the Prophet declares that the thing was so certain, as though it was seen by their own eyes. In order then to lead the Jews to the very scene itself, the judgments of God are here not only described, but as it were painted.

Stand, he says, *on the way, and look, thou inhabitant of Aroer.* This was another city of the Moabites, of which mention is made in many places; and then he mentions others, as we shall see. *Ask him,* he says, *who fleeth and her who escapes.* He, indeed, changes the gender of the nouns; but when he mentions many, and then one person, he did this for the sake of amplifying; because, on the one hand, he wished to shew that so great would be the number of exiles, that the whole land would become empty; and then, on the other hand, when he says that this and that person would flee, he means that they would be so scattered that they would not go in troops; but as it is usual in a disordered state of things, one would flee on this side, and another on the other side. *Ask him who fleeth,* or as we may render the words, *Ask all who flee;* and then, *ask her who escapes;* because not only men, but also women would flee, so that no sex would be spared. In short, he intimates, that those who dwelt in cities well fortified, would be all anxiety on seeing enemies irresistibly advancing through every part of the country.

20. Moab is confounded; for it is broken down: howl and cry; tell ye it in Arnon, that Moab is spoiled,	20. Pudefactus est Moab, quia contritus est; ululate et clamate, et annuntiate in Arnon, quoniam vastatus est Moab (*vel,* quòd vastatus est Moab; כי *enim hic explicativè accipitur, non causaliter;*)
21. And judgment is come upon the plain country; upon Holon, and upon Jahazah, and upon Mephaath,	21. Et judicium perveniet ad terram planam (*vel,* rectam, *hoc est,* ad ipsam planiciem,) ad Holon et ad Jazar et ad Mephaath;

22. And upon Dibon, and upon Nebo, and upon Beth-diblathaim,	22. Et super Dibon, et super Nebo, et super Beth-diblathaim (domum Diblathaim, *sed est nomen proprium urbis ;*)
23. And upon Kiriathaim, and upon Beth-gamul, and upon Beth-meon,	23. Et ad Cariathain, et ad Beth-gamoul, et ad Beth-meon ;
24. And upon Kerioth, and upon Bozrah, and upon all the cities of the land of Moab, far or near.	24. Et super Chirioth, et super Bozrah, et super omnes urbes terræ Moab remotas et propinquas.

We have stated why the Prophet describes so fully the ruin of the Moabites, and dwells so long on a subject in no way obscure ; it was not indeed enough merely to teach and to shew what was useful to be known, but it was also necessary to add goads, that the Jews might attend to these prophecies ; nay, it was necessary to drive as it were with a hammer into their minds what would have been otherwise incredible ; for they deemed it a fable that the Moabites could thus be broken, laid waste, and reduced to nothing. The Prophet then would have laboured in vain, or spoken ineffectually, had he described in simple and plain words what we here read. But he added vehemence to his words, as though he would drive in his words with a hammer and fasten them in the minds of the people.

He then says, that *Moab was ashamed, because he was smitten.* And then he turns again to address their neighbours, *Howl, cry, and declare in Aroer :* but the Prophet ironically exhorted others to howl and cry ; for, as we have said, it was not his purpose to shew that they deserved pity who had been the most cruel enemies to God's Church, but to shew that God's vengeance would be so dreadful as to call forth cryings and howlings through the whole neighbourhood. And then he adds, *Declare it in Aroer ;* and afterwards he names many cities ; as though he had said, that no corner of the land would be free from fear and anxiety, because the enemies, after having made an inroad into one part, would turn to another, so as to make no end of ravaging, until they had destroyed the whole country and all the people. Of these cities and of their situation there is no need of saying much, for it would be a useless labour. For in the last place, the Prophet sufficiently shews that what he had in view was what I have stated; for he says, *on all the cities of Moab, remote as well as near:* he intimates that no part of the land would be exempted from destruction; for the enemies having begun to attack it, would not cease until they had gone through every part, and desolation had spread everywhere, as though the whole country had been burnt with fire. It follows,—

25. The horn of Moab is cut off, and his arm is broken, saith the Lord.	25. Succisum est cornu Moab, et robor ejus confractum, dicit Jehova.

By another metaphor he expresses the same thing. By *horn* he means power, as all who are in any measure acquainted with Scripture well know that by this word is set forth power, strength, or any defence for the protection of a nation. He then says that the *horn of Moab was cut off;* and he adds afterwards as an explanation, that *his strength was broken.* Hence by this second clause we understand what the Prophet meant when he said, that the horn of Moab was cut off. But he again introduces God as the speaker, because the Moabites thought that their horn could not be broken. As then Jeremiah would not have obtained credit, had he spoken in his own name, he again brought forward God as declaring his own words. It now follows,—

26. Make ye him drunken; for he magnified *himself* against the Lord: Moab also shall wallow in his vomit, and he also shall be in derision.	26. Inebriate ipsum, quia adversus Jehovam magnificatus est, et complosit Moab in vomitu suo (*vel,* involvit se,) et ipse quoque in derisum (*vel,* in ludibrium: *adjungamus etiam alterum versum.*)
27. For was not Israel a derision unto thee? was he found among thieves? for since thou spakest of him, thou skippedst for joy.	27. Annon in risum fuit tibi Israel? an inter fures deprehensus fuit? quia ex quo sermo tuus de eo fuit, commovisti te.

The Prophet now addresses the Chaldeans, who were to be the executioners of God's vengeance: hence he says, *Make him drunk, because he has magnified himself against Jehovah,* that is, raised himself in his pride against God. Then the Prophet, as God's herald, encouraged the Chaldeans, fully to execute God's judgment, who had been chosen to be his servants. And the address had more force in it when the Prophet shewed that such a command was committed to him, as we have seen elsewhere; for the Prophets shewed how efficacious was their doctrine, when they besieged and stormed cities, when they gave orders to armies. This then is the course which Jeremiah now follows, when as God's herald he summons the Chaldeans, and commands them vigorously to perform what God approved and what he had decreed, even to *inebriate* the Moabites with evils. The rest to-morrow.

PRAYER.

Grant Almighty God, that we may learn, not only to consider thy judgments when they appear before our eyes, but also to fear them whenever they are announced, so that we may implore thy mercy, and also repent of our sins and patiently bear thy paternal chastisements, and never murmur when thou sparest for a time the ungodly, but wait with calm and resigned minds until the time comes when thou wilt execute vengeance on them, and when in the meantime thou wilt gather us at the end of our warfare into the blessed rest above, and give us to enjoy that inheritance which thou hast prepared for us in Heaven, and which has been obtained for us by the blood of thine only-begotten Son our Lord.—Amen.

Lecture One Hundred and Seventy-first.

We began yesterday to explain why the Prophet, denouncing on the Moabites the punishment they had deserved, directed his speech to the Chaldeans, even that his prophecy might have greater force and produce greater effect. The metaphor of drunkenness which he uses, is common; for when Scripture intimates that any are made miserable, as they say, to satiety, or more than what can be well borne, it compares them to those who are made drunk. For as a drunken man loses his senses, so they who are overwhelmed with miseries, are almost stunned with evils, so that they become deprived of reason and judgment. This then is the drunkenness which the Prophet now mentions. And following up the same idea, he adds, *And Moab is rolled in his own vomit.* Some by vomit understand intemperate joy, and render the words in the past tense, "And Moab shouted in his own vomit," that is, he luxuriated in his own abundance, and when he gorged himself with wine and with all kinds of luxuries, he loudly exulted; *and therefore he shall be also a reproach.* This contrast is not unsuitable, that Moab immediately exulted when in prosperity, and that therefore God would shortly punish him, so as to make him a reproach or a derision.

But I follow what has been generally approved, that Moab shall be rolled, or shall clap hands even in his own vomit: so that by vomit the Prophet means excessive grief. For the drunkard delights in drinking, but afterwards by vomiting he suffers the punishment of his intemperance, when his head, his stomach, his legs and other members shake and tremble. So also, it is no unsuitable comparison, when the Prophet calls sorrow, arising from calamity, vomiting. He then says, that when *Moab shall clap his hands*, or roll himself[1] (for the word is variously rendered) in his own miseries, he shall be even a *derision.* Why he says, that he would be a derision, we may learn from the next verse, for he says, *Has not Israel been a derision to thee?*

But the higher cause for the drunkenness mentioned here ought to be observed, even because Moab exalted himself against God. For after having spoken of the pride through which he exulted over God, he adds an explanation, *Has not Israel been a derision to thee?* See then how the Moabites acted proudly towards God, even because they treated his Church reproachfully. And this ought especially to be noticed; for God intimates by these words, that he is so

[1] The word has no other meaning than that of smiting, striking, or clapping the hand. A drunkard rejoices by clapping his hands, even in his filth, and thus makes himself an object of ridicule and derision; or he may strike his hands in agony: but it is by the first he renders himself ridiculous, the thing evidently intended here. It is observed justly by *Blayney*, that the first verb in the verse is in the singular number, used for the plural; and he regarded this verb to be the same; and his version is,—

And clap at Moab in his vomiting.

The objection to this is, the verb in this sense is not used without a preposition after it; see Lam. ii. 15: otherwise this would suit the passage: it was suggested by *Gataker.—Ed.*

connected with the faithful as to regard their cause as his own, as it is said elsewhere, " He that toucheth you, toucheth the apple of my eye." (Zech. ii. 8.) God then so takes the faithful under his own protection, that whatever injury is done to them, he counts it as done to him. This connection is well expressed by the Prophet, when he says, " The Moabites have raised themselves against God ;" and at the same time he shews the way and manner, even because they exulted over the Israelites. Were any one to object and say, that the Moabites injured mortal men only and not God ; the answer has already been given, even that God has so adopted his Church as to identify himself with it. Let us then know, that God, when he sees us suffering anything unjustly, regards the wrong as done to himself. As then the people of Israel had been a derision to the Moabites, the Prophet threatens them with a similar punishment for their pride.

And then he adds, *Has he been found among thieves?* It is, indeed, certain, that the people of Israel deserved very severe scourges, and that when they were subjected to so many adversities, a just reward was rendered to them for their iniquities. With regard to God this is certain ; but with regard to the Moabites, the people of Israel were innocent ; for these ungodly men could not object anything to the Israelites, for they were altogether like them, or even worse. God then compares here his chosen people with aliens, and says that the Israelites were not thieves. Under one thing he comprehends everything, as though he had said, " Of what wickedness have the Israelites been guilty, that you have thus become so enraged against them ?" We hence see what the words of the Prophet mean, even that the Moabites were impelled by nothing but cruelty and pride, when they so basely raged against the Israelites, and so disdainfully oppressed them ; for as I have already said, there was no cause why the Moabites should have been so hostile to the miserable people. Thus their crime was doubled, for they acted proudly towards God's people, and they acted thus without a cause ; for with regard to them, God's people were innocent.

By saying that they *were moved*, or excited *whenever they spoke of the Israelites*, he intimates that they were carried away by malevolence, so as to wish all kinds of evil to the miserable, and then, as far as they could, to lay snares for them. As then they thus raged furiously against the Israelites, the Prophet includes everything of this kind in the word "moved," or raised an uproar.[1] It follows—

28. O ye that dwell in Moab, leave the cities, and dwell in the rock, and be like the dove *that* maketh her nest in the sides of the hole's mouth.	28. Deserite urbes, et habitate in petra (*hoc est*, in rupibus) habitatores Moab, et erunt quasi columba, quæ nidulatur in transgressionibus (*hoc est,*) trans os fissuræ.

Here Jeremiah denounces exile on the Moabites; as though he had said, that such would be the desolation of their land, that they would be forced as wanderers to flee here and there. That he bids them to *leave their cities*, this is not done in the same way as when God commands his people what is right; but he only shews that he was armed with the sword of God, not only to speak with the mouth, but also to perform what he foretells; for the execution ought not to be separated from the prophecies, for the hand of God is joined with his mouth. When, therefore, he announces anything by his servants, the fulfilment also, as it has been stated, is included.

This is the import of the words, *Leave the cities, and dwell among the rocks;* that is, Hide yourselves in lurking-places, for no habitable land will afford you rest, or be a convenient place to flee to. *And they shall be*, he says, *like a dove which makes a nest in remote places beyond the clefts of the rocks*, or stones. He means the most deserted places. It is the same as though he had said, that it would not be simply an exile that God would allot to the Moabites, but that they would be taken away to regions unknown, and deserted by men. It follows—

29. We have heard the pride of Moab, (he is ex-	29. Audivimus superbiam Moab; superbit valde fastum ejus (*vel,* arrogantiam ejus)

[1] The *Vulg.* and the *Targ.* give the best version of these words,—
Surely for the abundance of thy words against him, thou shalt be quickly removed, *or*, led captive.
Then, in the following verse, Moab is bidden to quit his cities.—*Ed.*

ceeding proud,) his loftiness, and his arrogancy, and his pride, and the haughtiness of his heart.

et superbiam ejus (*nomen est etiam ejusdem significationis, et ab eadem radice, quemadmodum si quis diceret ferocitatem et ferocium, tantum pronuntiatione differunt istæ voces*) et altitudinem cordis.

Here the Prophet intimates by anticipation, that how much soever the Moabites might boast, they could not, by their boastings and their pride, so succeed that God should not appear against them as a Judge. We have said already, that as the Moabites had been long in a quiet state, what the Prophet denounced on them, appeared at the first hearing as incredible. It is then by way of anticipation that he says, that the Moabites were *proud*, did swell with *haughtiness*, and breathed much *arrogance*, that, in short, they manifested high and lofty spirits. When the Prophet says all this, and adds, that nothing would avail them, we see that he meets those doubts which might have possessed weak minds, so as to prevent them to believe his prophecy.

And when he uses the words, *We have heard*, he not only means by report, but that the Moabites loudly boasted, as it is usual with proud men; for they made, so to speak, a bellowing, and sought, even by their tongues alone, to strike others with terror. As then they proclaimed their wealth and their power, they sought in a manner to shake the very air, so that all might tremble at their voice alone. This seems to have been expressed by the Prophet, when he said, *We have heard*. In short, Jeremiah does not mean that the report of the pride of Moab had spread abroad, as rumours often fly respecting the haughtiness and boastings of men; but he intimates that the Moabites were heralds of their own power, so that they spoke in lofty terms of their own greatness, and thus their own tongues testified of their haughtiness and arrogance.[1] And hence it was that the

[1] Our version in Isaiah xvi. 6, where the same form of words occurs, is, "We have heard of," though here the "of" is dropped, and thus the meaning of *Calvin* is conveyed, which is favoured by the early versions.

The verse may be thus literally rendered,—

We have heard the arrogance of Moab;
Very arrogant *has been* his insolence and arrogance;
Yea, his arrogantness and the loftiness of his heart.

The word for "arrogance" means swelling; it is to grow big, and to claim

Prophet enlarged on their pride; Moab *is very proud,* he says; *we have heard his haughtiness, his pride and his arrogance,* (though it be the same word,) *and the loftiness of his heart,* or, as we may say in Latin, *et altos spiritus,* and his high sprits. It now follows—

30. I know his wrath, saith the Lord; but *it shall* not *be* so; his lies shall not so effect *it.*	30. Ego cognovi, dicit Jehova, insolentiam ejus; et mendacia ejus non rectitudo; non sic facient.

This verse is variously explained, at least the second clause. Some render it, "His indignation, and not what is right; then they add by itself, "his lies;" and lastly, "they have not done rightly," or as others, "they will not do anything fixed," which is more suitable, and comes near to the rendering which I have given. But I will not here discuss other interpretations, or try at large to disprove them, but it is sufficient for us to understand the real meaning of the Prophet.

In the first place, God is here introduced as saying, *I know his insolence.* The pronoun אני, *ani,* is emphatical, for in the last verse the Prophet had said, that the boastings of Moab were a terror, as they spoke loudly of their own strength and defences. As then they thus with open mouths sounded forth their own praises, they filled all their neighbours with terror; hence the Prophet said, *We have heard the pride of Moab.* Now God also on his part gives this answer, *I know,* he says, *his insolence;* as though he had said, "The Moabites do not thus boast, but that I am a witness; all these things ascend to my tribunal."

He afterwards adds, still in the person of God, *Not rectitude are his lies.* By the word עברתו, *obertu,* which some render, "his indignation," the Prophet means, I think, insolence. It signifies properly excess, as it comes from עבר, *ober,* to pass over. The noun is indeed often taken to express indignation, because anger keeps within no limits, but is, as Horace says, a momentary madness.[1] But on account

more than what belongs to us. Then "insolence" signifies to rise high, so as to look down on others with contempt. Arrogance is first, then insolence: and in the last line the two are inverted, and with this difference, the disposition is denoted in the last line, and the acting in the former.—*Ed.*

[1] Ira furor brevis est.—*Epist.* ii. *ad Loll.*

of what the passage seems to require, I render it insolence, and it is the most suitable word. And God having declared that the insolence of Moab was seen by him, mentions also his *lies.* The word בדים, *badim,* means branches of trees, and sometimes sons or children, they being members of the community; and hence some render it "sons" here, as though the Prophet had said, that after the Moabites had been cut off, there would be none remaining to continue their name in the world. As then there was to be no posterity to the Moabites, they think that בדים, *badim* here means sons or children. But this view cannot be admitted, because we shall hereafter see that there was to be some residue to the Moabites. We cannot then take בדים, *badim,* but as referring to their vain boastings, for they were nothing but lies.

But we must consider what Jeremiah says; the word כן, *ken,* means right; and I take the two words as being in apposition, "His lies are not right;" that is, there is no stability in his lies. For when an apposition is explained, one of the words is turned to an adjective, or a preposition is inserted: *Not right* then *are his lies;* that is, in his lies there is no rectitude, or in his lies there is no stability. But the rectitude of which the Prophet now speaks, refers not to justice or equity, but to stability; and that it has this meaning may be gathered from other places. Then he says, that the boastings which the Moabites indulged in were vain, because God would not establish what they thought, or as they commonly say, what they presumed.

And then he adds the reason; the particle כן, *ken,* is to be taken here adverbially; it is an adverb of likeness, "so," or thus, *they shall not so do;* that is, as they had conceived in their minds. It is a confirmation of the last clause; for why was there to be no stability in their lies? because God would break down the Moabites, so that their counsels would be vain, without any effect. We now then perceive the meaning of the words. Isaiah, in chap. xvi. 6, uses nearly the same expressions, but he does not add this confirmation, that they would not be able to do what they intended. He only says, "there shall no rectitude be in their boastings,"

לא כן בדיו, *la ken bediu,* having previously spoken of the loftiness of their heart and of their ferocity and insolence; for he mentions the third word with the other two.[1]

Now this verse may be accommodated to our use; whenever the ungodly indulge in boasting, and insolently arrogate all things to themselves, let us not fear and tremble, but bear in mind what the Prophet teaches us here, whose admonition is very necessary; for he shews that this pride is in derision with God, and that when the ungodly fulminate in a terrible manner, there will be no effect to their lies. It follows, —

31. Therefore will I howl for Moab, and I will cry out for all Moab; *mine heart* shall mourn for the men of Kir-heres.	31. Propterea super Moab ululabo, et ad Moab totum (*hoc est,* penitus ad totam gentem) clamabo, meditabor ad viros urbis testæ.

Some think the last word to be a proper name, though, according to etymology, it is "the city of potsherd." They therefore give this rendering, "the strong city." But Isaiah calls it "Kir-hareseth," קִיר־הֲרֶשֶׂת; he extends the word by adding a syllable to it; but the word, however, is the same. Then he says, *I will think of the men of Kir-cheres.* The word הגה, *ege,* is properly to complain, to whisper, to murmur; and hence some render the words not improperly, "I will mutter to the men of the city of potsherd."[2]

The Prophet does not relate here what he would do, as I have before reminded you; but that he might represent to the life the ruin of Moab, he mentions their howling, crying,

[1] The versions and the *Targ.* all differ as to this verse. The *Vulg.* is the best; it takes בדים, branches, and also limbs, in a metaphorical sense, signifying strength. I give the following rendering,—

30. I know, saith Jehovah, his excess, (*i.e.* of pride;)
But not so his strength, not so have they done.

The mixture of numbers, singular and plural, is common in the prophets—"his" and "they." The meaning seems to be, that however excessive was the pride and insolence of Moab, they had no power fully to effect their purposes.—*Ed.*

[2] This paragraph has been transplanted from the text.

The verbs here are imperatives in the *Sept.* and *Syr.*, "Howl ye," &c.; and in the future tense in the *Targ.*, "they shall howl," &c. The *Vulg.* is according to the Hebrew. The last verb is in the third person, "He (Moab) will mourn for the men of Kir-heres." This city was on the extremity of Moab northward, as Jazer was on its extremity southward.—*Ed.*

and complaints. He then says, I will howl, cry aloud, and with a trembling voice complain, as those who are grievously oppressed with evils; at one time they complain, cry aloud, and howl, and at another they mutter inwardly, grumble and murmur. Thus the Prophet assumes the character of such persons, in order that he might more fully set forth the extreme calamity of that nation. He afterwards comes to particulars:—

32. O vine of Sibmah, I will weep for thee with the weeping of Jazer: thy plants are gone over the sea, they reach *even* to the sea of Jazer: the spoiler is fallen upon thy summer-fruits, and upon thy vintage.

32. A fletu Jaezer flebo (*vel,* a planctu plangam) tibi (*id est,* super te) vitis Sibmah; propagines tuæ penetrarunt ultra mare (trajecerunt mare,) usque ad mare Jaezer (*hoc est, cives Jaezer, vel propagines*) attigerunt; super æstivales (*vel,* æstivos) fructus tuos (*vel,* messes *proprie,*) et super vindemias tuas irruit vastator.

Here the Prophet shews more clearly what he had said generally before, that Sibmah would weep for her vines, after having wept for Jazer. These were cities in the land of Moab, as it appears from other places. Some give this rendering, "In comparison with the weeping" or mourning, &c.; and מן, *men,* as it is well known, has this meaning; but as ב, *beth,* "in weeping," is adopted by Isaiah, instead of מן, *men,* there is no doubt but that the Prophet means a continued mourning, when he says, *From* (or with) *the weeping of Jazer I will weep for thee, vine of Sibmah;* that is, there will be no end to weeping; for after the Moabites had mourned for the destruction of the city Jazer, a new cause of weeping would arise, for other cities would be destroyed, and especially Sibmah.

Now the region of Sibmah was very fertile, especially on account of the abundance of vines. Then the Prophet includes the whole wealth of that city under the word *vine;* nay, he designates the citizens as its shoots or young branches. *I will weep,* he says, "*over thee, the vine* of the vine-bearing region of *Sibmah;* for *thy shoots,* that is, thy wealth, *have passed over the sea,* and the citizens of Jazer, who were thy neighbours." He afterwards repeats respecting the city of Jazer what he had said, because its calamity was connected with the other, and was the same. For God had involved these two cities in the same destruction. *Jazer* then *came even to the sea.* Now *a waster rushed in:* Isaiah has shouting, הידד, *eidad,* which is added presently here; but the word there has quite a different meaning, that all rejoicing would cease. The word here is שדד, *shidad,* and means a waster or spoiler. *A waster* then *has fallen,* that is, has come with great irresistible force, on thy vintages and harvests; that is, that he may scatter and consume all things. It follows,—

33. And joy and gladness is taken from the plentiful field, and from the land of Moab; and I have caused wine to fail from the wine-presses: none shall tread with shouting; *their* shouting *shall be* no shouting.

33. Et tolletur lætitia et exultatio ab agro fertili (*neque enim est hic proprium loci nomen; scio quidem montem Carmelum esse celebrem, sed hic accipitur appellativè, quia agitur de regione Moab; sicut explicativè continuo post additur proprium nomen regionis,*) a terra Moab (*inquit Propheta,*) et vinum e torcularibus cessare faciam (*loquitur adhuc in persona Dei,*) non calcabit cum cantico, cantico, non erit canticum.

He pursues the same metaphor or comparison; for he says that all places would be laid waste and desolate, which before had been valuable and highly regarded on account of their fruitfulness. *Cease* then *shall all rejoicing from the land of Moab,* however fruitful it might have been. And then he adds, *I will make the wine to cease from the presses;* that is, no one shall press the grapes, that from them the wine may flow. And he adds, הידד הידד, *eidad, eidad, shouting, shouting, for there will be no shouting.* Some render הידד, *eidad,* "signal," *celeuma,* (*vel celeusma,*) a Greek word, but used also in Latin: κέλευμα is said by the Greeks to be the shouting of sailors, especially when they drive to the shore; they then rouse one another in rowing, and also congratulate one another, because they are nigh to land; for to see the harbour is a cause of special joy to sailors, as though it were a restoration to life and safety. But this word κέλευμα is applied to other things, as it may be said that reapers sing a *celeusma* when they finish their work. The vine-dressers had also their songs; and they were sung by heathen nations, as Virgil says. "Now the worn-out vine-dresser sings at the extreme rows of vines."[1] By extreme rows or ranks he seems to mean the extreme parts of the vines; for ex-

[1] Jam canit extremos effœtus vinitor antes.—*Geor.* ii. 417.

treme rows (*antes*) are properly prominences or overhanging stones. Now when they had come to the end, they sang and congratulated themselves as to the vintage. It was then a common custom among all nations.

The Prophet, now alluding to this, says, "They who shall tread in the winepress shall not be as usual joyful, so as to have their shouting, shouting, הידד הידד, *eidad, eidad.*" He repeats the word, because men greatly exult at the vintage, and are excessive in their rejoicings. This is the reason why the Prophet mentions the word twice. He then adds, *there shall be no shouting,* לא הידד, *la eidad,* because there would be no vineyards. Isaiah uses other expressions, but the meaning is the same. It now follows,—

34. From the cry of Heshbon *even* unto Elealeh, *and even* unto Jahaz, have they uttered their voice, from Zoar *even* unto Horonaim, *as* an heifer of three years old: for the waters also of Nimrim shall be desolate.

34. A clamore Hesebon usque ad Elealeh, ad Jahaes edent (ediderunt, *ad verbum*) vocem suam; a Zoar ad Choronaim vitula triennis (*aut,* vitulam triennem;) quia etiam aquæ Nimrim in vastationem erunt (in ariditatem *scilicet.*)

He continues the same subject; and by many and various expressions confirms the same thing, in order that the faithful might know that the destruction of the Moabites was really foretold, and that they might feel more assured that God announced nothing but what he would presently execute.

At the cry of Heshbon even to Elealeh they shall *send forth their voice.* He means, as before, that there would be continued cryings and howlings sounding forth from every part, and spreading through every region. He then adds, *From Zoar to Horonaim.* We must bear in mind the situations of these cities; but we may suppose that the Prophet chose those cities which were opposite to each other. Then from one corner to the other continual crying would be heard, because there would be everywhere desolation and ruin. And then he comes to another part, from one city even to another there would be a similar cry. In short, he shews that no part in the whole land of Moab would be in a quiet state and free from miseries. This is the meaning.

But he compares the whole land of Moab, or the city

Horonaim, to an heifer three years old, on account of its lasciviousness. Some restrict the comparison to the city Horonaim, for they read the words in apposition, "to Horonaim, an heifer three years old," putting the last words in the accusative case: but others read them apart, "an heifer three years old" is Moab. And I prefer this construction, because he afterwards adds another city, even Nimrim. As, however, it is a matter of no great moment, I will not contend with any one who may take the other view. Whether then it be one city or the whole country, it is compared to *an heifer three years old,* because that nation had long luxuriated in its own pleasures. Now, an heifer three years old, as it is well known, frisks and leaps, because it knows not what it is to fear the yoke; and then it is not worn out, as the case is with cows, who are weakened by having often brought forth young; and further, the milk that is taken from them exhausts their strength. But an heifer three years old is in her vigour and prime. In short, the Prophet intimates that the Moabites lived well, and as it were unrestrained, for they had long exulted in their abundance; and as they had plenty of wine and bread, they gave themselves up to luxury.[1]

He then adds, *Surely even the waters of Nimrim shall be a desolation.* Some think Nimrim to have been a city, and it is elsewhere called Nimra. Its waters are also mentioned by Isaiah, as the brooks of the willows. We may hence conclude that these waters were perpetual and flowed continually. But the Prophet speaks metaphorically as before, for the meaning is, that nothing would be so safe in the land of Moab as not to be destroyed, that nothing would be so fruitful as not to be dried up. Then by *the waters of Nimrim* he means the abundance which was in the whole country. For the Chaldeans did not dry up that river or those lakes, for it is certainly unknown whether there was a river there or a lake. But it is probable that

[1] A reason more suitable to the passage has been given for this comparison,—that Moab in its distress is compared to an heifer lowing for want of pasture and especially of water, for it follows that the waters of Nimrim would be dried up. See Isaiah xv. 5, 6.—*Ed.*

there was there abundance of waters, which were not dried up by the coming of an hostile army; but, as I have said, he shews by these figurative expressions that the whole land of Moab would be laid waste. It follows—

35. Moreover, I will cause to cease in Moab, saith the Lord, him that offereth in the high places, and him that burneth incense to his gods.	35. Et cessare faciam (*id est* profligabo) ex Moab, inquit Jehova, eum qui offert in excelso, et qui adolet (*aut*, suffitum facit) diis suis.

In this verse the Prophet expresses what he had before referred to, that God would become in such a way the avenger of the pride and cruelty of the Moabites as to punish them for their superstitions. They had descended from a pious father, for they were the posterity of Lot; but they had renounced the worship of the only true God, and had defiled themselves with the pollutions of heathens. Justly then does God declare that he would be the avenger of idolatry, while executing punishment on the pride and cruelty of the Moabites.

Now this passage, as innumerable others, clearly shews that idolatry and all profanation of divine worship, cannot finally escape punishment. God may indeed for a time connive at it, but he must necessarily at last appear as the vindicator of his own glory in punishing superstitions. But if he spared not the Moabites, to whom the law had not been given, and who had been corrupted through many long years, how shall they now escape unpunished, to whom God's Word is daily propounded, and in whose ears it sounds? Let us then remember that superstitions cannot be endured, for God will at length vindicate his own glory with regard to these abominations; for every superstition is nothing less than a profanation of God's glory, which is thus transferred to idols and vain inventions.

PRAYER.

Grant, Almighty God, that since thou hast once deigned to receive us under thy protection, we may have thee as our defence against our enemies, and that the more cruel and ferocious they become, and that the more heavily thou chastisest them, we may thus find that thou carest for our salvation, and flee also to thee with greater confidence, and that when we have experienced thy mercy, we may more readily give thee continual thanks, through Christ Jesus our Lord.—Amen.

Lecture One Hundred and Seventy-second.

36. Therefore mine heart shall sound for Moab like pipes, and mine heart shall sound like pipes for the men of Kir-heres: because the riches *that* he hath gotten are perished.

36. Propterea cor meum propter Moab tanquam tibiæ resonabit, et cor meum ad viros Kir-cheres (*vel,* urbis testaceæ, *ut dictum fuit*) sicuti tibiæ resonabit, quoniam thesaurus quem fecerunt, perierunt (*ad verbum est,* residuum fecit, perierunt; *sed loquitur de thesauris reconditis, quemadmodum patet ex simili loco Isaiæ, capite* 15.)

HERE the Prophet, as it has been before stated, does not mourn the calamity of the people of Moab, but assumes the character of others, so that the event might appear more evident, it being set as it were before our eyes; for as we have said, the wealth of the Moabites was so great at that time, that it dazzled the eyes of all. It was then difficult for the faithful to form an idea of this vengeance of God, therefore the Prophet transfers to himself the feelings of others, and relates what the Moabites would do, when God had so grievously afflicted them.

My heart, he says, *shall sound like pipes.* Some think that mournful pipes are meant, but I know not whether or not they were instruments of this kind; and there are those who think that חללים, *chellim,* were bag-pipes, but what is too refined I leave. The Prophet simply means that such would be the trepidation, that the hearts of the Moabites would make a noise like pipes. He repeats the same thing in different words, that his *heart* would *make a noise,* or sound, *for the men of Kir-heres,* of which city we spoke yesterday.

He now adds, *for the residue which they have made,* or which Moab has made, for the verb is in the singular number; and then, *they have perished,* where also there is a change of number; but the reference is to the word "residue," יתרת, *iteret,* which included hidden treasures, as we have stated.[1] Whatever then the Moabites had gained for themselves, and whatever they thought would be always safe, the Prophet declares that it would perish. Isaiah adds, "their substance," פקותם, *pekotem*, and says, that they would carry it to the willows, that is, to deserted places; as though he had said, that all the wealth of the Moabites would be scattered, as though it were, as they say, a thing forsaken. It now follows—

37. For every head *shall be* bald, and every beard clipped: upon all the hands *shall be* cuttings, and upon the loins sackcloth.	37. Quia omni capiti calvitium, et omni barbæ rasura (*ad verbum* diminutio; גרע *significat diminuere, sed hic accipitur pro rasura,*) et super omnes manus incisiones, et super lumbos saccus.

The Prophet describes at large a very great mourning. They were wont in great sorrow to pull off their hair, to shave their beard, and to put on sackcloth, or to gird it round their loins, and also to cut their hands with a knife or with their nails. As these things were signs of grief, Jeremiah puts them all together, in order to shew that the calamity of Moab would not be common, but what would cause to the whole people extreme lamentation. *They shall make bald,* he says, *their heads; their beard they shall pull off,* or shave; for the word, to diminish, may signify either. Then he adds, the *incisions in the hands;* they shall tear their faces and their hands with their nails, or as some say, with a knife or a razor. As to sackcloth, it was also a sign of mourning. It is indeed certain that it was formerly the practice for men, as though it was innate in human nature, in great calamities to spread ashes on the head and to put on sackloth. But he has added other excesses which are not very congenial to nature, for it is not agreeable to humanity to pull off the beard, to make bald the head, or to tear the hands and the face with the nails. These things shew excesses, suitable neither to men nor to women,—not

[1] As to this clause, widely different are all the versions; the *Targ.* gives the general sense. The word יתרת is evidently plural, the ו being wanting. "Reserves," as given by *Blayney*, is an exact rendering,—

Because the reserves he had made have perished.

Connected with this word is another in Isaiah xv. 7, which means "deposits;" both signify the wealth or treasures they had laid up.—*Ed.*

to women on the ground of modesty, nor to men on the ground of manliness and strength of mind.

But mankind never control themselves, and whether they mourn or rejoice, they are ever led away to excesses, observing no moderation. There was also another evil connected with sackcloth and ashes; for when it was God's design to lead men by these symbols to humble themselves, to consider their sins and to flee to his mercy, they were diverted to another end, even that he who mourned might appear miserable to others, and make a display of his weeping and tears. In short, besides excess, there was also this common evil, even hypocrisy. For men ever turn aside to what is vain, and dissemble in all things. But in this place there is no reason to dispute about mourning, for the Prophet means only that the Moabites would become most miserable, exhibiting all the symptoms of sorrow. It follows—

38. *There shall be* lamentation generally upon all the house-tops of Moab, and in the streets thereof: for I have broken Moab like a vessel wherein *is* no pleasure, saith the Lord.

38. Super omnia tecta Moab, et in compitis ejus omnino planctus (*hoc est*, ubique; כלה *sumitur adverbialiter*,) quoniam confregi Moab tanquam vas quod non est in pretio (*ad verbum*, non desiderium in ipso, *tanquam vas quod contemnitur, quod non appetitur*,) dicit Jehova.

The Prophet at the beginning of the verse continues the same subject, that the Moabites would weep and lament throughout *all their houses* and in *all their streets.* The reason is added in the second clause, because God would bring a severe judgment on that nation.

By saying that there would be *lamentation on all the roofs*, he refers to what was customary at that time, for they had their walks on the roofs or tops of their houses. Then he says, that the Moabites, in order to be more seen and to excite pity, would ascend on the roofs, and cry, howl, and lament there. But we must observe what is added, that the calamity would come from God; for it would not have been sufficient to foretell adversity, except this was added, that God ascended his tribunal to execute his judgments when he thus chastised the people. He also compares the people of Moab to a *despised vessel*, in order to make a distinction between God's children and aliens; for God does also chastise his own people when they sin, but he ceases not to love them and to regard them as precious. Now he says that Moab would be a vessel despised and rejected.[1] It now follows,—

39. They shall howl, *saying*, How is it broken down! how hath Moab turned the back with shame! so shall Moab be a derision and a dismaying to all them about him.

39. Quomodo contritus est? ululabunt (*alii vertunt*, ulularunt:) quomodo vertit cervicem Moab; pudefactus est; et fuit Moab in derisum, et in terrorem omnibus qui sunt in circuitu.

The Prophet still speaks in the person of others, and according to their feelings and not his own. He then says, that *howling*, they would say, through wonder, *How is it that Moab has been so broken*, that all had turned their backs, that Moab had become ashamed? He indirectly intimates, that though no one could then know God's judgment, which he now foretells, yet God would by the event prove that he had said nothing but in earnest. This wonder then was expressed for this purpose, that the Jews might know, that though the calamity of Moab would fill all with astonishment, and make them cry out as respecting an extraordinary thing, "What can this mean?" yet the fulfilment of his prophecy would be certain.

This is the meaning of the words when he says, *Howling, they will cry out, How has Moab been broken? and how has he turned his neck*, or as they say, his back? *Moab is ashamed;* and then, *he is made a derision*, which we have observed before. He adds, *a terror*, though some read, "a bruising;" but more suitable is fear or terror. For the Prophet means, that Moab would be to others a derision, and that he would be to others a dread, being an example of God's awful judgment.[2] And he says that he would be *a terror to all around*, that is, to the whole surrounding country, as well as a laughter and a derision. It follows,—

[1] All the versions and *Targ.* read, "as a useless vessel;" but the Hebrew is, "as a vessel without delight in it," *i.e.*, as a vessel which has nothing pleasing or agreeable in it.—*Ed.*

[2] The literal rendering is as follows,—

How broken! they howled;
How has Moab turned the back ashamed!
Thus Moab has become a derision
And a terror to all around him.

The past tense is used for the future.—*Ed.*

40. For thus saith the Lord, Behold, he shall fly as an eagle, and shall spread his wings over Moab.	40. Quia sic dicit Jehova, Ecce tanquam aquila volabit, et expandet alas suas super Moab.

Here again he introduces God's name, for it was necessary to confirm an incredible prophecy by his authority. "God is he," he says, "who declares that enemies will come, who will fly through all the land of Moab." He now compares the Chaldeans to eagles; and there is here a name understood which is not expressed. *Fly will he like an eagle*, that is, the king of Babylon with his army.

The sum of what is said then is, that however widely extended might be the country of Moab, yet there would be no corner into which the Chaldeans would not penetrate, because they would nearly equal the eagles in swiftness. Hence he adds, *They will extend their wings*, not to cherish, as eagles spread their wings over their young ones; but by extension he means, that they would seize on all the land of Moab; so that hiding places would be sought in vain, because the Chaldeans would from one part to another take possession of every place, however remote the Moabites might think it to be, and however they might hope its distance would render it safe. He afterwards adds,—

41. Kerioth is taken, and the strong holds are surprised, and the mighty men's hearts in Moab at that day shall be as the heart of a woman in her pangs.	41. Captæ sunt urbes (*est hic etiam mutatio numeri, sed dura esset translatio ad verbum, ideo satis est sensum tenere;* captæ *ergo* sunt urbes, *hoc est,* unaquæque urbs capta est, *deinde,*) arces (*vel,* propugnacula) comprehensa sunt (*est iterum mutatio numeri,*) et fuit cor virorum Moab in die illa tanquam cor mulieris quæ angitur (*vel,* premitur anxietate.)

I have already reminded you, that the Prophet is not using too many words in this extended discourse, for it was necessary to confirm at large what all would have otherwise rejected. He then says, that *the cities of Moab were taken,* that *strongholds were seized.* He mentions these things expressly, because the country of Moab thought that it was defended by cities and strongholds; and they thus thought, "Should the Chaldeans come and make an irruption, there are many cities who will oppose them; they will then have to spend much time in overcoming these obstacles. It may then so happen, that being broken down with fatigue they will return to their own country, and we shall recover what we may have lost." With this confidence then the Moabites deceived themselves, when they looked on their well fortified cities and strongholds. For this reason the Prophet now says, *Taken are the cities, and seized on are the strongholds.*[1]

There was another thing of which the Moabites boasted, that they possessed military valour; and yet they had not of late made a trial of their strength, as they had been indulging themselves in sloth and pleasures. But as they had formerly performed deeds worthy of being remembered, they despised, as I have said, their enemies, arrogating to themselves the credit of great valour. The Prophet, on the other hand, declares that their courage would vanish away: *The heart,* he says, *of the men of Moab shall become effeminate in that day,* softer than the heart of a woman, when oppressed with evils. It might have appeared a complete comparison, when he said that the men of Moab would be soft and effeminate; but he wished to express something more, and hence he added, that they would become softer than women when in great trouble. And by these words he intimates, that it is in God's power to melt the hearts of men, and to break down their fierceness, so that they who were like lions are made like does. And this ought to be carefully noticed; because courage is not only a special gift, but it is also necessary that God should daily and constantly strengthen those whom he has once made brave; otherwise they who are courageous above others will soon lose their valour. It follows,—

42. And Moab shall be destroyed from *being* a people, because he hath magnified *himself* against the Lord.

42. Et contritus est (perditus, excisus) Moab, ut non sit populus; quia adversus Jehovam sese extulit (magnificatus est, *ad verbum.*)

[1] The literal rendering of the verse is as follows, the nominative case to the two verbs being Moab, taken here as the country,—

41. Taken it is,—the cities;
And the strongholds,—it is seized:
And become shall the heart of the valiants of Moab,
In that day, like the heart of a woman in distress.

In our language it would be, "as to its cities," and, "as to its strongholds."—*Ed.*

He repeats what we have before observed, that the calamity of Moab would be a just reward for his pride and indeed his sacrilege. The Prophet then says that though God's vengeance might seem extremely grievous, yet it was most just, because the Moabites had not only been cruel against their neighbours, but also reproachful against God. Here, then, he condemns them first for cruelty, and then for their impious pride, *because they exalted themselves against God.*

But we must bear in mind the reason noticed before; for the Moabites did not openly boast that they were equal or superior to God, but when they raised their crests against God's people, they became contumelious against God himself, who had promised to be the protector and the Father of his people. As then the Moabites thus despised the protection and promise of God, they are here justly condemned by the Prophet, that they *exalted themselves against God.* And this ought to be carefully noticed, so that we may not do any wrong to the godly, for God will at length shew that he is injured in their persons. And then also no common consolation may be hence derived, that all who molest us are carrying on war against God, and that all who injure us act sacrilegiously towards him. For the Prophet has before explained how the Moabites gloried against God, even because they regarded the children of Israel with derision. It follows,—

43. Fear, and the pit, and the snare, *shall be* upon thee, O inhabitant of Moab, saith the Lord.	43. Terror et fovea et laqueus super te, habitator Moab, dicit Jehova.
44. He that fleeth from the fear shall fall into the pit; and he that getteth up out of the pit shall be taken in the snare: for I will bring upon it, *even* upon Moab, the year of their visitation, saith the Lord.	44. Qui fugerit a facie terroris incidet in foveam; et qui ascenderit e fovea laqueo capietur; quoniam adducam super eam, super Moab, annum visitationis ipsorum, dicit Jehova.

By these words the Prophet shews, that though the Moabites should adopt many means of escape, yet they should be taken, for God's hand would everywhere entrap them. He mentions *terror* first, then the *pit,* and thirdly, the *snare,*[1] that is, "Thou wilt be so frightened that terror

[1] There is a striking alliteration in these words, fear, pit, snare—*peched, pechet, pech.*—*Ed.*

will compel thee to flee; but when thou fleest, pits will be in the way into which thou wilt fall: but if thou wilt rise from the pit, snares will surround thee, and thou wilt be taken." We then see that by these similitudes nothing else is meant but God's judgment, which impended over the Moabites, so that it could by no means be averted by them; for no ways could be found out by which they could escape, because fear would force them to flee, and would, as it is usually the case, deprive them of mind and thought, and thus they would be driven here and there, and could not move from any place without meeting with a pit, and, as it has been said, after the pit there would be the snare.

Now all this has not been expressed without reason, because we know with how many flatteries men are wont to delude themselves when God summons them to judgment; for they immediately look around here and there, and promise themselves impunity, and then they hope for light punishment, as though they were at peace with God. But the unbelieving harden themselves, as Isaiah says, as though they had made a covenant with death and a compact with hell. (Is. xxviii. 15.) As, then, the wicked set up security in opposition to God, the Prophet here shews that there are many ways in his hand, by which he can take the fugitives, and those who seem to think that they can escape through their own astuteness; and hence he said, *He who flees from terror*, that is, from present danger, *shall fall into the pit*, that is, when the Moabites shall now think themselves secure, they shall meet with new dangers, and new deaths will surround them.

But we must notice what is added at the end of the verse, *Because I will bring on Moab the year of their visitation.* Here God sustains the minds of the godly, that they might not faint on account of long delay. As, then, the faithful might have been worn out with weariness while God prolonged the time as to the Moabites, the Prophet says, "Come at length shall the year of their visitation." For as it has been stated elsewhere, by this mode of speaking God intimates that though he for a time passes by things and connives at them, he will at length shew himself to be the judge of the world. We would have God ever to act in haste; and hence, when he exhorts us to patience, all our feelings rebel. This happens, because we do not consider that the fitness of times is determined by his will. Hence he speaks now of *the year of visitation,* as though he had said, "I may for a time appear to disregard human affairs and to neglect my own, while my people are cruelly oppressed by the wicked; but the time of visitation will come." For by this word "visitation," God means that there are changes, or, as they commonly say, revolutions, which are fixed and certain. We now then understand the design of God, when he says, that he would bring a visitation on the Moabites. It follows,—

45. They that fled stood under the shadow of Heshbon, because of the force: but a fire shall come forth out of Heshbon, and a flame from the midst of Sihon, and shall devour the corner of Moab, and the crown of the head of the tumultuous ones.

45. In umbra Hesbon steterunt à fortitudine (*aut,* violentia) fugientes; quia ignis egressus est ex Hesbon, et flamma è medio Sion, et vorabit angulum Moab, et extremitatem et verticem filiorum tumultus.

He confirms what is said in the last verse, that the Moabites would in vain resort to their strongest cities, even *Heshbon* and *Sihon;* because a flame would thence break forth, which would consume the whole land. We hence see that God took away from the Moabites all their vain confidences, and shewed that no defences could stand against his power, when once he rose up for judgment.

The fleers, he says, *shall stand under the shadow of Heshbon,* thinking that there would be a safe refuge in that city, and in others.[1] But the particle כי, *ki,* seems not to me to be here causal, but rather an affirmative, or even an adversative; *but,* or *surely a fire has gone forth from Heshbon, and a flame from Sihon.* The Prophet, I doubt not, borrowed these words from Moses, for he says in Numbers xxi. 28, that

[1] The word "strength" is here omitted. Calvin's version is, "Under the shadow of Heshbon stood they who had fled from strength," or violence, *i.e.,* of their enemies. Some connect it with "stood," the fugitives "stood for strength," or, "without strength," which, perhaps, is preferable: they stood under the shadow or protection of Heshbon, and obtained no help; so far was this from being the case, that from Heshbon would go forth fire, that is, "the spoiler," or, destroyer, before often mentioned. Then כי would have its usual meaning, *for,* as giving a reason why the fugitives remained without strength or help, under the protection of Heshbon.—*Ed.*

a fire had gone forth from Heshbon; and there the expression is given as an old proverb. There is no doubt but that enemies had triumphed over that city when it was taken; for that whole song spoken by Moses is ironical, and in saying that fire had gone forth, he referred to their counsels, for they thought that city sufficiently strong against enemies. Now the Prophet says, that what had been formerly said of Heshbon would be again fulfilled, that it would be, as it were, the beginning of the fire. The meaning then, as I think, is, that the Moabites indeed thought, that they would have a quiet and agreeable shadow under the protection of the city Heshbon, and of the city Sihon; but what was to be? even that these two cities would become, as it were, the beginnings of the fire. How, or in what way? even because the probability is, that there those counsels were taken which provoked the Chaldeans. We indeed know that riches and power always produce haughtiness and false confidence in men; for in villages and small towns wars are not contrived; but the great cities gather the wood and kindle the fire; and the fire afterwards spreads and pervades the whole land.[1]

This, then, is what our Prophet means, when he says, that *fire went forth from Heshbon*, even contrary to the expectation of the people, for they thought that were all things to go to ruin, there yet would be safety for them in that city: *go forth,* he says, *shall fire* from the city *Heshbon, and a flame from the midst of Sihon, and it shall consume the corner of Moab,* and all his extremities; for by קדקד, *kadkad,* he means all parts. Extremity is elsewhere taken for a part; but he does not mean that fire would come to all parts or extreme corners, only as it were to touch them slightly: but he intimates that the whole land would be consumed by this fire; it would thus spread itself to its very extremities.[2]

[1] Most give a different explanation of this fire, that it designated "the spoiler" that was to come on Moab. That fire has often this meaning is evident. See Judges ix. 20.—*Ed.*

[2] The last clause is evidently a quotation from Numbers xxiv. 17: it is not literally the same, but the meaning is so. It is "corner" here and not "corners," as in Numbers; and the word there is קרקר, and not קדקד as here, only there are some copies which have the former word here. In that case, the passage would read thus,—

But as I have already said, the Prophet alludes to that old saying mentioned by Moses, (Numbers xxi. 27, 28.) Further, there is no doubt but that Heshbon and Sihon were then in the possession of that nation; for they had taken away many cities from the Israelites, and thus the children of Israel had been reduced to narrower limits. At length the tribe of Judah alone remained after the overthrow of the kingdom of Israel. When they were driven into Chaldea, it was an easy thing for the Moabites to make that their own which belonged to no one. Besides, as they had helped the Chaldeans and betrayed that miserable people, and had thus acted perfidiously towards their brethren, a reward was given to them. But when at length they themselves dreaded the power of the Babylonian monarchy, they began to change their minds, and endeavoured to obstruct the farther progress of the Chaldeans. Hence then a war was contemplated, and the occasion was given. He then speaks of Heshbon and Sihon as chief cities; and there is no doubt but that Sihon derived its name from a king who ruled there. For we know that there was a king bearing this name; but as he speaks here of a place, it is probable, that the king's name was given to the city in order to commemorate it.

He at length adds, that this *fire* and *flame* would devour the *top of the head of the sons of Saon*, or tumult. But he calls the Moabites tumultuous, because they before made a great noise, and were dreaded by their neighbours. As then all their neighbours had been frightened, in a manner, by their voice alone, he calls them sons of tumult, or tumultuous men, from the effect produced. It follows—

46. Woe be unto thee, O Moab! the people of Chemosh perisheth: for thy sons are taken captives, and thy daughters captives.	44. Væ tibi Moab! periit populus Chamos, quia tracti sunt (*vel*, rapti) filii tui in captivitatem, et filiæ tuæ in exilium.

And it shall devour the corner of Moab,
And destroy the sons (or children) of tumult.

שת in Numbers is probably for שאת, which means the same as the word here used, coming from the same root, and properly rendered "tumult."

This passage is omitted in the *Sept.*; the *Vulg.* renders קדקד, "verticem," the crown or top of the head; but the *Syr.* and *Targ.* drop the metaphor, and render it "chiefs" or nobles.—*Ed.*

Here the Prophet, as he comes to the end of his prophecy, suddenly exclaims, *Woe to thee!* as though he had said, that words failed him to express the grievousness of God's vengeance. There is then more force in this single expression, than if he had at large described the miseries of that nation. He then adds, *The people of Chemosh have perished.* The Prophet again intimates, that the Moabites vainly confided in their idol, Chemosh; they thought that there would be a sure safety to them from their god, who was, as they commonly say, a tutelar god. But the Prophet says, that their superstition would avail them nothing, for they and their idol would perish together. He exults over this fictitious god, that on the other hand he might extol the power of the only true God. For there is here an implied contrast between the God of Israel and Chemosh whom the Moabites worshipped.

He then adds, *Thy sons and thy daughters shall be carried away into captivity.* The Prophet does not seem here to continue the same subject; for he had said before that ruin or destruction was coming on the Moabites, but he now mitigates that punishment, and speaks only of exile. But as captivity is like death, as it abolishes the name of a nation, he speaks correctly and suitably. And then we must observe, that God, for a time, so executed his vengeance on the Moabites, that he left them some hope as to the future, according to what follows in the last verse—

47. Yet will I bring again the captivity of Moab in the latter days, saith the Lord. Thus far *is* the judgment of Moab.

47. Et reducam captivitatem Moab in fine dierum (*hoc est*, post longum tempus,) dicit Jehova. Hactenus judicium Moab.

Here, as we see, God gives place to his mercy, so that the Moabites should not wholly perish. At the same time, things which seem to be contrary agree together, even that destruction was nigh the people of Moab, and yet that some would remain alive, who would afterwards renew the name of the nation, as it was God's purpose to restore the Moabites to their former state. These things, as I have said, seem inconsistent, and yet they may be easily reconciled; for it was God's will so to destroy the Moabites, that those who died might not be without hope; and then, those who remained alive were not deemed to be among the living, but in exile they were like the dead. God, indeed, ever supported the godly with hope, even when they were driven into Babylon: but as to the Moabites, the living as well as the dead, had no hope. Why, then, was this promise given? not for the sake of the Moabites; but that the Jews might feel assured that God would at length be propitious to them; he promises pardon to the Moabites as it were accidentally, so to speak, and thus unavowedly stretches forth his hand to them, but with a design through this mercy to give to the Israelites a taste of his paternal favour. What remains we must reserve for the lecture to-morrow.

PRAYER.

Grant, Almighty God, that as thou wert formerly pleased to extend thy mercy to aliens, who were wholly estranged from thee, that the children of Abraham, whom thou didst adopt, might hence have a hope of deliverance,—O grant, that we may also, at this day, cast our eyes on the many proofs of thy goodness, manifested towards the ungodly and the unworthy, so as to make an application for our own benefit, and never to doubt but that however miserable we may be, thou wilt yet be ever propitious to us, since thou hast deigned to choose us for thy peculiar people, and hast promised to be ever our God and Father in Christ Jesus our Lord.—Amen.

Lecture One Hundred and Seventy-Third.

We began in our last lecture to explain what the Prophet has said of the restoration of Moab; and we said that some hope of mercy to the unworthy is left here. For though they had in various ways provoked the wrath of God, yet he was unwilling wholly to destroy them; and from that nation also Christ, the Redeemer of the world, derived his origin. Here, then, we have a memorable instance of God's favour, that he did not wholly obliterate that nation, which yet had deserved extreme punishment. We said further, that it was, as it were, accidental that the Prophet promised favour to the Moabites; for we know that the people of Israel were then a people distinct from other nations. God then so disposed of his favour, that when a few drops came to heathens, it was, as it were, adventitious. For it was not his will to cast indiscriminately to all the bread which he had designed for his own children, as Christ also says, that it is not right that the children's bread should be given to dogs. (Matt. xv. 26.) God, however, designed to shew some preludes of his mercy towards alien nations, when he so directed the promises of salvation to his chosen people as not wholly to exclude the heathens, as we have an example here in the Moabites. We shall hereafter see the same as to the Ammonites. Now follows—

CHAPTER XLIX.

1. Concerning the Ammonites, thus saith the Lord, Hath Israel no sons? hath he no heir? why *then* doth their king inherit Gad, and his people dwell in his cities?

1. Ad filios Ammon: Sic dicit Jehova, An filii non sunt Israeli? an hæres non est ei? quare hæreditate possidet rex eorum Gad et populus ejus in urbibus ejus habitat?

We have said that the Ammonites were not only contiguous to the Moabites, but had also derived their origin from Lot, and were thus connected with them by blood. Their origin was indeed base and shameful, for they were, as it is well known, the offspring of incest. There was, however, the bond of fraternity between them, because both nations had the same father. God had spared them when he brought up his people from Egypt; for in remembrance of the holy man Lot, he would have both peoples to remain uninjured. But ingratitude doubled their crime, for these impious men ceased not in various ways to harass the children of Abraham. For this reason, therefore, does Jeremiah now prophesy against them.

And we see here, again, the object of this prophecy and the design of the Holy Spirit in announcing it, even that the Israelites might know that they were not so completely cast away by God, but that there remained some remnants of his paternal favour; for if the Moabites and the Ammonites had been free from all evils, it would have been a most grievous trial; it would have been enough to overwhelm weak minds to see a people whom God had adopted, miserably oppressed and severely chastised, while heathen nations were remaining quiet in the enjoyment of their pleasures, and exulting also over the calamities of others. God, then, in order to mitigate the grief and sorrow which the children of Israel derived from their troubles and calamities, shews that he would yet shew them favour, because he would carry on war against their enemies, and become the avenger of all the wrongs which they had suffered. It was no common consolation for the Israelites to hear that they were still the objects of God's care, who, nevertheless, seemed in various ways to have poured forth his wrath upon them in a full stream. We now, then, see the reason why Jeremiah denounced destruction on the Ammonites, as he did before on the Moabites.

Then he says, *To the children of Ammon:*[1] *Are there no children to Israel? Hath he no heir?* It was a trial very grievous to the miserable Israelites to see a part of the inheritance promised them by God forcibly taken from them by the Ammonites; for what must have come to their minds but that they had been deceived by vain promises? But it had happened, that the Ammonites had deprived the children of Israel of a part of their inheritance. Hence the Prophet teaches us here, that though God connived for a time, and passed by this robbery, he yet would not suffer the Ammonites to go unpunished for having taken to themselves what justly belonged to others. Hence it is added, *Why doth their king inherit Gad?*

I know not why *Jerome* rendered מלכם, *melkam*, as though it were the name of an idol, as the word is found in the Prophet Amos.[2] But it is evident that Jeremiah speaks

[1] Literally it is, "To the children of Ammon thus saith Jehovah:" so the *Sept.*, the *Vulg.*, and the *Targ.* There are prophecies concerning Ammon in Ezek. xxi. 28-32; xxv. 2-7; Amos i. 13-15; and in Zeph. ii. 8-11.—*Ed.*

[2] "Milcom" is given by the *Sept.*, the *Vulg.*, and the *Syr.*; but "their king" by the *Targ.* In Amos i. 15, the *Vulg.* and *Syr.* are the same; but the *Sept.* have "kings," and the *Targ.* is the same as here. There

here of the king, for immediately after he adds, *his people. Their king*, then, he says, *inherits Gad.* Gad is not the name of a place, as some think, but Mount Gilead, which had been given to that tribe. The Prophet says that they possessed the country of the Gadites; for they had been ejected from their portion, and the children of Ammon had occupied what had been given by God to them. And this is confirmed by the Prophet Amos, when he says, "For three of the transgressions of the children of Ammon, and for four, I will not be propitious to them, because they have cut off the mountain of Gilead."[1] (Amos i. 13.) He speaks there metaphorically, because God had fixed the limits between the tribe of Gad and the children of Ammon, so that both might be satisfied with their own inheritance. But the children of Ammon had broken through and expelled the tribe of Gad from the cities of Mount Gilead. This, then, is what now our Prophet means, even that they had taken to themselves that part of the land which had been allotted to the children of Gad; for it immediately follows, *and his people dwell in his cities*, even in the cities which had been given by lot to that tribe; for we know that a possession beyond Jordan had been given to the children of Gad. We now, then, perceive the meaning of the words.

God, then, shews that he had not forgotten his covenant, though he had for a time suffered the Ammonites to invade the inheritance which he had conferred on the children of Israel; yet the Gaddites would at length recover what had been unjustly taken from them. For it was a robbery not to be endured, that the Ammonites should have dared to take to themselves that land, which was not the property of men, but rather of God himself, for he had called it his rest, because he would have his people to dwell there. And

was a king of Ammon, Jer. xxvii. 3; and there is one passage in which the possession of a country is ascribed to a heathen god, to Chemosh, see Judges xi. 24. But "inheriting" is more suitably applied to a king than to an idol; and the contrast in the next verse is with Israel and not with God, "Israel shall be heir," &c. Most probably, then, the king is meant, and not the idol.—*Ed.*

[1] The quotation is not literally given, but the meaning of the passage. —*Ed.*

though God inflicted a just punishment on the Gaddites when he expelled them from their inheritance, yet he afterwards punished the children of Ammon, as he is wont to chastise his own children by the hand of the wicked, and at length to render them also their just reward. It now follows—

2. Therefore, behold, the days come, saith the Lord, that I will cause an alarm of war to be heard in Rabbah of the Ammonites; and it shall be a desolate heap, and her daughters shall be burnt with fire: then shall Israel be heir unto them that were his heirs, saith the Lord.	2. Propterea ecce dies veniunt, dicit Jehova, et audire faciam (*vel*, faciam resonare) super Rabbath filiorum (*vel*, super filios) Ammon clangorem prælii, et erit in acervum vastitatis, et filiæ ejus igne comburentur, et possidebit Israel possessores suos, dicit Jehova.

God testifies here plainly that he would not suffer the Ammonites for ever to enjoy their unjust plunder. He says that *the days would come*, in order to sustain with hope the minds of his children: for the Prophet announced his prediction at a time when the Ammonites were in a state of security; and then, some years elapsed while that people enjoyed their spoils. He therefore holds here the minds of the faithful in suspense, that they might learn patiently to wait until the fixed time of God's vengeance came. For this reason, then, he says, that the *days* would *come* when God would *cause the trumpet of war to resound in Rabbah.* He speaks as of a thing extraordinary, for the Ammonites thought, as we shall see, that they should never be in any danger. As, then, they proudly trusted in their own strength, the Prophet speaks here of the trumpet of war in Rabbah, which was the metropolis of the whole land. Some think that it was Philadelphia, a name given to it by Ptolemy. Interpreters, however, do not agree; but the opinion mostly received is, that it was Philadelphia. Now, as to the main thing, there is no doubt but that it was then the chief seat of government, and the capital of the kingdom, because the Prophet, stating a part for the whole, includes the whole land when he speaks of this city.

He says that she would become *a heap of desolation.* But this was then wholly incredible, because Rabbah was so fortified that no one thought that it could be destroyed. But the Prophet now declares that the whole city would be demolished, so that neither walls nor private houses would remain, but that it would be a deformed mass of ruins. He adds, *her daughters shall be burned with fire.* By daughters he no doubt understands towns and villages; and hence is confirmed what I have said, that Rabbah was then the chief city of the whole land of Ammon. At the end of the verse he says, *Israel shall possess all who possess them.*[1] By these words Jeremiah again confirms what I have slightly referred to, that the calamity of the Ammonites would be a testimony as to God's paternal kindness towards his chosen people, because he resolved to avenge the wrongs done to them. As, then, God undertook the cause of the Israelites as his own, he sufficiently manifested the favour he had intended for his people, and for no other reason, but because he had gratuitously chosen them.

It may be asked, when was this prophecy fulfilled? God, indeed, under David, gave some indication of their future subjection, but Israel never possessed that land. Indeed, from that time Ammon had not been brought low until after the overthrow of Israel. It then follows that what Jeremiah predicted here, was not fully accomplished except under the kingdom of Christ. David humbled that nation, because he had received a great indignity from the king of Ammon; and he took also Rabbah, as it is evident from sacred history. (2 Sam. xii. 29, &c.; 1 Chron. xx. 1, 2.) He was yet satisfied with making the people tributary. From that time they not only shook off the yoke, but exercised authority within the borders of Israel; and that the Israelites had recovered what they had lost, we nowhere read.[2] Then Israel began to possess power over the Ammonites when the kingdom of Christ was established; by which all heathen nations were not only brought into subjection and under the yoke, but all unworthy of mercy were also reduced

[1] Literally it is, "And Israel shall inherit his inheritors." The Ammonites claimed to be the heirs, and Israel succeeded them as the right heir. This prophecy was fulfilled as recorded in 1 Macc. v. 6, 7, 28-36.—*Ed.*

[2] Except in 1 Macc. v. 6-8. The victories of the Maccabees were, no doubt, a literal accomplishment of this prophecy. See verses 33, 34; where the sound of the "trumpets" is expressly mentioned.—*Ed.*

to nothing. What is added at the end of the verse is not superfluous; for the Prophet introduces God as the speaker, because he speaks of great things, and of which it was difficult to be fully convinced. It now follows—

3. Howl, O Heshbon, for Ai is spoiled: cry, ye daughters of Rabbah, gird you with sackcloth; lament, and run to and fro by the hedges: for their king shall go into captivity, *and* his priests and his princes together.	3. Ulula Chesbon, quoniam vastata est Hai; vociferamini filiæ Rabbath, accingite vos saccis, plangite, discurrite per sepes, quoniam rex eorum in captivitatem profectus est, et sacerdotes ejus et principes cum ipso.

The Prophet now triumphs, as it were, over the land of Ammon, and, according to his accustomed manner, as we have before seen; for had the prophets spoken without metaphors, and simply narrated the things treated of by them, their words would have been frigid and inefficient, and would not have penetrated into the hearts of men. This, then, is the reason why the prophets adopted an elevated style, and adorned with grandeur their prophecies; for they never, like rhetoricians, affected eloquence, but necessity so urged them, that they represented to the eyes those things which they could not otherwise form a conception of in their minds. On this subject we have spoken often already; but I am again constrained briefly to touch on it, because those who are not well acquainted with Scripture, and do not understand the design of the Holy Spirit, may think that words only are here poured forth. But when we duly weigh what I have said, then we shall readily acknowledge that the Prophet did not, without reason, enlarge on what he had previously said.

Howl, thou Heshbon, he says, *for Ai is laid waste.* These were two neighbouring cities: hence he exhorts Heshbon to howl on seeing the overthrow of another city. He then adds, *Cry,* or cry aloud, *ye daughters of Rabbah.* He again repeats what he had before touched upon as to the city Rabbah. *Gird yourselves,* he says, *with sackcloth,* or put on sackcloth. He does not here exhort the citizens of Rabbah to repentance, but he speaks according to the customs of the people, as it has been stated elsewhere. Sackcloth was, indeed, a symbol of penitence; when the miserable wished humbly to flee to God's mercy, and to confess their sins, they put on sackcloth. But the unbelieving imitated the faithful without discretion or judgment. Hence it was, that they scattered ashes on their heads, that without any reason they put on sackcloth. What was then commonly done is now mentioned by Jeremiah ; *Put on sackcloth,* he says, *lament and run here and there by the fences.*

He afterwards adds in the third person, *for gone is their king into captivity.* He expressed this, that the Israelites might know, that though that kingdom flourished for a time, yet the day of which the Prophet had spoken would come, when the condition of the Ammonites would be nothing better than that of the Israelites ; whose king, as it was known, had been driven into exile, together with the priests and princes. The Prophet now denounces the same punishment on the Ammonites, that not only their king would be driven into another land, as a captive, but also their princes and their priests. It follows—

4. Wherefore gloriest thou in the valleys, thy flowing valley, O backsliding daughter? that trusted in her treasures, *saying,* Who shall come unto me?

4. Quid gloriaris reconditis tuis? defluxit profunditas tua (*ad verbum,* vallis tua ; *sed quoniam* עמק *significat profundum esse* ideo עמקים *sunt profunditates ;* cur *ergo* gloriaris in tuis profunditatibus? *sed non repugno quin transferamus,* quid gloriaris in vallibus tuis? defluvit vallis tua, *est idem nomen,*) filia aversatrix, quæ confidit in reconditis suis (in thesauris suis,) Quis veniet ad me?

As the minds of men continually vacillate, because they do not sufficiently consider the infinite power of God, the Prophet, that he might remove all obstacles which might have rendered his prophecy doubtful, now declares that the Ammonites gloried in vain in their valleys. Some understand by valleys a fertile land, well watered. But the Prophet, as I think, refers rather to fortified places. He then says, that they in vain *gloried in their deep valleys ;* as they were surrounded with mountains, so they thought that they could not be approached. He derides this vain confidence, *Why,* he says, *dost thou glory in thy valleys,* or, profundities? *Flown down has thy valley.* By saying, that the *valley,* or depth, had flown down, he alludes to its situation: for when any one considers a region situated among mountains, the land appears as flowing, like a river gliding between its banks. It is then a striking allusion to a deep place, when he says that the *valley flowed down.*[1] It was the same as though he had said, "Thy depth has vanished," or, "It shall not be to thee such a protection as thou thinkest." But the meaning is, that though the Ammonites, confiding in their defences, disregarded all attacks of enemies, they would yet be exposed to plunder; for their mountains and valleys would avail them nothing, notwithstanding the opinion they entertained, that they were so fortified, that they could not be assailed.

He calls Ammon a *rebellious*, or a backsliding *daughter*, though he mentions no particulars. But Ezekiel and also Amos and Zephaniah, these three, clearly shew why God was so severe towards the Ammonites, (Ezekiel xxv.; Amos i. 13; Zeph. ii. 9;) it was because they had uttered blasphemies against Him and his people, exulted over the miseries and calamities of the chosen people, and plundered them when they saw them overcome by their enemies. For these reasons, then, our Prophet now calls them a *rebellious* people: they had proudly exalted themselves against God, and exercised cruel tyranny as to the miserable Israelites, who were yet, as it has been stated, connected with them by blood.

[1] The verb means to flow out, and to flow away, to waste. The latter seems to be the meaning here, "wasted has thy valley." (See Lam. iv. 9.) It has a noun after it, when it means to flow out in the sense of abounding; but when used intransitively, it means to flow away in the sense of wasting,—

Why gloriest thou in deep valleys!
Flown away has thy deep valley,
O daughter, who hast turned aside,
Who hast trusted in thy treasures,
Who hast said in thine heart, "Who can come to me?"

The participle השובבה, "who hast turned aside," or away, is rendered "delicate," by the *Vulg.*, and "beloved," by the *Syr.*, and the idea of impudence or folly, is conveyed by the *Sept.* and *Targ.* How the word could be so rendered, it is difficult to say. The verb means to turn to or from. Being a reduplicate here, it means to turn away resolutely; hence "rebellious" would be no improper rendering. "Her" before "treasures," refers to "daughter," but in our language "thy" reads better, as adopted by the *Vulg.* and the *Syr.* There is an addition in several copies of the words, "Who hast said in thine heart," and all the versions have what corresponds with them.—*Ed.*

Who trusts in her secrecies, or hidden places: rendered by some, "in her treasures." But as אצר, *atser*, means to hide, the reference is, as I think, to strongholds; for the Prophet in the next words explains himself, *Who can come to me?* It appears, then, that the Ammonites thought themselves thus secure, because they were not exposed to their enemies, but protected by their mountains, as though they were in hiding places. This boasting sufficiently shews that they did not so much trust in their treasures as in their hidden places, because they dwelt in recesses. The meaning is, that though the Ammonites gloried that they were beyond the reach of danger, yet God would become the avenger of the cruelty which they had exercised towards their relations, the Israelites. It follows—

5. Behold, I will bring a fear upon thee, saith the Lord God of hosts, from all those that be about thee; and ye shall be driven out every man right forth; and none shall gather up him that wandereth.

5. Ecce ego adduco super te terrorem, dicit Dominator, Jehova exercituum, ab omnibus circuitibus tuis, et expellemini, quisque coram facie sua, et nullus erit qui colligat dispersos.

Jeremiah at length concludes his prophecy, by saying, that God would dissipate that foolish confidence through which the Ammonites were filled with pride, *because he would bring a terror* on them. He sets up terror in opposition to that security in which the Ammonites lay torpid; for they were inebriated, as it were, with their pleasures. And then the strongholds by which they thought themselves protected, so hardened their hearts, that they feared no danger. God then sets up this terror in opposition to the false arrogance by which they were inflated: *I bring*, then, *a terror from all around thee.* And this was not without reason added, for the Ammonites thought that they could, on some side, escape, if enemies pressed hard on them; and as there were many outlets, they thought it impossible that they should fall into the hands of enemies. But God declares that they would be in every way full of fear, for terror would surround and besiege them, so that they could not escape.

He then adds, *Ye shall be driven out, every one to his face,* or, before his face. This would be the effect of terror, because God would deprive them of all thought; for when we flee in haste, and only regard any opening that may present itself, it is evident that we are driven by terror. As we say in French, *Il court devant soi;* so the Prophet says here, *Ye shall be driven out, every one before his face*, that is, "ye shall flee wherever a place may be open to you." He shews that they would be so full of fear, that they would not consider which would be the best way, nor think of a safe retreat; they would, in short, think of nothing but of flight. And to the same purpose is what follows: *There will be none to gather the dispersed:* for when trembling seizes the hearts of the multitude, they can yet be recalled, when one who has more courage than the rest encourages them to stop, as we know that many armies have been in this way saved; for as to soldiers, when suddenly seized with fear, a leader has often been able to gather them again. But the Prophet, when he says, that there would be none to call them back from flight, intimates their destruction. He at length subjoins—

6. And afterward I will bring again the captivity of the children of Ammon, saith the Lord.	6. Et postea reducam captivitatem filiorum Ammon, dicit Jehova.

He now says the same thing of the children of Ammon, as he said before of the Moabites, that some hope yet remained for them, for God would at length shew mercy to that nation. But, as we have said, these promises were but adventitious, because God had chosen but one people to be a Father to them; and the children of Abraham must be viewed as distinct from all other nations. But though God built, as it were, a wall to separate his people from aliens, it was yet his will to give some preludes of his favour, and of the calling of the Gentiles. The Prophet, then, had here a regard to the kingdom of Christ. The promise, no doubt, extended itself to his coming; for he speaks of the calling of the Gentiles, which God deferred until he manifested his own Son to the world. It is the same then, as though the Prophet had said, that God's mercy would at length be shewed to the Ammonites in common with others;

that is, when God would gather his Church from the whole world, and unite, in one body, those who were before scattered. Nor is there a doubt but that the Prophet, speaking of the children of Ammon, intended to shew what was to be manifested through all parts of the world. And so it is, that on our calling is our salvation founded, for we see that the gospel has not been, without a design, proclaimed to the world; but as God had determined and settled this from the beginning, so we see that Jeremiah was a herald of our adoption. This, then, is the import of what is said. He afterwards passes over to the children of Edom. But I cannot now proceed farther.

PRAYER.

Grant, Almighty God, that as thou didst formerly give so many proofs how great and singular was thy love towards the children of Abraham, whom it had pleased thee to choose as thy people,—O grant that we at this day may also enjoy the same favour, since we have been admitted into a participation of the same union, and that we may be so chastised as never to lose the hope of thy mercy, but that we may so taste it as to meditate on that celestial kingdom, which has been obtained for us by the blood of thine only-begotten Son.—Amen.

Lecture One Hundred and Seventy-Fourth.

7. Concerning Edom, thus saith the Lord of hosts, *Is* wisdom no more in Teman? is counsel perished from the prudent? is their wisdom vanished?

7. Ad Edom (contra Edom) sic dicit Jehova exercituum, An non amplius sapientia in Theman? periitne consilium ab intelligentibus? computruit (*vel*, supervacua facta est) sapientia ipsorum?

Here Jeremiah turns to Idumeans, who were most inveterate enemies to the chosen people, though their origin ought to have disposed them to shew kindness to them, for they had descended from the same father, even Abraham. The Idumeans also gloried in their holy descent, and had circumcision in common with the Jews. It was then a most impious cruelty that the Idumeans entertained such bitter hatred towards their own blood. Hence our Prophet most severely reproved them, as also did Ezekiel and Obadiah. (Ezek. xxv. 12-14; Obad. 1, 8.)

He says first, *Is there not wisdom any more in Teman?* By these words he intimates, that though the Idumeans thought themselves safe through their own counsels, because they excelled in acuteness, it yet would avail them nothing, for the Lord would blind them and deprive them of a sane mind; for what is put here interrogatively is declared plainly by Obadiah, (verse 28,) even in God's name, "I will take away wisdom from Teman, and there shall be no understanding in Mount Esau." But as Obadiah had preceded Jeremiah, it was necessary that he should speak of this as of a future thing. But our Prophet, as the judgment of which Obadiah was a witness and a herald, was near at hand, boldly exults over the Idumeans, and laughs at their reproach, inasmuch as they were deprived of counsel and understanding when they had most need of them. Teman, no doubt, was the name of a mountain or of a region; and this we learn from the Prophet Habakkuk, "God shall come from Teman, and the holy one from Mount Paran." (Hab. iii. 3.) It was also a chief city, as we learn form other places; and our Prophet sets it forth as the seat of the kingdom, when he says, *Is there not wisdom in Teman?* and then, *Has counsel perished from the intelligent?*

I wonder that interpreters, skilful in the language and conversant in it, should render the last word "sons," for it is unsuitable to the place.[1] The word, no doubt, is derived from בון, *bun*, to understand, and not from בנה, *bene*, to build, whence the word, בנים, *benim*, sons, comes. For how can it suit this passage to say, *Is there no more wisdom in Teman? Has counsel perished from the children?* that is, as they understand it, "from the children of Esau." But this is frigid and forced; and the two clauses correspond much better when read thus, "Is there no more wisdom in Teman? has counsel perished from the intelligent?" that is, from those who have hitherto boasted of their intelligence and acuteness.

[1] So the *Vulg.* and the *Targ.*, while the *Sept.* and the *Syr.* have "prudent," or intelligent. The word is not in its regular form, the *iod* being wanted, and the *mem* before it being omitted, which is not uncommon. Discerning rather than "prudent," or "intelligent," is its meaning.—*Ed.*

He then adds, *Rotten has become their wisdom.* The verb סרח, *sarech,* means to be superfluous, but some render it here to be putrid, as it is in *Niphal.* I know not whether they have done this, because they did not know another meaning suitable to the context; but we may fitly render it thus, that their wisdom had become superfluous, that is, useless. We may also adopt another meaning, that their wisdom had been hitherto overflowing, that is, superabounded; for they had such wisdom, so as not only to act wisely for themselves, but also to shew to others what was right and useful. As then the Idumeans possessed so much wisdom as to direct others, and not to be wise only for themselves, the words would read well were they rendered, that their wisdom had abounded. But in that case the words would be ironical; for the Prophet seems to assign a reason for his astonishment.

I give then this explanation: he first says, *Is there wisdom no more in Teman?* He exclaims, as though the thing was very strange, "How can this be! is the very fountain of wisdom exhausted? Who could have thought that a city so renowned for wisdom would become so fatuitous as not to know her approaching calamity, so as to meet it, and apply in time the remedy?" And to the same effect he adds, *Has counsel perished from the intelligent?* At length he subjoins, *Abounded has their wisdom;* and this he says, in order to shew a reason for his astonishment.[1]

But we must notice the sameness and the difference between our Prophet and Obadiah. The latter foretold the blindness of that nation; but our Prophet, as though he

[1] Some maintain that the first clause only is a question, for there is no interrogatory particle prefixed to the other clauses,—

Is wisdom no longer in Teman?
Perished has counsel from the discerning,
Vanished has their wisdom.

Neither the versions nor the *Targum* put the two last lines as questions; nor the *Sept.* and the *Syr.* the first. The verb סרח is differently rendered, —by the *Sept.*, "departed;" by the *Vulg.*, "become useless;" by the *Syr.*, "taken away;" by the *Targ.*, "marred," or corrupted. The verb means to spread, to stretch out; and spreading here is in the sense of dissipating or scattering, and the verb here is passive. So "vanished" would convey the meaning. The first line is a question, and the two following contain the answer. A tautology cannot be otherwise avoided. —*Ed.*

wished to rouse from their torpor those who had been inattentive to the prophecy of Obadiah, exclaims, "How has wisdom perished from Teman, and counsel from the intelligent?" We must further observe, that this punishment was by God inflicted on the Idumeans, because they had applied all their thoughts to frauds and intrigues; and it seldom happens, but that they who excel in acuteness become very sharp and fraudulent. As then men are thus wont to abuse for the most part their knowledge, God blinds them, and shews that men cannot of themselves be wise, but as far as it is given them from above. As I have already said, the Prophet enlarges on this judgment, that he might the more effectually rouse the minds of men. For had the Idumeans been rustics, such as dwell among mountains, and had no report prevailed as to their wisdom, no one would have wondered that they were taken and subdued; for simple and unwary men are exposed to the intrigues of their enemies, and cannot escape them. But the Prophet, in order to set forth this judgment of God as wonderful, says that their wisdom had been as it were overflowing, that is, like an abundant treasure, for they administered counsel to others. As, then, the Idumeans so much excelled in intelligence, especially those who dwelt in the city Teman, the Prophet shews by this very circumstance that their blindness proceeded from the manifest vengeance of God, and that such a change did not happen by chance. It follows,—

8. Flee ye, turn back, dwell deep, O inhabitants of Dedan; for I will bring the calamity of Esau upon him, the time *that* I will visit him.

8. Fugite, conversi sunt, profundaverunt habitationem incolæ Dedan, quia interitum Esau adduxi super ipsum tempore visitationis ejus.

The Prophet shews here how great was the pride of that nation, and sets it as it were before their eyes. *Flee,* he says; the language is abrupt, yet the meaning is not ambiguous. The meaning is, that when any one warned the Idumeans to flee, none of them would move; nay, they would remain fixed in their own country, for they thought that they would have there a perpetual quietness. *The citizens of Dedan have made deep their habitation.* He names another city not far from Teman. He then adds, in God's name, *But I will bring destruction on Esau in the time of his visitation.*[1]

We now understand the design of the Prophet,—that he wished to set before our eyes how proudly the Idumeans trusted in their defences, as they never could be persuaded to flee. The Prophet then, as God's herald, declares that they would have to flee. But what did they do? They *made deep their habitation*, that is, they would remain quiet in their own country, as though they were fixed in the centre of the earth, and therefore unassailable. By saying then that they *made deep*, he sets forth their obstinacy, so that no one could terrify them, though he announced extreme dangers. But it was his purpose thus to strengthen confidence in his prophecy, because the greatest part of the faithful could form no judgment but according to the present aspect of things; and the Idumeans proudly laughed at all threatenings. That the faithful then might not think that the Idumeans would be safe, he afterwards adds, in God's name, " Behold, I will bring ruin on Esau." He mentions their father, and the Idumeans, we know, descended from Esau the first-born of Isaac; and hence they were of the same blood with the Israelites. But the Prophet, by bringing forward the name of a reprobate man, intended, no doubt, to renew the memory of a curse, for Esau had been rejected, and his younger brother Jacob succeeded in his place. Hence the Prophet, that he might gain more credit to his words, brought before the people what was well known to them, that Esau had been rejected by God; for on the rejection of Esau depended their gratuitous election and adoption.

And he says that God would be the avenger of that nation *at the time of visitation;* for as I have before reminded you, what we have read was not immediately fulfilled. When, therefore, the Israelites suffered extreme calamities, their hope might a hundred times have failed them, on seeing the

[1] The versions (except the *Syr.* and the *Targ.*) have the verbs here in the imperative mood; and they are so regarded by most critics, " Flee ye, turn back, dwell deep," &c. This is necessary on account of כי, *for*, which follows.—*Ed.*

Idumeans remaining still as it were asleep in their pleasures, and these judgments of God as it were buried ; for it might have come to their minds that all which Jeremiah had declared had passed away like smoke. Hence, to sustain their hope and patience, he sets before them here the *time* of visitation ; as though he had said, that the Idumeans also would have their turn, after God had patiently borne with their impiety and spared them for a long time. But of this we shall hereafter see. Now, as I have shewn elsewhere, the words which remind us of the time of God's visitations, ought to be noticed, that we may not by hastening fall headlong, as it is usually the case ; for they who are in a hurry, fall at the first step. That we may then learn to wait for the ripened time, let this remain fixed in our minds, that God has his settled seasons of visitations. It now follows—

9. If grape-gatherers come to thee, would they not leave *some* gleaning-grapes? if thieves by night, they will destroy till they have enough.

9. Si vindemiatores venissent contra te, non reliquissent uvas? si fures in nocte, nonne perdidissent quod sufficeret ipsis?

Interpreters have not only obscured, but also perverted this verse, and only said what is to no purpose, and have gone far from the meaning of the Prophet.[1] How so? because it did not occur to them to compare this with a passage in Obadiah. Obadiah is the true interpreter; nay, our Prophet has borrowed what we read here from him. For there a question is asked, "If thieves were to come to thee, if robbers (שׁודדי, *shaddi*, is added there, but is omitted by Jeremiah)—if robbers by night, how wouldest thou have been reduced to nothing?" But in the first place the rendering ought to be, "Had thieves come to thee, how wouldest thou have been reduced to nothing?" then he adds, "Would they not have stolen what would suffice them?" He afterwards adds the second clause, "If the grape-gatherers had come to thee, would they not have left grapes?" There is now then no ambiguity in the Prophet's words, if we read them interrogatively. But there is an implied contrast be-

[1] The interpreters probably referred to are the *Sept.* and the *Vulg.*, where the interrogative form is not used ; not so the *Syr.* and the *Targ.* —*Ed.*

tween the calamity threatened to the people and the other devastations. Were a thief of the night to plunder another's house, he would depart, loaded with his prey, and leave something behind; for in all plunder some things remain: so also as to grape-gatherers, some grapes remain, which escape the gatherers.

Then the Prophet here shews, that so great would be the destruction of that nation, that it would exceed all kinds of plundering; for when one strips his vines, he leaves some grapes; and when a thief enters a house, he does not carry all things away with him, being satisfied with his booty. But nothing, he says, shall be left remaining with the Idumeans. We hence see why the Prophet brings forward the two comparisons, that of the grape-gatherers and of the thieves.

We must at the sametime observe, that when God denounces his vengeance on the Israelites, he often adduces these comparisons, in order to shew that nothing would be left them, "When the olives are shaken, yet some fruit remains on the top of the trees; but thou shalt be wholly emptied." As God had said these things, the Israelites might have raised an objection and said, "What is our condition, and how miserable! for we are extremely afflicted; though God afflicts the Idumeans, yet he deals mildly with them, for God's wrath is less inflamed against them than against us." Lest then the faithful should be thus thrown into despair, our Prophet declares that the Idumeans would be wholly destroyed, so that not a grape would be left them, nor any of their furniture, for their enemies would lay desolate the whole land. Now follows a confirmation of this verse—

10. But I have made Esau bare, I have uncovered his secret places, and he shall not be able to hide himself his seed is spoiled, and his brethren, and his neighbours, and he *is* not.

11. Leave thy fatherless children, I will preserve *them* alive; and let thy widows trust in me.

10. Quia ego discooperio Esau, retego abscondita ejus, et occultari non poterit; vastatum est semen ejus (*aut,* vastabitur) et fratres ejus, et vicini, et non ipse (*quanquam alii vertunt,* et nemo erit, *et contexunt proximum versum,*)

11. Relinque pupillos tuos; ego vivificabo (*hoc est,* alam ipsos;) et viduæ tuæ in me sperent.

As to the beginning of the verse, the meaning of the Prophet is not obscure; for he means that such would be the destruction of the people of Edom, that they would be spoiled by enemies, that they would become wholly naked. But he speaks in the name of God: *Behold, I uncover Esau, and make open his hidden things.* By hidden things he means treasures, as it is evident from Obadiah. He then says that he would so expose the Idumeans to plunder, that there would be no hidden thing but that their enemies would seize and plunder it. This is the meaning.

He then confirms what I have said, that this plundering would not be like grape-gathering, or theft, or common robbery, because God would altogether empty the Idumeans of all that they had, even of all that they hid in the ground.

With regard to the end of the verse, some give this explanation, "There will be none to say:" there is then a word to be understood,—"there will be none to say, *Leave thy orphans to me, I will nourish* or sustain *them*, or I will be a father to them; *and thy widows, let them hope* or trust *in me*, or rest on me." For it is no small comfort to parents, when they know that their widows would have one to flee to, and also their orphans. When one dies and sees that his widow is destitute of every help, and sees that his orphans are miserable and needy, his paternal and conjugal love is grievously wounded. For is it more bitter than death itself, when the husband cannot provide any help for his widow, when he cannot provide any relief for his orphans. Hence some interpreters think that the ruin of this people is in this way exaggerated; that is, because no one would be found to bring comfort to parents, and to take as it were the place of the dead.

But the meaning would not be unsuitable, were the words deemed ironical, that the Prophet spoke in the person of God, *Leave to me thy orphans, I will nourish them, and let thy widows rest on me*, or trust in me: for it follows afterwards, *Behold, they to whom there was no judgment, have drunk of the cup*, &c. The passage then would not read amiss, if we consider that God taunts the Idumeans, and ironically declares that he would be a judge against them even after they were dead; for God's vengeance, we know, reaches to the third and the fourth generation. As then he had before declared, that the Idumeans would be destroyed, their seed, their brethren, and their neighbours, so he now confirms the same thing,—"What! dost thou expect that I should be a father or a protector to thy orphans? that I should bring aid to thy widow? This thou expectest in vain from me."

The Prophet, in a few words, very sharply goads the minds of the Idumeans, when God thus presents himself, and says by way of mockery, that he would be a protector to their orphans and widows; for they had indiscriminately vented their rage on orphans and women, and spared neither sex nor age. Then God shews here that there was no reason why they should expect any comfort as to their children, for he would be their avenger to the third and the fourth generation. And forced, no doubt, is what some say; at least I do not see how the words, *I will nourish them*, can comport with the rest of the context. This clause, then, I apply to God himself, because his vengeance would consume them with their brethren, their neighbours and their seed. And the irony is the most suitable to the whole passage; that is, that God meant to show, that he could bring no help to orphans or aid to widows, since they had been so cruel both to orphans and widows.[1] Then follows a confirmation—

[1] Neither of the two explanations here given are satisfactory, though the first especially has been adopted by many, such as *Henry* and *Scott.* It is difficult to know the meaning of the *Sept.;* the *Vulg.* and the *Syr.* are literally our version. The *Targ.* goes wide astray, representing this verse as addressed to the people of Israel, of whom there is no mention here. *Blayney* supposes a typographical mistake, joins עזב to the preceding verse, and puts ה to the next word, and gives this version,—

And there is nothing of him left.
11. Shall I preserve the life of thy fatherless children?
Or shall thy widows trust in me?

The questions he considers as strong negatives. The simpler view seems to be this: in the preceding verse the destruction not only of Esau, but also of his brethren and neighbours, is announced. His "seed" means his posterity, the nation, and he was *was not to be*, that is, as a kingdom. There would be still some "orphans" and "widows," and as "brethren" and "neighbours" would be destroyed as well as Esau himself, as to all grown up people, forming the nation, and thus orphans and

12. For thus saith the Lord, Behold, they whose judgment *was* not to drink of the cup have assuredly drunken; and *art* thou he *that* shall altogether go unpunished? thou shalt not go unpunished, but thou shalt surely drink *of it*.

12. Quia sic dicit Jehova, Ecce, quibus non erat judicium (*ad verbum*, quibus non judicium ipsorum,) ad bibendum calicem bibendo bibent; —tu verò ipse immunis eris? *vel*, immunis immunitatem adipisceris? *vel* tu, verò immunis evades?) non evades immunis, quia bibendo bibes.

He confirms the last verse, as I think,—that God's vengeance awaited the whole seed of Esau, because it would be unreasonable to deal more severely with God's people than with aliens, who had wholly shaken off the yoke. For I explain what is said here of the Church, *Those to whom it was not their judgment to drink the cup shall surely drink.* Some apply this to neighbouring nations who had not become so wicked as the Idumeans. But this exposition is frigid, and we ought always, as we have said elsewhere, to have regard to the design of the Prophet. What then was his object but to shew to the faithful, that there was no reason for them to despond, however grievously God might afflict them, because the punishment which he would inflict on the Idumeans would in no way be milder; for we know that we are greatly tempted by envy when we see that the state of the impious and the reprobate is better than that of God's children. And it was for this purpose that the thirty-seventh Psalm was composed, "Envy not the wicked, nor let their prosperity vex thee, because they shall soon perish." And David also, in Psalm lxxiii. 2, 3, confesses, that he in a manner staggered when he saw the wicked luxuriating in their pleasures, while the children of God were miserably treated. Then our Prophet in this place, as often elsewhere, had regard to the faithful, and wished to sustain them, lest they should succumb under their burden, when God afflicted them as well as the Idumeans. Hence he says, when speaking of the Idumeans, *Drinking they shall drink the cup whose*

widows would be left helpless, God was pleased to give the promise here stated:

Leave thy orphans, I will preserve *them*,
Thy widows also, in me let them trust.

The last verb is both masculine and feminine, and refers both to the orphans and widows. This is substantially the explanation given by Venema, and is the most satisfactory.—*Ed.*

judgment was not to drink, and shalt thou be exempted? that is, "I will not spare my people, and should I spare aliens? this cannot be."

We then see that it was a fruitful source of consolation to the faithful, when they heard that the wicked, who openly and avowedly disregarded God, could not escape his judgment.

But it may be now asked, how could he say that it was not the judgment of the Church to drink of the cup of God's wrath? He speaks comparatively, and this answer ought to suffice us. It is certain that the Israelites deserved all the evils which they suffered. God then justly chastised them; he did not act without reason or through sudden wrath, but executed what he had previously decreed. It was then God's judgment, even what he had determined and fixed; for judgment here is to be taken for God's decree, by which he apportions to each his own lot. It was not then a judgment to the Israelites to drink of the cup, when one compared them to the Idumeans,—how so? Here a new question arises, for the Israelites had been worse than all others. The Idumeans had departed wholly from God; all light had become extinct among them; and then the law had not been given them: before Jacob went down to Egypt, who was to be from thence delivered according to the prefixed time made known to Abraham, they dwelt in mountains separated from the land of Canaan. They therefore possessed no part of God's law, except that they had the empty symbol of circumcision. But the Israelites, on whom had always shone the doctrine of the law, were altogether inexcusable. Why then does the Prophet say that there was no judgment to them? My answer is, that the reference here is not to the persons of men, but on the contrary to the grace of God, through which he had been pleased to embrace the children of Israel. As then God had chosen that nation, what is regarded here is special adoption; for it is right in God to indulge his children, and it is right also in him to pardon them rather than aliens. When any one is offended with his own son, he will be reconciled to him; but an alien will not find pardon.

We now then see that the Prophet does not regard what

the people had deserved, nor consider how detestable had been their impiety, and of what grievous punishment they were worthy; but on the contrary, he refers to that grace of God through which he had chosen the seed of Jacob. He had indeed previously chosen the whole seed of Abraham; but the rejection of Esau followed, so that Jacob alone remained as the seed. Since then God had manifested himself as a father to the children of Jacob, the Prophet says that it was not their judgment to drink of the cup, because it was according to reason and common sense that God should forgive them rather than aliens, whom he had already rejected, and who were like putrid members: *They*, then, *whose judgment was not to drink the cup, drinking shall drink, and shalt thou escape free?* The meaning is, that if the green wood is burnt, what will become of the dry? as Christ said. (Luke xxiii. 31.) There is a similar consolation mentioned in 1 Peter iv. 17, 18, where those afflictions are mentioned to which the Church of God is now exposed. Now, as we are tender and delicate, and the minds of many may be harassed, Peter says, that if God be so severe towards his own, those of his own household, what will become of the wicked? what dreadful vengeance awaits them?

We hence perceive the drift of the Prophet's words, and what doctrine may be hence deduced, even that when we see God's judgment beginning at God's house, as the Prophet elsewhere says, (chap. xxv. 29,) and as also Peter says; that is, when God chastises his own children, and seems in the meantime to pass by the wicked, we ought patiently to wait for the visitation previously mentioned; and this ought always to be remembered by us, "If this be done in the green tree, what will be done in the dry?" We shall not then envy the wicked, when God defers and does not immediately execute his judgment; for the punishments inflicted by God on his servants are only temporary and limited, and intended as medicine, inasmuch as all we suffer are helps to our salvation, as Paul teaches us. (Rom. viii. 28.) As then God paternally chastises us, let us not shun his paternal hand; nor let us think that God deals more kindly with the wicked because he suspends his judgments, for at length they will be hurried into their own ruin, as the Prophet says here.

In speaking of *a cup*, the Prophet uses a phrase common in Scripture, for the Scripture by a metaphor calls punishment inflicted on men for their sins a cup; because God apportions to each his just measure. It is taken then as allowed, that calamities are not by chance, but proceed from God's hand, as though he gave a cup to drink. Now when he afflicts his own, they are constrained to drink as it were his wrath; it is therefore a sour and a bitter cup. But the wicked shall hereafter drink poison. Even medicine, though displeasing to the taste because of its bitterness, is yet wholesome; but poison kills men, though its taste is like medicine. This then is the comparison that is used here by Jeremiah; *Drinking, they shall drink the cup*, even God's servants, who yet ought to have been exempted through a singular privilege, even because God had chosen them to be his peculiar people; *shalt thou*, he says, *be exempted from drinking?* He addresses all aliens.

We have before seen another mode of speaking, "They shall drink to the dregs," as though he had said, "God will not only give thee to drink a bitter cup, but its bitterness will kill and destroy thee, for God will constrain thee to drink the very dregs." But still the meaning is the same, though the phrase is different. He then asserts that the Idumeans would not be exempt from God's judgment, and why? because God does not spare even his own children. Here then is suggested to us the best consolation when God in various ways afflicts us: let us know that it cannot be otherwise, but that it is a prelude to the last judgment, when salvation shall surely be our portion, for God purifies us now by temporal punishments, that we may be then free from final vengeance. But when the ungodly are secure, let us know that God's judgment is indeed hidden, but yet certain, and will shortly overtake them; for when they say, "Peace and security, then sudden destruction will come upon them." (1 Thess. v. 3.)

But the clock strikes.

PRAYER.

Grant, Almighty God, that as thou hast not only in thine eternal counsel adopted us as thy children, but hast also inscribed on our hearts a sure sign and pledge of thy paternal favour towards us, —O grant that we may accustom ourselves to bear thy scourges, and patiently to receive them without murmuring or complaining, but that we may ever look forward to the blessed rest and inheritance above, and at the same time dread the punishment that awaits the wicked, and that we may thus courageously persevere in our warfare, until thou at length gatherest us into that celestial kingdom which thine only-begotten Son has procured for us by his own blood.—Amen.

Lecture One Hundred and Seventy-fifth.

13. For I have sworn by myself, saith the Lord, that Bozrah shall become a desolation, a reproach, a waste, and a curse; and all the cities thereof shall be perpetual wastes.

13. Quia per me ipsum juravi, dicit Jehova, quòd in vastitatem, in opprobrium, in desertum, et in maledictionem erit Bosra; et omnes urbes ejus erunt in vastitates seculi (*id est,* perpetuas.)

HERE the Prophet confirms what he had already prophesied respecting the Idumeans; but to remove every doubt, he says, that God had *sworn;* and he introduces God as the speaker, in order that his word might be emphatical. He then declares that God had made an oath respecting the destruction of Bozrah. What is particular is put for what is general; for he includes the whole nation under the name of this city. Nor does he simply declare that the Idumeans would be laid waste and destroyed, but he accumulates words: *Bozrah,* he says, *shall be a waste;*[1] secondly, *a reproach;* thirdly, *a solitude,* or desert; and fourthly, *a curse.*

What the Prophet said was no doubt a thing difficult to be believed; for God did not without reason bring forth his own name. For as he would have us to use it seriously and reverently, so he does not interpose so precious a pledge except under the greatest necessity. It is then certain, that

[1] It is better to render it as in the *Syr.*, "astonishment;" then "reproach" comes after it; and the next word, חרב, is properly "a waste," and in the plural is rendered "wastes" at the end of the verse. There were two cities called Bozrah, one in Moab, chap. xlviii. 24, and one in Edom, Isaiah lxiii. 1.—*Ed.*

there was a weighty reason why God testified by an oath what we read here of the destruction of the people of Edom. Now I have said that what Jeremiah announced was hardly credible; and it was so, because there was no cause for war; and besides, the country was fortified by its own inclosures; for the Idumeans thought, as it seems, that they were impregnable. This, then, was the reason why God interposed an oath. At the same time his purpose was, as I have before reminded you, to consult the benefit of the faithful; for God makes an oath that he might apply a remedy to the weakness of our faith; for as we almost always vacillate, a simple testimony, without being sanctioned by an oath, would not be sufficient for us. This is then the reason for making an oath.

God is said to swear *by himself*, because there is none greater, as the apostle says, by whom he can swear. (Heb. vi. 13.) Men in doubtful and hidden things flee to God, who knows the heart, who is himself the truth, and from whom nothing is hid. And an oath, as we learn from many places of Scripture, is a part of divine worship. As then this honour peculiarly belongs to him, that is, that we should swear by his name, when he himself swears, he cannot derive authority from another, which may confirm his words: he therefore swears by himself. And we have heard what he declares by Isaiah, "I will not give my glory to another." (Isaiah xlii. 8.) God then prescribes to us the form of swearing, when he swears by himself. God is said to swear sometimes by his soul, or by his life, and he is said sometimes to lift up his hand. These expressions are not strictly proper, but transferred to God from men. But the mode of speaking used by Jeremiah ought especially to be observed, for we see how an oath is to be rightly made, even when it is made by an appeal to God's name, for he is alone the fit witness and judge in things doubtful and hidden.

There is therefore under the Papacy a base and an intolerable idolatry, for the Papists swear by dead saints. This is nothing else but to rob God of his right; for since he alone, as it has been stated, is the truth, so he alone is the fit judge when things are hidden and cannot be ascertained by human testimony. And we ought to notice the words used in swearing, that is, when men submit to God's judgment, and implore him as a judge. Whosoever then swears by the saints, it is the same thing as to make them to occupy the place of God, so as to make them the judges of the world, and to ascribe to them all power. "God is a witness to my soul," says Paul, (2 Cor. i. 23;) and then we have such words as these, "May God do this to me and add that." (Ruth i. 17; 1 Sam. xiv. 44; 2 Sam. iii. 35, &c.) By such expressions, as I have said, is set forth the authority and character of an oath. In short, we must bear in mind, that when necessity constrains us to swear, God is ever the sole judge, and that therefore his name is profaned when we swear by another.

Now what it is to be a *reproach* and a *curse*, is evident from other places, even when any one is set as it were in a theatre, that he might be an example of disgrace, or when any calamity gives an occasion for execrations and maledictions, "May God destroy thee as he destroyed the Idumeans:" this is to be a curse, as we have elsewhere seen.

He adds *cities*, and thereby intimates that this desolation would not be confined to one part, but be extended to all parts. He also says that they would be *perpetual wastes;* and thus he took away every hope of restoration. When he prophesied before against the Moabites and the Ammonites, he mingled some consolation, but as to Edom, every hope is cut off. The nation, no doubt, deserved a heavier vengeance, for it had a nearer connection with the Israelites—hence its cruelty was less to be borne. Besides, it appears that it exceeded in its barbarity all other nations; for it is not without reason said in the Psalms, "Remember, O Lord, the children of Edom, who said in the day of Jerusalem, Let it be erased, let it be wholly erased to its foundation." (Psalm cxxxvii. 7.) We hence learn that the Idumeans raged most cruelly against their own blood: and this was the reason why God declared that their cities would become perpetual desolations; for the word עולם, *oulam,* which some render "age," often means perpetuity. It follows—

14. I have heard a rumour from the Lord, and an ambassador is sent unto the heathen, *saying*, Gather ye together, and come against her, and rise up to the battle.

14. Auditum (*hoc est*, sermonem) audivimus à Jehova, et nuntius ad gentes missus est, Congregamini (*vel*, congregate vos,) et venite super eam, surgite ad prælium.

The Prophet again shews that God would be the author of the calamity of which he speaks; for if things were viewed by men, no one could have thought that the Idumeans could in so short a time be destroyed. It was therefore necessary for the faithful to raise upwards their minds. And this the Prophet had in view when he said that all this would be from God.

But most forcible are his words when he says, *We have heard a hearing;* some say, "a report," but improperly, as I think; for though שמועה, *shemuoe*, often means a report or rumour, yet here it ought to be taken for a proclamation, which God published as it were by his own heralds. For the similitude is taken from men, proclaiming war against their enemies by a solemn rite. Then Jeremiah says, that a *voice was heard* sent from above, because it was God's purpose publicly and openly to testify, that what we read here of the destruction of Edom would take place. We now then understand the meaning of the Prophet, when he says, *A hearing have we heard from Jehovah.*

Then follows immediately a confirmation, *a messenger*, or an ambassador, *is sent to the nations.* God, indeed, had no messenger or herald to proclaim war against the Idumeans, or to rouse up the Assyrians and Chaldeans; but the Prophets usually spoke thus, that men, being led to the very scene, might know that what was said was real, and would not be without its effect, as prophecies were as so many embassies. And according to this view, the prophets, as we have stated elsewhere, sometimes besieged and stormed cities, sometimes sounded the trumpet, even for this purpose, to shew that their doctrine was linked with its execution, for God never spoke by them to no purpose or in vain. The Prophet at the same time reminds us that the Chaldeans and the Assyrians were in God's hand, so that he could by a nod or a hiss rouse them to war, as it is said elsewhere, "God will hiss for the fly of Egypt." (Is. vii. 18.)

The Prophet then means, that the Chaldeans and the Assyrians would be ready to obey God, as though they were hired soldiers, and enlisted under his banner.

We now then see how forcible was this mode of speaking; for the faithful might hence learn, that it was in God's power to perform whatever he proclaimed by his servant, because he could by one word rouse, draw, arm, and lead to war the Assyrians and the Chaldeans, as he also says, *Be ye assembled, and come against her, and rise up to battle.* And he speaks of many nations, lest any one should think that the Idumeans would be able to resist, for he is not immediately conquered who is attacked by his enemies. But the Prophet meets this doubt, and says that there would be many nations, who, with their united strength, would come against the people of Edom, so that they would have no power to resist. Nearly the same words are found in Obadiah. It now follows—

15. For, lo, I will make thee small among the heathen, *and* despised among men.	15. Quia ecce parvum posui te inter gentes, contemptum inter homines.

Interpreters for the most part give this exposition, that the people of Edom would be contemptible, because God had determined to cast them down from their dignity, which they for a time possessed: and then they connect the next verse, in which the reason for this is given, "Thy terror deceived thee, the pride of thy heart," &c. But this passage may be taken otherwise,—that God derides the pride of that nation, which ought to have restrained itself, because it contended against nature, when it wished to elate itself so much. And it seems to me that this is the real meaning of the Prophet. I do not, indeed, pronounce the other view wrong, yet it behoves me to state what I prefer. I then think that there is to be understood here an implied comparison between the Israelites and the children of Edom, which is more clearly expressed by Malachi, (chap. i. 2, 3;) for God there extols his kindness towards the Israelites, because he gave them a rich and fruitful land, and sent away the posterity of Esau, and confined them within rough mountains. As then the Idumeans, ejected from so pleasant and desirable an inheritance as had been given to the children of Abraham, were confined as it were to rugged mountains, the Prophet derides their pride, because they tried in a way contrary and repugnant to nature to elevate themselves: *I made thee,* he says, *small among the nations, and contemptible among men.* And we know that less easily can that pride be borne, where there is no reason for boasting. When any one obscure from the lowest rank exalts himself above the most noble, all regard him with contempt, for it is a monstrous thing. It is for this reason that the Prophet now says, "What have you, O Idumeans, that ye are so proud! What do you possess? what is your glory? for God has humbled you. It is then the same as though a fly wished to exceed in bulk the elephant."

But if the other exposition be preferred, the meaning would be as follows, "Behold, I will make thee small and contemptible among the nations, because thou hast been very proud." But I have stated what I approve, even that God here brings against the Idumeans their folly, because they ought not to have boasted without reason, "Behold," he says; he shews, as by the finger, how mean and abject their condition was; *I have made thee small among the nations, and contemptible among men.* And, doubtless, were it a threatening, it would not have been sufficiently forcible; for the Prophet has hitherto been thundering against the Idumeans, and he goes on in the same strain. If then he had now put in what we read, referring to their smallness, it would have been frigid. I doubt not, then, but that the Prophet describes the state of that nation, such as it had been in comparison with that of the chosen people, and even of other nations; for though they were rich, had always been free from disturbance, and suffered no losses, yet they lived, as it has been stated, in mountains by no means fertile. It now follows—

16. Thy terribleness hath deceived thee, *and* the pride of thine heart, O thou that dwellest in the clefts of the rock, that holdest the height of the hill: though thou shouldest make thy nest as high as the

15. Superbia cordis tui, terror tuus, decepit te, quæ habitas in fissuris petræ (*vel,* rupis,) quæ occupas altitudinem collis (*id est,* collium, *mutatio est numeri, sicut etiam in* סלע, *nam significat rupes, plurali numero;*) quamvis extollas tanquam aquila nidum tuum, illinc detra-

eagle, I will bring thee down from thence, saith the Lord.	ham te (descendere faciam, *ad verbum,*) dicit Jehova.

Some render the first words thus, " Thine idol hath deceived thee ;" and others, " Thy folly hath deceived thee." The verb has, indeed, this meaning, though there is a different reading, for some put a point over the right side of the letter, and others on the left. But the most suitable meaning is thus conveyed, *Deceived thee has thy terror, the pride of thy heart.* Those who render the first word " idol," consider that superstition is referred to, that the false confidence which the Edomites placed in their idols had deceived them. But this seems to be a forced explanation. Why others have rendered the word " folly," I know not. The word properly means terror. The verb פלץ, *pelets,* means to terrify, and from this the noun is derived. And when the word is taken for an idol, it is so metaphorically, because idols terrify men, or because a terrible end awaits their worshippers. But I retain the proper meaning of the word. At the same time terror here is to be taken actively, because the Idumeans were a terror to other nations, and were thus blinded with pride on account of their conceit as to their power.

And the following words are explanatory, *the pride of thy heart ;* for they who despise others fill themselves with empty pride, and thus elevate their own hearts. As then the Idumeans had gained for themselves the repute of being a warlike people, the terror entertained for them inflated their own hearts with pride : but the Prophet says, that they were *deceived,* as they arrogated to themselves too much power. At the same time he continues the subject which I have stated, as though he had said, " How comes it, that as God has designed thee to be contemptible, thou takest to thyself such authority among the nations ? Thou fightest against nature, for thou hast hitherto in vain terrified thy neighbours : hence it is, that thou art swollen with pride ; but it is a mere delusion ; thou art greatly mistaken, and deceivest thyself in thus thinking of thy strength, since thy condition ought, on the contrary, to make thee humble." We now see how well the whole passage runs, and how aptly the words agree together. He then says that it was a foolish confidence, by which the people of Edom, whom God had made contemptible, were deceived.

He now adds, by way of concession, *Thou who dwellest in the fissures of rocks, and occupiest the heights of mountains.* In these words the Prophet concedes something to the Idumeans; but he afterwards adds, that the fortresses, by which they thought themselves to be protected, would come to nothing; *though thou raisest high thy nest as the eagle, thence will I,* says God, *draw thee down.* We hence see that the Prophet concedes to the Idumeans some reason for boasting on account of their mountains, because they presented on every side a defence against enemies; and yet he shews that all this would be useless to them; for he says, *though thou raisest high thy nest as the eagle,* that is, though thou ascendest, as they commonly say, above the very clouds, *thence will I draw thee down.*

Now this passage teaches us first, that all who trust in their own earthly defences deceive themselves; and, secondly, that all who arrogate to themselves more than what is just and right, contend, as it were, against God, and that it cannot, therefore, be otherwise but that God will lay them prostrate. We are then taught by this doctrine to cultivate humility. Humility has its roots fixed deeply within; so that the state of those who willingly submit themselves, becomes firm and permanent; for the root, which appears not on the surface, sustains the tree. So also that humility, which is not known by men, is our real and solid prop and support. Whosoever takes the wing and flies, and seeks, through his own presumption, to raise up himself, provokes God as it were designedly: and here the Prophet shews what end awaits all those who thus raise themselves on high, seeking to set their nest on a summit like the eagle; for God will draw them down and lay them prostrate, as he did to the Idumeans. It now follows—

17. Also Edom shall be a desolation: every one that goeth by it shall be astonished, and shall hiss at all the plagues thereof.	17. Et erit Edom in vastitatem, quisquis transierit super ipsam obstupescet, et sibilabit super omnes plagas ejus.

Here again the Prophet confirms what he had said. We have before stated how necessary was such a repetition, because no one could have thought that destruction was so nigh the Idumeans. He did not then repeat what he had said, in order to explain more clearly what might have been otherwise obscure, but to fix more fully in the hearts of the faithful what appeared incredible.

He then says that *Edom would become a waste ;* and then, that every one *passing by it* would be *astonished* and *hiss on account of all her wounds,* or strokes. Hissing may refer to derision, or to astonishment, or, at least, to wonder: for many hiss, or shake the head through mockery ; and others hiss through wonder, when any unusual thing happens. And as he had said before, *Whosoever shall pass through it shall be astonished,* I am disposed to refer this also to what is produced by wonder or amazement. It afterwards follows—

18. As in the overthrow of Sodom and Gomorrah, and the neighbour *cities* thereof, saith the Lord, no man shall abide there, neither shall a son of man dwell in it.

18. Secundum subversionem Sodomæ et Gomorræ et vicinarum ejus, dicit Jehova, non habitabit illic vir, et non manebit in ea filius hominis.

He expresses more at large what he had briefly included in one word : he had said, that Edom would become a *waste ;* but he now shews what sort of waste it would be, even such as that of *Sodom and Gomorrah, and other cities ;* for God, as it is well known, destroyed the five cities against which he fulminated.

And hence again we learn, that there was no hope left for the Idumeans ; as though the Prophet had said, that their final overthrow was inevitable, because God would have them wholly destroyed, and their memory obliterated. It is yet probable that there were some remnant of the nation ; but this was not inconsistent with this prophecy, because they who remained alive became so scattered, that they never formed one people, nor had any name. And though God might have chosen some from that nation, yet this favour remained hid, and, as it was unknown to men, it can hardly be taken to the account. However this may have been, we must bear in mind what I have before briefly referred to,—

that the Idumeans were so accursed, that their calamity was much severer than that of other nations; and this they had deserved by their unnatural cruelty and many contumelies towards the miserable Israelites, their own relatives. This, then, was the reason why Jeremiah compared the land to *Sodom* and *Gomorrah, and the other cities; no man shall dwell there,* that is, the country shall be desolate.

And yet it appears, from history, that that country was afterwards inhabited, for even the Romans placed there a garrison. But the Prophet, as I have already said, meant that none of the Idumeans would survive to possess the land, so as to become a nation. Though, then, other inhabitants might have afterwards possessed the land, this was nothing to the Idumeans; for that people had perished, and from that time no restoration followed: this was sufficient as a fulfilment of this prophecy. Nay, it was a harder thing, that their land should receive aliens and strangers, than if it had been left desolate.

But we must also bear in mind the common mode of speaking adopted by the Prophets; for when they adduce Sodom and Gomorrah as examples, they speak hyperbolically; and there is no need here to accumulate passages to prove this; for they who are in any tolerable measure acquainted with Scripture, must know that whenever mention is made of Sodom and Gomorrah, all pardon and alleviation of punishment are excluded. Isaiah, extolling God's mercy towards his chosen people, says, "Had not God left us a very small seed, we must have been as Sodom and like to Gomorrah." (Isaiah i. 9.) And this mode of speaking, as I have said, often occurs in Scripture; yea, even our Prophet threatened the Israelites with the destruction of Sodom and Gomorrah, (chap. xxiii. 14.) The words, no doubt, are used hyperbolically; for God had not fulminated against other lands or nations and sunk them in the deep, as he had done to Sodom and Gomorrah. But in comparisons all parts do not correspond.

Now, some one may ask, Why does God thus exceed due limits in speaking? To this I answer, that it is not done without just reason and necessity. We indeed see that men are indifferent to God's judgments; for such is their sloth and insensibility, that they disregard as a light thing, or deem as nothing, what God threatens. As then men are so brutish, being unmoved by God's threatenings, it is necessary that such indifference should be roused and awakened. He therefore sets Sodom and Gomorrah before their eyes; and as Jude also says, there an example of all the punishments which await the reprobate has been exhibited. (Jude 7.) God therefore designed to represent once for all, as in a mirror, how dreadful will be his vengeance on all the wicked. Since it is so, to the same end is this threatening, that God would destroy the Idumeans and all like them, as he did Sodom and Gomorrah, so that none would survive, though aliens might come and succeed the Idumeans and occupy their inheritance. I cannot now finish; we shall leave the other comparison.

PRAYER.

Grant, Almighty God, that as thou hast been pleased to stretch forth thine hand to us, we may be raised by faith above the world, and learn to submit to thee in true humility, and to know how miserable must be our condition and life, except we wholly recumb on thee alone, so that we may be made partakers of that glory which thou hast purchased for us in Heaven, and which thine only-begotten Son, our Lord, has obtained for us.—Amen.

Lecture One Hundred and Seventy-sixth.

19. Behold, he shall come up like a lion from the swelling of Jordan against the habitation of the strong: but I will suddenly make him run away from her; and who *is* a chosen *man, that* I may appoint over her? for who *is* like me? and who will appoint me the time? and who *is* that shepherd that will stand before me?

19. Ecce tanquam leo ascendet ab elevatione Jordanis ad tabernaculum fortitudinis; postquam quiescere fecero, faciam currere ab ea; et quis electus super eam præficiam? nam quis sicut ego? et quis contestabitur mecum? et quis hic pastor qui stet coram facie mea (*vel*, contra faciem meam.)

The Prophet here confirms what he had said, that such would be the violence of the Chaldean army, that the Idumeans would not be able to resist it. He then says, that the Chaldeans would come like lions, who ascend in great fury when compelled to change the place of their habitation; for so I explain what is said of the elevation of Jordan. The explanations are various; but the one I approve is, that Jeremiah compares the Chaldeans to lions, who every year, or at least when there was a great inundation, sought hiding-places on mountains or on elevated grounds, because they could not lie down on the plains. The elevation of Jordan is then to be taken for its swelling, that is, when it overflowed. We learn from many passages that the lions lodged around Jordan. As then they dwelt in the low plains, when the river swelled, they changed the place of their habitation. But this could not be without their rage being excited; for we know how savage these wild beasts are. Jeremiah had also a regard to the situation of Idumea, which was more elevated than Jordan and the country around it. He says the same also, in the next chapter, of the Babylonians. But it may be that he alluded in this place to what was common among the Idumeans, and this is probable.

The meaning then is, as I think, that as lions ascended to higher grounds when Jordan swelled and overflowed, so the Chaldeans would come to the Idumeans, and invade the country like furious wild beasts. This is one thing. Then he adds, *to the habitation of strength.* Jerome's rendering is, "to valiant beauty;" the word is so explained almost everywhere, but it is to be taken here for a strong dwelling. He alludes to the situation of that land, for it seemed impregnable, because it was surrounded, as it has appeared elsewhere, by mountains. The situation of Babylon was different, it being surrounded by the various streams of the Euphrates.

What follows is obscure, *when I shall have made him to rest, I will make him to run from her.* Some explain the particle כי, *ki,* differently. It is indeed a causative, but is often taken, as it is well known, as an adverb of time. But the meaning of the Prophet is ambiguous, and some have imagined that the chosen people are spoken of, as though the Prophet meant, that when the Lord gave rest to his people, he would then cause them to flee from the land of Edom. But this exposition is wholly inadmissible; and I wonder how they came to make such a mistake; for the Prophet, I have no doubt, means here that the Idumeans had a long time been at ease, but that a sudden calamity would come which would scatter them here and there, and force them to seek safety by flight; and this is the best meaning that we can elicit: *When,* therefore, *I shall have made her to rest,* or, from the time I shall have made her to rest, *I will make him to flee from her;* as though he had said, "I have hitherto suffered this nation to rest in its abundance, and thus to remain quiet; but I will suddenly disperse the inhabitants here and there, and they shall see their own land occupied by their enemies." In short, there is here a comparison between two conditions; for the Idumeans had long remained in their own dregs, for there was no one who caused them any trouble. God had then granted them a continual quietness; but now he declares that he would make all of them to flee, and that suddenly. And it was necessary that this should be distinctly expressed, that the Idumeans might not in future trust in their tranquil state, as hypocrites do, who usually abuse God's indulgence, and think, when he bears long with them, that they have escaped every danger. Lest then such confidence should deceive the Idumeans, the Prophet says that they would have to flee after having been long in a state of tranquillity.

The words may at the same time be explained otherwise; for רגע, *rego,* means to rend, to cut, to break; and it may be so taken here, "When I shall have made a rent;" for the Idumeans, as it has been stated, were fortified by defences on every side. God now intimates that he would make an irruption, which he compares to rending; and this explanation is not unsuitable.

It afterwards follows, *And who is the chosen* one, *that I may set him over her?* God now summons all the strong ones, that he might set them over Idumea, not as pastors or such as might care for the welfare of the land and provide for its safety, but such as would oppress it with tyrannical cruelty: *Who* then *is the chosen* one? At the same time God shews that all men of war are in his hand and at his disposal; as though he had said, "If the Idumeans think that they surpass all others in courage and strength, they are greatly mistaken; for I will find those who possess more courage, for I have ready at hand chosen men to set over them whenever I please, who will easily subdue the Idumeans, however superior they may think themselves to be in martial valour." Then God does not here ask a question as of a doubtful matter, *Who is the chosen one, that I may set him over her?* but he shews that it would be no difficult thing for him to destroy the Idumeans, because he would send for the chosen one from any part of the world he pleased, and set him over Idumea, not as a pastor, as I have said, but as a cruel tyrant.

He then adds, *For who is as I am?* He confirms the last clause; for God extols his own power, which is wont to be despised by the unbelieving. The sentence indeed seems to be a common truth, *Who is as I am?* for all allow this from the least to the greatest. The Prophet appears then to have announced something trite and ordinary by saying, that *none is like God;* for even the worst of men acknowledge this, and the least child confesses it, and it is the dictate of nature. But were any one duly to consider how great is the pride of men, he would find that this truth is not so common; for there is hardly one in a hundred who concedes to God what justly belongs to him. For when he comes forth either to promise salvation or to announce punishment, how little is any one moved? nay, they who hold this principle, that God can do all things, are yet carried away, when the least hinderance occurs, to vain imaginations, and at length become wholly lost. When any one is persuaded that God ought to be feared, if any occasion for a false confidence be presented, what he had at first entertained in his mind will be choked, and then wholly extinguished. In short, if we carefully consider how contemptibly men think of God, we shall understand that this truth is not in vain often repeated in Scripture, that God has none like him. For when any one dares to exalt himself against God, he immediately strikes all with terror; and yet the power of God is regarded as nothing. We see that even the faithful themselves deem the least thing stronger than God;

nay, they hesitate not to set up flies and insects, so to speak, in opposition to God, and even to make them equal to him. This is indeed very shameful, and yet it is what has usually prevailed perpetually in all ages.

We now, then, understand why God declares here as a great matter and as it were incredible, that *there is none like him.* And hence also we learn what the last clause means, when it is asked, *Where is the chosen one whom I may set over her?* for he follows up the subject by saying, *There is no one like me.* By these words he shews that the whole world is under his power.

He now adds, *and who will protest against me?* Some read, "Who will prescribe to me the time?" But they who thus render the words, obscure the meaning of the Prophet. The Prophet, I doubt not, means, that there is no one who will dare to dispute with God; or were any one to attempt this, it would be ridiculous, because God could with one breath dissipate all contentions which men might raise. When therefore he says, *Who will protest against me?* it is the same as though he said, "Who will make himself a party against me?" as it is commonly said. Who then will oppose himself to me? or, Who will dare to contend with me? or, Who will dare to dispute in judgment with me? I have therefore given this rendering, *and who will protest against me?* and this seems clearly to express the meaning of the Prophet.

He afterwards says, *and who is this pastor that stands before my face?* By the word *pastor*, he alludes to the comparison of a lion; for he thus compares the Idumeans to sheep. Though they were very ferocious, yet here their weakness is referred to. As, then, a sheep cannot defend itself against a lion, so the Prophet shews that the Idumeans would not possess sufficient courage to resist the attacks of the Chaldeans. In short, the Prophet means, that though the Idumeans had many protectors, yet there would be no one able to stand against God when he came forth armed to destroy that nation. The sum of what is said is, that there would be no one, by right or by strength, equal to God, to defend the Idumeans; for he said first, *Who will protest against me?* and then, *What shepherd will stand against me?* We now perceive the meaning of the Prophet, that as the Idumeans had to carry on war with God, it could not possibly be but that they must perish, for though they might get aids on every side, yet they could not, either by right or by strength, withstand God.[1] It follows—

20. Therefore hear the counsel of the Lord that he hath taken against Edom, and his purposes that he hath purposed against the inhabitants of Teman: Surely the least of the flock shall draw them out; surely he shall make their habitations desolate with them.	20. Propterea audite consilium Jehovæ, quod consultavit contra Edom, et cogitationes ejus, quas cogitavit contra habitatores Theman; Si non minores gregis eos dejecerint, si non perdiderint super eos habitacula ipsorum (*vel*, si non perdant super ipsos habitacula ipsorum.)

The Prophet proceeds with his subject respecting the Idumeans and their destruction; but he makes a preface in order to gain credit to his words. He then says that this was God's *counsel* and his *thoughts.* He speaks after the manner of men; for he transfers to God what does not properly belong to his nature; for God does not deliberate or consult, but has once for all decreed before the creation of the world what he will do; nor does he toss about his thoughts in all directions, as men do, who do not immediately see what is right or what ought to be done. Nothing of this kind belongs to God. But this way of speaking is sufficiently common, when what strictly applies to man is transferred to God. It ought at the same time to be observed, that this is not done without reason, for when God

[1] This verse is variously rendered in the versions and in the *Targum*, and also by commentators. The following rendering I deem plain and literal,—

> Behold, as a lion from the swelling of Jordan,
> Will he ascend to the strong habitation;
> For suddenly will I cause him to run from it:
> And he who is chosen will I appoint over her;
> For who is like me? and who can meet me?
> And who is he, the shepherd, who can stand before me?

The word ארגיעה, as in Prov. xii. 19, is "suddenly," or in a moment. "Him" is the lion, and "from it," the swelling of Jordan. "Over her" is Edom. "Who can meet me?" that is, to contend with me, or resist me, according to the *Sept.* The verb is יעד, though *Calvin* derived it from עוד. The "shepherd" is mentioned, because of the "lion," whom no shepherd can resist when he attacks the flock. God speaks of himself as identified with his chosen one.—*Ed.*

speaks by his servants, we ever raise doubts, "Is that said in earnest—can it be changed—is it revocable?" In short, we receive what is light and frivolous, and immediately give credit to it; but when God declares anything, we subject it to comments, and raise up a hundred disputes on every subject, "Oh, but this or that may happen; and it may be that God does not speak in earnest." As, then, men never acquiesce in God's word, as they ought to do, the Prophets borrow from common use these forms of speech, that God had thus thought, that he had thus decreed.

The meaning is, that whatever Jeremiah had hitherto predicted of the Idumeans, could not be retracted, for it was a settled decree, so fixed as though God had thought of it for a hundred or thousand years.

He now adds, *the inhabitants of Teman;* by whom he means the Idumeans. But the repetition deserves notice: he first mentions Edom, and then the inhabitants of Teman. And Teman and Seir are sometimes the same. *If not, cast them down,* &c.; the verb properly means to draw, and to draw in reproach and contempt, as when a carcase is drawn through the mire. Then the Prophet means here a throwing down, accompanied with reproach. And he says, *If not, draw them forth shall the least of the flock.* He speaks here otherwise than before; for he called the Chaldeans chosen, and extolled their strength, that he might strip the Idumeans of their vain confidence; but he now proceeds further and says, that there was no need of great valour to put that nation to flight, because even the least could lay them prostrate on the ground, and also draw them in disgrace through the land. Now, though the manner of speaking is different, yet the meaning remains the same, even that God would arm the Chaldeans with courage, so that they would easily destroy the land of Edom; and then, that though the Chaldeans should not, according to the estimation of men, excel in valour, they would yet be superior to the Idumeans, because victory was in God's hand, and he could work by means of flies as well as by men, and by children as well as by giants.

The formula of swearing is adopted, when he says, *If not,*

draw them, &c. It is an elliptical phrase, as it has often been observed ; such an obtestation as this is understood, " Believe me not hereafter," or, " Regard me not as God." In short, it is a form of an oath, which is a stronger affirmation than if he had simply said, "Draw them forth shall the least of the flock."

Some render the last clause, " If not, set shall they," &c. ; as though the verb came from שום, *shum*, to put, to set ; but it is from שמם, *shemem*, or ימם, *imem*, as some think, though rather שמם, *shemem*. The Prophet, I have no doubt, means, that they would destroy, or lay waste over them their dwellings. It follows—

21. The earth is moved at the noise of their fall ; at the cry, the noise thereof was heard in the Red sea.	21. A voce ruinæ ipsorum contremuit terra ; clamor vocis eorum in mari rubro auditus est.

The Prophet in many words dwells on the same thing, in itself sufficiently clear ; but as it was not easy to convince the Jews of what had been already said of the destruction of the Idumeans, the Prophet continues the same subject. He then says that the *earth trembled at the sound of their fall.* By these words he means that such would be the calamity, that it would terrify all neighbouring countries : as when a great mass falls, the earth shakes, so the fall of the Idumeans, who had long gloried in their wealth, could not but strike all their neighbours with terror. Lest the Jews should think that incredible which had been said, the Prophet says, that though the earth should tremble, yet God would overthrow that nation.

He then adds, *the cry of their voice was heard at the Red Sea.*[1] This sea, called now Red, was at some distance. The word סוף, *suph*, properly signifies weedy, a name given to it on account of the bulrushes it produced ; but the sea that is meant, is what is now called the Red Sea. I have said that the distance between these places was considerable, and what the Prophet means is, that so great and so dreadful would be the shaking of the land of Edom, that its noise

[1] The literal rendering is,—

The cry—at the Red Sea was heard its sound.

It is an instance of the nominative case absolute.—*Ed.*

would make this sea to tremble, though it was at some distance. It follows—

22. Behold, he shall come up and fly as the eagle, and spread his wings over Bozrah: and at that day shall the heart of the mighty men of Edom be as the heart of a woman in her pangs.	22. Ecce tanquam aquila ascendet, et volabit et expandet alas suas super Bosra, et erit cor fortium Edom die illo sicuti cor mulieris anxiæ.

He again speaks of the speedy coming of the Chaldeans, as though he had said, "When the state of that nation shall seem peaceable, when they rest secure in their own nest, then shall the Chaldeans suddenly come, or rather fly." For he compares them to eagles, in order to shew that it would be a very quick and ruinous expedition. At the time this prophecy was declared by the Prophet, no one could have suspected that the Chaldeans would become enemies to the Idumeans, for they were on the best terms with each other; nay, we know that they paid every attention to gain the favour of the Chaldeans. Hence it is said in the Psalms, "Remember, O Lord, the children of Edom, who said in the day of Jerusalem, Let it be cut down, let it be cut down." (Ps. cxxxvii. 7.) By these words is intimated the impious conspiracy of that nation with the Chaldeans. Nor is there a doubt but that they tried by all means to conciliate the Chaldeans for their own interest. Hence the Prophet here points out a sudden change, when he says that the Chaldeans would be like eagles, who would *expand their wings over Bozrah.* We have seen elsewhere that this was the chief city of that nation.

The heart, he says, *of the valiant men of Edom shall be like the heart of a sorrowful woman.* We have seen how great was the pride of the Idumeans. As then they thought themselves superior in valour and counsel, and all other things, the Prophet here shews that the *heart* of their *valiant* men would become effeminate; for it cannot be but the hearts of men are in God's hand. God then is alone he who can sustain and animate us and give us firmness; and he also, when he pleases, can debilitate our spirits; and these things he does every moment: and *that day* then is not expressed without reason; for God does not only impart to every one of us what valour he pleases, but also takes away, when he pleases, the courage which he had given. Hence it is, that the hearts of the brave become cowardly, and also, that the most timid become sometimes bolder than lions, even when it pleases God either to weaken or to strengthen the hearts of men.

But it ought to be noticed, that no hope is given here to the Idumeans as to any remnant. When the Prophet spoke before of other nations, he gave them some consolation; but here he does not mitigate God's vengeance: he dooms the Idumeans to final ruin, without giving them any hope; and for this reason, because God had for a long time borne with them, and they had most wickedly abused his forbearance. He had spared them from the time the children of Israel came up from Egypt; and when they denied a passage to them, the children of Israel made a long circuit with great inconvenience, that they might not touch their land. It was a singular favour shewn to them. And had they had the least drop of humanity in them, they must have acknowledged such a kindness; on the contrary, they had ever cruelly treated their own brethren, and never ceased to do so, though often warned. It is no wonder then that God should now give them up to ruin, and announce predictions full of despair. This ought to be carefully observed, so that we may learn not to make light of God's patience when he bears long with us, but in due time to repent, lest when he rises for judgment he should utterly destroy us. It now follows—

23. Concerning Damascus. Hamath is confounded, and Arpad; for they have heard evil tidings: they are faint-hearted; *there is* sorrow on the sea; it cannot be quiet.

23. Ad Damascum: Pudefacta est Chemath, et Arphad, quia rumorem malum audierunt, liquefacti sunt; in mari pavoris ad quiescendum non potest (*hoc est*, quod quiescere non potest.)

Jeremiah speaks here of the kingdom of Syria, which he means by *Damascus*, where the kings, as it is well known, resided. The Syrians had been from the beginning very hostile to the Israelites; and histories, well known, record that they had continual wars for many years. At length the kings of Israel confederated with the Syrians for the purpose of attacking their brethren the Jews. Hence it was, that the Syrians caused great troubles to the Jews, and were friends to the Israelites until both kingdoms were subverted by the Chaldeans. It is hence probable that this prophecy was announced while the kingdom was yet standing, or at least before its final overthrow; for it was much weakened before it was wholly cut off, as it has been stated elsewhere.

It was necessary to make this preface, in order that we might know the design of God in proclaiming this prophecy against the Syrians, even because they had been from the beginning enemies to the Israelites, and also, because they had united their strength with them for the purpose of oppressing the Jews. They had therefore always been like the fans of the Devil in the work of consuming the church of God. God then shews here that the calamity which awaited them, was a just reward for the impious cruelty which they had exercised towards the chosen people. This we must bear in mind.

He now says, that *Hamath is confounded;* this is considered to have been Antioch in Syria. There were many celebrated cities of this name; but Hamath towards Cilicia was the most renowned. He then says that the city *Hamath*, that is, Antioch, was *ashamed* as well as *Arpad*, which was also an opulent city. He adds, *because they heard a bad report*, or an adverse rumour. By these words he intimates that the kingdom of Syria would be terrified by a report only. No one could have thought such a thing, for when they had united themselves with the Israelites, they thought that they had power enough to drive away their enemies. As then they supposed themselves to be thus strong, so as to be beyond danger, the Prophet derides their confidence, and says that they would be so terrified by mere report, that they would be ashamed as though conquered by enemies.

He then adds, that they *would be melted;* for מוג, *mug*, means to be dissolved or melted. But there is here a different reading; many copies have בים דאגה, *beim dage*, connected with this; and they who read thus are forced to wrest the words of the Prophet. This reading literally is,

"They are ashamed in the sea, dread to rest," or, make to rest, "it cannot," or could not. We see how harsh is the expression; they, however, elicit this meaning, that these cities would be dissolved, as he who sails on the sea and cannot through dread make his heart tranquil. But, as I have already said, the words of the Prophet are thus perverted. Now, if we read for בּ, *beth*, כ, *caph*, which denotes likeness, the meaning would be very suitable, *as a sea of dread*, or a turbulent sea (a noun in the genitive case instead of an adjective, a common thing in Scripture) *which cannot rest* or be still.[1]

As to the general meaning of the passage, there is not much difference; for the Prophet intends to shew that the Syrians would be like a turbulent sea, which is tossed here and there, so that the waves conflict together. If any one prefers to refer this to sailors, the meaning would be still materially the same. The sum of what is said then is, that as the Syrians had been terrible to all, so they would be frightened at the mere report of war, and so much so as to melt away and not be able to stand their ground, like the sea, which, when a tempest rages, has no rest, but is driven in all directions. He afterwards adds,—

24. Damascus is waxed feeble, *and* turneth herself to flee, and fear hath seized on *her;* anguish and sorrows have taken her, as a woman in travail.

24. Remissa est (*vel*, debilitata) Damascus; convertit se ad fugam; et tremor apprehendit eam; angustia et dolores tenuerunt eam tanquam parturientem.

As the clock strikes, I will not proceed further.

PRAYER.

Grant, Almighty God, that as thou settest before our eyes memorable judgments which ought to benefit us at this day, so that we may be kept under thy yoke and under the fear of thy law,—

[1] There are several copies in which the כ, *caph*, is found, and it is evidently the most suitable reading,—

Confounded is Hamath and Arpad;
For an evil report have they heard,—they melt away;
Like the sea the agitation, the quieting none can effect.

The melting away was through fear. They were moved or agitated, and, like the sea, they could not rest or be still. אל may be often rendered none or nothing.—*Ed.*

O grant, that we may not grow hard at such threatenings, but anticipate thy wrath, and so submit to thee, that whatever thou denouncest on the ungodly may turn to our comfort, and for a cause of joy, when we know that the salvation of thy church is thus promoted, of which thou hast been pleased to regard and acknowledge us as members in thy Son our Lord.—Amen.

Lecture One Hundred and Seventy-seventh.

24. Damascus is waxed feeble, *and* turneth herself to flee, and fear hath seized on *her;* anguish and sorrows have taken her, as a woman in travail.

24. Debilitata est Damascus; convertit se ad fugam (*vel,* ad fugiendum;) terror apprehendit eam; et angustia et dolores tenuerunt eam, sicut parturientem.

The Prophet goes on with the same subject, for as the kingdom of Syria had flourished, and had been eminent in wealth and power, it was hardly credible that it could so soon be overthrown. This, then, is the reason why the Prophet, according to his usual manner, describes at large the ruin of that kingdom in order to confirm what he said.

He then says, *relaxed,* or weakened, *is Damascus.* This verb, indeed, sometimes means to cease: he means that she was broken in strength. But under the name of this city, he includes, as it was stated yesterday, the whole kingdom of Syria, which was celebrated for its riches, largeness, and number of men. *She turns,* he says, *to flight.* By these words he intimates that no safety remained for the Syrians except by fleeing into other countries. And it is a miserable safety when men cannot otherwise secure it than by a voluntary exile. He adds the reason, *Trembling has laid hold on her, anguish and pangs have seized her as a woman in travail.* Whenever this comparison occurs in Scripture, some sudden and unexpected evil is intended. The Prophet then no doubt means that the ruin of Syria would be sudden; and he says this, that it might not trust in its own power, and that others might not think her to be beyond danger, because they saw that it was fortified by the number of its men, and by the abundance of all other things. It now follows,—

25. How is the city of praise not left, the city of my joy!

25. Quomodo non est relicta urbs laudis? civitas gaudii mei?

Some think "my" to be redundant, and therefore render it "the city of joy;"[1] but they seem to be induced by no good reason; for they think it absurd that it should be called a city of joy to the Prophet, since he ought not to have regarded Damascus with any love or kindness. But the prophets, we know, do not always speak according to their own feelings, but assume the persons of others. We might then fitly read the words as they are, *the city of my joy!* Besides, Jeremiah very cuttingly exults over Damascus, when he thus expresses his wonder at its destruction: "How can this be," he says, "that *the city of praise,* that is, a celebrated city, and *the city of my joy,* that is, a spectacle so noble as to cause joy to all,—how can it be that this city should not be left, that is, should not be spared? For by "left" he does not mean forsaken by its inhabitants, or reduced to solitude; for by "left" he means untouched or safe.[2]

But we must ever bear in mind what we have often stated, that the prophets, when they thus speak in astonishment, do not adopt an elevated style as rhetoricians do, to shew their eloquence, but have always a regard to what is profitable. It was necessary powerfully to impress the minds of men, when the Prophet spoke of the ruin of so great a city. Then this astonishment includes what they call an

[1] So the versions, (except the *Sept.*) and also the *Targ.*, the י *iod* being regarded as paragogic. So *Grotius.—Ed.*

[2] The *Syr.* rendered it "spared;" the *Vulg.* has left out the negative *not*. There are two difficulties, the verb עזב is not used in the sense of sparing, though *Gataker* labours to shew this; then the connexion: the next verse begins with a "therefore." Take the verb here in its usual sense, and then "therefore" will have its force. He asks, Why was not this city, under the circumstances previously mentioned, forsaken or abandoned, notwithstanding its being a celebrated and a joyous city? But as it was not forsaken, "therefore," he says, "her young men shall fall in her streets," &c.

Venema's view is different; his version is,—

Why not? forsaken has been the city of praise,
The city of my joy.

That is, Why should not Damascus be compelled to flee, since Jerusalem had been forsaken, the city of praise and of his joy. "Therefore," in this sense, refers to the slaughter of those who would not flee.—*Ed.*

anticipation; for it obviated a doubt which might have prevented credit from being given to this prophecy. This might have immediately occurred to every one, "How can it be that Damascus is to perish?" Then the Prophet anticipates this, and shews, that though this was contrary to the judgment commonly formed, yet, as the Lord had so decreed, the destruction of that city was certain. We now then perceive the design of the Prophet. It afterwards follows,—

26. Therefore her young men shall fall in her streets, and all the men of war shall be cut off in that day, saith the Lord of hosts.	26. Propterea cadent electi ejus (*aut*, robusti juvenes, בחורים, *enim propria sunt electi, sed transfertur hoc nomen ad eos qui sunt in pleno vigore aut flore ætatis*) in compitis ejus; et omnes viri militares silebunt (*alii vertunt*, excidentur, *te metaphoricè accipitur illo sensu hoc verbum*) in die illo, inquit Jehova exercituum.

Here the Prophet in a manner corrects himself, and declares, that though the ruin of Damascus would astonish all, yet it was certain; and so I explain the particle לכן, *lacen.* It is regarded by the Hebrews as a particle assigning a reason—therefore, for this cause. They then think that a reason is here expressed why God had decreed to destroy that city, even because it had formerly made war with the Israelites, and then with the Jews, and thus it had not ceased to persecute the Church of God. But it is to be taken here in a simpler way, as an affirmative, according to its meaning in many other places. The Prophet then checks here the astonishment which he had expressed, as though he had said, "However this may be, yet it is so appointed by God, though all should be astonished at the destruction of Damascus, yet *fall shall its young* men, &c." The meaning is, that no power under heaven was such as could resist God. Then Damascus, as it was devoted to destruction, could not avoid that judgment, though it was, according to the opinion of men, impregnable.

And this passage deserves particular notice, for when hinderances occupy our minds, and are presented to our thoughts, we ought ever to set up this as our shield, "Whatever God has appointed must be fulfilled." Though, then, heaven and earth may seem united to impede the celestial decree, let us know that we ought to acquiesce in God's word, and this particle "yet," or nevertheless, לכן, *lacen*, ought always to be remembered by us. For we have said that it was Jeremiah's purpose, in a manner, to bring into subjection whatever men might plan in their own minds; for this alone is sufficient, God has decreed what he declares. It follows,—

27. And I will kindle a fire in the wall of Damascus, and it shall consume the palaces of Ben-hadad.	27. Et accendam ignem in muro Damasci, et consumet palatia Ben-hadad.

Here God himself speaks, and declares that he would be the author of the destruction of which Jeremiah prophesied. And he employs the similitude of fire, because there is nothing more violent or more dreadful than burning; for we know that the greatest cities are soon consumed and reduced to ashes when fire begins to blaze. God then compares the destruction of the city to burning, though no fire was applied to destroy the walls and the palaces of the king; but the Prophet means by this metaphor, that such would be the destruction of the city, as though it was consumed by fire. He at the same time reminds the faithful of God's judgment, that they might know that whatever happened to the Syrians proceeded from his hand; because such calamities would have availed but little, except this doctrine was also added, that just punishments are inflicted by God on the wickedness of men.

But when he speaks of the *palaces of Ben-hadad*, he briefly points out the cause why God would deal so severely with the Syrians. We have said already that they had been always hostile to God's chosen people. They first tried to overthrow the kingdom of Israel; afterwards they confederated with the kings of Israel, but it was for the purpose of overthrowing the kingdom of Judah; and many were the confederacies for this end. But Ben-hadad, as we read in the first book of Kings, grievously distressed the Israelites. We indeed learn from the history of those times, that there were many kings of Syria who bore this name, for it was a common name, as the kings of Egypt were called Pharaohs; and other kings also took a popular name, as the emperors of Rome called themselves Cæsars. But we read that the last Ben-hadad was the son of Hazael, who was also the king of Syria; and as I have said, it was not a private name. Since, then, sacred history clearly shews that there were many who were called Ben-hadad, the Prophet, I have no doubt, refers to the first who began to disturb and harass the Israelites. He then points out the cause why God had determined to destroy Damascus, for he had in his forbearance borne for a long time with the Syrians. But when he saw that they did not repent, but on the contrary added sins to sins, at length ascending his tribunal, he says, that the *fire* which he would apply to the walls of Damascus, would also consume the palaces of Ben-hadad, that is, the palaces whence so many evils had proceeded, and so much cruelty, by which the miserable Church had been distressed. This is the meaning. It now follows,—

28. Concerning Kedar, and concerning the kingdoms of Hazor, which Nebuchadrezzar king of Babylon shall smite, thus saith the Lord, Arise ye, go up to Kedar, and spoil the men of the east.

28. Ad Kedar, et regna Hazor, quæ percussit Nabuchadrezar, rex Babylonis, sic dicit Jehova, Surgite, ascendite adversus Kedar, et perdite filios Kedem (*vel*, orientis).

There is here another prophecy added respecting the Kedareans, who inhabited a part of Arabia. There is elsewhere mention made of them, and it is probable that they were neighbours to the Syrians and not far from Judea; for David complained (if he was the author of that psalm) that he dwelt among the children of Kedar, "Woe to me, because I am compelled to dwell in Mesech and with the children of Kedar," (Psalm cxx. 5.) Whoever, then, composed that psalm, it is a probable conjecture that the Kedareans, though not contiguous to Judea, were not yet far distant; and we have said that they were the inhabitants of Arabia. And the Prophet adds, *the children of Kedem;* so some render the word, as though it were the name of a nation; and Moses tells us that Kedem was one of the sons of Ishmael. It may be that for this reason Jeremiah joined this people to the Kedareans, (Gen. xxv. 13-15.) But I am, however, inclined to the opinion, that he mentions here *the children of the East,* that is, with respect to Judea; not that they were nigh the Persians or other oriental nations, but he only points out a land to the east of Judea.

But why God took vengeance on that people, the cause is not expressed. It may yet have been that they formerly had much injured the Israelites; God therefore having long spared them at length appeared as their severe judge. And though the reason was unknown, yet it did good to the Jews to know, that God's hand was extended to every part of the world to execute vengeance; for they might have hence concluded that they were justly punished, because they had rebelled against God; for we know that a servant who wilfully and disdainfully disobeys his master, deserves double punishment. (Luke xii. 47.) When the Jews then saw that these barbarians, who were like wild beasts, could not escape God's vengeance, they might have thought within themselves how just must have been God's judgments executed on them, who had knowingly and wilfully despised him. This then was one of the benefits to be derived from this prophecy.

And then, as we have elsewhere said, this general rule ought to be borne in mind, that when changes happen in the world, it is necessary, as men's thoughts and feelings are evanescent, that this warning should be given, that God so rules in all these changes, that chance has no place in them. For when calamities, like a deluge, spread over the whole world, then we think, as it has been stated, that such a confusion happens by chance, and without any cause. For when God afflicts some portion, the difference may lead us to some reflection,—"One part is afflicted and another escapes;" but when evils overwhelm the whole world, then, there being no difference, we think that all things are in a state of confusion, nor can we collect our thoughts so as to know, that God so takes vengeance on all, that he yet regulates his judgments, as it is right, according to his infinite and incomprehensible wisdom and justice. As then this adjustment which God makes, as to his judgments, is not evident to the mind and perception of men, it was necessary, when God was at the same time fulminating through the whole world, that the Jews should be reminded to be ever attentive to the operations of his hand. They saw themselves ruined, they saw the same thing happening to the Egyptians and to all other contiguous nations ; at length Assyria was to have its turn, then Chaldea, and afterwards the Medians and Persians. As then no part was to remain untouched, who would not have thought that all things revolved, as it were, through blind and uncertain fate? God, therefore, did not, without reason, forewarn the faithful, lest they should think, that in so great vicissitudes and violent changes, all things were indiscriminately mixed together, but that they might know that God, from heaven, regulated and overruled all these confusions. This is the reason why the Prophets so particularly spoke of the calamities of all nations.

Let us come now to the Kedareans: *To Kedar*, he says, *and the kingdoms of Hazor.* These kingdoms, no doubt, included a large country, for it is hardly credible that Hazor was the name of a city ; for who would have said, *the kingdoms of Hazor*, had it been only the name of a city? It is, indeed, certain, that there was a city of this name, as it is mentioned by Joshua. But here it means a large region, contiguous to the Kedareans. And he says that all these nations had been *smitten by Nebuchadnezzar*, because these barbarous men were probably but little known to the Jews. It must yet be observed, that they had not been as yet smitten by Nebuchadnezzar, that is, at the time the Prophet spoke of their destruction. But Jeremiah spoke thus, in order to confirm his prophecy, as though he had said, that what many disregarded, and even treated with disdain, was at length really fulfilled. For when he threatened ruin to these remote nations, it is probable that he was derided by his own people ; and hence he says, that he had not spoken in vain, but that by the event itself his vocation was proved, because these were smitten as he had predicted.

And this is the prophecy, *Arise ye, ascend against Kedar, and destroy the children of the East.*[1] Here the Prophet speaks of the Babylonians, and in the person of God, as his

[1] It is " Kedem" in the *Sept.*, and " East" in the other versions and the *Targum.—Ed.*

herald. And we have said that God's servants commanded and ordered what was future with supreme authority, in order to gain more reverence and honour to their words or doctrine. For prophecies were despised by ungodly men, and they insultingly said, that they were only words. Hence the servants of God, to shew that their words had accomplishment connected with them, assumed the person of God. Thus they boldly commanded the greatest kings, as Jeremiah does here, *Arise ye ;* for whom does he here address ? the king of Babylon, that greatest of monarchs, and also the Assyrians as well as the Chaldeans : and he commanded them to *arise* and to *ascend,* as though he had them ready for his service, even because he did not speak except by God's command.

And such mode of speaking ought to be especially observed, that we may learn to embrace whatever is announced in God's name, as though the thing itself were already before our eyes, and that we may also know that the power of the whole world, is in such a way under God's control, that all the kingdoms of the earth are ready to fulfil his word. When, therefore, God himself speaks, we ought so to regard the efficacy of his word, as though heaven and earth were ready to obey and to fulfil what he has commanded. It follows,—

29. Their tents and their flocks shall they take away: they shall take to themselves their curtains, and all their vessels, and their camels ; and they shall cry unto them, Fear *is* on every side.	29. Tentoria ejus (tabernacula ejus) et greges ejus tollent, et cortinas ejus, et omnia vasa ejus, et camelos ejus sument sibi, et clamabunt contra eos, Terror undique.

The Prophet, in speaking of tents and curtains, had regard to the way of living adopted by that nation ; for the Arabs, we know, dwelt in cabins and tents, as they do at this day, and they were also shepherds. They had no cultivated fields, but led their flocks through the deserts ; and they had a great number of camels. This is the reason why the Prophet mentions *tents, curtains, camels,* and *flocks,* while speaking of the Kedareans ; for they dwelt not in a fertile country, they possessed no arable lands, nor had they much other wealth, neither cities nor palaces. The sum of what is said is, that the Kedareans were doomed to destruction, and were therefore exposed as a prey to their enemies.

But as this was difficult to be believed, he adds, *They shall cry to them, Terror on every side.* By these words the Prophet means, that there would be so much dread, that all would suffer their possessions to be plundered, not daring to make any resistance, because terror on every side would lay hold on them. They who read, "They shall call them terror on every side," think that this is said metaphorically of the soldiers, as they were terrible. Some also say, "The king of Babylon shall call" or summon "terror on every side against them." But the former explanation is the most probable, that when enemies called or cried out, *Terror, terror*, as conquerors, they would overcome them by their voice alone. This is, as I think, the real meaning of the Prophet. It now follows,—

30. Flee, get you far off, dwell deep, O ye inhabitants of Hazor, saith the Lord; for Nebuchadrezzar king of Babylon hath taken counsel against you, and hath conceived a purpose against you.

30. Fugite, abite procul valdè (profundaverunt ad habitandum incolæ Hasor, dicit Jehova); quia consultavit super vos Nabuchadnezar rex Babylonis consilium, et cogitavit contra vos cogitationem.

Jeremiah continues here the same subject, but more clearly expresses what he had said, *Flee*, he says, *depart far away.* What follows I read as a parenthesis, *Deep have they made to dwell, the inhabitants of Hazor*. Then Jeremiah proceeds with his subject, *because consulted against you has Nebuchadnezzar, the king of Babylon*, &c. He then bids them to *flee* to a distance, because Nebuchadnezzar had resolved to destroy them. By *counsel* and *thought* or purpose, the Prophet means the secret means by which he subdued the people when they feared no such thing. As then these shepherds lived securely on their mountains, Nebuchadnezzar prepared his forces, and divided them ; and thus were these taken by his counsel and craft less than by strength. What the Prophet says here of the *counsel* and *device* of Nebuchadnezzar is not superfluous, because he indirectly touched on the sloth of that nation, who exercised no vigilance and thought, their desert being a sufficient cover to them. As then they thus lived securely, the Prophet here reminds them that they would have to do with a cunning enemy, who would contrive and form his counsels at home, and then would execute in due time what he had long meditated.

But a parenthesis follows, *Deep have they made ;* to make more clear the sense, an adversative particle must be considered as understood, *Though deep have they made to dwell ;* for without this exception the prophecy would have been less credible. For Kedareans were on every side fortified, because no one envied them, as they were not only frugal men, but also barbarous and contented with an austere and wretched living. As then they thought themselves thus safe, some one might have raised this objection and said, " Why dost thou bid them to flee ? wherefore should they flee ? for there is no one so foolish as to attack them." So also the Scythians laughed at Alexander when he attacked them. " What is your object ? you think that you have to do with men ; we are wild beasts : and then if you seek wealth and riches, you will not find them with us." Such then was the state of those nations mentioned here. When, therefore, the Prophet bids them to flee, because Nebuchadnezzar would suddenly attack them, he at the same time adds, *Though deep have they made to dwell.*[1] He had before used this mode of speaking : to make deep to dwell, means to have a safe and hidden standing, remote from all danger. They are then said to be deep in their dwellings who dwell in fortified cities, or who inhabit deserts, or who are hid in some poor country, as the Kedareans and their neighbours. But the Prophet says, that this would not prevent the Babylonians from invading their land, and taking possession of it. It follows,—

31. Arise, get you up unto the wealthy nation, that dwelleth without care, saith the Lord, which have neither gates nor bars, *which* dwell alone.

31. Surgite, ascendite contra gentem securam, habitatorem (eum qui habitat) in fiducia, dicit Jehova ; non portæ nec vectes ei, solus habitat.

[1] This verb is deemed by most to be in the imperative mood, like the two foregoing verbs ; and it is so given in the *Sept.*, the *Vulg.*, and the *Targ.* In the *Syr.* all the verbs are in the past tense, which is not consistent with the context. *Blayney's* version is,—

Flee ye, move off apace,
Retire deep for to dwell, &c.

The meaning is, as he says, that they should go into deep caverns to hide themselves from their enemies. See Judges vi. 2 ; 1 Sam. xiii. 6.—*Ed.*

He confirms the last verse, repeating what he had already said, *Arise, ascend;* but he adds, *against a quiet nation.* This was the *deep* dwelling of which he had spoken; for the Kedareans, as they thought themselves to be as it were in another world, were secure; and hence he says, *against a secure nation.* The word שליו, *sheliu,* means delicate, as we have seen elsewhere, but in this place its meaning is secure. For though there might be no joys there, it is yet said to be a secure nation, גוי שליו, *gui sheliu,* a nation which feared nothing. And then he explains himself, *a dweller in confidence,* one without fear and anxiety.

And he gives the reason, because they had no need of *gates* and *bars,* and they *dwelt alone.* Some interpreters think that the pride of the Kedareans is denoted, because they would not protect themselves in the usual way, and regarded gates and bars as nothing. But the Prophet's meaning is different, that as they were barbarians and shepherds and beyond the reach of envy, they thought that no enemy would ever come to them. For what are the causes of wars but avarice and ambition? and who would wish to rule over barbarous nations living on their mountains? and then wealth cannot be found in a wild uncultivated country. As then the Kedareans were such, the Prophet says that they *dwelt securely,* though they were not fortified by gates and bars, but lived alone. He then says that they lived alone, not because they thought much of themselves as being solitary, and regarded themselves as being above kings—for solitude often produces pride and obstinacy; but the meaning of the Prophet, as I have said, is quite different, even because the Kedareans thought that they had no need of friends and assistants, because they depended not on their neighbours for aid, but were contented with their own deserts. And at the same time they did not think that any enemy would disturb them, as there was no cause and no occasion.

We now then perceive again why the Prophet says, that they *made deep to dwell,* that is, that they had their dwelling deep, even because poverty and the absence of all riches were to them a sort of safe fortress: as they had no splendour and no dignity, they thought themselves exempt from the common lot of other men. But nevertheless he says that the Chaldeans would come and plunder them of what they had. It follows,—

32. And their camels shall be a booty, and the multitude of their cattle a spoil: and I will scatter into all winds them *that are* in the utmost corners; and I will bring their calamity from all sides thereof, saith the Lord.	32. Et erunt cameli eorum in direptionem, et copia pecorum ipsorum in prædam; et dispergam eos ad omnem ventum, extremos anguli, et ab omnibus lateribus ejus adducam perditionem ipsorum, dicit Jehova.

The explanation shall be given to-morrow.

PRAYER.

Grant, Almighty God, that though the things related to us to-day from thy Prophets, concerning ancient nations, may seem as grown out of use, O grant that we may however be seriously impressed whenever we read of thy judgments as executed on any part of the world, so that we may learn at this day wholly to submit to thee and flee to thy mercy, and that whatever may happen to us, we may never doubt but that thou wilt be propitious to us, if we seek thee with a sincere heart, and with unfeigned faith in Christ Jesus, our Lord.—Amen.

Lecture One Hundred and Seventy-eighth.

In the verse we read yesterday, Jeremiah again repeated that the Kedareans would be so plundered by their enemies that nothing would remain for them. He therefore speaks again of camels and of cattle: he says that the *abundance of cattle* and the *camels* would be for a *spoil* and *plunder*. But why he names camels and cattle rather than fields and vineyards, I briefly explained yesterday. For when a fertile country is the subject, whether abounding in corn or in vines, the Prophets spoke of such possessions; but when, as now, a reference is made to a country abounding in cattle and also mountainous, the Prophet speaks only of camels and of cattle; for the mode of living in that nation, as it has been stated, was austere and hard, and almost below the condition of man. When food for their cattle failed them, they went elsewhere, and carried in their waggons all their furniture.

It now follows, *I will disperse them to every wind.* Here Jeremiah predicts the scattering of that nation. It sometimes happens that a country is plundered by enemies, when yet the inhabitants, stripped of their goods, remain there and live in poverty. But together with poverty, Jeremiah declares that there would be no ordinary exile, for the words are emphatical, *I will scatter them to every wind.* There is here an implied contrast between that people and chaff; for as the chaff is carried away in all directions by blasts of wind, so would be, as Jeremiah shews, the scattering of that people. And he mentions also *the utmost corners* קצוצי פאה, *kotsutsi pae. Jerome* usually renders the words, "shorn of hair," but very improperly; for there is no reason why the other people mentioned before should be thus called; for in chap. vii. and xxv. Jeremiah did not speak of the Kedareans, and yet he called many nations קצוצי פאה *kotsutsi pae.* The verb קצץ *kotsets,* whence this word comes, means to cut off; and פאה *pae,* signifies the extremity of anything.[1] This phrase then is the same as though he mentioned those bordered by an extremity or a corner. And this is most suitable to this passage; for it was not probable that they who dwelt in recesses should be thus scattered. When any wealthy country is plundered by enemies, they flee here and there in all directions; for instance, were a part of Italy laid waste, they would flee to those parts who could receive fugitives; but when a nation dwells in an extreme corner, where could it betake itself, when routed by enemies? The Prophet therefore enhances the misery of exile when he says, that people at the extremities would become fugitives, so as to be scattered through all parts of the world.

He adds, *and from all its sides will I bring their destruction.* He confirms the same thing; for when an evil enters on one side, neighbours may assist; but when calamity urges on every side, miserable men must then of necessity be scattered; and they must seek some distant exile, as there is no part that can shew them hospitality. All this then refers to their scattering. It afterwards follows,—

[1] See vol. i. p. 506.—*Ed.*

33. And Hazor shall be a dwelling for dragons, *and* a desolation for ever: there shall no man abide there, nor *any* son of man dwell in it.

33. Et erit Hazor in habitationem draconum, vastitas usque in perpetuum (in seculum;) non habitabit illic vir, et non manebit illic (*aut,* peregrinabitur in ea) filius hominis.

Here Jeremiah concludes his prophecy concerning the Kedareans; he says that their land would be deserted. The Prophets often make use of this way of speaking, that the land, deserted by its inhabitants, would become the habitation of dragons. And this is more grievous than when the land remains empty; for when dragons succeed men, it is a dreadful thing. Hence, that God's judgment might produce more impression on men's feelings, the Prophets often declare that a deserted place would become the dwelling of dragons. He adds what imports the same thing, *A waste shall it be for an age:* but עולם, *oulam,* means perpetuity. And it is added, *Not dwell there shall a man, nor live there shall a son of man.* There seems indeed to be a superfluity of words, for it would have been sufficient in one sentence to say, that the land would be deserted and not inhabited. But he first assigns it to dragons: then he adds that it would be a waste or solitude; and lastly, he says that no one would dwell there, and not only so, but having mentioned *man,* he adds the *son of man.* Some indeed think that by *man* the nobles are referred to, and that by the *son of man,* or Adam, we are to understand the common people, the multitude. But as we have said elsewhere, this is too refined. It is a repetition which increases the effect, though in the second clause he speaks more generally and expresses the thing more clearly, as though he had said, that no one of the human race would become an inhabitant of that land.[1] It now follows,—

34. The word of the Lord that came to Jeremiah the prophet against Elam, in the beginning of the reign of Zedekiah king of Judah, saying,
35. Thus saith the Lord of hosts,

34. Qui fuit sermo Jehovæ ad Jeremiam, prophetam, contra Elam, principio regni Zedechiæ, regis Jehudah, dicendo,
35. Sic dicit Jehova exercituum,

[1] The difference in the two clauses is properly distinguished by *Blayney,* in his version,—

There shall not a man dwell there,
Nor shall a son of man sojourn therein.—*Ed.*

Behold, I will break the bow of Elam, the chief of their might.	Ecce ego frango arcum Elam, principium fortitudinis ipsorum.

By Elam some interpreters understand Persia, and it is the most common opinion. I however think that the Elamites were not the same with the Persians ; I should rather say that they were the Parthians, were it not that Luke, in Acts ii. 9, makes them a distinct people from the Parthians. At the same time it is not right, as it seems to me, to regard the Persians as generally designated by Elam ; for the Persians were remote from the Jews, and the Jews never received any injury from that people. There was therefore no reason why the Prophet should denounce punishment on them. The country of Elymais was known as bordering on the Medes, and contiguous to the Persians. But that people must have joined the Assyrians and Chaldeans against the Jews. As then the Babylonians had them as auxiliaries, it was God's purpose to avenge the injury done to his people. Besides, Pliny also speaks of Elamites as being contiguous to the Nabatheans ; but they were occupying, as it were, the middle place between Persia and Judea. They were indeed, as he shews elsewhere, a maritime people ; for he speaks often of Elymais, but names the Elamites only once. However this may have been, they were orientals as the Persians were, but not so far from Judea ; and as they were, at it has been said, near the Medes, the probability is that they joined themselves with the enemies of the Church, when Nebuchadnezzar drew with him the vast forces which he had everywhere gathered, that he might extend his dominion far and wide ; for we shall see in what follows that God was grievously displeased with the Elamites.[1] We hence conclude that they were very hostile to the chosen people, whose cause God here undertakes.

This much as to the name: when, therefore, Jeremiah speaks here of the Elamites, let us know that a particular nation is referred to, and one distinct from the Persians, and

[1] They were the descendants of Elam the son of Shem, Gen. x. 22. They were a powerful kingdom in the days of Abram, Gen. xiv. 1. Isaiah speaks of them as hostile to the people of Israel, Isaiah xxii. 6. Shushan is said to have been in the province of Elam, Dan. viii. 2.—*Ed.*

then that this nation assisted the Chaldeans in oppressing the Jews. Let us now see what the Prophet declares respecting them.

He says, first, that this word came to him *in the beginning of the reign of Zedekiah.* Nebuchadnezzar, then, greatly harassed the Jews, while yet they remained in their obstinacy; and it is probable that the Elamites formed a part of the Chaldean army. When, therefore, the Jews considered how various were their enemies, and when they did not expect that they would ever be punished, it was a trial that must have greatly distressed the minds of the godly. What Jeremiah then declared, no one could have thought of, that is, that the Elamites would not escape unpunished, because they so furiously attacked the chosen people under the banner of King Nebuchadnezzar. This, then, was the reason why the Prophet specified the time: *this word,* then, *came in the beginning of the reign of Zedekiah.*

Then God, in the first place, declares that he would *break the bow of Elam.* The Parthians and other Orientals, we know, were very skilful archers; for every nation possesses its own peculiar excellency in connexion with war. Some excel in the use of one kind of weapons, and others in the use of another kind. Formerly light infantry were in high repute among the Italians; the Gauls excelled in mailed horsemen. Though, now, all things are changed, yet still every nation differs as to its peculiar art in war. Now historians testify that the Orientals were very skilful in the use of the bow and arrow. It is, then, no wonder that the Prophet speaks of the *bow* of this people, and calls it *the chief part of their strength,* as they excelled in this sort of fighting. The Parthians were indeed much dreaded by the Romans; they pretended to flee, and then they turned back and made an impetuous attack on their enemies. They had also arrows dipped in poison. By these means they conquered large armies. For the Romans laid by their darts and fought hand in hand, and carried on a standing fight, so to speak; but when the Parthians kept discharging their arrows, they almost always fought unsuccessfully with them. I refer to this, that we may know that the bow was not without reason called the *chief of their might*, for it was by it that they were superior to other nations, though they could not fight hand in hand nor with drawn swords. It afterwards follows—

36. And upon Elam will I bring the four winds from the four quarters of heaven, and will scatter them toward all those winds; and there shall be no nation whither the outcasts of Elam shall not come.

36. Et adducam contra Elam quatuor ventos a quatuor finibus cœlorum, et dispergam eos ad omnes ventos istos; et non erit gens ad quem non veniat quispiam profugus (*est mutatio numeri, sed quæ sensum non obscurat*, quispiam ex iis qui expulsi fuerint) ab Elam.

He now adds that *four winds* would come, which would dissipate the whole people. God himself speaks, in order that the word might be more powerful and have more weight. *I will rouse up*, he says, *four winds.* And we know that the air is in a moment put in motion whenever it pleases God; and when Scripture extols the power of God, it does not without reason refer to the winds; for it is not a small miracle when the whole world is on a sudden put in motion. It is now tranquil, and then in half an hour the winds rise and conflict together in mid air. And God alludes to what is usual in nature: as then he suddenly rouses up winds which make, as it were, the whole world to shake and tremble; so he says he would raise up winds from the four ends of the world. But he speaks metaphorically; by winds he understands enemies, who would on all sides unite their powers to oppress the Elamites. *I will bring*, he says, *on Elam the four winds from the four quarters of the world.* By the last words he expresses more clearly what I have just said, that God alludes to that formidable power which is daily presented to our eyes in nature. As, then, a sudden change disturbs the whole earth when winds arise, so God declares that he would rouse up four winds from the four quarters of the heavens. And he calls them the *quarters of the heavens;* for though the winds arise from the earth, yet their blowing is not perceived until they ascend into mid air: and though sometimes they seem to be formed above the clouds, they yet arise from the earth; for the origin of the wind is cold and dry-exhalation.

We now understand the reason why the Prophet speaks

of the winds. There is yet no doubt but that he denotes some enemies by the four winds; but this prophecy was not fulfilled as long as the Persian monarchy ruled and flourished. It is, then, probable that the destruction denounced by the Prophet took place many ages after, even when the soldiers of Alexander contended about the supremacy; for we know how grievously distressed were all the Orientals when Alexander made an irruption into those countries. It was, indeed, a horrible tempest. But as he enjoyed the empire of the east but for a short time, what is said by the Prophet here was not then fulfilled. But those countries were afterwards so miserable, torn by intestine wars, that the Prophet does not without reason compare those contrary and opposite movements to four winds; for never has there been a fiercer emulation between enemies, and each of them had strong armies. Hence, then, it was, that that land was not oppressed by one enemy, but exposed to various and almost innumerable calamities. This is the reason that leads me to interpret this prophecy as fulfilled in the calamities which followed the death of Alexander the Great.

I will scatter them, he says, *to these four winds;* that is, as one wind breaks out at one time, and another at another time, so the Elamites shall flee here and there. For no one ruled long peaceably in the East, till almost all the soldiers of Alexander were consumed by mutual slaughters. Then Seleucus obtained Syria, and exercised the cruellest tyranny. But, as I have said, before Seleucus obtained peace and security, the whole of that part of the world had been inundated with blood. This is the reason why the Prophet says that the Elamites would be scattered to *these four winds.*

The end of the verse remains: *and there shall be no nation to which some of the fugitives from Elam shall not come.* We cannot, certainly, shew from histories when this was fulfilled which the Prophet now says; but it is probable that that people were scattered at the time when the chiefs contended about the supremacy, that is, those who obtained power under Alexander. At the same time there would be nothing unreasonable were we to say that the Prophet spoke hyperbolically; and no doubt he exceeds due limits when he says

"There shall be no nation to which some of the fugitives from Elam shall not come." He indeed understands all the neighbouring nations. But it may also have been that they did not flee to the Asiatics, but rather departed towards the Persian sea or to the Indies. We have already stated why the servants of God sometimes introduced hyperbolical expressions into their teaching, even because they had to do with men who were slow and stupid, who would not hear God when speaking in a simple manner, and could hardly be moved when he thundered. It now follows—

37. For I will cause Elam to be dismayed before their enemies, and before them that seek their life; and I will bring evil upon them, *even* my fierce anger, saith the Lord; and I will send the sword after them, till I have consumed them.

37. Et expavefaciam Elam coram hostibus ipsorum, et coram his qui quærunt animam ipsorum; et adducam super eos malum excandescentiæ iræ meæ, dicit Jehova; et emittam post eos gladium usque dum consumpsero ipsos.

This verse especially shews that the Elamites were of the number of those who had inhumanly raged against God's people, for he did not without reason set forth the severity of his vengeance towards them. We must, then, bear in mind that the Elamites had been among the chief of God's enemies, or at least had been in no ordinary way cruel, delighting in slaughters. Hence he says, *I will dismay*, or affright, &c. The verb חתת, *chetat*, means to tear in pieces, or to break; it may therefore be rendered, "I will break." They who render it "I will lay prostrate," do not seem to know the difference between *consternere*, to lay prostrate, and *consternare*, to dismay. But the most suitable meaning is, that God would terrify the Elamites, for he had spoken before of their flight and exile.

He then mentions the cause of their dread, even because *God* would dismay them and frighten them before their enemies, so that they would not be able to stand before them. By these words he intimates, that however warlike the Elamites were, they yet would not stand their ground when it seemed good to God to render to them their reward, for in his hand are the hearts of men. Though, then, the Elamites were brave, yet the Prophet declares that they would be so faint-hearted *at the sight of enemies*, as immediately to flee away, even because God would terrify them.

He afterwards adds, *I will send the sword after them.* He means by this clause that he would not be content with terrifying them, but that when they began to flee, he would take them, because he would follow them, that is, urge on their enemies. And it ought ever to be observed, that what proceeds from men is ascribed to God, because men, however little they may think of it, yet execute his purpose, and are not only the proclaimers of his wrath, but also the instruments of it.

But he mentions *the evil of the indignation of his wrath.*[1] This mode of speaking seems indeed harsh; but we have elsewhere stated, that the Prophets did not without reason join together these words, which appear somewhat harsh. Now wrath does not in a strict sense belong to God, for no feelings of this kind appertain to him. But when heat of wrath or indignation is mentioned, it doubles its vehemence in order to shake off the torpor of men, who would otherwise, as I lately said, be wholly insensible and indifferent. In short, by *indignation* the Prophet means no other thing than that vengeance is dreadful, and ought to astonish all mortals, so that they ought to fall down immediately as it were lifeless, as soon as they hear that God is displeased with them. In the meantime he shews what I have stated, that God was grievously offended with that people whom he threatens with extreme punishment, for he says, *until I shall have consumed them.* We see what I have said, that this people were not slightly chastised, according to what has been mentioned of others: it hence follows that their wickedness had been very atrocious. The two clauses seem however to be inconsistent, —that God would scatter the Elamites through all nations,— and that he would consume them, for dispersion and consumption widely differ. But consumption refers to the body of the nation or to its name, as though he had said, that no Elamites would survive, because they would be merged in other nations, and disappear like chaff. It follows—

[1] "The indignation of his wrath" is in apposition with "evil." So the *Vulg.*, the *Syr.*, and the *Targ.*

And I will bring on them evil,
The burning of my wrath, saith Jehovah.

The evil was the effect of God's high displeasure.—*Ed.*

38. And I will set my throne in Elam, and will destroy from thence the king and the princes, saith the Lord.	38. Et statuam solium meum in Elam; et perdam illinc regem et principes, dicit Jehova.

He confirms what I have just referred to as to their consumption; but he at the same time adds, that God would be in such a way the avenger as though his tribunal was erected in that land. He threatens that he would *destroy the king and the princes;* and this, as I have explained, was the consumption; for though some individuals would remain alive, yet the name of the people would not survive, the whole race as such would become extinct.

But these words ought to be noticed—that God would *erect* his *throne.* God is said to erect his throne when he rules; but his kingdom is not to be taken always in a good sense. God is properly said to rule or reign among the faithful, whom he governs by his Spirit. So God's kingdom begins and has its origin when regeneration takes place. But sometimes, as I have already said, God is said to reign in the midst of his enemies, as we have seen respecting the Egyptians. He then erected his throne when he executed his recorded judgment on the Elamites, for though the Elamites were blind, yet God's power was made really evident, and by the effect he proved that he was the King of that people whose wickedness he punished with so much severity. In short, as God is said to be silent, to sleep, or to lie down, when he does not execute his vengeance; so in this place he is said to erect his throne when he discharges the office of a Judge. It follows—

39. But it shall come to pass in the latter days, *that* I will bring again the captivity of Elam, saith the Lord.	39. Et erit in posteritate dierum (*hoc est,* diebus sequentibus, *vel* successu dierum) convertam (*vel,* reducam) captivitatem Elam, dicit Jehova.

Here God mitigates the severity of the prediction, because he would at length gather some of the Elamites and restore them, so that they might again obtain some place or honour. He says not in the *end of days,* but after many days, *It shall be in course of time that I will restore the captivity of Elam.* If it be asked when this was fulfilled, doubtless there has not been a restoration of that nation recorded in history. But the Prophet no doubt gives here a hope to the Elamites, which he gave before to other nations, even that they should be united again under Christ as their head. Though then the Elamites were not afterwards known, yet they have found out that this was not said in vain; nor does the Holy Spirit without reason mention them by the mouth of Luke among others who were converted to Christ. (Acts ii. 9.) For though the Elamites were almost unknown, yet he connects them with the Medes and Parthians, "Parthians and Medes and Elamites." This then was the time of which Jeremiah had prophesied, when he said that the Elamites would again be gathered together, that they might not be perpetually captives. And though they might not have then returned into their own country, yet it was a condition far better and more desirable when they obtained a name and a place in the Church than if they had enjoyed every other blessing in the world. And we know that it is said of Christ, that God would gather under his hand all things scattered both in heaven and earth. (Col. i. 20.) A part of this scattering was God's vengeance on the Elamites. Gathered then have been Elamites with others; and thus God at that time stretched forth in a manner his hand to them through Christ the Mediator, and opened to them the door of hope as to eternal life.

PRAYER.

Grant, Almighty God, that as thou didst favour despairing men with some consolation when justly and extremely indignant with them,—O grant that whenever we at this day provoke thy wrath, we may at the same time taste of thy paternal mercy, and learn to flee to thee, and to put our hope in thine only-begotten Son, so that we may never despond, but ever look forward to that gathering, whose beginning is now seen, and whose final and complete accomplishment awaits us in heaven, through the same Christ our Lord.—Amen.

CHAPTER L.

Lecture One Hundred and Seventy-ninth.

1. The word that the Lord spake against Babylon, *and* against the land of the Chaldeans, by Jeremiah the prophet.

1. Sermo quem loquutus est Jehova super Babylone, super terra Chaldæorum, in manu Jeremiæ prophetæ.

Our Prophet has been hitherto speaking of neighbouring nations who had cruelly harassed the chosen people; and it was some consolation when the children of Abraham understood that God undertook their cause and would be the avenger of those wrongs which they had suffered. But this of itself would have been no great consolation, yea, it might have been viewed as nothing by many, while there was no hope of restoration; for it would have been but a small consolation to have others as associates in misery. If, indeed, Jeremiah had only taught that none of the nations who had troubled God's Church would escape unpunished, the Jews might have raised an objection, and said, that they were not freed from their own calamities, because the monarchy of Babylon still flourished, and that they were buried as it were in a perpetual grave. It was therefore necessary that what we read here should be predicted. And though this prophecy is given last, we ought to notice that the Prophet had from the beginning expressly spoken, as we have seen, of the calamity and destruction of Babylon. But this prophecy is given as the conclusion of the book, to mitigate the sorrow of the miserable exiles; for it was no small relief to them to hear that the tyranny by which they were oppressed, and under which they did live as it were a lifeless life, would not be perpetual. We now then understand why the Prophet spoke of the Babylonians and of their destruction.

But a longer preface would be superfluous, because those acquainted with Scripture well know that the Jews were at length so reduced by the Babylonians that their very name seemed to have been obliterated. As then they were reduced to such extremities, it is no wonder that the Prophet here affirms that the Babylonians would be at length punished, and that not only that God might shew himself to be the avenger of wickedness, but also that the miserable exiles might know that they were not wholly repudiated, but on the contrary that God had a care for their salvation. We now perceive the design of this prophecy.

The word of Jehovah, he says, *which he spoke concerning Babylon, concerning the land of the Chaldeans, by the hand of*

Jeremiah the Prophet. He testifies in his usual manner that he did not bring forward what he himself had invented, but that God was the author of this prophecy. He at the same time declares that he was God's minister; for God did not descend from heaven whenever it pleased him to reveal his favour to the Jews, but, as it is said in Deuteronomy, he was wont to speak by his servants. (Deut. xviii. 18.) In short, Jeremiah thus recommends the things he was about to say, that the Jews might reverently receive them, not as the fictions of men, but as oracles from heaven. It follows—

2. Declare ye among the nations, and publish, and set up a standard; publish, *and* conceal not: say, Babylon is taken, Bel is confounded, Merodach is broken in pieces; her idols are confounded, her images are broken in pieces.

2. Nuntiate in gentibus, audire facite (*hoc est,* promulgate,) et tollite signum, promulgate, ne taceatis (*ad verbum,* ne occultetis,) dicite, Capta est Babylon, pudefactus est Bel, contritus est Merodach, pudefacta sunt simulachra ejus, contrita sunt idola ejus.

He predicts the ruin of Babylon, not in simple words, for nothing seemed then more unreasonable than to announce the things which God at length proved by the effect. As Babylon was then the metropolis of the East, no one could have thought that it would ever be possessed by a foreign power. No one could have thought of the Persians, for they were far off. As to the Medes, who were nearer, they were, as we know, sunk in their own luxuries, and were deemed but half men. As then there was so much effeminacy in the Medes, and as the Persians were so far off and inclosed in their own mountains, Babylon peaceably enjoyed the empire of the whole eastern world. This, then, is the reason why the Prophet expresses at large what he might have set forth in a very few words.

Tell, he says, *among the nations, publish, raise up a sign,* and again, *publish.* To what purpose is such a heap of words? even that the faithful might learn to raise up their thoughts above the world, and to look for that which was then, according to the judgment of all, incredible. This confidence shews that Jeremiah did not, in vain, foretell what he states; but he thundered as it were from heaven, knowing whence he derived this prophecy. And his proclamation was this, *Babylon is taken, Bel is confounded, and Merodach is broken.* I know not why some think that Merodach was an idol: for as to Bel, we know that the Babylonians trusted in that god, or rather in that figment. But the Prophet mentions here evidently the name of a king well known to the Jews, in order to shew that Babylon, with all its defences and its wealth, was already devoted to destruction: for we know that men look partly to some god, and partly to human or temporal means. So the Babylonians boasted that they were under the protection of Bel, and dared proudly to set up this idol in opposition to the only true God, as the unbelieving do; and then in the second place, they were inebriated with confidence in their own power: and hypocrisy ever rules in the unbelieving, so that they arrogate to themselves much more than what they ascribe to their idols. It is then the same thing as though he had said, that Babylon was taken, that Bel was confounded, and that the kingdom was broken, or broken in pieces.[1]

The name *Merodach*, as I have said, was well known among the Jews, and mention is made of a father and of a son of this name, by Isaiah and in sacred history. (Is. xxxix. 1; 2 Kings xx. 12.) It is no wonder, then, that the Prophet should name this king, though dead, on account of the esteem in which he was held, as we have seen in the case of the kingdom of Syria, he mentioned Ben-hadad, though no one supposes that he was then alive; but as Ben-hadad distinguished himself above other kings of Syria, the Prophet introduced his name. For the same reason, in my opinion, he names Merodach here.

[1] Most consider that "Merodach" here was a false god; first probably a king, afterwards deified. As "confounded," or put to shame, is applied to Bel, the other verb חת, should be rendered "dismayed" or terrified, a meaning which it often has,—

Taken is Babylon,
Confounded is Bel,
Terrified is Merodach;
Confounded are her images,
Terrified are her idols.

The word for "images" means labour, and refers to the labour and pains taken by those who made them; and the word for "idols" means a trunk or log of wood from which they were made.—*Ed.*

The sum of the whole is, that though Babylon thought itself safe and secure through the help of its idol, and also through its wealth and warlike power, and through other defences, yet its confidence would become vain and empty, for God would bring to shame its idol and destroy its king. He again returned to the idols, and not without reason ; for he thus called the attention of his own nation to the only true God, and also reminded them how detestable was the idolatry which then prevailed among the Chaldeans. And it was necessary to set this doctrine before the Jews, and to impress it on them, that they might not abandon themselves to the superstitions of heathens, as it happened. But the Prophet designedly spoke of images and idols, that the Jews might know that it was the only true God who had adopted them, and that thus they might acquiesce in his power, and know that those were only vain fictions which were much made of through the whole world by the heathens and unbelieving. It now follows—

3. For out of the north there cometh up a nation against her, which shall make her land desolate, and none shall dwell therein: they shall remove, they shall depart, both mna and beast.

3. Quoniam ascendet contra eam gens ab aquilone, quæ ponet terram in vastitatem, et (ut) non sit habitator in ea ab homine usque ad bestiam; fugerunt, abierunt.

Let what I have before said be borne in mind, that the Prophet makes use of many words in describing the ruin of Babylon ; for it was not enough to predict what was to be ; but as weak minds vacillated, it was necessary to add a confirmation. After having then spoken of the power of Babylon and its idols, he now points out the way in which it was to be destroyed—a nation would come from the north, that is, with reference to Chaldea. And he means the Medes and Persians, as interpreters commonly think ; and this is probable, because he afterwards adds that the Jews would then return. As then Jeremiah connects these two things together, the destruction of Babylon and the restoration of God's Church, it is probable that he refers here to the Medes and Persians. If, at the same time, we more narrowly view things, there is no doubt but that this prophecy extends further, and this will appear more evident as we proceed.

He simply says now that a *nation* would *come from the north,* which would *turn the land to a waste.* This clause shews that this prophecy could not be fitly confined to the time when Babylon was taken by Cyrus ; for we know that it was betrayed by two Satraps during a siege ; and that it was at a time when a feast was held, as though there was peace and security, as Daniel testifies, with whom heathen writers agree. Now Xenophon testifies that Cyrus exercised great forbearance and humanity, and that he used his victory with such moderation, that Babylon seemed as though it had not been taken. It had, indeed, changed masters, but such was the change that the citizens readily submitted to it. But it was afterwards more hardly dealt with, when Darius recovered it by the aid of Zopyrus ; for Babylon had revolted from the Persians, and shook off the yoke. Darius having in vain stormed it, at length recovered it by the help of one man ; for Zopyrus, having cut off his nose, and mutilated his ears and his face, pretended, in this deformed manner, to be a fugitive, and complained of the cruelty and barbarity of his king, with whom yet he was most intimate. The city was soon afterwards taken by treachery in the night. Then about four thousand of the Persians were hung in the middle of the Forum, nor did Darius spare the people. The Prophet then seems to include this second destruction when he predicted that the whole land would be made desolate. Nor ought this to be deemed unreasonable, for the Prophets so spoke of God's judgments, that they extended what they said further than to the commencement, as was the case in the present instance.

When, therefore, Babylon was taken by the Persians, it received the yoke ; and she which ruled over all other nations, was reduced to a state of servitude. For the Persians, as it is well known, were very inhuman, and Isaiah describes them so at large. In the meantime, the city, as I have said, retained its external appearance. The citizens were robbed of their gold and silver, and of their precious things, and were under the necessity of serving strangers: this was bitter to them. But when Darius punished their perfidy and hung so many of the chief men, about four thousand, and also shed indiscriminately the blood of the people, and subjected the city itself to the plunder of his soldiers, then doubtless what the Prophet says here was more fully accomplished. It was yet God's purpose to give only a prelude of his vengeance, when he made the Babylonians subject to the Medes and Persians. It now follows—

4. In those days, and in that time, saith the Lord, the children of Israel shall come, they and the children of Judah together, going and weeping: they shall go, and seek the Lord their God.

4. Diebus illis et tempore illo (*sed* עת *propriè significat condictum aut præfixum tempus,*) dicit Jehova, venient filii Israel ipsi, et filii Jehudah simul, eundo et flendo venient, et Jehovam Deum suum quærent.

The Prophet now explains more clearly the purpose of God, that in punishing so severely the Chaldeans, his object was to provide for the safety of his Church. For had Jeremiah spoken only of vengeance, the Jews might have still raised an objection and said, "It will not profit us at all, that God should be a severe judge towards our enemies, if we are to remain under their tyranny." Then the Prophet shews that the destruction of Babylon would be connected with the deliverance of the chosen people; and thus he points out, as it were by the finger, the reason why Babylon was to be destroyed, even for the sake of the chosen people, so that the miserable exiles may take courage, and not doubt but that God would at length be propitious, as Jeremiah had testified to them, having, as we have seen, prefixed the term of seventy years. He was derided by the Jews, who had so habituated themselves to hardness of heart, that they counted as nothing, or at least regarded as fables, all the reproofs and threatenings of God, and also gave heed, as we have seen, to the flatteries of the false prophets.

Jeremiah now promises that God would be their liberator after the time of exile had passed, of which he had spoken. Thus we perceive the design of this passage, in which the Prophet, after having referred to the destruction of Babylon, makes a sudden transition, and refers to God's mercy, which he would shew to the Jews after they had suffered a just punishment: *In those days,* he says, *and at that time*—he adds the appointed time, that the Jews might not doubt but that the Chaldeans would be subdued, because God had appointed them to destruction.

He says, *Come shall the children of Israel, they and the children of Judah together;* and he says this, that they might still suspend their desires. He commends here the greatness of God's favour, because the condition of the Church would be better after the exile than it was before. The ten tribes, as we know, had separated from the kingdom of Judah; and that separation was as it were the tearing asunder of the body. For God had adopted the seed of Abraham for this end, that they might be one body under one head; but they wilfully made a defection, so that both kingdoms became mutilated. The kingdom of Israel became indeed accursed, for it had separated from the family of David, and this separation was in a manner an impious denial of God. As then the children of Israel had alienated themselves from the Church, and the kingdom of the ten tribes had become spurious, their condition was doubtless miserable (though the Jews as well as the Israelites were alike inebriated with their own lusts).

But what does our Prophet now say? They shall return together, *the children of Israel and the children of Judah;* that is, God will not only gather the dispersed, but will also apply such a remedy, that there will no more be any separation; but that on the contrary a brotherly concord will prevail between the ten tribes and the tribe of Judah, when God shall restore them again to himself. We now then perceive what the Prophet had in view: there is, indeed, here an implied comparison between their former state and that which they could yet hardly hope for, after their return from exile; for there is nothing better than brotherly concord, as it is said in the Psalms, "How good and how pleasant it is for brethren to dwell together in unity." (Psalm cxxxiii. 1.) For the kingdom and the priesthood, the pledges, as it were, of the people's safety, could not stand together, without the union of the Israelites with the Jews.

But they had been long alienated from one another, so that the chief favour of God had been extinguished by this separation. The Prophet says now, that they would *come together.*

And he adds, *Going and weeping they shall come.* This may seem contrary to what is said in the Psalms, " Going they shall go, and weep as those who sow ; but coming they shall come with joy, carrying their handfuls." (Psalm cxxvi. 6.) The Prophet says here, that they shall *come with tears.* How can these two things be consistent ? even because weeping may be taken for that which flows from joy or from admiration ; for we know that tears gush out not only through sorrow, but also through rejoicing ; and further, when anything unexpected happens, tears will flow from our eyes. We can then take the Prophet's words in this sense, that they would come weeping, because they would then find God merciful to them. But it is better to regard sorrow as simply meant ; and the two things may be thus reconciled,—that the Jews would come with joy, and also with sorrow, not only because the memory of their exile could not be immediately obliterated from their minds, but because it behoved them to remember their sins : they saw the Temple overthrown, the land wasted—sights sufficient to draw tears a hundred times from the hardest. On one side there were reasons for joy ; and on the other, reasons for tears. We know that there were tears shed ; for the Prophet Haggai expressly tells us, that the old men, who had seen the former Temple, were much cast down, because there was then no such glory as they had seen. (Haggai ii.)

However this may have been, the Prophet means, that though the return would not be without many troubles, yet the Jews would come ; *coming,* he says, they shall *come,* that is, going they shall go, *and weep,* as it is said in the Psalms, that they would come through desert and dry places. (Psalm lxxxiv. 6.) The meaning then is, that though the journey would be hard and laborious, yet the Jews would return with alacrity into their own country, so that no labours would so fatigue them as to make them to desist from their course.

He subjoins the main thing, that they would come to *seek their God.* Their change of place would have been useless, had they not come animated with the desire of worshipping God; for the worship had ceased during the time of exile, as it is said again in another Psalm, "How shall we sing songs to our God in a foreign land?" (Psalm cxxxvii. 4.) Then the Prophet here reminds them, that God's favour would be real and complete, because the Jews would not only return to their own country, so as to possess it, but that they would also set up the worship of God, and dwell as it were under his protection. It follows,—

5. They shall ask the way to Zion, with their faces thitherward, *saying*, Come, and let us join ourselves to the Lord in a perpetual covenant *that* shall not be forgotten.

5. Sion interrogabunt viam (*hoc est*, interrogabunt de via) versus Sionem, illuc facies eorum: Venite, et copulate vos Jehovæ fœdere perpetuo, quod oblivione non delebitur (*subaudiendum est relativum pronomen, quod omissum est.*)

He explains himself more at large, that they would *ask* those they met *the way*, that *their faces* would be towards *Sion*, that they would also exhort one another to seek God and join themselves to him by a perpetual covenant. The Prophet includes here all the tribes, and says that the Jews and the Israelites would not only return into their own country, to partake of the produce of that rich and fruitful land, but that they would also render to God the worship due to him, and then that nothing would be so vexatious to them but that they would be able to overcome all difficulties and all obstacles.

He says first, that they would *ask the way*—a proof of perseverance; that they would *ask the way to Sion*, that is, ask how they were to proceed that they might come to Sion. By these words, the Prophet, as I have just said, denotes their constancy and indefatigable resolution, as though he had said, that though they journeyed through unknown lands, yea, through many devious places, they would yet be in no way disheartened so as not to inquire of those they met with until they came to Sion. This is one thing. Then he adds to the same purpose, *Thither their faces.* We indeed know, that plans are often changed when adverse events impede us; for he who undertakes an expedition, when he sees his course very difficult, turns back again. But the Prophet declares here that there would be no change of mind that would cause the Jews to relinquish their purpose of returning, because *their faces* would be towards *Sion*, that is, they would turn their eyes thither, so that nothing would be able to turn them elsewhere. There is added, in the third place, an exhortation, *Come ye; and they shall join themselves to Jehovah* their God, by *a perpetual covenant.* Here the Prophet first shews, that the Jews would be so encouraged as to add stimulants to one another; and hence it is said, *Come ye;* and, secondly, he adds, *they shall cleave* (there is here a change of person) *to Jehovah by a perpetual covenant which shall not by oblivion be obliterated.*[1]

He again repeats what he had said, that the exiles would not return to their own country, that they might there only indulge themselves, but he mentions another end, even that they might join themselves to God. He means, in short, that God would do for them something better and more excellent than to allure them by earthly pleasures.

But we must notice the words, *they shall cleave* (so it is literally) *to Jehovah by a perpetual covenant;* for there is an implied contrast between the covenant they had made void and the new covenant which God would make with them, of which Jeremiah spoke in chapter xxxi. God's covenant was, indeed, ever inviolable; for God did not promise to be the God of Abraham for a certain term of years; but the adoption, as Paul testifies, remains fixed, and can never be

[1] The two verbs are rendered by the versions, except the *Syr.*, and by the *Targ.*, in the future tense, "They shall come and be joined," &c.; and one MS., says *Blayney*, has יבאו. This would read better. Then the verse would run thus—

To Zion will they ask the way,
Hither their faces;
They shall come and be joined to Jehovah,
By an everlasting covenant, *which* shall not be forgotten.

"Hither," and not "thither," for the Prophet was at Jerusalem: and so the particle means, and it is so given in the *Sept.* and *Vulg.* The last clause requires "which" in our translation, though not in *Welsh*, for, like the Hebrew, it can do without it—*nad anghofir*, literally the Hebrew. What is here predicted was literally accomplished, as recorded by Nehemiah, (ix. 38; x. 29.)—*Ed.*

changed. (Rom. xi. 29.) Then on God's part it is eternal. But as the Jews had become covenant-breakers, that covenant is called, on this account, weak and evanescent: and for this reason the Prophet said, " In the last days I will make a covenant with you, not such as I made with your fathers, for they have broken, he said, that covenant." (Chapter xxxi. 31, 32.) Jeremiah now repeats the same thing, though more briefly, that the Jews would return to favour with God, not only for a moment, but that his covenant might continue and remain valid; and the way by which this would be done is expressed in chapter xxxi., even because God would inscribe his law on their inward parts, and engrave it on their hearts. For it is not in man's power to continue so constant as that God's covenant should never fail; but what the Prophet omits here must be supplied from the former passage, that when the Jews returned, God's covenant would again become so valid and fixed, that it would never fail, even because their hearts would be renewed, so that they would be faithful to God, and never become apostates any more like their fathers.

He then adds, This covenant *shall not be forgotten.* We hence conclude, that the perpetuity of which he speaks, was founded rather on the mere benevolence of God than on the virtue of the people. He calls then the covenant which God would never forget, perpetual, because he would remember his mercy towards the chosen people; and though they were unworthy to receive such a favour, yet he would continue perpetually his mercy towards them to the coming of Christ; for the passage clearly shews that this prophecy cannot be otherwise explained than of Christ's spiritual kingdom. The Jews indeed returned to their own country, but it was only a small number; and besides, they were harassed by many troubles; God also visited their land with sterility, and they were lessened by various slaughters in wars: how then came the prophets thus to extol in such high terms the favour of God, which yet did not appear among the people? even because they included the kingdom of Christ; for whenever they spoke of the return of the people, they ascended, as we have said, to the chief deliverance. I do not yet follow our interpreters, who explain these prophecies concerning the spiritual kingdom of Christ allegorically; for simply, or as they say, literally, ought these words to be taken,—that God would never forget his covenant, so as to retain the Jews in the possession of the land. But this would have been a very small thing, had not Christ come forth, in whom is founded the real perpetuity of the covenant, because God's covenant cannot be sèparated from a state of happiness; for blessed are the people, as the Psalmist says, to whom God shews himself to be their God. (Ps. cxliv. 15.) Now, then, as the Jews were so miserable, it follows that God's covenant did not openly appear or was not conspicuous; we must therefore come necessarily to Christ, as we have elsewhere seen, that this was commonly done by the Prophets. The Prophet now enters on a new argument,—

6. My people hath been lost sheep; their shepherds have caused them to go astray, they have turned them away *on* the mountains: they have gone from mountain to hill, they have forgotten their resting-place.

6. Grex perditus fuit populus meus, pastores eorum errare fecerunt ipsos, per montes abierunt, a monte in collem profecti sunt, obliti sunt accubitus sui.

As the clock strikes, I must stop here.

PRAYER.

Grant, Almighty God, that we may not be inebriated with the sweetness of earthly blessings which thou bestowest continually on us, but learn to ascend to the hope of celestial life and eternal felicity, and in the meantime have such a taste of thy blessings, that we may know that thou art an inexhaustible fountain of all felicity, so that we may cleave to thee with a sincere heart and in perfect integrity, until we shall at length be brought to the full fruition of that kingdom, which thine only-begotten Son has procured for us by his own blood.—Amen.

Lecture One Hundred and Eightieth.

The Prophet in the sixth verse compares God's people to lost sheep: he therefore says, that the Jews *wandered on the mountains* and *went from mountain to hill.* He throws the blame on the shepherds, by whom the miserable people had been led astray. Notwithstanding, God does not extenuate the fault of the people; nor did he accuse the pastors as though their wickedness and perfidy absolved the people; but on the contrary, he commends the greatness of his own grace, that he had mercy on a flock that was lost and without hope.

We now then understand the design of the Prophet when he thus spoke in the person of God, *My people have become lost sheep, and the shepherds have seduced them, on the mountains have they made them to go astray, from mountain to hill have they gone;* and he says, that they had *forgotten their lying down;*[1] for when there is no fixed station, the sheep have no place to rest. Flocks, we know, return in the evening to their folds. But the Prophet says that the Jews, when scattered, forgot their lying down, because they had no settled habitation. It afterwards follows,—

7. All that found them have devoured them; and their adversaries said, We offend not, because they have sinned against the Lord, the habitation of justice; even the Lord, the hope of their fathers.

7. Omnes qui invenerunt eos comederunt, et adversarii eorum dixerunt, Non peccamus, quia scelerati fuerunt contra Jehovam; habitaculum justitiæ et expectatio (*vel*, spes) patrum ipsorum, Jehova.

Jeremiah goes on with the same subject; for he tells us how miserable was the condition of the people until God looked on them to relieve them from their evils. And this comparison, as I have before said, more fully sets forth the favour of God, because he raised up his people as it were from hell at a time when they were reduced to despair.

He says first, *All who found them devoured them;* that is,

[1] I render the verse thus,—

6. Lost sheep have become my people;
Their shepherds have caused them to err,
Having turned them here and there on the mountains;
From mountain to hill have they gone;
They have forgotten their resting-place.

The meaning of שׁוֹבְבִים is given by the *Sept.* and *Vulg.*, "causing them to wander;" the verb שׁב is to turn; being here a reduplicate, it means to turn much, or again and again, or here and there; and this is confirmed by what follows—they went, through the teaching of their pastors, from "mountain to hill," that is, from one form of idolatry to another; and "forgotten their resting-place," which was God.—*Ed.*

all who came in contact with them thought them a prey. He, in short, means that they were plundered by all who met them; and then that enemies were so far from sparing them that they gloried in their cruelty towards them. Hence he adds, *Their enemies said, We sin not, because they have acted wickedly against Jehovah.* By these words the Prophet intimates, that their enemies indulged in greater wantonness, because they thought that what they did would not be punished. Almost the same sentiment is found in Zechariah, where it is said, "All who devoured them sinned not, and they who devoured them said, Blessed be the Lord who has enriched us." (Zech. xi. 5.) But we must more closely consider the design of the Holy Spirit. The Prophet indeed shews that the Jews were reduced to extremities, so that they were not only cruelly treated by their enemies, but were also exposed to the greatest contempt. He, however, reminded them at the same time of their duty to repent, for when the whole world condemned them, it was but right that God should call them to an account for their sins. As then he had set over them all men as their judges, he indirectly touched and goaded their consciences, so that they might know that they had to do with God. When therefore Zechariah said, "All who devoured thee said, Blessed be the Lord," he meant, that the sins of the people were so manifest to all, that all the heathens declared that they deserved extreme punishment; for by the words, "Blessed be the Lord who hath enriched us," he intimated that heathens, in spoiling and plundering the Jews, would be so far from feeling any shame, that they would rather glory in being enriched with prey as it were by the hand of God. So also in this place, *All who found them devoured them, and their enemies said, We sin not,*—and why? *because they have acted wickedly against Jehovah.*

In short, the Prophet means, that the Jews would not only be exposed to the rapacity, avarice, and cruelty of enemies, but also to the greatest contempt and reproach. At the same time he exhorted them to repent; for if they were thus condemned by the judgment of the whole world, it was not unreasonable to direct their thoughts to the tribunal of

God. Nor was it a strange thing that the unbelieving referred to God, for it is what we commonly meet with in all the prophets ; and it was ever a principle held by all nations, that there is some supreme Deity ; for though they devised for themselves various gods, yet they all believed that there is one supreme God. So the name, Jehovah, was known in common by all nations: and hence the Prophet here introduced the Chaldeans as speaking, that the Jews had *acted wickedly against Jehovah ;* not indeed that they ascribed to God his honour, but because this opinion, that there is some God, was held by all ; and this God they all indiscriminately worshipped according to their own forms of religion, but they still thought that they worshipped God.

What follows, interpreters explain as though the Prophet in the person of enemies intended to exaggerate the sin of the chosen people; they therefore connect the words thus, "They have been wicked against Jehovah, who is the habitation of justice, and has always been the hope of their fathers." If we take this meaning, it is no wonder that their sin is amplified, because the Jews had forsaken not some unknown God, whose favour and power they had not experienced, but because they had been perfidious against the God who had by many proofs testified his paternal love towards them. It was then an impiety the more detestable, because they had thus dared to forsake the only true God.

But I approve of a different meaning,—that the Prophet answers by God's command, that their enemies deceived themselves, when they thus confidently trod under foot the chosen people, and thought that everything was lawful for them. The Prophet, I doubt not, now checks the wantonness of which he speaks, as though he had said, "Ye think that this people are wholly rejected by me, and hence there are no limits to your cruelty; but I have so adopted them, that my covenant can never be rendered void." We may better understand what Jeremiah means by a similar example: when Isaiah answered King Hezekiah that God would be the defender of the city, when they recited to him the words of Sennacherib or of Rabshakeh, who brought his orders, (Isa. xxxvii. 24,) he said, " But he thinks not that I have founded Sion."[1] That answer seems to me to be wholly like this passage. Sennacherib said, " I will go up and take the city and the temple ;" he, in short, triumphed as though he was a conqueror ; but God, on the other hand, restrained his confidence in these words, " But that impious and proud enemy knows not that I have created Sion, and have been from the beginning its maker: can I then now bring upon it such a destruction as would wholly cut off the memory of it ? Many cities have indeed perished, and there is no place so illustrious which may not sometime be destroyed ; but the condition of the holy city (says God) is different." And he adds the reason, Because he had created it. So in this place, *Jehovah is the habitation of justice and the hope of their fathers.* For God's enemies almost always form their judgment according to the present state of things ; for in prosperity they are inflated with so much pride that they dare insolently to utter blasphemies against God. For though the Chaldeans had spoken thus, that they sinned not, because the Jews had been wicked, there is yet no doubt but that their boasting was insulting to God, as it is said in Is. xxxvii. 22, 23, " The virgin, the daughter of Zion, hath despised and derided thee, and drawn out the tongue against thee ; me, the God of hosts, he says, hath he despised." By these words God shews that he was derided in the person of his Church. For this reason, then, God himself now comes forth and declares that he is the habitation of justice and the hope of his chosen people, in order that the Chaldeans might not promise themselves prosperity perpetually.

We hence see that these sentences are set in opposition one to another rather than connected together, and spoken in the person of the ungodly. The Chaldeans said, " We sin not, because they have acted wickedly against Jehovah ;" then the Prophet responds and shews that they deceived themselves if they thought that God's covenant was abolished, because he for a time chastised his people, as it is said by

[1] *Calvin*, in his exposition of Isa. xxxvii. 26, applies what is said to Sion, and not to Sennacherib, as it is commonly done.—*Ed.*

Isaiah, "What shall the messengers of the nations declare?" or, "What shall be told by the messengers of the nations? that God hath founded Sion." (Isa. xiv. 32.) When he spoke of the deliverance of the people and city, he added this acclamation, that it would be a memorable benefit, the report of which would be known among all nations, that is, that God had founded Sion, that it had been wonderfully delivered as it were from present destruction.

He first calls God the *habitation of justice;* and he alludes, as I think, to the tabernacle; and then he more clearly expresses himself, that *God was the hope of their fathers.* The Jews were indeed unworthy of being protected by God; but he speaks not here of their merits, but, on the contrary, God himself affirms the perpetuity of his covenant, and the constancy of his faithfulness, in opposition to the ungodly. For since the Chaldeans had already possessed the greater part of the country, and had taken all the cities except Jerusalem, they thought that the people were forsaken by their God; and this tended to cast reproach on God himself. Hence he declares here, that though the Jews had been wicked, yet his covenant was so far from being extinct, that he was a *habitation,* that is, like a place of refuge. And he calls him the *habitation of justice,* that is, firm or faithful; for justice is not to be taken here in its proper sense, but, as in many other places of Scripture, it means firmness or rectitude; as though he had said, "God has once extended his wings to cherish his people, (as it is said elsewhere;) he will therefore be always a sure habitation."

He had also been the hope of their fathers, according to what is said by Isaiah, that he had created Sion from the beginning; but he renews the memory of his covenant, as though he had said, "It is not to-day that I have first received this people into favour, but I made a covenant with their father Abraham, which will remain fixed." So, also, he says in this place, that he was the hope of their fathers, even because he had adopted the whole race of Abraham, and shewed them mercy through all ages. Then the Prophet indirectly infers that it would not be possible for their enemies perpetually to possess power over them, because

God, after having chastened his people, would again gather the dispersed, and thus heal all their evils.[1]

A useful doctrine may be hence gathered, that whenever the Church seems to be so oppressed by enemies as to exclude any hope of restoration, this ought always to be borne in mind by us, that as God has once chosen it, it cannot be but that he will manifest his faithfulness even in death itself, and raise from the grave those who seem to have been already reduced to ashes. Let this passage, then, come to our minds, when the calamities of the Church threaten utter ruin, and nothing but despair meets us; and when enemies insolently arrogate everything to themselves, and boastingly declare that we are accursed. But God is a *habitation of justice*, and was the *hope of our fathers;* let us, then, recumb on that grace which he has once promised, when he deigned to choose us for himself, and to adopt us as his peculiar people. Such is the import of the passage. It follows,—

8. Remove out of the midst of Babylon, and go forth out of the land of the Chaldeans, and be as the he-goats before the flocks.	8. Fugite e medio Babylonis, et e Chaldæa egredimini, et sitis tanquam hirci ante gregem.

This verse confirms the exposition which I have given; for God does not now reprove his people, nor does he condemn their sins; but on the contrary, he exhorts them to entertain good hope, though they were overwhelmed with extreme miseries. He then pursues the same subject when he bids them to *flee from Babylon and to go forth from Chaldea;* for he promises deliverance to the faithful, and at the same time reminds them of the coming ruin of the Chaldean empire, so that they who went the farthest off would best

[1] The most approved exposition is the first, which makes the latter words to be in apposition with Jehovah, as given in the Versions, though the last clause seems to be a separate sentence,—

Because they have sinned against Jehovah,
The habitation of righteousness;
And the hope of their fathers *was* Jehovah.

By calling God the habitation of righteousness, what is implied is, as *Lowth* suggests, that they would not have been banished, had they not justly deserved to be so treated, God being the seat or dwelling-place of justice or righteousness. And in addition to this, he had been the hope of their fathers. See ch. xl. 3, where we have an example of what their enemies alleged.—*Ed.*

consult their own safety. For the Prophet intimates that all found in Chaldea would be exposed to the violence of enemies; hence he bids them to flee and to go forth quickly. But as I have before said, he promises a free exit to the Jews; for he would have in vain exhorted them to depart had they been shut up, for we know that they had been confined as within inclosures. Had they then been thus captives, the Prophet would have spoken in mockery by saying to them, *Flee* and *go forth*. But he shews that their captivity would not be perpetual, because God would remove all obstacles and open a way for the miserable exiles to return to their own country.

He bids them to be as *he-goats before the flocks:* by which he means that they were to hasten with all confidence. For the he-goats possess more boldness than sheep, and they go before the flock because no fear restrains them. So God takes away every fear of danger from the Jews when he bids them to be *as he-goats before the flock;* as though he had said that they were no more to fear, lest the Chaldeans should punish them for avowing their wish to return to their own country; for it was a capital offence to speak of their return as long as the Chaldeans ruled over the Jews. But God now promises a change, for he would dissipate the terror by which they had been for a time restrained. It follows,—

9. For, lo, I will raise, and cause to come up against Babylon, an assembly of great nations from the north country: and they shall set themselves in array against her; from thence she shall be taken: their arrows *shall be* as of a mighty expert man; none shall return in vain.

9. Quia ecce ego excito (excitans, *ad verbum*, et adducens) et adduco super Babylonem congregationem gentium magnarum e terra aquilonis, et ordinabunt contra eam (aciem *scilicet*,) unde capietur; sagittæ ejus tanquam fortis prudenter agentis; non redibit frustra.

Here, again, God declares that enemies would come and overthrow the monarchy of Babylon; but what has been before referred to is here more clearly expressed. For he says, first, that he would be the leader of that war—that the Persians and Medes would fight under his authority. *I*, he says (the pronoun אנכי, *anki*, is here emphatical,) *I am he*, says God, who *rouse* and *bring*, and then he adds, *an assem-*

bly of great nations. The Chaldeans, as we know, had devoured many kingdoms, for Babylon had subjugated all the neighbouring nations. Except, then, this had been distinctly expressed, they might have disregarded the prophetic threatenings. But Jeremiah speaks here of the assembly of great nations, lest the Chaldeans, relying on their power, the largeness of the monarchy, and the multitude of their men, should promise themselves victory, and thus lie asleep in their indulgences. God then, in these words, shortly intimates that there would be ready at hand those who in number and power would surpass the Chaldeans.

He afterwards adds, *They will set in order against her.* Something is to be here supplied—that they would set the battle in order. Now, by this expression, the Prophet sets forth the boldness of the Persians and Medes, as they would be immediately ready for the conflict; they would not long consult, but quickly advance to the fight. In short, he refers to the quickness and boldness of the Persians and Medes, when he says, *They shall set in order against her;* for they who distrust their own strength, take convenient positions, or contrive ambushes, or withdraw for a time until they know all the plans of their enemies; but the Prophet says that the Persians would by no means be such, because they would be prepared for battle at the first onset, and have the army set in order against the Babylonians.

It follows, *thence taken shall be* Babylon. The word משם, *mesham,* means from that place. But the Prophet intimates that the Persians would become conquerors by one battle only, so that the Chaldeans would no more dare to resist. We indeed know that those once put to flight, do often prepare new forces and renew the battle; this is indeed usually the case, and it seldom happens that any one is conquered in one battle. But the Prophet here declares that Babylon would be taken at one time; as soon, he says, as the fight begins, the enemies shall not only overcome, but shall by one assault take Babylon, so as to make it captive.

We now, then, perceive the design of the Prophet; but, doubtless, this prophecy was a derision to the unbelieving, for he seemed to speak of a thing impossible: thus he sang a fable to the deaf. But God, however, did not without reason predict that Babylon would be so taken, that it would, as it were, in one moment fall into the hands of enemies. We said, indeed, yesterday, that it was long besieged and taken by treachery in the night; but we also said that this prophecy is not to be confined to one period; for Babylon was often taken. It was taken through the contrivance of Zopyrus, as we said yesterday, when it thought itself sufficiently strong to resist, and Darius had nearly despaired. We shall therefore find nothing inconsistent in this prophecy, when we consider how great and how supine was the security of that people even at the time when they were suddenly overthrown.

He now adds, *Its arrows as of a valiant man;* some render it, "as of a bereaving man," because some put the point on the right side and some on the left. The word שכל, *shecal,* means to act prudently, to be prosperous, and also to be bereaved. But I agree with those who take the first sense, for it immediately follows, *it shall not return in vain.* Those who render the word "bereaved," understand thereby that the arrows of the Persians would be deadly or fatal. But the context does not correspond, for an explanation is afterwards given, that it would not return in vain. It seems, then, that by this word Jeremiah denotes their dexterity, as though he had said that the Persians would be so skilful in throwing arrows, that they would not discharge one arrow in vain; as those who are well exercised in that art always aim directly at an enemy, and never shoot their arrows here and there without effect. So then the Prophet says that the arrows of the Persians would be those of men shooting skilfully, who know how to take a right aim.[1] And he calls them *valiant* or strong; for it is not enough to send arrows straight against an enemy, except there be also nerve and strength to shoot them; for arrows might touch one, but not penetrate into his body, or hardly hurt his skin. But

[1] Their arrows, like those of a skilful warrior.—*Blayney.* In the next line there is an instance of לא being in the sense of *none,*—"None shall return empty," or void; *i.e.,* without effecting its purpose. See Isa. lv. 11. —*Ed.*

the Prophet refers to both these things—that arrows would be hurled with sufficient force to strike and wound the Chaldeans—and that they would also have always a direct aim, so that no one would miss its object. It afterwards follows,—

10. And Chaldea shall be a spoil: all that spoil her shall be satisfied, saith the Lord.	10. Et erit Chaldæa in prædam; quicunque prædati fuerint ipsam, saturabuntur, dicit Jehova.

Here he mentions the effect of the victory, that he might more fully confirm what he had said; for it is sometimes the case, that they who are conquered flee to their cities. The country is indeed laid waste, but the enemies depart with their spoils. But the Prophet here says, that the whole of Chaldea would be plundered: he further adds, that the plunderers would be *satiated*, as though he had said, "The enemies shall not only seize on all sides, as it sometimes happens, on what may fall into their hands, but they shall heap together all the treasures of Chaldea until they shall be satiated." He means, in short, that Chaldea would be wholly emptied; for these two things ought to be deemed as set in opposition the one to the other,—that the enemies would be filled to satiety, and that the Chaldeans would be reduced to poverty. Then the satiety of which the Prophet speaks, implies that the Chaldeans would be brought to extreme penury and want. It follows,—

11. Because ye were glad, because ye rejoiced, O ye destroyers of mine heritage, because ye are grown fat as the heifer at grass, and bellow as bulls;	11. Certè lætati estis (*in futuro quidem tempore,* lætabimini,) et exultabitis quum diripietis hæreditatem meam; multiplicabimini (*hoc est,* augescetis) tanquam vitula herbæ, et hinnietis tanquam equi fortes:
12. Your mother shall be sore confounded; she that bare you shall be ashamed: behold, the hindermost of the nations *shall be* a wilderness, a dry land, and a desert.	12. Pudefacta est mater vestra valdè, erubuit genitrix vestra; ecce postremum gentium, desertum, vastitas, solitudo.

God shews here, that though the Chaldeans insolently exulted for a time, yet their joy would not continue; and at the same time he points out the cause of their ruin, even because they dealt so arrogantly with the people of God. He then says in the former clause, *Ye exulted and rejoiced in plundering my heritage;* and then he adds, *Ye became fat* (for to be multiplied means here to become fat) *as a heifer*, well fed, or *of the grass;* for some think that the word is used for דשאה, *deshae;* but some render it, "herbified," or fed on grass; while others derive the word from דוש, *dush*, to thresh or tread out corn.[1] It is then added, *Ye neighed like strong horses*, or ye bellowed like bulls, as some render the words; for אבירים, *abirim*, sometimes mean bulls, and sometimes strong horses; and the verb צהל, *tzal*, means to cry aloud, but is taken sometimes in the sense of neighing, as we have seen in the fifth chapter, "Every one neigheth on his neighbour's wife;" the Prophet said so in condemning the people for their lusts; and they who apply this passage to bulls are obliged to change the meaning of the verb—for bellowing, and not neighing, is what belongs to bulls.[2]

Now it was necessary, for two reasons, for the Prophet to speak thus; first, it was hardly credible, that the Chaldeans, after so many and so remarkable victories, could be broken down and laid prostrate by new enemies; for they had been terrible to the whole world, they had subdued all their neighbours, they had extended on all sides their borders; it was then the same as though they had set their nest in the clouds. Then the Prophet says here, that though they exulted and gave loose reins to their joy, yet this state of things would not be perpetual, because they should at length be brought to shame. This is one thing. And the second reason why the Prophet spoke thus was, because God intended that it should be testified to his own people, that though he permitted so much liberty to the Chaldeans, he had not yet forgotten his covenant; and for this reason he mentioned the word heritage. Though then the calamity of his people was apparently a sort of repudiation, as though God designed to have nothing more to do

[1] Several copies have דשה, threshing. Being allowed to eat at pleasure, the threshing heifer became fat and frisky. It is so taken by *Blayney* and *Henderson*, though not countenanced by the Versions or the *Targ.—Ed.*

[2] Jeremiah having twice before (chapters viii. 16; xlvii. 3) used the word for steeds or horses, we may conclude that he means the same here. *—Ed.*

with them, yet he says that they were his own heritage; and thus he shews, that God would give a specimen of his favour towards the Jews, by thus severely chastising the Chaldeans. This then is the reason why he says, *Ye have rejoiced in plundering my heritage, but your mother is ashamed.* He expresses here more than if he had said, "Ye shall at length lie down confounded with shame;" but he names their mother, that he might intimate the destruction of the whole of that monarchy, which had been so terrible to all the neighbouring nations.[1]

PRAYER.

Grant, Almighty God, that though we cease not daily to provoke thy wrath by our many sins, we may yet, with confidence, flee to thy mercy, and that though thou seemest for a time to cast us away, we may not yet cast away hope, founded on thy eternal word, but that, relying on that Mediator in whom we always find the price of expiation, we may not hesitate to call on thee as our Father; and may we, in the meantime, find thee by experience to be such towards us, so that we may cheerfully look forward to that celestial inheritance, which has been obtained for us by the blood of thy only-begotten Son.—Amen.

Lecture One Hundred and Eighty-first.

We explained yesterday why the Prophet denounced shame and reproach on the Babylonians, even because they had arrogantly exulted over the children of God. And he says that Babylon would be *the extremity of the nations.*

[1] The connexion of these two verses will be more evident, if we render כי *when,* as proposed by *Gataker,* and not *surely,* as by *Calvin,* nor *because,* as in our version,—

11. When ye shall rejoice, when ye shall exult,
Ye plunderers of mine heritage,
When ye shall skip as a fed heifer,
And neigh like steeds,
12. Ashamed greatly *shall be* your mother,
Confounded *shall* she *be* who bare you;
Behold, the last of the nations *shall she be,*
A desert, a dry land, and a wilderness.

The reference seems to be to the rejoicings of Babylon, when it was taken. —*Ed.*

The Chaldeans had flourished in power and wealth, and possessed the empire of the East. It was then an extraordinary revolution to be reduced to the lowest condition, to be, as it were, the dregs of all the nations. And to the same purpose he adds, *a barren land, a desert, and a solitude.* It now follows,—

13. Because of the wrath of the Lord it shall not be inhabited, but it shall be wholly desolate: every one that goeth by Babylon shall be astonished, and hiss at all her plagues.	13. Ab indignatione Jehovæ non habitabitur (*hoc est*, præ indignatione, *aut*, propter indignationem,) et erit vastitas tota; quisquis transierit per Babylonem stupebit, et sibilabit super omnibus plagis ejus.

Jeremiah again repeats that the destruction of Babylon would be an evidence of God's vengeance, because the Chaldeans had unjustly raged against the Church. But the name of God seems also to have been designedly mentioned, that the faithful might more readily receive this prophecy: for had they thought that what Jeremiah said came from man, they would have hardly believed his words, for what he said exceeded the comprehension of men. He then mentioned the indignation of God, that the faithful might know that it was absurd to form an opinion concerning the ruin of Babylon according to the present aspect of things, because God would do a work there beyond the common course of things.

He then says, that it would become *a waste*, so that *every one passing through it* would be astonished, and yet would not pity it. This way of speaking often occurs in the Prophets, when they wish to describe a waste exceeding what is common. In the meantime, what follows ought to be noticed, that this arrangement would excite no commiseration, but rather mockery, which the Prophet denotes by the the word *hissing.* It then follows,—

14. Put yourselves in array against Babylon round about; all ye that bend the bow, shoot at her, spare no arrows: for she hath sinned against the Lord.	14. Ordinate contra Babel per circuitum; quicunque tenditis arcum projicite (*vel*, jaculamini) super eam, (contra eam,) ne parcatis sagittæ; quia contra Jehovam sceleratè egit.

The Prophet now turns to address the Medes and Persians, and instigates them, in the name of God, to destroy Babylon. We have already said, why the Prophets assume authority over all nations, even that they might shew that God's power is connected with his word. For men do not easily apprehend the efficacy of God's word, and think that the air is to no purpose beaten by an empty sound. Hence the Prophets shew that God has his hand extended whenever he speaks, so that nothing is announced in vain. This then is the reason why the Prophet now, as before, commands the Persians and Medes strenuously to exert themselves in attacking Babylon.

He says, first, *Set in order*, that is, the battle, or the assault; set in order *against Babylon;* and then, *around*, so that no escape might be open to them. He adds, *All ye who bend the bow*, for this mode of fighting was common among the Medes and Persians, as it appeared elsewhere; and the Orientals still follow the same practice, for they throw darts at their enemy, and move here and there, for they do not engage in pitched battles. He afterwards says, *Throw* or shoot *at her*, *spare not the arrow;* the singular is here used for the plural. He adds the reason, *because they have acted wickedly against God.*[1]

Though the iniquity of Babylon was manifold, there is yet no doubt but that God here undertakes the cause of his Church. Then, of all the sins of the Chaldeans, the chief was this, that they had oppressed the Church of God; for we know with what favour God regards his children, so that he who hurts them toucheth the apple of his eye, as he testifies elsewhere. (Zech. ii. 8.) This singular effect of love Jeremiah sets forth when he says, that the Chaldeans had *acted wickedly against Jehovah*, even because they had tyrannically oppressed his Church.

Now God will have nothing, as it were, apart from his children: and hence we learn a useful doctrine,—that the salvation of his Church is so precious in the sight of God, that he regards the wrong done to the faithful as done to himself. Thus there is no reason why we should torment ourselves, when the ungodly harass us, because God will at length really shew that our salvation is not less dear to him than their own eyes are to men. It afterwards follows,—

[1] Or literally, "Because against Jehovah has she sinned."—*Ed.*

15. Shout against her round about: she hath given her hand: her foundations are fallen, her walls are thrown down; for it *is* the vengeance of the Lord: take vengeance upon her; as she hath done, do unto her.

15. Vociferamini contra eam per circuitum; dedit manum suam; ceciderunt fundamenta ejus, diruti sunt muri ejus, quia ultio Jehovæ hæc; ultionem sumite de ea; quemadmodum fecit, facite ei.

Jeremiah proceeds in exhorting the Persians and the Medes, not that he had ever spoken to them; but this mode of speaking, as it has been said, availed to confirm the minds of the godly, so that they might feel assured that what had proceeded from the mouth of Jeremiah was not vain. Here, then, he assumes the person of God himself, and with authority commands the Persians and the Medes as to what they were to do. He says again, *Cry aloud against her*. By crying aloud or shouting, he means the cry of triumph which soldiers send forth when a city is taken, or rather, as I think, the encouraging cries, by which soldiers rouse one another when they make an attack; for battles are never without shoutings, nor the storming of cities. God then bids the soldiers to animate one another in their usual way to make a strenuous effort. *Shout*, he says, and then adds, *all around*.

He then says, *She hath given her hand*. By these words he intimates that Babylon would not be able to resist. Hands are wont to be given as a token of union; but he is also said to give his hand who confesses himself to be conquered. In this sense we may take the words of Jeremiah, that Babylon had *given her hand*, because she could not defend herself against the Medes and Persians. But as we know that the city was taken by treachery, in this manner also was fulfilled what Jeremiah had announced, when two Satraps, in order to revenge private wrongs, sent for Cyrus: for thus it happened that Babylon, or those within it, willingly stretched forth the hands.

It is added, *her foundations have fallen, and her walls have been overthrown*; not that Cyrus attacked the city with warlike engines, for he entered in by the fords; but still the soldiers readily mounted the walls. Jeremiah then speaks figuratively, as though he had said, that the Chaldeans were mistaken in thinking that they had strong fortresses, because the walls would avail them nothing, however high and wide they were. And we know what ancient historians relate of these walls and towers. The event was almost incredible ; for no one could have thought it possible that a city so fortified could be taken by assault. But the Prophet derides this confidence, and declares that the *walls would be overthrown*, together with their *foundations*.[1] But as it was a thing difficult to be believed, he again adds a confirmation, that it would be *the vengeance of Jehovah ;* as though he had said, that the destruction of Babylon ought not to be estimated according to the thoughts of men, because God would there put forth his wonderful power. In the meantime, he animates again the Persians and the Medes to take vengeance, and to render to the Babylonians what they had deserved. The Prophet in short intimates that the Persians and the Medes would be armed to execute God's vengeance on the Babylonians.

But we must notice the last clause, *Do to her as she has done* to others ; for we hence learn, what we have also observed elsewhere, that a reward is rendered to every one, so that they who have been cruel to others, do find how dreadful is God's judgment. God does not always execute his judgment by men ; but still this is ever true, "Woe to thee who plunderest, for thou shalt be plundered ;" and also this, "Judgment without mercy shall be to him who hath shewed no mercy ;" and still further, "With what measure any one measures, the same shall be rendered to him." (Isa. xxxiii. 1 ; James ii. 13 ; Matt. vii. 2.) This truth, then, remains fixed and unchangeable. But God in various ways renders to the ungodly their reward ; for he sometimes punishes them by the hand of man, and sometimes he suspends his judgment. Here he shews that the Persians and the Medes would be the executioners of his vengeance, even as the Chaldeans themselves had been as it were his scourges when he chastised his people for their sins ; for he had employed the Chaldeans in carrying on war against the Jews. But God has many ways by which he calls each one to an

[1] Rather "battlements" or ramparts, as given by the *Sept. ;* for it is not proper to say that "foundations" have fallen.—*Ed.*

account. Thus at length he punished the Chaldeans, because they indulged only their avarice and ambition in oppressing the Jews; for it was not their purpose to punish the Jews as they deserved; but their own lust, as I have just said, led them to cruelty and slaughter. It was, therefore, but just that they should in their turn be chastised by God's hand. It follows,—

16. Cut off the sower from Babylon, and him that handleth the sickle in the time of harvest: for fear of the oppressing sword they shall turn every one to his people, and they shall flee every one to his own land.	16. Excidite seminantem è Babylone, et qui apprehendit falcem tempore messis; coram gladio opprimente, quisque ad populum suum respiciet, quisque ad terram suam fugiet.

He still addresses the Medes and the Persians, and bids them *cut off* from *Babylon* both the *sowers* and the *reapers;* but by stating a part for the whole he includes also all others. Husbandmen in a manner preserve the life of men, as other arts and occupations are not capable of doing so. Were there no sowing and reaping, all would of necessity perish. When, therefore, the Prophet bids them take away those who sowed and reaped, it was the same as though he had said, "Strike with the sword and kill all the inhabitants, so that nothing may remain but the land reduced to solitude." He then commands the Chaldeans to be slain, so that no husbandmen should remain to sow and reap.

This, indeed, was not fulfilled by Cyrus, as we have elsewhere seen. But what I then reminded you of ought to be borne in mind, that the Prophet extends his threatenings much further, for Babylon was often smitten by God's hand, and at length wholly destroyed. The assault of Cyrus was a prelude, but other calamities followed, when it was more severely oppressed.

He adds, *From the face of the oppressing* or wasting *sword every one shall flee to his people and to his own land.* As that country was wealthy, many strangers had come there, and they had also drawn together captives from all parts. Thus many foreigners no doubt dwelt in Chaldea when the empire flourished. There were there many husbandmen and many artificers. The Chaldeans ruled, and yet many were content with small means, and even paltry;

or it may be that the Chaldeans compelled conquered nations to do servile work in agriculture and in works of art. The Prophet now says, that in the revolution which was to happen, each would look to his own land and flee there, as there could be no delight in a country deserted and desolate. Then *from the face of the oppressing sword shall every one look to his own people and to his own land ;* and those who before pretended to be wholly devoted to the Chaldeans, would forsake them in their necessity, because nothing would be better for them than to consult their own safety. It follows,—

17. Israel *is* a scattered sheep ; the lions have driven *him* away : first the king of Assyria hath devoured him, and last this Nebuchadrezzar king of Babylon hath broken his bones.

17. Grex dispersus (*vel,* agnus dispersus *aut* hædus ; שה *significat interdum gregem, interdum etiam significat singulos agnos, vel singulas oves ;* grex *ergo* dispersus fuit) Israel ; leones expulerunt eum ; primus voravit eum rex Assyriæ, et hic postremus contrivit ossa ejus Nabuchadrezer rex Babylonis.

Here the Prophet more clearly shews what he had briefly referred to, even that God was thus incensed against the Babylonians, because he had undertaken the cause of the people whom he had chosen. Then Jeremiah's design was to shew to the faithful, that though God severely chastised them for a time, he had not wholly divested himself of his paternal regard towards them, because he would at length make it openly evident that they to whom he had been so rigid were dear to him. He then mitigates the severity of punishment, that the Jews might not succumb to despair, but call upon God in their miseries, and hope that he, after having turned them, would at length be propitious to them.

The sum of what is said is, that whatever punishments God inflicts on his Church are temporary, and are also useful for salvation, being remedies to prevent them from perishing in their vices. Let us then learn to embrace the promises whenever we are wounded with extreme sorrow under the chastisements of God : let us learn, I say, to look to his mercy ; and let us be convinced of this, that though signs of his wrath may appear on every side, yet the punishments we suffer are not fatal, but on the contrary, medicinal. For this reason, the Prophet exhorted the faithful of his time to be patient, by shewing that God, after having been a Judge, would be again a Father to them.

He then says that *Israel* was like a *scattered flock,* or a straying sheep, which is the same thing. He expresses how they became so, *the first* who *devoured* them was *the king of Assyria ;* for we know that the kingdom of Israel was overthrown by the Assyrians, and the land of Judah was also very much pillaged by them ; a small portion remained. Then God says, that the people had been consumed by the calamities which the Assyrians had occasioned. But he compares what remained to bones, as though a wild beast devoured a sheep, and left only the bones. There was then no flesh or skin in Israel after the Assyrians had cruelly treated them, and that often. But as the kingdom of Judah remained, he says that it was like bones ; and hence he adds, *and this last, Nebuchadnezzar, the king of Babylon, hath broken his bones,*[1] that is, hath broken in pieces and devoured the bones which remained.

We now perceive the meaning of the Prophet. Moreover, he exaggerates the miseries of the chosen people, that he might in a manner open a way for mercy. God, then, here assumes the feeling of man, who is touched with a sad spectacle, when he sees a miserable and harmless sheep devoured, and the bones cast away, and then sees another wild beast, still more savage, who breaks the bones with his teeth and devours them. Since God then thus speaks, there is no doubt but that he meant to express with what tender feeling he regarded his chosen people, and that he also meant to give the godly the hope of salvation. It afterwards follows,—

18. Therefore thus saith the Lord of hosts, the God of Israel, Behold, I will punish the king of Babylon and his land, as I have punished the king of Assyria.

18. Propterea sic dicit Jehova exercituum, Deus Israel, ecce ego visito super regem Babylonis, et super terram ejus, quemadmodum visitavi regem Assyriæ.

What I have said may hence with more certainty be in-

[1] Literally, "and boned him;" which is to be taken in a privative sense, "and unboned him." There are similar words in Hebrew : to neck is to break the neck. (Ex. xiii. 13.) To tail is to cut off the tail. (Josh. x. 19.) To root is to root up. (Ps. lii. 5.) The *Vulg.* here is *exossavit.—Ed.*

ferred—that the similitude which God employed was intended for this end, that having assumed the person of one in sorrow, he might represent as it were to their eyes his sympathy. He then shews that he would be the avenger of the cruelty which the Chaldeans had practised, as he had already been the avenger of all the evils which the Assyrians had done to his people.

We must bear in mind the time—for the meaning of this passage depends on history. The Assyrians were stronger than the Chaldeans when they harassed the kingdom of Israel: for we know that in the time of Hezekiah the king of Babylon sent to him to seek his favour, and to allure him to a confederacy. While then the monarchy of Assyria was formidable, the Assyrians were very hostile to the Israelites and also to the Jews: what followed? Nineveh was overthrown, and Babylon succeeded in its place; and so they who had ruled were constrained to bear the yoke, and thus Babylon made the Assyrians captive to itself. God now refers to this judgment, which was known to all. The Assyrians themselves did not indeed think that the God of Israel was the avenger of his people, but yet it was so. Hence God here declares that he had already given a manifest proof of the solicitude which he had for the welfare of his people: as then he had punished Assyria, so he declares that he would take vengeance on the Babylonians. And thus, by an example, he confirms what might have appeared incredible. For who could have thought that that monarchy could so suddenly fall? And yet it happened beyond what any could have anticipated. God here repeats what had taken place, that the faithful might feel assured that the judgment which the Assyrians had experienced, awaited the Babylonians. This is the plain meaning of the Prophet. It follows,—

19. And I will bring Israel again to his habitation, and he shall feed on Carmel and Bashan, and his soul shall be satisfied upon mount Ephraim and Gilead.

19. Et reducam Israelem ad caulas suas, et pascetur in (monte) Carmel et Basan, et in monte Ephraim et Gilead; satiabitur anima ejus.

Jeremiah pursues here the same subject, and sustains the

minds of the faithful in their miseries, lest they should wholly despond. It is then the same as though he stretched forth his hand to the shipwrecked, or gave support to those lying down as it were lifeless; for exile to God's children was not only sad, but was like death, because they perceived the vengeance of God as though they had been wholly repudiated. It was therefore necessary to give them some consolation, that they might not altogether despair. The object, then, of our Prophet now is, to encourage the Jews to bear patiently their troubles, and not to think the stroke inflicted on them to be fatal. Hence God promises a restoration to their own country, which would be an evidence of pardon and of mercy; for when God gathered his people, it was the same as though he had openly shewed that their adoption remained unchanged, and that the covenant which seemed for a time to fail was still valid.

We now then see why Jeremiah spoke of the restoration of the people; and then he adds, *to their own folds*, or to their own habitation. This mode of speaking, we know, is found everywhere in the Prophets, for they compare God to a shepherd, and the Church to a flock of sheep. This similitude then is sufficiently common, nor could God better express how much he was concerned for the welfare of his people, than by setting himself forth as their shepherd, and by testifying that he would take care of his flock. But as we said at the beginning of the book, Jeremiah had a special reason for using this similitude, because he was from a town of pastures, and had been from his childhood among shepherds: there is therefore no wonder that he often uses expressions to which he had been accustomed; for education in a great measure forms the language of men. Though then the Prophet speaks according to the usual phraseology of Scripture, there is yet no doubt but that he retained, as it has been said elsewhere, his own habitual mode of speaking.

He then says, that after the people had been gathered, they would inhabit rich and fertile mountains, even *Carmel* and *Bashan.* The fruitfulness of these mountains is spoken of in many places, but it is not necessary to quote them.

The meaning however is, that God, after having again gathered his chosen people, would be as it were a faithful shepherd to them, so that they might feel assured that there would be not only a free return to their own country, but that God would be also the guardian of their safety, so as ever to protect them, to exercise care over them, to defend them against their enemies.

But that God might more fully set forth his kindness, he adds, *and satisfied shall be his soul.* Soul here is to be taken for desire, as in many other places. Now the former doctrine ought to be borne in mind, that God is never so angry or displeased with his Church but that he remembers his covenant. Then, as to the faithful, after they have undergone their temporary punishment, God at length stretches forth his hand to them; nor is he once only propitious to them, but continues his mercy, and so cherishes them, that he is not less solicitous for their welfare than a shepherd is, to whom his flock is not less dear than his own life, so that he watches in the night, endures cold and heat, and also exposes himself to many dangers from robbers and wild beasts in order that he might protect his flock. But the Prophet points out as by the finger the very fountain of all this when he adds,—

20. In those days, and in that time, saith the Lord, the iniquity of Israel shall be sought for, and *there shall be* none; and the sins of Judah, and they shall not be found: for I will pardon them whom I reserve.

20. In diebus illis et tempore illo, dicit Jehova, quæretur iniquitas Israel, et nulla erit, scelus Jehudah, et non invenietur; quia propitius ero his quos fecero residuos.

As I have already said, the Prophet now shews the primary cause why God purposed to deal so kindly and mercifully with his people, even because he would remit their sins. And doubtless whatever is said of the remission of sins is cold and unmeaning, except we be first convinced that God is reconciled and propitious to us. The unbelieving indeed seek no other thing than to be relieved from their evils, as the sick who require nothing from their physician but that he should immediately remove pain. If the sick man thirsts, "Take away thirst," he will say. In short, they regard only the symptom, of the disease they do not say a word. Such is the case with the ungodly, they neglect the chief thing, that God should pardon them and receive them into favour. Provided they are exempted from punishment, this is enough for them. But as to the faithful, they can never be satisfied until they feel assured that God is propitious to them. In order, then, to free from disquietude and all misgivings the minds of the godly, our Prophet says that God would be propitious, so that he would bury all the sins of Israel and Judah, so that they might no more be remembered or come to judgment.

This passage is remarkable, and from it we especially learn this valuable truth, that when God severely chastises us, we ought not to stop at the punishment and seek only a relief from our troubles, but on the contrary we ought to look to the very cause of all evils, even our sins. So David, in many places, when he seeks from God a relaxation of evil, does not only say, "Lord, deliver me from mine enemies; Lord, restore to me my health; Lord, deliver me from death;"—he does not simply speak thus, but he earnestly flees to God and implores his mercy. And on the other hand, when God promises deliverance from punishment, he does not simply say, "I will restore you from exile or captivity, I will restore you to your own country;" but he says, "I will forgive you your sins." For when the disease is removed, the symptoms also which accompany the disease disappear. So also it happens in this case, for when God shews that he is propitious to us, we are then freed from punishment, that is, what we have for a time suffered, or what awaited us, had not God spared us according to his infinite mercy and goodness.[1]

[1] The idea of this verse is rightly given in these words: the punishment for iniquity and sins would not be exacted, because God would pardon the remnant; hence they appeared not. The removal of punishment, the restoration from exile, would shew that iniquity and sins no longer existed, God having fully pardoned them, and thus obliterated them.

The iniquity of Israel was false worship, the worship of the calves, and the sins of Judah were especially idolatry and the rejection of God's messages by his prophets. For these evils more particularly they were banished, and their exile proved a remedy for them, as they never afterwards fell into these sins.—*Ed.*

PRAYER.

Grant, Almighty God, that since thou hast been so merciful towards thine ancient people, and however grievously thou mightest have been offended, yet thou didst preserve some remnant to whom thou gavest tokens of thy mercy,—O grant that it may please thee so to allure us also at this day; and however we may deserve a thousand times to be condemned by thee, yet deign to receive us in thine only-begotten Son, and through him shew thyself reconciled to us to the end of our life; and be thou our Father in death itself, so that we may live and die to thee, and acknowledge this to be the only true way of salvation, until we shall at length enjoy that celestial inheritance which has been obtained for us by the blood of the same, thine only-begotten Son. —Amen.

Lecture One Hundred and Eighty-second.

In the last lecture we began to explain what the Prophet says, that when God redeemed his people he would be so propitious as to blot out all their sins. We said also that the Prophet shews that the people had for just reasons been treated with severity. Here then we have to observe the justice of God in all his judgments. For the Prophet reminds us that the Jews could not have been reconciled to God, except they acknowledged that they had been justly punished. And hence we learn also a useful doctrine, that whenever God smites us with his rods, we are not only to seek that relief may be given us from external evils or sorrow, but that God may also forgive us. The reason also is to be observed, for the Prophet teaches us that there would be no iniquity because God would be propitious. We hence learn that there were also just reasons why God chastised his people, but that as he designed to forgive their sins he became their deliverer. Let us then know that we are counted just before God, not because he sees no iniquities in us, but because he freely forgives them. It is, in short, the only true way of being reconciled to God, when he buries as it were our sins so as never to call them to judgment.

Moreover, that this favour properly belongs to the kingdom of Christ may be gathered from the thirty-first chapter, where the Prophet, having spoken of the new covenant, lays down this as the principal thing, " I will pardon their iniquities," (ver. 34;) and he uses here the same verb. This promise then ought not to be confined to that short time when the people returned from their Babylonian exile, but ought on the contrary to be extended to the kingdom of Christ, for it was then that this prophecy was fully accomplished, because our sins do not appear before God when he is reconciled to us.

Yet the Prophet intimates that this favour would not be general, for he adds that God would be propitious only to the *remnant;* and it was needful to express this, because the faithful after their return might have otherwise desponded, when they saw that a few only of the people were restored. Had their restoration been indiscriminately promised, the faith of the godly might have faltered on seeing that almost the whole people disregarded the favour offered to them; for a part only of the tribe of Judah availed themselves of the kindness of Cyrus and Darius; and the ten tribes chose rather to dwell in Chaldea and in other places. And it was not only once that God restricted the promise given here; for it is said by Isaiah, " Were thy people as the sand of the sea, a remnant only shall be saved." (Isa. x. 21, 22.) The people gloried in their number and boasted of what had been said to Abraham, " Number if thou canst the stars of heaven and the sand of the sea, so shall thy seed be. (Gen. xv. 5.) God then shews that the Jews were greatly mistaken when they thought that they would be always in a safe state. Hence the Prophet says here that God would not be propitious indiscriminately to all, but to those whom he would *make the remnant.* And God also intimates that it was to be ascribed to his gratuitous goodness that any remained alive, according to what is said in Isaiah i. 9, " Except some seed had been left to us, we must have been as Gomorrah, and like to Sodom," God then declares here that the remnant would not otherwise be saved than through his gratuitous mercy, as Paul also says, that the Jews were not to hope for salvation, except through the free mercy of God. (Rom. xi. 5.) And he especially noticed this passage and similar passages, because the Jews then in opposing the

Gospel raised the objection, that they were the seed of Abraham, and the chosen people; but Paul gave them this answer, that it was not a new thing that God gathered a small remnant from his people; and he assigns as the cause his gratuitous election. It now follows,—

21. Go up against the land of Merathaim, *even* against it, and against the inhabitants of Pekod: waste and utterly destroy after them, saith the Lord, and do according to all that I have commanded thee.	21. Super terram exasperantium ascende super eam (*sed abundat*) et super habitatores visitationis (et habitatores visitationis;) occide et disperde post eos, dicit Jehova; et fac omnia quæ præcepi tibi.

The Prophet here undertakes the office of a herald, and animates the Persians and the Medes to make war with Babylon. This prophecy indeed never came to these nations, but we have stated why the Prophets proclaimed war and addressed at one time heathen nations, at another time the Jews—now one people, then another; for they wished to bring the faithful to the very scene of action, and connected the accomplishment with their predictions. By this mode of speaking, the Prophet then teaches us, that he did not scatter words into the air, but that the power of God was connected with the word which he spoke, as though God had expressly commanded the Medes and the Persians to execute his vengeance on Babylon. And doubtless Jeremiah did not thus speak according to his own thoughts, nor did he thus speak in the person of man; but on the contrary, he introduced God as the speaker, as it appears from the end of the verse.

He then says, *Ascend on the land of the exasperating;* others read, "of bitterness," but improperly. God indeed calls the Chaldeans rebellious, for though they were for a time the scourges of his wrath, they yet had cruelly treated many nations, being impelled only by their own pride and avarice; he justly calls them "the exasperating," and then adds, *Slay the inhabitants of visitation.* Some regard פקוד, *pekud,* as a proper name; and they first imagine that it was a town of some note in Chaldea, which is groundless; and then they give a frigid explanation by saying that it was some mean and obscure place. There is then no doubt but that the Prophet calls the Chaldeans the *inhabitants of visitation*, because God's vengeance awaited them, nay, it was even suspended over their heads, as he afterwards declares. But this way of speaking frequently occurs in the Prophets.[1]

He afterwards adds, *and destroy after* or behind *them.* There is an alliteration in the words החרם אחריהם, *echerem acheriem ;* and he means that the slaughter would be extreme, so that the Medes and Persians would not cease to destroy until they had extinguished the name of Babylon. Yet we know that this was not done by Cyrus and Darius ; for as we have already stated several times, the city was taken by fraud and treachery in the night, and the king and the princes were slain, for Darius, or rather Cyrus, spared the rest of the people ; for though Darius had the name of being king, yet Cyrus was by far the most renowned, as he was a valiant soldier, and only on account of his fame accompanied his father-in-law and uncle. As then the sword did not destroy all the Chaldeans when Babylon was taken, we conclude that the Prophets, when they denounced slaughter and destruction on Babylon, did not confine what they said to that time, but included also other slaughters ; for Babylon was often taken. It revolted from the Persians ; and when it was recovered, it suffered very severe punishment ; for, by way of reproach, those who were first in power

[1] Merathaim and Pekod are appellatives, and not proper names, in the early versions, and the first is so in the *Targ.* and rendered "rebellious ;" but by the *Sept.* "bitterly ;" by the *Vulg.* "rulers ;" and by the *Syr.* "exasperating." The most probable derivation of the word is from מרה, to rebel, with a dual termination, doubly rebellious, *i.e.*, very rebellious. As to "Pekod," the versions give it the idea of visiting by way of punishment : "Avenge thou with the sword," is the *Sept. ;* "Visit her inhabitants," the *Vulg. ;* "Assail ye her and her inhabitants," the *Syr. ;* the *Targ.* has "the inhabitants of Pekod." It is better to take both words as appellatives :—

21. Against the land of the most rebellious, against her ascend,
And to the inhabitants of visitation ;
Slay and utterly destroy their posterity, saith Jehovah,
And do according to all that I have commanded thee.

As to Babylon being "rebellious," see verses 24 and 33. "Inhabitants of visitation" were such as were to be visited, *i.e.*, with judgment ; see verse 31. The repetition, "against her," is emphatical. "Posterity," *i.e.*, children, or young men, as in verse 30. See 1 Kings xvi. 3.—*Ed.*

and authority were hung, and there was also great cruelty exercised towards men and women. There is no doubt then but that the Prophets, in speaking of the destruction of Babylon, referred to God's judgments inflicted at various times. However this may have been, we learn that though God may long connive, or suspend extreme judgments, yet the ungodly cannot possibly escape his hand, though they may long be spared.

He then adds, *Do to them as I have commanded thee.* This prophetic mode of speaking ought also to be noticed; for the Medes and the Persians never thought that they fought under the authority of God; why then is the word "commanded" used? even because God rules by his secret power ungodly men, and leads them wheresoever he pleases, though nothing of the kind is ever thought of by them. To explain the matter more fully, we must observe that God commands in two ways; for he commands the faithful when he shews to them what is right and what they ought to follow. Thus daily God may be said to exercise his authority or right of ruling, when he exhorts us to do our duty, when he sets his law before us. And it is the proper way of commanding, or of exercising authority, when God expresses what he would have us to do, or what he requires from us. But God commands the unbelieving in another way; for though he does not declare to them what he would have them to do, he yet draws them, willing or unwilling, wherever he pleases. Thus, by his secret operation, he induced Cyrus and Darius to take up arms against Babylon.

We now then understand what the Prophet meant by this expression; for he did not mean that Darius and Cyrus obeyed God from the heart, because they knew not that he was the leader and author of that war; no such thing ever entered into their minds. The former mode of commanding, as I have said, is peculiar to the Church; for God is pleased to bestow on us a peculiar privilege and favour, when he shews to us what is right, and prescribes the rule of life. But yet his hidden providence, by which he influences the ungodly, takes the place of a command, as it is said, "The king's heart is in the hand of God." (Prov. xxi. 1.) But

Solomon speaks of a king rather than of common men, because, if there be any liberty among mankind, it belongs to kings, for they seem exempt from every yoke; and Solomon declares that the hearts of kings are ruled by God. Though then Darius and Cyrus were carried away by their own cupidity when they made war, yet God, as we shall hereafter see more clearly, guided their hearts. So also he is said to command the heavens and the earth—not that the heavens, being without ears and reason, hear his voice, but because God powerfully moves and influences the heavens; for when he intends to punish us, he commands the heaven not to rain. This command of God the heaven executes, and the earth also obeys God; but there is no word of command given to them,—what then? it is God's providence which is hid from us. It follows,—

22. A sound of battle *is* in the land, and of great destruction.

22. Vox prælii in terra et contritio magna.

The Prophet continues the same style of speaking, for he says that there would be *the voice* or the sound *of battle.* Could he rouse up the Medes and the Persians? not indeed by his own power, but here he exalts the efficacy of his doctrine; as though he had said, that the vengeance he denounced on the Babylonians would be in readiness when the time came, as Paul says that the ministers of the gospel had vengeance ready at hand for all those who despised it. We now then see why the Prophet mentions the word *battle,* and says that *breaking,* or ruin, would be *great in the land.* It now follows,—

23. How is the hammer of the whole earth cut asunder and broken! how is Babylon become a desolation among the nations!

24. I have laid a snare for thee, and thou art also taken, O Babylon, and thou wast not aware: thou art found, and also caught, because thou hast striven against the Lord.

23. Quomodo excisus est et contritus malleus universæ terræ? quomodo redacta est (fuit) in vastitatem Babylon inter gentes?

24. Illaqueavi te, atque etiam (*vel* atque, ideo, גם, *hic ponitur loco rationalis particulæ,* ideo) capta es Babylon, et tu nescivisti; inventa es atque adeò deprehensa, quoniam contra Jehovam te miscuisti (litigasti.)

Here, in the first place, Jeremiah asks in astonishment how it happened that *the hammer of the whole earth was broken*, when it had before broken all nations. God afterwards gives an answer, even because "I am he who have taken Babylon." The question availed to rouse the people to a greater attention. We neglect God's judgments or are blind to them, even because we do not carefully consider them; for little things often excite us, when that which God works in an unusual manner is deemed by us as nothing. As then our apathy as to the works of God is so great, it is necessary to stimulate us. And this is what is done now by Jeremiah, when he says in astonishment, *How?* for he intimates that to cut down Babylon would be incredible, for no one could have thought that that monarchy could have ever fallen; for it had arrived to the highest eminence, and was surrounded on all sides by so many fortresses, that no danger could be feared. In short, all thought that Babylon could not be endangered without a concussion of heaven and earth.

Then the Prophet here wonders at a thing unusual, and says, *How is the hammer of all the earth broken and shattered to pieces?*[1] and then, *How has Babylon become a waste among the nations?* for it had subjugated to itself not only the neighbouring nations, but the remotest parts of the earth. And in this manner he animated the faithful to entertain hope, lest they should despond, for the power of that monarchy was terrible.

He then immediately answers in the person of God, *I have ensnared thee, and therefore thou Babylon art taken.* Here God declares, that though it could not be possible that Babylon and its empire should fall through human means, yet its destruction was in his hand. *Thou*, he says, *art*

[1] The first verb, נגדע, means to cast off as well as to cut off; the breaking is expressed by the following verb. According to order often found in the Prophets, the final act, casting off, is first mentioned, and then the previous act, the breaking of it,—

23. How has the hammer of all the earth
Been cast off and broken!
How has Babylon become a wonder among nations!

"A wonder" or astonishment, for so the word is evidently to be taken here, according to the *Syr.*, though rendered "extinction" by the *Sept.*, and "desert" by the *Vulg.* and *Targ.* *Blayney* and *Henderson* render it "astonishment."—*Ed.*

taken, even because *I ensnared thee;* as though he had said, that the Chaldeans would not have to do with men, because he himself would carry on the war and guide and direct the Persians and the Medes, and also endue them with power: He would, in short, fight himself until he had overcome the Babylonians.

When he says, *thou knewest not*, he not only reproves the insensibility of that people, but at the same time derides their security, as though he had said, "Thou thinkest thyself beyond the reach of harm, but thou wilt find that no one can escape my hand." We now then perceive the meaning of the Prophet. It is indeed true that the unbelieving, when God punishes them for their wickedness, do not acknowledge his hand; but the Prophet means another thing, —that though Babylon trusted in its strength and feared nothing, it would yet be taken, because it could not evade the snares.

He adds, *Thou art found and therefore caught;* and he states the reason, because she had *contended* with God. We shall presently explain how Babylon contended or litigated with or against God, even because God had taken under his protection and patronage the Israelites. This, then, is said with reference to the Church, as I shall presently explain more at large. It must be here briefly observed, that God so undertakes the cause of his people, as though he himself were injured, according to what he promises that they would be to him as the apple of his eye. (Zech. ii. 8.) It now follows,—

25. The Lord hath opened his armoury, and hath brought forth the weapons of his indignation: for this *is* the work of the Lord God of hosts in the land of the Chaldeans.

25. Aperuit Jehova thesaurum suum, et protulit vasa iræ suæ, quia opus hoc Domini, Jehovæ exercituum, est in terra Chaldæorum.

The Prophet here expresses more clearly what he had touched upon, even that this war would not be that of the Persians, but of God himself. He then says, that God had *opened his treasure*, even because he has various and manifold ways and means, which cannot be comprehended by men, when he resolves to destroy the ungodly. That monarchy was impregnable according to the judgment of men;

but God here says that he had hidden means by which he would lay waste Babylon and reduce it to nothing. Then what is by a similitude called the *treasure* of God, means such a way as surpasses the comprehension of men, that is, when God executes his judgments in a way hidden and unexpected.

As, then, the faithful could hardly conceive what Jeremiah said, he raises up their thoughts to God's providence, which ought not to be subjected to human judgment; for it is absurd in men to judge of God's power according to the perceptions of the flesh ; it is the same as though they attempted to include heaven and earth in the hollow of their hand. God himself says, that he takes heaven and earth in the hollow of his hand. When, therefore, men seek to comprehend the power of God, it is like a fly attempting to devour all the mountains. Hence the Prophet reproves this presumption to which we are all by nature inclined, even to determine according to the comprehension of our minds what God is about or ought to do, as though his power were not infinite.

This is the reason why the Prophet says, God *hath opened his treasury;* and then, *he hath thence brought forth the instruments of his wrath,* that is, from his treasury, even in a way and manner which was then incomprehensible.[1] And subjoined is the reason, *Because this is the work of God* alone, *the God of hosts, in the land of the Chaldeans.*[2] Here the Prophet briefly concludes, intimating, that the faithful ought quietly to wait until what he taught came to pass, even because it was the work of God. And there is nothing more absurd than for men to seek to measure God's power, as it has been said, by their own judgment. It follows,—but I cannot explain the verse now.

[1] "Treasury" here means an armoury or arsenal, as rendered by *Blayney:* and then "instruments" signify weapons, drawn from the armoury. —*Ed.*

[2] Literally it is,—

For a work—this the Lord Jehovah of hosts has
In the land of the Chaldeans.—*Ed.*

PRAYER.

Grant, Almighty God, that since thou hast been pleased to set before us thy judgments on the unbelieving, we may not only fear thee, but also learn to cast on thee the hope of our salvation, so that we may make progress in the truth, that we may neither be insensible as to thy threatenings, nor tremble in our extreme evils, but so learn to raise up to thee our eyes, that we may, during the whole course of our life, call on thee through Christ Jesus our Lord.—Amen.

Lecture One Hundred and Eighty-third.

23. Come against her from the utmost border, open her storehouses; cast her up as heaps, and destroy her utterly: let nothing of her be left.	23. Venite contra eam a fine, aperite apothecas ejus, calcate eam tanquam acervos, et disperdite eam, ne sint ei reliquiæ.

THE Prophet again addresses the Persians and the Medes, and encourages them to come against Babylon. We stated yesterday that the prophets are wont to speak with authority, because they sustained the person of God; and we mentioned how necessary this mode of speaking was, for the world does not acknowledge that God speaks effectually.

Then he says first, *Come ye against her;*[1] and then, *Open her storehouses.* The word מאבס, *meabes,* means a corn-house or a repository of any kind: hence some render it "granaries." But it seems to me that the word is thus too much restricted, for the Prophet no doubt speaks of the treasures of Babylon. Now storehouses, (*apothecas,*) the Greeks call those repositories which contain all sorts of things, not only wine and oil, but goods of merchants, and also money. We call them in French, *Arrières-boutiques,* or, *magasins.* But this word is to be extended to wine, to every kind of fruit, and then to treasures, and also to arms; for they were repositories of arms, of weapons of every kind. It is the same as though Jeremiah had said, that nothing would be so hidden among the Chaldeans but that the Medes and the Persians would find it out.

[1] It is added, "from the extremity," *i.e.*, of heaven, according to a parallel passage in Isa. xiii. 5. They were to come from the farthest parts of the earth then known.—*Ed.*

He then adds, *Tread her as heaps.* The word ערמים, *oremim*, means not heaps of stones, but on the contrary, of sheaves. Then he intimates that the Persians and the Medes would act cruelly, and tread them as corn is trodden on the floor.[1] He lastly says, *Destroy her utterly, that there may be to her no remnant.* He seems indirectly to set this in contrast with what God promised always to his people, that there would be some remnant. He then says that nothing would remain when God had executed his vengeance on the Chaldeans. The sum of what is said is, that the punishment of which the Prophet speaks would be such as would obliterate the very name of the Babylonian monarchy. This, as we said yesterday and also previously, was not completed in one day. But when the Prophets speak of God's judgments, they do not regard only the preludes, but their words extend to the last judgment that awaits all the reprobate. It now follows,—

27. Slay all her bullocks; let them go down to the slaughter: woe unto them! for their day is come, the time of their visitation.	27. Occidite omnes juvencos ejus; descendant ad mactationem: væ illis! quia venit dies eorum, tempus visitationis eorum.

He goes on with the same subject; he bids the Persians and the Medes to slay every strong man in Chaldea; for by *bullocks* he no doubt means by a metaphor all those who excelled in strength, or in power, or in wealth. The sum of what he says is, that the vengeance of which he now speaks, would not only be against the common people, but also against the highest and the choicest among them. He includes then the nobles as well as all the men of war; for he refers not only to strength of body, but also to power and authority.

Slay, then, he says, *all her bullocks,* that is, whatever is most valued in Chaldea: that was to perish when the day of vengeance came.[2] He afterwards says, *let them descend*

[1] The most approved rendering is, "Cast (or throw) her up as heaps," *i.e.*, of rubbish, according to chap. li. 37. It is said that the verb here never means to tread under foot, "Make her, of a goodly, stately city, nothing but heaps of earth, stones, and rubbish." *Gataker.—Ed.*

[2] The *Sept.* and *Syr.* take פרי here as signifying fruit, *i.e.*, of the womb—children, offspring; and what is said in Isa. xiii. 16-18, favours this meaning, as well as what is said in verse 21 of this chapter, if we

to the slaughter. We must ever bear in mind what I have said, that the Prophet gave orders as though he had the Medes and the Persians under his own hand and authority, because the whole world is subject to God's word. He says, *Woe to them! for their day is come, and the time of their visitation.* This was added, because the faithful might have disputed with themselves and said, "How can it be that Babylon should perish so quickly?" For God seemed to have favoured that monarchy for a long time, as though he intended to protect it perpetually. Hence the Prophet speaks here of the time of visitation, so that the faithful might not doubt respecting this prophecy, because God had not as yet put forth his hand. He then reminded them that God has his fixed times, and that he does not every day visit nations, that is, that he does not execute his judgments every moment, but at the time which he has appointed. Whenever, then, the ungodly securely exult and triumph, let us ever remember this truth, that the time is not yet come for God to execute his judgment; how so? because there is a fixed time of visitation, and that is dependent on God's will. Let us then learn to bear patiently all our trials until it shall please God to shew that he is the judge of the world. It follows,—

28. The voice of them that flee and escape out of the land of Babylon, to declare in Zion the vengeance of the Lord our God, the vengeance of his temple.

28. Vox fugientium et qui evaserint è terra Babylonis ad annuntiandum in Sion vindictam Jehovæ Dei nostri, vindictam templi ejus.

The Prophet again shews, that God in punishing Babylon, would give a sure proof of his favour towards his Church. For this prophecy would have been uninteresting to the faithful, did they not know that God would be an enemy to

render אחריהם, "their posterity." The *Vulg.* and the *Targ.* render the word here "valiants," expressing the meaning of "bullocks." The first version is the most suitable,—

Slay ye all her fruit (or offspring;)
Let them descend to the slaughter.

It is descending to the slaughter that led critics to render פרי bullocks, but we find this expression unconnected with bullocks in chap. xlviii. 15; where "chosen young men" are said to "descend to the slaughter." To descend denotes degradation, and to ascend dignity. The *Targ.* has, "Let them be delivered to the slaughter."—*Ed.*

that great monarchy, because he had undertaken the care of their safety. Then the Prophet often calls the attention of the faithful to this fact, that God's vengeance on the Babylonians would be to them a sure proof of God's favour, through which he had once embraced them, and which he would continue to shew to them to the end.

This, then, was the design of the Prophet, when he said, *The voice of fleers and of those who escape from the land of Babylon*, &c.; as though he had said, "Babylon is on many accounts worthy of destruction, but God in destroying it will have a regard to his own people, and will effectually shew that he is the Father of the people whom he has adopted." Jeremiah afterwards exhorts the faithful to shew their gratitude. There are here, then, two things; the first is, that when God destroyed Babylon, the people would hence with certainty perceive how dear they were to God; and secondly, from this truth flows an exhortation, that the faithful were not to be mute at such a singular benefit of God, but were to proclaim their deliverance. Hence he says, *The voice of fleers and of those who escape from the land of Babylon, to announce in Sion*, &c. By saying *in Sion*, he shews for what end God intended to gather his people, even that he might again be worshipped as formerly in his own Temple.

He adds, *to announce in Sion the vengeance of our God*. The vengeance of God is to be taken here in an active sense, signifying the vengeance which God would execute. The vengeance of the Temple, which immediately follows, is to be taken passively, as meaning the vengeance by which God would avenge the indignity offered to the Temple. God then takes vengeance, and God's Temple is defended from contempt and reproach.

We now then see the meaning of this passage. The Prophet first teaches us, that God would have a regard to his people in so rigidly punishing Babylon; and secondly, he adds an exhortation, lest the faithful should be unthankful to God, but acknowledge that God, for the sake of their deliverance had undertaken war against that monarchy; and lastly, he shews the end, even that the people who had been scattered, as it is said in Psalm cxlvii. 2, "God is he who gathers the dispersed of Israel," might again be collected together. As, then, the Jews were as a mutilated body among the Chaldeans, the Prophet shews that that monarchy would be dispersed, in order that the faithful might again be gathered, and that all might worship God together in the Temple, or on mount Sion. It follows,—

29. Call together the archers against Babylon: all ye that bend the bow, camp against it round about; let none thereof escape: recompense her according to her work; according to all that she hath done, do unto her: for she hath been proud against the Lord, against the Holy One of Israel.

29. Convocate contra Babylonem potentes, omnes qui intendunt arcum; obsidete eam in circuitu, ne sit evasio; reddite ei secundum opus suum, secundum omnia quæ fecit facite ei; quia contra Jehovam superbè egit, contra sanctum Israelis.

The Prophet adopts various modes of speaking, and not without reason, because he had to thunder rather than to speak; and then as he spoke of a thing incredible, there was need of no common confirmation; the faithful also, almost pining away in their miseries, could hardly entertain any hope. This is the reason why the Prophet dwells so long and so diffusely on a subject in itself not obscure, for there was not only need of amplifying, but also of great vehemence.

Then, as though he had many heralds ready to obey, he says, *Call together the mighty against Babylon.* Some read "many," but the word רבים, *rebim,* means both; and I think that "the mighty" or strong are meant here. Why some render it "arrows" I know not. It is, indeed, immediately added, *all who bend the bow,* כל־דרכי קשת, *cal-dereki koshet.* But the word, without anything added to it, never means an arrow. They refer to a place in Gen. xxi. 20, where Ishmael is said to be "an archer," רבה, *rebe;* but the word "bow" follows it. We cannot then take רבים, *rebim,* here but as signifying many or the mighty; and the latter is the most suitable word. Then the Prophet bids the strong and the warlike to come together, and then he mentions them specifically,—*all who bend the bow,* even all skilful archers. For the Persians excelled in this art, they were archers of the first order. It was indeed a practice common among eastern nations, but the Persians surpassed all others.

The Prophet then points them out when he bids *archers* to assemble.[1]

He adds, *encompass* or besiege *her around, that there may be no escape.* This also was a thing difficult to be believed, for Babylon was more like a country than a city. Then one could have hardly thought that it could have been besieged around and at length taken, as it happened. Therefore the Prophet here testifies that what exceeded the opinion of all would take place. But he had said before that this would be the work of God, that the faithful might not form a judgment according to their own measure, for nothing is more absurd, as it has been said, than to measure the power of God by our own understanding. As then the Prophet had before declared that the siege of Babylon would be the work of God, he bids them now, with more confidence, to *besiege it around, that there might not be an escape.*

It is then added, *Render to her according to her work; according to what she has done, do to her.* By these words the Prophet shews that the vengeance which God would execute on the Chaldeans would be just, for nothing is more equitable than to render to one what he had done to others. "With what measure ye mete to others," says Christ, "it shall be rendered to you." (Luke vi. 38.) As, then, nature itself teaches us that that punishment is most just which is inflicted on the cruel themselves, hence the Prophet reminds us here that God would be a just avenger in his extreme violence against the Babylonians. But he looks farther, for he assumes this principle, that God is the judge of the world. Since he is so, it follows that they who unjustly oppress others must at length receive their own reward; as also Paul says, that the judgment of God, otherwise obscure, will be made evident, when he shall give relief and rest to the miser-

[1] The early versions and the *Targ.* render רבים, "many:" and the rendering of the *Sept.* and *Vulg.* is to this effect,—

Proclaim ye to the many at Babylon,
To all who bend the bow,—
" Encompass her around,
Let there be no escape," &c.

The first part is a charge like what we find in the second verse; and the second states what they were to do. "Proclaim ye to," is literally, "Make ye to hear,"—"Make ye the many at Babylon to hear," &c.—*Ed.*

able who are now unjustly afflicted, and when he shall render their reward to oppressors. (2 Thess. i. 6, 7.) The Prophet then takes occasion of confidence from this truth to animate the faithful and to encourage them to entertain hope. How so? Since God is the judge of the world, the Jews ought to have considered what sort of people the Babylonians had been; nay, they had already sufficiently experienced how cruel and barbarous they were. As, then, the avarice and cruelty of the Chaldeans were sufficiently apparent, the Prophet here reminds them, that as God is in heaven, it could not be otherwise but that he would shortly call them to judgment, for otherwise he would not be God. Surely he would not be the judge of the world, were he not to regard the miserable unjustly oppressed, and bring them help, and stretch forth his hand to relieve them; and were he not also, on the other hand, to punish the avaricious and the proud and the cruel. We now understand the meaning of the Prophet.

He adds, in the last place, *because she has acted proudly against Jehovah, against the Holy One of Israel.* By saying that the Babylonians had *acted proudly,* he means that they had not only been injurious to men, but had been also insolent towards God himself; for the verb here used denotes a sin different from that which happens through levity or want of thought. When any one sins inconsiderately, he is said to have erred; but when one sins knowingly, it is a deliberate wickedness, and he is said to be proud; and this we learn from Psalm xix. 12; for David there sets pride in opposition to errors: "errors," he says, "who can understand?" and then he asks God to cleanse him from all pride. David indeed had not designedly raised his horns against God, but he yet feared lest the wantonness of the flesh should lead him to pride. When, therefore, the Prophet now says that the Chaldeans had *acted proudly towards God,* it is the same as though he accused them of sacrilegious pride, even that they designed to be insolent towards God himself, and not only cruel to his people.

But an explanation follows, *against the Holy One of Israel.* The Babylonians might have raised an objection, and said, that it was not their purpose to act proudly towards God. But the Prophet here brings forward the word *Israel,* as though he had said, "If there be a God in heaven, our religion is true; then God's name dwells with us. Since, then, the Babylonians have basely oppressed the people whom God has chosen, it follows that they have been sacrilegious towards him." And he meant the same thing when he said before, *the vengeance of Jehovah our God.* Why did he add, *our God?* that the Jews might know that whatever wrongs they had suffered, they reached God himself, as though he were hurt in his own person. So also in this place the Prophet takes away from the Babylonians all means of evasion when he says, that they had *acted proudly towards the Holy One of Israel.* When, therefore, the ungodly seek evasions and say that they do not contend with God, their pretences are disproved, when they carry on war with his Church, and fight against his faithful people, whose safety he has undertaken to defend. For God cannot be otherwise the protector of his Church than by setting himself up as a shield in its defence whenever he sees his people unjustly attacked by the reprobate. It follows,—

30. Therefore shall her young men fall in the streets, and all her men of war shall be cut off in that day, saith the Lord.

30. Propterea cadent electi ejus (*vel,* adolescentes,) in plateis ejus, et omnes viri militiæ ejus (*hoc est,* omnes viri bellicosi) redigentur ad silentium (*alii vertunt,* compescentur; nam דמם significat utrumque) in die illo, dicit Jehova.

He confirms the same thing, and shews that the destruction of Babylon would be such, that everything valuable would be destroyed. *Fall,* he says, *shall her strong men in the streets;* which is worse than if he had said, "They shall fall in battle." Babylon was so taken that all her armed men were slain in the middle of the city. Cyrus indeed spared, as it has been already said, the common people; but he slew all the chief men and the armed soldiers. As the Babylonians were taken while keeping a feast, as we read in Daniel, hence Jeremiah mentions *the streets.* He afterwards adds,—

31. Behold, I *am* against thee, O *thou* most proud, saith the Lord God

31. Ecce ego contra te, superbe, dicit Dominus Jehova exercituum,

of hosts: for thy day is come, the time *that* I will visit thee.

quia venit dies tuus, tempus visitationis tuæ.

Jeremiah, in order more fully to confirm what he had said, again introduces God as the speaker. And we have stated how necessary this was, because he could have hardly gained credit otherwise to his prophecy; but when he introduced God, he removed every doubt. *Behold,* he says, *I am against thee, O proud one.* He again calls the Babylonians *proud,* even because they had not been led to war by levity or folly, or vain ambition, but because they had assailed God and men without any reverence and without any regard to humanity.

He says that the *time had come,* because the faithful would have otherwise interrupted him and said, "How is this, that God so long delays?" That they might then sustain and cherish hope until the time which God had prescribed for his vengeance, he says, that the *day had come, and the time of visitation.* Whenever this mode of speaking occurs, let us know that all the natural instincts of our flesh are checked; for there is no one of us who does not immediately jump to take vengeance when we see the faithful oppressed, when we see many unworthy things done to our brethren, when we see innocent blood shed, and the miserable cruelly treated by the ungodly. When, therefore, all these instances of barbarity happen, none of us can contain himself; hence God puts on us a bridle, and exhorts us to exercise patience, when he says, that the time of visitation is not yet completed.

As long then as God delays, let us know that the fit time is not yet come, because he has a fixed day of visitation, unknown to us. It follows,—

32. And the most proud shall stumble and fall, and none shall raise him up; and I will kindle a fire in his cities, and it shall devour all round about him.

32. Et impinget superbus et cadet, et nemo qui eum erigat; et accendam ignem in urbibus ejus, qui consumet omnia quæ sunt in circuitu (per circuitus ejus, *ad verbum.*)

The Prophet continues the same subject: as then he had announced in God's name that the time of visitation would come when God would rise up against the Chaldeans, he now adds, *stumble shall the proud, and fall.* The verb כשל,

cashel, means also to fall; but as it is added, ונפל, *vanuphel, and fall,* it ought to be rendered *stumble* here. *Stumble,* then, *shall the proud, and fall*—for the Prophet denotes a gradation. Some render the words, "Fall shall the proud and tumble down:" but more suitable is the rendering I have given, that the *proud would stumble,* and then that he *would fall. And no one,* he says, *shall raise him up.* By these words, God intimates, that though Babylon had many nations under its authority, yet there would be no help given to it, when the time of visitation came. It indeed often happens that many busy themselves, and make every effort to assist the wicked, but without any success. When, therefore, God declares that there would be no one to raise up Babylon when fallen, the meaning is not, that courage would be wanting to all, but that the efforts of all would be of no avail, even because God, when Babylon fell, would be against her, so that were the whole world to unite for her relief, all their attempts would be useless.

And for the same purpose, he adds, *I will kindle a fire which will consume* or devour *all his cities.* God calls slaughter, by a metaphor, fire; for slaughter, like fire, raged so as to consume the whole monarchy—not only the city, but also all the neighbouring nations—for the war reached even to Asia. Cyrus, as it is well known, passed over the sea and depopulated Phrygia. In short, though victory might have been mild, yet it was no doubt like fire, as it devoured all the neighbouring nations. It follows,—

33. Thus saith the Lord of hosts; the children of Israel and the children of Judah *were* oppressed together: and all that took them captives held them fast; they refused to let them go.

34. Their Redeemer *is* strong; the Lord of hosts *is* his name: he shall throughly plead their cause, that he may give rest to the land, and disquiet the inhabitants of Babylon.

33. Sic dicit Jehova exercituum, Oppressi fuerunt filii Israel et filii Jehudah pariter; et omnes qui captivos ceperunt prævaluerunt contra ipsos, et renuerunt ipsos dimittere.

34. Redemptor (inquit) eorum fortis, Jehova exercituum nomen ejus; litem litigando litigabit, (*hoc est,* disceptando disceptabit causam ipsorum,) ut terram ipsam reddat tranquillam, (*ut alii vertunt, sed ego potius ita interpretor,* ut terram scindat,) et contremiscere faciat habitatores Babylonis.

Our Prophet returns again to his former subject—that God, in destroying the Babylonian monarchy, would have a regard to his chosen people. But the comparison made here is very important; for in the first place, the Prophet refers to an occasion of diffidence and even of despair, which might have closed up the way against all his prophecies. For this objection might have always been made, "We are driven into exile, we are in a far country, and in places distant from one another; it is the same as though we were in another world, and we can hardly move a foot without our conquerors being enraged against us." Thus the Jews, according to the aspect of things at that time, could not otherwise than despair of returning to their own country. This, then, is the reason why the Prophet says here, by way of concession, "It is, indeed, true that the children of Judah and the children of Israel are oppressed with cruel tyranny:" as when we wish to secure faith, we state what seems to be opposed to us, and then dissipate it; so now the Prophet does in this place, as though he had said, "I see what his own mind may dictate to every one, even that the children of Judah, as well as the children of Israel, are held captive, and shut up by such fastnesses that no way of escape is open to them."

When he speaks of the children of Israel and of the children of Judah, we must remember that the ten tribes had been led into exile, and also that the whole kingdom had been destroyed; and at length, after a considerable time, the Chaldeans took possession also of the kingdom of Judah. Hence then it was, that both the Israelites and the Jews became subject to a cruel oppression. He therefore adds, *They who led them captive have prevailed*, or, as some render the last word, "have held them;" for חזק, *chesek*, means to hold, to lay hold; but the Prophet seems to mean another thing, even that their conquerors so prevailed as securely to rule over them; and hence it is added, *they have refused to let them go;* and we learn the same thing from the next verse, in which the strength and power of God is set in opposition to the power of their enemies. As far as things appeared to men, there was certainly no way of deliverance for the people. The Prophet then concedes what might have taken away every hope from them.

But he immediately after removes this ground of despair, and says, *Their redeemer is strong.* He then sets this *strong*, חזק, *chesek*, in opposition to the verb used before, "prevailed" or ruled, החזיקו בם, *echesiku beem*, "prevailed" or domineered "over them," so that they were stronger. But now, on the other hand, he calls the *Redeemer of Israel strong;* for were you only to consider, he seems to say, how great the power of Babylon is, you might despond; but can God, in the meantime, do nothing? Is there any power on earth which can overrule him? Since then their redeemer was strong, he would prove superior to the Chaldeans.

He afterwards adds what is of the same import, *His name is Jehovah of hosts;* that is, neither Babylon nor all other nations have so much power as can resist the infinite power of God, for he is always like himself, and perfect; he is the God of hosts. He at length adds, *Their strife by litigating he will litigate,* or, by pleading he will plead the cause of his people, even so as to *cut off* or destroy *the land.* The verb, רגע, *rego,* means indeed sometimes to rest, and so almost all give this rendering, "so as to make to rest the land:" but as I take "land" and "the inhabitants of Babylon" to be the same, I doubt not but that this verb is to be taken here in its proper sense. Then it is, *so as to cut off* or destroy *the land,*[1] *and to make to tremble the inhabitants of Babylon.* He then speaks of the Chaldeans in mentioning the land, and afterwards explains himself by adding, the inhabitants of Babylon.

PRAYER.

Grant, Almighty God, that, as thou hast deigned once to take us under thy protection, we may always raise up our eyes to thine

[1] The versions, except the *Syr.* and the *Targ.*, give a similar meaning to this verb: but there is no instance of the verb in Hiphil having this meaning, though it would be the most suitable to this place. At the same time we may consider the land of Chaldea to be meant, if we regard the stillness or quietness as referring to the check produced by God's restraining power,—

So as to render the land still,
And to terrify the inhabitants of Babylon.

The promise is to make the land quiet so as not to oppose the return of the Jews, and for the same purpose, to terrify Babylon.—*Ed.*

infinite power, and that when we see all things not only confounded, but also trodden under foot by the world, we may not yet doubt but that thy power is sufficient to deliver us, so that we may perpetually call on thy name, and with firm constancy so fight against all temptations, that we may at length enjoy in thy celestial kingdom the fruit of our victory, through Jesus Christ our Lord.—Amen.

Lecture One Hundred and Eighty-fourth.

35. A sword *is* upon the Chaldeans, saith the Lord, and upon the inhabitants of Babylon, and upon her princes, and upon her wise *men*.

35. Gladius super Chaldæos, et super habitatores Babylonis, et super principes ejus, et super sapientes ejus.

The Prophet proceeds with the same subject, and employs the same manner of speaking. He denounces war on the Chaldeans as a celestial herald; and then that what he says might have more force and power, he sets the Persians and the Medes before us in the act of assailing and destroying Babylon. He therefore says now in general, *A sword on the Chaldeans;* and, secondly, he mentions the *inhabitants of Babylon,* for that city was the seat and head of the kingdom, as it is well known; but as the power of that monarchy was deemed by men unassailable, the Prophet adds, that though the chief men excelled in counsel and strength, and in the art of war, yet a *sword would be* upon them; and in the last place, that though Babylon had its diviners, their knowledge would yet be in vain. He, indeed, uses an honourable name, yet he no doubt refers to astrologers and soothsayers, and other kinds of prophets. For we know that the whole nation was given to many superstitions; but they boasted themselves to be the chief of all astrologers; and hence soothsayers, who practise their impostures, are called Chaldeans, and it was formerly a common designation.

Then the Prophet means, that neither power nor warlike skill, nor knowledge of any kind, would be a defence to the Chaldeans, nor the arts in which they gloried, even though they thought that they were familiarly acquainted with

God; for by the stars they were wont to divine whatever was to be. It follows,—

36. A sword *is* upon the liars; and they shall dote: a sword *is* upon her mighty men; and they shall be dismayed.	36. Gladius super divinos ejus, et infatuabuntur; gladius super fortes ejus, et conterentur (*vel*, expavescent.)

He repeats the same thing, but in other words; and in the first clause he mentions diviners whom he before called wise men; and he calls them now by their true and proper name; for בדים, *bedim*, mean mendacious men as well as falsehoods. He then calls those now impostors to whom he conceded before the name of wise men. But when he called them wise men, he spoke according to the common opinion, and he was unwilling to contend with the Chaldeans as to the character of their wisdom: he, however, at the same time made known the impositions of those who boasted that they had a familiar intercourse with God and angels, whilst they pronounced by the stars what was to be.[1] That art itself is indeed worthy of praise, were men to preserve moderation. But as the curiosity of men is insatiable, so they wandered here and there, and overleaped all limits, and thus perverted the whole order of nature. The Chaldeans, then, were not genuine, but, on the contrary, spurious astrologers.

This is the reason why the Prophet calls them now liars; for we have before seen, that it was a mere imposition, when the Chaldeans held that the whole life of man is subject to the influence of the stars. Hence he exhorted the faithful to fear no dangers from the stars. It is then no wonder that the Prophet now charges all the diviners with falsehoods, who yet proudly arrogated to themselves the name of wise men, *they shall be infatuated*, he says. The verb יאל, *ial*, means indeed to begin, but in *Niphal* it means to become foolish, or to be infatuated.[2]

[1] The word is rendered "diviners" by the *Vulg.*, the *Syr.*, and the *Targ.*; it is left out by the *Sept.* Some derive it from ברא, to feign, to devise, to invent, the א being left out in בדים: others say that it comes from בד, alone, solitary, separate, so that בדים were the recluse, retirement or seclusion being often the habit of impostors. It is connected, in Isaiah xliv. 25, with קסמים, diviners, prognosticators.—*Ed.*

[2] Events would prove, that they were foolish and ignorant, being not able to foretell the ruin of their own nation, notwithstanding their boast in the knowledge of futurity.—*Ed.*

Then he says, *The sword shall be on her valiant men;* whom before he called chief men or princes, שרים, *sherim,* he now calls strong, גברים, *geberim,* or those who excelled in valour. The amount of the whole is,—that whatever wisdom Babylon arrogated to itself would become folly, and that the valour in which it prided, would vanish away. For he says, that they would *be broken in pieces.* The verb חתת, *chetat,* means to be broken, but as we have elsewhere seen, it is often applied to the mind, and then it means to dread, or to be terrified. He then says, that the valiant would not be able to stand when the sword was upon them, for they would become, as it were, lifeless, or, at least, they would become so effeminate as to think of nothing but flight.

37. A sword *is* upon their horses, and upon their chariots, and upon all the mingled people that *are* in the midst of her; and they shall become as women; a sword *is* upon her treasures; and they shall be robbed.

37. Gladius super equos ejus, et super currus ejus, et super multitudinem ejus (*aut,* vulgus promiscuum; ערב *significat examen animalium sicuti apum, et transfertur etiam ad homines, et tunc accipitur pro vulgo ignobili;* super multitudinem *ergo,*) quæ est in medio ejus; erunt in mulieres (*hoc est,* erunt similes mulieribus;) gladius super thesauros ejus, et spoliabuntur (expositi erunt in prædam.)

The Prophet, indeed, changes the gender of the pronouns, and seems to refer to the king; but there is no ambiguity in the meaning. He then declares that the horses as well as the chariots would perish; for the sword would consume all the things used in war. And at the beginning he generally declared that destruction was nigh all the Chaldeans, so he repeats the same now, *on all the promiscuous multitude, which is in the midst* of Babylon. He says that they would be without courage, for the Lord would dishearten them by terror, as it will be hereafter stated again. Then he joins, *and on her treasures, and they shall be a prey* to enemies. It follows,—

38. A drought *is* upon her waters; and they shall be dried up: for it *is* the land of graven images, and they are mad upon *their* idols.

38. Siccitas super aquas ejus et arescent; quia terra sculptilium est, et iis idolis (*propriè,* in terroribus, *vel,* terriculamentis) gloriantur (*vel,* insaniunt.)

Here the same word is used in a different sense: he had often before used the word חרב, *chereb,* "sword;" but now by changing only a point, he uses it in the sense of waste, or drought.[1] But as he mentions waters, the Prophet, no doubt, means drought; nor was it without reason that he mentioned this, because the Euphrates, as it is well known, flowed near the city, and it was also divided into many streams, so that there were many islands, as it were, made by the skill and hand of men. Thus the city was in no ordinary way fortified, for it was difficult of access, being on one side surrounded by so large a river: it had also trenches full of water, and it had many channels. But Cyrus, as Xenophon relates, when attempting to take the city, used the same contrivance, and imitated those who had fortified Babylon, but for a different purpose; for he diverted the streams, so that the river might be forded. Thus, then, he dried up that great river, which was like a sea; so that Babylon was taken with no great trouble. Cyrus, indeed, entered in by night, and unexpectedly invaded Babylon, while they were securely feasting, and celebrating a festival, as we find in the book of Daniel. However, the way by which Cyrus contrived to take the city was, by dividing the Euphrates into many streams. Hence it was, that the Prophet, in order that the Jews might see, as it were, with their own eyes, spoke nothing without reason, having not only predicted the slaughter and destruction of the city, but shewed also the very way in which it was done, as though the event had been portrayed before them.

The reason is added, *because it is the land of carvings*, or gravings. God, indeed, took vengeance on Babylon for other things, as it has before appeared; but the Prophet here speaks of carvings, that the Israelites might know that there is no certain salvation anywhere else except in the one true God, who had revealed himself to them. Jeremiah, in short, means, that when any country is destitute of God's help, though it may excel in arms, in number, in wealth, and in

[1] It is so rendered by the *Vulg.* and the *Targ.*, omitted by the *Sept.*, and rendered "sword" by the *Syr.*, and also by *Blayney* and *Henderson.* The same incongruity exists as to the treasures; but the sword here means those who wielded it, the soldiers of Cyrus: they spoiled the treasures, they turned the streams of the rivers.—*Ed.*

wisdom, yet everything under heaven is of no avail without the blessing and favour of God. He has spoken of princes and of wise men, and he has named chariots, horses, and treasures,—all these have been mentioned for the purpose I have just stated, even to shew, that were we supplied with all that may seem necessary to defend us, except God protected us, whatever the world may offer would be all in vain; for we shall at length find, that without God neither arms, nor chariots, nor wisdom nor counsel, nor any other helps, can avail us anything.

It follows, that Chaldea *gloried in images.* The word אימים, *aimim,* means terrors, and giants are called by this name in Deut. ii. 10, because they inspire terror by their aspect. But this name is no doubt applied to images, because they are only bugbears, *des épovantailz,* as we say in French.[1] As then they are mere scarecrows, which only frighten children, they are called אימים, *aimim.* And he says, that they *gloried in,* or doted on them—for הלל, *elal,* means both, in *Hithpael,* as it is found here. It means to boast or to elate one's-self, and also to be mad or to dote. Either sense would not be unsuitable to this place; for the unbelieving gloried in their idols, and at the same time were mad: yet the first meaning seems to me the best, that they *gloried in their idols,* as it is said in Psalm xcvii. 7, "Let them perish who trust in images and glory in them." Though the verb there is indeed different, yet the meaning is the same.

It was not, indeed, without reason, that the Prophet reproaches the Chaldeans, that they gloried in their idols, because they thereby robbed God of his honour; for what is ascribed to idols is taken away from God. He intimates, in short, that the Chaldeans would be justly punished as guilty of sacrilege, because they had impiously transferred the glory of God to their own idols. And this passage teaches us, that when God is purely worshipped among us, and when true religion flourishes, it will be our best protection. We shall then be more impregnable than if we had all the power and wealth of the world: nothing can hurt us, if

[1] That the Babylonians had large idols or images, which were of terrific size, is evident from Dan. iii. 1.—*Ed.*

we give to God his due honour, and strive to worship him in sincerity and truth. It now follows,—

39. Therefore the wild beasts of the desert, with the wild beasts of the islands, shall dwell *there*, and the owls shall dwell therein: and it shall be no more inhabited for ever; neither shall it be dwelt in from generation to generation.	39. Propterea habitabunt *aves* sylvestres cum bestiis sylvestribus, et habitabunt filiæ struthionum; nec habitabitur amplius in seculum; non erit (inquam) in habitationem usque ad ætatem et ætatem.

The birds of the forest with the beasts of the forest, are rendered by some, "the satyrs with the fairies;" but איים, *aiim*, as well as ציים, *tsiim*, are, on the contrary, birds or beasts of the forest. Some render איים, *aiim*, "cats." I hold no controversy as to these words—let there be a free judgment to every one; but, as we have elsewhere seen, the Prophet means birds and beasts of the forest, rather than satyrs and fairies. Then he adds, *the daughters of the ostriches*, rendered by some "of the owls;" but about this name also I will not contend. Some then render יענה, *ione*, "owl," and refinedly explain that "daughters" are mentioned, because these birds forsake their young, when they howl through want or famine; but this is fictitious. I then take the daughters of the ostriches or of the owls, according to the usual manner of the language, to mean the very birds themselves.[1]

The Prophets usually speak thus, when they give no hope. We have said before, that Babylon was not then so laid waste, but that men dwelt there, who afterwards lived in great luxury; for the city, under Cyrus and his son, was always populous; and then, after its revolt, it was again inhabited; and when Alexander subdued Asia, Babylon was full of people, and flourished in luxury and wealth; and when he died there, he left the city very opulent. We hence, then, conclude, that what Jeremiah declares here, was not immediately fulfilled. But as the light or moderate punishments which the unbelieving suffer now are certain preludes of final

[1] As to the two first words, the versions and the *Targ.* widely differ. According to *Bochart*, the first word, ציים, means "wild cats," and the second, איים, "jackals." The *Vulg.*, the *Syr.*, and the *Targ.* render the other word, יענה, the same, "the ostrich;" and this is the general opinion.—*Ed.*

and eternal destruction; so the Prophets, when speaking of God's vengeance, ever extend what they say to the last overthrow; and this also appears more clearly from the next verse, where it is said,—

40. As God overthrew Sodom and Gomorrah, and the neighbour *cities* thereof, saith the Lord; *so* shall no man abide there, neither shall any son of man dwell therein.

40. Secundum subversionem Dei in Sodomam et Gomorram et vicinos ejus, dicit Jehova, non habitabit illic vir, et non morabitur in ea filius hominis.

This verse confirms and explains the previous verse. But that the design of the Prophet may be more evident, we must remember what Jude in his epistle (ver. 7) says, that the destruction of Sodom is as it were a mirror in which we behold God's vengeance on all the ungodly. God overthrew Sodom; but he does not proceed in the same way with other lands and nations; yet the same is the lot of all the unbelieving, of the despisers of God, and reprobates; for they are exposed to his vengeance, which they cannot escape, though it may be for a time suspended. When, therefore, the Prophet says now that Babylon would be overthrown, as Sodom was overthrown, he does not mean that this would be after seventy years, when taken by Cyrus and Darius, nor when retaken after its revolt, nor when taken by Alexander; for it remained a long time after this, even to the reign of Augustus Cæsar. As, then, it has been so, it follows that our Prophet does not speak of its first, second, or third assault, but that he had in view what I have already stated,—that when God summons the wicked to judgment, it is a certain prelude of eternal and final destruction. His way with the godly is another; for though God may sink them down to the grave, nay, to the centre of the earth, yet hope is still left them; hence their death is never like the destruction of Sodom. And to the same purpose is what we have already quoted from Isaiah, "Except a seed had been left us, we should have been as Sodom, and like to Gomorrah." (Isa. i. 9.) That exception shews the difference between God's children and the reprobate, even because he often delivers them from ruin.

We now then understand the Prophet's meaning when he says that Babylon would become desolate and solitary, so that *no one would dwell there, nor remain;*[1] and that *from age to age,* or from generation to generation.

Moreover, we learn from what is here said, that the unbelieving are overwhelmed with despair even under the least punishment, because they see nothing but the vengeance of God; for though God does not immediately slay them, yet the least puncture denotes what impends over them; nay, he inflicts a deadly wound when he seems only to touch them lightly. There is then only one consolation, which can sustain us in our miseries, even to know that we are separated from the Sodomites through the mercy of God alone; because we have deserved the same destruction, and the Lord has spared us according to his infinite goodness. This, then, is the meaning. It follows,—

41. Behold, a people shall come from the north, and a great nation, and many kings shall be raised up from the coasts of the earth.	41. Ecce populus veniet ab aquilone, et gens magna, et reges multi (*aut,* validi) excitabuntur à lateribus terræ.

The Prophet again shews whence destruction was to come on the Babylonians. He does not indeed mention Cyrus, as Isaiah does (chap. xliv. 28; xlv. 1), nor does he mention the Persians; but he evidently points out the Medes, when he says that a *people* would *come from the north.* He adds, a *great nation and many* or powerful *kings;* and lastly, *from the sides of the earth.* It is indeed certain that the war was carried on under the banner and command of Cyrus and Darius. Cyrus was the chief, but Darius, on account of his age, was deemed the king. To whom then does Jeremiah refer, when he says *many kings,* if we so render the words? even to the satraps or princes, of whom a great number Darius brought with him; for Cyrus came from remote mountains, and from a barbarous nation; but the kingdom of Darius was very wide. There is then no doubt but that he brought with him many kings, who yet obeyed his authority. But we may take רבים, *rebim,* in the sense of being strong. However this may be, the Prophet means that the Chaldeans would have to carry on war, not with one nation or one king, but with many nations and

[1] Rather "sojourn," according to the *Sept.—Ed.*

with many kings, or certainly with mighty kings. Hence he mentions the *sides* of the earth, by which phrase he reminds us that the army would come, not from one country but from remote parts; and though the distance might be great, yet the Prophet says, that they would all come together to attack the Chaldeans.

We now see that what afterwards happened is represented as in a picture, in order that the event itself might confirm the Jews, not only in the truth announced by Jeremiah, but also in the whole law and worship of God; for this prophecy was ratified to the faithful when they found that Jeremiah, a faithful interpreter of the law, had thus spoken. And then his doctrine availed also for another purpose, even that the people might know that they rebelled against God when they obstinately resisted the holy Prophet; for we know that they were extremely disobedient. They were then proved, by what happened, to have been guilty of having contended with God in their pertinacious wickedness and contempt. There was afterwards given them a sure ground of hope; for as Jeremiah had spoken of the destruction of Babylon, so, on the other hand, he had promised a return to the Jews. They had then reason to look for restoration, when they saw fulfilled what Jeremiah had spoken.

By the word *raised,* he expresses something more than by the word *come:* he says that people would *come,* and adds, that they would be *raised up* or roused; he intimates that they would not come of themselves, but by the hidden influence of God, because this war was not carried on merely by men. Cyrus indeed, led by insatiable avarice and ambition, was guided by his own inclination to undertake this war; and he made no end of his cruelty, until he at length miserably died, for he never ceased to shed innocent blood everywhere. But yet the Lord made use of these kings and nations to destroy Babylon: they were in reality the scourges of God, and accordingly he says, that they were *roused from the sides of the earth,* that is, from the most distant places.

42. They shall hold the bow and the lance: they *are* cruel, and will not shew mercy: their voice shall roar like the sea, and

42. Arcum et scutum apprehendent, crudelis ipse (*hoc est,* omnes erunt crudeles,) et non tangentur misericordia; vox eorum tanquam mare sonabit (*vel,*

they shall ride upon horses, *every one* put in array, like a man to the battle, against thee, O daughter of Babylon.

tumultuabitur,) et super equos ascendent; paratus est quisque tanquam vir (*hoc est*, parati erunt) ad prœlium contra te, filia Babylonis.

Jeremiah again speaks especially of armour, to intimate that the Babylonians would not be able to sustain the assault of their enemies. He then says that they would be armed with the *bow* and the *shield;*[1] and adds, that they would be *cruel.* It is certain that the Persians were very bloody; for it was a barbarous nation; and where barbarity rules, there is no feeling of mercy. Cyrus indeed wished to appear a magnanimous prince, and not a savage; but it is sufficiently evident that he was very cruel, though Xenophon in his Life speaks of him otherwise; but he is not a true historian, for he tells many false things in favour of Cyrus. But when any one reads all that has been recorded, he will readily find out that Cyrus was a barbarian, who delighted in slaughter and carnage.

As to the Medes, they were given to luxuries, and were not a warlike nation. Darius, however, brought with him many princes, those whom he had overcome in uncultivated countries, and such as also possessed some valour. Though, then, the king of the Medes was effeminate as well as his people, yet he had with him many warlike men. And the same thing is expressed also by Isaiah; and you ought to compare this prophecy with that of Isaiah (chap. xiii. 17:) for the two Prophets wholly agree, though Isaiah was dead when Jeremiah uttered this prophecy and wrote it.

He says that *their voice* would be *tumultuous as the sea,* or would sound or roar as the sea, when moved by some violent storm. And all these things were said, that the Babylonians might know that all their defences would be of no avail, when God should arm the Persians and the Medes for their destruction. For had that war been carried on only by men, the Chaldeans would have never thought that their enemies would be victorious; and doubtless they would have never been so, had not the Lord roused them and determined by their means to execute vengeance on the

[1] Rather "spear" or lance; so the *Sept.* and *Syr.*, though the *Vulg.* and *Targ.* have "shield."—*Ed.*

Chaldeans. He says that they would be *prepared as a man for war.* Interpreters do not seem to me to understand the meaning of the Prophet; for though Jeremiah uses the word "prepared" in the singular number, yet he speaks of the whole people. But how does he say they would be prepared? even *like a man.* Here he sets forth the union of the whole army, for they would all come to battle, like one man attacking his own enemy. It is indeed difficult for the minds of all to be so directed in battle, that they should unitedly attack an enemy and fight as it were with one hand, and that they should not look on one another, and yet make an united assault. This, then, is what the Prophet means when he says, that they would be *prepared* against the Chaldeans *as one man.*

He then adds, *against thee, daughter of Babylon.* He intimates that they would be not only sufficiently strong against ordinary enemies, but also against the city itself. For had not this been added, Babylon would have ever been considered as an exception; for it was deemed impregnable on account of the multitude of men, the height and breadth of its walls, its towers, and all other defences. Now, then, God shews that though Babylon proudly exulted in its forces, and thought itself exempt from every danger, yet the Persians and the Medes would possess sufficient power by which they would easily overcome it. What follows I cannot finish to-day; it is therefore better to stop here.

PRAYER.

Grant, Almighty God, that since thou teachest us by the example of the ungodly to fear thy name, we may learn to submit our necks to thy word, and willingly, and as it becomes us, submissively to receive thy yoke, that while we strive to glorify thy name, being safe under thy protection, we may disregard all the attacks of our enemies, and all the assaults and onsets of Satan, who is the captain of all our enemies, until we shall at length enjoy our victory in the celestial kingdom, through Christ our Lord.—Amen.

Lecture One Hundred and Eighty-fifth.

43. The king of Babylon hath heard the report of them, and his hands waxed feeble: anguish took hold of him, *and* pangs, as of a woman in travail.

43. Audivit rex Babylonis famam ipsorum, et dissolutæ sunt manus ejus; anxietas apprehendit (*vel*, corripuit) eum, dolor tanquam parturientem.

The Prophet means by these words, that as soon as the report of war reached the Chaldeans, they would be so disheartened through fear as to become like a conquered people. As they had subjected to themselves many nations, they had acquired the name of being a warlike people; but the Prophet delcares here that they would have no courage, and that therefore there would be no need of much valour to attack them, as they would of themselves give way and flee. The sum of what is said is, that the Persians and the Medes would gain the victory before they fought, for there would be no need of an attack, as their enemies would flee as being without any courage.

The Prophet at the same time intimates that in God's hand are the hearts of men, as I have often said, so that they who seem to excel in great boldness, melt as wax in a moment. For no doubt the Chaldeans were not wanting in courage to fight until God had rendered them effeminate, so that they took to flight through fear as soon as they heard the report respecting their enemies. It is, indeed, true that this was not immediately the case, for we know that they had long sustained a siege, and that Belshazzar was slain in the night, while they were securely and joyfully feasting as in the greatest quietness and peace; but they were at length taken, so that they had neither wisdom nor confidence; for the king and his princes were slain, and the city was in a moment taken, as though all the men were turned into logs of wood or into statues of stone. It follows,—

44. Behold, he shall come up like a lion from the swelling of Jordan unto the habitation of the strong: but I will make them suddenly run away from her: and

44. Ecce tanquam leo ascendet (ascendens) à tumore Jordanis (ab altitudine, *vel*, elevatione, *propriè*, גאון *etiam significat metaphoricè superbiam*) ad habitaculum forte, quum quiescere fe-

who *is* a chosen *man, that* I may appoint over her? for who *is* like me? and who will appoint me the time? and who *is* that shepherd that will stand before me?

cero, (*vel,* postquam irruptionem fecero,) currere faciam eos ab ipsa; et quis electus quem super eam præficiam? quis enim similis mei? et quis contestabitur mecum? et quis ille pastor qui consistat coram me (*vel,* ad faciem meam)?

We have explained nearly the same words in the last chapter; for the Prophet not only used the same similitude respecting the Idumeans, but also added all the words which are found here; nay, the Prophet brings forward nothing new to the end of the chapter, but only repeats what we have seen before.

He first compares either Darius or Cyrus to a lion, who, at the overflowing of Jordan, removes to another place. This passage, like the former, is indeed variously explained. Some read, "for the pride of Jordan." But as it appears from other places that lions had their dens near the banks of Jordan, I have no doubt but that the Prophet here compares Cyrus to a lion, forced to leave his own lair because of the inundation of that river. We know how savage a beast is the lion; but when he is forced to change his dwelling and to move to another place, his fury rages the more. It is the same, then, as though he had said, that not any sort of lion would attack the Babylonians, but a lion furious through rage. He then adds, *to the strong habitation.* When he spoke of the Idumeans, the allusion might have been to their country, which was elevated, and they had also mountains as their fortresses. But as Babylon was also strongly fortified, and nearly impregnable on account of the various streams of the Euphrates, what the Prophet says is also suitable, that *a lion* would *come,* though there were hindrances which might impede his course; for when a lion rambles, being not hungry nor forced by any necessity, he can turn here and there as he pleases; but when rage drives and constrains him, he will then surmount all obstacles. So also the Prophet says, that how confident soever Babylon might be in its fortresses, yet Cyrus would break through them, for he would be like a lion, who, at the overflowing of Jordan, removes elsewhere, as he can no longer find his wonted dwelling.

We now perceive the meaning of the words,—that the Babylonians would have to do, not with an idle but a terrible enemy, and with one who would surmount all obstacles, as when fury excites a lion when necessity drives him as it were headlong.

What follows is obscure. Some render the words thus, "When I shall make Israel to rest, then I will make them to flee from her." In the former place (chap. xlix. 19), we read "him," in the singular, ארי׳צנו, *aritsnu ;* but here the Prophet uses the plural number, "them," ארי׳צם, *aritsem ;* it is yet certain that the meaning is the same. Some, at the same time, apply this to the Jews, that God would remove them from Babylon, purposing to give them rest, that is, by dwelling securely in their own country ; but as there is no mention made here of his people, this view is forced and far-fetched. I omit other explanations, for the meaning of the Prophet seems to me to be simply this, *When I shall make an irruption,* or, after I shall have made them rest, *I will make them to flee.* He speaks, as I think, of the Chaldeans ; and the particle כי, *ki,* is to be taken as an adverb of time, *when,* or *after.* It is, indeed, often a causative, but it has sometimes this meaning.

Now, these two clauses may be thus explained : *When I shall make an irruption,* or, when I shall have made them rest ; for רגע, *rego,* means both to break and to rest. It is here in the active or causative conjugation, in *Hiphil.* If, then, we read, "After I shall have made them to rest," the sense will be that the Babylonians had been long tranquil, as there was no one who infested them or disturbed their peace ; and we know that men having long rested in their idleness and sloth, become almost stupified, so that they are touched with no fear. God then shews that the Babylonians were greatly mistaken, if they thought that the rest which they had previously enjoyed would be perpetual ; for he would make them to flee from the city, though they had been long there in a tranquil state. The other sense is by no means unsuitable, "When I shall break," or make an irruption, then all will flee away, that is, leave the city, which was before like a paradise. There is still no doubt but that the Prophet here denounces on the Babylonians a sudden overthrow, which would drive the people here and there in all directions.[1]

It now follows, *Who is the chosen* one *whom I shall set over her?* God here in a manner deliberates as to the person whom he should make the leader of the war against the Chaldeans; and by these words he intimates that there would be ready for him the best general, and one especially active and also excelling in the art of war. And we know that even the unwilling are made to serve God, when he employs the ungodly as his scourges. In short, God shews that though the Babylonians might have brave leaders and most skilful in war, there yet would be prepared leaders, to whom he would commit the office of taking that city. And thus he teaches us at the same time that men are ruled by his hand, so that he chooses them according to his will and directs them to any work he pleases, *Who is the chosen* one, he says, *whom I shall set over her?*

And he adds, *and who is like me?* Here the Prophet shews that the Babylonians in vain trusted in their own defences; for after having tried all things, they would find that whatever was set up against God and his invincible power, would be mere smoke. This sentence often occurs; and however common it may appear, yet, if we examine ourselves, we shall find that the Holy Spirit does not so often enforce it without reason; for after we have confessed that none is equal to God or can add to his power,—as soon as any trial assails us, this confession vanishes, and we tremble as though God was nothing, and had no power to bring us help. Diffidence, then, which often creeps in when we are in difficulties or dangers, sufficiently shews that we do not attribute to God the praise due to his power. He does not then exclaim here, as in other places, without reason, *Who is like me?* as though he had said, that the Babylonians would foolishly seek auxiliaries here and there; for when they had made the utmost exertions, whatever

[1] See note on chap. xlix. 19, pp. 87-92.—*Ed.*

they might think the most useful would all vanish away, so that they would be destitute of all remedies.

He adds, *And who will protest against me?* Some give this frigid version, *Who will prescribe to* me the time? but they wholly pervert the meaning of the Prophet; for God in this place declares, that men would in vain contend or litigate with him. It is the same as if he had said, "Though all men were to rise up against me, yet I will not allow them to litigate with me; and this they would also do in vain." In short, God intimates that men would in vain clamour against his judgments, for he would nevertheless perform what he has decreed. He does not yet claim for himself that absolute power about which the sophists prattle, while they separate it from justice; but he intimates that the causes are not always manifest to men when he executes his judgments; for it is not without reason that the Scripture testifies that God's judgments are a deep abyss; but by such an expression it is not meant that anything in God's judgments is confused or in disorder,—what then? even that God works in an extraordinary manner, and that hence his judgments are sometimes hidden from men.

Then God briefly shews, that though the Babylonians were to dispute, and start many objections, all this would be useless, because he would execute what he had decreed, and that without debating.

Let us then learn from these words, that when God's works have the appearance of being unreasonable, we ought humbly to admire them, and never to judge them according to our computation; for God is not to be judged by us. Therefore, as I have already said, we are then only wise, when we humbly adore him in all his works, without disputing with him; for when we adduce all possible things, he will close our mouth with one word, and check all our presumption; nay, he will ever overcome us by being silent, for his justice will always overthrow whatever may come to our minds. But we must bear in mind what I have stated, that God never so acts by his absolute power as to separate it from his justice; for this would be as it were to wound himself; for these things are undivided, his power and justice, though justice often does not appear. However this may be, his sole and simple will is to us the rule of all justice.

It follows, *And who is that shepherd who will stand before me?* He alludes to the similitude he had used, for he compared himself before to a lion. He says now, "Since I shall go against Babylon like a lion, what shepherd will dare to oppose me?" We see that there is to be understood a contrast between a lion and a shepherd; for God would be like a lion to destroy Babylon; hence, by pastor, he denotes any adversary who might come forth to defend the Chaldean flock. It follows,—

45. Therefore hear ye the counsel of the Lord, that he hath taken against Babylon; and his purposes, that he hath purposed against the land of the Chaldeans; Surely the least of the flock shall draw them out; surely he shall make *their* habitation desolate with them.

45. Propterea audite consilium Jehovæ quod consultavit contra Babylonem, et cogitationes quas cogitavit contra terram Chaldæorum; Si non traxerint eos parvuli gregis; si non perdiderint super eos habitaculum.

The Prophet confirms his previous doctrine, and uses an oath, for he had already spoken sufficiently at large of the destruction of Babylon, and his words might seem otherwise superfluous, because the subject had been explained with abundant clearness. But he introduces God here as making an oath, for the particles, "if not," אם לא, *am la*, shew the sentence to be elliptical; and we know that this form of swearing is common in Scripture. Then God swears, that the Babylonians were already given up to destruction, so that even the *least of the flock* would be superior to them.

But it is not without reason that the Prophet speaks here of the *counsel* of God and of his *thoughts;* for we know that men through their own vanity are held suspended or in doubt, so that they do not firmly acquiesce in God's word, at least they vacillate so as to have no stability of faith. As, then, men think in themselves that possibly a thing may happen otherwise than according to the words of the prophets, Jeremiah does here meet such thoughts, and bids men to *hear* the *counsel* of God and his *thoughts.* It is, indeed, a mode of speaking transferred from men, when he speaks of the thoughts of God; for we know that God does not deliberate on what he is about to do, as the case is with men. But this manner of speaking so frequently occurs, that it ought to be familiar to us. However this may be, he intimates that God did not in vain announce terror when speaking of Babylon, but that the irrevocable decree was declared which God had formed. Hence he says, that he had already taken counsel, so that men need not deliberate any more, nor call into question his fixed decree, nor dispute concerning his thoughts. There is, then, no reason for men to revolve things in themselves, and to adopt different views; because events must be, he says, as I have predicted; God then has commanded me to announce this prophecy as brought forth from his counsel, which can by no means be changed. This is the reason why he mentions God's counsel and thoughts.

He adds, *If they shall not draw them forth;* some read, "cast them out." But סחב, *sacheb,* means to draw; and there is no doubt but that the Prophet denotes by this verb contempt and reproach; as carcases are drawn through the mud, or a dead dog is drawn and cast into a river; so now, he says, *Draw forth the Babylonians shall the least of the flock.* But how can these things agree together, that there was to be the choicest leader, and that yet the least of the flock would be the conquerors? God intimates, that though he would endow Cyrus with warlike valour, yet if it pleased him, there would be means by which he could destroy the Babylonians, were he to send sheep or lambs as their enemies. He means, in a word, that the Babylonians would be unwarlike, when God deprived them of their courage.

If they will not upset over them their tabernacle. Some read as though the verb were שום, *shum,* "If they will not set," &c.; others derive the word from ישם, *ishem;* but it comes rather from שמם, *shemem; If,* then, *they will not upset over them their tabernacle,* that is, when the Babylonians shall be laid prostrate, even their houses shall fall and overwhelm them. In short, God sets forth here a final ruin, from which the Babylonians could never be restored; for it is an evidence of hopeless despair, when houses are upset, so that their masters are buried in their ruins. It follows,—

46. At the noise of the taking of Babylon the earth is moved, and the cry is heard among the nations.

46. A voce captæ Babylonis contremuit terra, et clamor in gentibus, (*vel*, per gentes,) auditus est.

This is to anticipate an objection; for many might have said, "How can it be, that Babylon should thus fall, on whose monarchy so many and so wide countries are dependent?" As, then, such an event appearing so unreasonable, might occur to them, the Prophet meets the objection, and answers by way of anticipation, that though the earth shook, yet this would surely take place. He shews, at the same time, how great the calamity would be, for it would, by its noise, make the whole world to tremble: it would be thus better known how grievous was to be God's vengeance on the Babylonians; for it was not to be without the shaking of the whole earth. Now follows,—

CHAPTER LI.

1. Thus saith the Lord, Behold, I will raise up against Babylon, and against them that dwell in the midst of them that rise up against me, a destroying wind.

1. Sic dicit Jehova, Ecce, ego excitans contra Babylonem, et contra habitatores cordis qui insurgunt contra me, ventum corrumpentem (*vel*, dissipantem.)

He proceeds with the same subject. Jeremiah seems, indeed, to have used more words than necessary; but we have stated the reason why he dwelt at large on a matter so clear: His object was not only to teach, for this he might have done in a few words, and have thus included all that we have hitherto seen and shall find in the whole of this chapter; but as it was an event hardly credible, it was necessary to illustrate the prophecy respecting it with many figures, and to inculcate with many repetitions what had been already said, and also to confirm by many reasons what no one hardly admitted.

He then says, *Behold, I will*, &c. God is made the speaker, that the word might have more force and power. *Behold*, he says, *I will raise up a destroying wind* against the Chaldeans. The similitude of wind is very appropriate, for God thus briefly reminded them how easy it was for him to destroy the whole world even by a single blast. The wind is, indeed, indirectly set in opposition to instruments of war; for when any one seeks to overcome an enemy, he collects many and strong forces, and procures auxiliaries on every side; in short, he will not dare to attempt anything without making every possible preparation. As, then, men dare not attack their enemies without making strenuous efforts, God here extols his own power, because it is enough for him to raise up a *wind.* We now, then, perceive the design of the similitude, when he says, that he would raise up a wind that would destroy or scatter the Chaldeans.

In the following words there is an obscurity; literally, they are, *the inhabitants of the heart;* for as the word ישבי, *ishebi,* is in construction, another word necessarily follows it, as for instance, the country of the Chaldeans. But the relative ה, *He,* referring to Babylon, ought to have been put down. Yet as the words occur, we are compelled to read, *and against the inhabitants of the heart.* Some will have the relative, אשר, *asher,* to be understood, but that is harsh, for it is an unnatural mode of speaking. They, however, give this rendering of אשר לב, *asher leb,* "those who in heart rose up against me." But what if we read the words *inhabitants of the heart* metaphorically, as meaning those who gloried in their own wisdom? for the Babylonians, as it is well known, thought other men dull and foolish, and were so pleased with their own astuteness, as though they were fortified by inclosures on every side. They dwelt then in their own heart, that is, they thought themselves well fortified around through their own wisdom. In this sense the Prophet seems to call the Babylonians *the inhabitants of the heart.*[1]

[1] The *Targ.* and the versions widely differ from one another. The cabbalistic solution is very frivolous, by which the two words לב and קמי are made one, and made to signify "Chaldeans," according to what was called "Athbash," by which *aleph,* the first letter, was taken for *tau,* the last letter, and *beth,* the second, for *shin,* the last but one; and so on through the whole alphabet. But *Blayney* and others, such as *Gataker* and *Venema,* give a satisfactory explanation of the words. The word

He adds, at the same time, that they *rose up against God*, even because they had cruelly treated his people, and nearly destroyed them. And we know that God undertook the cause of his Church, and therefore complained that war was made on him by the ungodly, whenever they molested the faithful. It is also at the same time generally true, that all who arrogate to themselves wisdom rise up against God, because they rob God of the honour due to him. But it ought properly to be referred to the union which exists between God and his Church, when he charges the Chaldeans, that they *rose up* against him. It follows,—

2. And will send unto Babylon fanners, that shall fan her, and shall empty her land: for in the day of trouble they shall be against her round about.

2. Et mittam contra Babylonem ventilatores, qui ventilent ipsam (*ad verbum*, et ventilabunt ipsam,) et exinanient terram ejus (*vel*, spoliabunt; בקק *enim significat propriè exinanire, evacuare, ut vulgo dicunt; et significat etiam spoliare et prædari;* qui *ergo* exinanient terram;) quia erunt contra eam in circuitu in die mali (*hoc est*, in die adversa.)

Here he explains himself more clearly, without the metaphor he had used. He no longer uses the similitude of wind when he declares that he would send *fanners*. At the same time some take זארים, *zarim*, in the sense of aliens, who would banish her; but this would be harsh. I then doubt not but that the Prophet alludes to the wind before mentioned. He does not indeed continue that metaphor; but yet what he says corresponds with it. Instead of wind he now mentions fanners, or winnowers; but this cannot be understood except of enemies. A clearer explanation is still found in the word *empty*, after having said that the Persians and the Medes would *fan* or winnow Babylon. He compares her, no doubt, to chaff. As then the chaff, when ventilated, falls on the ground, so he says a similar thing would happen to the Babylonians.

But he adds, *And shall make empty her land*, that is, the land of Babylon. He says that the whole country would be

לב, the heart, often means the middle of anything, as "the heart of heaven," in Deut. iv. 11 means the midst of heaven; and "the heart of the seas," in Psalm xlvi. 2, means the midst of the seas. So here, "the heart of my adversaries," means the centre of the country of his adversaries, *i.e.*, Babylon,—

Against the inhabitants of the metropolis of my adversaries.—*Ed.*

so plundered, that nothing would be left remaining. And he confirms this declaration, *because they shall be,* he says, *around her.* By this expression he intimates that there would be no escape for the Chaldeans.

It often happens that men stealthily escape, when pressed by their enemies; for though enemies may watch all passages, yet they often do not find out all hiding-places. But the Prophet says, that their enemies would so surround them, that the Chaldeans would not be able to take with them anything which they might save from their enemies' hands. He adds, *in the day of evil.* By this phrase he intimates again, that the Chaldeans were already devoted by God to destruction. It is, then, the same thing as though he had said, that as soon as her enemies came, it would be all over with Babylon and the whole nation,—how so? for it would be the day of her utter ruin. It follows,—

3. Against *him that* bendeth let the archer bend his bow, and against *him that* lifteth himself up in his brigandine: and spare ye not her young men; destroy ye utterly all her host.

3. Ad tendentem qui tendit arcum suum (ידרך *est hic vox supervacua,* qui tendit *igitur* arcum suum,) et qui se extollit lorica sua, et (*copula hic abundat;*) ne parcatis electis ejus, interficite omnem exercitum ejus.

Interpreters give various expositions of this verse. Some understand a soldier of light armour by *him who bends the bow;* and by him who *elevates himself in his coat of mail,* they understand a heavy-armed soldier. There is also another difference; some take אל, *al,* for לא, *la,* when it is said ואל יתעל, *veal itol,* because a copulative follows; and the words seem not to be well connected, if we read thus, "As to him who raises himself up in his coat of mail, and spare ye not," &c.; and hence they take negatively the particle אל, *al,* instead of לא *la,* "and that he may not raise up himself in his coat of mail." But it is probable that the copulative in the second place is redundant. The simple meaning would therefore be, *As to him who bends the bow, and who raises himself up in his coat of mail.*[1]

[1] It is singular that אל is omitted in the *Sept.* and the *Syr.*, and retained in its negative sense in the *Vulg.* and the *Targ.*, which makes no sense consistently with the context. There is evidently אשר understood before the first verb, as is often the case when the verb is in the future tense. Then the literal rendering would be this,—

I do not, indeed, give such a refined interpretation as some do, respecting the light and heavy armed soldiers. I doubt not, then, but that he points out the archers, and those clad in mail. If, however, any one prefers the other explanation, let him enjoy his own opinion. As to the main point, it is evident that the Prophet exhorts the Persians and the Medes not to spare the young men among the Chaldeans, but to destroy their whole army, so that no part of it should be left remaining.

PRAYER.

Grant Almighty God, that since thou wert formerly so solicitous respecting the salvation of thy people as to undertake war, for their sake, against a most powerful nation,—O grant, that we also, at this day, may know, that we shall be safe and secure under the protection of thy hand, and that we may so experience thy power, that there may be to us a just reason for glorying in thee, and that our enemies may be confounded, in order that thy glory may shine forth more and more, and that the kingdom of thine only-begotten Son may also be thus promoted.—Amen.

Lecture One Hundred and Eighty-sixth.

4. Thus the slain shall fall in the land of the Chaldeans, and *they that are* thrust through in her streets.	4. Et cadent vulnerati in terra ejus (in terra Casdin) et transfixi (*vel*, confossi) in compitis ejus.

He proceeds with what we began yesterday to explain,—that the time was nigh when God would take vengeance on the Babylonians. As, then, this could not be without great destruction in a city so very populous, and as it could not be overthrown except calamity extended itself through the whole country, hence, he says, that though Babylon should prepare great and powerful armies, it would yet be in vain,

At him who bends let the bender bend his bow,
And at him who glories in his coat of mail;
And spare ye not her chosen men,
Utterly destroy all her host.

There is here perfect consistency. They who take אל as a negative say, that the first part is addressed to the Chaldeans, and the second to their enemies; but this would be strangely abrupt.—*Ed.*

because *they shall fall*, he says, *wounded everywhere in the land;* and then he adds, *and pierced through in her streets.* By these words he means, that the Chaldeans would be slain not only in the open fields, but also in the midst of the city. He afterwards adds,—

5. For Israel *hath* not *been* forsaken, nor Judah, of his God, of the Lord of hosts; though their land was filled with sin against the Holy One of Israel.	5. Quoniam non viduatus est Israel, et Jehudah à Deo suo, à Jehova exercituum; quin potius (*eadem est particula* כי *causalis, quæ tamen* hic *plus aliquid exprimit, ergo* quin potius) terra ipsorum plena est peccato propter sanctum Israel.

The Prophet shews here the cause why God had resolved to treat the Babylonians with so much severity, even because he would be the avenger of his own people. He also obviates a doubt which might have disturbed weak minds, for he seemed to have forsaken his people when he suffered them to be driven into exile. As this was a kind of repudiation, as we have seen elsewhere, the Prophet says now, that *Israel had* not been *wholly widowed, nor Judah, by his God;* as though he had said, that the Jews and the Israelites were indeed, for a time, like widows, but this was not to be perpetual. For, as we have said, the divorce was temporary, when God so forsook his Temple and the city, that the miserable people was exposed to plunder. As long, then, as the will of their enemies prevailed, God seemed to have forsaken his people. It is of this widowhood that the Prophet now speaks; but he yet testifies that Israel would not be wholly widowed by Jehovah his God.

He indeed alludes to that spiritual marriage, of which frequent mention is made; for God had, from the beginning, united the Church to himself, as it were, by a marriage-bond; and the people, as it is well known, had been so received into covenant, that there was contracted, as it were, a spiritual marriage. Then the Prophet now says, that they were not widowed; in which he refers to the hope of deliverance; for it could not have been denied but that God had repudiated his people. But he shews that their chastisement would not be perpetual, because God would at length reconcile to himself the people from whom he had been alienated, and would restore them to the ancient condition and honour of a wife. He speaks of both kingdoms.

Then he adds, *by Jehovah of hosts.* By this title he sets forth the power of God, as though he had said, that as God is faithful in his promises, and constantly keeps his covenant, so he is not destitute of power, so as not to be able to save his people and to rescue them, when it pleases him, from death itself. He confirms this truth, when he says, *for the land* of the Chaldeans *is filled with sin on account of the Holy One of Israel,* as though he had said, that the land was abominable, because it carried on war against God. For when he speaks of the *Holy One of Israel,* he shews that God had such a care for his people that he was prepared, when the suitable time came, to shew himself as their avenger. We now perceive what the Prophet means when he says, that Chaldea was *filled with sin,* even because it provoked God when it thought that the wrong was done only to men.[1] It follows,—

6. Flee out of the midst of Babylon, and deliver every man his soul: be not cut off in her iniquity; for this *is* the time of the Lord's vengeance; he will render unto her a recompence.	6. Fugite è medio Babylonis, et servate quisque animam suam, (*vel,* eripite,) ne excidamini (*vel,* pereatis) in iniquitate ejus; quia tempus hoc ultionis Jehova, mercedem ipse rependet ei.

He goes on with the same subject, but illustrates it by various figures; for otherwise he would not have penetrated into the hearts of the godly. Were any at this day to predict the destruction of Rome, it could hardly be believed; and yet we know that it has in our life been stormed, and now it hangs as it were by a thread, though hitherto it has been supported and fortified by the greatest forces. But the dignity of the city so confounded the minds of men, that it

[1] The explanation of the last clause is, according to the Jewish commentators, not generally taken. The "land," by most is deemed to be the land of Israel and Judah. The word אשם, means not only guilt, but also guilt's penalty—judgment; and this seems to be its meaning here,—

For not widowed is Israel, nor Judah,
By his God, by Jehovah of hosts;
Though their land has been filled
With judgment by the Holy One of Israel.

But if we render מ *before* or *against,* then the last line would be,—

With guilt (or sin) before the Holy One of Israel.—*Ed.*

was hardly credible that it could have been so soon subverted. How, then, was it possible for such a thing to have happened at that time? for Babylon was the mistress of the East. The Assyrians had previously possessed the empire; but they had been subdued, and had, as it were, been brought under the yoke. As, then, Babylon now flourished in power so great and invincible, Jeremiah seemed to be fabling when he spoke of its approaching destruction. It was hence necessary that what he said should be confirmed, as it is now done. And so he now turns to foreigners and guests, and exhorts them to flee lest they should perish in the accursed city.

Flee, he says, *from the midst of Babylon.* But there was then no safer place in the land; for had all the regions of the world been shaken, yet Babylon would have been deemed beyond any danger. But he says that all guests were to flee from the midst of it, if they wished to save their lives. Then he adds, *lest ye perish in her iniquity.* He assigns a reason why those who then dwelt in Babylon could not be safe except they fled, even because God was about to punish the city for its iniquities. He then sets the iniquity of Babylon in opposition to the multitude of its men, as well as to its wealth and defences, and other means of strength. Babylon was populous; it might also be aided by many auxiliaries; and there were ready at hand those who might hire their services. As, then, there was nothing wanting to that city, the Prophet here shews that wealth and abundance of people, and all other helps would be of no moment, because it was God's will to punish her iniquity. This is the reason why Jeremiah now says, *lest ye perish in her iniquity;* that is, "do not mingle with those ungodly men whom God has given up to destruction."

And for the same purpose he adds, *For it is the time of the vengeance of Jehovah.* Here, again, he obviates an objection; for as God had suspended his judgment, no one thought it possible that a fire could so soon, and, as it were, in a moment be kindled to destroy Babylon. Then the Prophet says, that it was *the time;* by which he intimates, that though God does not immediately execute his judgments, yet he does not lie down as it were idly, so as to forget what he has to do, but that he has his own times. And this doctrine deserves to be noticed, because through our intemperate zeal we make much ado, except God brings us help as soon as we are injured; but if he delays even a short time, we complain and think that he has forgotten our welfare. And even saints, in depositing familiarly their cares and anxieties in his bosom, speak thus, "Arise, O Lord, why sleepest thou?" (Psalm xliv. 23.) As, then, we are by nature inclined to impatience, we ought to observe what Scripture so often inculcates, even this—that God has his certain and fixed times for punishing the wicked. Hence Jeremiah now teaches us, that the *time of God's vengeance* was come.

He then adds, *A reward will he render to her;* as though he had said, that though Babylon would not have to suffer punishment immediately, yet she would not escape from God's hand, for the reward which God would render her was already prepared. And this doctrine arises from a general principle, that God will ever render to every one his just reward. We now, then, perceive the design of the Prophet.

We have said that the words were addressed to the strangers and the guests who were in Chaldea, or in the city Babylon. They then pervert this passage, who think that the faithful are here exhorted immediately to depart from Babylon, that is, to withdraw themselves from superstitions and the defilements of the world; for the Prophet means no such thing. A passage might, however, be made from one truth to another. It now follows,—

7. Babylon *hath been* a golden cup in the Lord's hand, that made all the earth drunken: the nations have drunken of her wine; therefore the nations are mad.	7. Calix aureus Babylon in manu Jehovæ, inebrians totam terram; è vino ejus biberunt gentes, propterea insanierunt gentes.

Here again he anticipates an objection which might have been made; for we know that the kingdoms of the world neither rise nor stand, except through the will of God; as, then, the Prophet threatens destruction to Babylon, this objection was ready at hand. "How comes it, then, that this city, which thou sayest is accursed, has hitherto so greatly flourished? for who hath honoured Babylon with so great dignity, with so much wealth, and with so many victories? for it has not by chance happened that this monarchy has been elevated so high; for not only all Assyria has been brought under its yoke, but also the kingdom of Israel, and the kingdom of Judah is not far from its final ruin." To this the Prophet answers, and says, that *Babylon was a cup in God's hand to inebriate the earth;* as though he had said, that God was by no means inconsistent with himself when he employed the Babylonians as his scourges, and when he now chastises them in their turn. And he shews also, that when things thus revolve in the world, they do not happen through the blind force of chance, but through the secret judgments of God, who so governs the world, that he often exalts even the ungodly to the highest power, when his purpose is to execute through them his judgments.

We now, then, understand the design of this passage; for otherwise what the Prophet says might seem abrupt. Having said that the *time of God's vengeance* had already come, he now adds, *A golden cup is in God's hand;*—to what purpose was this added? By what has been stated, it appears evident how aptly the words run, how sentences which seem to be wide asunder fitly unite together; for a doubt might have crept in as to this, how could it be that God should thus bestow his benefits on this city, and then in a short time destroy it. As, then, it seems unreasonable that God should vary in his doings, as though he was not consistent with himself, the Prophet on the other hand reminds us, that when such changes happen, God does in no degree change his purposes; for he so regulates the government of the world, that those whom he favours with remarkable benefits, he afterwards destroys, they being worthy of punishment on account of their ingratitude, and that he does not without reason or cause use them for a time as scourges to chastise the wickedness of others. And it is for this reason, as I think, that he calls it *a golden cup;* for God seemed to pour forth his benefits on the Babylonians as with a full hand. When, therefore, the splendour of that city and of the monarchy was so great, all things were there as it were golden.

Then he says, that it was *a golden cup*, but *in the hand of God.* By saying that it was in God's hand, he intimates that the Babylonians were not under the government of chance, but were ruled by God as he pleased, and also that their power, though very great, was yet under the restraint of God, so that they did nothing but by his permission, and even by his command.

He afterwards adds how God purposed to carry this cup in his hand, a cup so splendid as it were of gold; his will was that it should *inebriate the whole earth.* These are metaphorical words; for the Prophet speaks here, no doubt, of punishments which produce a kind of fury or madness. When God then designed to take vengeance on all these nations, he inebriated them with evils, and this he did by the Babylonians. For this reason, therefore, Babylon is said to have been the golden cup which God extended with his own hand, and gave it to be drunk by all nations. This similitude has also been used elsewhere, when Jeremiah spoke of the Idumeans, " All drank of the cup, yea, drank of it to the dregs, so that they were inebriated," (chap. xlix. 12.) He there also called the terrible punishment that was coming on the Idumeans the cup of fury. Thus, then, were many nations inebriated by the Babylonians, because they were so oppressed, that their minds were infatuated, as it were, with troubles; for we know that men are stupified with adversities, as though they were not in a right mind. In this way Babylon inebriated many nations, because it so oppressed them that they were reduced to a state of rage or madness; for they were not in a composed state of mind when they were miserably distressed.[1]

To the same purpose is what is added: *The nations who drank of her cup became mad.* Here he shews that the

[1] Some render the last word "reel," or stagger, and perhaps more consistently with the comparison of drunkenness. The verb in *Hithpael*, as here, means to be moved violently, either through rage or joy. Moved or agitated is the rendering of the versions and the *Targum*. To be moved with joy is to exult or to glory; and so *Blayney* renders it, and connects the end of this verse with the following, *i.e.*, that the nations gloried because of the fall of Babylon,—

Therefore shall nations glory, [saying,]
Babylon is suddenly fallen, &c.—*Ed.*

punishments were not ordinary, by which divers nations were chastised by the Babylonians, but such as deprived them of mind and judgment, as it is usually the case, as I have just said, in extreme evils.

Moreover, this passage teaches us, that when the wicked exercise their power with great display, yet God overrules all their violence, though not apparently ; nay, that all the wicked, while they seem to assume to themselves the greatest license, are yet guided, as it were, by the hand of God, and that when they oppress their neighbours, it is done through the secret providence of God, who thus inebriates all who deserve to be punished. At the same time, the Prophet implies, that the Babylonians oppressed so many nations neither by their own contrivance, nor by their own strength ; but because it was the Lord's will that they should be inebriated : otherwise it would have greatly perplexed the faithful to think that no one could be found stronger than the Babylonians. Hence the Prophet in effect gives this answer, that all the nations could not have been overcome, had not the Lord given them to drink the wine of fury and madness. It follows,—

8. Babylon is suddenly fallen and destroyed : howl for her ; take balm for her pain, if so be she may be healed.

8. Subito cecidit Babylon et confracta est ; ululate super eam ; tollite resinam (*alii*, balsamum) ad dolorem ejus, si forte sanetur.

The Prophet now declares that the fall of Babylon would be sudden, that the faithful might understand that God could accomplish in one moment what he had decreed. For when the prophets spoke of God's judgments, the people questioned among themselves, how could that be which surpassed the common ideas of men. That men, therefore, might not estimate God's power according to their own thoughts, he introduces this word, *suddenly ;* as though he had said, that God had no need of warlike forces ; for though he makes no preparations, yet he can subvert every power that exists in the world.

He then adds, *Howl for her ;* and this is said, because it could not be but that many nations would either bewail the ruin of so great a monarch, or be astonished at her, and thus many things would be said. He then says, that though the whole world were to howl for Babylon, it would yet fall and be suddenly broken, whenever it pleased God. And he says, by way of irony, *Take balm, if peradventure it can be healed.* The word צרי, *tsari,* is, by some, rendered *balsam,* but it means rosin, for we know that it was deemed precious in Judea; and the Prophet no doubt accommodated what he said to what was commonly known. As then that medicament was in common use among the Jews, he now says, *Take rosin.* As there is hardly any country which has not its peculiar remedies; so we see that Jeremiah refers not to what was usually done at Babylon, or to medicaments used by the Chaldeans, but to what was commonly used in his own country, as it appears from other places. Now rosin was a juice which flowed from trees, and it was a thick juice. The best rosin which we now use is from the terebinth; but in these parts they have what proceeds from the fir, for here the terebinth is not found. But Judea had a most valuable rosin, as we learn from many parts of Scripture. And under this one thing is included everything, *Take rosin;* as though he had said, "Let physicians come together (otherwise she will perish) from every place, if *peradventure she can be healed.*" This is said ironically, that the faithful might know that the diseases of Babylon would be incurable.

We have said elsewhere, that Babylon was not wholly demolished when taken by Cyrus, and that the people were not then driven away. They dwelt there as usual, though made tributary, as they were afterwards, under the dominion of the Persians. Babylon was also grievously oppressed, when punished for its revolt, until what Jeremiah and others prophesied was fulfilled. Then the time of which he speaks ought not to be confined to one calamity only, which was only a prelude to others still greater. He afterwards adds,—

9. We would have healed Babylon, but she is not healed: forsake her, and let us go every one into his own country; for her judgment reacheth un-

9. Curavimus Babylonem (*idem est quidem verbum,* רפא, *quod significat sanare et mederi, quia non semper est in medico relevetur ut æger, nec semper fœliciter succedit, ideo dicit Propheta,* medicati sumus, *vel,* remedia attulimus ad curandum Babylonem,) et non sanata

to heaven, and is lifted up *even* to the skies.	fuit; derelinquite eam, et proficiscamur quisque in terram suam; quia pertigit ad cœlos judicium ejus, et elevatum est usque ad nubes.

The Prophet assumes different characters; he speaks here in the person of those who of themselves brought help to the Babylonians. And many, no doubt, would have been ready to assist them, had King Belshazzar wished to accept aid; and we know also, that the city had a large army. He compares, then, the nations subject to the Babylonians, and also the hired and foreign soldiers, to physicians, as though he had said, "Babylon has been, with great care, healed." As when a great prince is taken ill, he sends here and there for the best and most skilful physicians; but when the disease is incurable, they all strive in vain to save his life: so now the Prophet speaks, using a metaphor; but he speaks in the person of those who either had set to hire their services, or had come from a sense of duty to heal Babylon. "See," they said, "the fault is not with us, for we have faithfully and carefully done our best to heal her, but she has not been healed."

He then adds, *Leave her, and let us depart, every one to his own land.* This was the language of foreign soldiers and mercenaries. When they saw that the safety of the city was hopeless, they began to counsel one another, "What do we? Ought we not rather to consult our own safety? for our efforts are wholly useless. It is then time for every one to return to his own country, for the end of Babylon is come." But the change of person has much more force than if the Prophet had spoken thus, "The time shall come when the auxiliaries shall flee away, for they will see that it would be all in vain to defend her." But when he compares them to physicians, this similitude more fully illustrates the case; and then when he speaks in their person, this renders what is said still more emphatical.

He at length adds, *For her judgment has reached to the heavens, and has been elevated to the clouds.* Jeremiah could not have properly addressed what he said to the unbelieving, if you explain this of God being adverse and hostile to the Babylonians; for it never occurred to the hired soldiers, that

Babylon perished through the just judgment of God. But the Prophet, according to a usual mode of speaking, says, *Her judgment* (that is, her destruction) *reached to the heavens, and has been elevated to the clouds;* that is, no aid shall be found under heaven, which can deliver Babylon,—how so? because it will be the same as though destruction came from heaven itself, and from the clouds. For when danger is nigh either from behind or from before us, we can turn aside either to the right hand or to the left, so that we may escape the evils which men may bring on us: but when heaven itself seems to threaten our heads, then an escape is attempted in vain. This then is the reason why the Prophet says that the judgment of Babylon had reached to the heavens and had been elevated to the clouds.[1] It follows,—

10. The Lord hath brought forth our righteousness: come, and let us declare in Zion the work of the Lord our God.

10. Eduxit (*vel,* protulit; egredi fecit, *ad verbum*) Jehova justitias nostras: venite et narremus in Sion opus Jehovæ, Dei nostri.

The Prophet here addresses the faithful, and especially shews, that the ruin of Babylon would be a sure evidence of God's paternal favour towards his Church. And it was no common consolation to the faithful, in their extreme miseries, to know, that so dear and precious to God was their salvation, that he would by no means spare the Babylonians, whom the whole world regarded as half gods; for, as I have said, the power of that monarchy filled the minds of men with astonishment. When the faithful, then, knew that the Babylonians were to perish, because they had oppressed and cruelly treated them, an invaluable consolation, as I have said, must hence have been conveyed to them. The Prophet then reminds us here, that it would be a singular testimony as to God's favour to his Church, when he subverted

[1] Another view has been given of this clause: It is a mode of speaking to express the greatness of a thing; see Psalm xxxvi. 5; Ezra ix. 6. The judgment or punishment of Babylon would be so great, that it might be compared to what may reach to the heavens, and to the ethereal regions; for such is the meaning of the last word, and is rendered "stars," by the *Sept.,*—

For to the heavens has reached her judgment,
And it has risen up to the ethereal regions.

By "heavens," are often meant the skies.—*Ed.*

Babylon, and he also exhorts the faithful to gratitude: for it is the design of all God's benefits, that his name may be celebrated by us, according to what David says: "What shall I render to the Lord for all the benefits which he has bestowed on me? The cup of salvation will I take and call on the name of the Lord." (Psalm cxvi. 12, 13.)

He then says, first, *Brought forth hath Jehovah our righteousness.* Here, some anxiously toil to untie a knot, where there is none; for fearing lest the word, righteousness, should be laid hold on for the purpose of setting up merits, they say that righteousness is the remission of sins. Then they thus explain the words of the Prophet,—"God has at length unfolded his mercy towards us, and it is our righteousness when all our iniquities are buried." But this is forced. When the Prophet speaks here of righteousnesses, he does not mean the merits by which the Jews were to obtain what had been promised to them; but righteousnesses he calls their good cause with regard to the Babylonians. For righteousness has various meanings; and when a comparison is made between men, God is said to bring forth our righteousness, when he vindicates our integrity from the calumnies of the wicked. So Jacob said, "The Lord will bring forth my righteousness as the dawn." (Gen. xxx. 33.) But in this sense our righteousness has a reference to our adversaries. So whenever David asked of God to regard his righteousness, he no doubt compared himself with his enemies. And righteousness here is to be taken simply with reference to the Babylonians. For though God had punished the Jews as they deserved, yet as to the Babylonians they were cruel tyrants and wicked robbers. The cause, then, of the chosen people was just, with regard to them. This is the reason why he says, that God *brought forth* their *righteousnesses*. The rest to-morrow.

PRAYER.

Grant, Almighty God, that since thou didst formerly put forth thy wonderful power, to help thy miserably afflicted people,—O grant, that at this day the same power may be put forth in our behalf, and that the same evidence of thy grace and paternal favour may be shewn to us, by raising up thy terrible hand to destroy all the ungodly who cruelly oppress thine innocent people, that being delivered by thine hand, we may learn ever to give thanks to thee, in the name of thine only-begotten Son.—Amen.

Lecture One Hundred and Eighty-seventh.

We began yesterday to explain the words of the Prophet, when he says, that the *righteousnesses* of the people had been brought to light; and we said, that the word righteousnesses does not refer to God, as though the Jews had deserved a reward, but is, on the contrary, to be understood of a just cause as to the Chaldeans, who, being impelled by avarice and pride alone, had made war against the Church, and without any right, had tyrannically oppressed the people. As far, then, as it was God's will to defend his people, it was a just cause. Nor is there any need of having here a long dispute respecting this,—how could the people be just, who had, by so many iniquities, provoked the wrath of God; for, as we have already said, he does not treat now of their merits, but of a right which depended on the faithfulness and protection of God.

The Prophet now exhorts the faithful to gratitude; he would have them at the same time to rise up to the hope of deliverance, and to cherish the promises which he had given them, when he says, *Come*, as though he would set before their eyes the gift of redemption. He also shews the end, even that the people were to celebrate the grace of God, as though he had said, that the people, after having obtained mercy, ought to have this in view, to worship God again in his Temple; as though he had said, that when God restored his Church, his pure and true worship should, at the same time, be restored; for the design of his grace is religion, and not the honour or dignity of the people. This is the reason why he says, *Come and let us declare in Sion the work of Jehovah our God.* Now, when Peter treats of a better redemption, he says, that those who are delivered from the kingdom of darkness ought to set forth the unspeakable praises of God. (1 Pet. ii. 9.) We must then understand, that God has appeared to us as a Redeemer, in the person of his only-begotten Son, in order that we may celebrate his mercy, which we have experienced, according also to what is said in the song of Zacharias, " He delivered us from the hand of our enemies, that we may all our life worship him in holiness." (Luke i. 74, 75) It now follows,—

11. Make bright the arrows; gather together the shields: the Lord hath raised up the spirit of the kings of the Medes: for his device *is* against Babylon, to destroy it; because it *is* the vengeance of the Lord, the vengeance of his temple.	11. Polite sagittas (parate, *ad verbum*,) implete (*vel*, perficite) clypeos; suscitat Jehova spiritum regum Mediæ, quia super Babylonem cogitatio ejus ad perdendum eam, quia ultio Jehovæ hæc, ultio Templi ejus.

These words might have been addressed to the Medes as well as to the Babylonians. If the latter meaning be approved, that is, that the Prophet addresses the Babylonians, the words are a taunt, as though he had said, that they were to no purpose spending their labours in preparing their armies, because God would be stronger than they, and that the Medes would carry on war under his banner and authority. Nor would what I have also stated, be unsuitable, that is, that the Prophet bids the Medes to prepare themselves and to put on their arms, that they might fight courageously against the Babylonians.[1]

He now adds the main thing,—that the *kings of the Medes would come against Babylon*, because they had been called from above; and he mentions the word *spirit*, that he might more fully express that men's minds are ruled and turned by the secret power of God, and also that whatever power or boldness is found in them, proceeds altogether from God; as though he had said, that God would so prepare the Medes and the Persians, that he would not only strengthen their arms, hands, and feet, for the war, but would also lead them, and overrule their passions—that he would, in short, turn their spirit here and there, according to his will. He does

[1] The second clause in the versions and the *Targ.* is, " Fill the quivers," *i.e.*, with arrows. But the word means " shields :" hence some render the verb in the sense of filling up or completing. " Complete the shields," *i.e.*, their number, or rather, more consistently with sharpening or polishing the arrows, " Fill up," or mend, " the shields." So *Venema* and *Parkhurst.—Ed.*

not now speak of the wind, as before ; nor does he point out the enemies generally, but expressly names the Medes. For though Cyaxares, or Darius, as he is called by Daniel, was not a very prudent man, nor skilful in war, yet, as he was higher in dignity, the Prophet here mentions the Medes rather than the Persians. Cyrus excelled in celerity, and was also a man of singular wariness, activity, and boldness : but as he was by no means wealthy, and ruled over a rustic nation, and the limits of his kingdom were confined, the Prophet rightly speaks here of the Medes only, whose power far exceeded that of the Persians.

But we hence learn, that Jeremiah did not speak as a man, but was the instrument of the Spirit ; for it was an indubitable seal to his prophecy, that he predicted an event a long time before the war took place. Cyrus was not yet born, who was the leader in this war : nor was Darius as yet born ; for seventy years elapsed from the time the Prophet spoke to the taking of Babylon. We then see that this passage is a sure proof of his faithfulness and authority.

He afterwards adds, that God's *thought respecting Babylon* was *to destroy her*. He still speaks after the manner of men, and at the same time obviates an objection which might have disturbed weak minds, because Babylon not only remained safe and secure for a long time, but also received an increase of power and dignity. The minds then of the godly might have desponded, when there seemed to be no accomplishment of this prophecy. Hence the Prophet calls attention to the *thought* of God, as though he had said, that though God did not immediately put forth his hand, it was yet enough for the faithful to know what he had decreed. In short, the Prophet reminded them, that they ought to acquiesce in God's decree, though his work was yet hid.

And he again confirms the Jews, by adding, that it would be his *vengeance*, even that of God, because he disregarded not his *Temple*. By these words he intimates that the worship, according to the law, was pleasing to God, because the Jews became a distinct people from heathen nations, when the rule as to religion was prescribed to them. Then the Prophet intimates, that though any sort of religion pleased men, there is yet but one which is approved by God, even that which he himself has commanded. The case being so, we may conclude, that God cannot long endure his worship to be scoffed at. For we know how scornfully and proudly the Chaldeans spoke of the Temple, so that they not only uttered blasphemies, but also heaped every reproach they could think of on the Temple. Since that religion was founded on God's word, it follows that it could not be but that he must have at length risen and vindicated the wrongs done to him by the Chaldeans. We now perceive the meaning of the Prophet, when he says, that it would be the *vengeance of God;* and he adds, *because God will avenge his temple.* He confirms the Jews, when he declares that God would be the vindicator of his own worship; and he, at the same time, shews, that the worship according to the law, which had been taught by Moses, was the only worship in the world which God approved. It afterwards follows,—

12. Set up the standard upon the walls of Babylon, make the watch strong, set up the watchmen, prepare the ambushes: for the Lord hath both devised and done that which he spake against the inhabitants of Babylon.

12. Super muros Babylonis tollite vexillum, roborate custodiam (*vel,* augete,) parate (*vel,* statuite, *potius*) custodes, disponite insidias; quia etiam cogitavit Jehova, etiam fecit quod loquutus est super habitatores Babylonis.

These words seem to have been addressed to the Chaldeans rather than to the Medes or the Persians, as some expound them; for this is favoured by the context; for as he bids them first to raise a standard on the walls, so he adds, *Increase the watch,* which refers to the citizens of Babylon, and then he says, *set the watchmen.* All this cannot apply to the Persians and the Medes, but must be referred to the besieged, as being most suitable to them. I do not then doubt but that the Prophet here treats, with a taunt, all the efforts the Chaldeans would make for the defence of their city. For not only they who attack a city raise a standard, but also they who are besieged, and this as a sign of confidence, in order to shew that they possess sufficient courage to check their enemies, and to sustain all their attacks. It was then the design of the Prophet to shew, that however strenuously the Chaldeans might defend themselves, yet all their exertions would be in vain, because God would, without labour, destroy the city.

Raise, he says, *the banner on the walls of Babylon, and strengthen*, or increase *the watch;* and afterwards, *set watchmen*, so that every one might watch with more care than usual. He says at last, *set in order the ambushes.* "When all things have been tried by you, your labour will be without any advantage, for *the Lord hath spoken.*" When the particle גם, *gam*, is repeated, it ought to be rendered *as* and *so—for as the Lord hath thought, so will he do what he hath said*, &c. He says again that God had *thought*, lest the faithful should imagine that He heedlessly casts forth threatenings; for this thought often occurs to the mind, that God terrifies without effecting anything. Hence the Prophet, that he might more fully confirm his prophecy, says, that the thing had been meditated upon by God; and we said yesterday that God does not deliberate with himself like men; but as we cannot otherwise understand the certainty and unchangeableness of his secret counsel, nor form an idea of the validity of his decrees, the word *thought* is mentioned. The Prophet, in short, means, that he brought forth nothing but what God had decreed. For words are often heedlessly uttered, and the reality and the words are not always connected; but Jeremiah testifies that he had taken what he announced from the hidden and immutable counsel of God. Then he adds, *what he hath spoken* or said; and this refers to his doctrine or his prediction. It follows,—

13. O thou that dwellest upon many waters, abundant in treasures, thine end is come, *and* the measure of thy covetousness.

13. Quæ habitas super aquas multas (*vel*, magnas,) quæ multa es in thesauris, (*id est*, dives, *vel*, locuples) venit finis tuus, mensura cupiditatis tuæ.

The word שכנתי, *shekenti*, is to be taken here for שכנת, *shekenet*, a dweller; and the passage is more clear when we take it as the title of Babylon. And he says that she was a *dweller among waters*, because the Euphrates not only flowed by the city, (and we know that it was a very large river,) but it surrounded it; and it was indeed divided above Babylon into many streams, so that it made as it were many islands, and thus access to the city was more difficult. This circumstance served not only for a defence to it, but also for other advantages. For these streams or channels were navigable; and the land also was made more fertile by the irrigation they supplied. Thus these streams contributed to its wealth as well as to its defence in time of war. And though Babylon was deemed on this account impregnable, and was also a very fertile land, yet the Prophet says here that its *end was come.*

Now, except he had made this preface, that Babylon was situated among the rivers or many waters, and that it was also a city full of wealth, all this might have seemed a hinderance to prevent God from executing on it his vengeance; for this objection was ready at hand, "How can Babylon be taken, which is seated between many waters? for without great force and number of soldiers it cannot but remain in safety, since it is protected by so many rivers." Then another objection might have been brought forward, that Babylon was an opulent city, so that it could hire auxiliaries on every side, and that having such abundance of money, it would never be unprotected. Hence the Prophet here mentions these two things; but what he says ought to be taken adversatively, as if he said, "Though thou dwellest among many waters, and art great in treasures, that is, hast large treasures, yet *thine end is come.*"

He adds, *the measure of thy cupidity.* Some render אמת, *amet,* "end," but improperly; and the Prophet has not without reason introduced the word אמת, *amet,* which properly means a cubit, but is to be taken here for measure. *Jerome* renders it "a foot," a word in use in his age. But the meaning is sufficiently clear, that though Babylon had exhausted all the wealth of the world as an insatiable gulf, yet *the measure of her cupidity* would come. For the cupidity of that nation was unlimited, but God at length brought it to an end—not that they were amended, but that God checked their coveting. And according to this sense the Prophet says, that though they had been hitherto devouring the wealth of many countries, yet the *measure of her cupidity was come,* even because the Lord would take away, together with the monarchy, the power and opportunity of doing wrong. For the Chaldeans were able to act licentiously, when they had so many nations subject to them; but the *measure* of their cupidity was come, when God in a manner cut off their strength, not that they then desisted, or that their rapacious disposition was amended—for they changed not their nature; but cupidity is to be referred here to its exercise, even because their power was then taken from them, so that they could not carry on their plunders as they had used to do. He afterwards adds,—

14. The Lord of hosts hath sworn by himself, *saying*, Surely I will fill thee with men, as with caterpillars, and they shall lift up a shout against thee.

14. Juravit Jehova exercituum per animam suam, Nisi implevero te homine sicut locusta (*hoc est*, hominibus sicut locustis, *aut* bruchis,) qui canunt super te הידד, (*id est*, canticum vindemiale, *cujus ante facta fuit mentio.*)

The Prophet more fully confirms what he had said by introducing God as making an oath; and it is the most solemn manner of confirmation when God swears by his own name. But he speaks of God in the language of men when he says that he *swears by his own soul;* for it is a kind of protestation when men swear by their own souls, as though they laid down or pledged their own life. Whoever then swears by his own soul, means that as his own life is dear to him, he thus lays it down as a pledge, that were he to deceive by perjury, God would be an avenger and take it away. This is suitable to men, not to God; but what does not properly belong to God is transferred to him; nor is this uncommon, as we have seen in other places. And the more familiar is the manner of speaking adopted by God, the more it ought to touch men when he makes himself like them, and in a manner assumes their person as though he lived in the midst of them.

But we must still remember why the Prophet introduces God as making an oath, even that all doubtfulness might be removed, and that more credit might be given to his prophecy; for it not only proceeded from God, but was also sealed by an oath. *If I shall not fill Babylon*, he says, *with men as with locusts.*

The multitude of enemies is here opposed to the multitude of the citizens, which was very large. For we have said elsewhere that Babylon surpassed all other cities, nor was it less populous than if it were an extensive country. As then it was full of so many defenders, it might have been objected and said, "Whence can come such a number of enemies as can be sufficient to put to flight the inhabitants? for were a large army to enter, it would yet be in great danger in contending with so vast a multitude." But the Prophet compares here the Persians and the Medes to locusts; and we know that Cyrus collected from various nations a very large army, nay, many armies. Fulfilled then was what had been predicted by the Prophet, for Cyrus made up his forces not only from one people, but he brought with him almost all the Medes, and also led many troops from other barbarous nations. Hence then it happened, that what had been said by Jeremiah was proved by the event.

He also adds, that they would be victorious; for by the *vintage song*, or shout, he no doubt means a song or shout of triumph. But this song, הידד, *eidad*, was then in use among the Jews. Then as they did after vintage sing in token of joy, so also conquerors, exulting after victory over their enemies, had a triumphant song. And the Greek translators have rendered it κέλευσμα, or κελευμα, which is properly the song of sailors; when they see the harbour they exult with joy and sing, because they have been delivered from the dangers of the sea, and also have completed their sailing, which is always perilous, and have come to the harbour where they more fully enjoy life, where they have pleasant air, wholesome water, and other advantages. But the simple meaning of the Prophet is, that when the Persians and the Medes entered Babylon, they would become immediately victorious, so that they would exult without a contest and without any toil, and sing a song of triumph. The Prophet now confirms his prophecy in another way, even by extolling the power of God,—

15. He hath made the earth by his power, he hath established the world by his wisdom, and hath stretched out the heaven by his understanding.	15. Qui fecit terram in virtute sua, qui statuit (*alii vertunt*, paravit) orbem in sapientia sua, et in sua intelligentia extendit cœlos;

16. When he uttereth *his* voice, *there is* a multitude of waters in the heavens: and he causeth the vapours to ascend from the ends of the earth: he maketh lightnings with rain, and bringeth forth the wind out of his treasures.

16. Ad vocem dando copiam aquarum in cœlis, qui attollit (et attollit, *ad verbum*) elevationes a fine (*vel*, extremitate) terræ; fulgura in pluviam facit, educit ventum de thesauris suis.

The Prophet commends here, as I have already said, in high terms, the power of God; but we must bear in mind his purpose, for abrupt sentences would be otherwise uninteresting. His object was to encourage the Jews to entertain hope; for they were not to judge of Babylon according to its splendour, which dazzled the eyes of all; nor were they to measure by their own notions what God had testified. He bids the faithful to raise all their thoughts above the world, and to behold with admiration the incomprehensible power of God, that they might not doubt but that Babylon would at length be trodden under foot; for had they fixed their eyes on that monarchy, they could have hardly believed the words of prophecy; for the Prophet spoke of things which could not be comprehended by the human mind.

We now then understand why the Prophet set forth the power of God, even that the faithful might learn to think of something sublimer than the whole world, while contemplating the destruction of Babylon, for that would not be effected in a way usual or natural, but through the incredible power of God. The same words are also found in the tenth chapter; and the five verses we meet with here were there explained. But Jeremiah had then a different object in view, for he addressed the Jewish exiles, and bade them firmly to persevere in the worship of God: though religion was oppressed, and though the victorious Chaldeans proudly derided God, he yet bade them to stand firm in their religion, and then said, "When ye come to Babylon, say, Cursed are all the gods who made not the heaven and the earth." (Chap. x. 11.) And there, indeed, he used a foreign language, and taught them to speak in the Chaldee, that they might more plainly profess that they would persevere in the worship of the only true God. He afterwards added what he now repeats, even that the power of God was not diminished, though he had chastised for a time his own people. But now, as we have said, he speaks in sublime terms of the power of God, in order that the faithful might know that what the judgment of the flesh held as impossible, could easily be done by that God who can do all things.

He says first, *He who made the earth.* He does not mention God's name; but the expression is more emphatical, when he says, *the Maker of the earth;* as though he had said, "Who can be found to be the creator of the heaven and the earth except the only true God?" We hence see more force in the sentence than if God's name had been expressed; for he thus excluded all the fictitious gods, who had been devised by the heathens; as though he had said, "The only true God is He who made the earth." Then he says, *by his power.* He speaks of God's power in connexion with the earth, as it is probable, on account of its stability.

He afterwards adds, *Who hath constituted the world by his wisdom, and by his knowledge extended the heavens.* The wisdom of God is visible through the whole world, but especially in the heavens. The Prophet indeed speaks briefly, but he leads us to contemplate God's wonderful work in its manifold variety, which appears above and below. For though it may seem a light matter, when he says, that the world was constituted by the wisdom of God, yet were any one to apply his mind to the meditation of God's wisdom in the abundance of all fruits, in the wealth of the whole world, in the sea, (which is included in the world,) it could not, doubtless, be, but that he must be a thousand times filled with wonder and admiration: for the more carefully we attend to the consideration of God's works, we ourselves in a manner vanish into nothing; the miracles which present themselves on every side, before our eyes, overwhelm us. As to the heavens, what do we see there? an innumerable multitude of stars so arranged, as though an army were set in order throughout all its ranks; and then the wandering planets, not fixed, having each its own course, and yet appearing among the stars. Then the course of the sun, how much admiration ought it to produce in us!—I say, not in those only who understand the whole system of astronomy, but also in those who see it only with their own eyes; for when the sun, in its daily course, completes so great and so immense a distance, they who are not amazed at such a miracle must be more than stupid; and then the sun, as it is well known, has its own course, which is performed every year, and never passes in the least beyond its own boundaries; and the bulk of that body is immense (for, as it is well known, it far exceeds the earth,) and yet it rolls with great celerity and at the same time in such order as though it advanced by degrees quietly. Surely it is a wonderful specimen of God's wisdom. The Prophet, then, though he speaks in an ordinary way, yet supplies the godly with materials of thought, so that they might apply their minds to the consideration of God's works. Some explain the words, that God expands the heavens whenever they are covered with clouds; but this is wholly foreign to the meaning of the Prophet; for there is no doubt but that he points out in this verse the perpetual order of nature, as in the next verse he speaks of those changes which sometimes happen.

PRAYER.

Grant, Almighty God, that since thou hast deigned once to receive us under thy protection, we may learn to recumb on the power of thy hand, and that as so many terrors on every side meet us through the assaults and cruelty of our enemies, we may yet continue firm, and persevere in calling on thy name, until thou appearest as our Redeemer, not only once, but whenever we may need thy help, until thou gatherest us at length into that blessed rest, which has been prepared for us in heaven, through Christ our Lord.—Amen.

Lecture One Hundred and Eighty-eighth.

In our last Lecture, we stopped where the Prophet commends the power of God, as manifested in his ordinary works. Having previously spoken of creation, and briefly shewn, that both in heaven and on earth there are many clear evidences of God's wonderful wisdom as well as of his power, he now comes to the rains and winds. We have further said, that there is a difference between a fixed order of nature and those changes which are daily observed; for were the appearance of the heavens and the earth always the same, God's power and wisdom could not appear so wonderful; but when the heavens are covered with clouds, when the air is now tranquil, and then disturbed by winds, when storms suddenly arise, and then rains follow, God thus vividly sets forth his manifold wisdom and power.

This, then, is the reason why the Prophet, after having briefly touched on what we have seen, adds, as evidences of God's power and wisdom, those things which appear to us in their various changes. He then says, that by *his voice alone he gives abundance of waters in the heavens,* and then that *he raises vapours from the extremity of the earth,* that he *creates lightnings and the rain,* which yet seem to be contrary things. At last he says, that he *brings the winds out of his treasures.* Philosophers indeed mention the causes of these things, but we ought to come to the fountain itself, and the original cause, even this, that things are so arranged in the world, that though there are intermediate and subordinate causes, yet the primary cause ever appears eminently, even the wisdom and power of God. Winds arise from the earth, even because exhalations proceed from it; but exhalations, by whom are they created? not by themselves: it hence follows, that God is their sole author. And he calls hidden places *treasures*: as when one draws out this or that from his storehouse, so he says that winds come forth from hidden places, not of themselves, but through God, who holds them as though they were shut up. I pass by these things by only touching on them, because I have already reminded you that we have before explained, in the tenth chapter, what is here literally repeated.[1] It now follows,—

17. Every man is brutish by *his* knowledge; every founder is confounded by the graven image: for his molten image *is* falsehood, and *there is* no breath in them.

17. Infatuatus est omnis homo à scientia, pudefactus omnis conflator à sculptili; quia mendacium est fusile, et non est spiritus in ipsis.

[1] See vol. ii. pp. 31-38.—*Ed.*

This verse is usually explained, as though the Prophet pointed out how men glide into errors and fancies, even because they seek to be wise according to their own notions; and Paul, in the first chapter to the Romans, assigns it as the cause of idolatry, that men become vain in their own wisdom, because they follow whatever their own brains suggest to them. This doctrine is in itself true and useful; for men have devised idols for themselves, because they would not reverently receive the knowledge of God offered to them, but rather believed their own inventions: and as mere vanity is whatever man imagines according to his own thoughts, it is no wonder that those who presumptuously form their own ideas of God, become wholly foolish and infatuated. But it is evident from the context, that the Prophet means here another thing, even that the artificers who cast or forge idols, or form them in any other way, are wholly delirious in thinking that they can, by their own art and skill, make gods. A log of wood lies on the ground, is trodden under foot without any honour; now when the artificer adds form to it, the log begins to be worshipped as a god; what madness can be imagined greater than this? The same thing may be said of stones, of silver, and of gold; for though it may be a precious metal, yet no divinity is ascribed to it, until it begins to put on a certain form. Now when a melter casts an idol, how can a lump of gold or silver become a god? The Prophet then upbraids this monstrous madness, when he says, that men are in their knowledge like brute beasts, that is, when they apply their skill to things so vain and foolish. But he mentions the same thing twice, according to the common usage of the Hebrew style; for we know that the same thing is often said twice for confirmation by the prophets.

After then having said that *men are infatuated by knowledge,* he adds, that they were *made ashamed by the graven image.* There seems to be an impropriety in the words; for פסל, *pesal,* "graven," does not well agree with צרף, *tsareph,* "the caster," or founder; but the Prophet, stating a part for the whole, simply means, that all artificers are foolish and delirious in thinking that they can by their own hand and skill cast or forge, or in any way form gods. And to prove this he says, that there is *no spirit* or breath *in them;* and this was a sufficient proof; for we know that God is the fountain of life, and hence he is called by Moses "the God of the spirits of all flesh." (Numb. xvi. 22.) Whatever life, then, is diffused through all creatures, flows from God alone as the only true fountain. What, then, is less like divinity, or has less affinity to it, than a lump of gold or of silver, or a log of wood, or a stone? for they have no life nor vigour. Nothing is more fading than man, yet while he has life in him, he possesses something divine; but a dead body, what has it that is like God? But yet the form of a human body comes nearer to God's glory than a log of wood or a stone formed in the shape of man. It is not, then, without reason that the Prophet condemns this madness of all the heathens, that they worshipped fictitious gods, in whom yet there was no spirit.[1] It follows,—

18. They *are* vanity, the work of errors: in the time of their visitation they shall perish.	18. Vanitas ipsi, opus illusionum, tempore visitationis ipsorum peribunt.

As he had called idols a lie, so now in the same sense he declares that they were *vanity,* even because they were nothing real, but vain pomps, or phantoms, or masks; and he afterwards expresses himself more clearly by saying that they were *the work of illusions.* But he does not seem to take the word תעתעים, *totoim,* in a passive but in an active sense. He then means that it was a deceptive work, which was a snare to men; as though he had said, that they were the work of imposture, or impostures.

This passage, and such as are like it, ought to be carefully noticed; because the Papists seem to themselves to find a way to escape when they confess their images are not to be worshipped, but that they are books for the unlearned. They who are moderate in their views have recourse to this evasion. This was once suggested by Gregory, but very foolishly; and they who wish to appear more enlightened than others under the papacy repeat the same saying, that images ought to be tolerated, because they are the books of

[1] See note in vol. ii. p. 38.—*Ed.*

the ignorant. But what does the Holy Spirit, on the other hand, declare here, and also by the Prophet Habakkuk? that they are *the work of impostures*, even mere snares or traps. (Hab. ii. 18.) All, then, who seek instruction from statues or pictures gain nothing, but become entangled in the snares of Satan, and find nothing but impostures. And doubtless, whatever draws us away from the contemplation of the only true God, ought justly to be deemed an imposture or a deception; for who by the sight of a picture or a statue can form a right idea of the true God? Is not the truth respecting him thus turned into falsehood? and is not his glory thus debased? For we have then only the true knowledge of God, when we regard him to be God alone, when we ascribe to him an infinite essence which fills heaven and earth, when we acknowledge him to be a spirit, when, in short, we know that he alone, properly speaking, exists, and that heaven and earth, and everything they contain, exist through his power. Can a stone or wood teach us these things? No; but on the contrary, I am led by the stone to imagine that God is fixed and confined to a certain place. And then the life of God, does it appear in the stone or in the wood? Besides, what likeness has a body, and that lifeless, to an infinite spirit? It is, then, not without reason that he complains, as it is recorded by Isaiah, that he is thus wholly degraded: "To whom have ye made me like? for I contain the earth in my fist, and ye confine me to wood or stone." (Isa. xl. 12, 18.) If, in a word, the minds of men received no other error from idols than the thought that God is corporeal, what can be more preposterous?

We hence see that the Prophet does not here say without cause, that all idols are vanity, and the work of imposture or deception.

He lastly adds, that all fictitious gods would perish *at the time of visitation*. In this clause he exhorts the faithful to patience, and in a manner sustains their minds, that they might not despond; for it was not a small trial to see the monarchy of Babylon flourishing, when yet it had no other protection than that of idols. As, then, the Babylonians thought that fictitious gods were the guardians and defenders of their safety, and that through them they had subdued all their neighbours, they became thus more and more addicted to their superstitions, the reward of which they regarded all their wealth and power. Inasmuch as the minds of the godly could not have been otherwise than shaken by such a trial, the Prophet here supports them, and reminds them to wait for the time of visitation when the the idols were to perish. However, a reference may be intended to the Babylonians as well as to the idols, when he says, *They shall perish at the time of their visitation*, that is, when the Chaldeans shall be visited. But it is probable that the time of visitation refers here especially to idols, because the Prophet had spoken before of all the wicked and reprobate. However this may be, we understand that his object was to shew that however prosperous idolaters might be for a time, yet the hand of God was to be patiently borne until the suitable time came, which is here called the time of visitation. And the metaphor refers to the notions of men, for we think that God dwells idly in heaven and turns away his eyes from us, while he spares the ungodly. Hence the Prophet calls the judgment of God a *visitation*, because he then shews really, by evident proofs, that he does not disregard the affairs of men. It now follows,—

19. The portion of Jacob *is* not like them; for he *is* the former of all things; and *Israel is* the rod of his inheritance: the Lord of hosts *is* his name.	19. Non sicut ipsi (*vel,* sicut ipsa, *si ad idola referimus*) portio Jacob: quia fictor omnium ipse, et virga hæreditatis ejus, Jehova exercituum nomen ejus.

Had the Prophet only said that idols were mere impostures and mockeries, it would have been indeed something; but this part of his teaching would have been cold and uninteresting, had he not, on the other hand, proclaimed the glory of the one and only true God. We ought, indeed, to know that idols are nothing, that men are most foolishly deceived, and are wholly infatuated, when they imagine that there is in them some divinity. But the main thing is, that the true God himself is brought before us, and that we are taught to direct all our thoughts to him. This, then, is what is now done by the Prophet; for after having exposed the folly of the heathens in worshipping idols, and having shewn that the whole is nothing but deception and falsehood, he now says, *Not as they,* the fictitious gods, *is the portion of Jacob;* that is, the God who had revealed himself to the chosen people is very far different from all idols.

And, doubtless, the vanity which the Prophet before mentioned cannot be adequately understood, except the true God be known. For though some of the ancient philosophers ridiculed the grossest errors of the common people, yet they had nothing fixed or certain on which they could rest, like him, who, when asked, "What was God?" requested time to consider, and who after several delays confessed that the more he inquired into the nature of God, the more absorbed were all his thoughts. And this must necessarily be the case with men until they are taught what God is, which can never be done until he himself represents himself and his glory as it were in a mirror.

This is then the reason why the Prophet, while setting the only true God in opposition to idols and all the inventions of mortals, calls him *the portion of Jacob,* because the law was as it were the representation of the glory of God. As then he had plainly shewn himself there, as far as it was needful for the salvation of the chosen people, the Prophet, in order to invite men to the true knowledge of the true God, calls him *the portion of Jacob,* as though he had set the law as a mirror before their eyes. *The portion of Jacob* then *is God,* who is not like fictitious gods; how so? because he is the framer of all things. It is indeed by a few words that he makes the distinction between the only true God and the fictitious gods; but in this brief sentence he includes what I have before explained, even that God is the fountain of life, and the life of all, and then that his essence is spiritual and also infinite; for as he has created the heaven and the earth, so of necessity he sustains both by his power.

We then see that the Prophet speaks briefly but not frigidly; and from this passage we learn a useful doctrine, even that God cannot be comprehended by us except in his works. As then vain men weary themselves with speculations, which have not in them, so to speak, any practical knowledge, it is no wonder that they run headlong into many delirious things. Let us then be sober in this respect, so that we may not inquire into the essence of God more than it becomes us. When therefore we seek to comprehend what God is, or how to attain the knowledge of him, let us direct all our thoughts, and eyes, and minds to his works.

So also by this passage, when the Prophet calls God the worker or framer of all things, is exposed the vanity of all superstitions; and how? because we hence learn that the power which made not the heaven and the earth, is vain and worthless; but the only maker of heaven and earth is God, then he is God alone. Since he is the only true God, it follows that the inventions or figments of men are altogether delirious, and are therefore the artifices and impostures of the devil to deceive mankind. We hence see that the doctrine of the Prophet is exclusive, when he says that God is *the maker of all things;* for where the maker of all things is not found, there certainly no divinity can be.

He adds, *the rod of his inheritance.* This seems to refer to God, but in the tenth chapter the word *Israel* is introduced; otherwise these five verses literally agree, but in that passage the Prophet says that Israel was the *rod of God's inheritance.* Here the rod means a measuring pole; for the similitude is taken from lands being measured; for the ancients used poles of certain length for measuring. Hence the Hebrews called an inheritance the rod of inheritance, because it was what had been measured and had certain limits: as when one possesses a field, he knows how many acres it contains, it having been measured. But both things may be fitly and truly said, even that Israel is the rod of God's inheritance, and also that God himself is a rod of inheritance; for there is a mutual union. For as God favours us with this honour, to make us his inheritance, and is pleased to have us as his own, so also he offers himself to us as an inheritance. David says often, "The Lord is my portion," and "The Lord is the portion of mine inheritance," that is, my hereditary portion. So in this place the meaning would not be unsuitable were we to apply the words to God. As, however, the word *Israel* is found in the former place, it may be deemed as understood here.[1]

He says at last, *Jehovah of hosts is his name.* There is implied a contrast here; for he does not honour God with this character, as though it was a common or ordinary name; but he claims for him his own right, and thus distinguishes him from all idols. By saying, then, that this name belongs only to the true God, even the God of Israel, he intimates that by this distinction he differs from all idols, and that men are sacrilegious when they transfer any power to idols, and expect safety from them, and flee to them. As then this name belongs only to God, it follows that in Him dwells a fulness of all power and might. Since it is so, then wholly worthless is everything that the world has ever imagined respecting the number and multitude of gods. It now follows,—

20. Thou *art* my battle-axe *and* weapons of war: for with thee will I break in pieces the nations, and with thee will I destroy kingdoms;

21. And with thee will I break in pieces the horse and his rider; and with thee will I break in pieces the chariot and his rider;

22. With thee also will I break in pieces man and woman; and with thee will I break in pieces old and young; and with thee will I break in pieces the young man and the maid;

23. I will also break in pieces with thee the shepherd and his flock; and with thee will I break in pieces the husbandman and his yoke of oxen; and with thee will I break in pieces captains and rulers.

20. Malleus tu mihi, vasa (*vel,* instrumenta) prœlii, (*aut,* bellica,) et conteram (*vel,* contrivi) per te gentes, et perdam (*vel,* perdidi, *malo in prœterito tempore accipere utrunque verbum, rationem postea dicam*) per te regna;

21. Et contrivi per te equum et ascensorem ejus, et contrivi per te currum et ascensorem ejus;

22. Et contrivi per te virum et mulierem, et contrivi per te senem et puerum, et contrivi per te adolescentem et virginem;

23. Et contrivi per te pastorem et gregem ejus, et contrivi per te agricolam et jugum ejus, et contrivi per te duces et principes.

The Prophet here obviates the doubts of many; for as he had spoken of the destruction of Babylon, it might have

[1] Though the Hebrew here is exactly the same as in ch. x., except that "Israel" is omitted here, yet the *Vulg.*, the *Syr.*, and the *Targ.* give a different version; but in the *Sept.* it is the same. But many copies have "Israel" here, which is no doubt the correct reading.—*Ed.*

been readily objected, that the monarchy which was fortified by so many defences, and which had subjugated all the neighbouring nations, was impregnable. Hence the Prophet here shews that the power and wealth of Babylon were no hinderances that God should not destroy it whenever he pleased; for it is an argument derived from what is contrary. We have before seen that God roots up what he has planted, (ch. xlv. 4;) and then we have seen the metaphor of the potter and his vessels. When the Prophet went down to the potter, he saw a vessel formed and then broken at the will and pleasure of the potter (ch. xviii. 2-4.) So also now God shews that the destruction was as it were in his hand, because the Chaldeans had not raised themselves to eminence through their own power, but he had raised them, and employed them for his own purpose. In short, he compares the Babylonians in this passage to a formed vessel, and he makes himself the potter: "I am he who has raised Babylon to so great a height; it therefore belongs to me to pull it down whensoever it pleases me." We now understand the design of this passage, though the Prophet employs different words.

He says that Babylon was a *hammer and weapons of war to break in pieces* the nations. The verb נפץ, *nuphets,* means to break in pieces, and carelessly to scatter here and there, and also violently to scatter. He says then, "I have by thee scattered the nations, and by thee have destroyed kingdoms." But as the Chaldeans had enjoyed so many victories and had subjugated so many nations, he adds, *I have by thee broken in pieces the horse and his rider, the chariot and its rider;* and then, *I have broken in pieces men and women, old men and children, the young men and the maidens, the shepherds and also their flocks.* He enumerates here almost all kinds of men. He then mentions *husbandmen* and *yokes of oxen,* or of horses; and lastly, he mentions *captains and rulers.*[1] All these things are said by way of conces-

[1] Many render this passage in the future tense, according to all the Versions and the *Targ.*, and consider Cyrus to be intended by the "hammer;" but they render בך, *by,* or *with thee,* contrary to the *Targ.* and the Versions, which is rendered *in thee, i.e.,* Babylon; and *for thee* in the *Syr.* And this seems to be the view most consistent with the whole passage,

sion; but yet the Prophet reminds us that no difficulty would prevent God to destroy Babylon, because Babylon in itself was nothing. According to this sense, then, it is called a hammer. In short, the Prophet takes away the false opinion which might have otherwise disturbed weak minds, as though Babylon was wholly invincible. He shews at the same time that God executed his judgments on all nations by means of Babylon. Thus the faithful might have been confirmed; for otherwise they must have necessarily been cast down when they regarded the formidable power of Babylon; but when they heard that it was only a hammer, and that they would not have been broken in pieces by the Babylonians had they not been armed from above, or rather had they not been driven on by a celestial power, it then appeared that the calamity which the Jews had suffered was nothing more than a punishment inflicted by God's hand. When, therefore, they heard this, it was no small consolation; it kept them from succumbing under their miseries, and from being swallowed up with sorrow and despair. But it now follows,—

24. And I will render unto Babylon, and to all the inhabi-	24. Et rependam Babyloni et omnibus habitatoribus Chaldææ omnia mala

especially verse 24. Babylon was the "hammer" which God had employed, (ch. L. 23,) but he would hereafter employ, as it were, a hammer, or a scatterer, in Babylon itself,—

20. A scatterer (or a hammer) art thou to me,
A weapon of war;
But I will scatter in thee nations,
And destroy in thee kingdoms;
21. And I will scatter in thee the horse and its rider,
And I will scatter in thee the chariot and its rider;
22. And I will scatter in thee the husband and the wife,
And I will scatter in thee the old and the child,
And I will scatter in thee the young man and the maid;
23. And I will scatter in thee the shepherd and his flock,
And I will scatter in thee the ploughman and his team,
And I will scatter in thee the governors and princes.

Then comes, naturally, a summary of the whole,—

24. And I will render to Babylon
And to all the inhabitants of Chaldea,
All the evil which they have done in Sion,
Before your eyes, saith Jehovah.

Then in the two following verses Babylon is still addressed.

"Scatter" is according to the *Sept.*, the *Syr.*, and the *Targ.*; "dash against one another" is the *Vulg.*—*Ed.*

tants of Chaldea, all their evil that they have done in Zion in your sight, saith the Lord.

ipsorum quæ intulerunt in Sion (contra Sion, quæ fecerunt in Sion, *ad verbum*,) in oculis vestris, (*vel*, coram oculis vestris,) dicit Jehova.

The Prophet, after having reminded the Jews that all that they had suffered from the Babylonians had been justly inflicted on account of their sins, and that God had been the author of all their calamities, now subjoins, *I will render to Babylon and to the Chaldeans* what they have deserved. It may, however, appear strange at the first view, that God should here threaten the Babylonians; for if their services depended on his command, they seemed doubtless to have deserved praise rather than punishment; nay, we know what the Holy Spirit declares elsewhere, "I gave Egypt as a reward to my servant Nebuchadnezzar, because he has faithfully performed my work," (Ezek. xxix. 20;) for Nebuchadnezzar had afflicted the Jews, therefore he obtained this, says Ezekiel, as his reward. It seems then an inconsistent thing when God declares that the Chaldeans deserved punishment because they had afflicted the Jews. But both declarations agree well together; for when God declared by Ezekiel that he gave Egypt as a reward to his servant Nebuchadnezzar, he had a regard to the Jews and to their perverseness, because they had not as yet been sufficiently humbled; nay, they thought that it was by chance that they had been subdued by the Babylonians. God then declares that he had executed his judgment on them by the hand of Nebuchadnezzar. It was afterwards necessary that the faithful should be raised up in their extreme distress; and this was regarded by our Prophet when he said—*Behold, I will render to Babylon and to the Chaldeans all their evils.* They then obtained Egypt for a short time, but afterwards all the evils they had brought on other nations recoiled on their own heads.

But this promise was in a peculiar manner given to the Church; for though the vengeance executed on the Chaldeans was just, because they exercised extreme cruelty towards all nations; yet God, having a care for his own Church, thus undertook its cause; therefore he speaks not here generally of the punishment inflicted on the Chaldeans for their cruelty; but God, as I have said, had a regard to his own Church. Hence, he says, I will render to the Babylonians and to all the Chaldeans, all the evil *which they had done in Sion.* We now see that this punishment had a special reference to the chosen people, in order that the faithful might know that they had been so chastised by God, that yet the memory of his covenant had never failed, and that thus in the midst of death they might have some hope of salvation, and that they might feel assured that God would at length be merciful; not that God would ever restore the whole body of the people; but this promise, as it has been elsewhere stated, is addressed only to the remnant. Yet fixed remains the truth, that God, after having broken in pieces the Jews and other nations by means of one nation, would yet be the avenger of his Church, because he could never forget his covenant. He adds, *before your eyes,* that the faithful might with calmer minds wait for the vengeance of which they themselves would be eye-witnesses.

PRAYER.

Grant, Almighty God, that since thou hast favoured us with the light of thy Gospel, in which we see thy glory, and into which we may be also transformed, except prevented by our unbelief,—O grant, that with fixed eyes we may ever study that knowledge which once for all has been made known to us, until at length, having followed the way there set before us, we shall come to the fulness of that celestial glory which has been obtained for us by the blood of thine only-begotten Son.—Amen.

Lecture One Hundred and Eighty-ninth.

25. Behold, I *am* against thee, O destroying mountain, saith the Lord, which destroyest all the earth: and I will stretch out mine hand upon thee, and roll thee down from the rocks, and will make thee a burnt mountain.

25. Ecce ego ad te, mons perditionis, dicit Jehova, perdens omnem terram; et extendam manum meam super te, et devolvam te e rupibus, et ponam te in montem combustionis.

THERE is no doubt but that the Prophet speaks of Babylon. But it may seem strange to call it a mountain, when that city was situated in a plain, as it is well known; nay, it has no mountains near it. It was a plain, so that streams might be drawn here and there in any direction. Hence they think that the city was called a mountain on account of the height of its walls and also its great buildings. And this is probable, as though the Prophet called it a great mass; for historians tell us that its walls were very high, about two hundred feet, and a foot commonly exceeded three fingers. Then the towers were very high. In short, Babylon was a prodigy for the quantity of its bricks, for the walls were not built with squared stones, but formed of bricks. Their breadth also was incredible; for chariots drawn by four horses could go along without touching one another. Their breadth, according to Strabo and also Pliny, was fifty feet. Then this metaphor was not used without reason, when the Prophet, regarding in one respect the state of the city, called Babylon a *mountain*, as though Ninus, or Semiramis, or others, had contended with nature itself. The beginning of Babylon was that memorable tower mentioned by Moses, but then the work was left off. (Gen. xi.) Afterwards, either because such a beginning inflamed the desire of men, or because the place was very pleasant and fertile, it happened that a city of great size was built there. In short, it was more like a country than a city; for, as Aristotle says, it was not so much a city as a country or a province. This much as to the word *mountain*.

Now God himself declares war against Babylon, in order that more credit might be given to this prophecy; for the Prophet had no regard to the Chaldeans, but to his own nation, and especially to the remnant of the godly. The greater part derided his prophecy, but a few remained who received the Prophet's doctrine with becoming reverence. It was then his object to consult their good and benefit; and, as we shall see at the end of this chapter, he wished to lay up this treasure with them, that they might cherish the hope of restoration while they were as it were lost in exile. God then does here encourage them, and declares that he would be an enemy to the Babylonians.

Behold, he says, *I am against thee, O mountain of perdition.* The mountain of perdition is to be taken in an active sense, for destroying mountain, as also a clearer explanation follows, when he says that it had *destroyed all the earth*. For the Babylonians, as it is well known, had afflicted all their neighbours, and had transferred the imperial power of the Medes to their own city. When they subdued the Assyrians they extended their power far and wide, and at length advanced to Syria, Judea, and Egypt. Thus it happened that the Babylonians enjoyed the empire of the east till the time of Cyrus; and then the monarchy was possessed by the Persians. But our Prophet had respect to the former state of things; for he said that the Chaldeans had been like a hammer, which God had employed to break in pieces all the nations; and, according to the same meaning, he now says that all the earth had been destroyed by the Babylonians.

But God here declares that he would be their judge, because he would *extend his hand over Babylon*, and *roll it down from the rocks*. He proceeds still with the same metaphor; for as he called Babylon a mountain on account of its great buildings, and especially on account of its high walls and lofty towers, so now he adopts the same kind of language, *I will cast thee down*, or rather roll thee, *from the rocks*, and *make thee a mountain of burning*. He thus intimates that Babylon would become a heap of ashes, though this was not immediately fulfilled; for as we have said, it was so taken as not to be entirely laid waste. For in the time of Alexander the Great, many years after, Babylon was standing, and there Alexander died. It then follows that it was not reduced to solitude and ashes by Darius and Cyrus. But we have already untied this knot, that is, that the Prophet does not only speak of one vengeance of God, but includes others which followed. For Babylon soon after revolted and suffered a grievous punishment for its perfidy, and was then treated with great contempt. Afterwards, Seleucus tried in various ways to destroy it, and for this end Seleucia was built, and then Ctesiphon was set up in opposition to Babylon. Babylon then was by degrees reduced to that solitude of which the Prophet here speaks. Pliny says that in his time the temple of Bel was there, whom they thought to have been the founder of the city; but he afterwards adds that the other parts of the city were deserted. If Jerome, as he says, visited it, we ought to believe what he had seen; and he says that Babylon was a small ignoble town, and ruins only were seen there. There is, then, nothing unreasonable in this prophecy, for it ought not to be restricted to one calamity only; for God ceased not in various ways to afflict Babylon until it was wholly laid waste, according to what our Prophet testifies. According to this view, then, he says that Babylon would become a *mountain of burning*, or a burnt mountain,[1] for ruins only would remain; and in the same sense he immediately adds,—

26. And they shall not take of thee a stone for a corner, nor a stone for foundations; but thou shalt be desolate for ever, saith the Lord.	26. Et non tollent ex te lapidem ad angulum, et lapidem ad fundamenta; quia solitudines perpetuæ eris, dicit Jehova.

He confirms the former verse, that when Babylon was destroyed, there would be no hope of restoration. It often happens, that those cities which have been wholly destroyed are afterwards built up again; but God says that this would not be the case with Babylon, for it was given over to perpetual destruction. By *corner* and *foundations* he understands the strength of the buildings. He then says, that there was no hope that the stones would be again fitted together, for the building of the city, for Babylon would become a perpetual waste or desolation.

We have, indeed, said, that the walls of Babylon were not made of stones but of bricks: but the Prophet simply speaks according to the common manner, in order to shew that its ruin would be for ever.[2] We have also said elsewhere that a difference is commonly made by the prophets between the people of God and the reprobate, that God promises to his Church a new state as a resurrection from death, but that

[1] *Blayney* views "the mountain" differently, as a metaphor for a nation, or a prince, rising above others in power: and "the rocks" he considers to be the strongholds of this mountain.—*Ed.*

[2] Though the greatest part of the walls and towers was built of bricks, yet there were stones no doubt used. Some understand, by "stone," a king or a prince, and consider that an intimation is given that Babylon would not hereafter have a king of its own, but be tributary.—*Ed.*

he denounces on the unbelieving perpetual desolation. This course is now followed by our Prophet when he says, that the desolations there would be *for ever*, because there is no hope of pardon or of mercy to the unbelieving. It afterwards follows,—

27. Set ye up a standard in the land, blow the trumpet among the nations, prepare the nations against her, call together against her the kingdoms of Ararat, Minni, and Ashchenaz; appoint a captain against her; cause the horses to come up as the rough caterpillars.

27. Tollite signum in terra, clangite tuba in gentibus, sanctificate (*vel,* præparate) super eam gentes, congregate contra eam regna Ararath, Minni, et Aschenaz, præficite super eam ducem (*alii putant esse nomen proprium, et relinquunt* טפסר *sed accipitur haud dubie pro duce,*) educite equum tanquam locustam (*vel,* bruchum) horribilem (*vertit Hieronymus,* aculeatum; *alii vertunt,* horripilantem; *sed vox illa asperior est, et tamen propriè signatur horror ille, dum pili exurgunt ob metum, vel, ob iracundiam.*)

The Prophet here confirms what he had before taught, even that Babylon, however proud on account of its strongholds, would not yet escape God's hand. Had he used a simple mode of speaking, hardly any one would have ventured to look for what the Prophet said. It was then necessary to introduce figurative expressions, of which we have before spoken. Here, then, with the highest authority, he commands the nations to raise up war against Babylon.

We must observe, as I have before reminded you, that by such modes of speaking, the effect of prophetic doctrine is set forth. For the unbelieving deride whatever they hear, because the voice of God is the same to them as though it were a sound flowing through the air. Hence the Prophet shews that he was endued with the power of God, and that the hand of God was connected with his mouth, so that he fulfils whatever he predicts. *Raise,* he says, *a standard.* This might have appeared ludicrous, for we know that the Prophet was despised, not only at Jerusalem, but also in his own town where he had been born: by what right, then, or on what ground does he now boldly command all nations, and bid the banners to be raised? But as I have said, he shews that a false judgment would be formed of what he said, except the people thought that God himself spoke.

Sound with the trumpet, he says, *among all nations,* and then, *sanctify against her the nations;* and further, *assem-*

ble, literally, " make to hear," but it means, in *Piel*, to collect, to assemble. As to the word *Ararat*, it may be taken for Armenia. I know not why some have taken Minni to be the lower Armenia, for there is no creditable author for such an opinion. Nor is it certain what country the Prophet designates by *Ashchenaz*. But it is evident from histories, that the great army which Darius, or Cyrus under the authority of Darius, led with him, had been collected from various and even remote nations. For he brought with him the Hyrcanians and the Armenians, and some from many unknown places. As, then, heathen authors declare that this army was collected indiscriminately from many nations and almost unknown, it is nothing strange that the Hebrew names are at this day unknown. And there is no doubt but that the Prophet here indirectly intimates some great shaking of the world, as though he had said, that even barbarous nations, the name of whom hath not hitherto been heard of, would come like an overwhelming flood to destroy Babylon. He will hereafter speak of the Medes ; but here he treats the subject in a different way, as though he had said, that so great would be the multitude of enemies, that Babylon, notwithstanding its largeness, would be easily overthrown. We now perceive the Prophet's design as to these obscure words.

He says afterwards, *Set up a leader against her*. This is to be understood of Cyrus, whose vigour was especially apparent in that war. Nor is there a doubt but that he led his uncle and father-in-law to undertake the war. For those historians fable, who say that Cyrus was cast away by his grandfather, and that he was brought up privately by Astyages, and that he afterwards made war with his grandfather. All these things have been invented. For it is quite evident that Darius, the king of the Medes, was the chief in that war, and Daniel is our best witness on this point. Heathen writers imagine that there was no king of the Medes except under the authority of Cyrus. But Cyrus did not rule until after the death of his father-in-law, or his uncle, whose daughter he had married. It then follows, that he was the general, so that he carried on the war under the authority of Darius. Cyrus then was, as it were, the hired soldier of his uncle and father-in-law, but at length he obtained the kingdom of the Medes and the whole empire of the East. Of this leader, then, I understand this passage, when the Prophet says, *Set up* or appoint *a leader against* Babylon:[1] and he adds, *Bring forth*, or make to ascend, *the horse as the locust.* This refers to their number; as though he had said, Bring forth against Babylon horses without number, who shall be as locusts. He compares them to locusts, not for strength or skill in war, but only with regard to their number. But as the locusts are frightful, he applies to them the word סמר, *samer*, "dreadful," as though he had said, They are, indeed, locusts as to their abundance, but they are at the same time dreadful, as though they had on them frightful hairs. It afterwards follows,—

28. Prepare against her the nations, with the kings of the Medes, the captains thereof, and all the rulers thereof, and all the land of his dominion.	28. Præparate contra eam gentes, regna Medorum, duces ejus, et principes ejus, et totam terram ditionis ejus.

He now repeats what he had said of preparing the nations; but he mentions them first generally, and then he comes to specify them particularly. He then bids the *nations* to be sent for, and then he shews who they were, even the *kingdoms of the Medes.*[2] There was, indeed, but one kingdom, but many kings were subject to it. Then, on account of the many provinces over which satraps ruled, and also on account of many tributary countries, the Prophet was not satisfied to use the singular number, but calls them in the plural number, the *kingdoms of the Medes;* for that monarchy had extended itself far and wide, so that many kings were subject to Darius.

[1] The Versions and the *Targ.* all differ as to the word טפסר, rendered by *Calvin*, "leader." It is translated "commander" by *Blayney*. *Parkhurst* says that it is a Chaldee word, from טפס, to reduce to order, and סר, a ruler. Then it means a commanding officer, a captain, or a general. It occurs only here and in Nahum iii. 17.—*Ed.*

[2] The Hebrew is, "the kings of Media;" but the *Sept.* and *Syr.* have "the king of Media;" which is required by "his dominion" at the end of the verse: the pronoun affixed to "captains" and "rulers" is "her," referring to Media.—*Ed.*

And it tended, in no small degree, to shew the certainty of this prophecy, that Jeremiah declared, before Cyrus or even Darius was born, that the Medes would come. But we have stated, that though Cyrus, being singularly active and a good warrior, carried on the war, yet Darius was the first in authority. Then Babylon obeyed the Medes for a time; but as Darius was now old, Cyrus succeeded him; and then the monarchy was transferred to Persia; and laws issued thence until the time of Alexander the Great, who, together with his catamite, burnt the tower. Nor is there a doubt but that many memorable transactions were deposited there. But Alexander being drunk, seized a torch and burnt the tower; for he thought that the memory of the Oriental monarchy could thus be abolished.

We now then perceive why the Prophet expressly mentions here the Medes; and he adds, *the captains and princes.* He includes, no doubt, under these names, all the satraps and kings. At length he adds, *the whole land of its dominion,* or jurisdiction; and by this word he designates the kingdoms already mentioned. It now follows,—

29. And the land shall tremble and sorrow: for every purpose of the Lord shall be performed against Babylon, to make the land of Babylon a desolation without an inhabitant.	29. Et contremuit terra, et doluit (*similitudo sumpta est à parturientibus,*) quia stabilita fuit super Babylon cogitationes (*in plurali numero ponit cum tamen verbum sit singulare, hoc est,* stabilitæ sunt cogitationes) Jehovæ ad ponendum terram Babylonis in solitudinem, ita ut non sit habitator (*vel,* qui illic habitet.)

The Prophet no doubt endeavoured to remove all doubts from the minds of the godly, which would have otherwise weakened confidence in his doctrine. It might have occurred to the minds of all, that the whole world would sooner come to nothing than that Babylon should fall. Though it were so, says the Prophet, that the whole earth trembled, yet Babylon will be destroyed. Hence, he says, *Tremble shall the land and be in pain,* even *because confirmed,* &c. There is here a striking contrast between the moving of the earth and the stability of God's purpose. The verb means properly to rise, but it is taken in many places in the sense of confirming or establishing, and necessarily so in this passage. He then says, *Tremble shall the land,*[1] even *because confirmed shall be the thoughts of God respecting Babylon.*

But he mentions thoughts in the plural number, as though he had said, that whatever God had appointed and decreed would be unchangeable, and that the whole earth would sooner be shaken than that the truth of God should lose its effect. Then this verse contains nothing else but a confirmation of the whole prophecy. But the Prophet shews, that if even all the hindrances of the world were in favour of the perpetuity of Babylon, yet what God had decreed respecting its destruction, would be fixed and unchangeable. It afterwards follows,—

30. The mighty men of Babylon have forborne to fight, they have remained in *their* holds: their might hath failed; they became as women: they have burnt her dwelling-places; her bars are broken.

30. Cessarunt fortes Babylonis ad pugnandum (*hoc est.* destiterunt pugnare fortes Babylonis,) sederunt in munitionibus, deficit (*vel,* elanguit) virtus ipsorum, fuerunt in mulieres, accenderunt habitacula ejus, confracti sunt vectes ejus.

The Prophet shews here, as by the finger, the manner of the destruction of Babylon, such as it is described by heathen authors. He then says, that the *valiant* men *of Babylon,* even those who had been chosen to defend the city, *ceased to fight.* For the city was taken rather by craft than by open force; for after a long siege, Cyrus was laughed to scorn by the Babylonians; then they securely held a feast. In the meantime two eunuchs of Belshazzar passed over to Cyrus; for, as Xenophon relates, the tyrant had slain the son of one, and by way of disgrace castrated the other. Hence, then, it was that they revolted from him; and Cyrus was instructed by them how he could take the city. The fords were dried up, when Belshazzar suspected no such thing, and in the night he heard that the city was taken. Daniel gives a clearer description; for he says that there was held a stated feast, and that the hand of a writer appeared on the

[1] The "earth" here is evidently the land of Chaldea or Babylon,—
And tremble shall the land and be in pain;
For confirmed respecting Babylon shall be the purposes of Jehovah,
To set the land of Babylon a waste,
Without an inhabitant.—*Ed.*

wall, and that the king, being frightened, had heard from Daniel that the end of his kingdom was near at hand, and that the city was taken that very night. (Dan. v. 25-30.) Hence the Prophet says now that the valiant men desisted, so that they did not fight. He indeed speaks of what was future, but we know what was the manner of the prophets, for they related what was to come as though it had already taken place.

He afterwards adds, that they *sat down in their fortresses*, for the city was not taken by storm—there was no fighting; but the forces passed silently through the fords, and the soldiers entered into the middle of the city; the king was slain together with all his satraps, and then all parts of the city were taken possession of. We now, then, see that the Spirit of God spoke by the mouth of Jeremiah, as of a thing that had already taken place.

He then adds, that *their valour had failed* or languished, even because terror stupified them when they heard that the city was taken. So also true became what is added, that they *became women*, that they were like women as to courage, for no one dared to oppose the conquerors. Fighting might have still been carried on by so large a multitude, yea, they might have engaged with their enemies in hundred or in thousand of the streets of the city, for it would have been easy in the night to distress them: but the Prophet says, that they all became women as to courage. At last, he adds, that *burnt by enemies were the palaces*, and that *the bars of the gates were broken;* for no one dared to summon to arms after it was heard that the city was taken. It follows,—

31. One post shall run to meet another, and one messenger to meet another, to shew the king of Babylon that his city is taken at *one* end.	31. Cursor in occursum cursoris cucurrit (*vel*, curret, *ad verbum*) et nuntius in occursum nuntii ad nuntiandum regi Babylonis, quòd capta sit urbs ejus ab extremitate.

This also was fulfilled according to the testimony of heathen authors, as well as of Daniel. They do not indeed repeat these words, but according to the whole tenor of history we may easily conclude that messengers ran here and there, for the Babylonians never thought that the enemy could so suddenly penetrate into the city, for there was no entrance. We have seen how high the walls were, for there were no muskets then, and the walls could not have been beaten down. There were indeed battering-rams; but what was the breadth of the walls? even fifty feet, as already stated, so that four horses abreast could pass without coming into contact. There was then no battering-ram that could throw down walls so thick. As to the fords, the thing seemed incredible; so that they kept a feast in perfect security. In such an irruption, what our Prophet testifies here must have necessarily happened. But it is quite evident that he was the instrument of the Holy Spirit; for Cyrus was not as yet born when this prophecy was announced. We hence then know, that the holy man was guided from above, and that what he said was not produced in his own head, but was really celestial; for he could not have divined any such thing, nor was it through probable conjecture that he was able thus to speak and lead the Jews, as it were, into the very scene itself.

Nor is there a doubt but that his authority was afterwards confirmed when the fathers told their children, "So have we heard from the mouth of the Prophet what we now see with our eyes; and yet no man could have conjectured any such thing, nor have discovered it by reason or clear-sightedness: hence Jeremiah must have necessarily been taught by the Spirit of God." This, then, is the reason why God designed that the destruction of Babylon should be, as we see, so graphically described.

He then says, *A runner ran to meet a runner*, and then, *a messenger to meet a messenger, to tell the king of Babylon that his city was taken at its extremity.*[1] Had this been said of a small city, it might have appeared ridiculous: why are these runners? one might say. But it has been sufficiently shewn, that so extensive was that city, that runners, passing through many fields, might have come to the king, and convey the news that the city was taken at one of its extremities.

[1] It seems to have been taken at its two extremities: hence the runners met each other at the king's palace, from both ends of the city, and each said, that it was taken at its end.—*Ed.*

And heathen writers cannot sufficiently eulogize the contrivance and skill of Cyrus, that he thus took possession of so great a city; for he might have only secured one half of it, and Belshazzar might have retained the other half, and might have bravely contested with Cyrus and all his forces; and he would have no doubt overcome him, had it not been for the wonderful and unusual expedition of Cyrus. This haste, then, or expedition of Cyrus, is what the Prophet now sets forth, when he says that *messengers ran to the king to tell him that the city was taken.* He now adds, respecting other things, what no one could have divined,—

32. And that the passages are stopped, and the reeds they have burnt with fire, and the men of war are affrighted.	32. Et vada capta sunt, e stagna exusta sunt igni, et viri prœlii (*hoc est,* bellicosi) conterriti sunt.

This verse most clearly proves that Jeremiah was God's herald, and that his language was under the guidance of the celestial Spirit; for he sets forth the manner in which Babylon was taken, as though he had witnessed it with his own eyes.

He says that *the fords were taken,* and that the *pools were burnt with fire.* We do not read that Cyrus had made use of fire; and some render pools, reeds, but there is no reason to constrain us so to render the word; for the Prophet speaks metaphorically. Their object was to give a literal rendering, by saying that reeds were burnt; but the Prophet shews, speaking hyperbolically, that the fords of the Euphrates were dried up, as though one burned wood by applying fire to it. This, indeed, is not suitable to water; but he, by a hyperbole, expresses more fully the miracle which might have otherwise exceeded human comprehension. He then says, that the fords were dried up, and then adds, that the pools were burnt. The same thing is expressed twice, but in a different way; and as I have already said, he states hyperbolically, that such was the skill of Cyrus and his army, that he made dry the fords and the pools, as though one collected a large heap of wood and consumed it with fire.[1] We now perceive the design of the Prophet.

[1] The word אגמים, properly pools, is probably a metonomy for what they grow, even reeds or bulrushes, especially as the same word, in some-

He afterwards adds, that the *men of war were broken in pieces.* For though the fords were made dry, that is, the streams which were drawn from the Euphrates, yet the guards of the city might have still kept possession of a part of it, and have manfully resisted, so as to prevent the soldiers of Cyrus from advancing farther; but the city was so craftily taken, that the Babylonians were so terrified as not to dare to raise up a finger, when yet they might have defended a part of the city, though one part of it was taken.

PRAYER.

Grant, Almighty God, that as thou didst formerly testify thy favour towards thy Church by not sparing the greatest of monarchies,—O grant that we may know thee at this day to be the same towards all thy faithful people who call upon thee ; and as the power and cruelty of our enemies are so great, raise thou up thine hand against them, and shew that thou art the perpetual defender of thy Church, so that we may have reason to magnify thy goodness in Christ Jesus our Lord.—Amen.

Lecture One Hundred and Ninetieth.

33. For thus saith the Lord of hosts, the God of Israel, The daughter of Babylon *is* like a threshing floor : *it is* time to thresh her : yet a little while, and the time of her harvest shall come.	33. Quoniam sic dicit Jehova exercituum, Deus Israel, filia Babylonis tanquam area, tempus calcandæ ejus; adhuc paulisper, et veniet messis ei.

By this similitude the Prophet confirms what he had before said, even that God would be the avenger of his Church, and would justly punish the Babylonians, but at the suitable time, which is usually called in Scripture the time of visitation. He then compares Babylon to a *threshing-floor,* not indeed in the sense which interpreters have imagined, but because the threshing-floor only serves for the time of

what another form, אגמון, clearly means a reed. See Isaiah ix. 14 ; xix. 15. But what these reeds were, authors are at a loss to know. It is said in the thirtieth verse, that they "burnt her habitations ;" may it not have been, that they were such as were made of reeds ? Then the whole verse appears intelligible ; the passages (that is, the entrances from the river, whose streams were diverted) were seized on, and such houses as were in part built of reeds were set on fire ; hence the men were frightened.—*Ed.*

harvest, and is afterwards closed up and not used. Babylon, then, had been for a long time like a threshing-floor, because there had been no treading there, that is, no noise or shouting. But God declares that *the time of harvest would come,* when the threshing-floor would be used. Oxen did then tread the corn; for the corn was not beaten out with flails, as with us and in most places in France, though the inhabitants of Provence still use the treading. In Judea they tread out the corn on floors, and oxen were used for the purpose. Now, the reason for the similitude seems evident; for the time would come when God would smite Babylon, as oxen after harvest tread out with their feet the corn on the threshing-floor, which for the rest of the year is not wanted, but remains closed up and quiet. Hence I have said that what we have before seen as to the time of visitation is confirmed; for it was strange at the first view to promise deliverance to the Jews, while yet Babylon was increasing more and more and extending the limits of its monarchy. (Isa. xxviii. 24-26.) God shews in that passage that it was no matter of wonder if he did not daily exercise his judgments in an equal degree; and he bids us to consider how husbandmen act, for they do not sow at the same time wheat and barley and other kinds of grain; nor do they always plough, or always reap, but wait for seasonable times. "Since, then, husbandmen are endowed with so much care and foresight as I have taught them, why may not I also have my times rightly distributed, so that there may be now the harvest, and then the treading or threshing? and should I not at one time sow wheat, and at another cumin?" for the Prophet adds these several sorts. The same is the mode of reasoning in this place, though the Prophet speaks more briefly.

He then says that Babylon would be like a threshing-floor, and how? because it had been as a place closed up and wholly quiet; for God had spared the Chaldeans, and, as we shall hereafter see, they had been so inebriated with pleasures that they feared no danger.

And then immediately he explains himself,—it is *time to tread* or thresh *her*. Then Babylon became like a threshing-floor, for she had not been trodden or threshed for a long time, as the threshing-floor is not used for nine or ten months through the whole year. But he adds, *yet a little while, and come will her harvest.*

We learn from this and other passages that treading or threshing was in use among the Jews and other eastern nations only during harvest. In other places, corn is often kept in the ears for five and six years. Some thresh the corn after six, or eight, or nine months, as it suits their convenience. But there are many countries where the corn is immediately threshed; it is not stored up, but is immediately conveyed to the threshing-floor, and there it is trodden by oxen or threshed with flails. As then it was usual immediately to tread the corn, hence God declares that the time of harvest would come when Babylon would be trodden, as the threshing-floor is trodden after harvest.[1]

We must observe that *a little while* is not to be understood according to the notions of men; for though God suspends his judgments, he yet never delays beyond the time; on the contrary, he performs his work with all due celerity. The Prophet Haggai says, "Yet a little while, and I will shake the heaven and the earth." (Hag. ii. 7.) But this was not fulfilled till many years after. But we must remember what is in Habakkuk,—"If the vision delays, wait for it, for it will come and will not be slow." (Hab. ii. 5.) He says that prophecies delay, that is, according to the judgment of men, who make too much haste, and are even carried away headlong by their own desires. But God performs his work with sufficient celerity, provided we

[1] By identifying the time of threshing and the time of harvest, it is that we can see the meaning of this verse. Mention is first made of threshing or treading—the punishment prepared for Babylon; then it is said that what led to that—the harvest, would shortly come. The verb "come" is to be understood in the third line, it being given only in the last,—

33. For thus saith Jehovah of hosts, the God of Israel,—
Babylon *shall be* like a threshing-floor;
Come shall the time of threshing her;
Yet a little while, and come to her shall the time of harvest.

The order as to threshing and harvest is similar to what is often found in the prophets,—the last thing, being the main thing, is mentioned first, and then what precedes or leads to it.—*Ed.*

allow him to arrange the times according to his own will, as it is just and right for us to do. Whenever, then, the ungodly enjoy ease and securely indulge themselves, let this fact come to our own minds, that the threshing-floor is not always trodden, but that the time of harvest will come whenever it pleases God. This is the use we ought to make of what is here said. It follows,—

34. Nebuchadnezzar the king of Babylon hath devoured me, he hath crushed me, he hath made me an empty vessel, he hath swallowed me up like a dragon, he hath filled his belly with my delicates, he hath cast me out.

34. Comedit me, contrivit me Nabuchadnezer rex Babylonis; posuit me (locavit, *ad verbum*) vas inane; diglutivit me tanquam draco, implevit ventrem suum deliciis meis, ejecit me.

Here is mentioned the complaint of the chosen people, and this was done designedly by Jeremiah, in order that the Jews might feel assured that their miseries were not overlooked by God; for nothing can distress us so much as to think that God forgets us and disregards the wrongs done to us by the ungodly. Hence the Prophet here sets the Israelites in God's presence, that they might be convinced in their own minds that they were not disregarded by God, and that he was not indifferent to the unjust and cruel treatment they received from their enemies. For this complaint is made, as though they expostulated with God in his presence.

He then says, *Devoured me and broken me in pieces has Nebuchadnezzar, the king of Babylon.*[1] The word, *to eat*, or devour, was enough; but Jeremiah wished to express something more atrocious by adding the word, *to break in pieces*;[2] for he intimates that Babylon had not been like a man who devours meat set before him, but that she had been a cruel wild beast, who breaks in pieces the very bones.

[1] The pronoun after the verbs in this verse is in the plural number, *us*, according to the present Hebrew text, but according to the *Keri* and several copies, it is in the singular number, *me*. The authority as to MSS. is nearly equal; only the latter reading is favoured by the versions and the *Targ.*, and also by the verse which follows.—*Ed.*

[2] The common meaning of the verb is, violently to disturb, but it is evidently used in the sense of breaking, crushing, or breaking in pieces, in Isa. xxviii. 28: and this is the most suitable sense here, as it follows "devouring."—*Ed.*

We now, then, understand the design of the Prophet; he amplifies the savageness of the king of Babylon, by saying that God's people had not only been devoured by him as men swallow down their food, but that they had also been torn in pieces by his teeth, as though he had been a lion, or a bear, or some other wild animal; for these not only devour their prey, but also with their teeth break in pieces whatever is harder than flesh, such as bones.

For the same purpose he adds, *He has set me an empty vessel,* that is, he has wholly exhausted me, as when one empties a flagon or a cask. Then he says, he has *swallowed me like a dragon.*[1] It is a comparison different from the former, but yet very suitable; for dragons are those who devour a whole animal; and this is what the Prophet means. Though these comparisons do not in everything agree, yet as to the main thing they are most appropriate, even to shew that God suffered his people to be devoured, as though they had been exposed to the teeth of a lion or a bear, or as though they had been a prey to a dragon.

He adds, *Filled has he his belly with my delicacies,* that is, whatever delicate thing I had, he has consumed it. He then says, *he has cast off the remnant,* like wolves and lions and other wild beasts, who, when they have more prey than what suffices them, choose what is most savoury; for they choose the head of man that they may eat the brain; they suck the blood, but leave the intestines and whatever they do not like. So also the Prophet says here of the miserable Jews, that they had been so devoured that the enemy, having been satiated, had cast off the remainder.[2]

We hence learn that God's people had been so exposed to plunder, that the conqueror was not only satisfied, but cast away here and there what remained; for satiety, as it is well known, produces loathsomeness. But the Prophet refers to the condition of the miserable people; for their wealth

[1] Or a sea-monster, or a whale, who devours smaller fish whole and entire.—*Ed.*

[2] The last verb is left out by the *Sept.*, rendered "cast out," by the *Vulg.*; "destroyed," by the *Syr.*; "made to emigrate," by the *Targ.* The verb properly means to drive out or away; and their ejection from the land is what is meant.—*Ed.*

had been swallowed up by the Chaldeans, but their household furniture was plundered by the neighbouring nations; and the men themselves had been driven into exile, so that there came a disgraceful scattering. They were then scattered into various countries, and some were left through contempt in the land; thus was fulfilled what is said here, "He has cast me out," even because these wild beasts, the Chaldeans, became satiated; meat was rejected by them, because they could not consume all that was presented to them.

By these figurative terms, as it has been stated, is set forth the extreme calamity of the people; and the Prophet no doubt intended to meet such thoughts as might otherwise have proved very harassing to the Jews. For as they found no end to their evils, they might have thought that they had been so cast away by God as to become the most miserable of men. This is the reason why our Prophet anticipates what might have imbittered the minds of the godly, and even driven them to despair. He then says, that notwithstanding all the things which had happened, yet God had not forgotten his people; for all these things were done as in his sight.

With regard to us, were God not only to double the calamities of his Church, but also to afflict it in an extreme degree, yet what the Prophet says here ought to afford us aid, even that God's chosen people were formerly so consumed, that the remainder was cast away in contempt; for the conqueror, though insatiable, could not yet consume all that he got as a prey, because his cupidity could not contain it. It now follows,—

35. The violence done to me and to my flesh *be* upon Babylon, shall the inhabitant of Zion say; and, My blood upon the inhabitants of Chaldea, shall Jerusalem say.

35. Violentia mea (*sed passivè accipitur, alii vertunt,* rapinam, *quod idem est*) et caro mea contra Babylonem, dicet (*vel,* dicat) habitatrix Sion, sanguis meus contra habitatores Chaldææ, dicat Jerusalem.

36. Therefore thus saith the Lord, Behold, I will plead thy cause, and take vengeance for thee: and I will dry up her sea, and make her springs dry.

36. Propterea sic dicit Jehova, Ecce ego litigans litem tuam (*hoc est,* disceptans causam tuam, *vel,* cognitor causæ tuæ,) et vindicans vindictam tuam; et arefaciam mare ejus, et exsiccabo fontem ejus.

Jeremiah goes on with the same subject; for, after having shewn that the calamities of the people were not unknown to God, he now, in an indirect way, exhorts the faithful to deposit their complaints in the bosom of God, and to apply, or appeal to him, as their defender. The design, then, of the Prophet is, (after having explained how grievously the Jews had been afflicted,) to shew them that their only remedy was, to flee to God, and to plead their cause before him.

And this passage is entitled to particular notice, so that we may also learn in extreme evils, when all things seem hopeless, to discover our evils to God, and thus to unburden our anxieties in his bosom. For how is it, that sorrow often overwhelms us, except that we do not follow what God's Spirit prescribes to us? For it is said in the Psalms, "Roll thy cares into God's bosom, and he will sustain thee, and will not give the righteous to a perpetual change." (Psalm lv. 23.) We may, then, by prayer, unburden ourselves, and this is the best remedy: but we murmur, and sometimes clamour, or at least we bite and champ the bridle, according to a common proverb; and, in the meantime, we neglect the chief thing, and what the Prophet teaches us here.

We ought, then, carefully to mark the design of what is here taught, when it is said, *my violence and my flesh* be *upon Babylon.* When he adds, *Say will* (or let) *the daughter of Sion,* he no doubt shews that the faithful have always this consolation in their extreme calamities, that they can expostulate with God as to their enemies and their cruelty. Then he says, *my plunder* or violence; some render it "the plunder of me," which is harsh. But the meaning of the Prophet is not ambiguous, for it follows afterwards, *my flesh.* Then violence was that which was done by enemies. But the people is here spoken of under the name of a woman, according to what is commonly done, *Let the inhabitress of Sion say, My plunder and my flesh.* By the second word the Prophet shews sufficiently plain what he understood by plunder. *My flesh,* he says, (even that which the Chaldeans had devoured and consumed,) be *on Babylon.* This is of the greatest weight, for by these words he intimates, that though the Chaldeans thought that they had exercised with impunity their cruelty towards the Jews, yet their innocent blood cried, and was opposed to them as an enemy.

To the same purpose he afterwards adds, *Let Jerusalem say, My blood is upon the Chaldeans.*

Then follows a clearer explanation, when God promises that he would be the avenger of his chosen people, and that whatever the Jews had suffered would be rendered to Babylon: *Therefore thus saith Jehovah, Behold, I will litigate thy quarrel.* By this passage we are taught to present our complaints to God, if we wish him to undertake our cause; for when we are silent, he will in his turn rest, as he considers us unworthy of being helped. But if we cry to him, he will doubtless hear us. Then we must remember the order of things, for the Prophet says on the one hand, *Let Jerusalem cry, let the daughter of Sion say;* and on the other hand he says, Therefore God will come and hear the cry of his people.

He says, first, *Behold, I will plead thy cause,* and then, *I will vindicate* or avenge *thy vengeance.* These are hard words to Latin ears; but yet they contain more force and power than if we were to follow the elegance of the Latin tongue. It is then better to retain the genuine terms than to study neatness too much.

In short, God promises to be the defender of his people, and by using the demonstrative particle, he doubtless removes every doubt, as though the thing was now present. We know that more than seventy years had elapsed since God had spoken thus; for as it has been already stated, it was not after the taking of the city that Jeremiah prophesied against the Chaldeans: but though God suspended his judgment and vengeance for seventy years after the destruction of the city, yet this was said, *Behold, I,* as though he brought the faithful to witness the event; and this was done for the sake of certainty.

Now, we hence learn, that though God humbles his people, and suffers them even to be overwhelmed with extreme miseries, he will at length become the avenger of all the wrongs which they may have endured; for what has been said of the destruction of the people has a reference to us ; nay, what is here said, has not been left on record except for our benefit. And further, let us learn, as I have before reminded you, to prepare our minds for patience whenever God seems to forsake us. Let us, at the same time exercise ourselves constantly in prayer, and God will hear our groans and complaints, and regard our tears.

It is afterwards added, *I will make dry her sea ;* for Babylon, as it has been already stated, was surrounded by the streams of the Euphrates ; and there was no easy access to it. The Prophet then compares the fortifications of Babylon to a *sea* and a *fountain.* For who would have thought that the Euphrates could be dried up, which is so large a river, and has none equal to it in all Europe ? Even the Danube does not come up to the largeness of that river. Who then would have thought it possible that such a river could be made dry, which was like a sea, and its fountain inexhaustible ? God then intimates by these words, that such was his power, that all obstacles would vanish away, and that he was resolved at the same time to execute his judgment on the Babylonians. It afterwards follows,—

37. And Babylon shall become heaps, a dwelling-place for dragons, an astonishment, and an hissing, without an inhabitant.	37. Et erit Babylon in acervos, habitaculum draconum, stupor et sibilum, absque habitatore.

He confirms what he had said, that when God raised his hand against Babylon, such would be its destruction, that the splendour, which before astonished all nations, would be reduced to nothing. Perish, he says, shall all the wealth of Babylon—its towers and its walls shall fall, and its people shall disappear ; in short, *it shall become heaps of stones,* as he said before, that it would become a mountain of burning. It is then for the same purpose that he now says that it would become heaps. But we must bear in mind what we observed yesterday, that it would become such heaps that they would not be fit for corners, that they could not be set in foundations ; for the ruins would be wholly useless as to any new building.

He says that it would become *an astonishment and a hissing.* Moses also used these words, when he threatened the people with punishment, in case they transgressed the law of God. (Deut. xxviii. 37.) But these threatenings extend to all the ungodly, and the despisers of God. Then God fulfilled as to the Babylonians what he had denounced by Moses on all the despisers of his law. It then follows,—

38. They shall roar together like lions: they shall yell as lions' whelps.	38. Rugient tanquam leones, rugient (*est quidem alium verbum sed ejusdem sensus*) tanquam catuli leonum.

Here, by another figure, Jeremiah expresses what he had said of the destruction of Babylon, even that in the middle of the slaughter, they would have no strength to resist: they would, at the same time, perish amidst great confusion; and thus he anticipates what might have been advanced against his prophecy. For the Babylonians had been superior to all other nations; how then could it be, that a power so invincible should perish? Though they were as lions, says the Prophet, yet that would avail nothing; they will indeed roar, but roaring will be of no service to them; they will roar as the whelps of lions, but still they will perish.

We now, then, understand the object of this comparison, even that the superior power by which the Babylonians had terrified all men would avail them nothing, for nothing would remain for them in their calamity except roaring.[1] It follows,—

39. In their heat I will make their feasts, and I will make them drunken, that they may rejoice, and sleep a perpetual sleep, and not wake, saith the Lord.	39. In calore ipsorum ponam convivia ipsorum, et inebriabo eos, ut exultent, et dormiant somnum perpetuum, et non expergiscantur, dicit Jehova.

[1] Taking this verse in connexion with the following, *Gataker* and *Lowth* give somewhat another view,—that the Babylonians roared like lions and shouted with exultation *before* the city was taken. It is said by *Herodotus*, that " they ascended the walls, and capered, and loaded Darius and his army with reproaches." They roared with rage at their enemies, and excited themselves as whelps when beginning to hunt for themselves, full of life and animation,—

Together as young lions shall they roar.
And rouse themselves as whelps of lionesses.

There is a ו wanting before the last verb, which is supplied by the *Vulg.*, *Syr.*, and the *Targ.*; and it is rendered necessary by the tense of the verb.—*Ed.*

Here, also, he describes the manner in which Babylon was taken. And hence we learn, that the Prophet did not speak darkly or ambiguously, but so shewed, as it were by the finger, the judgment of God, that the prophecy might be known by posterity, in order that they might understand that God's Spirit had revealed these things by the mouth of the Prophet: for no mortal, had he been a hundred times endowed with the spirit of divination, could ever have thus clearly expressed a thing unknown. But as nothing is past or future with God, he thus plainly spoke of the destruction of Babylon by his Prophet, that posterity, confirmed by the event, might acknowledge him to have been, of a certainty, the instrument of the Holy Spirit. And Daniel afterwards sealed the prophecy of Jeremiah, when he historically related what had taken place; nay, God extorted from heathen writers a confession, so that they became witnesses to the truth of prophecy. Though Xenophon was not, indeed, by design a witness to Jeremiah, yet that unprincipled writer, whose object was flattery, did, notwithstanding, render service for God, and sealed, by a public testimony, what had been divinely predicted by Jeremiah.

In their heat, he says, *I will make their feasts,* that is, I will make them hot in their feasts; for when the king of Babylon was drunk, he was slain, together with his princes and counsellors. I will inebriate them that they may exult, that is, that they may become wanton. This refers to their sottishness, for they thought that they should be always safe, and ridiculed Cyrus for suffering so many hardships. For he lived in tents, and the siege had been now long, and there was no want in the city. Thus, then, their wantonness destroyed them. And hence the Prophet says that God would make them hot, that they might become wanton in their pleasures; and then, that they might *sleep a perpetual sleep,* that is, that they might perish in their luxury:[1]

[1] "In their heat," that is, as it appears, of rage, while they were roaring like lions. The word rendered "feasts" by *Calvin* and in our version, properly means drinking, and it is so rendered in the early versions, and more suitably here,—

In their heat I will set *for them* their drink,
And will make them drunk, that they may leap for joy;

though they had despised their enemy, yet they should never awake; for Babylon, as we observed yesterday, might have resisted for a long time, but it was at once taken. The Babylonians were not afterwards allowed to have arms. Cyrus, indeed, suffered them to indulge in pleasures, but took away from them the use of arms, deprived them of all authority, so that they lived in a servile state, in the greatest degradation: and then, in course of time, they became more and more contemptible, until at length the city was so overthrown, that nothing remained but a few cottages, and it became a mean village. We hence see that whatever God had predicted by his servant Jeremiah was at length fulfilled, but at the appropriate time,—at the time of treading or threshing, as it has been stated. It follows,—

40. I will bring them down like lambs to the slaughter, like rams with he-goats.	40. Educam (*ad verbum est,* descendere faciam) eos tanquam agnos ad mactationem, tanquam arietes cum hircis.

This is a comparison different from the former, when the Prophet said that they would be like lions, but as to roaring only. But he now shews how easy would that ruin be when it should please God to destroy the Babylonians. Then as to their cry, they were like lions; but as to the facility of their destruction, they were like lambs led to the slaughter. God does not mean here that they would be endued with so much gentleness as to give themselves up to a voluntary death; but he means, that however strong the Babylonians might have previously been, and however they might have threatened all other nations, they would then be women in courage, and be led to the slaughter as though they were lambs or rams.

This is a comparison which occurs often in the prophets, for sacrifices were then daily made; and then the prophets considered the destruction of the ungodly as a kind of sacrifice; for as sacrifices were offered under the Law as evidences of piety and worship, so when God appears as a judge and takes vengeance on the reprobate, it is the same as though

And they shall sleep a perpetual sleep,
And shall not awake, saith Jehovah.

It is a clear allusion to the feast celebrated in Babylon the very night it was taken.—*Ed.*

he erected an altar, and thus exhibited an evidence of the worship that is due to him; for his glory and worship is honoured, yea, and celebrated by such sacrifices. Then the destruction of all the ungodly, as we have said, may be justly compared to sacrifices; for in such instances the glory of God shines forth, and this is what especially belongs to his worship. It at length follows,—

41. How is Sheshach taken! and how is the praise of the whole earth surprised! how is Babylon become an astonishment among the nations!	41. Quomodo capta est Sesak, et comprehensa laus totius terræ? quomodo facta est Babylon in vastitatem (*vel*, in stuporem) inter cunctas gentes?

Here the wonder expressed by the Prophet tended to confirm what he had said, for he thus dissipated those things which usually disturbed the minds of the godly, so as not to give full credit to his predictions. There is indeed no doubt but that the godly thought of many things when they heard Jeremiah thus speaking of the destruction of Babylon. It ever occurred to them, "How can this be?" Hence Jeremiah anticipated such thoughts, and assumed himself the character of one filled with wonder—*How is Sheshach taken?* as though he had said, "Though the whole world should be astonished at the destruction of Babylon, yet what I predict is certain; and thus shall they find who now admit not the truth of what I say, as well as posterity."

But he calls Babylon here Sheshach, as in chapter xxv. Some think it to be there the proper name of a man, and others regard it as the name of a celebrated city in Chaldea. But we see that what they assert is groundless; for this passage puts an end to all controversy, for in the first clause he mentions Sheshach, and in the second, Babylon. That passage also in chapter xxv. cannot refer to anything else except to Babylon; for the Prophet said, "Drink shall all nations of God's cup of fury, and after them the king of Sheshach," that is, when God has chastised all nations, at length the king of Babylon shall have his turn. But in this place the Prophet clearly shews that Sheshach can be nothing else than Babylon. The name is indeed formed by inverting the alphabet. Nor is this a new notion; for they had this retrograding alphabet in the time of Jerome. They put ת, *tau*, the last letter, in the place of א, *aleph*, the first; then ש, *shin*, for ב, *beth:* thus we see how they formed Sheshach. The ש, *shin*, is found twice in the word, the last letter but one being put for ב, *beth*, the first letter but one; and then כ, *caph*, is put in the place of ל, *lamed*, according to the order of the retrograde alphabet. There is no good reason for what some say, that the Prophet spoke thus obscurely for the sake of the Jews, because the prophecy was disliked, and might have created dangers to them; for why did he mention Sheshach and then Babylon in the same verse?

Many understand this passage enigmatically; but there is no doubt but that that alphabet was then, as we have stated, in common use, as we have *Ziphras*, as they call it, at this day. In the meantime, though the Prophet was not timid, and encouraged his own people to confidence, it yet pleased God that this prophecy should in a manner be hidden, but not that it should be without evidence of its certainty, for we shall see in the last verse but one of this chapter that he commanded the volume to be thrown into the Euphrates, until the event itself manifested the power of God, which for a long time remained as it were buried, until the time of visitation came of which he had spoken.

PRAYER.

Grant, Almighty God, that since thou art pleased at this day to receive us for thy people, we may enjoy the same favour to the end, and be sheltered under thy wings; and though we deserve to be wholly cast away, yet, if thou chastisest us for a time, deal with us with moderate severity, and chastise us in judgment, and not with extreme rigour; and then, after darkness, let thy serene face appear, until we shall at length enjoy that full light to which thou invitest us daily through Christ Jesus our Lord.—Amen.

Lecture One Hundred and Ninety-first.

42. The sea is come up upon Babylon: she is covered with the multitude of the waves thereof.	42. Ascendit contra Babylonem mare, multitudine fluctuum ejus cooperta est (*vel*, obruta.)

The Prophet here employs a comparison, in order more fully to confirm his prophecy respecting the destruction of

Babylon; for, as it was incredible that it could be subdued by the power or forces of men, he compares the calamity by which God would overwhelm it to a deluge. He then says that the army of the Persians and of the Medes would be like the sea, for it would irresistibly overflow; as when a storm rises, the sea swells, so he says the Medes and the Persians would come with such force, that Babylon would be overwhelmed with a deluge rather than with the forces of men. We now then understand the Prophet's meaning, when he says that Babylon would be *covered with waves* when the Medes and the Persians came. It then follows,—

43. Her cities are a desolation, a dry land, and a wilderness, a land wherein no man dwelleth, neither doth *any* son of man pass thereby.

43. Erunt urbes ejus in vastitatem, terra deserti et siccitatis (*aut*, vastitatis) terra; non transibit per eam quisquam (omnis homo,) et non habitabit in illa quisquam (et non transibit in illa, *hoc est*, per illam) filius hominis.

He repeats what he had previously said, but we have before reminded you why he speaks so largely on a subject in itself not obscure. For he might have comprehended in a few words all that he had said in the last chapter and also in this; but it was difficult to convince men of what he taught — it was therefore necessary to dwell at large on the subject.

He says now that the *cities* of Babylon, that is, of that monarchy, would *become a desolation.* He seems to have hitherto directed his threatenings against the city itself; but now he declares that God's vengeance would extend to all the cities under the power of the Chaldean nation; and he speaks at large of their desolation, for he says that it would be a *land of desert, a land of drought,* or of filthiness, so that *no one would dwell in it.* And though he uses the singular number and repeats it, yet he refers to cities, *Pass through it shall no man, dwell in it shall no man.*[1] He in-

[1] The *Sept.* and the *Syr.* remove the incongruity that is in this verse; they supply כ before the "land" that occurs first, and omit the second "land." Then the verse would read thus,—

43. Become have her cities a desolation,
Like a land of drought and a wilderness;
Dwell in them shall no man,
And pass through them shall no son of man.

The second "land" is omitted in two MSS.; and one has "in her," instead of "in them."—*Ed.*

deed speaks of the whole land, but so that he properly refers to the cities, as though he had said, that so great would be the destruction, that however far and wide the monarchy of Babylon extended, all its cities would be cut off. It afterwards follows,—

44. And I will punish Bel in Babylon, and I will bring forth out of his mouth that which he hath swallowed up: and the nations shall not flow together any more unto him; yea, the wall of Babylon shall fall.	44. Et visitabo super Bel in Babylone, et extraham quod voravit ab ore ejus; et non confluent ad ipsum amplius gentes; etiam murus Babylonis cecidit.

God again declares that he would take vengeance on the idols of Babylon; not that God is properly incensed against idols, for they are nothing but things made by men; but that he might shew how much he detests all superstitious and idolatrous worship. But he speaks of Bel as though it was an enemy to himself; yet God had no quarrel with a dead figure, void of reason and feeling; and such a contest would have been ridiculous. God, however, thus rises up against Bel for the sake of men, and declares that it was an enemy to himself, not because the idol, as we have said, of itself deserved any punishment.

But we hence learn how detestable was that corruption and that false religion. It appears evident from heathen writers that Bel was the supreme god of the Chaldean nation; nay, that idol was worshipped throughout all Assyria, as all testify with one consent. They thought that there had been a king skilful in the knowledge of the stars, and hence he was placed by erring men among the gods. But we learn from the prophets that this was a very ancient superstition; and it is hardly probable that there had been any king of this name—for otherwise Isaiah and Jeremiah, when predicting the ruin of this idol, would not have been silent on the subject. That common opinion, then, does not appear to me probable; but I think that on the contrary this name was given to the idol according to the fancies of men; for no reason can be found why heathen nations so named their false gods. It is indeed certain that divine honour was given to mortals by the Greeks and the Romans, and by barbarous nations. But the worship of Bel was more ancient than the time when such a thing was done. And in such veneration was that idol held, that from it they called some of their precious stones. They consecrated the eye-stone to the god of the Assyrians, because it was a gem of great price. (*See Plin.* lib. xxxvii. cap. 10.)

Jeremiah, then, now declares that Bel would be exposed to God's vengeance, not that God, as we have said, was angry with that statue, but he intended in this way to testify how much he abominated the ungodly worship in which the Chaldeans delighted. Nor did he so much regard the Chaldeans as the Jews; for I have often reminded you that it was a hard trial, which might have easily endangered the faith of the people, to think that the Chaldeans had not obtained so many and so remarkable victories, except God had favoured them. The Jews might on this account have had some doubts respecting the temple and the law itself. As then the Babylonians triumphed when success accompanied them, it was necessary to fortify the minds of the godly, that they might remain firm, though the Babylonians boasted of their victories. Lest the faithful should succumb under their trials, the prophets supplied a suitable remedy, which is done here by Jeremiah. God then declares that he would *visit Bel;* for what reason and to what purpose? that the Jews might be convinced that that idol could do nothing, but that they had been afflicted by the Babylonians on account of their sins. That true religion, then, might not be discredited, God testified that he would some time not only take vengeance on the Chaldeans themselves, but also on their idol, which they had devised for themselves; *I will* then *visit Bel in Babylon.*

And he adds, *and I will bring* or, draw *out of his mouth what he has swallowed.* The word בלע, *belo,* means indeed what is devoured; but the Prophet refers here to the sacred offerings by which Bel was honoured until that time. And there is no doubt but that many nations presented gifts to that idol for the sake of the Chaldean nation, as we find that gifts were brought from all parts of the world to Jupiter Capitolinus when the Roman empire flourished; for when the Greeks, the Asiatics, or the Egyptians, wished to obtain some favour, they sent golden crowns, or chandeliers, or some precious vessels ; and they sought it as the highest privilege to dedicate their gifts to Jupiter Capitolinus. So, then, there is no doubt but that many nations offered their gifts to Bel, when they wished to flatter the Chaldeans. And hence the Prophet declares that when God visited that idol, he would make it disgorge what it had before swallowed. This is indeed not said with strict propriety ; but the Prophet had regard to the Jews, who might have doubted whether the God of Israel was the only true God, while he permitted that empty image to be honoured with so many precious offerings ; for this was to transfer the honour of the true God to a dead figure. Then he says, *I will draw out*, as though Bel had swallowed what had been offered to it,—*I will draw out from its mouth what it has swallowed.* Though the language is not strictly correct, yet we see that it was needful, so it might not disturb the minds of the Jews, that almost all nations regarded that idol with so much veneration.

He afterwards expresses his meaning more clearly by adding, *the nations shall no more flow together.*[1] We hence then see what he meant by the voracity of Bel, even because there was a resort from all parts to this temple, for the nations, seeking to ingratiate themselves with the Babylonians, directed their attention to their god. We, indeed, know that the temple of Bel remained even after the city was conquered ; there is yet no doubt but that the predictions of Jeremiah and of Isaiah have been accomplished. For Isaiah says, "Lie prostrate does Bel, Nebo is broken." (Isa. xlvi. 1.) He names some other god, who is not made known by heathen writers ; but it is sufficiently evident from this testimony that Bel was in high repute. He afterwards says that it would " be a burden to the beasts even to weariness." We hence learn that Bel was carried away, not that it was worshipped by the Medes and the Persians,

[1] " The long processions of pilgrims," observes *Henderson*, " moving slowly along, are fitly expressed by נהר, which properly signifies, *to flow as a river.*"—*Ed.*

but because all the wealth was removed, and probably that idol was made of gold.

It afterwards follows, *Even the wall of Babylon has fallen.* We have said elsewhere that this prophecy ought not to be restricted to the first overthrow of Babylon, for its walls were not then pulled down except in part, where the army entered, after the streams of the Euphrates had been diverted. However, the ancient splendour of the city still continued. But when Babylon was recovered by Darius, the son of Hystaspes, then the walls were pulled down to their foundations, as Herodotus writes, with whom other heathen authors agree. For Babylon had revolted together with the Assyrians when the Magi obtained the government; but when Darius recovered the kingdom, he prepared an army against the Assyrians who had resorted to Babylon; and their barbarous cruelty is narrated, for they strangled all the women that they might not consume the provisions. Each one was allowed to keep one woman as a servant to prepare food and to serve as a cook; but they spared neither matrons nor wives, nor their own daughters. For a time the Persians were stoutly repulsed by them. At length, through the contrivance of Zopyrus, Darius entered the city; he then demolished the walls and the gates, and afterwards Babylon was no better than a village. Then also he hung the chief men of the city, to the number of three or four thousand, which would be incredible were we not to consider the extent of the city; for such a slaughter would be horrible in a city of moderate size, even were men of all orders put to death. But it hence appears what an atrocious cruelty it must have been, when all the chief men were hung or fixed to crosses; and then also the walls were demolished, though they were, as it has been elsewhere stated, of incredible height and width. Their width was fifty feet; Herodotus names fifty cubits, but I rather think they were feet; and yet their feet were longer than common.

As, then, Jeremiah now says, that *the wall of Babylon had fallen,* there is no doubt but his prophecy includes this second calamity, which happened under Darius; and this confirms what I have referred to elsewhere. It now follows,—

45. My people, go ye out of the midst of her, and deliver ye every man his soul from the fierce anger of the Lord.	45. Exite è medio ejus, popule mî, et servate quisque animam suam ab excandescentia iræ Jehovæ.

Here the Prophet exhorts the Israelites to flee from Chaldea and Assyria. Yet this exhortation was intended for another purpose, to encourage them in the hope of deliverance ; for it was hardly credible that they should ever have a free exit, for Babylon was to them like a sepulchre. As then he exhorts them as to their deliverance, he intimates that God would be their redeemer, as he had promised. But he shews that God's vengeance on Babylon would be dreadful, when he says, Flee from the *indignation of God's wrath.*

We must, however, observe, that the faithful were thus awakened, lest, being inebriated with the indulgences of the Chaldeans, they should obstinately remain there, when God stretched forth his hand to them; for we know what happened when liberty to return was given to the Israelites—a small portion only returned ; some despised the great favour of God ; they were so accustomed to their habitations, and were so fixed there, that they made no account of the Temple, nor of the land promised them by God. The Prophet, then, that he might withdraw the faithful from such indulgences, says, that all who, in their torpor, remained there, would be miserable, because the indignation of God would kindle against that city. We now perceive the object of the Prophet.

It appears, indeed, but a simple exhortation to the Jews to remove, that they might not be polluted with the filth of Babylon, but another end is also to be regarded, proposed by the holy Prophet. This exhortation, then, contains in it a promise of return, as though he had said, that they were not to fear, because liberty would at length be given them, as God had promised. In the meantime, a stimulant is added to the promise, lest the Israelites should be delighted with the pleasures of Chaldea, and thus despise the inheritance promised them by God ; for we know how great was the pleasantness of that land, and how great was the abundance it possessed of all blessings; for the fruitfulness of that land is more celebrated than that of all other countries. No wonder, then, that the Prophet so strongly urged the Jews to return, and that he set before them the vengeance of God to frighten them with terror, in case they slumbered in Chaldea. And he afterwards adds,—

46. And lest your heart faint, and ye fear for the rumour that shall be heard in the land; a rumour shall both come *one* year, and after that in *another* year *shall come* a rumour, and violence in the land, ruler against ruler.

46. Et ne fortè mollescat cor vestrum, et timeatis in rumore (*hoc est,* ob rumorem) qui audietur in terra; veniet in anno rumor, et postea in anno (altero, *subaudiendum est* anno posteriore) rumor, et violentia in terra, et dominator super dominatorem.

Here the Prophet in due time anticipates a danger, lest the Jews should be disturbed in their minds, when they saw those dreadful shakings which afterwards happened; for when their minds were raised to an expectation of a return, great commotions began to arise in Babylon. Babylon, as it is well known, was for a long time besieged, and, as is usual in wars, every day brings forth something new. As, then, God, in a manner, shook the whole land, it could not be, especially under increasing evils, but that the miserable exiles should become faint, being in constant fear; for they were exposed to the wantonness of their enemies. Then the Prophet seasonably meets them here, and shews that there was no cause for them to be disturbed, whatever might happen.

Come, he says, *and rise shall various rumours;* but stand firm in your minds. Interpreters confine these rumours to the first year of Belshazzar; but I know not whether such a view is correct. I consider the words simply intended to strengthen weak minds, lest they should be overwhelmed, or at least vacillate, through trials, when they heard of grievous commotions.

But there is a doctrine here especially useful; for when God designs to aid his Church, he suffers the world to be, in a manner, thrown into confusion, that the favour of redemption may appear more remarkable. Unless, then, the faithful were to have some knowledge of God's mercy, they could never endure with courageous minds the trials by which God proves them, and while Satan, on the other hand, seeks to upset their faith. There is the prelude of this very thing to be seen in the ancient people: God had promised to be their redeemer; when the day drew nigh, war suddenly arose, and the Medes and the Persians, as locusts, covered the whole land. We know what various evils war brings with it. There is, then, no doubt but that the children of God sustained many and grievous troubles, especially as they were exiles there; they must have suffered want, they must have been harassed in various ways. Now, as the event of war was uncertain, they might have fainted a hundred times, had they not been supported by this prophecy. But, as I have said, so now also God deals with his Church; for when a deliverer appears, all things seem to threaten ruin rather than to promise a joyful and happy deliverance. It is then necessary, that these prophecies should come to our minds, and that we should apply, for our own benefit, what happened formerly to our fathers, for we are the same body. There is, therefore, no reason for us at this day to wonder, if all things seem to get worse and worse, when yet God has promised that the salvation of his Church will ever be precious to him, and that he will take care of her: how so? because it is said, *Let not your heart be faint, fear ye not when rumours arise*, one after another; when one year brings tumults, and then another year brings new tumults, yet let not all this disturb your minds.[1]

[1] Some, as *Blayney*, following the *Syr.*, connect this verse with the preceding: The Jews are bidden to leave Babylon, that they might escape the wrath of God, and lest their hearts should faint at the evil rumours that would spread there,—

> And lest your heart faint,
> And ye be afraid of the rumour rumoured in the land,—
> For it shall come in one year, the rumour, &c.

But if פן, rendered *lest*, be taken, as it is sometimes, a dissuasive particle, then the rendering would be as follows,—

> And let not your heart be faint,
> Nor be ye afraid of the rumour rumoured in the land;
> When it shall come in one year, the rumour,
> And afterwards in a year, the rumour,
> And violence *shall be* in the land, ruler against ruler.

The reference seems to be to the commotions in Babylon before the liberation of the Jews.—*Ed.*

And Christ seems to allude to these words of the Prophet, when he says, "Wars shall arise, and rumours of wars: be ye not troubled." (Matt. xxiv. 6.) These words of Christ sufficiently warn us not to think it strange, if the Church at this day be exposed to violent waves, and be tossed as by continual storms: why so? because it is right and just that our condition should be like that of the fathers, or at least approach to it. We now, then, understand the design of the Prophet, and the perpetual use that ought to be made of what is here taught.

He afterwards adds, *Violence in the land*, and a *ruler upon* or after a *ruler*. This refers to Cyrus, who succeeded Darius, whom some call Cyaxares. They, indeed, as it is well known, both ruled; but Darius, who was older, had the honour of being the supreme king. Afterwards Cyrus, when Darius was dead, became the king of the whole monarchy. And Darius the Mede lived only one year after Babylon was taken. But I doubt not but that the Prophet here bids the Jews to be of good courage and of a cheerful mind, though the land should often change its masters; for that change, however often, could take away nothing from God's authority and government. It afterwards follows,—

47. Therefore, behold, the days come, that I will do judgment upon the graven images of Babylon; and her whole land shall be confounded, and all her slain shall fall in the midst of her.

47. Propterea ecce dies veniunt, et visitabo super simulachra Babylonis; et tota terra ejus pudefiet, et omnes occisi ejus (*vel*, interfecti) cadent in medio ejus.

He repeats a former sentence, that *God would visit the idols of Babylon.* He does not speak now of Bel only, but includes all the false gods. We have already said why God raised his hand against idols, which were yet mere inventions of no account. This he did for the sake of men, that the Israelites might know that they had been deceived by the wiles of Satan, and that the faithful might understand that they ought not to ascribe it to false gods, when God for a time spared the ungodly. However wanton, then, they might be, in their prosperity, yet when they perished together with their idols, the faithful would then learn by experience, that idols obtained no victory for their worshippers.

When, therefore, the Prophet now says, *Behold, the days are coming, and I will visit,* &c., he no doubt intended to support the minds of the godly, who otherwise would have been cast down. And it was the best support, patiently to wait for the time of visitation, of which he now speaks; *I will visit,* he says, *all the images of Babylon;* and then he adds, *her whole land shall be ashamed.* He speaks of the land, because the dominion of that monarchy extended far, so that it was difficult to travel through all its regions, and enemies could hardly have access to them. At length he adds, *all her slain shall fall in the midst of her.*[1] He then speaks first of the country, and then he adds, that however fortified the city might be, yet its walls and towers would be of no moment, for conquerors would march through her very streets, and everywhere kill those who thought themselves hid in a safe place, and set, as it were, above the clouds. He then adds,—

48. Then the heaven and the earth, and all that *is* therein, shall sing for Babylon: for the spoilers shall come unto her from the north, saith the Lord.

48. Et jubilabunt contra Babylonem cœli et terra, et omnia quæ in eis sunt; quia ab aquilone veniet illi vastatores, (*est mutatio numeri,*) dicit Jehova.

That he might more fully convince the Jews of the truth of all that he has hitherto said of the destruction of Babylon, he declares that God would effect it, and that it would be applauded by all the elements. *Shout,* he says, *shall heaven and earth;* which is a kind of personification—for he ascribes knowledge to heaven and earth. It might, indeed, be more refinedly explained, that angels and men would shout for joy, but it would be a frigid explanation; and the Prophet removes every ambiguity, by adding, *and all that is in them:* he includes, no doubt, the stars, men, trees, fishes, birds, fields, stones, and rivers. And the expression is very emphatical when he says, that all created things, though without reason and understanding, would yet be full of joy, so that they would, in a manner, rejoice and sing praise. If such would be the feeling in dead creatures, when God put forth his hand against Babylon, would it be possible

[1] Rather,

And all her slain, they shall fall in the midst of her.—*Ed.*

for that city to remain safe, which was so hated by heaven and earth, and which was accursed by birds and wild beasts, by trees, and everything void of understanding!

We hence see that the Prophet heaps together all kinds of figures and modes of speaking, in order to confirm weak minds, so that they might confidently look forward to the destruction of Babylon. He at the same time intimates that Babylon was hated by all creatures, because it had reached to the highest pitch of wickedness. He then shews the cause by the effect, as though he had said that Babylon was hated by heaven and earth, so that heaven and earth seemed as though they deemed themselves in a manner polluted by the sight of that city. As long, then, as Babylon stood, heaven and earth sighed: but, on the contrary, when God appeared as an avenger, then heaven and earth, and all things in them, would shout with joy. Could it then be that God, the judge of the world, would always connive at its sins? If heaven and earth could not endure it, and Babylon was so loathsome to all, and joy would arise from its destruction, could God possibly allow that city, filled with so many sins, and detested by heaven and earth, to escape with impunity his judgment?

We now, then, more fully understand why the Prophet says that triumph and joy would be in heaven and earth, and among all created things.

He says, *because;* but the particle כי, *ki,* may be taken for an adverb of time: then he says, *when from the north shall come wasters.* He alludes to the Medes, for the Persians were eastward. But as the Medes were nigher, and also their monarch far wealthier, the Prophet refers especially to the Medes when he says that evil would come from the north. For the Medes were north of Chaldea, as the Persians were eastward.

PRAYER.

Grant, Almighty God, that since thou not only testifiest to us that thou wilt be the Redeemer of thy Church, into which thou hast been pleased to introduce us, but hast also really manifested thyself to us in thine only-begotten Son,—O grant that we may patiently bear all the contests and afflictions by which thou now provest our faith, and that we may perseveringly fight under the cross, until, having gone through all our trials, we shall at length enjoy eternal glory, when we shall find thee to be our complete Redeemer, through the same Christ Jesus our Lord.—Amen.

Lecture One Hundred and Ninety-second.

49. As Babylon *hath caused* the slain of Israel to fall, so at Babylon shall fall the slain of all the earth.

49. Sicuti Babylon ut caderent (*hoc est*, fecit ut caderent, *subaudiendum est aliquid*,) interfecti Israelis, sic Babyloni cadent interfecti totius terræ.

The words literally read thus, "As Babylon, that they might fall, the slain of Israel, so for Babylon they shall fall, the slain of all the lands." Some, omitting the ל, *lamed*, in the second clause, render the passage thus, "As the slain of Israel have fallen through Babylon, so by Babylon shall they fall:" and others render the last like the first, "through Babylon." But the simpler rendering is that which I have given, even that this would be the reward which God would render Babylon, that they would fall everywhere through its whole land, as it had slain the people of Israel. For the Prophet no doubt had this in view, to alleviate the sorrow of the godly by some consolation; and the ground of consolation was, that God would be the avenger of all the evils which the Babylonians had brought on them. For it is a heavy trial when we think that we are disregarded by God, and that our enemies with impunity oppress us according to their own will. The Prophet, then, testifies that God would by no means suffer that so many of the Israelites should perish unpunished, for he would at length render to the Babylonians what they deserved, even that they who destroyed others should in their turn be destroyed.

We may now easily gather what the Prophet means, "As Babylon," he says, "has made many in Israel to fall, so now the Babylonians themselves shall fall." To render ל, *lamed*, by "through," or, on account of, is improper. Then he says the Babylonians themselves shall fall, the slain of the whole land. By the whole land, I do not understand the whole world, as other interpreters, but Chaldea only. Then everywhere in Chaldea, they who had been so cruel as to shed innocent blood everywhere would perish.[1] And though that saying is generally true, Whoso sheddeth man's blood shall be punished; yet the word is especially addressed to the Church. God, then, avenges all slaughters, because he cannot bear his own image to be violated, which he has impressed on men. But as he has a paternal care for his Church, he is in an especial manner the avenger of that cruelty which the ungodly exercise towards the faithful.

In short, the Prophet means, that though God may suffer for a time the ungodly to rage against his Church, yet he will be at the suitable season its avenger, so that they shall everywhere be slain who have been thus cruel.

But we hence learn that we ought by no means to despair when God allows so much liberty to the ungodly, so that they slay the miserable and the innocent, for the same thing happened formerly to the ancient people. It was the Church of God in which the Chaldeans committed that carnage of which the Prophet speaks: the children of God were then slain as sheep. If the same thing should happen to us at this day, there would be no reason for us to despond, but to wait for the time of vengeance of which the Prophet speaks here; for experience will then shew how precious to God is the life of all the godly. It now follows,—

50. Ye that have escaped the sword, go away, stand not still: remember the Lord afar off, and let Jerusalem come into your mind.	50. Qui evasistis è gladio, abite, ne stetis; recordamini è longinquo Jehovæ, et Jerusalem ascendat in cor vestrum.

The Prophet again bids the faithful quickly to flee from Chaldea; but he says, *They who remain from the sword.* He

[1] This verse may be deemed as the shouting song at the fall of Babylon,—

"As Babylon *made* to fall the slain of Israel,
So for Babylon have fallen the slain of all the land."

It is said before, in verse 47, that her slain should fall in the midst of her land. "For Babylon" means, on account of what she had done. But if it be "in Babylon," as in the *Sept.*, the meaning is, within the borders of Babylon; and the intimation is, that there would be none led captive, but slain in the land, except "all" be taken, as is often the case, as signifying a large number.—*Ed.*

then intimates that the slaughter would be such, that it would include many of God's people, and that they would be destroyed. And we know that many among them deserved such a sad end; but the Prophet now turns to address those who had been preserved through God's special favour. He then bids them to *depart* and not to stand still or stay.

Now, we said yesterday what was the object of this exhortation, even that the faithful might feel assured of their free return to their own country, from which, nevertheless, they thought they were perpetually excluded; for they had wholly despaired of deliverance, though it had been so often promised. This exhortation, then, contains a promise; and in the meantime the Prophet reminds us, that though God inflicted a temporary punishment on the chosen people, yet his vengeance on the Babylonians would be perpetual. For God not only tempers his rigour towards the faithful when he chastises them, but he also gives them a happy issue, so that all their afflictions become helps to their salvation, as Paul also teaches us. (Rom. viii. 28.) In short, the punishments inflicted by God on his children are so many medicines; for he always consults their safety even when he manifests tokens of his wrath. But the case with the ungodly is different; for all their punishments are perpetual, even those which seem to have an end. How so? because they lead to eternal ruin. This is what the Prophet means when he bids those who *remained, to flee from Chaldea,* according to what we observed yesterday, when he said, *Flee ye from the indignation of God's wrath.* There is, then, an implied comparison between the punishment which brings ultimate ruin on the reprobate, and the temporary punishment inflicted by God on his children.

He bids them to *remember Jehovah from afar.* Some apply this to the seventy years, but, in my view, in a sense too restricted. I then doubt not but that the Prophet bids them to entertain hope and to look to God, however far they may have been driven from him, as though he were wholly alienated from them. The Israelites had then been driven into distant lands, as though God never meant to restore them. As, then, the distance was so great between Chaldea and Judea, what else could come into the minds of the miserable exiles but that God was far removed from them, so that it was in vain for them to seek or call upon him? The Prophet obviates this want of faith, and raises their confidence, so that they might not cease to flee to God, though they had been driven into distant lands: *Be*, then, *mindful of Jehovah from afar.*

Then he adds, *Let Jerusalem ascend on your heart;* that is, though so many obstacles may intercept your faith, yet think of Jerusalem. The condition of the people required that they should be thus animated, for they might otherwise, as it has been said, have a hundred times despaired, and have thus become torpid in their calamities. Then the Prophet testifies that an access to God was open to them, and that though they were removed far, he yet had a care for them, and was ready to bring help whenever called upon And for the same reason he bids them to *direct their minds to Jerusalem*, so as to prefer the Temple of God to all the world, and never to rest quiet until God restored them, and liberty were given them of worshipping him there.

Now this passage deserves special notice, as it applies to us at this day; for when the scattering of the Church takes place, we think that we are forsaken by God, and we also conclude that he is far away from us, so that he is sought in vain. As, then, we are wont, being inclined to distrust, to become soon torpid in our calamities, as though we were very remote from God, and as though he did not turn his eyes to look on our miseries, let us apply to ourselves what is here said, even to *remember Jehovah from afar;* that is, when we seem to be involved in extreme miseries, when God hides his face from us and seems to be afar off; in short, when we think ourselves forsaken, and circumstances appear as proving this, we ought still to contend with all such obstacles until our faith triumphs, and to employ our thoughts in remembering God, though he may be apparently alienated from us. Let us also learn to direct our minds to the Church; for however miserable our condition may be, it is yet better than the happiness which the ungodly seek for themselves in the world. When, therefore, we see the ungodly flattering themselves as to their possessions, when we see them pleased and delighted as though God were dealing indulgently with them, let then *Jerusalem come to our minds,* that is, let us prefer the state of the Church, which may be yet sad and deformed, and such as we would shun, were we to follow our own inclinations. Let then the condition of the Church come to our minds, that is, let us embrace the miseries common to the godly, and let it be more pleasant to us to be connected with the children of God in all their afflictions, than to be inebriated with the prosperity of those who only delight in the world, and are at the same time accursed by God. This is the improvement which we ought to make of what is here taught. It now follows,—

51. We are confounded, because we have heard reproach: shame hath covered our faces; for strangers are come into the sanctuaries of the Lord's house.

51. Pudefacti sumus, quia audivimus opprobrium; operuit ignominia facies nostras, quia venerunt extranei in sanctuaria domus Jehovæ.

It is thought that these words were spoken by the Prophet to the faithful, to confirm them as to their return. But I rather think that they were spoken by way of anticipation. They who think that they were spoken as a formula to the Israelites, that they might with more alacrity prepare themselves for their return, suppose a verb understood, "Say ye, we are confounded (or ashamed), because we have heard reproach;" even that sorrow would wound the minds of the faithful, to the end that they might nevertheless go through all their difficulties. But as I have said, the Prophet here repeats what the faithful might have of themselves conceived in their own minds; and he thus speaks by way of concession, as though he said, "I know that you have in readiness these words, 'We are ashamed, we are overwhelmed with reproaches; strangers have entered into the sanctuary of God: since the temple is polluted and the city overthrown, what any more remains for us? and doubtless we see that all things supply reasons for despair.'"

As, then, the thoughts of the flesh suggested to the faithful such things as might have dejected their minds, the Prophet meets them and recites their words. He then says, as in their person, *We are confounded, because we have heard reproach;* that is, because we have been harassed by the reproaches of our enemies. For there is no doubt but that the Chaldeans heaped many reproaches on that miserable people; for their pride and their cruelty were such that they insulted the Jews, especially as their religion was wholly different. As, then, the ears of the people were often annoyed by reproaches, the Prophet declares here that they had some cause according to the flesh, why they could hardly dare to entertain the hope of a return.

To the same purpose is what he adds, *Shame hath covered our faces, because strangers have come into the sanctuaries of Jehovah.* For it was the chief glory of the chosen people that they had a temple where they did not in vain call upon God; for this promise was like an invaluable treasure, "I will dwell in the midst of you; this is my rest, here will I dwell." (Ps. cxxxii. 13, 14.) As, then, God was pleased to choose for himself that throne and habitation in the world, it was, as I have said, the principal dignity of the people. But when the temple was overthrown, what more remained for them? it was as though religion was wholly subverted, and as though God also had left them and moved elsewhere; in short, all their hope of divine aid and of salvation was taken away from them.

We now, then, understand why the Prophet speaks thus according to the common thoughts of the people, even that they were *covered with shame, because strangers had come into God's sanctuaries;* for that habitation, which God had chosen for himself, was polluted. And he says "sanctuaries," in the plural number, because the temple had many departments, as the tabernacle had; for there was the vestibule or the court where they killed the victims; and then there was the holy place, and there was the holy of holies, which was the inner sanctuary. It was then on this account that he said that the *sanctuaries* of the house of God were possessed by strangers; for it was a sad and shameful pollution when strangers took possession of God's temple, where even the common people were not admitted; for though the whole of the people were consecrated to God, yet none but the priests entered the temple. It was therefore a dreadful profanation of the temple, when enemies entered it by force and for the sake of degrading it. What then remained for the people, except despair? "This is your glory," said Moses, "before all nations; for what people so noble, what nation so illustrious, as to have gods so near to it!" (Deut. iv. 6-8.) When, therefore, God ceased to dwell familiarly with the Jews, all their glory fell, and they were overwhelmed with shame. But after the Prophet recited these complaints, he immediately subjoins a consolation,—

52. Wherefore, behold, the days come, saith the Lord, that I will do judgment upon her graven images; and through all her land the wounded shall groan.

52. Propterea ecce dies veniunt, dicit Jehova, et visitabo super sculptilia ejus; et in tota terra ejus clamabit vulneratus (*vel*, occisus, *hoc nomen* חלל, *jam sæpius vidimus.*)

The design of the Prophet is, as I have reminded you, to raise up the minds of the godly that they might not succumb under their trials, on seeing that they were exposed to shame and were destitute of all honours. He then says that the time would come when God would take vengeance on the *idols* of Babylon. And thus God claims for himself that power which seemed then to have almost disappeared; for the temple being overthrown, the Babylonians seemed in a manner to triumph over him, as God's power in the temple was overcome. Then as the ruin of it, as we have said, seemed to have extinguished God's power, the Prophet applies a remedy, and says that though the temple was overthrown, yet God remained perfect and his power unchangeable. But among other things he bids the faithful patiently to wait, for he invites their attention to the hope of what was as yet hidden.

We now see how these things agree, and why the Prophet uses the particle "therefore," לכן, *laken : Therefore, behold, the days are coming*, that is, though ye are confounded, yet God will give you a reason for glorying, so that ye shall again sing joyfully his praises. But he says, "the days will come;" by these words he reminds us that we are to cherish the hope of the promises until God completes his work; and thus he corrected that ardour by which we are seized in the midst of our afflictions, for we wish immediately to fly away to God. The Prophet, then, here exhorts the faithful to sustain courage until the time fixed by God ; and so he refers them to God's providence, lest they assumed too much in wishing him to act as their own minds led them. *Come* then *shall the days when I shall visit the graven images of Babylon ; and groan* or cry, &c. ; for the word אנק, *anak*, means to cry. Some render thus, "groan shall the wounded ;" and they render the last word "wounded," because they think it improper to say that the slain cry or groan. But the Prophet means that the cry in that slaughter would be great, that is, that while the Babylonians were slain, a great howling would be everywhere. It follows,—

53. Though Babylon should mount up to heaven, and though she should fortify the height of her strength, *yet* from me shall spoilers come unto her, saith the Lord.

53. Si ascenderit Babylon in cœlos, et si munierit excelsum fortitudinis suæ (*vel*, munierit fortitudinem suam in excelso, *quod mihi magis placet*,) à me venient vastatores ei, dicit Jehova.

The Prophet again teaches us, that however impregnable Babylon might be, there was yet no reason to fear but that God would be its judge ; for it is by no means right to measure his power by our thoughts. And nothing does more hinder or prevent us from embracing the promises of God, than to think of what may be done naturally, or of what is probable. When, therefore, we thus consult our own thoughts, we exclude the power of God, which is superior to all the means that may be used.

Hence the Prophet says here, that though Babylon ascended above the heavens, and in the height fortified strength for itself, yet *from me*, he says, *shall come wasters to it.*[1] There is to be understood here a contrast between God and men ; for if there be a contest between men, they fight one with

[1] The idea seems to be, if Babylon ascended the heavens, or the skies, and fortified there a high place for her strength, yet to this place desolators would come,—

Though Babylon mounted the skies,
And though she fortified the height *as* her strength,
From me would come to her destroyers, saith Jehovah.—*Ed.*

another; but the way of God is different, for he can thunder from heaven, and thus lay prostrate the highest mountains. We now, then, perceive the purpose of the Prophet by saying, that *desolators* would come from God to destroy Babylon, were it to ascend above the clouds. It follows,—

54. A sound of a cry *cometh* from Babylon, and great destruction from the land of the Chaldeans.

54. Vox clamoris è Babylone, et confractio magna è terra Chaldæorum.

Jeremiah in a manner exults over Babylon, in order that the faithful, having had all obstacles removed or surmounted, might feel assured that what the Prophet had predicted of the fall of Babylon would be confirmed. He then brings them to the very scene itself, when he says, that there would be the *voice of a cry from Babylon*, and that there would be *great breaking* or distress *from the land of the Chaldeans.* We, at the same time, may render שבר, *shober*, here "crashing," so that it may correspond with the previous clause: he had said, *The voice of a cry from Babylon;* now he says, *a crashing from the land of the Chaldeans.* They call that sound crashing, which is produced by some great shaking; as when a great mass falls, it does not happen without a great noise. This, then, is properly what the Prophet means. We have already stated why he used these words, even that the faithful might have before their eyes the event itself, which as yet was incredible. It follows,—

55. Because the Lord hath spoiled Babylon, and destroyed out of her the great voice; when her waves do roar like great waters, a noise of their voice is uttered.

55. Quia perdens Jehova Babylonem (*hoc est* perdet, *aut* vastabit *propriè est* שדד) et perdet (*nunc aliud est verbum*) ex ea vocem magnam (*vel,* magnificam;) et sonuerunt fluctus eorum tanquam aquæ magnæ, editus est sonitus vocis eorum.

The reason for the crashing is now added, even because God had resolved to lay waste Babylon, and to reduce it to nothing. Jeremiah again calls the faithful to consider the power of God. He then says, that it would not be a work done by men, because God would put forth his great power, which cannot be comprehended by human minds. He then sets the name of God in opposition to all creatures, as though he had said, that what exceeds all the efforts of men, would yet be easily done by God. He, indeed, represents God here as before our eyes, and says that Babylon would perish, but that it was God who would lay it waste. He thus sets forth God here as already armed for the purpose of cutting off Babylon. *And he will destroy from her the magnificent voice*, that is, her immoderate boasting.

What follows is explained by many otherwise than I can approve; for they say that the waves made a noise among the Babylonians at the time when the city was populous; for where there is a great concourse of men, a great noise is heard, but solitude and desolation bring silence. They thus, then, explain the words of the Prophet, that though now waves, that is, noises, resounded in Babylon like great waters, and the sound of their voice went forth, yet God would destroy their great or magnificent voice. But I have no doubt but that what the Prophet meant by their great voice, was their grandiloquent boasting in which the Babylonians indulged during their prosperity. While, then, the monarchy flourished, they spoke as from the height. Their silence from fear and shame would follow, as the Prophet intimates, when God checked that proud glorying.

But what follows I take in a different sense; for I apply it to the Medes and the Persians: and so there is a relative without an antecedent—a mode of speaking not unfrequent in Hebrew. He then expresses the manner in which God would destroy or abolish the grandiloquent boasting of the Babylonians, even *because their waves*, that is, of the Persians, *would make a noise like great waters;* that is, the Persians, and the Medes would rush on them like impetuous waves, and thus the Babylonians would be brought to silence and reduced to desolation.[1] When they were at peace, and no

[1] This is the meaning given by the *Targum*. *Venema* and *Horsley* would put a colon or a period after אבד,—

55. For Jehovah is laying waste Babylon and destroying her:
From her comes a loud voice!
And roar do their waves like great waters,
Going forth is the tumult of their voice.

According to the preceding verse, the destruction of Babylon is represented as *then* taking place,—

54. A voice of howling from Babylon!
And of great destruction from the land of the Chaldeans!

The commotions and tumults, arising from the invasion of enemies, seem

enemy disturbed them, they then gave full vent to their pride; and thus vaunting was the speech of Babylon as long as it flourished; but when suddenly the enemies made an irruption, then Babylon became silent or mute on account of the frightful sound within it. We hence see why he compares the Persians and the Medes to violent waves which would break and put an end to that sound which was before heard in Babylon. It follows,—

56. Because the spoiler is come upon her, *even* upon Babylon, and her mighty men are taken; every one of their bows is broken: for the Lord God of recompences shall surely requite.

56. Quia venit super eam, super Babylonem, vastator; et deprehensus est fortis ejus (deprehensi sunt, *vel*, capti, fortes ejus;) confractus est arcus eorum, quia Deus retributionum Jehova reddendo reddet.

He confirms the former verse; for as the thing of which he speaks was difficult to be believed, he sets God before them, and shews that he would be the author of that war. He now continues his discourse and says, that *desolators shall come against Babylon.* He had ascribed to God what he now transfers to the Medes and the Persians. He had said, *Jehovah hath desolated* or wasted, שדד יהוה, *shedad Jeve;* he says now, *coming is a desolator,* שודד, *shudad.* Who is he? not God, but Cyrus, together with the united army of the Persians and the Medes; yea, with vast forces assembled from many nations. Now that the same name is given to God and to the Persians, this is done with regard to the ministration. Properly speaking, God was the desolator of Babylon; but as in this expedition he employed the services of men, and made the Persians and the Medes, as it were, his ministers, and the executioners of his judgment, the name which properly belongs to God is transferred to the ministers whom he employed. The same mode of speaking is also used when blessings are spoken of. He is said to have raised up saviours for his people, while yet he himself is the only Saviour, nor can any mortal assume that name without sacrilege. (Judges iii. 15; 2 Kings xiii. 5.)

to be set forth in verse 55; and the beginning of the following, the 56th, ought to be rendered in the present tense, the first verb being a participle.—*Ed.*

For God's peculiar glory is taken away, when salvation is sought through the arm of men, as we have seen in chapter xvii. But though God is the only author of salvation, yet it is no objection to this truth, that he employs men in effecting his purposes. So also he converts men, illuminates their minds by the ministers of the gospel, and also delivers them from eternal death. (Luke i. 17.) Doubtless were any one to arrogate to himself what Christ is pleased to concede to the ministers of his gospel, he could by no means be endured; but as I have already said, we must bear this in mind, that though God acts by his own power and never borrows anything from any one, nor stands in need of any help, yet what properly belongs to him is, in a manner, applied to men, at least by way of concession. So now, then, the Prophet calls God the desolator, and afterwards he honours with the same title the Persians and the Medes.

He adds, that *the valiant men of Babylon were taken*, according to what we have before seen, that the city was so taken that no one resisted. Then he adds, that *their bow was broken.* Here is a part stated for the whole; for under the word *bow* he includes all kinds of armour. But as bows were used at a distance, and as enemies were driven from the walls by casting arrows, the Prophet says that there would be no use made of bows, because the enemies would shew themselves in the middle of the city before the watchmen saw them, as we know that such was really the case. We now perceive why the Prophet mentions the bow rather than swords or other weapons.

The reason follows, *Because Jehovah is the God of retributions, and recompensing her recompences*, that is, he will recompense. The Prophet here confirms all that he had said, and reasons from the nature or character of God himself. As then the fall of Babylon would hardly be believed by the faithful, the Prophet does not ask what God is in himself, but declares that he is the God of retributions, as though he had said, that it belonged to God, and that it could not be separated from his nature, to be the God of retributions, otherwise his judgment would be nothing, his justice would be nothing. For if the reprobate succeeded with impunity, and if the righteous were oppressed without any aid, would not God be like a stock of wood or an imaginary thing? For why has he power, except that he may exercise justice? But God cannot be without power.

We now, then, see how forcible is this confirmation, with which the Prophet closes his discourse: for it is the same as if he had said, that no doubt could possibly be entertained as to the fall of Babylon, because God is the God of retributions. Either there is no God, he says, or Babylon must be destroyed; how so? for if there be a God, he is the God of retributions; if he is the God of retributions, then recompensing he will recompense. Now, it is well known how wicked Babylon was, and in what various ways it had provoked the wrath of God. Then it was impossible for it to escape his hand unpunished, since it had in so many ways sought its own ruin.

PRAYER.

Grant, Almighty God, that when thou hidest at this day thy face from us, the miserable despair we apprehend may not overwhelm our faith, nor obscure our view of thy goodness and grace, but that in the thickest darkness thy power may ever appear to us, which can raise us above the world, so that we may courageously fight to the end, and never doubt but that thou wilt at length be the defender of thy Church, which now seems to be oppressed, until we shall enjoy our perfect happiness in heaven, through Christ our Lord.—Amen.

Lecture One Hundred and Ninety-third.

57. And I will make drunk her princes, and her wise *men*, her captains, and her rulers, and her mighty men: and they shall sleep a perpetual sleep, and not wake, saith the King, whose name *is* the Lord of hosts.

57. Et inebriabo principes ejus et sapientes ejus et duces ejus et præfectos ejus et fortes ejus; et dormient somnum perpetuum, et non expergefient, dicit rex, cujus nomen est Jehova exercituum.

Jeremiah pursues the same subject. He said yesterday that desolators would come to destroy Babylon. He now confirms this by a similitude; and God himself speaks, *I will inebriate* the princes and captains as well as the soldiers and all the counsellors. He seems here to allude to that feast of which Daniel speaks, and of which heathen authors have written. (Dan. v. 1.) For while the feast was celebrated by the Babylonians, the city was that night taken, not only through the contrivance and valour of Cyrus, but also through the treachery of those who had revolted from Belshazzar. As, then, they were taken while at the feast, and as the king was that night slain together with his satraps, God seems to refer to this event when he declares, that when he had inebriated them, they would be overtaken with perpetual sleep; for death immediately followed that feasting. They had prolonged their feast to the middle of the night; and while they were sitting at table, a tumult arose suddenly in the city, and the king heard that he was in the hand of his enemies. As, then, feasting and death followed in close succession, it is a striking allusion given by the Prophet, when God threatens the Babylonians with perpetual sleep, after having inebriated them.

But he mentions here the *rulers* and the *captains*, as well as the *counsellors* and *the wise* men. We, indeed, know that the Babylonians were inflated by a twofold confidence, —they thought themselves endued with consummate wisdom, and also that they possessed warlike valour. This is the reason why the Prophet expresses so distinctly, that all the captains and rulers in Babylon, however superior in acuteness and prudence, would yet be overtaken with perpetual sleep before they rose from their table. And we must observe that Jeremiah had many years thus prophesied of Babylon; and hence we conclude that his mind as well as his tongue was guided by the Spirit of God, for he could not have possibly conjectured what would be after eighty years: yet so long a time intervened between the prediction and its accomplishment, as we shall presently see.

Moreover, the Prophet uses here a mode of speaking which often occurs in Scripture, even that insensibility is a kind of drunkenness by which God dementates men through his hidden judgment. It ought, then, to be noticed, that whatever prudence and skill there is in the world, they are in such a way the gifts of God, that whenever he pleases the wisest are blinded, and, like the drunken, they either go astray or fall. But we must bear in mind what I have already said, that the Prophet alludes to that very history, for there was then an immediate transition from feasting to death. It now follows,—

58. Thus saith the Lord of hosts, The broad walls of Babylon shall be utterly broken, and her high gates shall be burnt with fire; and the people shall labour in vain, and the folk in the fire, and they shall be weary.

58. Sic dicit Jehova exercituum, Murus Babylonis latitudinis (*hoc est, latus*) dissipando dissipabitur, et portæ ejus excelsæ igne comburentur, et laborabunt populi ad nihilum, et gentes in igne, et fatigabuntur.

The Prophet again introduces God as the speaker, that what he said might obtain more attention from the Jews; and for this reason he subjoined a eulogy to the last verse, and said that the *king* spoke, *whose name is Jehovah of hosts.* We have stated elsewhere what is the design of such expressions, even that men may rise above everything seen in the world when God's power is mentioned, that they may not try to contain it in their own small measure. Then the Prophet now again repeats the name of God, that the Jews might receive with becoming reverence what he announced.

And what he says is, *The wall of Babylon,* however *wide* it may be, *shall* yet *be surely demolished.* We have said that the walls were fifty feet wide, and the feet were indeed long, though Herodotus, as I have said, mentions cubits and not feet. The width, indeed, was such that four horses abreast meeting, could pass, there being space enough for them. It hence, then, appears, that their thickness was so great, that the Babylonians confidently disregarded whatever had been predicted by the Prophet; for no engines of war could have ever beaten down walls so thick, especially as they were made of bricks and cemented by bitumen. As, then, the material, beside the thickness, was so firm and strong, this prophecy was incredible. It did not indeed reach the Babylonians, but the Jews themselves regarded as a fable all that they had heard from the mouth of the Prophet. Yet God did not in vain refer to width of the wall, in order that the faithful might feel assured that the walls of Babylon could not possibly resist him, however firm they might be in their materials and thickness. *The wall,* he says, *shall surely be demolished.*

He afterwards mentions the *gates,* which Herodotus says were of brass when Darius took them away. He, indeed, means the doors, but the Prophet includes the framework as well as the brazen doors. He then says, they shall *be consumed with fire.* The Babylonians might have laughed at this threatening of Jeremiah, for brass could not have been consumed with fire, even if enemies had been permitted to set fire to them—for brass could not have been so soon melted. But as the Prophet had predicted this by God's command, so at length his prophecy was verified when he was dead, because it was proved by the event that this proceeded from God; for when the doors were removed, the gates themselves were demolished; and it may have been that Darius put fire to them, that he might the sooner destroy the gates and the towers, which were very high, as well as the walls.

He afterwards adds, *Labour shall the people in vain, and the nations in the fire; they shall be wearied.* So this passage is commonly explained, as though the Prophet had said, that when the walls of Babylon had begun to burn, and the gates to be consumed with fire, there would be no remedy, though the Babylonians might greatly weary themselves and fatigue themselves in attempting to quench the fire. But this exposition seems to be forced and unnatural. I therefore take the words, though future, in the past tense. And as the walls of Babylon had not been erected without great labour, and a vast number of men had been hired, some to bring bitumen, others to heap up the earth, and others to make the bricks, the Prophet in this place intimates that all this labour would be in vain, even because it was spent for the fire,—that whatever they did who had been either hired for wages or forced by authority to erect the walls, was labour for the fire; that is, they laboured that their work might eventually be consumed by fire. This seems to me to be the real meaning of the Prophet. He then says that *the people had laboured in vain*, or for nothing, and why? because they *laboured for the fire*. The second clause is in my view an explanation of the former.[1] It now follows,—

59. The word which Jeremiah the prophet commanded Seraiah the son of Neriah, the son of Maaseiah, when he went with Zedekiah the king of Judah into Babylon in the fourth year of his reign. And *this* Seraiah *was* a quiet prince.

59. Sermo quem præcepit Jeremias propheta Seraiæ filio Neriæ, filii Mahesiæ, quum profectus est pro Zedechia (*vel*, à Zedechia,) rege Jehudah, Babylonem, anno quarto regni ipsius; Seraiah autem princeps quietis.

This is a remarkable sealing of the whole of what we have hitherto found said respecting the destruction of Babylon; for the Prophet not only spoke and promulgated what the Spirit of God had dictated, but also put it down in a book; and not contented with this, he delivered the book to Seraiah the son of Neriah, when he went to Babylon by the command of Zedekiah the king, that he might read it there, cast it into the Euphrates, and strengthen himself in the hope of all those things which had been divinely predicted.

He says first that he *commanded Seraiah* what he was to do, even to read the volume and to throw it into the Euphrates, as we shall hereafter see. But he points out the time and mentions the disposition of Seraiah, that we might not think it strange that the Prophet dared to give an authoritative command to the king's messenger, which a man of another character would have refused. As to the time, it was the fourth year of the reign of Zedekiah; seven years before the city was taken, being besieged the ninth year and taken the eleventh. Then seven years before the destruction and ruin of the city, Seraiah was sent

[1] The ו before ויגעו is evidently conversive, and may be rendered *so that*, or *therefore*,—

Thus saith Jehovah of hosts,
The wall of Babylon, the broad one,
It shall be utterly laid in ruins;
And her gates, the lofty ones,
They shall be consumed with fire:
So that peoples had laboured for vanity,
And nations for the fire, and wearied themselves.

Several MSS. have חמת, wall, and so it is in the *Sept.*, as required by "broad," which is in the singular number. "For vanity" is for a vain object; and "for the fire" means for what was to be consumed by fire. The last words may be rendered "though they wearied themselves."—*Ed.*

by the king to Babylon. There is no doubt but that the message was sent to pacify the king of Babylon, who had been offended with the fickleness and perfidy of King Zedekiah; an ambassador was then sent to seek pardon. But what the Jews say, that Zedekiah went to Babylon, is wholly groundless; and we know that Sederola, whence they have taken this, is full of all kinds of fables and trifles; and on such a point as this, sacred history would not have been silent, for it was a thing of great moment; and then the particle את, *at,* expresses no such thing, but may be rendered in this sense, that the messenger was sent *for*, or *by*, or *in the place of* Zedekiah. Let us then be satisfied with this simple and obvious explanation, that Seraiah was the king's messenger sent to remove the offences taken by the Babylonians.[1] And this happened *in the fourth year of Zedekiah.*

Now, by calling Seraiah *a prince of quietness*, I doubt not but that a reference is made to his gentleness and meekness; and I wonder that in so plain a thing interpreters have toiled so much. One renders it, even the Chaldean paraphrast, "the prince of the oblations," as though he was set over to examine the presents offered to the king. Others imagine that he was a facetious man who amused the king in his fears; and others think that he was called "prince of quietness," because he preserved the city in a quiet state. But all these things are groundless.[2] No other view, then, seems to me right, but that he was a prince of a quiet disposition. Therefore the word "quietness" ought not to be referred to any office, but a noun in the genitive case used

[1] The *Vulg.* and *Syr.* have "with," but the *Sept.* and *Targ.* give it the meaning of "from;" and את has often the meaning of מאת; see Gen. iv. 1; xliv. 4; L. 9, 29. So *Gataker*, *Venema*, and *Blayney*.—*Ed.*

[2] The variety in the early versions is remarkable; the *Sept.* and the *Targ.* have "the prince of gifts" or presents; the *Vulg.*, "the prince of prophecy;" and the *Syr.*, "the prince of warfare." A similar phrase is found in 1 Chron. xxii. 9; Solomon is said to be "a man of rest," איש מנוחה. The meaning most suitable to this passage is that of *Calvin* and of our version. So thought *Gataker;* but *Lowth* and *Parkhurst* regarded the words as pointing out his office as the king's chief chamberlain, "the prince of the resting-place," or chamber; but the objection to this is, that the word is never used in this sense; it means not the rest of sleep, but the rest of peace and quietness.—*Ed.*.

instead of an adjective. He was, then, a quiet prince, or one of a placid disposition. And this commendation was not without reason added, because we know how haughtily the princes rejected everything commanded them by the servants of God. Seraiah might have objected, and said that he was sent to Babylon, not by a private person, and one of the common people, but by the king himself. He might then have haughtily reproved the Prophet for taking too much liberty with him, " Who art thou, that thou darest to command me, when I sustain the person of the king? and when I am going in his name to the king of Babylon? and then thou seekest to create disturbances by ordering me to read this volume. What if it be found on me? what if some were to suspect that I carry such a thing to Babylon? would I not, in the first place, carry death in my bosom? and would I not, in the second place, be perfidious to my king? for thus my message would be extremely disliked."

As then Seraiah might have stated all these things, and have rejected the command which Jeremiah gave him, his gentleness is expressly mentioned, even that he was a meek man, and who withheld not his service—who, in short, was ready to obey God and his servant. What, in a word, is here commended, is the meekness of Seraiah, that he received the Prophet with so much readiness,—that he suffered himself to be commanded by him, and that he also hesitated not to execute what he had commanded, when yet it might have been a capital offence, and it might especially have been adverse to his mission, which was to reconcile the king of Babylon. And surely it is an example worthy of being noticed, that Seraiah was not deterred by danger from rendering immediate obedience to the Prophet's command, nor did he regard himself nor the office committed to him, so as to reject the Prophet, according to the usual conduct of princes, under the pretext of their own dignity; but laying aside his own honour and forgetting all his greatness, he became a disciple to Jeremiah, who yet, as it is well known, had been long despised by the people, and had sometimes been nearly brought to death. It was, then, a remarkable instance of virtue in Seraiah, that he received with so much modesty and readiness what had been said to him by the Prophet, and that he obeyed his command, to the evident danger of his own life. It now follows,—

60. So Jeremiah wrote in a book all the evil that should come upon Babylon, *even* all these words *that are* written against Babylon.

61. And Jeremiah said to Seraiah, When thou comest to Babylon, and shalt see, and shalt read all these words,

62. Then shalt thou say, O Lord, thou hast spoken against this place, to cut it off, that none shall remain in it, neither man nor beast, but that it shall be desolate for ever.

63. And it shall be, when thou hast made an end of reading this book, *that* thou shalt bind a stone to it, and cast it into the midst of Euphrates:

64. And thou shalt say, Thus shall Babylon sink, and shall not rise from the evil that I will bring upon her; and they shall be weary. Thus far *are* the words of Jeremiah.

60. Et scripsit Jeremias omne malum, quod venturum erat contra Babylonem in libro uno, omnes sermones istos scriptos contra Babylonem.

61. Et dixit Jeremias ipsi Seraiæ, Quum ingressus fueris Babylonem, et conspexeris eam, tunc leges omnes sermones istos,

62. Et dices, Jehova, tu loquutus es contra locum hunc, ad excidendum ipsum, ut non sit in eo habitator, ab homine ad bestiam, quia vastationes perpetuæ erit (*hoc est*, erit in vastationes perpetuas, *vel* redigetur.)

63. Et erit quum finem feceris legendo librum hunc, alligabis ad ipsum lapidem, et projicies in medium Euphratem:

64. Et dices, Sic mergetur Babylon, et non exurget à facie mali quod ego immitto contra eam, et volabunt (*aut*, fatigabunt.) Huc usque sermones Jeremiæ.

Here we see, on one hand, what courage the Prophet had, who dared to command the king's messenger; for though Seraiah was a meek man, so as to render himself submissive, yet Jeremiah exposed himself to danger; for he might have been timid, though he was neither proud nor arrogant; and thus, as men are wont to do when terrified, he might have referred to the king what he had heard from the Prophet. Then Jeremiah did what we here read, not without danger; and hence appears his firmness. We then see that he was endued with the spirit of invincible courage, so as to discharge his office freely and intrepidly.

On the other hand, we have to observe not only the meekness of Seraiah, but also his piety, together with his modesty; for except he had in him a strong principle of religion, he might have adduced plausible reasons for refusing. As, then, he was so submissive, and dreaded no danger, it is evident that the real fear of God was vigorous in his soul.

And these things ought to be carefully noticed; for who of our courtly princes can be found at this day who will close his eyes to all dangers, and resolutely disregard all adverse events, when God and his servants are to be obeyed? And then we see how pusillanimous are those who profess to be God's ambassadors, and claim to themselves the name of Pastors. As, then, teachers dare not faithfully to perform their office, so on the other hand courtly princes are so devoted to themselves and to their own prudence, that they are unwilling to undertake duties which are unpopular. On this account, then, this passage, with all its circumstances, ought to be carefully noticed.

Jeremiah, then, *wrote in a book all the evil which was to come on Babylon*, even *all those words*, (he refers to the prophecies which we have seen;) *and Jeremiah said to Seraiah*,[1] &c. Here the boldness of Jeremiah comes to view, that he hesitated not to command Seraiah to read this book when he came to Babylon and had seen it. To see it, is not mentioned here without reason, for the splendour of that city might have astonished Seraiah. Then the Prophet here seasonably meets the difficulty, and bids him to disregard the height of the walls and towers; and that however Babylon might dazzle the eyes of others, yet he was to look down, as from on high, on all that pomp and pride: *When thou enterest* the city, *and hast seen it, then read this book*. The verb קרא, *kora*, means to call, to proclaim, and also to read. Then Seraiah must have read this book by himself; nor do I doubt but that the words ought to be so understood, as we shall see. It was not then necessary for Seraiah to have a pulpit, or in a public way to read the book to an assembled people; but it was sufficient to read it privately by himself, without any witnesses; and this may be gathered from the context.

And thou shalt say, Jehovah, thou hast spoken against this place. It hence appears that Seraiah was commanded to read the book, not for the benefit of hearers, for they would have been doubly deaf to the words of Seraiah. And it is not probable that the Hebrew language was then familiar to the Chaldeans. There is a great affinity, as it is well known, in the languages, but there is also some difference.

[1] That the connexion may appear more evident, the 60th verse and the first sentence in the 61st ought to be put within a parenthesis; for "the word which Jeremiah commanded Seraiah," mentioned in the 59th verse, is what follows, "When thou comest to Babylon," &c.—*Ed.*

But we conclude, from this passage, that the reading was in a chamber, or in some secret place; for Seraiah is bidden to fix all his thoughts on God, and to address his words to him. He did not then undertake the work or office of a preacher, so as openly to proclaim all these things to the Babylonians. But having inspected the city, he was to read the book by himself, that is, what had been written.

And this also deserves to be noticed; for however courageous we may be, yet our constancy and boldness are more apparent when we have to do with men than when we are alone, and God is the only witness; for when no one sees us, we tremble; and though we may have previously appeared to have manly courage, yet when alone, fear lays hold on us. There is hardly one in a hundred who is so bold as he ought to be when God alone is witness. But shame renders us courageous and constrains us to be firm, and the vigour which is almost extinct in private is roused in public. As, then, ambition almost always rules in men, this passage ought to be carefully noticed, where the Prophet commands Seraiah to deal alone with God, and, though no mortal was present, to strengthen himself, by relying on the certain and infallible fidelity of God; *Thou shalt* then *say, Jehovah*, &c. And it is doubtless a real experiment of faith, when we consider within ourselves the promises of God, and go not forth before the public to avow our firmness; for when any one in silence acknowledges God to be true, and strengthens himself in his promises, and so disregards the false judgments of all, that were he alone in the world, he would not yet despond,—this is a true and real trial of faith.

Thou shalt then *say, Jehovah, thou hast spoken against this place.* The design of the words was, that Seraiah might feel assured that God was true, and embrace in his presence what he read, and not doubt but that the word, which came from God, would, in due time, be accomplished: how so? because God is true. The word *Jehovah,* then, ought to be regarded as emphatical; *and thou shalt say, Thou, Jehovah, hast spoken against this place;* that is, neither Jeremiah, nor any other mortal, is the author of this prophecy; but thou, O Lord, has dictated to thy servant whatever is contained in this volume.

To destroy it, so that there should not be an inhabitant in it, neither man nor beast: how so? *because it shall be reduced to desolations,* or the particle כי, *ki,* may be taken adversatively, *but it shall be reduced to perpetual desolations.*[1]

He afterwards adds, *And when thou hast made an end of reading, thou shalt tie a stone to it and cast it into the Euphrates, and shalt say, Thus sink shall Babylon.* Here is added an external symbol to confirm the faith of Seraiah. We must yet bear in mind, that this was not said to Seraiah for his own sake alone, but that the people might also know, that the king's messenger, who had been sent for the sake of conciliating, was also the messenger of God and of the Prophet, who might have otherwise been despised by the people. When, therefore, the faithful knew this, they were in no ordinary way confirmed in the truth of the prophecy. Jeremiah, then, not only consulted the benefit of Seraiah alone, but that of all the godly; for though this was unknown for a long time, yet the messenger afterwards acknowledged that this command had been given him by Jeremiah, and that he took the book and cast it into the Euphrates. This, then, was given as a confirmation to all the godly.

As to the symbols by which God sealed the prophecies in former times, we have spoken elsewhere; I therefore pass them by slightly now: only we ought to bear in mind this one thing, that these signs were only temporary sacraments; for ordinary sacraments are permanent, as the holy supper and baptism. But the sign mentioned here was temporary, and referred, as they say, to a special action: it yet had the force and character of a sacrament, as to its use, the confirmation of this prophecy. Seraiah was then bidden to *tie a stone* to the book, and then to *cast it into the Euphrates:* why so? that the volume might not swim on the surface of the water, but be sunk down to the bottom; and the application follows, *Thou shalt say,* &c. We see that words ought ever to be connected with signs. We hence conclude how fatuous the Papists are, who practise many ceremonies,

[1] Literally the words are,—

For desolations of perpetuity shall it (or she) be.

Babylon is sometimes referred to as masculine, and sometimes as feminine.—*Ed.*

but without knowledge. They are, indeed, dead and empty things, whatever signs men may devise for themselves, except God's word be added. *Thou shalt* then *say, Thus sink shall Babylon, and shall not rise from the evil which I shall bring upon her.* In short, Seraiah was commanded, as the Prophet's messenger, to predict by himself concerning the fall of Babylon; but it was for the sake of all the godly, who were afterwards taught what had been done.[1]

The conclusion follows, *Thus far the words of Jeremiah.* We have said that the prophets, after having spoken in the Temple, or to the people, afterwards collected brief summaries, and that these contained the principal things: from these the prophetic books were made up. For Jeremiah did not write the volume as we have it at this day, except the chapters; and it appears evident that it was not written in the order in which he spoke. The order of time is not, then, everywhere observed; but the scribes were careful in this respect, that they collected the summaries affixed to the doors of the Temple; and so they added this conclusion, *Thus far the words of Jeremiah.* But this, in my view, is not to be confined to the prophecies respecting the fall of Babylon; for I doubt not but that the scribe who had collected all his prophecies, added these words, that he had thus far transcribed the words of Jeremiah.

We hence conclude that the last chapter is not included in the prophetic book of Jeremiah, but that it contains history only as far as was necessary to understand what is here taught: for it appears evident that many parts of the prophecy could not be understood without the knowledge of this history. As to the book of Lamentations, we know that

[1] *Calvin* takes no notice here of the verb which closes this sentence, ויעפו; but in his version he renders it, "and they shall fly," or they shall be wearied. Critics know not what to make of it: it is omitted in the *Sept.*, and rendered by the *Vulg.*, "and it shall be dissolved;" by the *Syr.*, "but they shall be thrown down;" and by the *Targ.*, "and they shall fail." It is left out in no MS. *Blayney*, following the *Sept.*, omits it. The best explanation is given by *Junius* and *Tremelius*, "though they may weary themselves," that is, the citizens of Babylon: their attempt to rise and resist their enemies would be ineffectual, however much they might toil in the effort.

The emendator, *Houbigant*, proposes to read the word, ויספו, "and they shall come to an end." This agrees nearly with the *Targ.*, "and they shall fail."—*Ed.*

it was a work distinct from the prophecies of Jeremiah: there is, then, no wonder that it has been added, *Thus far the words of Jeremiah.*

PRAYER.

Grant, Almighty God, that since thou hast deigned to choose us for thy people, we may not doubt but that our enemies will be before thee like Babylon, so that when thou hast chastised us, thou wilt at length, by a fatal and perpetual destruction, so lay them prostrate, that they shall rise up no more; and when thou hast killed the body, manifest thyself as our deliverer, until we shall at length be gathered into that celestial kingdom which has been prepared for us by thine only-begotten Son.—Amen.

[The last chapter, as it is historical, and all its parts have been elsewhere handled, holy Calvin did not expound in his Lectures, that he might not burden the hearers with superfluous repetitions: however, to render the book complete, we here add it.]

CHAPTER LII.

1. Zedekiah *was* one and twenty years old when he began to reign; and he reigned eleven years in Jerusalem; and his mother's name *was* Hamutal, the daughter of Jeremiah of Libnah.

2. And he did *that which was* evil in the eyes of the Lord, according to all that Jehoiakim had done.

3. For through the anger of the Lord it came to pass in Jerusalem and Judah, till he had cast them out from his presence, that Zedekiah rebelled against the king of Babylon.

4. And it came to pass, in the ninth year of his reign, in the tenth month, in the tenth *day* of the month, *that* Nebuchadrezzar king of Babylon came, he and all his army,

1. Viginti et unius anni erat Sedechias quando regnavit, et undecim annis regnavit in Jerusalem, et nomen matris ejus Hamutal filia Jeremiæ de Libnah.

2. Et fecit malum in oculis Jehovæ, secundum omnia quæ fecerat Jehoiakim:

3. Nempe propter furorem Jehovæ qui fuit contra Jerusalem et Jehudah, donec projiceret eos à facie sua, rebellavit Sedechias contra regem Babylonis.[1]

4. Fuit autem anno nono regni ejus, mense decimo, decima mensis, venit Nabuchadrezer rex Babylonis, ipse et universus exercitus ejus adversus Jerusalem, et castrametati sunt

[1] The best rendering of this verse is by *Venema*,—
Therefore the height of the wrath of Jehovah (that is, the extreme wrath of Jehovah) was on Jerusalem and Judah, until he cast them from his presence: and Zedekiah rebelled against the king of Babylon.
The same words, in 2 Kings xxiv. 20, ought to be rendered in the same way.—*Ed.*

against Jerusalem, and pitched against it, and built forts against it round about.

contra eam, et ædificaverunt contra eam munitionem undique.

5. So the city was besieged unto the eleventh year of king Zedekiah.

5. Venitque civitas in obsidionem usque ad undecimum annum regis Sedechiæ.

6. And in the fourth month, in the ninth *day* of the month, the famine was sore in the city, so that there was no bread for the people of the land.

6. Mense quarto, nona mensis, invaluit fames in urbe, (*adeo*) ut non esset panis populo terræ.

7. Then the city was broken up, and all the men of war fled, and went forth out of the city by night, by the way of the gate between the two walls, which *was* by the king's garden; (now the Chaldeans *were* by the city round about;) and they went by the way of the plain.

7. Et dirupta fuit urbs, et omnes viri bellatores fugerunt, exieruntque de urbe nocte per viam portæ (*quæ erat*) inter duos muros, qui (erant) juxta hortum regis (Chaldæi autem erant juxta urbem per circuitum) abieruntque per viam solitudinis.

8. But the army of the Chaldeans pursued after the king, and overtook Zedekiah in the plains of Jericho; and all his army was scattered from him.

8. Persecutus verò est exercitus Chaldæorum regem, apprehenderuntque Sedechiam in desertis Jericho; quia omnis exercitus ejus dispersus est ab eo.

9. Then they took the king, and carried him up unto the king of Babylon to Riblah, in the land of Hamath; where he gave judgment upon him.

9. Comprehenderunt igitur regem, et duxerunt eum ad regem Babylonis in Riblatah, in terram Chamath, qui disceptavit cum eo judiciis.

10. And the king of Babylon slew the sons of Zedekiah before his eyes: he slew also all the princes of Judah in Riblah.

10. Et jugulavit rex Babylonis filios Sedechiæ in oculis ejus, et etiam omnes principes Jehudah jugulavit in Riblatah:

11. Then he put out the eyes of Zedekiah; and the king of Babylon bound him in chains, and carried him to Babylon, and put him in prison till the day of his death.

11. Oculos autem Sedechiæ excæcavit, et vinxit catenis, adducique fecit eum rex Babylonis, Babylonem, et posuit eum in domo carceris[1] usque ad diem quo mortuus est.

12. Now, in the fifth month, in the tenth *day* of the month, (which *was* the nineteenth year of Nebuchadrezzar king of Babylon,) came Nebuzar-adan, captain of the guard, *which* served the king of Babylon, into Jerusalem,

12. Mense autem quinto, decima mensis[2] (is annus erat decimus nonus annus regis Nabuchadrezer regis Babylonis) venit Nebuzaradan princeps militum, qui stabat[3] coram rege Babylonis, in Jerusalem,

[1] Literally, "in the house of visitations," that is, of punishments.—*Ed.*

[2] It is "the seventh" in 2 Kings xxv. 8. This discrepancy is accounted for by *Blayney* and others, by supposing a typographical mistake of putting the numeral ז, *seven*, for י, *ten*, or *vice versa.*—*Ed.*

[3] It is עבד, "served," in 2 Kings xxv. 8; but the meaning is the same. To stand before one is a phrase which designates the office of one who serves. See Luke i. 29. It would be better, in rendering this part of the verse, to change the place of the verb, to come,—"Nebuzar-adan, the prince of the executioners, who stood before the king of Babylon, came to Jerusalem."—*Ed.*

13. And burnt the house of the Lord, and the king's house; and all the houses of Jerusalem, and all the houses of the great *men*, burnt he with fire.

13. Et incendit domum Jehovæ et domum regis, atque cunctas domos Jerusalem, et omnem domum magnam combussit igni:[1]

14. And all the army of the Chaldeans, that *were* with the captain of the guard, brake down all the walls of Jerusalem round about.

14. Omnesque muros Jerusalem undique destruxerunt totus exercitus Chaldæorum, qui erat cum magistro militum.

15. Then Nebuzar-adan, the captain of the guard, carried away captive *certain* of the poor of the people, and the residue of the people that remained in the city, and those that fell away, that fell to the king of Babylon, and the rest of the multitude.

15. De pauperibus autem populi, et de reliquo populo qui remanserant in urbe, et de transfugis qui transfugerunt ad regem Babylonis, et de reliquiis multitudinis transmigrare fecit Nebuzaradan magister militum.[2]

16. But Nebuzar-adan, the captain of the guard, left *certain* of the poor of the land for vine-dressers, and for husbandmen.

16. De pauperibus verò terræ reliquit Nebuzaradan magister militum vinitores et agricolas.

17. Also the pillars of brass that *were* in the house of the Lord, and the bases, and the brazen sea that *was* in the house of the Lord, the Chaldeans brake, and carried all the brass of them to Babylon.

17. Et columnas æreas quæ erant in domo Jehovæ, et bases et mare æreum quod erat in domo Jehovæ confregerunt Chaldæi, et detulerunt omne æs eorum Babylonem.

18. The caldrons also, and the snuffers, and the bowls, and the spoons, and all the vessels of brass wherewith they ministered, took they away.

18. Lebetes quoque et scopas et psalteria et pelves et cochlearia et omnia vasa ærea quibus ministrabant, tulerunt.

19. And the basons, and the firepans, and the bowls, and the caldrons, and the candlesticks, and the spoons, and the cups; *that* which *was* of gold *in* gold, and *that* which *was* of silver *in* silver, took the captain of the guard away.

19. Et hydrias et thuribula et pelves et ollas et candelabra, et mortariola et cyathos, quæ aurea, aurea, et quæ argentea, argentea,[3] tulit magister militum.

[1] The literal rendering is, "even every great house burnt he with fire." This clause qualifies the former one.—*Ed.*

[2] Though in the parallel passages in chapter xxxix. 9, and in 2 Kings xxv. 11, the words, "Some of the poor of the people," are not found, yet the *Vulg.*, the *Syr.*, and the *Targ.*, retain them here, and they are found in all the MSS. except one. Some of the poor of the city were evidently left, as well as some of the poor of the land. In the following words, the *Vulg.* for the most part is followed, which is not correct: the words should be, "et reliquum populum," and, "et reliquias multitudinis." And the last words should be, "even the remnant (or remainder) of the multitude," that is, of the people that formerly inhabited the city. See chapter xxxix. 9.—*Ed.*

[3] "Which gold, gold, and which silver, silver:" אשר, "which," repeated, may be rendered here, "some;" and the repetition of "gold," and of "silver," is the same as to say, that some of the vessels were pure gold, and that some were pure silver: then the version would be this, "some gold of gold," *i.e.*, pure gold, "and some silver of silver," *i.e.*, pure silver, there being no mixture in either.—*Ed.*

20. The two pillars, one sea, and twelve brazen bulls that *were* under the bases, which king Solomon had made in the house of the Lord: the brass of all these vessels was without weight.

21. And *concerning* the pillars, the height of one pillar *was* eighteen cubits; and a fillet of twelve cubits did compass it; and the thickness thereof *was* four fingers; *it was* hollow.

22. And the chapiter of brass *was* upon it; and the height of one chapiter *was* five cubits, with net-work and pomegranates upon the chapiters round about, all *of* brass: the second pillar also and the pomegranates *were* like unto these.

23. And there were ninety and six pomegranates on a side; *and* all the pomegranates upon the net-work *were* an hundred round about.

24. And the captain of the guard took Seraiah the chief priest, and Zephaniah the second priest, and the three keepers of the door:

25. He took also out of the city an eunuch, which had the charge of the men of war; and seven men of them that were near the king's person, which were found in the city; and the principal scribe of the host, who mustered the people of the land; and threescore men of the people of the land, *that were* found in the midst of the city.

26. So Nebuzar-adan, the captain of the guard, took them, and brought them to the king of Babylon to Riblah.

27. And the king of Babylon smote them, and put them to death in Riblah, in the land of Hamath. Thus Judah was carried away captive out of his own land.

28. This *is* the people whom Nebuchadrezzar carried away captive: In the seventh year three thousand Jews, and three and twenty:

29. In the eighteenth year of Nebuchadrezzar he carried away captive from Jerusalem eight hundred thirty and two persons:

30. In the three and twentieth year of Nebuchadrezzar, Nebuzar-

20. Columnas duas, mare unum, et boves duodecim æreos, qui erant sub basibus quas fecerat rex Solomo in domo Jehovæ, non erat pondus æris eorum omnium (*nempe*) vasorum istorum.

21. Quod ad columnas, octodecim cubitorum erat altitudo columnæ unius, et filum duodecim cubitorum circuibat eam, cujus crassitudo (*quæ*) erat quatuor digitorum; (erat) vacua.

22. Capitellum autem quod erat super eam æreum; altitudo verò capitelli unius, quinque cubitorum erat, et reticulum, et malogranata super capitellum per circuitum, omnia ærea et similia erant columnæ secundæ et malogranata.

23. Fuerunt autem malogranata nonaginta et sex ad plagam (unam) omnia malogranata, centum super reticulum per circuitum.

24. Tulit quoque magister militum Seraiah sacerdotem primum, et Sephaniah sacerdotem secundum, et tres custodes liminis.

25. Et de urbe tulit eunuchum unum, qui erat præpositus super viros bellatores, et septem viros ex iis qui videbant faciem regis, qui inventi sunt in urbe, et scribam principem militiæ, qui colligebat ad militiam populum terræ, et sexaginta viros de populo terræ, qui inventi sunt in medio urbis.

26. Tulit, inquam, eos Nebuzar-adan magister militum, et deduxit eos ad regem Babylonis in Riblatha:

27. Et percussit eos rex Babylonis, et interfecit eos in Riblatha in terra Chamath; et translatus est Jehudah de terra sua.

28. Iste est populus quem transferre fecit Nabuchadrezer, anno septimo, Judæos tria millia et viginti tres.

29. Anno decimo octavo Nabuchadrezer transferre fecit de Jerusalem animas octingentas triginta duas.

30. Anno tertio et vigesimo Nabuchadrezer, transferre fecit Nebuzar-

adan, the captain of the guard, carried away captive of the Jews seven hundred forty and five persons: all the persons *were* four thousand and six hundred.

31. And it came to pass, in the seven and thirtieth year of the captivity of Jehoiachin king of Judah, in the twelfth month, in the five and twentieth *day* of the month, *that* Evil-merodach king of Babylon, in the *first* year of his reign, lifted up the head of Jehoiachin king of Judah, and brought him forth out of prison,

32. And spake kindly unto him, and set his throne above the throne of the kings that *were* with him in Babylon,

33. And changed his prison-garments; and he did continually eat bread before him all the days of his life.

34. And *for* his diet, there was a continual diet given him of the king of Babylon, every day a portion, until the day of his death, all the days of his life.

adan magister militum, Judæorum animas septingentas quadraginta quinque; omnes animæ quatuor millia et sexcentæ.[1]

31. Fuit autem tricesimo septimo anno transmigrationis Jehoiakin regis Jehudah, duodecimo mense, vicesima quinta mensis, elevavit Evil-merodach rex Babylonis, anno regni sui, caput Jehoiakin regis Jehudah, et eduxit eum de domo carceris;

32. Loquutusque est eum eo bona, et posuit thronum ejus super thronum regum, qui erant secum in Babylone;

33. Et mutavit vestimenta carceris ejus, et comedebat panem coram eo semper omnibus diebus vitæ suæ.

34. Et portio ejus, portio perpetua dabatur ei a rege Babylonis, per singulos dies ejus, usque ad diem quo mortuus est, omnibus diebus vitæ ejus.

[1] The number here given is to be restricted to the years here specified, that is, the *seventh*, the *eighteenth*, and the *twenty-third* of Nebuchadnezzar's reign. We read of other captivities; that is, in the *third* year of Jehoiakim's reign, (Dan. i. 1,) which was the *first* of Nebuchadnezzar; and in the *eighth* year of his reign, (2 Kings xxiv. 12,) when Jehoiachin was taken prisoner, and with him not less than ten thousand people, (2 Kings xxiv. 14.)

We have no account of the number in the first captivity, when Daniel was taken to Babylon. The largest number was in the *eighth* year of Nebuchadnezzar's reign, even *ten* thousand. The amount of *three* captivities mentioned here, the last of which must have been after the murder of Gedaliah, is *four* thousand *six* hundred. All these being men, and of full age, there must have been many women and children. It has been thought that all, taken captive all these times, could not have been less than fifty thousand.—*Ed.*

Laus Deo.

PRELECTIONS OF JOHN CALVIN

ON

THE LAMENTATIONS OF JEREMIAH.

PREFACE.

I UNDERTAKE now to explain THE LAMENTATIONS OF JEREMIAH. We must inquire when the Book was composed by the Prophet, and also what was the object of the author. Grossly mistaken was *Jerome*, who thought that it is the ELEGY which JEREMIAH composed on the death of Josiah; for we see nothing here that is suitable to that event. There is indeed mention made in one place of a king, but what is said there cannot be applied to Josiah; for he was never driven into exile, but was buried at Jerusalem with his fathers. From the whole contents of the Book we may justly conclude, that it was written after the city was destroyed, and the people led into exile.

Some think that JEREMIAH, before this calamity happened, historically described it, and that he thus prophesied of what was future and yet unknown. But this is by no means probable; for JEREMIAH here sets before the eyes of all, those things which they knew as facts; and we shall easily discover that his manner of stating things is wholly different from that used in prophetic writings. There is, then, no doubt but that JEREMIAH, after the city was destroyed and the Temple burnt, bewailed the miserable state of his own nation, not after the manner of heathens, but that he might shew that even in so disastrous a state of things some benefit might be derived from what he says. And this is what ought to be especially noticed; for except we bear this in mind, the

Book will lose its peculiar interest: but if we direct our minds to that desolation, which wholly dejected not only the people in general, but also the Prophet himself, so that he lost all hope, we may surely hence derive no small benefit. It is an easy thing to extol in high terms the favour of God in prosperity, and also to exhort those who have reasons to hope well to entertain confidence, and to bring forward God's promises, that the minds of the godly may recumb on them; but when things are in a state of despair, and God seems to have forsaken his Church, since prophecy still remains in its force, and God appears as stretching forth his hand to the miserable, and to such as are almost in a hopeless state, we hence derive much benefit, and this is the chief use of what is taught here. But we see that Jeremiah, when the kingdom had fallen, when the king with all his children was exposed to extreme disgrace, when in short the covenant of God seemed wholly abolished, still continued to discharge his office, which he certainly did not do in vain.

When, therefore, he understood that his teaching would not be without fruit, he was thus induced to speak first of God's judgments; secondly, to exhort the people to repentance; thirdly, to encourage them to hope; and lastly, to open the door for prayer to God, so that the people in their extremities might venture to flee to God's mercy; which could not have been done without faith.

We now in a measure understand for what purpose this Book was written by JEREMIAH: his object was to shew that though nothing in the land appeared but desolation, and the Temple being destroyed, the Covenant of God appeared as made void, and thus all hope of salvation had been cut off, yet hope still remained, provided the people sought God in true repentance and faith; and he thus proceeded in the course of his calling, and made it evident that his doctrine would not be without benefit.

He indeed bewails, as I have said, the extreme calamity of his people; but he mingles with his lamentations the doctrine of repentance and faith: For, on the one hand, he shews that the people suffered a just punishment for the many iniquities, of which they could not have been healed;

and then, on the other hand, he gives them some intimations of God's mercy, that in death itself the Jews might seek life, nay, that in the lowest depths they might know that God would be propitious to them. He at length by his own example stimulates them to pray; but prayer is founded on faith. It then follows, that JEREMIAH, when the people had become wholly alienated from the worship of God, yet spent his labour in collecting together the remnant. Though, then, the whole Church was not only in the greatest disorder, but also reduced as it were almost to nothing, yet JEREMIAH constructed some sort of building out of the ruins. This is the substance of this Book.

The Greek Translators call this Book Θρήνους, LAMENTATIONS, and very properly, as also the Hebrews call it קינות, *kinut;* though the common name or title is איכה, *aike,* from the first word in it. But when they wish to express what the Book contains, they call it קינות, *kinut,* LAMENTATIONS.

Let us now proceed to the words; for what I have now briefly touched upon, can be more fully explained as we go on.

CHAPTER I.

Lecture First.

1. How doth the city sit solitary *that was* full of people! *how* is she become as a widow! she *that was* great among the nations, *and* princess among the provinces, *how* is she become tributary!	1. Quomodo sedet solitaria civitas, quæ abundavit populo! facta est tanquam vidua, quæ magna fuit in gentibus! quæ dominata est in provinciis, redacta est ad tributum!

THE Prophet could not sufficiently express the greatness of the calamity, except by expressing his astonishment. He then assumes the person of one who on seeing something new and unexpected is filled with amazement. It was indeed a thing incredible; for as it was a place chosen for God to dwell in, and as the city Jerusalem was not only the royal throne of God, but also as it were his earthly sanctuary, the city might have been thought exempted from all danger. Since it had been said, "Here is my rest for ever, here will I dwell," (Ps. cxxxii. 14,) God seemed to have raised that city above the clouds, and to have rendered it free from all earthly changes. We indeed know that there is nothing fixed and certain in the world, and that the greatest empires have been reduced to nothing; but the state of Jerusalem did not depend on human protection, nor on the extent of its dominion, nor on the abundance of men, nor on any other defences whatever, but it was founded by a celestial decree, by the promise of God, which is not subject to any mutations. When, therefore, the city fell, uprooted from its foundations, so that nothing remained, when the Temple was disgracefully plundered and then burnt by enemies, and further, when the king was driven into exile, his children slain in his presence, and also the princes, and when the people were scattered here and there, exposed to every contumely and reproach, was it not a horrible and monstrous thing?

It was not, then, without reason that the Prophet exclaimed, *How!* for no one could have ever thought that such a thing would have happened; and then, after the event, no one with a calm mind could have looked on such a spectacle, for innumerable temptations must have come to their minds; and this thought especially must have upset the faith of all—"What does God mean? How is it that he has promised that this city would be perpetual? and now there is no appearance of a city, and no hope of restoration in future." As, then, this so sad a spectacle might not only disturb pious minds, but also upset them and sink them in the depths of despair, the Prophet exclaims, *How!* and then says, *How sits the city solitary,* which had much people! Here, by a comparison, he amplifies the indignity of the fact; for, on the one hand, he refers to the flourishing state of Jerusalem before the calamity, and, on the other hand, he shews how the place had in a manner been turned into darkness. For this change, as I have said, was as though the sun had fallen from heaven; for the sun has no firmer standing in heaven than Jerusalem had on earth, since its preservation was connected with the eternal truth of God. He then says that this city had many people, but that now it was sitting *solitary.* The verb to sit, is taken in Hebrew in a good and in a bad sense. Kings are said to sit on their thrones; but to sit means sometimes to lie prostrate, as we have before seen in many places. Then he says that Jerusalem was lying solitary, because it was desolate and forsaken, though it had before a vast number of people.

He adds, *How is she become,* &c.; for the word *how,* איכה, *aike,* ought to be repeated, and applied to both clauses. *How,* then, *is she become as a widow, who was great among the nations!*[1] He says that Jerusalem had not only been full of citizens, but had also extended its power through many nations; for it is well known that many contiguous nations were tributary to it under David and Solomon. And to the same purpose is what follows, *She who ruled among provinces is become tributary!* that is, is become subject to a tribute. This phrase is taken from Deuteronomy xxviii., for the prophets were wont freely to borrow expressions from Moses, that chief teacher and prophet, as we shall presently see again.

We now then see the meaning of the Prophet. He wonders at the destruction of the city Jerusalem, and regarded it as a prodigy, which not only disturbed the minds of men, but in a manner confounded them. And by this mode of speaking he shews something of human infirmity; for they must be void of all feeling who are not seized with amazement at such a mournful sight. The Prophet then spoke

[1] The word is not repeated in the early Versions, nor by *Blayney* and *Henderson.* The word איכה, means properly, "Whence thus?" and it may be rendered, "How *is* this?" and the passage would be more emphatic,—

1. How *is* this? alone sits the city, *that was* full of people!
   Like a widow is she *that was* great among nations!
   A princess among provinces is under tribute!
2. Weeping she weeps in the night, and her tear on her cheek!
   None to her a comforter of all her lovers!
   All her friends have deceived her, they are become her enemies!

These were the various things which created astonishment in the Prophet. —*Ed.*

not only according to his own feelings, but also according to those of all others; and he deplored that calamity as it were in the person of all. But he will hereafter apply a remedy to this astonishment. For when we thus exaggerate evils, we at the same time sharpen our grief; and thus it happens that we at length become overwhelmed with despair; and despair kindles rage, so that men clamour against God. But the Prophet so mourned, and was in such a way amazed, that he did not yet indulge his grief nor cherish his amazement; but as we shall see, he restrained himself, lest the excess of his feelings should carry him beyond due bounds. It then follows,—

2. She weepeth sore in the night, and her tears *are* on her cheeks; among all her lovers she hath none to comfort *her:* all her friends have dealt treacherously with her; they are become her enemies.	2. Plorando ploravit noctu, et lachrymæ ejus super genas ejus, non est ei consolator ex omnibus amicis ejus, et omnes socii ejus perfidè egerunt cum ea, fuerunt illi inimici.

Jeremiah still pursues the same subject, for he could not have spoken briefly and in a few words of things so bitter and mournful; and he seems to have felt deeply the ruin of his own country. And when we wish to penetrate into the hearts of those whose sorrow we desire to alleviate, it is necessary that they should understand that we sympathize with them. For when any one stronger than another seeks to mitigate another's grief, he will be disregarded if what he adduces seems to proceed from an unfeeling barbarity. Had, then, Jeremiah spoken as it were in contempt, he could have hardly hoped for any fruit from his teaching, for the Jews would have thought him void of all human feelings. This, then, is the reason why he bewails, as one of the people, the calamity of the city. He did not, however, dissemble in any degree in the history he related; but we know that God's servants, while they speak in earnest, do not yet forget prudence; for they regard in this respect what is useful; and their doctrine ought in a manner to be so regulated as to produce effect on the hearers.

He then says that the weeping of Jerusalem was continual; for he says first, *Weeping she wept,* and then, *in the night;* by which words he means that there was no intermission.

For the night is given us for rest, and God intends some relaxation to men by the interchange of nights and days. When, therefore, the Prophet says that Jerusalem, *weeping, wept in the night,* he intimates that her sorrow, as I have stated, was continual. Then he adds, *her tears are on her cheeks.* Some render it jaws, but improperly; the word לחי, *lachi,* indeed means a jaw, but it is to be taken for cheeks, or cheek-bones. Then he means that tears were so profuse as to wet the whole face. It is possible in weeping to restrain tears; but when they flow over the whole face and cover the cheeks, it is an evidence of great mourning. This, then, is the reason why the Prophet says that tears were on her cheeks; for he wished to shew that tears were profusely shed.

He says further, *She has no comforter.* And this circumstance ought to be noticed, for nothing is more seasonable in grief than to have friends near us to shew us kindness, to be partakers of sorrow, and to apply the consolations which may be had. But when no one feels for us in our evils, our sorrow is much more increased. The Prophet then says that there was no one seeking to soothe the griefs of Jerusalem. He adds, *of all thy friends.* Had Jerusalem been always forsaken, she could have borne it better when no comforter was present. For we see that miserable men are not thus soft and tender when very grievous calamities happen to them; they do not look here and there for friends to come to them, and why? because they have always been disregarded. It is, then, nothing new to them, even in the greatest adversities, to have no one to shew them any tokens of kindness. But when they who have had many friends, and thought that they would be always ready to bring them aid—when they see themselves forsaken, their sorrow becomes much more grievous. This, then, is what the Prophet means in saying, that of many friends there were none to comfort Jerusalem in her miseries.

There is not yet a doubt but that he indirectly reproved Jerusalem; and by אהבים, *aebim,* he understood *lovers,* as we have seen in other places; for as they thought themselves safe by means of ungodly treaties, the prophets say that they were like harlots who everywhere prostitute themselves and make gain by their lasciviousness, and allure lovers on every side. It was, therefore, right in the Prophet to remind the Jews in this place of that wickedness, even that they had conciliated at one time the Egyptians, at another, the Assyrians, like an impudent woman, who is not satisfied with her own husband, but draws lovers from all quarters. However this may be, he no doubt understands by *friends* those who confederated with them; and who were these? even those with whom the Jews had connected themselves, having disregarded God; for they had been sufficiently warned by the prophets not to form connexions with the heathens. But, at the same time, Jeremiah sets forth the atrocity of the thing by saying that there was none of all her friends a comforter to Jerusalem, because all her friends had *acted perfidiously*. It follows,—

3. Judah is gone into captivity because of affliction, and because of great servitude; she dwelleth among the heathen, she findeth no rest: all her persecutors overtook her between the straits.

3. Migravit (*tanquam in exilium*) Jehudah præ afflictione et præ magnitudine servitutis; ipsa sedet in gentibus, (*ad verbum*, sedens in gentibus,) non invenit requiem, (*vel, in præsenti tempore*, non invenit;) omnes apprehensores ejus apprehenderunt eam inter angustias.

Interpreters apply this, but in my view improperly, to the captivity of the people; on the contrary, the Prophet means that the Jews had been scattered and sought refuges when oppressed, as they were often, by the tyranny of their enemies, and then by degrees he advances to their exile; for he could not have said all things at the same time. Let, then, the order in which he speaks be observed: before he bewails their exile, he says that Judah had been *scattered;* for many, fleeing the cruelty of enemies, went into voluntary exile. We have before seen that many concealed themselves with the Moabites; nor is there a doubt but that many went into Egypt: in short, there was no country in which some of the Jews were not fugitives.

The real meaning, then, of the Prophet here is, that the Jews had *migrated*, that is, had left their own country and fled to other countries, because they were subjected to miseries and cruel servitude.

Some take the words in a passive sense, even that Judah migrated, because they had inhumanly oppressed their servants. But I suspect what has led them astray, they thought that exile is meant here; and then one mistake produces another; for it would have been absurd to say, that the Jews had migrated into exile on account of affliction, and had migrated willingly; for we know that they were violently driven by the Chaldeans. They did not, then, willingly migrate. When these two things could not be connected, they thought that the cruelty of the Jews is what is referred to, which they had exercised towards their own brethren. But the migration of which the Prophet speaks is improperly applied, as I have said, to the captivity; but on the contrary, he means those who had removed into different parts of the world, because this was more tolerable than their condition in their own country. And we hence learn how severely they had been harassed by the Chaldeans, for they had willingly fled away, though, as we know, exile is hard. We then conclude that it was a barbarous and a violent oppression, since the Prophet says, that the Jews thus went into exile of their own accord, and sought hiding-places either in Egypt or in the land of Moab, or among other neighbouring nations.[1]

[1] *Blayney* and *Horsley* agree in this view; but *Gataker*, *Henry*, and *Henderson* take the previous view, that is, that Judah went to exile on account of the oppression they practised, and the multiplied servitude they exacted, especially the servitude or slavery to which servants were subjected, as recorded in Jer. xxxiv. What confirms this view is the word "Judah," which, as it implies the greater part, could not be applied to the comparatively few who voluntarily migrated.

3. Removed is Judah for oppression and for much servitude;
She dwells among nations without finding rest;
All her pursuers seized her in the straits.

The *Targum* paraphrases "oppression" by mentioning orphans and widows, and "servitude," by referring to what servants were subjected to, as related in Jer. xxxiv. These were sins for which the Jews had often been threatened with banishment. "Pursuers" rather than "persecutors;" and to be "seized in (or, between) the straits," is, as Lowth says, a metaphor taken from hunters, who drive the game to narrow places, from which there is no escape.

Houbigant proposes to connect "oppression and servitude" with the following words, and not with the preceding,—

Removed is Judah; for oppression and for much servitude,
She dwells among the nations without finding rest.—*Ed.*

He afterwards adds another evil, that they never *found rest;* and lastly, that they had been *taken* by their enemies *between straits,* so that no escape was possible. It must have been a sad condition for the people to live in a foreign land; for we know that such a precarious life differs but little from death; and there were no contiguous nations by whom the Jews were not hated. When they then fled to such people, it was no small evil. But when they had nowhere a quiet abode, the indignity was still greater, and this is what the Prophet now refers to. But when we flee and tremblingly turn here and there, it is one of the greatest of evils to fall into the hands of enemies, and to be taken by them when we are enclosed as it were between two walls, or in a narrow passage, as some explain the word. It follows,—

4. The ways of Zion do mourn, because none come to the solemn feasts: all her gates are desolate; her priests sigh, her virgins are afflicted, and she *is* in bitterness.

4. Viæ Sion lugentes à non venientibus (*ad verbum;* quia non sint qui veniant) ad solennitatem; omnes portæ ejus solitariæ (vastatæ, שׁוֹמֵמִין;) sacerdotes ejus plorantes, virgines ejus afflictæ, et ipsa amaritudo ei (*hoc est,* ipsa in amaritudine, *ut vertit Hieronymus.*)

Jeremiah refers here to another cause of sorrow, that the worship of God had ceased, it having been interrupted; nay, it seemed to have become extinct for ever. He then says that the *ways of Sion mourned,* because none came to the feasts. The words are figurative, for we know that feelings belong not to ways; but the Prophet ascribes feeling to what is inanimate. And this sort of personification is more emphatical than if he had introduced the people as mourning. But when the Jews saw that God's worship had fallen, it was more grievous than to find themselves bereaved of children or of wives, or plundered of all their goods; for the more precious God's worship was to them, and the more religion was thought of, in which consisted the eternal salvation of their souls, the more severe and mournful was it to see the Church so scattered, that God could no longer be worshipped and invoked.

It is indeed true that God's worship was not tied to ceremonies; for Daniel never ceased to pray, and he was heard no less in his exile than if he came to the sacrifices with great solemnity to make an offering in the Temple. This is no doubt true; but as God had not in vain instituted these duties and rites of religion, the Prophet exhibits the thing itself by its symbols. As, then, feasts were testimonies of God's grace, it was the same as though the Jews were called together by a standard being lifted up, and as though God appeared in the midst of them. Hence the Prophet, referring to these external symbols, shews that the worship of God had in a manner ceased.

Her gates are solitary, or desolate; *her priests are in mourning, her virgins in afflictions; she is in bitterness.*[1] Now this passage reminds us, that when God afflicts his Church, however grievous it may be to see innocent men slain, blood shed promiscuously, the sexes, men and women, killed indiscriminately; and though it be a sad spectacle to see houses robbed and plundered, fields laid waste, and all things in a confusion, yet when all these things are compared with the abolition of God's worship, this passage reminds us that all these things ought to appear light to us. Though David greatly deplored his condition, because he was banished from the Temple, and did not as usual lead thither the assembly, when he was not the only one ejected from the sanctuary of God; yet when the sanctuary itself was destroyed, together with the altar, when there were no sacrifices, no thanksgiving, no praises; in short, no prayer, it was surely much more bitter.

This lamentation of the Prophet ought then to be carefully noticed, when he says, that *the ways of Sion mourned,* that no one went up *to the feasts.* What follows I pass over; I shall hereafter dwell more on these things when we advance towards the end of the narrative.

5. Her adversaries are the chief, her enemies prosper; for the Lord hath afflicted her for the multitude of her transgressions: her children

5. Fuerunt inimici ejus in caput; hostes ejus feliciter egerunt (fuerunt in pace, שלו;) quia Jehova afflixit eam super magnitudine scelerum

[1] Participles are used throughout this verse, which express the present state of things,—

The ways of Sion *are* mourning, for none *are* coming to the feasts;
All her gates *are* made desolate, her priests *are* sighing;
Her virgins *are* afflicted, and she, bitterness *is* to her.—*Ed.*

are gone into captivity before the enemy. | ejus; parvuli ejus profecti sunt in exilium coram adversario.

He first says that her *enemies had become the head;* and by this expression he doubtless means power; and this way of speaking he borrowed from Moses, for these are his words, "Thou shalt be the head and not the tail, in a high place, not obscure." (Deut. xxviii. 13.) He then says, that *enemies were the head,* that is, ruled over them. And the opposite of that is to be understood, even that they had become the tail, that is, were under the feet as it were of their enemies. And he says that her enemies had *acted successfully,* even *because Jehovah had afflicted her.* He here laments after the common practice, as ungodly men are wont to do; but he mixes instruction with his mourning, and shews that God, in a state of things so turbulent and confused, appeared as a righteous judge. He then recalled them to the consideration of God's hand, when he said that her enemies had acted successfully, because God had *afflicted her. Jerome* renders the words, "because Jehovah hath spoken." He derives the verb from הגה, *ege,* which means to speak or to meditate. But this is an evident mistake, as we shall find another presently in this very chapter. There is no doubt but that the Prophet intimates that the cause of all evils was, that God had afflicted her, even on account of the greatness of her impieties, or of her sins. He now then begins to shew that there is no reason why the Jews should be swallowed up with grief and despair, if only they considered whence their evils proceeded. He thus begins to call their attention to God's judgment. This indeed of itself would not have been sufficient; but he afterwards points out a fruitful source of consolation. But we shall see these things mentioned in their due order.

PRAYER.

Grant, Almighty God, that as the deformity of thy Church at this day is sufficient to dishearten us all, we may learn to look to thine hand, and know that the reward of our sins is rendered to us, and that we may not doubt but that thou wilt be our physician to heal our wound, provided we flee to thy mercy; and do thou so retain us in the assurance of thy goodness and paternal care, that we may not hesitate, even in extreme evils, to call on thee in the name of thine only-begotten Son, until we shall find by experience that never in vain are the prayers of those, who, relying on thy promises, patiently look for a remedy from thee alone, even in extreme evils, and also in death itself. —Amen.

Lecture Second.

We began yesterday to explain the passage where the Prophet says, that the enemies of Jerusalem had become *the head* and had *been successful.* It was a trial which must have grievously assailed the minds of the faithful, when they saw their enemies having fortune, as they commonly say, as it were in their own hand; for it appeared as though God shewed himself favourable to them. Hence the Prophet assigns the reason, lest the faithful should fall off from religion and the fear of God, and says that the whole of this proceeded from the just vengeance of God, it being his purpose to afflict his own Church; and he states not this alone, but adds, *on account of the greatness of her iniquities.* For ungodly men sometimes acknowledge that they have to do with God, but yet they murmur and think that God is unjust and cruel. Hence the Prophet not only taught the Jews that God was the author of the calamities which had happened, but at the same time reminded them that they were worthy of such a reward, not only because they had transgressed, but because they had added sins to sins; for this is what he means by *the greatness of iniquities.* But he will presently repeat this sentence and enlarge upon it: it is then enough now to state his object. It was for this cause, then, as he says, that *her little ones went into captivity before the adversary.*

It was, indeed, an indignity, calculated to imbitter the minds of the faithful, to see not only their young men but also infants so cruelly treated. For men always think that they have some just cause to contend with God, and especially when the case of infants is brought forward; who, then, is not disposed to say that God's vengeance exceeds its due limits? "If his purpose be," say they, "to punish men for their wickedness, why does he not restrain his wrath as to the innocent? for how have miserable infants sinned?" But the Prophet here checks such audacity, and says that God had just reasons for extending his vengeance even to the little ones.[1] It now follows,—

6. And from the daughter of Zion all her beauty is departed: her princes are become like harts *that* find no pasture, and they are gone without strength before the pursuer.	6. Et egressus est à filia Sion omnis decor ejus; fuerunt principes ejus tanquam cervi qui non inveni-unt pascuum; et profecti sunt abs-que virtute coram persequutore.

He continues the same subject. He says here that the daughter of Sion was denuded of all her ornaments. Now, we know what was the honour or dignity of that people; for Moses, in order to set forth the greatness of God's grace, exclaims, "What nation so illustrious under heaven!" (Deut. iv. 7.) As, then, the singular gifts of God had been conferred on that people, it was a very sad spectacle to see that city, which once possessed the highest glory, robbed of all its honour and covered with disgrace, as we shall hereafter see. He then says that all her *glory* was taken away from the daughter of Sion.

Now, there is no need to enumerate all the kinds of honour or glory which belonged to the city Jerusalem. But it may be said first, that God had chosen there a habitation for himself; and then a sacerdotal kingdom was there, —the people were holy to God—they were his heritage,— there God had deposited his covenant,—he deemed all the Jews his children, and his will was that they should in return count him as their Father. As, then, they had been enriched with so many ornaments and so superior, it is no wonder that the Prophet deplored the state of the city when stripped of all its glory.

[1] 5. Become have her oppressors the head,
Her enemies have prospered;
For Jehovah has afflicted her
For the number of her transgressions;
Her children are gone into captivity
Before the face of the oppressor.

The word צר, is not an "adversary," but an oppressor, one who straitens and oppresses another.—*Ed.*

He then adds, that *her princes were like famished harts:* for harts, as they are by nature swift, when pressed by want run as though they were flying. Since then the swiftness of that animal is so great, the Prophet says that the princes, who were wont to walk with so much gravity and to carry the appearance of great authority, had become swift, like harts oppressed with hunger; for they also laboured under the want of everything.[1] He adds that at length they *went away,* that is, they fled *before their pursuers without strength.* He intimates by these words that they dared not to contend with their enemies, but that they were so frightened that they fled, and thus proved that they were wholly disheartened and lifeless. It follows,—

7. Jerusalem remembered in the days of her affliction, and of her miseries, all her pleasant things that she had in the days of old, when her people fell into the hand of the enemy, and none did help her: the adversaries saw her, *and* did mock at her sabbaths.

7. Recordata est Jerusalem diebus afflictionis suæ et penuriæ suæ, omnium desiderabilium suorum, quæ fuerunt à diebus antiquis, cum caderet populus ejus in manu hostis et nullus auxiliator ei; viderunt hostes, subsannarunt (*vel,* riserunt) super sabbatho (*vel,* cessatione) ejus.

He confirms the former verse when he says, that *Jerusalem remembered her desirable things* when she was afflicted by God's hand, and reduced to extreme want. And he intimates by these words, that when Jerusalem was in its splendour, it did not sufficiently consider the blessings of God; for the despisers of God cram themselves with whatever flows from his bounty, and yet do not acknowledge him; for ingratitude is like an abyss which absorbs all the fulness of God's blessings. Then the Prophet intimates that when Jerusalem flourished in wealth and in abundance of all things, when it was adorned with singular gifts, she became as it were inebriated, and never considered as she ought to have done, the benefits which God had bestowed on her. And now, when she was reduced to want and surrounded with extreme miseries, she *remembered her desirable things,* even the glory before mentioned; for by desirable things he means those gifts in which Jerusalem excelled

[1] The idea here is somewhat different; the princes are compared to harts reduced and enfeebled by famine, so that they were driven by their enemies like a herd of tame cattle.—*Ed.*

as long as God manifested himself as a bountiful Father towards it.

I wonder how all have given this version, "Jerusalem remembered the days," &c. Some rightly explain the passage, but all agree in giving a wrong version. But the meaning is sufficiently evident, *Jerusalem remembered her desirable things in the days of her affliction and of her want*, or of her groaning, or of her transmigration; for some derive the word from רוד, *rud*, which means to complain, or to migrate. Hence they render it "exile," or migration. But others render it "complaint." Others, again, derive it from מרד, *mered*, which sometimes means to fail, and render it "want," or indigence. Why some have translated it "iniquities," I know not, and there is no reason for such a version. I do not approve of "complaint;" exile or want is the best word.[1]

The days of affliction he more clearly expresses, when he says, *When the people fell into the hand of the enemy, and there was no helper*. We now see what the Prophet means, even that Jerusalem was as it were roused from her lethargy when God afflicted her. For as the drunken, after being satiated, so sleep in their excess that they know and feel nothing, but seem half dead; so prosperity inebriated Jerusalem for a long time; but being at length awakened, she perceived whence she had fallen. As long, then, as she stood in her high place of honour, she did not consider God's indulgence towards her; but after she was stripped of all her blessings, and became deeply afflicted, she then *remembered her desirable things*, that is, she at length began to perceive what she had lost, because she had fallen from the grace of God.

We may hence gather a useful doctrine; for what the

[1] The versions and the *Targ.* are evidently wrong here, and are not consistent with one another. There is no meaning except ב be considered as understood before ימי, "days." The only difference among critics is about the meaning of מרוד. There is no different reading. It is rendered "rejections—ἀπωσμῶν," by the *Sept.*, "prevarication" by the *Vulg.*, and "punishment" by the *Syr.* *Parkhurst* and *Blayney* derive it from ירד, to come down, to descend. It means the descendings or abasements to which Jerusalem had been subjected, and has the same meaning in chap. iii. 19. "In the days of her affliction and of her abasements."—*Ed.*

Prophet relates of Jerusalem is seen almost in all mankind; but we must beware lest this should be true of us. For God has not only in a common manner dealt liberally hitherto with us, but he has also been pleased to favour us with evidences of favour even more than paternal; he has separated us from the unbelieving, and has bestowed on us many of his blessings. Let us now, then, take heed lest we become stupid while God deals liberally with us; but on the contrary, let us learn to appreciate the blessings of God, and consider the end for which they have been given us, otherwise what is said here of Jerusalem will happen to us; for being too late awakened, we shall know that we were happy when God shewed himself a father to us. We see the same thing exemplified in Adam the first man; for though God adorned him with excellent gifts, yet being not content with his lot, he wished to exalt himself beyond due limits; after he fell and was reduced to extreme want, he then began to know what he had previously been, and what he had become through his fall. (Gen. i. 26, 27; iii. 6, 7.) But as this testimony of the Prophet is peculiarly suitable to the Church, let us know that we are warned by the example of Jerusalem; so that when God shews to us his bounty, his gifts ought as they deserve, to be valued, lest when too late we shall at length begin to acknowledge how desirable had been our previous condition. Then, in a word, Jeremiah here reproves the stupidity of the people, who did not know how desirable was their state, until they were deprived and plundered of all their blessings. He also says, *from the days of old.* By these words he probably intimates that the course of God's kindness had been perpetual; for God had not for a short time been bountiful to that people, but had shewed them favours successively and continually.

When her people fell, &c. It was a heavier misery, because they had so long flourished. It is added, *Seen her have enemies, they laughed at her Sabbath,* or at her cessation, which I do not dislike. But they who render it "leisure," or idleness, either pervert or too much obscure the meaning of the Prophet. In the word "cessation," there is an irony, for the enemies did not simply laugh at cessation, but did so in mockery, as they took this opportunity to taunt them for their religion. We know that the Sabbaths of the Jews were always hated by the heathens; and they were thereby subjected to many reproaches; for by way of reproach they called the Jews Sabbatharians. And when they wished ignominiously to traduce the whole service of God, as under the law, they named it "Sabbaths." There is, then, no doubt but that the heathens reproachfully taunted the Jews because they observed the Sabbath; "See, now is the time to worship God." And we also see that God upbraided the Jews in a similar way by saying, "Until the land shall enjoy its Sabbaths." (Lev. xxvi. 43.) For when the Jews had the opportunity and leisure (when no enemies molested them) to observe the worship of God, they contemptuously profaned the Sabbaths. As, then, God's worship had been so disgracefully neglected by them, God said, "The land itself shall in your stead keep the Sabbath;" how? it shall not be ploughed, it shall not bring forth fruit. (Lev. xxvi. 34, 35.) That cessation was called by God Sabbath, but not without a taunt; for he cuttingly reproved the Jews for having violated the Sabbaths, as was also done by Jeremiah, (chap. xvii. 22, 27.)[1]

It then appears to me probable that taunts were cast by enemies against the Jews, that they might now have a long and a continual Sabbath, while the city was deserted and no one dwelt there. For it would have been cold and unmeaning to say that the enemies laughed at the cessation of it. The Prophet would have no doubt used a different word, if his purpose had been to point out the blasphemy

[1] There are in this verse four lines, while there are only three in all the rest; but there is no ground for supposing an interpolation, as some have thought; for it is found in every Hebrew copy and in the versions, and the *Targum*. As to the last word, it is rendered by the *Sept.*, "habitation," or according to the Alexandrian copy, "emigration;" by the *Vulg.* "sabbaths;" and by the *Syr.* "sorrow." The word is nowhere found to signify the Sabbath. It is either from שבה, to lead captive, as *Parkhurst* thinks, and means captivity, emigration; or from שבת, to cease, to come to an end, according to *Blayney* and *Henderson*, and may be rendered "discontinuance," *i.e.*, as a nation or a state, or "ruin." But the former meaning agreeing with the *Sept.* is to be preferred,—

When fall did her people, and she had no helper,
See her did oppressors, they laughed at her captivity.—*Ed.*

of enemies as to God's worship. *The enemies* then *saw and laughed at her cessation;* but this cessation they called by way of reproach Sabbatharian. It follows,—

8. Jerusalem hath grievously sinned; therefore she is removed: all that honoured her despise her, because they have seen her nakedness; yea, she sigheth, and turneth backward.	8. Peccatum peccavit Jerusalem (*hoc est,* sceleratè egit;) propterea in migrationem (*vel,* commotionem) facta est (*hoc est,* reddita fuit instabilis;) omnes qui honore eam persequebantur, spreverunt eam, quia viderunt turpitudinem (*vel,* fœditatem) ejus; etiam ipsa gemens, et conversa est retrorsum.

Here the Prophet expresses more clearly and strongly what he had briefly referred to, even that all the evil which the Jews suffered proceeded from God's vengeance, and that they were worthy of such a punishment, because they had not lightly offended, but had heaped up for themselves a dreadful judgment, since they had in all manner of ways abandoned themselves to impiety. This is the substance of what is said. We hence learn that the Prophet did not compose this song to lament the calamity of his own country as heathens were wont to do. An example of a heathen lamentation we have in Virgil:—

"Come is the great day and the unavoidable time
Of Dardania: we Trojans have been; Ilium has been,
And the great glory of the Teucrians: cruel Jupiter has to Argos
Transferred all things: the Danai rule in the burnt city."[1]

He also repeats the same sentiment in other words:—

"O country! O Ilium, the house of the gods! and the famous for war,
The camp of the Dardanidans! cruel Jupiter has to Argos
Transferred all things."[2]——

He thus mourns the destruction of Troy; but he complains of the cruelty of God, and calls him cruel Jupiter, because he was himself enraged, and yet the speaker was Pantheus the priest of Apollo. We hence see how the unbelieving, when they lament their own calamities, vomit

[1] "Venit summa dies et ineluctabile tempus
Dardaniæ: fuimus Troes; fuit Ilium et ingens
Gloria Teucrorum: ferus omnia Jupiter Argos
Transtulit: incensa Danai dominantur in urbe."
Virg. Æn. 2.

[2] "O patria! O divûm domus Ilium! et inclyta bello
Mœnia Dardanidum! ferus omnia Jupiter Argos
Transtulit."——
Æn. 2.

forth blasphemies against God, for they are exasperated by sorrow. Very different is the complaint of the Prophet from that of the ungodly ; for when he deplores the miseries of his people, he at the same time adds that God is a righteous avenger. He does not then accuse God of cruelty or of too much rigour, but reminds the people to humble themselves before God and to confess that they justly deserved all their evils.

The unbelieving do indeed sometimes mingle some words, by which they seem to give glory to God ; but they are evanescent, for they soon return to their perverseness. They are sometimes moderate, "If thou art turned by any entreaties." In that case they expostulate with God, as though he were deaf to the prayers of his servants. At length they break out into open blasphemies,—

> "After it seemed good to the gods to subvert the affairs of Asia
> And the undeserved nation of Priam."[1]——

They regarded the nation which had been cut off unworthy of such a punishment ; they called it an undeserved nation. Now, then, we perceive what is the difference between the unbelieving and the children of God. For it is common to all to mourn in adversities ; but the end of the mourning of the unbelieving is perverseness, which at length breaks out into rage, when they feel their evils, and they do not in the meantime humble themselves before God. But the faithful do not harden themselves in their mourning, but reflect on themselves and examine their own life, and of their own accord prostrate themselves before God, and willingly submit to the sentence of condemnation, and confess that God is just.

We hence now see how the calamity of the Church ought to be lamented by us, even that we are to return to this principle, that God is a just avenger, and does not punish common offences only, but the greatest sins, and that when he reduces us to extremities, he does so on account of the greatness of our sins, as also Daniel confessed. For it was

[1] "Postquam res Asiæ, Priamique evertere gentem
Immeritam visum Superis."——
Virg. Æn. 3.

not in few words that he declared that the people were worthy of exile and of the punishment which they suffered; but he accumulated words, "We have sinned, we have acted impiously, we have done wickedly, we have been transgressors." (Dan. ix. 5.) Nor was the Prophet satisfied without this enumeration, for he saw how great the impiety of the people had been, and how mad had been their obstinacy, not for a few years, but for that long time, during which they had been warned by the prophets, and yet they repented not, but always became worse and worse. Such, then, is the mode of speaking adopted here.

He says that *she was made a commotion*, that is, that she was removed from her country. There seems to be implied a contrast between the rest which had been promised to the Jews, and a wandering and vagrant exile; for, as we have seen, the Jews had not only been banished, but they had nowhere a quiet dwelling; it was even a commotion. This may at the same time be referred to the curse of the law, because they were to be for a commotion—for even the unbelieving shook their heads at them. But the word נידה, *nide,* ought properly to be applied to their exile, when the Jews became unfixed and vagrant.[1] It is added, that she was *despised* and treated reproachfully by *all who* before esteemed and *honoured* her. This also did not a little increase the grievousness of her calamity; she had been repudiated by her friends, by whom she had before been valued and honoured. The reason is mentioned, *because they saw her nakedness.* But the word properly means turpitude or ignominy. It is at length added, that *she even groaned and turned backward;* that is, that she was so oppressed with grief, that there was no hope of a remedy; for to turn backward means the same as to be deprived of all hope of restoration.[2] It now follows,—

[1] "Fluctuation," by the *Sept.;* "instable," by the *Vulg.;* "vagrant," or wandering, by the *Targ.;* and "horror," by the *Syr.* The verb means to remove; and the reference here is evidently to banishment, and not to uncleanness, as some take it, because the noun is sometimes so taken, persons being *removed* from society on account of uncleanness.—*Ed.*

[2] "To turn back" or backward, is a phrase which some regard as expressive of shame, as those who feel shame recede from the public view and hide themselves.—*Ed.*

9. Her filthiness *is* in her skirts; she remembereth not her last end; therefore she came down wonderfully: she had no comforter. O Lord, behold my affliction; for the enemy hath magnified *himself*.

9. Ignominia ejus in fimbriis ejus, non est recordata finis sui; et descendit mirabiliter, nemo consolator ei; vide, Jehova, afflictionem meam, quia magnificè se effert hostis (*ad verbum*, magnificatus est hostis.)

He continues here, as I think, the same subject; he had said at the end of the last verse that turpitude or baseness had been seen at Jerusalem; and now he says that it was on the very *fringes* or skirts. The Prophet seems to allude to menstruous women who hide their uncleanness as much as they can; but such a thing is of no avail, as nature must have its course. In short, the Prophet intimates that the Jews had become filthy in no common degree, being so afflicted that their uncleanness appeared on their skirts. This seems to be the Prophet's meaning. Interpreters think that Jeremiah speaks of the sins of the people, but they are mistaken; for I doubt not but that the reference is to their punishment. They say that filthiness was on the skirts, because the people had shamelessly prostituted themselves to all kinds of wickedness, and that they remembered not their end, because they had become altogether foolish, according to what is said in the song of Moses, "O that they were wise, and would foresee their end!" (Deut. xxxii. 29.) But let any one duly consider the design of the Prophet, and he will readily agree with me that he speaks not of guilt, but on the contrary of punishment.[1]

The Prophet then says that the reproach of the Jews was on their skirts, because they could not hide their disgrace. For shame often makes men to hide their evils and silently to bear them, because they are unwilling to expose themselves to the mockery of their enemies. But the Prophet says that the miseries of the people could not be kept hidden, but that they appeared to all, as the case is with women subject to an overflow—it issues forth to the extremities of their garments.

And when he says that *she remembered not her end*, I understand this to mean, that the Jews were so overwhelmed

[1] "She carries the marks of her sins in the greatness of her punishment," is Lowth's remark, which seems to favour this view.—*Ed.*

with despair, that they did not raise up their thoughts to God's promises; for it is no ordinary source of comfort, and what even common sense dictates to us, to take breath in extreme evils, and to extend our thoughts farther, for misery will not always oppress us—some change for the better will happen. As then men are wont thus to sustain themselves in adversities, he says that the Jews *remembered not their end;* that is, they were so demented by their sorrow, that they became stupified, and entertained no hope as to the future. In short, by these words, he denotes extreme despair; for the Jews were so stupified that they could not raise up their minds to any hope.

And the reason is expressed, because they had *come down wonderfully,* that is, because they had been cast down in an extraordinary manner. A noun is here put instead of an adverb, and in the masculine gender, פלאים, *pelaim;* sometimes we have פלאות, *pelaut,* but in the same sense. He then says that the Jews had sunk as it were miraculously; but by a miracle he means a prodigy, the word being taken in a bad sense; then *miraculously has Jerusalem come down.* It hence followed that it succumbed under its miseries, so that it could not turn its thoughts to any hope, nor think of another end; but became stupid in its miseries, as men usually become desperate, when they think that there is no deliverance for them. He repeats what he had said before, that *there was no comforter.*

These things ought to be carefully observed, for Satan at this day uses various means to lead us to despair. In order to avert us from all confidence in the grace of God, he sets before us extreme calamities. And when sorrow lays such hold on our minds, that the hope of grace does not shine forth, from that immoderate sorrow arises impatience, which may drive us to madness. Hence it comes that we murmur, and then clamour against God. As, then, at this day Satan supplies materials to harass our minds, that we may succumb under our griefs, let us bear in mind what the Prophet says, that Jerusalem, which was then the only true Church of God in the world, was overwhelmed with so many and so great evils, that she *remembered not her end.* This, indeed, ought to be understood of external circumstances, for God no doubt sustained the minds of the godly, and always so mitigated their grief that they had regard to their end. But the reference is to the people in general, and also to the outward appearance of things, when the Prophet says that the Jews remembered not their end.

He now encourages them to pray, and suggests words to them, for he speaks as in the person of all: *See, Jehovah, my affliction, for the enemy hath highly exalted himself.* Though the Prophet here represents the Church, yet he exhorts them no doubt, according to the obligations of his office, to entertain good hope, and encourages them to pray, for true and earnest prayer cannot be offered without faith ; for when the taste of God's grace is lost, it cannot be that we can pray from the heart ; and through the promises alone it is that we can have a taste of God's paternal goodness. There is, then, no doubt but that the Prophet here promises a sure deliverance to the Jews, provided they turned to God, and believed and were fully persuaded that he would be their deliverer.

We now, then, see what is the right way of teaching, even that men are to be humbled, and that their just condemnation is to be set before them, and that they are also to be encouraged to entertain hope, and a hand is to be stretched out to them, that they may pray to God, and not hesitate in extreme evils not only to hope for but even to request aid from him. This is the order observed by the Prophet ; we must learn in adversities ever to come down to ourselves, and to acknowledge our guilt ; and then when we are sunk deep, we must learn to elevate our minds by faith, that thence prayer may arise by which our salvation is to be attained.

One thing has escaped me ; the Prophet, in order to obtain favour, says, that enemies had *greatly exalted* themselves. And this deserves a special notice ; for what seems to occasion despair to us, ought, on the contrary, to encourage us to entertain good hope, that is, when enemies are insolent and carry themselves with great arrogance and insult us. The greater, then, is their pride and the less tolerable, with more confidence may we call on God, for the Holy Spirit has not in vain taught us this truth, that God will be propitious to us when enemies thus greatly exalt themselves, that is, when they become beyond measure proud, and immoderately indulge themselves in every kind of contempt. It follows,—

10. The adversary hath spread out his hand upon all her pleasant things: for she hath seen *that* the heathen entered into her sanctuary, whom thou didst command *that* they should not enter into thy congregation.

10. Manum suam extendit hostis ad omnia desiderabilia ejus; quia vidit gentes quum ingressæ sunt sanctuarium ipsius, de quibus præceperas, ne ingrederentur in congregationem tibi (*hoc est,* quæ tibi sacrata est.)

The Prophet again deplores the profanation of all sacred things; and this complaint, as I have said, proceeded from the bitterest sorrow; for though it was a sad thing for the faithful, to lose all their property, to wander in exile and to suffer the want of all things, yet it must have been more grievous to them to see the Temple polluted, and all religion exposed to shame. This calamity, then, the Prophet again deplores, when he says that *enemies had stretched forth their hand against all desirable things.* Now, by desirable things, he does not mean riches, nor anything that belongs to the condition of an earthly and fading life, but those invaluable treasures which God had deposited with the chosen people. The enemy, then, had *extended his hand* against the altar, against the table, against the ark of the covenant, against all the sacred vessels.

Then this indignity was increased, *because* Jerusalem *saw the heathens entering into her sanctuary;* for the pronoun is in the feminine gender. But the sanctuary of Jerusalem was God's Temple; for, though properly speaking, it was alone God's sanctuary, it was yet at the same time the sanctuary of the people, because God had not caused the Temple to be built for his own benefit, but rather for the benefit of his people. What God, then, had consecrated for himself is rightly called the sanctuary of the people. He still increases the indignity, because God *had forbidden the heathens to enter the sanctuary;* but they had violently rushed in there. They did not, however, enter for the sake of worshipping God, for it was his command to keep them from the holy assembly; but they had by force entered for the purpose of violating the Temple, and also of abolishing the whole worship of God, and of exposing religion to all kinds of mockery.[1]

PRAYER.

Grant, Almighty God, that as at this day we see thy Church miserably afflicted, we may direct our eyes so as to see our own sins, and so humble ourselves before thy throne, that we may yet cease not to entertain hope, and in the midst of death wait for life; and may this confidence open our mouth, that we may courageously persevere in calling on thy name, through Christ our Lord.—Amen.

Lecture Third.

11. All her people sigh, they seek bread; they have given their pleasant things for meat to relieve the soul: see, O Lord, and consider; for I am become vile.

11. Totus populus ejus gementes, quærentes panem, dederunt desiderabilia sua (*hoc est*, quicquid habebant pretiosum) pro cibo ad revocandum animam: vide, Jehova, et aspice, quia facta sum vilis (*aut*, contempta.)

The Prophet here complains that all the citizens of Jerusalem were constantly groaning through want and famine. He first says, that *all were sighing.* The word "people" is collective, and hence he uses the plural number, נאנחים, *nanechim.* Then he says that they were all sighing; but he expresses also the reason, because they were *seeking bread.* To seek bread is indeed common to all; but by this word he intimates extreme want, as though he had said, that they begged their bread. He then compares them to beggars, who go about here and there to seek bread.

He says also, that they *gave the most precious things for meat,* to *recover the soul.* Here he refers more clearly to famine, for he says that in a manner they suffered want. Others render the last clause, "to refresh the soul," which

[1] The verse may be thus rendered,—

His hand has the oppressor expanded over all her desirable things;
Indeed she saw it: nations entered her sanctuary;
Though thou hast commanded this, "They shall not come to thine assembly."

"The desirable things" were sacred things, and might be so rendered. To expand the hand over them was to seize them, to take possession of them.—*Ed.*

is not unsuitable. But the Prophet no doubt meant to denote a deficiency as to the support of life, when he said, that they gave whatever precious thing they had to restore their souls, as it were from death to life.

A prayer follows, *See, Jehovah, and look, for I am become vile.* We said yesterday, that the complaints which humbled the faithful, and, at the same time, raised them to a good hope, and also opened the door to prayers, were dictated by the Spirit of God. Otherwise, when men indulge in grief, and torment themselves, they become exasperated; and then to be kindled by this irritation is a kind of madness. The Prophet, therefore, in order to moderate the intensity of sorrow, and the raging of impatience, recalls again the faithful to prayer. And when Jerusalem asks God *to see and to look,* there is an emphasis intended in using the two words; and the reason given does also more fully shew this, because she had become *vile;*[1] so that the Church set nothing else before God, to turn him to mercy, but her own miseries. She did not, then, bring forward her own services, but only deplored her own miseries, in order that she might obtain the favour of God. It follows,—

12. *Is it* nothing to you, all ye that pass by? behold, and see if there be any sorrow like unto my sorrow, which is done unto me, wherewith the Lord hath afflicted *me* in the day of his fierce anger.

12. Non ad vos omnes qui transitis per viam? Aspicite et videte, an sit dolor sicut dolor meus, qui factus est mihi, quia afflixit me (*vel,* dolore affecit) Jehova in die excandescentiæ iræ suæ.

The beginning of the verse is variously explained. Some read it interrogatively, " Is it nothing to you who pass by the way?" Others more simply, " I see that I am not cared for by you; to you my sorrow is nothing." Some again read thus, " Let it not be a sorrow to you;" and others, " Let not sorrow be upon you," that is, let not what I have happen to you; so that it is a prayer expressive of benevolence.

What I prefer is the interrogation, *Is it nothing to you who pass by the way?* for the letter ה, *He,* the note of a question, is often omitted. But were it read affirmatively, the meaning would not be unsuitable: "It does not concern you who

[1] That is, she was treated as vile or worthless: " dishonoured" is the *Sept.—Ed.*

pass by," as though Jerusalem, in its lamentations, felt grieved that all those who passed by were not touched either with pity or with sorrow.[1]

But she addressed those who *passed by*, that she might more fully set forth the greatness of her calamity. For had she directed her words to neighbours alone, there would not have been so much force in them; but when she spoke to strangers, she thus shewed that her calamity was so great, that it ought to have roused the sympathy of men from the remotest parts, even while on their journey. And she asks them to *look* and *see*. The order is inverted, for she said before, "See, Jehovah, and look." Then Jerusalem asked God, first to turn his eyes to see her calamities, and then attentively to notice them: but now for another purpose she says, *look ye and see*, that is, consider how evident is my calamity, which otherwise might have been in a measure hidden from you. *Look ye*, she says, *is there a sorrow like my sorrow?* she adds, *which is come to me:* some render the words actively, "which Jehovah has brought on me;" but the other version is more correct, for it is more literal. Jerome's rendering is, "who has gleaned me;" and עלל, *olal*, means sometimes to glean, nor do I wish to reject this interpretation. But what follows is incorrectly rendered, as in a former instance, by Jerome, "of which Jehovah has spoken:" for he derived the verb, as before stated, from הגה, *ege;* but it comes from יגה, *ige*, as it is evident from the letter ו, *vau*, being inserted. There is then no doubt but that the Church intimates that God was the author of that sorrow which she deplored.

And it is necessary to know this, lest men should be carried away into excesses in their mourning, as it frequently happens. For the majesty of God imposes a check, when we perceive that we have to do with him. Simple and bare knowledge of this is not, indeed, sufficient, for, as it has been said, the ungodly, while they know that their sorrows proceed from God, yet murmur against him: but it is never-

[1] It is evidently taken as לו by the *Sept.*, the *Vulg.*, and the *Targ.*; but as a negative by the *Syr.*, and the sentence is taken as a question: and this gives the best meaning.—*Ed.*

theless the beginning of patience and meekness when we have a regard to God. It was, then, for this reason that Jerusalem said that she had been afflicted by God.

And it is added, *In the day of the indignation of his wrath.* Here the Prophet wished to express the grievousness of God's vengeance, by mentioning *the indignation of wrath.* Some render חרון, *cherun,* "fury;" but as the word "fury" is too harsh, the word "indignation," or great heat (*excandescentia*) is not unsuitable. We must, however, bear in mind the design of the Prophet, which was to shew that God's vengeance had been so dreadful, as though his wrath had all been on a flame against Jerusalem: and this is more fully confirmed in the following verse,—

13. From above hath he sent fire into my bones, and it prevaileth against them: he hath spread a net for my feet; he hath turned me back; he hath made me desolate *and* faint all the day.

13. E sublimi misit ignem in ossa mea, et dominatus est in ipso (*est mutatio numeri, refertur quidem ad ossa, sed perinde est ac si diceret,* dominatus est ignis in unoquoque ossium;) extendit rete suum pedibus meis, convertet me retrorsum; dedit me (reddidit me, *vel,* posuit) vastam (*vel,* desolatam) toto die dolentem (*vel,* infirmam.)

The Prophet proceeds with the same subject, that God's vengeance had raged most dreadfully against Jerusalem. But employing a metaphor she says, that *fire* had been sent to her *bones.* They who interpret bones of fortified places, weaken the meaning of the Prophet. I take bones in their proper sense, as though it was said, that God's fire had penetrated into the inmost parts. This way of speaking often occurs in Scripture. By bones is denoted strength or valour. Hence David sometimes deplored, that his bones were vexed or troubled. (Psalm vi. 2.) And Hezekiah said in his song "As a lion he hath broken my bones." (Isa. xxxviii. 13.) In the same sense the Prophet now says, that *fire* had been *sent by God, which ruled in his bones,* that is, which not only burnt the skin and the flesh, but also consumed the bones. רדה, *rede,* means also to take away or to receive: but as the former rendering is most commonly taken, I am disposed to follow it—that *fire ruled in his bones.*

There is another similitude added, that God had *spread a net before her feet;* and thus he had taken away every means of escape. She intimates (for it is Jerusalem who speaks) that she had been ensnared by God's judgments, so that she was bound over to ruin, as though she had fallen into toils or snares. It is stated in the third place, that she was *desolate all the day, so that she sorrowed perpetually.* By *all the day* is meant continually. It is then said, that she sorrowed without end, beyond measure, because she had been turned back by the nets of God, and her bones had been consumed by celestial fire: for the expression *from above,* ממרום, *memerum,* is emphatical, for the Prophet means that it was no common or human burning; because what is ascribed to God exceeds what is human or earthly. It is, then, as though he had said, that it had been such a vengeance as betokened the dreadful power of God; for it was the same as though God had thundered from heaven. We now perceive the import of the words. It follows,—

14. The yoke of my transgressions is bound by his hand; they are wreathed, *and* come up upon my neck: he hath made my strength to fall; the Lord hath delivered me into *their* hands, *from whom* I am not able to rise up.

14. Ligatum est (*hic vertit Hieronymus,* vigilavit, *nam hallucinatus est in puncto duntaxat* נשקד, *et legendum est* נשקר, *quia est punctum sinistrum, quod significat ligare,* ligatum est *igitur*) jugum iniquitatum mearum in manu ejus; implicitæ sunt (*vel,* perplexæ,) ascenderunt super collum meum; corruere fecit (*vel,* debilitavit) robur meum; dedit me Dominus in manus eorum (*est in regimine, et tamen nulla sequitur additio, quæ respondeat, sed apparet aliquid esse subaudiendum,* in manus *ergo* hostium) ex quibus non potero surgere.

Here, again, Jerusalem confesses that God had been justly displeased. She had ascribed to God's vengeance the evils which she suffered; but now she expresses the cause of that displeasure or wrath. Hence she says, that the *yoke* of her *iniquities* had been *bound* in God's hand. Though interpreters explain the words, yet they touch not the meaning of the Prophet; for they consider not that there is a continued metaphor. We ought then to bear in mind the two clauses,—that God's hand held the yoke tied, and also that the yoke was bound around the neck of Jerusalem. As when a husbandman, after having tied a yoke to oxen, holds a rein, and folds it round his hand, so that the oxen not only cannot throw off the yoke, but must also obey the hand which holds the reins; so also it is said, that the yoke of iniquities was fastened: "I bear the yoke," she says, "but it is tied, and so fastened, that it cannot be shaken off; and then, however furious I may be, or kick, God holds the tied yoke by his own hand so as to constrain me to bear it."

We now, then, see the design and import of the Prophet's words, that God was justly incensed against Jerusalem, and had justly used so much severity. Expressed at the same time is the atrocity of the punishment, though wholly just; for, on the one hand, Jerusalem complains that a yoke was laid on her neck, tied and fastened, and also that it was tied by the hand of God, as though she had said, that she was under such a constraint, that there was no relaxation. On the one hand, then, she bewails the grievousness of her calamity; and on the other, she confesses that she fully deserved what she suffered; and thus she accused herself, lest any should think that he clamoured against God, as is commonly the case in sorrow.[1]

It is added, *He hath made to fall*, or weakened, &c. The verb כשל, *cashel*, in *Hiphil*, means, as it is well known, to stumble, or to cause to stumble or fall. *He hath*, then, *weakened my strength; the Lord hath given me up into the hand* of my enemies, from whom *I shall not be able to rise;*

[1] All the versions agree in rendering נשקד in the sense of watching; and when they agree, there is a strong presumption that they are right. And all agree as to על being a preposition, and not a noun, "yoke," except the *Vulg.*, which hardly gives any meaning. The Rabbins have invented a new meaning for the verb, which it has in no other place, and some have followed them. It is rendered impersonally by the *Sept.*, "there has been watching," but by the *Vulg.*, "he hath watched." To "watch over transgressions," is similar to "watch upon (or over) the evil," in Dan. ix. 14; it is to watch over them in order to punish them. The whole verse I render thus,—

> 14. He hath watched over my transgressions, by his hand they are twined;
> His yoke *is* upon my neck, he hath made to fail my strength;
> Yea, given me hath the Lord into the hands *of the oppressor*, I cannot stand.

The word "hands" is in a construct form, which shews that there is a word left out. "I cannot stand," *i.e.*, against the oppressor; I cannot resist. The future is used in the sense of the present; literally it is, "I shall not be able to stand," or resist. So it is exactly in Welsh; it is the future, but understood as expressing what is present.

In the first line, "his hand" is connected in all the versions with "twined," or wreathed together.—*Ed.*

that is, he hath so subjugated me, and so laid me prostrate under the hands of my enemies, that there is no hope of rising again. Were any one to ask, "Why then does she pray, and again will pray often?" the answer is, that when she says here, that she will not be able to rise again, the reference is made to the outward state of things: in the meantime, the grace of God is not taken to the account: and this goes beyond all human means. She then says, that according to the thoughts of the flesh, she had no hope, because there appeared to be no means of rising. But yet she did not despair, but that God would at length, by his almighty power, cause her to rise from fatal ruin. And this is a mode of speaking that ought to be borne in mind; for hope sees things which are hidden. But at the same time the faithful speak according to the common appearance of things, and when they seem to despair, they regard what falls under their own observation and judgment. So then Jerusalem now says that she could not rise, except God manifested his extraordinary power, which far exceeds all human means. It follows,—

15. The Lord hath trodden under foot all my mighty *men* in the midst of me; he hath called an assembly against me to crush my young men: the Lord hath trodden the virgin, the daughter of Judah, *as* in a winepress.

15. Calcavit omnes fortes meos Dominus in medio mei; vocavit super me diem (*hoc est*, edixit statum diem, *alii vertunt*, congregationem; *et* מועד, *tam cœtum ipsum significat, quam condictum tempus*,) ad conterendos adolescentes meos (*vel*, electos;) torcular calcavit Adonai super virginem (*vel*, puellam,) filiam Jehudah.

She first says, that *all* her *valiant* men had been *trodden under foot.* Now we know how much the Jews trusted in their men even to the very time when they were wholly subdued. As then they had shewed so much insolence and pride towards the prophets, it hence became a cause of greater sorrow, when Jerusalem herself saw that she was destitute of every protection, and that her valiant men were trodden under foot. She says, *in the midst of me.* And this ought to be observed; for if they had fallen on the field of battle, if they had been taken in the fields by their enemies, such a thing would not have been so grievous: but that they had been thus laid prostrate in the very bosom of the city, was indeed a token of vengeance from above. We now see that this circumstance was not superfluous, that all the valiant men of Jerusalem were laid prostrate in *the midst* of her.

It is then said that it was the *fixed time*, when God *destroyed her chosen men*, or her youth. Should it seem preferable to take מועד, *muod*, as meaning a congregation, I do not object; yet I do not approve of this meaning, for it seems forced. It agrees better with the context to regard it as the fixed time, the time before appointed by God to destroy all the strong men.[1]

There is then another metaphor used,—that God had *trodden the winepress as to the daughter of Sion.* This figure occurs elsewhere, as in Isa. lxiii. 1, "Who is this that cometh from Edom? and why are his garments red?" For the Prophet wonders how God could come forth from Edom, sprinkled with blood. God answers, "The winepress have I trod alone;" that is, because he had avenged the wrongs done to his people. For we know that the Idumeans had always been incensed against the miserable Jews. Then God, in order to shew that he was the defender of his Church, says that he came from Edom, and was sprinkled and even made wet with blood. As when any one is red with wine after having toiled in the winepress, so also is the representation in this place. We have also seen in Jer. li. 33, that Babylon was like a threshing-floor. The metaphor, indeed, is different, but bears a likeness to the present. As, then, God is said to tread, or to thresh, when he afflicts any land, so he is said to tread the winepress, as here.[2] It follows,—

[1] If the word be rendered "assembly," or congregation, the meaning is, the assembly of the Chaldeans, and an allusion, as *Gataker* says, is made to the calling of the people to their feasts. It is rendered "time" by the *Sept.* and the *Vulg.*, but "assembly" by the *Syr.* To call against or upon one a fixed time, is no suitable expression. Our version is no doubt right; and with it agree *Blayney* and *Henderson.*—*Ed.*

[2] The words are as follows,—

The winepress has the Lord trodden as to the virgin, the daughter of Judah.

The ל sometimes means "as to," or, with respect to. "The daughter of Judah" is in apposition with "virgin."—*Ed.*

16. For these *things* I weep: mine eye, mine eye runneth down with water, because the comforter that should relieve my soul is far from me; my children are desolate, because the enemy prevailed.

16. Propter id ego plorans, oculus meus, oculus meus, descendunt aquæ, (*hoc est*, defluit in aquas,) quia remotus est à me consolator, qui animam revocet, (*vel*, recreat animam, משיב;) fuerunt filii mei desolati, quia prævaluit hostis.

He describes at large the calamities of Jerusalem. But it is no wonder that the Prophet thus lengthened his discourse; for we know that those who are heavily oppressed never satisfy themselves with mourning and lamentations. If, indeed, we duly consider how great the evils were, the Prophet will not appear to us wordy, nor will his prolixity be wearisome to us. For when any one compares the flourishing state of Jerusalem with that desolate ruin which the Prophet laments, it will surely appear to him that no words, however many, can fully express what it really was; nay, though the expressions may seem hyperbolical, yet they do not exceed the greatness of that calamity. This point is briefly adverted to, lest any one should be wearied with those various modes of expression which the Prophet employs, when yet he might have at once said that Jerusalem was destroyed.

He says, *For this will I weep.* He throughout sustains the person of a woman; for Jerusalem herself speaks, and not Jeremiah. *I*, she says, *for this will weep; mine eye! mine eye! it shall descend into waters.* Others read, "Waters will descend from mine eyes;" but such a rendering is too loose. I do not, then, doubt but that Jerusalem says that her eyes would be like fountains of waters. She indeed speaks in the singular number, and repeats the words, *mine eye! mine eye! it shall descend*, or flow as waters, that is, as though they were two fountains, *because alienated from me*, or far from me, is *a comforter, to revive my soul.*[1] By these words she intimates that she was fainting, and as it

[1] Though the *Sept.* and *Vulg.* do not repeat the "eye," yet the *Targ.* has "my two eyes," and the *Syr.*, "mine eyes." The repetition is in most copies, and it is very emphatical. See a similar instance in Jer. iv. 9.

16. For these things I weep: mine eye! mine eye! it brings down water;
For far from me is a comforter, a restorer of my life;
Become desolate are my sons, for the enemy has prevailed.—*Ed.*

were dying, and that there was no one present to administer comfort, so that her soul might be revived. As it appeared before, that it is deemed an extreme evil when there is no friend to do the duty of humanity by alleviating sorrow; so now again Jerusalem repeats the same complaint, and says that all her *sons were destroyed, because the enemy had prevailed.* It follows,—

17. Zion spreadeth forth her hands, *and there is* none to comfort her; the Lord hath commanded concerning Jacob, *that* his adversaries *should be* round about him: Jerusalem is as a menstruous woman among them.

17. Expandit Sion in manibus suis (*id est,* manus suas, *vel,* complosit manibus suis, *alii vertunt,* confregit,) nullus consolator ei; mandavit Jehova super Jacob per circuitus ejus adversarios ejus; facta est Jerusalem in abominationem inter ipsos (*vel,* tanquam immunda, *vel,* menstruata, נדה, *enim vocatur mulier menstruata apud Mosen.*)

The Prophet first says that *Jerusalem had expanded her hands,* as a token of sorrow, or that she might seek friends from every side; for when we wish to move men to pity, we stretch forth our arms. I wonder how it came to the minds of some to say that Jerusalem had broken bread with her hands. This is extremely puerile. Some have rendered the words, that she had broken with her hands, understanding thereby that she had clapped with her hands. It is, however, a harsh mode of speaking. I retain the most suitable sense, that *Jerusalem had expanded her hands.* The word פרש, *peresh,* means also to disperse, or scatter; but the Prophet no doubt means the expansion of the hands, as though Jerusalem had said that she was like a woman lamenting her calamities, and seeking friends on every side to give her some consolation. And we may gather the meaning of the Prophet from the passage itself, *Sion,* it is said, *by spreading hands calls her friends, and no one is a comforter:* these clauses ought to be read together, that is, that Sion expanded her hands, and yet no one responded to alleviate her sorrow by consolation.

It follows, that *Jehovah had commanded respecting Jacob, that through his circuits adversaries should afflict him.* The Prophet again reminds us that these evils did not happen through men, but that God had resolved in this manner to punish the obstinate impiety of the people. Lest, then, the

Jews should give vent to their sorrow, and ascribe it to the Chaldeans, as it was commonly done, he recalls their attention to God himself, and says that the Chaldeans, however cruel they were, yet did nothing merely through their own impulse, but through God's command. He adds, *through the circuits,* that the Jews might know that there was no escape, for God held them all as though they were shut up. For we can in various ways escape from the hands of men; but when God is our enemy, we in vain seek hiding-places. The Prophet then teaches us that subterfuges did not avail the Jews, because God on every side kept them shut up.

He says at length that *Jerusalem was like a menstruous woman,* or was an abomination; for נדה, *nede,* may be rendered uncleanness, or abomination, and is often a noun substantive; and I am disposed so to render it, even that Jerusalem was regarded as filth, as though the Prophet had said that there was no humanity or moderation in the enemies of the Jews, because they were not counted as men, but as offscourings, as an abominable filth.[1]

Now, if such a thing happened to the ancient Church, let us not wonder if at this day also God should deal with us more severely than we wish. It is, indeed, a very bitter thing to see the Church so afflicted as to have the ungodly exulting over its calamities, and that God's children should be as the refuse and filth of the world. But let us patiently bear such a condition; and when we are thus contemptuously treated by our enemies, let us know that God visits us with punishment, and that the wicked do nothing except through the providence of God, for it is his will to try our faith, and

[1] The same word, נדה, occurs in verse 8, only there is a י in it; and the phrase in its form is similar. The Versions, except the *Syr.*, and also the *Targ.*, give to it there the idea of wandering, but here of uncleanness. There seems to be no reason for this change; and the end of the next verse favours the idea of wandering: Jerusalem had become a wanderer, or a fugitive, among her oppressors,—

17. Expanded hath Sion her hands, no comforter is to her;
Commanded has Jehovah as to Jacob, *Let* those around him *be* his oppressors;
Become has Jerusalem a wanderer among them.

The word נד is a fugitive, a wanderer, and as Jerusalem is feminine, ה is added, a feminine termination. "Jerusalem" here, as in verse 8, means its citizens.—*Ed.*

thus to shew himself a righteous judge: for if we rightly consider in how many ways, and how obstinately we have provoked his wrath, we shall not wonder if we also be counted at this day an abomination and a curse. It follows,—

18. The Lord is righteous; for I have rebelled against his commandment: hear, I pray you, all people, and behold my sorrow; my virgins and my young men are gone into captivity.	18. Justus ipse Jehova, quia os ejus exacerbavi: Audite agedum omnes populi, videte dolorem meum; virgines meæ et adolescentes mei profecti sunt in captivitatem.

Jerusalem again acknowledges, and more clearly expresses, that she suffered a just punishment. She had before confessed that her enemies were cruel through God's command; but it was necessary to point out again the cause of that cruelty, even that she had too long provoked the wrath of God.

She says, first, that God was *just*, or righteous,[1] *because she had provoked his mouth.* By the *mouth* of God we are to understand the prophetic doctrine, as it is well known. But the phrase is emphatical, for when the word of God was proclaimed by the mouth of prophets, it was despised as an empty sound. As, then, prophetic doctrine has not its own majesty ascribed to it, God calls whatever his servants declare his *mouth.* This mode of speaking is taken from Moses, and often occurs in his writings. *Jehovah,* then, *is just;* how so? *because I have provoked his mouth.* And it was more grievous and less excusable to provoke the mouth of God than simply to offend God. The ungodly often offend God when they labour under ignorance; but when the Lord is pleased to open his mouth to recall the erring, and to shew the way of salvation, and then men rush headlong, as it were designedly, into sins, it is certainly a mark of extreme impiety. We hence understand why the Prophet mentions the *mouth* of God, or the teaching of the prophets, even to exaggerate the wickedness of Jerusalem, which had so obstinately disregarded God speaking by his prophets.

The greatness of her sorrow is again deplored; and what follows is addressed to all nations, *Hear, I pray, all ye people;*

[1] "Righteous he, Jehovah:" the pronoun is used instead of the verb *is,* —a common thing in Hebrew.—*Ed.*

see my sorrow. And what was the reason for this great sorrow? *because,* she says, *my virgins and my young men have been driven into captivity.* This might seem a light thing; for a previous account has been given of other calamities, which were far more severe; and exile in itself is but a moderate punishment. But we must bear in mind what we have before stated, that the Jews dwelt in that land, as though they had been placed there by the hand of God, that Jerusalem was to be a perpetual rest, which had been granted them from above; in short, that it was as it were a pledge of the eternal inheritance. When, therefore, they were driven into captivity, it was the same as though God had cast them down from heaven, and banished them from his kingdom. For the Jews would not have been deprived of that land, had not God rejected them and shewed his alienation from them. It was then the same as repudiation. It is therefore no wonder that Jerusalem so much lamented because her sons and her daughters were driven into exile.

PRAYER.

Grant, Almighty God, that as thou hast hitherto dealt so mercifully with us, we may anticipate thy dreadful judgment; and that if thou shouldest more severely chastise us, we may not yet fail, but that being humbled under thy mighty hand, we may flee to thy mercy and cherish this hope in our hearts, that thou wilt be a Father to us, and not hesitate to call continually on thee, until, being freed from all evils, we shall at length be gathered into thy celestial kingdom, which thine only-begotten Son has procured for us by his own blood.—Amen.

Lecture Fourth.

19. I called for my lovers, *but* they deceived me: my priests and mine elders gave up the ghost in the city, while they sought their meat to relieve their souls.

19. Clamavi ad amicos meos, ipsi deceperunt me: sacerdotes mei et seniores mei in urbe obierunt, quia quæsierint cibum sibi et refocillarunt (*ad verbum, hoc est,* ut refocillarent) animam suam (*ad verbum,* ut redire facerent, *quemadmodum Gallicè dicimus,* faire revenir le cœur.)

Here the people of God complain in the person of a woman, as we have before seen, that in their calamity they were left destitute of every comfort. And it is a circumstance which increases grief, when no one is present to shew any kindness to the miserable ; for it is no small alleviation of sorrow, when friends offer their kind services, and as far as they can, endeavour to mitigate the severity of the evil.

The Church of God now says, that she was so forsaken by friends as to be left alone to pine away in her mourning and sorrow. There may, however, be here an allusion to shameful and impure connexions ; for by this term, *friends*, the Spirit often points out the Egyptians as well as others in whom the Israelites had foolishly trusted ; for in this manner, we know, they had turned aside from conjugal fidelity. God had bound them to himself, that they might acquiesce in his favour alone ; and so to acquiesce was their spiritual chastity. Rightly, then, does Scripture compare both the Egyptians and the Assyrians to harlots, whenever the Israelites sought aid from them. But as this explanation seems too refined, I am content to view what is said simply as a complaint, that the people of God, though looking in all directions, yet could find no comfort in the world. *I cried,* she said, *to my friends ; they deceived me.*

It is then added, *My priests and mine elders expired in the city.* Had they been slain in battle, it would have been no wonder ; for they who go against an enemy, go as it were to meet death. But God's people here deplore a more grievous evil, that the priests died in the city, not through the enemies' sword, but through famine, which is as it were the extreme of evils. It is then said, that the priests as well as the elders perished through famine, because they could not find food. And when it is said that they *sought food to refresh the soul,* there is a contrast to be understood between ordinary food and a remedy for the famine ; for we naturally seek food whenever we feel hungry ; but the Prophet refers here to something more than this, even that the priests and the elders sought food, because long abstinence urged them ; and it was very sad, that the priests, who excelled in honour, and also the elders, were thus reduced to want. Had such a thing happened to the common people, it would not have been so wonderful ; for the long siege of the city had consumed all their provisions. But when the priests, and those who had wealth, were thus oppressed with hunger, we may conclude that the want which the Prophet wished to describe was extreme. It follows,—

20. Behold, O Lord, for I *am* in distress; my bowels are troubled: mine heart is turned within me; for I have grievously rebelled: abroad the sword bereaveth, at home *there is* as death.

20. Vide Jehova, quia afflictio mihi, (*vel*, angustia,) viscera mea conturbata sunt (*alii*, contracta;) eversum est cor meum inter me, quia rebellando rebellavi; foris orbat gladius, domi tanquam mors.

The people turn again to pray God: and what has been before said ought to be remembered, that these lamentations of Jeremiah differ from the complaints of the ungodly; because the faithful first acknowledge that they are justly chastised by God's hand, and secondly, they trust in his mercy and implore his aid. For by these two marks the Church is distinguished from the unbelieving, even by repentance and faith. To sigh and to mourn in adversities, and to lament also their miseries, are common to both; but the children of God differ greatly from the ungodly, because they humble themselves under his mighty hand, and confess that they deserve to suffer punishment; and further, they cast not away the hope of salvation, but implore his mercy. Then the Prophet introduces again the people as praying God to look on them. For the ungodly pour forth their complaints into the air; and when at any time nature dictates to them that they ought to address God, yet no prayer arises from a sincere heart.

There is no doubt but that the Prophet here shewed to the faithful how they were to lament their common miseries, even so as patiently to bear the chastisements of God, and also to seek deliverance from him, though they had provoked his wrath. For when we see that we are pressed down by God's hand, we do not murmur, but the knowledge of our sins humbles us, and faith moderates our mourning, which would otherwise exceed moderation. And when we thus humbly flee to God, we in a manner unburden our sorrows into his bosom, as it is said in the Psalms, "Cast (or roll) on God thy cares." (Ps. lv. 22.)

He then says first, *See, Jehovah, for affliction* is *to me.*

He then expresses the manner of the affliction, *because his bowels were bound*, or troubled. The word is from חמר, *chemer*, which is doubled. Some derive it from חמור, *chemur*, an ass, and so render it "bound," as when a burden is fastened on an ass. But more probable is the opinion of those who derive the word from mortar or cement, for as cement is made by mixing water with lime and sand, and stirring them together, so by a metaphor the bowels are said to be stirred or troubled;[1] and this explanation agrees better with what follows—for it is added, *my heart is overturned.* The reason is given, because the people by *rebelling had rebelled*, that is, had been very rebellious against God. We have said that the complaints of the godly differ from those of the ungodly, for they not only pray to God, but make also a sincere confession, so as to make it evident that they are justly chastised by God's hand. At the beginning of the verse the faithful prayed, and now again they declare that they deserved what they suffered, because they had been very rebellious. Then Jeremiah proceeds with what he had begun to say respecting the grievousness of their punishment, *Abroad*, or without, he says, *the sword bereaves, and at home it is like death ;* that is, "When we go abroad, the sword meets us ; and when we hide ourselves at home, there also many deaths surround us." He uses the particle of likeness, *as*, or like ; as though he had said that nothing met them at home but what was deadly.[2] It now follows,—

21. They have heard that I sigh ; *there is* none to comfort me : all mine enemies have heard of my trouble ; they are glad that thou hast done *it :* thou wilt bring the day *that* thou hast called, and they shall be like unto me.

21. Audierunt quòd sum gemens, (*hoc est*, quòd sim in luctu,) nec quisquam consolator mihi ; omnes inimici mei audierunt malum meum, gavisi sunt quòd tu feceris, et adduxeris diem, quem tu vocasti ; atqui erunt sicuti ego.

The verb שמעו, *shemou*, is put down twice, but at the beginning without a nominative case:. hence the sentence is

1 "Troubled," or disquieted, is the rendering of all the versions, and also of the *Targ.* As it is a reduplicate, the verb means greatly troubled or greatly disturbed, or violently agitated.—*Ed.*

2 The rendering of the *Sept.* is,—

Abroad the sword has bereaved me, as death at home.

To the same purpose is the *Syr.* and *Arab.* Having before referred to death by famine, he now adds the devastation of the sword.—*Ed.*

defective, until in the second clause the word איבי, *aibi*, is expressed. Jeremiah evidently says, that enemies had *heard* of the evils under which the people laboured, even that they were *sighing*, and that no one shewed them any kindness; for it is commonly the case that sympathy is manifested towards the miserable. By this circumstance he amplifies the grievousness of their punishment, there being no one, as before said, to administer any consolation. But it is repeated, that *enemies had heard;* for as there is nothing more bitter than reproaches, we seek in adversities to withdraw ourselves in a manner from the observation of men; but our evil is especially doubled, when we become a spectacle to enemies; for they derive joy from our adversities, and then exult over us. When, therefore, the chosen people said, that *enemies* had *heard,* they thus shewed that nothing could be added to their miseries: *They have heard,* then, that I was sighing and that no one comforted me. Who had heard? all mine enemies; and they *have rejoiced that thou hast done* it.

Jeremiah seems to intimate, that their enemies, being fully persuaded that God was displeased with his people, did on this account more freely rejoice; and at the same time they believed that it was all over with those miserable people with whom God was displeased. But I know not whether this view is well grounded. I indeed do not reject it, nor will I dispute with any one who may hold that the enemies rejoiced, because they thought that God was become the enemy of that people, whom he had before chosen and also protected: nor is this view unsuitable; for the reprobate then fully triumph when they can boast that God is adverse to us. But when no such thought comes to their minds, they yet cease not to rejoice when they see that we are oppressed and afflicted. Though, then, they may not think of God's hand, yet they rejoice that it is *done;* that is, they rejoice that we are distressed, though they understand not who the author is. We may then take the meaning simply to be, that the enemies of the Church rejoiced at that calamity, without considering who the author of it was.

But why is it expressed that *God had done it?* even to

shew that while the ungodly think that fortune is unfavourable to us, it is our duty to cast our eyes on God, for we ought not to judge of things according to their blindness. As, then, they ascribe not to God the glory due to him when they do not acknowledge him as judge, it ever behoves us to see by the eyes of faith what is hid from the natural perceptions of men, even that nothing happens to us except through the righteous judgment of God. Though, then, enemies had not wisdom to know how it was that the Church was afflicted, yet it behoved the Church itself to use by means of faith such a language as this, that God had *done* it; *they rejoiced that thou hast done it.*

And it follows, *Thou hast brought the day which thou hast called,* or proclaimed; for קרא, *kora,* has sometimes this meaning.[1] In short, the faithful now confess not only that they were afflicted by God's hand, but also that what the prophets had so often threatened, and what had been despised, was now fulfilled. For we have seen with what pertinacity that people rejected the threatenings given by the prophets: God had often exhorted them to repent, and also had proclaimed or fixed a time for them, but without effect. Therefore the faithful now reflect on what had not been sufficiently known before, even that the day was brought which had been often proclaimed. And thus they confessed, not only that they were worthy of punishment, but that it was the proper time for them to be chastised, as they had not repented after having been so often warned.

He adds, *But they themselves shall be as I* am. Here the future tense may be considered as optative, for presently a prayer follows which confirms this view. But we may also take the meaning to be simply this,—that the faithful

[1] Our version is wrong in rendering this clause in the future tense. The reference is not to the day of vengeance to the Babylonians, but to the day of vengeance which God had brought on his own people. The versions, except the *Syr.*, give the verb in the past tense.

There are here two instances of כי being carried on to the next clause,—

21. Heard have they that I sigh, *that* I have no comforter:
All mine enemies have heard of my evil; they have rejoiced
That thou hast done it, *that* thou hast brought the day thou hast announced;
But they shall be like myself.—*Ed.*

began to take courage, as they looked forward to the time when God would render to the wicked according to their proud and disdainful exultations. It follows,—

22. Let all their wickedness come before thee; and do unto them as thou hast done unto me for all my transgressions: for my sighs *are* many, and my heart *is* faint.

22. Veniet (*aut*, veniat) omnis malitia eorum in conspectum tuum, et facias illis, quemadmodum fecisti mihi super omnibus sceleribus meis; quia multa suspiria mea, et cor meum debile (*vel*, mœstum.)

Here, no doubt, the faithful regarded as a part of their comfort the judgment which God would at length execute on the ungodly; and there is no doubt but that this kind of imprecation had been suggested to God's children by the Holy Spirit, in order to sustain them when pressed down by heavy troubles; not that God gave them thus loose reins to desire vengeance on their enemies, but that while those perished who indulged their malice, the faithful might derive from their ruin a hope of deliverance; for the vengeance of God on the reprobate brings with it a token of paternal favour towards the elect.

And that we may better understand what this imprecation means, we must first bear in mind that we cannot complain of enemies, except they are also enemies to God. For should I hurt any one, and should he, impelled by wrath, vex me, there could be no access for my complaint to God, and in vain could I seek a covering from this example; why? because whenever we go before God, it is necessary, as I have said, that our enemies should be also his enemies. But, secondly, it would not be sufficient, except our zeal were also pure; for when we defend our own private cause, something excessive will necessarily be in our prayers. Let us, then, know that we are not to pronounce an imprecation on our enemies, except, first, they are God's enemies; and, secondly, except we disregard ourselves, and plead not our own cause, but, on the contrary, undertake the cause of public safety, having laid aside all turbulent feelings; and especially, except our fervour arises from a desire to glorify God. With these qualifications, then, we may adopt the form of prayer given us here by the Prophet. But as this subject has been explained elsewhere, and often and very fully, I touch on it here but briefly.

He then says, *Let all their wickedness come before thee; do to them as thou hast done to me.* Here, again, the faithful take upon themselves the blame for all the evils they were suffering; for they do not expostulate with God, but pray only that he would become the judge of the whole world, in order that the ungodly might also at length have their turn, when God would be pacified towards his children. But they afterwards more clearly express that they had deserved all that they had suffered—*for all my sins.* Then they add, *because my sighs are many and my heart is weak.* We, in short, see that the faithful lay humbly their prayers before God, and at the same time confess that what they had deserved was rendered to them, only they set before God their extreme sorrow, straits, griefs, tears, and sighs. Then the way of pacifying God is, sincerely to confess that we are justly visited by his judgment, and also to lie down as it were confounded, and at the same time to venture to look up to him, and to rely on his mercy with confidence. Now follows the second elegy,—

CHAPTER II.

1. How hath the Lord covered the daughter of Zion with a cloud in his anger, *and* cast down from heaven unto the earth the beauty of Israel, and remembered not his footstool in the day of his anger!

1. Quomodo obnubilavit in iracundia sua Dominus filiam Sion, projecit a cœlo in terram decorem Israel, et non recordatus est scabelli pedum suorum in die iracundiæ!

The Prophet again exclaims in wonder, that an incredible thing had happened, which was like a prodigy; for at the first sight it seemed very unreasonable, that a people whom God had not only received into favour, but with whom he had made a perpetual covenant, should thus be forsaken by him. For though men were a hundred times perfidious, yet God never changes, but remains unchangeable in his faithfulness; and we know that his covenant was not made to depend on the merits of men. Whatsoever, then, the people might be, yet it behoved God to continue in his purpose, and not to annul the promise made to Abraham. Now, when Jerusalem was reduced to desolation, there was as it were an abolition of God's covenant. There is, then, no wonder that the Prophet here exclaims, as on account of some prodigy, *How can it be that God hath clouded* or darkened, &c.

We must, however, observe at the same time, that the Prophet did not mean here to invalidate the fidelity or constancy of God, but thus to rouse the attention of his own nation, who had become torpid in their sloth; for though they were pressed down under a load of evils, yet they had become hardened in their perverseness. But it was impossible that any one should really call on God, except he was humbled in mind, and brought the sacrifice of which we have spoken, even a humble and contrite spirit. (Ps. li. 19.) It was, then, the Prophet's object to soften the hardness which he knew prevailed in almost the whole people. This was the reason why he exclaimed, in a kind of astonishment, *How has God clouded*, &c.[1]

Some render the words, "How has God raised up," &c., which may be allowed, provided it be not taken in a good sense, for it is said, *in his wrath;* but in this case the words to raise up and to cast down ought to be read conjointly; for when one wishes to break in pieces an earthen vessel, he not only casts it on the ground, but he raises it up, that it may be thrown down with greater force. We may, then, take this meaning, that God, in order that he might with

[1] The verb here is in the future tense, and the clause might be thus rendered,—

Why should the Lord in his wrath becloud the daughter of Sion?

And if ישבה, in chap. i. 1, be in the future tense, as it may be, that clause may be rendered in the same way,—

Why should sit alone the city *that was* full of people?

Then follows here, as in the former instance, a description of what had happened to Sion,—

He hath cast from heaven to earth the glory of Israel,
And not remembered his footstool in the day of his wrath.

At the same time, the clauses may both be rendered as proposed in a note on chap. i. 1, and the tenses of the verbs be preserved. The verb here is clearly in the future tense, and the verb in the former instance may be so; and the future in Hebrew is often to be taken as the present, as the case is in Welsh.

How this! in his wrath becloud does the Lord the daughter of Sion! —*Ed.*

greater violence break in pieces his people, had raised them up, not to honour them, but in order to dash them more violently on the ground. However, as this sense seems perhaps too refined, I am content with the first explanation, that God had *clouded the daughter of Sion in his wrath;* and then follows an explanation, that he had *cast her from heaven to the earth.* So then God covered with darkness his people, when he drew them down from the high dignity which they had for a time enjoyed. He had, then, *cast on the earth all the glory of Israel, and remembered not his footstool.*

The Prophet seems here indirectly to contend with God, because he had not spared his own sanctuary; for God, as it has been just stated, had chosen Mount Sion for himself, where he designed to be prayed to, because he had placed there the memorial of his name. As, then, he had not spared his own sanctuary, it did not appear consistent with his constancy, and he also seemed thus to have disregarded his own glory. But the design of the Prophet is rather to shew to the people how much God's wrath had been kindled, when he spared not even his own sanctuary. For he takes this principle as granted, that God is never without reason angry, and never exceeds the due measure of punishment. As, then, God's wrath was so great that he destroyed his own Temple, it was a token of dreadful wrath; and what was the cause but the sins of men? for God, as I have said, always preserves moderation in his judgments. He, then, could not have better expressed to the people the heinousness of their sins, than by laying before them this fact, that God *remembered not his footstool.*

And the Temple, by a very suitable metaphor, is called the footstool of God. It is, indeed, called his habitation; for in Scripture the Temple is often said to be the house of God. It was then the house, the habitation, and the rest of God. But as men are ever inclined to superstition, in order to raise up their thoughts above earthly elements, we are reminded, on the other hand, in Scripture, that the Temple was *the footstool* of God. So in the Psalms, "Adore ye before his footstool," (Ps. xcix. 5;) and again, "We shall adore in the place where his feet stand." (Ps. cxxxii. 7.) We, then, see that the two expressions, apparently different, do yet well agree, that the Temple was the house of God and his habitation, and that yet it was only his footstool. It was the house of God, because the faithful found by experience that he was there present; as, then, God gave tokens of his presence, the Temple was rightly called the house of God, his rest and habitation. But that the faithful might not fix their minds on the visible sanctuary, and thus by indulging a gross imagination, fall into superstition, and put an idol in the place of God, the Temple was called the footstool of God. For as it was a footstool, it behoved the faithful to rise up higher and to know that God was really sought, only when they raised their thoughts above the world. We now perceive what was the purpose of this mode of speaking.

God is said *not to have remembered his Temple*, not because he had wholly disregarded it, but because the destruction of the Temple could produce no other opinion in men. All, then, who saw that the Temple had been burnt by profane hands, and pulled down after it had been plundered, thought that the Temple was forsaken by God; and so also he speaks by Ezekiel, (chap. x. 18.) Then this oblivion, or not remembering, refers to the thoughts of men; for however God may have remembered the Temple, yet he seemed for a time to have disregarded it. We must, at the same time, bear in mind what I have said, that the Prophet here did not intend to dispute with God, or to contend with him, but, on the contrary, to shew what the people deserved; for God was so indignant on account of their sins, that he suffered his own Temple to be profaned. The same thing also follows respecting the kingdom,—

2. The Lord hath swallowed up all the habitations of Jacob, and hath not pitied: he hath thrown down in his wrath the strong holds of the daughter of Judah; he hath brought *them* down to the ground: he hath polluted the kingdom and the princes thereof.

2. Perdidit Dominus, non pepercit (*hoc est*, non parcendo, absque venia) omnia habitacula Jacob; diruit in excandescentia sua munitiones filiæ Jehudah; detraxit ad terram: profanavit regnum ejus et principes ejus.

He pursues the same subject, but in other words. He

first says, that *God had without pardon destroyed all the habitations of Jacob;* some read, "all the beauty (or the ornament) of Jacob." But the other rendering is more suitable, that he had destroyed all the *habitations* of Jacob; and then that he had *demolished in his indignation,* &c. The word is derived from what means excess; but we know that all words signifying wrath are transferred to God, but they do not properly belong to him. God, then, *in his violent wrath had demolished all fortresses,* and *cast them to the ground;* and afterwards, that he had *profaned,* &c.

This profanation of the kingdom, and of the princes, corresponds with the former verse, where he said that God had not remembered his footstool; for we know that the kingdom was sacerdotal and consecrated to God. When, therefore, it was polluted, it follows that God in a manner exposed his name to reproach, because the mouth of all the ungodly was thus opened, so that they insolently poured forth their slanders. That God, then, spared not the kingdom nor the Temple, it hence followed that his wrath against the Jews was dreadful. Now, as he is a righteous judge, it follows, that such was the greatness of the sins of the Jews, that they sustained the blame for this extreme sacrilege; for it was through their sins that God's name was exposed to reproach both as to the Temple and the kingdom.

PRAYER.

Grant, Almighty God, that as thou settest before us at this day those ancient examples by which we perceive with what heavy punishments thou didst chastise those whom thou hadst adopted, —O grant, that we may learn to regard thee, and carefully to examine our whole life, and duly consider how indulgently thou hast preserved us to this day, so that we may ever patiently bear thy chastisements, and with a humble and sincere heart flee to thy mercy, until thou be pleased to raise up thy Church from that miserable state in which it now lies, and so to restore it, that thy name may, through thine only-begotten Son, be glorified throughout the whole world.—Amen.

Lecture Fifth.

3. He hath cut off in *his* fierce anger all the horn of Israel: he hath drawn back his right hand from before the enemy, and he burned against Jacob like a flaming fire, *which* devoureth round about.

3. Confregit in excandescentia iræ suæ omne cornu Israelis: retraxit (*vel*, redire fecit) retrorsum dexteram suam à facie inimici, et exarsit in Jacob tanquam ignis, flamma devoravit in circuitu.

JEREMIAH expresses the same thing in various ways; but all that he says tends to shew that it was an evidence of God's extreme vengeance, when the people, the city, and the Temple, were destroyed. But it ought to be observed, that God is here represented as the author of that calamity: the Prophet would have otherwise lamented in vain over the ruin of his own country; but as in all adversities he acknowledged the hand of God, he afterwards added, that God had a just reason why he was so grievously displeased with his own people.

He then says, that *every horn* had been *broken* by God. We known that by *horn* is meant strength as well as excellency or dignity; and I am disposed to include both here, though the word breaking seems rather to refer to strength or power. But the whole clause must be noticed, that God had *broken every horn of Israel in the indignation of his wrath.* The Prophet intimates that God had not been angry with his people as though he had been offended by slight transgressions, but that the measure of his wrath had been unusual, even because the impiety of the people had so burst forth, that the offence given to God could not have been slight. Then, by *indignation of wrath* the Prophet does not mean an excess, as though God had through a violent impulse rushed forth to take vengeance; but he rather intimates that the people had become so wicked, that it did not behove God to punish in an ordinary way an impiety so inveterate.

He then adds, that God had *withdrawn his right hand from before the enemy,* and that at the same time he had *burned like a fire,* the flame of which had *devoured all around.* The Prophet here refers to two things; the first is, that though God had been accustomed to help his people, and to oppose their enemies, as they had experienced his aid in the greatest dangers, yet now his people were forsaken and left destitute of all hope. The first clause, then, declares, that God would not be the deliverer of his people as formerly, because they had forsaken him. But he speaks figuratively, that God had *drawn back his right hand;* and God's right hand means his protection, as it is well known. But the Prophet's meaning is by no means obscure, even that there was hereafter no hope that God would meet the enemies of his people, and thus preserve them in safety, for he had drawn back his hand.[1] But there is a second thing added, even that God's hand *burned like fire.* Now it was in itself a grievous thing that the people had been so rejected by God, that no help could be expected from him ; but it was still a harder thing, that he went forth armed to destroy his people. And the metaphor of fire ought to be noticed ; for had he said that God's right hand was against his people, the expression would not have been so forcible; but when he compared God's right hand to fire which burned, and whose flame consumed all Israel, it was a much more dreadful thing.[2]

Moreover, by these words the Israelites were reminded that they were not to lament their calamities in an ordinary way, but ought, on the contrary, to have seriously considered the cause of all their evils, even the provoking of God's wrath against themselves; and not only so, but that God was angry with them in an unusual degree, and yet justly, so that they had no reason to complain. It follows,—

4. He hath bent his bow like an enemy: he stood with his right	4. Extendit arcum suum tanquam inimicus, stetit dextera ejus tanquam

[1] *Gataker, Henry, Blayney,* and *Henderson,* consider "the right hand" as that of Israel—that God drew back or restrained the right hand of Israel, so that he had no power to face his enemies. But *Scott* agrees with *Calvin;* and favourable to the same view are the early versions, except the *Syr.*, for they render the pronoun, "his own—suam:" the *Targ.* also takes the same view. Had the word been "hand," it might have been applied to Israel; but it is "the right hand," which commonly means protection, or rather God's power, as put forth to defend his people and to resist enemies. This is farther confirmed by what is said in the following verse, that God "stood with his right hand as an adversary." See Ps. lxxiv. 11.—*Ed.*

[2] The last clause may be literally rendered thus,—

And he burned in Jacob as fire, the flame devoured around.—*Ed.*

hand as an adversary, and slew all *that were* pleasant to the eye in the tabernacle of the daughter of Zion: he poured out his fury like fire.	adversarius, et occidit omnes desiderabiles aspectu (oculo) in tabernaculo filiæ Sion (*vel,* in tabernaculum filiæ Sion); effudit tanquam ignem iracundiam suam.

He employs now another metaphor, that God, who was wont to defend his people, now took up arms against them; for stating a part for the whole, he includes in the *bow* every other weapon. When, therefore, he says that God had bent his bow, it is the same as though he said that he was fully armed. The bow, then, as we have before seen, means every kind of weapon. He then adds, that his *right hand stood as an adversary.* Here he more plainly describes what he had before touched upon, even that God had not only given up his people to the will of their enemies, but that he himself had held up a banner to their enemies, and went before them with an armed hand. Nor is there a doubt but that by the right hand of God he means all their enemies; for it was necessary carefully to impress this fact on the minds of the people, that the war had not been brought by the Chaldeans, but that God had resolved thereby to punish the wickedness of the people, and especially their desperate obstinacy, for he had omitted nothing to restore the people to the right way.

Whenever, then, there is mention made here of God, let us know that the people are reminded, as I have already said, that they had to do with God, lest they should forget this, or think that it was adverse fortune, or dream of some other causes of evils, as men are wont in this respect to be very ingenious in deceiving themselves. And we shall see this more clearly hereafter, where it is said, that God had thought to destroy the wall of Jerusalem; but this thought was the same as his decree. Then the Prophet explains there more fully what is yet here substantially found, even that God was brought forward thus before the people, that they might learn to humble themselves under his mighty hand. The hand of God was not indeed visible, but the Prophet shews that the Chaldeans were not alone to be regarded, but rather that the hidden hand of God, by which they were guided, ought to have been seen by the eyes of faith. It was, then, this hand of God that stood against the people.

It then follows, *He slew all the chosen men;* some read, "all things desirable;" but it seems more suitable to consider men as intended, as though he had said, that the flower of the people perished by the hand of God *in the tabernacle of the daughter of Sion;* though the last clause would unite better with the end of the verse, that *on the tabernacle of the daughter of Sion God had poured forth his wrath,* or his anger, *as fire.*

He repeats the metaphor which he had used in the last verse; and this is what we ought carefully to notice; for God threatens by Isaiah that he would be a fire to devour his enemies: "The light of Israel shall be a fire, and his Holy One a flame of fire, and it shall devour all briers and all kinds of wood." (Isa. x. 17.) There God threatened the Chaldeans, as though he had said that his vengeance would be dreadful, when as a patron and defender of his people he would contend with the Chaldeans. He there calls himself the light of Israel and the Holy One; and hence he said that he would be a fire and a flame as to the Chaldeans. But what does he say here? even that God had poured forth his wrath as fire, that its flame had devoured all around whatever was fair to be seen in Israel. We hence see that the people had provoked against themselves the vengeance of God, which would have been otherwise poured forth on their enemies; and thus the sin of the people was doubled. It follows,—

5. The Lord was as an enemy: he hath swallowed up Israel, he hath swallowed up all her palaces; he hath destroyed his strong holds, and hath increased in the daughter of Judah mourning and lamentation.

5. Fuit Dominus tanquam hostis, perdidit Israelem, perdidit omnia palatia ejus, corrupit munitiones ejus, auxit in filia Jehudah fletum et lamentationem.

These words might seem superfluous, since the Prophet has often repeated, that God was become an enemy to his own people; but we shall hereafter see, that though they were extremely afflicted, they yet did not rightly consider whence their calamity arose. As, then, they had become so stupified by their evils, that they did not turn their eyes to God, they were on this account often urged and stimulated, that they might at length understand by their evils that God was a judge. Now, as it was difficult to convince them of this truth, the Prophet did not think it enough briefly to touch on it, but found it necessary to dwell on it at large, so that the people might at length be roused from their insensibility.

He then says that God himself *was to them as an enemy*, lest the Israelites should fix their eyes on the Chaldeans, and thus think that they had been the chief movers of the war. He therefore says, that they had undertaken that war through the secret influence of God, and had carried it on successfully, because God endued them with his own power. And hence the faithful ought to have concluded, that nothing could have been more grievous than to have God as their adversary; for as long as they had suffered themselves to be defended by the hand of God, they were victorious, we know, over all their enemies, so that they could then brave all dangers with impunity. The Prophet now reminds them, that as they had been successful and prosperous under the defence and protection of God, so now they were miserable, for no other reason but that God fought against them. But we ought at the same time to bear in mind the truth, which we have noticed, that God is never angry with men without reason; and since he was especially inclined to shew favour to his people, we must understand that he would not have been thus indignant, had not necessity constrained him.

He has destroyed Israel, he says; *he has destroyed all his palaces;* and afterwards, *he has dissipated* or demolished *all his fortresses;* and finally, *he has increased in the daughter of Judah mourning and lamentation;* תאניה ואניה *tanie veanie*, words derived from the same root, but joined together for the sake of amplifying, not only in this place, but also in the twenty-ninth chapter of Isaiah, and in other places. The meaning is, that God had not put an end to his vengeance, because the people had not resolved to put an end to their obstinate wickedness. He afterwards adds,—

6. And he hath violently taken away his tabernacle, as *if it were of* a garden; he hath destroyed his places of the assembly: the Lord hath caused the solemn

6. Et transtulit (*vel*, dissipavit, *vel* evertit) tanquam hortum tabernaculum suum (*alii vertunt*, tabernaculum suum tanquam hortum,) perdidit testimonium suum, oblitus est Jehova in Sion conven-

feasts and sabbaths to be forgotten in Zion, and hath despised, in the indignation of his anger, the king and the priest.

tus solennis (*vel*, sacrificii) et sabbathi, et repulit in excandescentia iræ suæ (*diversæ quidem sunt voces, sed ego non adeò scrupulosè distinguo*) regem et sacerdotem.

Then he says first, that *his tabernacle had been overthrown by God.* They who render it "cottage" extenuate too much what is spoken of; nor does the Prophet simply compare the sanctuary of God to a cottage. Then I take tabernacle in a good sense. With regard to the verb חמס, *chemes*, as it means to migrate, they properly render it, as I think, who give this version, that God had removed his tabernacle; nor do I disapprove of repeating the word tabernacle. God, then, had removed his tabernacle, as though it were a cottage in a garden. Watchmen, as it appears from the first chapter of Isaiah, had then cottages in their gardens, but only for a time, as is the case at this day with those who watch over their vineyards; they have, until the time of vintage, small chests in which they conceal themselves. The Prophet then says, that though God's tabernacle was honourable, and of high dignity, it was yet like a cottage in a garden. It is not, however, a simple comparison, as before stated, and therefore I reject the opinion of those who render it cottage, for it is not suitable, and it would be unmeaning. *God,* then, *hath removed his tabernacle as a garden,* that is, the sanctuary where he dwelt. And how did he remove it? even as a garden-cottage. And as watchers of gardens were wont to construct their little cots of leaves of trees and slight materials, so the Prophet, in order to increase commiseration, says, that the sacred habitation of God was like a cottage in a garden, because it was removed from one place to another; and thus he intimates that God regarded as nothing what he had previously adorned with singular excellencies.[1]

[1] The word שכו is rendered by the versions in the sense of סכו, "his tabernacle;" but by so doing they make it the same in effect with מועדו, "his place of meeting," in the following clause. The verb חמס never means what *Calvin* says, to migrate or to remove, but to cast off, or to throw down, that is, with force or violence. Then שׂך, a fence or inclosure, is what suits the verb,—

6. And he has thrown down as that of a garden his inclosure,
He has destroyed his assembling-place;

He then adds, that God had *destroyed his testimony.* By the word מועד, *muod,* he means the same throughout; but some confine it to the ark of the covenant, and of this I do not disapprove. We must yet bear in mind the design of the Prophet, which was to shew that by the entire ruin of the Temple the covenant of God was in a manner abolished. It is, indeed, certain, that God had not forgotten his faithfulness and constancy, but this abolition of his covenant refers to what appeared to men. He then says, that the sanctuary which was, as it were, the testimony of God's favour, had been overthrown. Now, as he repeats again the word מועד, *muod,* it may be that he thus refers to the Tabernacle, either because the holy assemblies met there, or because it had been solemnly dedicated, that God might there hold intercourse with his people. For מועד, *muod,* means a fixed time, it means an assembly, it means a festival, and sometimes it means a sacrifice; and all these significations are not unsuitable: yet when he says that God had *destroyed his testimony,* I apply this to the Tabernacle itself, or, if it seems to any preferable, to the ark of the covenant; though the former is the most suitable, because it was a place consecrated, as it has been stated, for mutual intercourse.

He afterwards says, that God had *forgotten the assembly,* the sacrifice, or the tabernacle; for it is the same word again, but it seems not to be taken in the same sense. Then I think that מועד, *muod,* is to be taken here for the assembly. As he had previously said, that the place where the holy assemblies met had been overthrown or destroyed, so now he says, that God had no care for all those assemblies, as though they had been buried in perpetual oblivion; for he mentions also the *Sabbath,* which corresponds with the subject. God, then, had forgotten all the assemblies as well as the Sabbath. There is, again, as to this last word, a part stated for the whole, for this word was no doubt intended to

Forgotten hath Jehovah in Sion the assembly and the Sabbath;
And has cast off, in the foaming of his wrath, the king and the priest.

The "inclosure," or fence, refers to the courts which surrounded the Temple; hence the place where the people assembled was destroyed. God had regarded it no more than the fence of a common garden. There is "fence" understood after כ, no uncommon thing in Hebrew.—*Ed.*

include all the festivals. The meaning of the passage then is, that the impiety of the people had been so great, that God, having, as it were, forgotten his covenant, had inflicted such a dreadful punishment, that religion, for a time, was in a manner trodden under foot.

He says, in the last place, that *the king and the priest* had been rejected by God. We have already said, that these were as two pledges of God's paternal favour; for, on the one hand, he who reigned from the posterity of David was a living image of Christ; and on the other hand, there was always a high-priest from the posterity of Aaron to reconcile men to God. It was then the same as though God shewed himself in every way propitious to the chosen people. Then their true happiness was founded on the kingdom and the priesthood; for the kingdom was, as it were, a mark of God's favour for their defence, and the priesthood was to them the means by which reconciliation with God was obtained. When, therefore, God wholly disregarded the king and the priest, it became hence evident, that he was greatly displeased with his people, having thus, in a manner, obliterated his favours. It follows,—

7. The Lord hath cast off his altar; he hath abhorred his sanctuary: he hath given up into the hand of the enemy the walls of her palaces; they have made a noise in the house of the Lord, as in the day of a solemn feast.

7. Abominatus est Dominus altare suum, repulit (*vel,* rejecit procul ab animo suo) sanctuarium suum, tradidit in manum hostis muros palatiorum ejus, vocem ediderunt in domo Jehovæ tanquam in die sacri conventus (*vel,* solennis; *iterum ponitur nomen* מועד, *tamen accipitur vel pro conventu vel pro die festo.*)

He proceeds with the same subject, and adopts similar words. He says first, that God had *abominated his altar;*[1] an expression not strictly proper, but the Prophet could not otherwise fully shew to the Jews what they deserved; for had he only spoken of the city, of the lands, of the palaces, of the vineyards, and, in short, of all their possessions, it would have been a much lighter matter; but when he says that God had counted as nothing all their sacred things,—the altar, the Temple, the ark of the covenant, and festive days,—when, therefore, he says, that God had not only dis-

[1] Our version, "cast off," gives the real meaning of the verb.—*Ed.*

regarded, but had also cast away from him these things, which yet especially availed to conciliate his favour, the people must have hence perceived, except they were beyond measure stupid, how grievously they had provoked God's wrath against themselves; for this was the same as though heaven and earth were blended together. Had there been an upsetting of all things, had the sun left its place and sunk into darkness, had the earth heaved upwards, the confusion would have hardly been more dreadful, than when God put forth thus his hand against the sanctuary, the altar, the festal days, and all their sacred things. But we must refer to the reason why this was done, even because the Temple had been long polluted by the iniquities of the people, and because all sacred things had been wickedly and disgracefully profaned. We now, then, understand the reason why the Prophet enlarged so much on a subject in itself sufficiently plain.

He afterwards adds, He *hath delivered all the palaces,* &c.; as though he had said, that the city had not been taken by the valour of enemies, but that the Chaldeans had fought under the authority and banner of God. He, in short, intimates that the Jews had miserably perished, because they perished through their own fault; and that the Chaldeans had proved victorious in battle, and had taken the city, not through their own courage or skill, but because God had resolved to punish that ungodly and wicked people.

It follows in the last place, that the *enemies had made a noise in the temple of God as in the day of solemnity.* Here also the Prophet shews, that God would have never suffered the enemies insolently to exult and to revel in the very Temple, had not the Israelites deserved all this; for the insolence of their enemies was not unknown to God, and he might have easily checked it if he pleased. Why, then, did he grant so much license to these profane enemies? even because the Jews themselves had previously polluted the Temple, so that he abhorred all their solemn assemblies, as also he declares by Isaiah, that he detested their festivals, Sabbaths, and new moons. (Isa. i. 13, 14.) But it was a shocking change, when enemies entered the place which

God had consecrated for himself, and there insolently boasted and uttered base and wicked calumnies against God! But the sadder the spectacle, the more detestable appeared the impiety of the people, which had been the cause of so great evils. For we ought ever to remember what I have often stated, that these circumstances were noticed by the Prophet, that the people might at length acknowledge themselves guilty as to all these evils, which they would have otherwise ascribed to the Chaldeans. That, then, the Chaldeans polluted the Temple, that they trod under foot all sacred things, all this the Prophet shews was to be ascribed to the Jews themselves, who had, through their own conduct, opened the Temple to the Chaldeans, who had exposed all sacred things to their will and pleasure. It follows,—

8. The Lord hath purposed to destroy the wall of the daughter of Zion; he hath stretched out a line, he hath not withdrawn his hand from destroying: therefore he made the rampart and the wall to lament; they languished together.	8. Cogitavit Jehova ut perderet murum filiæ Sion, extendit lineam, non retraxit manum suam à dissipatione; itaque luxit antemurale, et murus; pariter corruerunt (*vel*, eversi sunt.)

The verb to *think*, has more force than what is commonly assigned to it; for it would be very flat to say, that God *thought to destroy;* but to think here means to resolve or to decree.[1] This is one thing. And then we must bear in mind the contrast between this and those false imaginations, by which men are wont to be drawn away, so as not to believe that God is present in adversities as well as prosperity. As, therefore, men go wilfully astray through various false thoughts, and thus withdraw themselves, as it were, designedly from God, the Prophet says here that the *walls of Jerusalem* had not *fallen* by chance, but had been overthrown through a divine decree, because God had so determined, according to what we have seen in many places throughout the book of Jeremiah: " See, these are the thoughts which God has thought respecting Jerusalem, which he has thought respecting Babylon." The Prophet, then, in these instances,

[1] The verb is often used in this secondary sense, to purpose or resolve or determine, as the result of thinking. The *Vulg.* and the *Targ.* very improperly retain its primary meaning, but the *Syr.* gives that of resolving or determining.—*Ed.*

taught what he now confirms in this place, that when the city Jerusalem was destroyed, it was not what happened by chance ; but because God had brought there the Chaldeans, and employed them as his instruments in taking and destroying the city : *God*, then, *has thought to destroy the wall of the daughter of Sion.* It is, indeed, true, that the Chaldeans had actively carried on the war, and omitted nothing as to military skill, in order to take the city : but the Prophet calls here the attention of the Jews to a different thought, so that they might acknowledge that they suffered justly for their sins, and that God was the chief author of that war, and that the Chaldeans were to be viewed as hired soldiers.

He afterwards adds, that God had *extended a line* or a rule, as it is usually done in separating buildings.[1] And then he says, *He hath not drawn back his hand from scattering ; and so it was, that the ramparts and the walls mourned, and fell down together.*[2] We now see that what the Prophet had in view was to lead the Jews fully to believe that the destruction was not to be ascribed to the Chaldeans, but, on the contrary, to God. Added at the same time must be another part of what is here taught, that God would not have been so displeased with the holy city which he had chosen, had not the people extremely provoked him with their sins. It now follows,—

9. Her gates are sunk into the ground ; he hath destroyed and broken her bars ; her king and her princes *are* among the Gentiles : the law *is* no *more ;* her prophets also find no vision from the Lord.

9. Demersæ sunt in terra portæ ejus, perdidit et confregit vectes ejus, rex ejus et principes ejus in gentibus (*vel*, ad gentes ;) nulla lex, etiam prophetæ non reperiunt visionem à Jehova.

He again relates in other words what he had said, that

[1] It was the line of destruction as mentioned in Isa. xxxiv. 11, designed to point out what was to be destroyed.—*Ed.*

[2] The verbs אבל, to mourn, and אמל, to be faint, to fail, when applied to inanimate things, mean to be desolate and to decay. This clause then ought to be thus rendered,—

So that he has made desolate the rampart and the wall,
They are become wholly decayed together.

The connexion shews that the ו here must be rendered, "so that ;" and as the last verb has the last letter doubled, the word "wholly" ought to be introduced.—*Ed.*

the walls of Jerusalem had fallen. But he now speaks of the gates and says, that they had *sunk into the ground,* or had become fixed in the ground; for it may be explained in both ways; as though he had said, that the gates had been no hinderance to the enemies so as to prevent them to enter the city. He thus derides the foolish confidence of the people, who relied on their defences and thought the city impregnable. He then says that the *gates had sunk,* or had become fixed *in the ground.*

He then says that God had *destroyed and broken her bars;* for no doubt the gates had firm and strong bars. He then says that neither the gates nor the bars were found sufficient, when God stretched forth his hand to the Chaldeans, to lead them into the city. He afterwards adds, that both the king and the princes had been driven into exile; for when he says, *among the nations,* or to the nations, he intimates that there was no more a king, for he and the royal seed and the princes were gone into banishment. The rest I defer until to-morrow.

PRAYER.

Grant, Almighty God, that since so many tokens of thy wrath meet us at this day, we may without delay return to thee, and so submit to thee in true repentance, as to strive at the same time to be reconciled to thee; and as a Mediator has been given to us to lead us to thee,—O grant that we may by a true faith seek him, and follow wherever he may call us, that having been purified from all pollutions, we may be glorified by thee our Father, and may so call on thee, that we may find thy grace present in all our evils.—Amen.

Lecture Sixth.

AMONG the calamities of Jerusalem which the Prophet deplores, he mentions this as one, that there was *no law* or doctrine. The Chaldee Paraphraser thought that the reference is to punishment, but he perverts the words of the Prophet. There follows afterwards an amplification; after having said, *there is no law,* he adds, *her prophets also have not found a vision from Jehovah.* There is then no doubt but that the Prophet means that among the miseries of the people this was the greatest, that they were without doctrine or teaching, and without prophets. The word תורה, *ture,* is indeed used often by way of excellency to designate the law, but it signifies also doctrine or instruction; and the meaning here is the same, as though the Prophet had said, that the Jews had been so forsaken by God, that they found no consolation in their evils. This may be better understood by a similar complaint in the Psalms: "Our signs we see not, there is not a Prophet any more, there is no more any one who understands." (Ps. lxxiv. 9.) The faithful there say, that they were in a hopeless state, because God shewed them no signs of his favour; and signs were given when God appeared propitious to them. Now, as God had testified that there would be always faithful teachers to guide the people, they therefore complained that there was no Prophet, that there was no one any more who had a vision. And so in this place the Prophet says, that there was *no law,* and that *the prophets* were without *a vision,* even because God, as though wearied, had given up the care of the people: for his paternal favour could not have been better known than by this evidence, that he sent them prophets; and it is certain that all prophecies ceased when the people were driven into exile.

A long time after, Daniel began to exhort the faithful to hope for a return; and on this account it is said by Isaiah, "Comfort ye, comfort ye my people, will our God say." (Isa. xl. 1.) There Isaiah indicates that there would be a temporary silence; for all the prophets would be mute, that the people might lie in a hopeless state, and for this reason, because they had long abused God's patience, and had disregarded that singular blessing, when God manifested by his servants that he was solicitous for their wellbeing and safety, as he had often said, that he rose up early and extended his hand to them by the prophets. As, then, the gift of prophecy was to the people a sure pledge not only of God's favour, but also of the solicitude which he entertained for them; so when he withheld prophets from the people, he departed from them, having forsaken as it were his station among them.[1]

We now then understand what the Prophet meant by saying, that there was *no doctrine* any more, and that the *prophets* of Jerusalem *found no vision* any more *from Jehovah;* for God, after his word had been long profaned, became silent, and deigned not for a time to open his sacred mouth, because he had seen that he had been treated with derision.

Now this passage teaches us, that nothing is more desirable in evils, and that there is no better remedy, than to have God's promise, that he will at length be merciful to us. For when any promise of God is set before us, it is like a small light kindled in darkness. Though then our misery were like a thick darkness, yet when God shews some token of favour by his promises, that ought to be sufficient to give us hope and joy. On the other hand, when no promises of God occur to us, it is a sure token of reprobation, unless that he sometimes thus tries us, as we read here. But the faithful also themselves, when they perceive no evidence of God's paternal favour in his promises, are as it were in a hopeless state, and sunk in the lowest depths. Hence it is then only that we arise from death to life, and find support so as not to be overwhelmed with despair, when God is pleased to speak to us. It now follows,—

10. The elders of the daughter of Zion sit upon the ground, *and* keep silence: they have cast up dust upon their heads; they have girded themselves with sackcloth: the virgins of Jerusalem hang down their heads to the ground.

10. Sedent ad terram, silent senes filiæ Sion, attollunt pulverem super caput suum, accincti sunt saccis; demiserunt (*vel*, demittunt) ad terram caput suum virgines (*aut*, puellæ) Jerusalem.

The Prophet here strikingly represents the grievousness of the people's calamity, when he says, that *the elders*, as in

[1] "No law." *Gataker* understood this to refer to the fact, that the law written on the tables of stone, deposited in the temple, was lost, having been destroyed by the Chaldeans. Others say, "no law" was observed respecting God's worship, the temple having been destroyed. The law, moral, ceremonial and judicial, was given to Israel, and formed the condition on which they were to inherit the land. When banished, because they kept not the law, they had in exile as it were no law; the covenant respecting the land, dependent on the law, was during the exile made void or suspended.—*Ed.*

hopeless despair, were lying *on the ground*, that they *cast dust on their heads*, that they were *clad in sackcloth*, as it was usually done in very grievous sorrow, and that the *virgins* bent their *heads down to the ground*. The meaning is, that the elders knew not what to do, and led others to join them in acts of fruitless and abject lamentation. We indeed know that young women are over-careful as to their form and beauty, and indulge themselves in pleasures; and that when they roll themselves with their face and hair on the ground, it is a token of extreme mourning. This is what the Prophet means.

They were wont indeed to put on sackcloth as a token of repentance, and to cast dust on their heads; but their minds were often so confused, that they only thus set forth their mourning and sorrow, and had no regard to God; and hypocrites, when they put on sackcloth, pretended to repent, but it was a false pretence. Now in this place the Prophet does not mean that the elders by adopting these rites professed to repent and humbly to solicit pardon; but refers to them only as tokens of sorrow; as though he had said, that the elders had no resources, and that the young women had no hope nor joy. For the elders did lie down on the ground, as it is usual with those who have no remedy. We now understand the meaning of the Prophet.[1] It follows,—

11. Mine eyes do fail with tears, my bowels are troubled, my liver is poured upon the earth, for the destruction of the daughter of my people; because the children and the sucklings swoon in the streets of the city.

11. Defecerunt in lachrymis oculi mei, conturbata sunt viscera mea, effusum est ad terram jecur meum, propter contritionem filiæ populi mei, dum evanuit parvulus et sugens ubera in compitis urbis.

The Prophet himself now speaks, and says that his *eyes were consumed with tears*, while weeping on account of the calamities of the people: even in the deepest grief tears at length dry up; but when there is no end of weeping, the sorrow, which as it were never ripens, must necessarily be

[1] The verse may be thus rendered,—

10. They sit on the ground, they are silent, the elders of the daughter of Sion;
They have cast dust on their head, they have girded on sackcloth;
They have bent to the ground their head, the daughters of Jerusalem.
—*Ed.*

very bitter. Jeremiah then expresses now the vehemence of his grief when he says that his *eyes failed through shedding tears.* He said in chap. ix., " Who will give me eyes for fountains ?" that is, who will make my eyes to turn into fountains, that they may continually flow ? and this he said, because he saw how dreadful a vengeance of God impended over the obstinate. But now, when he sees accomplished what he had dreaded, he says, that his eyes were consumed with weeping.

To the same purpose is what he adds, that his *bowels were disturbed.* It is the same verb as we have seen before, חמרמרו, *chemermeru ;* which some render " bound," as we also said then. I know not why one expositor has changed what he had elsewhere said rightly ; he puts here, " swollen have my bowels." But I see no reason why the verb should be taken here in a different sense, for it immediately follows, *my liver is poured forth on the ground.* He may, indeed, have included other parts of the intestines by stating a part for the whole. The word here properly means the liver, as when Solomon says, "He hath pierced my liver." (Prov. vii. 23.) But Jeremiah, in short, shews that all his faculties were so seized with grief, that no part was exempt. He then says that his *liver was poured forth,* but in the same sense in which he said that his bowels were disturbed. They are indeed hyperbolical expressions ; but as to the meaning, Jeremiah simply expresses his feelings ; for there is no doubt but that he was incredibly anxious and sorrowful on account of so great a calamity ; for he not only lamented the adversity in no ordinary way, but he also considered how wicked was that obstinacy in which the people had hardened themselves for almost fifty years ; for he had spent himself in vain, not for a short time, but for nearly fifty years he never ceased to speak to them. He then, no doubt, thought within himself what the people had deserved, so that he had no common dread of God's vengeance. This, then, was the reason why he said that his bowels were disturbed and his liver poured forth.[1]

[1] The verbs here are all in the past tense, and the versions so render them. Our version is wrong, as well as that of *Blayney* and *Henderson,*

He, however, mentions the cause of his sorrow, even *the breach* or destruction *of the daughter of his people;* and he mentions one thing in particular, because *the little one and he who sucked the breasts vanished away in the streets of the city;* for so I render the verb עטף, *otheph,* which properly means to cover; but its secondary meaning is to vanish away, as we shall again presently see. It was, indeed, a miserable sight, when not only men and women were everywhere slain, but when, through famine, little children also fainted. We, indeed, know that infants move our pity, for the tears of a child in hunger penetrate into our inmost souls. When, therefore, little children and those who hung on their mothers' breasts, cried through the streets of the city, it must have touched the most iron hearts. It was then not without reason that Jeremiah referred to this in particular, that *little children and sucklings vanished away,* not in a deserted and barren land, but in the very *streets of the city.* It follows,—

12. They say to their mothers, Where *is* corn and wine? when they swooned as the wounded in the streets of the city, when their soul was poured out into their mother's bosom.	12. Matribus suis dicunt, Ubi triticum et vinum? cum evanescunt (in evanescendo ipsos, *ad verbum*) tanquam vulneratus (*aut,* mortuus; dum evanescunt *ergo* tanquam vulnerati, *aut,* mortui; *est numeri enallage*) in compitis urbis (*iterum repetit,*) et cum se effundit (*vel,* effunditur) anima eorum in sinum matrum ipsorum.

There is either a personification in the words of the Prophet, or he speaks now of another party, for he cannot refer now to children sucking their mothers' breasts, for they could not have expressly said, *Where is corn and wine?* and the use of wine is not allowed to infants. Then the words of the Prophets extend further, for not infants, but children somewhat grown up, could have thus spoken. And in this view there is nothing unreasonable or forced, for he spoke of little children, and to little children he joined in-

in rendering them in the present tense; for the Prophet is describing how he felt when he witnessed the destruction of Jerusalem,—

11. Consume with tears did my eyes, agitated were my bowels,
Poured out on the ground was my liver, for the breach of the daughter of my people,
When faint did the child and the suckling in the streets of the city.
—*Ed.*

fants.[1] And now he refers only to one party, even that children, who could now speak, complained to their mothers that there was no bread nor wine, that is, no means of support, no food.

If, however, any one prefers a personification, I do not object; and this view would not be unsuitable, that even infants by their silence cried for food; for the tears of children speak more efficaciously than when one gives utterance to words.

However this may be, the Prophet intimates that such was the scarcity, that children died in the bosom of their mothers, and in vain sought food and cried that they were without support. He then says that they *said to their mothers*;[2] by which expression he means that their complaints were the more pitiable, because their mothers could afford them no help. And we know how tender and affectionate are the feelings of mothers, for a mother would willingly nourish her own child, not only with her own milk, but even, if possible, with her life. When, therefore, the Prophet says that children cried to their mothers, he means to represent a sad spectacle, and which ought justly to produce horror in the minds of all. *Where is bread and wine?* he says, even *when they vanished away* (some say "fainted," but I prefer, as I have said, this rendering) *as a dead man in the streets*; and further, *when they poured out*, a sadder thing still,—*when they poured out their souls into the bosom of their mothers.* It now follows,—

13. What thing shall I take to witness for thee? what thing shall I liken to thee, O daughter of Jerusalem? what shall I equal to thee,	13. Quid contestabor tibi (*vel*, adducam tibi testes, *vel*, testificabor tecum?) quid simile tibi faciam, filia Jerusalem (*vel*, cur? מה *potest trans-*

[1] That young children and infants are spoken of, is evident from the end of the verse; the one died in the streets, and the other in the mother's bosom. The question, "Where is corn," &c., is to be understood of the children, young boys and girls.—*Ed.*

[2] To correspond with the former verse, the versions render this, "They said to their mothers." The verb is, indeed, in the future tense, and it might be rendered, "To their mothers would they say;" for the Hebrew future may be thus rendered,—

12. To their mothers would they say, "Where is corn and wine?"
When they fainted as one wounded in the streets of the city,
When they poured out their life into the bosom of their mothers.—*Ed.*

that I may comfort thee, O virgin daughter of Zion? for thy breach *is* great like the sea; who can heal thee?

ferri utroque modo;) quid (*vel,* cur) æquabo tibi quicquam (*est repetitio, sed diverso verbo*) ut te consoler, virgo filia Sion? quia magna sicut mare contritio tua; quis sanabit te?

When we wish to alleviate grief, we are wont to bring examples which have some likeness to the case before us. For when any one seeks to comfort one in illness, he will say, "Thou art not the first nor the last, thou hast many like thee; why shouldest thou so much torment thyself; for this is a condition almost common to mortals." As, then, it is an ordinary way of alleviating grief to bring forward examples, the Prophet says, "What examples shall I set before thee? that is, why or to what purpose should I mention to thee this or that man who is like thee? or, *What* then *shall I call thee to witness,* or testify to thee?" But I prefer this rendering, "To what purpose should I bring witnesses to thee, who may say that they have seen something of a like kind? for these things will avail thee nothing."[1]

The Prophet, then, means that comforts commonly administered to those in misery, would be of no benefit, because the calamity of Jerusalem exceeded all other examples, as though he had said, "No such thing had ever happened in the world; God had never before thundered so tremendously against any people; were I, then, to seek to bring examples to thee, I should be utterly at a loss; for when I compare thee with others in misery, I find that thou exceedest them all." We now, then, perceive the meaning of the Prophet: he wished by this mode of speaking to exaggerate the grievousness of Jerusalem's calamity, for she had been afflicted in a manner unusual and unheard of before; as though he had said that the Jews had become miserable beyond all other nations. *Why* then *should I bring witnesses before thee? and why should I make any one like thee? why should I make other miserable people equal to thee?* He adds the reason or the end (for the ו, *vau,* here ought to be so rendered) *that I might comfort thee,* that is, after the usual manner of men.

[1] The simpler rendering would be, "What shall I testify (or declare) to thee?" So the *Sept.*: or, "What shall I call thee to witness?"—*Ed.*

He afterwards adds, *because great as the sea is thy breach* or breaking; that is, "Thy calamity is the deepest abyss: I cannot then find any in the whole world whom I can compare to thee, for thy calamity exceeds all calamities; nor is there anything like it that can be set before thee, so that thou art become a memorable example for all ages."

But when we hear the Prophet speaking thus, we ought to remember that we have succeeded in the place of the ancient people. As, then, God had formerly punished with so much severity the sins of his chosen people, we ought to beware lest we in the present day provoke him to an extremity by our perverseness, for he remains ever like himself. But whenever it may happen that we are severely afflicted and broken down by his hand, let us still know that there is yet some comfort remaining for us, even when sunk down in the lowest depth. The Prophet, indeed, exaggerates in this place the evils of the people; but he had previously begun to encourage the faithful to entertain hope; and he will again repeat the same doctrine. But it was necessary for the Prophet to use such words until those who were as yet torpid in their sins, and did not sufficiently consider the design of God's vengeance, were really humbled. He adds,—

14. Thy prophets have seen vain and foolish things for thee; and they have not discovered thine iniquity, to turn away thy captivity; but have seen for thee false burdens, and causes of banishment.

14. Prophetæ tui viderunt tibi vanitatem et insulsitatem (*vel*, insipidum,) et non aperuerunt super iniquitate tua (*hoc est*, non revelarunt tibi; *aut*, manifestarunt iniquitatem tuam,) ut converterent captivitatem tuam (*alii vertunt*, aversionem tuam, *vel*, defectionem) et viderunt tibi prophetias vanitatis, et expulsiones.

Here the Prophet condemns the Jews for that wantonness by which they had, as it were, designedly destroyed themselves, as though they had wilfully drunk sweet poison. They had been inebriated with those fallacies which we have seen, when impostors promised them a prosperous condition; for we have seen that false prophets often boldly declared that whatever Jeremiah threatened was of no account. Since, then, the Jews were inebriated with such flatteries, and disregarded God's judgment, and freely indulged themselves in their vices, the effect was, that God's wrath had been always and continually kindled by them. Now, then, Jeremiah reproves them for such wantonness, even because they wilfully sought to be deceived, and with avidity cast themselves into snares, by seeking for themselves flatterers as teachers. Micah also reproves them for the same thing, that they sought prophets who promised them a fruitful vintage and an abundant harvest. (Mic. ii. 10.) The meaning of Jeremiah is the same.

He says that *prophets had prophesied*, or had seen *vanity for them;* but the verb refers to prophecies, as prophets are called seers. He then says that *the prophets had seen vanity and insipidity.*[1] This availed not to extenuate the fault of the people; and Jeremiah does not here flatter the people, as though they had perished through the fault of others; and yet this was a common excuse, for most, when they had been deceived, complained that they had fallen through being led astray, and also that they had not been sufficiently cautious when subtle men were laying snares for them. But the Prophet here condemns the Jews, because they had been deceived by false prophets, as it was a just reward for their vainglory and ambition. For they had very delicate ears, and free reproofs could not be endured by them; in a word, when they rejected all sound doctrine, the devil must have necessarily succeeded in the place of God, as also Paul says, "that those were justly punished who were blinded by God so as to believe a lie, because they received not the truth." (2 Thess. ii. 11, 12.)

We now perceive the design of the Prophet: he says that the Jews had indeed been deceived by the false prophets; but this had happened through their own fault, because they had not submitted to obey God, because they had rejected sound doctrine, because they had been rebellious against all his counsels. At the same time, not only their crime

[1] So it means when applied to eatables, but folly or absurdity when applied to words. It comes from נבל, to fall, in the sense of decaying or degenerating. It is what is neither wise nor true. Hence it is rendered "foolishness" by the *Sept.;* "foolish" by the *Vulg.;* and "without substance" by the *Targ.*,—

Thy prophets, they have seen vanity and folly.

What they had seen were both "vain," useless, and "foolish," absurd.—*Ed.*

seems to have been thus exaggerated, but also their shame was brought before them,—because they had dared to set up these impostors against Jeremiah as well as other servants of God; for they had boasted greatly of these their false prophets whenever they sought to exult against God. How great was this presumption! When the false prophets had promised them security, they immediately triumphed in an insolent manner over Jeremiah, as though they were victorious. As, then, their wickedness and arrogance had been such against God, the Prophet justly retorts upon them, "Behold now as to your false prophets; for when they lately promised to you prosperity of every kind, I was inhumanly treated, and my calling was disdainfully repudiated by you; let now your false prophets come forward: be wise at length through your evils, and acknowledge what it is to have acted so haughtily against God and against his servants." We now understand why the Prophet says, "They have seen for you vanity and insipidity."

He adds, *they have not opened*, or revealed, &c. The preposition על, *ol*, is here redundant; the words are, "they have not revealed upon thine iniquity." There is, indeed, a suitableness in the words in that language, that they had not applied their revelations to the iniquities of the people, for they would have been thus restored to the right way, and would have thus obviated the vengeance of God.

Now, this passage ought to be carefully noticed: Jeremiah spake of the fallacies of the false prophets, which he said were insipid: he now expresses how they had deceived the people, even because they *disclosed not their iniquities.* Let us then know that there is nothing more necessary than to be warned, that being conscious of our iniquities we may repent. And this was the chief benefit to be derived from the teaching of the prophets. For the other part, the foretelling of future things would have had but little effect had not the prophets preached respecting the vengeance of God,—had they not exhorted the people to repentance,—had they not bidden them by faith to embrace the mercy of God. Then Jeremiah in a manner detects the false doctrines of those who had corrupted the prophetic doctrine, by saying that they *had not disclosed iniquities.* Let us then learn by this mark how to distinguish between the faithful servants of God and impostors. For the Lord by his word summons us before his tribunal, and would have our iniquities discovered, that we may loathe ourselves, and thus open an entrance for mercy. But when what is brought before us only tickles our ears and feeds our curiosity, and, at the same time, buries all our iniquities, let us then know that the refined things which vastly please men are insipid and useless. Let, then, the doctrine of repentance be approved by us, the doctrine which leads us to God's tribunal, so that being cast down in ourselves we may flee to his mercy.

He afterwards adds, *that they might turn back thy captivity;* some prefer, "thy defection"—and this meaning is not unsuitable; but the Prophet, I have no doubt, refers to punishment rather than to a crime. Then the captivity of the people would have been reversed had the people in time repented; for we obviate God's wrath by repentance: "If we judge ourselves," says Paul, "we shall not be judged." (1 Cor. xi. 31.) As, then, miserable men anticipate God's judgment when they become judges of themselves, the Prophet does not without reason say that the false prophets had not disclosed their iniquities, so that they might remain quiet in their own country, and never be driven into exile. How so? for God would have been thus pacified, that is, had the people willingly turned to him, as it is said in Isaiah, "And be converted, and I should heal them." (Isa. vi. 10.) Conversion, then, is said there to lead to healing; for as fire when fuel is withdrawn is extinguished, so also when we cease to sin fuel is not supplied to God's wrath. We now, then, perceive the meaning of the Prophet; he, in short, intimates that people had been destroyed because they sought falsehoods, while the false prophets vainly flattered them; for they would have in due time escaped so great evils, had the prophets boldly exhorted the people to repentance.[1]

[1] The verb rendered "turn back," means also to turn away or aside,

He then adds, *And they saw for thee prophecies of vanity and expulsions.* Though the word משאת, *meshat,* is often taken in a bad sense for a burden, that is, a hard prophecy which shews that God's vengeance is nigh, yet it is doubtful whether the Prophet takes it now in this sense, since he speaks of prophecies which gave hope of impunity to the people; and these were not משאות, *meshaut,* that is, they were not grievous and dreadful prophecies. But when all things are well considered, it will be evident that Jeremiah did not without reason adopt this word; for he afterwards adds an explanation. The word משאה, *meshae,* is indeed taken sometimes as meaning any kind of prophecy, but it properly means what is comminatory. But now, what does Jeremiah say? *They saw for thee burdens* which thou hast escaped. For to render odious the doctrine of the holy man, they called whatever he taught, according to a proverbial saying, a burden. Thus, then, they created a prejudice against the holy man by saying that all his prophecies contained nothing but terror and trouble. Now, by way of concession, the Prophet says, "They themselves have indeed been prophets to you, and they saw, but saw at length burdens."

While, then, the false prophets promised impunity to the people, they were flatterers, and no burden appeared, that is, no trouble; but these prophecies became at length much more grievous than all the threatenings with which Jeremiah had terrified them; and corresponding with this view is what immediately follows, *expulsions.* For the Prophet, I doubt not, shews here what fruit the vain flatteries by which the people had chosen to be deluded had produced: for hence it happened, that they had been expelled from their country and driven into exile. For if the reason was asked, why the people had been deprived of their own inheritance, the obvious answer would have been this, because they had chosen to be deceived, because they had hardened

and this is the meaning given it here by the *Syr.*, and most suitable to the passage,—

And they discovered not thine iniquity, to turn aside thy captivity.

That is, as the *Syr.* expresses it, to avert it.—*Ed.*

themselves in obstinacy by means of falsehoods and vain promises. Since, then, their exile was the fruit of false doctrine, Jeremiah says now that these impostors saw burdens of vanity, but which at length brought burdens; and then they saw מדוחים, *meduchim*,[1] expulsions, even those things which had been the causes of expulsion or exile.

PRAYER.

Grant, Almighty God, that though thou chastisest us as we deserve, we may yet never have the light of truth extinguished among us, but may ever see, even in darkness, at least some sparks, which may enable us to behold thy paternal goodness and mercy, so that we may especially be humbled under thy mighty hand, and that being really prostrate through a deep feeling of repentance, we may raise our hopes to heaven, and never doubt but that thou wilt at length be reconciled to us when we seek thee in thine only-begotten Son.—Amen.

Lecture Seventh.

15. All that pass by clap *their* hands at thee; they hiss and wag their head at the daughter of Jerusalem, *saying*, *Is* this the city that *men* call The perfection of beauty, The joy of the whole earth?

15. Plauserunt super te manibus suis (*id est*, comploserunt manus suas) omnes transeuntes per viam, sibilarunt, et moverunt caput suum super filia Jerusalem, An hæc urbs de qua dixerunt, perfecta decore, gaudium totius terræ?

The Prophet here reminds the Jews of the miseries by which they had been already in an extreme measure afflicted, so that these words seem redundant and somewhat unkind; for unseasonable is reproof when one lies down, as it were, worn out with evils. As this was the condition of the people, the Prophet ought not to have made more bitter their grief. But we have already referred to the reason

[1] There seems to be a mistake in this word of a ד for an ר, two letters very similar; for the *Targ.*, the *Syr.*, and the *Arab.*, must have so read the word, as they render it in the sense of what is deceptive, fallacious, or imaginary. It is in the last rendered "phantasms." The word occurs in Jer. xxii. 14, and is applied to chambers through which air or wind passed freely. It may be rendered here winds or airy things. Such was the character of their prophecies. This is far more suitable to the passage than expulsions or rejections, as given by the *Sept.* and *Vulg.*—*Ed.*

for this, even because the Jews, though they mourned and were extremely sorrowful in their calamities, did not yet consider whence their evils came. It was therefore necessary that they should be more and more awakened; for it is but of little profit for any one to suffer evils, except he has regard to God's judgment. We hence perceive the design of the Prophet, why he so much at large speaks of the miseries which were seen by all, and could not escape the notice of the Jews, who were almost overwhelmed with them; for it was not enough for them to feel their miseries, except they also considered the cause of them.

He then says, *All who have passed by clapped their hands and hissed and moved the head*, either in token of mockery, or of abhorrence, which is more probable. He then says, that they *moved* or shook *the head at the daughter of Jerusalem*,[1] *Is this the city of which they said, It is perfect in beauty, and the joy of the whole earth?* I know not why some render כלילת, *calilat*, a crown; it comes, as it is well known, from כלל, *calal*, which means fulness, or anything solid. He then says, that Jerusalem had been *perfect in beauty*, because God had adorned it with singular gifts; he had especially favoured it with the incomparable honour of being called by his name. Hence Jerusalem was in a manner the earthly palace of God, that is, on account of the Temple; and further, it was there that the doctrine of salvation was to be found; and remarkable was this promise, "From Sion shall go forth the law, and the word of God from Jerusalem." (Isa. ii. 3.) God had also promised to Ezekiel, that this city would be the fountain and origin of salvation to the whole world. (Ezek. xlvii. 1-12.) As, then, Jerusalem had been adorned with so remarkable gifts, the Prophet introduces here strangers, who ask, "Could it be that a city so celebrated for beauty had become a desolation?"

He calls it also *the joy of the whole earth;* for God had poured there his gifts so liberally, that it was a cause of joy to all. For we delight in beautiful things; and wherever

[1] Jeremiah relates what had taken place, the verbs being in the past tense. Our version is not correct in rendering the verbs in the present tense. The old versions follow the Hebrew.—*Ed.*

God's gifts appear, we ought to have our hearts filled with joy. Some give a more refined explanation—that Jerusalem had been the joy of the whole earth, because men have no peace except God be propitious to them; and there God had deposited the testimony and pledge of his favour: and thus Jerusalem made glad the whole world, because it invited all nations to God. This, at the first view, is plausible; but it seems to me more refined than solid. I am, therefore, content with this simple view, that Jerusalem was the joy of the whole earth, because God had designed that his favour should appear there, which might justly excite the whole world to rejoice.[1] It afterwards follows,—

16. All thine enemies have opened their mouth against thee; they hiss and gnash the teeth: they say, We have swallowed *her* up: certainly this *is* the day that we looked for; we have found, we have seen *it*.

16. Aperuerunt[2] super te os suum cuncti hostes tui, sibilarunt et frenduerunt dente (*vel*, dentibus;) dixerunt, Devorabimus; utique hic dies quem expectavimus; invenimus, vidimus.

Here, also, the Prophet introduces enemies as insolently exulting over the miseries of the people. He first says, that they had *opened the mouth*, even that they might loudly upbraid them; for he is not said to open the mouth who only speaks, but who insolently and freely utters his calumnies. God is, indeed, sometimes said emphatically to open his mouth, when he announces something that deserves special notice; and so Matthew says, that Christ opened his mouth when he spoke of true happiness. (Matt. v. 2.) But in this place and in others the enemy is said to open his mouth, who, with a full mouth, so to speak, taunts him whom

[1] The words may be rendered, "the joy of the whole land," *i.e.*, the land of Israel; which was strictly true.—*Ed.*

[2] This verse begins with פ, and the next with ע; thus the alphabetical order is deranged. The same thing occurs in the two next chapters, though in the first chapter the usual order of the letters is preserved. Many conjectures have been made on the subject, but no satisfactory reason has been assigned. The *Targ.* and the early versions, except the *Syr.*, follow in the three places the present text; only the *Sept.*, very strangely, prefix the letters in their alphabetical order, and yet give the verses as they now are. When, added to this, we find the *meaning* favours the present arrangement, we cannot but conclude that it was the original one, though the reason why Jeremiah changed, as to these two letters, even in three instances, the alphabetical order, cannot now be discovered.—*Ed.*

he sees worn out with evils. Hence, he refers to petulance or insolence, when he says, that enemies had *opened their mouth.*

He then adds, that they had *hissed.* By hissing he no doubt means scoffing or taunting; for it immediately follows, that they had *gnashed with* their *teeth*, as though he had said, that enemies not only blamed and condemned them, but had also given tokens of extreme hatred; for he who gnashes with his teeth thus shews the bitterness of his mind, and even fury; for to gnash the teeth is what belongs to a wild beast. The Prophet then says, that enemies had not only harassed the people with taunts and scoffs, but had also cruelly and even furiously treated them. Now we know that to men of ingenuous minds, such a treatment is harder than death itself: for it is deemed by many a hard thing to fall in battle—and we see how men of war expose themselves to the greatest danger; but a disgraceful death is far more bitter. The Prophet, then, no doubt, amplifies the miseries of the people by this circumstance, that they had been harassed on every side by taunts. And he mentions this on purpose, because reproofs by the prophets had not been received by them; for we know how perversely the Jews had rebelled against the prophets, when they reproved them in God's name. As, then, they would not have borne the paternal reproofs of God, they were thus constrained to bear the reproaches of enemies, and to receive the just reward of their pride and presumption. Nor is there a doubt, as I have said, but that the Prophet related reproaches of this kind, and the scoffs of enemies, that the people might at length know that they had been exposed to such evils, because they had proudly rejected the reproofs given them by the prophets.

He says, that enemies spoke thus, *We have devoured; surely this is the day which we have expected;* as though they triumphed when they saw that they got the victory, and that they could do with the people as they pleased. And as I have said, this in itself was a very bitter thing to the people; but when the Prophet related, as in the person of the enemies, what was already sufficiently known to them, the people ought to have called to mind the reason why they had been so severely afflicted ; and this is what the Prophet clearly sets forth in the next verse ; for he adds,—

17. The Lord hath done *that* which he had devised; he hath fulfilled his word that he had commanded in the days of old: he hath thrown down, and hath not pitied: and he hath caused *thine* enemy to rejoice over thee; he hath set up the horn of thine adversaries.

17. Fecit Jehova quod cogitaverat, complevit sermonem suum quem præceperat à diebus antiquis: diruit (*vel*, evertit) et non pepercit ; et exhilaravit super te inimicum, et extulit cornu hostium tuorum.

Had the Prophet related only the boastings of enemies, the people would have probably become more hardened in their sorrow. But now, on the other hand, he assumes a different character. After having represented how insolently the enemies conducted themselves, he now says, *Jehovah hath done what he had determined ;* and thus from the taunts of enemies he calls the attention of the people to the judgment of God. For when enemies insult us, we indeed feel hurt, but afterwards grief in a manner blunts our feelings. Our best remedy then is, not to have our thoughts fixed on the insolence of men, but to know what the Scripture often reminds us, that the wicked are the scourges of God by which he chastises us. This, then, is the subject which the Prophet now handles. He says that God had *done,* &c. ; as though he had said, that however enemies might exceed moderation, yet if the people attended to God there was a just cause why they should humble themselves.

He says, first, that *Jehovah had done what he had determined :* for the word to *think* is improperly applied to God, but yet it is often done, as we have before seen. He then says, that he had *fulfilled the word* which he had formerly commanded ; for had the Prophet touched only on the secret counsel of God, the Jews might have been in doubt as to what it was. And certainly, as our minds cannot penetrate into that deep abyss, in vain would he have spoken of the hidden judgments of God. It was therefore necessary to come down to the doctrine, by which God, as far as it is expedient, manifests to us what would otherwise be not only hidden, but also incomprehensible ; for were we to inquire into God's judgments, we should sink into the deep. But when we direct our minds to what God has taught us, we find that he reveals to us whatever is necessary to be known; and though even by his word, we cannot perfectly know his hidden judgments. yet we may know them in part, and as I have said, as far as it is expedient for us. This, then, is the reason why the Prophet, after having spoken of God's counsels and decrees, adds *the word.*

Let us then hold to this rule, even to seek from the Law and the Prophets, and the Gospel, whatever we desire to know respecting the secret judgments of God; for, were we to turn aside, even in the smallest degree, from what is taught us, the immensity of God's glory would immediately swallow up all our thoughts; and experience sufficiently teaches us, that nothing is more dangerous and even fatal than to allow ourselves more liberty in this respect than what behoves us. Let us then learn to bridle all curiosity when we speak of God's secret judgments, and instantly to direct our minds to the word itself, that they may be in a manner inclosed there. Moreover, the Prophet was also able, in this manner, more easily to check whatever the Jews might have been otherwise ready to object: for we know that they were always wont to murmur, and that as soon as the prophets spake, they brought forward many exceptions, by which they attempted to confute their doctrine.

As, then, they were an unteachable people, Jeremiah did not only speak of God's hidden judgments, of which some doubt might have been alleged; but, in order to cut off every occasion for disputes and contentions, he mentioned *the word* itself; and thus he held the Jews as it were convicted; for, as it is said by Moses, they could not have objected and said, "Who shall ascend into heaven? who shall descend into the deep? who shall pass over the sea?" (Deut. xxx. 12-14;) for in their mouth was God's word, that is, God had sufficiently made known his judgments, so that they could not complain of obscurity. We now then perceive another reason why the Prophet joined the word to God's judgments and decrees or counsel.

But he says that this *word* had been published *from ancient days;* and here he touches on the untameable obstinacy of the people; for had they been admonished a few days or a short time before, they might have expostulated with God; and there might have been some specious appearance that God had as it were made too great haste in his rigour. But as prophets had been sent, one after another, and as he had not ceased for many years, nay, for many ages, to exhort them to repentance, and to threaten them also that they might repent, hence their inveterate impiety more fully betrayed itself. This is the reason why the Prophet now mentions the *ancient days*, in which God had published his word.

He at length adds, *he hath subverted and not spared.* He does not here charge God with too much rigour, but rather he reproves the Jews, so that from the grievousness of their punishment they might know how intolerable had been their iniquity. He would then have them to judge of their sins by their punishment, for God does not act unjustly towards men. It hence follows, that when we are severely afflicted by his hand, it is a proof that we have been very wicked.

He then concludes that it was God who had *exhilarated their enemies, and raised up their horn.*[1] By these words he confirms the doctrine on which I have already touched, that we ought to turn our eyes to God, when men are insolent to us and exult over our miseries; for such a reproach might otherwise wholly overwhelm us. But when we consider that we are chastised by God, and that the wicked, however petulantly they may treat us, are yet God's scourges, then we resolve with calm and resigned minds to bear what would otherwise wear us out by its acerbity. It follows,—

18. Their heart cried unto the Lord, O wall of the daughter of Zion, let tears run down like a river day and night: give thyself no rest; let not the apple of thine eye cease.	18. Clamavit cor eorum ad Dominum; Mure filiæ Sion, deducas tanquam fluvium lachrymas (*vel*, tanquam fluvius) die et nocte; ne des requiem tibi, ne sileat (*hoc est*, ne quiescat) pupilla oculi tui.

He means not that their *heart* really *cried to God*, for there was no cry in their heart; but by this expression he

[1] Literally it is,—
And he hath made to rejoice over thee the enemy,
He hath exalted the horn of thine oppressors.—*Ed.*

sets forth the vehemence of their grief, as though he had said, that the heart of the people was oppressed with so much sorrow, that their feelings burst forth into crying; for crying arises from extreme grief, and when any one cries or weeps, he has no control over himself. Silence is a token of patience; but when grief overcomes one, he, as though forgetting himself, necessarily bursts out into crying. This is the reason why he says that their *heart cried to Jehovah.*

But we must observe, that the piety of the people is not here commended, as though they complained of their evils to God in sincerity and with an honest heart: on the contrary, the Prophet means that it was a common cry, often uttered even by the reprobate; for nature in a manner teaches this, that we ought to flee to God when oppressed by evils; and even those who have no fear of God exclaim in their extreme miseries, "God be merciful to us." And, as I have said, such a cry does not flow from a right feeling or from the true fear of God, but from the strong and turbid impulse of nature: and thus God has from the beginning rendered all mortals inexcusable. So, then, now the Prophet says, that the Jews *cried* to God, or that *their heart cried;* not that they looked to God as they ought to have done, or that they deposited with him their sorrows and cast them into his bosom, as the Prophet encourages us to do; but because they found no remedy in the world—for as long as men find any comfort or help in the world, with that they are satisfied. Whence, then, was this crying to God? even because the world offered them nothing in which they could acquiesce; for it is indigenous, as it were, in our nature (that is, corrupt nature) to look around here and there, when any evil oppresses us. Now, when we find, as I have said, anything as a help, even an empty spectre, to that we cleave, and never raise up our eyes to God. But when necessity forces us, then we begin to cry to God. Then the Prophet means that the people had been reduced to the greatest straits, when he says that their *heart cried to God.*

He afterwards turns to the *wall* of Jerusalem, and ascribes understanding to an inanimate thing. *O wall* of Jerusalem, he says, *draw down tears as though thou wert a river;* or, as a river; for both meanings may be admitted. But by stating a part for the whole, he includes under the word *wall*, the whole city, as it is well known. And yet there is still a personification, for neither houses, nor walls, nor gates, nor streets, could shed tears; but Jeremiah could not, except by this hyperbolical language, sufficiently express the extent of their cry. This was the reason why he addressed the very *wall* of the city, and bade it to *shed tears like a river.*[1]

There seems to be some allusion to the ruins; for the walls of the city had been broken down as though they were melted. And then the Prophet seems to allude to the previous hardness of the people, for their hearts had been extremely stupified. As, then, they never had been flexible, whether addressed by doctrine, or exhortations, or threatenings, he now by implication brings forward in contrast with them the walls of the city, as though he had said, "Hitherto no one of God's servants could draw even one tear from your eyes, so great was your hardness; but now the very walls weep, for they dissolve, as though they would send forth rivers of waters. Therefore the very stones turn to tears, because ye have hitherto been hardened against God and all prophetic instruction."

He afterwards adds, *Spare not thyself, give not thyself rest day or night, and let not the daughter of thine eye,* or the pupil of thine eye, *cease,* literally, be silent; but to be silent is metaphorically taken in the sense of ceasing or resting. He intimates that there would be, nay, that there was now, an occasion of continual lamentation; and hence he exhorted them to weep *day and night;* as though he had said, that sorrow would continue without intermission, as there would

[1] The meaning suggested by the *Vulgate* is the most appropriate. The words may be rendered thus,—

Cried has their heart to the Lord,
"O the wall of the daughter of Sion!"—
Bring down like a torrent the tear, day and night;
Give no rest to thyself,
Let not cease the daughter of thine eye.

Their exclamation was, "O the wall," &c. Then follow the words of Jeremiah to the end of the chapter; but the daughter of Sion, not the wall, is exhorted to weep and repent. "The daughter of the eye," may be the tear, as suggested by *Blayney* and approved by *Horsley;* and it would be more suitable here.—*Ed.*

be no relaxation as to their evils. But we must bear in mind what we have before said, that the Prophet did not speak thus to embitter the sorrow of the people. We indeed know that the minds of men are very tender and delicate while under evils, and then that they rush headlong into impatience; but as they were not as yet led to true repentance, he sets before them the punishment which God had inflicted, that they might thereby be turned to consider their own sins. It follows,—

19. Arise, cry out in the night; in the beginning of the watches pour out thine heart like water before the face of the Lord: lift up thy hands toward him for the life of thy young children, that faint for hunger in the top of every street.

19. Surge, Clama nocte principio excubiarum (custodiarum, *ad verbum, sed significat vigilias nocturnas;*) effunde tanquam aquas cor tuum coram facie Domini; attolle ad ipsum manus tuas propter animam parvulorum tuorum, qui deficiunt fame in capite omnium compitorum.

The Prophet now explains himself more clearly, and confirms what I have lately said, that he mentioned not the calamities of the people except for this end, that those who were almost stupid might begin to raise up their eyes to God, and also to examine their life, and willingly to condemn themselves, that thus they might escape from the wrath of God.

The Prophet then bids them to *rise* and *to cry.* Doubtless they had been by force constrained by their enemies to undertake a long journey: why then does he bid them to *rise,* who had become fugitives from their own country, and had been driven away like sheep? He regards, as I have said, the slothfulness of their minds, because they were still lying torpid in their sins. It was then necessary to rouse them from this insensibility; and this is what the Prophet had in view by saying, *Rise.*[1] And then he bids them to *cry at the beginning of the watches,* even when sleep begins to creep on, and the time is quieter; for when men go to bed, then sleep comes on, and that is the main rest. But the Prophet bids here the Jews to cry, and in their uneasiness to utter their complaints at the very time when others take their rest. Yet he did not wish them heedlessly to

[1] The simpler meaning, as stated by *Gataker*, is, "Rise" from thy bed; for she is exhorted to cry in the night.—*Ed.*

pour forth into the air their wailings, but bade them to present their prayers to God. Then as to the circumstances of that time, he repeats what we have already seen, that so great was their mass of evils, that it allowed the people no relaxation; in short, he intimates that it was a continual sorrow.

But, as I have said, he would have the Jews not simply to cry, but after having exhorted them to *pour out their hearts like waters,* he adds, *before the face of Jehovah.* For the unbelieving make themselves almost hoarse by crying, but they are only like brute beasts; or if they call on God's name, they do this, as it has been said, through a rash and indiscriminate impulse. Hence the Prophet here makes a difference between the elect of God and the reprobate, when he bids them to pour forth their hearts and their cries *before* God, so as to seek alleviation from him, which could not have been done, were they not convinced that he was the author of all their calamities; and hence, also, arises repentance, for there is a mutual relation between God's judgment and men's sins. Whosoever, then, acknowledges God as a judge, is at the same time compelled to examine himself and to inquire as to his own sins. We now understand the meaning of the Prophet's words.

For the same purpose he adds, *Raise up to him thy hands.* This practice of itself is, indeed, not sufficient; but the Scripture often points out the real thing by external signs. Then the elevation of the hands, in this place and others, means the same thing as prayer; and it has been usual in all ages to raise up the hands to heaven, and the expression often occurs in the Psalms, (Ps. xxviii. 2; cxxxiv. 2;) and when Paul bids prayers to be made everywhere, he says, "I would have men to raise up pure hands without contention." (1 Tim. ii. 8.) God has no doubt suggested this practice to men, that they may first go beyond the whole world when they seek him; and, secondly, that they may thus stimulate themselves to entertain confidence, and also to divest themselves of all earthly desires; for except this practice were to raise up our minds, (as we are by nature inclined to superstition,) every one would seek God either at his feet or by his side. Then God has planted in men this feeling, even to raise upwards their hands, in order that they may go, as I have said, beyond the whole world, and that having thus divested themselves of all vain superstition, they may ascend above the heavens. This custom, I allow, is indeed common among the unbelieving; and thus all excuse has been taken away from them. Though, then, the unbelieving have been imbued with gross and delirious fantasies, so as to connect God with statues and pictures, yet this habit of raising up the hands to heaven ought to have been sufficient to confute all their erroneous notions. But it would not be enough to seek God beyond this world, so that no superstition should possess our minds, except our minds were also freed from all worldly desires. For we are held entangled in our lusts, and then we seek what pleases the flesh, and thus, for the most part, men strive to subject God to themselves. Then the elevation of the hands does also shew that we are to deny ourselves, and to go forth, as it were, out of ourselves whenever we call on God. These are briefly the things which may be said of the use of this ceremony or practice.

But we must remember what I have referred to, that the Prophet designates the thing itself by an outward sign, when he bids them to *raise up the hands* to God. He afterwards shews the necessity of this, *because of the soul of thy little ones, who faint in famine;*[1] but the ב, *beth*, is redundant here, —*who*, then, *through famine faint* or fail, and that openly. For it might have happened that those who had no food pined away at home, and thus fainted because no one gave them aid, because their want was not known. But when infants in public places breathed out their souls through famine, hence was evident that extreme state of despair, which the Prophet intended here to set forth by mentioning *at the head of all the streets.* It follows,—

20. Behold, O Lord, and consider to whom thou hast done this. Shall the women eat their fruit, *and* children of a span long? shall the priest	20. Vide, Jehova, et aspice cui feceris sic; an comedent mulieres fructum suum (*hoc est*, fœtus suos,) parvulos educationis? an occidetur

[1] Rather, "who fainted through famine;" for he refers to what had taken place.—*Ed.*

and the prophet be slain in the sanctuary of the Lord?	in sanctuario Domini sacerdos et propheta?

Here, also, Jeremiah dictates words, or a form of prayer to the Jews. And this complaint availed to excite pity, that God had thus afflicted, not strangers, but the people whom he had adopted. Interpreters do, indeed, give another explanation, " See, Jehovah, To whom hast thou done this?" that is, Has any people been ever so severely afflicted? But I do not think that the comparison is made here, which they seek to make, but that the people only set before God the covenant which he had made with their fathers, as though they said, " O Lord, hadst thou thus cruelly raged against strangers, there would have been nothing so wonderful; but since we are thine heritage, and the blessed seed of Abraham, since thou hast been pleased to choose us as thy peculiar people, what can this mean, that thou treatest us with so much severity?"

We now, then, perceive the real meaning of the Prophet, when, in the person of the people, he speaks thus, *See, and look on, Jehovah, to whom thou hast done this;* for thou hast had to do with thy children: not that the Jews could allege any worthiness; but the gratuitous election of God must have been abundantly sufficient to draw forth mercy. Nor do the faithful here simply ask God to *see*, but they add another word, *Look on.* By the two words they more fully express the indignity of what had happened, as though they said, that it was like a prodigy that God's people should be so severely afflicted, who had been chosen by him: *see,* then, *to whom thou hast done this.*

And this mode of praying was very common, as we find it said in the Psalms, " Pour forth thy wrath on the nations which know not thee, and on the kingdoms which call not on thy name." (Ps. lxxix. 6.) And a similar passage we have before observed in our Prophet. (Jer. x. 25.) The sum of what is said is, that there was a just reason why God should turn to mercy, and be thus reconciled to his people, because he had not to do with aliens, but with his own family, whom he had been pleased to adopt. But the rest I shall defer until to-morrow.

PRAYER.

Grant, Almighty God, that as thy Church at this day is oppressed with many evils, we may learn to raise up not only our eyes and our hands to thee, but also our hearts, and that we may so fix our attention on thee as to look for salvation from thee alone; and that though despair may overwhelm us on earth, yet the hope of thy goodness may ever shine on us from heaven, and that, relying on the Mediator whom thou hast given us, we may not hesitate to cry continually to thee, until we really find by experience that our prayers have not been in vain, when thou, pitying thy Church, hast extended thy hand, and given us cause to rejoice, and hast turned our mourning into joy, through Christ our Lord.—Amen.

Lecture Eighth.

We explained yesterday the complaint of the Prophet, when he set before God his own covenant. For it might have appeared unreasonable that God should deal with so much severity with the Church which he had adopted. Hence the Prophet said, *See, Jehovah, to whom thou hast done this.* He now mentions some things calculated to produce horror, and thus to obtain pardon from God, *Should women eat their own fruit?* that is, their own fœtus, *the infants of nursings?* This, as I have said, was a horrible thing: for we see that mothers often forget their own life in their concern for the safety of their infants. That a child, then, should be devoured by its mother, was a most abominable thing; and yet we know that it was done. It hence appears, that the Israelites, when blinded by God, had fallen into this barbarity: for it happened in the siege of Samaria, as sacred history declares; and the Prophet now mentions the same thing as having taken place in his time, and he repeats the same in the fourth chapter. And Josephus also says, that when the city was besieged by Titus, the state of things was such, that mothers agreed to eat their own children, and that they cast lots who should first slay their child, and that they stole a leg or an arm from one another. Though it was so inhuman a thing, yet the Prophet seeks to turn God to mercy by adducing so great an enormity. He then says, that it was by no means right, that *mothers should eat their own children, the children of nursings*, or nurturings.[1]

He afterwards adds, *Should the priest and the prophet be slain in the sanctuary of the Lord?* This was another indignity, by which he sought to lead God to shew mercy. We indeed know that the priests and the prophets were deemed sacred; and in the Psalms, where Abraham, Isaac, and Jacob are referred to, God, in order to shew how much they were to be regarded, says, "Touch not my Christs, and to my prophets do no harm." (Ps. cv. 15.) As, then, the priests and the prophets were especially under the protection of God, what is here said was an intolerable atrocity. But when the profanation of the Temple was added, it was still a greater prodigy. Jeremiah then complains, not only that the priests and the prophets were slain, but that they were slain in the sanctuary. It now follows,—

21. The young and the old lie on the ground in the streets: my virgins and my young men are fallen by the sword; thou hast slain *them* in the day of thine anger; thou hast killed, *and* not pitied.

21. Jacuerunt in terra per compita puer et senex; virgines meæ et adolescentes mei ceciderunt gladio; occidisti in die iræ tuæ; mactasti et non pepercisti.

Here he relates in the person of the Church another calamity, that the young and the aged were lying prostrate in the streets; and he joins children to the old men, to shew that there was no difference as to age. Then he says that

[1] *Educationum.* Our version is nearly the *Vulg.* It is paraphrased by the *Sept.*, "who suck the breasts;" and the *Targ.* is, "who are clad in silks." *Blayney* rightly says, that טפח is the open palm of the hand; and he gives this as the literal rendering of the words, "children of palms;" that is, children of sufficient age to be carried about. His version of this line is, "Little ones dandled on the hands." *Horsley* approves of this meaning.

The previous word, פרים, has been a difficulty to most, the final *mem* being masculine. "Fruit," in the sense of offspring, is applied to men as well as to women. We may take the final *mem* in נשים, as a pronoun, "their wives;" the same are meant as in verse 18, "their voice," *i.e.*, the citizens of Jerusalem. Thus the construction will be quite grammatical.

Should their own wives eat their offspring,
Infants dandled on the hands!
Should they be killed in the sanctuary of the Lord,
The priest and the prophet!

It is the language of humble expostulation.—*Ed.*

dead bodies were lying promiscuously in public places. He adds, that *virgins* and *young men* had *fallen by the sword;* by which he confirms the previous clause, for there is nothing new said here, but only the manner is shewn by which they had been slain; for slain by the sword had been the young men and young women without any distinction; the enemies at the same time had not spared the old, while they killed the very flower of the people.

But the Prophet at the same time shews that all this was to be ascribed to God, not that the Jews might expostulate with him, but that they might cease vainly to lament their calamities, and in order that they might on the contrary turn to God. Hence he does not say that the young and the old had been slain by the enemies, but by God himself. But it was difficult to convince the Jews of this, for they were so filled with rage against their enemies, that they could not turn their thoughts to the consideration of God's judgments. This, then, is the reason why the Prophet makes God the author of all their calamities; *Thou,* he says, *hast slain in the day of thy wrath; thou hast killed and not spared.* And though the people seem here in a manner to contend with God, we must yet bear in mind the design of the Prophet, even to teach the people to look to God himself, so that they might know that they had to do with him. For there ought to be a passing from one truth to another, so that men, conscious of their sins, should first give glory to God, and then humbly deprecate the wrath which they have deserved. It follows at length,—

22. Thou hast called, as in a solemn day, my terrors round about; so that in the day of the Lord's anger none escaped nor remained: those that I have swaddled and brought up hath mine enemy consumed.

22. Vocasti tanquam ad diem festum terrores meos undique, et non fuit in die indignationis Jehovæ superstes ac residuus; quos enutrivi et educavi, hostis meus consumpsit eos (*sed abundat relativum.*)

Here he uses a most appropriate metaphor, to shew that the people had been brought to the narrowest straits; for he says that *terrors* had on every side surrounded them, as when a solemn assembly is called. They sounded the trumpets when a festival was at hand, that all might come up to the Temple. As, then, many companies were wont to come to Jerusalem on feast-days—for when the trumpets were sounded all were called—so the Prophet says that terrors had been sent by God from every part to straiten the miserable people: *thou hast*, then, *called my terrors all around*,—how? *as to a feast-day*, the day of the assembly; for מועד, *muod*, means the assembly as well as the place and the appointed time.[1]

But we must ever bear in mind what I have already referred to, that though enemies terrified the Jews, yet this was to be ascribed to God, so that every one might acknowledge for himself, that the Chaldeans had not come by chance, but through the secret impulse of God. He afterwards adds, *in the day of Jehovah's wrath* (he changes the person) *there was none alive*, or remaining; nay, he says *the enemy has consumed those whom I had nursed and brought up*. Here he transfers to enemies what he had before said was done by God, but in this sense, that he understood God as the chief author, and the Chaldeans as the ministers of his vengeance. Now follows,—

CHAPTER III.

1. I *am* the man *that* hath seen affliction by the rod of his wrath.	1. Ego vir videns afflictionem in virga indignationis ejus.

The word עברה, *obere*, properly means assault, passing over limits; but what is peculiar to man is often in Scripture ascribed to God. Here also he changes the person, for

[1] The verb for calling or summoning is in the future tense, and must be so, to preserve the alphabetical character of the elegy, but it is rendered as in the past tense by all the versions, but the reason why does not appear. The future in Hebrew is often to be rendered as a subjunctive, potential, or optative: so here,—

Shouldest thou summon, as on a festival day,
My terrors all around!—
And there was not, in the day of Jehovah's wrath,
A fugitive or a survivor;
Whom I dandled and brought up,
My enemy has consumed them.

The first two lines are a kind of expostulation: "My terrors" mean my terrifiers, according to the *Vulg.*, the abstract for the concrete.—*Ed.*

he spoke before of the people under the person of a woman, as it is often done; but now the Prophet himself comes before us. At the same time there is no doubt but that by his own example he exhorted all others to lamentation, which was to be connected with true repentance. And this chapter, as we shall see, is full of rich instruction, for it contains remarkable sentiments which we shall consider in their proper places.

Some think that this Lamentation was written by Jeremiah when he was cast into prison; but this opinion seems not probable to me; and the contents of the chapter sufficiently shew that this ode was composed to set forth the common calamity of the whole people. Jeremiah, then, does not here plead his own private cause, but shews to his own nation what remedy there was for them in such a state of despair, even to have an immediate recourse to God, and on the one hand to consider their sins, and on the other to look to the mercy of God, so that they might entertain hope, and exercise themselves in prayer. All these things we shall see in their due order.

The Prophet then says that he was *an afflicted man,* or a man who saw affliction. This mode of speaking, we know, is common in Scripture—to see affliction—to see good and evil—to see life and death. He then says that he had *experienced* many afflictions, and not only so, but that he had been given up as it were to miseries,—how? *by the rod of his fury.* He does not mention the name of God, but Jeremiah speaks of him as of one well known, using only a pronoun. Now, then, at the very beginning, he acknowledges that whatever he suffered had been inflicted by God's hand. And as all the godly ought to be convinced of this, that God is never angry without just reasons, there is included in the word *wrath* a brief confession, especially when it is added, *by the rod,* or staff. In short, the Prophet says that he was very miserable, and he also expresses the cause, for he had been severely chastised by an angry God.

2. He hath led me, and brought *me into* darkness, but not *into* light.	2. Me deduxit et proficisci fecit in tenebras, et non in lucem.

The letters of the alphabet are tripled in this chapter,

which I had omitted to mention. In the first two chapters each verse begins with the successive letters of the alphabet, except that in the last chapter there is one instance of inversion, for Jeremiah has put פ, *phi*, before ע, *oin;* or it may be that the order has been changed by the scribes; but this is uncertain. Here then, as I have said, each letter is thrice repeated. Then the first, the second, and the third verse begins with א, *aleph;* and the fourth begins with ב, *beth*, and so he goes on to the end.[1]

He confirms here the last verse, for he shews the cause or the manner of his afflictions, *for he had been led into darkness and not into light.* This kind of contrast has not the same force in other languages as it has in Hebrew. But when the Hebrews said that they were in darkness and not in the light, they amplified that obscurity, as though they had said that there was not even a spark of light in that darkness, it being so thick and obscure. This is what the Prophet now means. And we know what is everywhere understood in Scripture by darkness, even every kind of lamentation: for the appearance of light exhilarates us, yea, the serenity of heaven cheers and revives the minds of men. Then darkness signifies all sorts of adversities and the sorrow which proceeds from them. He afterwards adds,—

3. Surely against me is he turned; he turneth his hand *against me* all the day.	3. Utique contra me vertetur, convertet manum suam quotidie (*vel*, toto die, *quanquam in duobus verbis videtur futurum tempus debere resolvi in præteritum, vel saltem Propheta actum continuum designat, ut sæpe fieri solet.*)

Now he says that *God was an adversary to him;* for this is what the verb ישב, *isheb*, means, *he is turned against me.* As an enemy, when intending to fight, comes to meet one

[1] The verses in this chapter are needlessly multiplied: It would have been better had each verse contained a letter, for the length of this chapter is the same with the two foregoing; the only difference is, that the lines, or alternate lines, begin with the same letter three times, as follows,—

א I am the man who hath seen affliction,
Through the rod of his indignation;
א Me hath he led and caused to walk
In darkness and not in light;
א Surely against me he turns,
Upset *me* does his hand all the day.

The three next lines, or alternate lines, begin with ב, and so on to the end of the alphabet.—*Ed.*

from the opposite side, so the Prophet says of God, who had become an enemy to him; and he teaches the same thing in another way when he says that he perceived that the hand of God was against him: *He turns,* he says, *against me his hand daily,* or all the day, כל-היום, *cal-eium.* But the Prophet simply means constancy, as though he had said that there was no truce, no cessation, because God manifested the rigour of his vengeance without limit or end. He afterwards adds,—

4. My flesh and my skin hath he made old; he hath broken my bones.	4. Senio confecit carnem meam (senescere fecit, *ad verbum*) et pellem meam (*vel,* cutem;) confregit ossa mea.

These, as it evidently appears, are metaphorical words. Illness often makes people to look old, for from pain proceeds leanness: thus the skin is contracted, and the wrinkles of old age appear even in youths. As, then, sorrows exhaust moisture and strength, hence he is said to grow old who pines away in mourning. This is what the Prophet now means. *God,* he says, *has made my flesh and my skin to grow old,* that is, he hath worn me out, within and without, so that I am almost wasted away.

He then adds, *He hath broken my bones.* This seems to be hyperbolical; but we have said elsewhere that this simile does not in every instance express the greatness of the sorrow which the faithful feel under a sense of God's wrath. Both David and Hezekiah spoke in this way; nay, Hezekiah compares God to a lion, "As a lion," he says, "has he broken my bones." (Isa. xxxviii. 23.) And David says at one time that his bones wasted away, at another that they were broken, and at another that they were reduced to ashes; for there is nothing more dreadful than to feel that God is angry with us. The Prophet, then, did not only regard outward calamities, but the evidence of God's vengeance; for the people could see nothing else in their distresses except that God was their enemy—and this was true; for God had often exhorted them to repentance; but upon those whom he had found incurable, he at length, as it was just, poured forth his vengeance to the uttermost. This, then, was the reason why the Prophet said, that God had *broken* his *bones.* He then adds,—

5. He hath builded against me, and compassed *me* with gall and travail.	5. Ædificavit contra me, et circumdedit felle et molestia.

The words, as translated, may seem harsh, yet they have no common beauty in Hebrew. The Prophet says he was *blocked up* and straitened as it were by walls; and as we shall see, he repeats this comparison three times; in other words, indeed, but for the same purpose.

God, he says, *hath built against me,* as, when we wish to besiege any one, we build mounds, so that there may be no escape. This, then, is the sort of building of which the Prophet now speaks: God, he says, holds me confined all around, so that there is no way of escape open to me.

He then gives a clearer explanation, that he was *surrounded by gall*[1] or poison *and trouble.* He mentions poison first, and then, without a figure, he shews what that poison was, even that he was afflicted with many troubles. He afterwards adds,—

6. He hath set me in dark places, as *they that be* dead of old.	6. In tenebris jacere me fecit tanquam mortuos seculi.

Here he amplifies what he had before said of poison and trouble; he says that he was *placed in darkness,* not that he might be there for a little while, but remain there for a long time; *he hath made me,* he says, *to dwell in darkness.* But the comparison which follows more clearly explains the Prophet's meaning, *as the dead of ages.* The word עולם, *oulam,* may refer to future or past time. Some say, *as the dead for ever,* who are perpetually dead. But the Scripture elsewhere calls those *the dead of ages* who have been long buried, and have decayed, and whose memory has become nearly extinct. For as long as the dead body retains its form, it seems more like a living being; but when it is reduced to ashes, when no bone appears, when the whole skin

[1] The *Sept.*, the *Targ.*, and the *Arab.* render this "my head;" but the *Vulg.* and the *Syr.*, "gall." It occurs again in verse 19, and is rendered "gall" by the *Targ.* and all the versions. He was "surrounded with gall," with what was bitter to him, and "with faintness," with what made him to faint. Hence, in the next verse, he represents himself as being like the dead.—*Ed.*

and nerves and blood have perished, and no likeness to man remains, there can then be no hope of life. The Scripture then calls those *the dead of ages,* who have wholly decayed. So also in this place the Prophet says, that he *dwelt in darkness,* into which he had been cast by God's hand, and that he dwelt there as though he had been long dead, and his body had become now putrid.

This way of speaking appears indeed hyperbolical; but we must always remember what I have reminded you of, that it is not possible sufficiently to set forth the greatness of that sorrow which the faithful feel when terrified by the wrath of God. He then adds,—

7. He hath hedged me about, that I cannot get out; he hath made my chain heavy.	7. Sepsit me, ut non egrediar; aggravavit compedem meum.

Here he says, first, that he was held *shut up;* for גדר, *gidar,* is to enclose, and גדרה, *gidare,* means a fence or a mound, or an enclosure of any kind. He then says, that he was shut up as it were by a fence, so that he could not go forth; literally, it is, *and I shall not go forth;* but the conjunction here is to be taken as denoting the end. He has *shut me up,* he says, or he has enclosed me, *that I might not get out.*

It then follows, *He hath made heavy my fetter.* His meaning is, that he was not only bound with fetters, but so bound that he could not raise up his feet, as though he had said, that he not only had fetters, but that they were so heavy that he could not even move his feet.

8. Also when I cry and shout, he shutteth out my prayer.	8. Etiam si clamem et vociferer, clausit precationem meam (*vel,* precationi meæ.)

The Prophet describes here the extremity of all evils, that it availed him nothing to cry and to pray. And yet we know that we are called to do this in all our miseries: "The strongest tower is the name of the Lord, to it will the righteous flee and shall be safe." (Prov. xviii. 10.) Again, "Whosoever shall call on the name of the Lord shall be saved." (Joel ii. 32.) And Scripture is full of testimonies of this kind; that is, that God graciously invites all the faithful to himself: "He shall call upon me, and I will hear him." (Ps. xci. 15.) "In the day when I call, answer me speedily." (Ps. cii. 2.) "Before they call, I will answer." (Isa. lxv. 24.) In short, there is no need to collect all the passages; but we may be content with this one thing, that when God claims to himself this prerogative, that he answers prayers, he intimates that it is what cannot be separated from his eternal essence and godhead; that is, that he is ready to hear prayer. And hence the Psalmist concludes, "To thee shall all flesh come." (Ps. lxv. 3.) When, therefore, Jeremiah complains that his prayers were in vain, and without any fruit or effect, it seems strange and inconsistent. But we know that God holds the faithful in suspense, and so hears as to prove and try their patience, sometimes for a long time. This is the reason why he defers and delays his aid.

It is no wonder, then, that God did not hear the prayers of his servant, that is, according to the judgment of the flesh. For God never rejects his own, nor is he deaf to their prayers and their sighs; but the faithful often speak according to what the flesh judges. As, then, the Prophet found that he obtained nothing by prayer, he says that his *prayer was shut out*, or that the door was closed against him, so that his prayer did not come to God.

Now, this passage is worthy of special notice; for except God immediately meets us, we become languid, and not only our ardour in prayer is cooled but almost extinguished. Let us, then, bear in mind, that though God may not help us soon, yet our prayers are never repudiated by him; and since we see that the holy fathers experienced the same thing, let us not wonder, if the Lord at this day were to try our faith in the same manner. Let us, therefore, persevere in calling on Him; and should there be a longer delay, and our complaint be that we are not heard, yet let us proceed in the same course, as we shall see the Prophet did. It follows,—

9. He hath enclosed my ways with hewn stone; he hath made my paths crooked.	9. Sepivit (*idem est verbum quod ante vidimus*) vias meas lapide quadrato, semitas meas pervertit.

Other metaphors are used. Some think that the Prophet

refers to the siege of Jerusalem, but such a view is not suitable. The metaphors correspond with one another, though they are somewhat different. He had said before, that he was enclosed by God, or surrounded as with a mound; and now he transfers this idea to his ways. When the life of man is spoken of, it is, we know, compared to a way. Then the Prophet includes under this word all the doings of his life, as though he had said, that all his plans were brought into straits, as though his way was shut up, so that he could not proceed: "Were I to proceed in any direction, an obstacle is set before me; I am compelled to remain as it were fixed." So the Prophet now says, his *ways were enclosed*, because God allowed none of his counsels or his purposes to be carried into effect.

And to the same purpose he adds, that God had *perverted his ways*, that is, that he had confounded all his doings, and all his counsels.

But these words are added, *with a squared stone.* The verb גזז, *gizaz*, means to cut; hence the word גזית, *gizit*, signifies a polished stone, or one trimmed by the hammer. And we know that such stones are more durable and firmer than other stones. For when unpolished stones are used, the building is not so strong as when the stones are squared, as they fit together better. Then the Prophet intimates that the enclosures were such that he could by no means break through them, as they could not be broken. He, in short, means that he was so oppressed by God's hand, that whatever he purposed God immediately reversed it. We now, then, perceive what he means by saying, that all his *ways* were *subverted* or overturned by God.[1] This is not to be understood generally, for it is God who directs our ways. But he is said to pervert our ways, when he disconcerts our counsels, when all our purposes and efforts are rendered void; in a word, when God as it were meets us as an adversary, and impedes our course; it is then that he is said

[1] "Subverted" is the *Vulg.*, "obstructed" the *Sept.*, and "rendered oblique" the *Syr.* The meaning is, "turned aside." He had built as it were a wall of hewn stones across his way, and thus he turned aside his goings or his paths, so that he was constrained to take some other course. —*Ed.*

to pervert our ways. But this ought not to be understood as though God blinded men unjustly, or as though he led them astray. The Prophet only means that he could find no success in all his counsels, in all his efforts and doings, because he had God opposed to him. Here I stop.

PRAYER.

Grant, Almighty God, that as thou didst in former times so severely chastise thy people, we may in the present day patiently submit to all thy scourges, and in a humble and meek spirit suffer ourselves to be chastised as we deserve; and that we may not, in the meantime, cease to call on thee, and that however slowly thou mayest seem to hear our prayers, we may yet persevere continually to the end, until at length we shall really find that salvation is not in vain promised to all those who in sincerity of heart call on thee, through Christ our Lord.—Amen.

Lecture Ninth.

10. He *was* unto me *as* a bear lying in wait, *and as* a lion in secret places.	10. Ursus insidians fuit mihi (ipse mihi,) leo in latebris.

Harsh is the complaint when Jeremiah compares God to a bear and a lion. But we have said that the apprehension of God's wrath so terrified the faithful, that they could not sufficiently express the atrocity of their calamity; and then borne in mind must also be what we have stated, that they spoke according to the judgment of the flesh; for they did not always so moderate their feelings, but that something fell from them worthy of blame. We ought not, then, to make as a rule in religion all the complaints of holy men, when they were pressed down by the hand of God; for when their minds were in a state of confusion, they uttered much that was intemperate. But we ought, on the other hand, to acknowledge how great must be our weakness, since we see that even the strongest have thus fallen, when God exercised severity towards them.

Though, then, it does not seem that it was said in due honour, that God did *lie in wait* as *bears* for travellers, or as *lions* in their dens; yet, if we consider how much the faithful dreaded the tokens of God's wrath, we shall not wonder at this excess. It is then certain that the Prophet brings before us here not only evidences of the fear of God, of religion and humility, but also of the corrupt feelings of the flesh; for it cannot be, but that the infirmity of men will betray itself in extreme evils. He adds, what is of the same import,—

11. He hath turned aside my ways, and pulled me in pieces: he hath made me desolate.	11. Vias meas pervertit et scidit me (*vel*, dissipavit, *vel*, laceravit.) posuit me vastatam (*vel*, quasi vastitatem.)

In this verse also the Prophet shews how grievously the faithful are disturbed when they feel that God is adverse to them. But he uses the same figure as yesterday, though the word סורר, *surer*, is different: what he used yesterday was עוה, *oue*, but in the same sense.

He then says that his *ways* had been *perverted;*[1] and for this reason, because he had been disappointed in his purpose; whatever he did was made void, because God by force prevented him. When we undertake to do anything, a way is open to us; but when there is no success, our way is said to be perverted. And this is done by God, who has all events, prosperous as well as adverse, in his own hand. As, then, God directs our ways when he blesses our counsels and our actions; so, on the other hand, he perverts them, when all things turn out unsuccessfully, when our purpose is not done and events do not answer our expectations.

He afterwards adds, *He hath torn me* or broken me. The verb פשח, *peshech*, means properly to cut, but here to tear or scatter. It follows lastly, *he hath made me a waste.* In this expression he includes the other two things; for he who is reduced to desolation, does not hold on his way, nor find any exit; he is also drawn here and there, as though he was torn into several parts. We hence see that the Prophet here complains of extreme evils, for there was no hope of deliverance left. He adds,—

12. He hath bent his bow, and set me as a mark for the arrow.	12. Extendit (*vel*, intendit) arcum suum, et statuit me quasi signum sagittæ.

[1] The word, having the last letter doubled, means to turn aside again and again, "He has often turned aside my ways."—*Ed.*

Here the Prophet introduces another metaphor, that God had shot him with arrows, as he was made a mark to them. Jeremiah has elsewhere often used the word מטרא, *methera*, for a prison; but here it means a mark at which arrows are levelled, and such is its meaning in Job xvi. 12, where there is a similar complaint made. The meaning is, that the people, in whose name Jeremiah speaks, had been like marks, because God had directed against them all his arrows. It is, indeed, a fearful thing when God aims at us, that he may discharge his darts and arrows in order to hit and wound us. But as God had so grievously afflicted his people, that he seemed to have poured forth all his vengeance, the Prophet justly complains that the people had been like marks for arrows.

13. He hath caused the arrows of his quiver to enter into my reins.	13. Induxit in renes meos filios pharetræ suæ (*id est*, sagittas.)

He goes on with the same metaphor; he said in the last verse that God had levelled his bow; he now adds, that his *arrows had penetrated into his reins*, that is, into his inward parts. But we must bear in mind what the Prophet meant, that God had dealt so severely with the people, that no part, even the innermost, was sound or untouched, for his arrows had perforated their very reins. He afterwards adds,—

14. I was a derision to all my people, *and* their song all the day.	14. Fui risus (*vel*, ludibrium) toti populo meo, pulsatio (*vel*, canticum, *quod pulsatur ab organo et instrumento musico*) quotidie (*vel*, toto die.)

The Prophet again complains of the reproaches to which God had exposed the Jews. We have said that of all evils the most grievous is reproach, and experience teaches us that sorrow is greatly embittered when scoffs and taunts are added to it; for he who silently bears the most grievous sorrows, becomes broken in heart when he finds himself contumeliously treated. This, then, is the reason why the Prophet again amplifies the miseries of the people, because they were exposed to the scoffs of all men. But it may seem a strange thing that the Jews were derided by their own people. This is the reason why some think that the

Prophet complains of his own private evils, and that he does not represent the whole people or the public condition of the Church. But it may also be said in reply, that the Prophet does not mean that the people were derided by themselves, which could not be; but it is the same as though he had said, that their state was so disgraceful, that while they looked on one another, they had a reason for taunting, if this their condition was allowed to continue.

In short, the Prophet does not mean what was actually done, but he simply complains that their calamity was liable to all kinds of reproaches, so that any one looking on Jerusalem might justly deride such a disgraceful spectacle. And it was, as we have said, a most equitable reward, for they had not ceased to reproach God. Then rendered to them was what they had deserved, when God loaded them in turn with dishonour.

He afterwards adds, that he was *their song*, that is, of derision; for it is a confirmation of the former clause, and the same complaint is also found in Job. He says that he was their song *daily* or all the day. This constancy, as it has been said, proved more clearly the grievousness of the evil.

15. He hath filled me with bitterness, he hath made me drunken with wormwood.	15. Satiavit me amaritudinibus, saturavit me felle.

Some render the last word "wormwood," but this word seems not to me to suit the passage, for though wormwood is bitter, yet it is a wholesome herb. I therefore take it in this and like places for poison or gall; and ראש, *rash*, as we shall see, is joined with it. To satiate, is also a metaphor very common. Then the Prophet means that he was full of bitterness and gall; and he thus had regard to those calamities from which so much sorrow had proceeded.

We hence also gather that the faithful were not free from sorrow in their evils, for bitterness and gall sufficiently shew that their minds were so disturbed that they did not bear their troubles with sufficient patience. But they struggled with their own infirmity, and their example is set before us that we may not despond when bitterness and gall lay hold on our minds; for since the same thing happened to the best servants of God, let us bear in mind our own infirmity, and at the same time flee to God. The unbelieving nourish their bitterness, for they do not unburden their souls into the bosom of God. But the best way of comfort is, when we do not flatter ourselves in our bitterness and grief, but seek the purifying of our souls, and in a manner lay them open, so that whatever bitter thing may be there, God may take it away and so feed us, as it is said elsewhere, with the sweetness of his goodness. He adds,—

16. He hath also broken my teeth with gravel-stones, he hath covered me with ashes.	16. Confregit (*vel*, contrivit) lapillo dentes meos, involvit me (fœdavit me, *alii autem*, versavit) in pulvere.

Many renderings are given of these words: there is, however, no over-statement here; for, as it has been often said, the grief of the people under such a mass of evils could not be sufficiently expressed. The Prophet, no doubt, extended here his hand to the weak, who would have otherwise lain down as dead; for under such evils the ruin of the whole nation, the fall of the city, and the destruction of the temple, it could not be but such thoughts as these must have occurred. Now, as to any one unacquainted with such a trial, he would soon succumb, had no remedy been presented to him. The Prophet then dictates for all the godly such complaints as they might, so to speak, pour forth confidently and freely into the bosom of God.

We hence see that here is even expressed whatever might occur to the minds of God's children, so that they might not hesitate in their straits to direct their prayers to God, and freely confess whatever they suffered in their souls. For shame closes up the door of access; and thus it happens that we make a clamour as though God were far away from us; hence impatience breaks out almost to a rage. But when an access to God is opened to us, and we dare to confess what burdens our minds, this, as I have said, is the best way for obtaining relief and comfort. We must then understand the design of the Prophet, that he suggests words to the faithful, that they might freely cast their cares and sorrows on God, and thus find some alleviation.

For this reason, he says that his *teeth* had been *broken by a little stone* or pebble.[1] The same expression, if I mistake not, is found in Job. It is a metaphor taken from those who press stones instead of bread under their teeth; for when grit lies hid in bread, it hurts the teeth. Then inward and hidden griefs are said to be like small stones, which break or shatter the teeth. For the Prophet does not speak here of large stones, but on the contrary he speaks of pebbles or small stones, which deceive men, for they lie hid either in bread or in meat, or in any other kind of food. As, then, the teeth are hurt by pressing them, so the Prophet says that his sorrows were most bitter, as that part, as it is well known, is very tender; and when any injury is done to the teeth, the pain spreads instantly almost through the whole body. This is the reason why he says that his teeth were broken.

Then he adds, that he was *covered with dust*, or that he was lying down or dragged along in the dust. The expression is taken from those who are drawn by way of reproach along the ground, as a carcase is, or some filthy thing which we abhor.[2] Thus the Prophet complains that there was nothing short of extreme evils. He adds,—

17. And thou hast removed my soul far off from peace: I forgat prosperity.	17. Et remota fuit à pace anima mea, oblitus sum boni.

By saying that his *soul was remote from peace*, he means that no good remained; for by peace, as it is well known, the Hebrews understood every kind of prosperity. And he explains himself by another clause, that he had *forgotten*

[1] The word means grit or gravel, rendered "pebble" by the *Sept.*, and "stones" by the *Syr.* and the *Targ.* It is rendered "gravel" in Prov. xx. 17. The verb only occurs here and in Ps..cxix.; and to wear out, is its most suitable meaning,—

And he hath worn out with grit my teeth.—*Ed.*

[2] The verb rendered "covered," is found only here, and is translated "fed" by the *Sept.* and *Vulg.*; "tumbled" or laid low, by the *Targ.*; and "besprinkled," by the *Syr.* As he had said, that his food had been as it were grit, he could not have said that he was fed with ashes. Therefore the *arg.* or the *Syr.* is the most suitable, that God had laid him low in ashes, *Tr* that he had besprinkled or covered him with ashes.—*Ed*

every good; and this forgetfulness ought to be understood, so to speak, as real or entire; for if there had been any reason for rejoicing, it would not have been forgotten; for all are naturally pleased with what is pleasant, nay, they with avidity seek what delights them. It would then be contrary to nature to forget things good and pleasant to us. But the Prophet means here a privation. Hence the forgetfulness of which he speaks is nothing else but alienation from everything good, as though he had said (as the previous clause shews) that he was far removed from every hope of peace.

But the expression is much more emphatical, when he says, that his soul was far removed from peace. By *soul* he does not mean himself only, (for that would be frigid,) but he understands by it all things connected with him, as though he had said, " Wherever I look around me, I find no peace, and no hope appears to me." Hence it was, that all the faculties of his soul were far removed from all experience of good things. It follows,—

18. And I said, My strength and my hope is perished from the Lord.	18. Et dixi, Periit fortitudo mea, et spes mea à Jehova.

This verse shews what I have before reminded you of, that the Prophet does not here speak as though he was divested of every sin, and prescribed a perfect rule for prayer. But, on the contrary, in order to animate the faithful to seek God, he sets before them here an instance of infirmity which every one finds true as to himself. It was yet a most grievous trial, because the Prophet almost despaired; for since faith is the mother of hope, it follows, that when any one is overwhelmed with despair, faith is extinct. Nevertheless the Prophet makes this declaration, *Perished,* he says, *has my strength and my hope from God.*[1]

[1] The word "strength" is rendered "victory" by the *Sept.*, "end" by the *Vulg.*, "splendour" by the *Syr.*, and "valour" by the *Targ.* It means superiority, excellency, rather than strength,—

And I said, Perished hath my excellency,
And my expectation from Jehovah.

Whatever he had that was excellent had perished; and perished also had every good he expected from Jehovah. The meaning is not, that these things perished from Jehovah, but that his excellency and his expectation from Jehovah had perished.—*Ed.*

He does not speak through some inconsiderate impulse, as though he was suddenly carried away, as many things happen to us which we have had no thought of; but he speaks what was, as it were, fixed in his mind. As he said, "Perished has my hope and strength from Jehovah," it is evident that his faith was not slightly shaken, but had wholly failed: but the expression, *I said*, renders the thing still stronger; for it means, as it is well known, a settled conviction. The Prophet was then fully persuaded that he was forsaken by God; but what does this mean? We ought indeed to maintain this, that faith sometimes is so stifled, that even the children of God think that they are lost, and that it is all over with their salvation. Even David confesses the same thing; for it was an evidence of despair, when he declared, "I said in my haste, Vanity is every man." (Ps. cxvi. 11.) He had almost failed, and he was not master of himself when he was thus agitated. There is no doubt but that the Prophet also expressly reminded the faithful that they ought not to despair, though despair laid hold on their minds, or though the devil tempted them to despair, but that they ought then especially to struggle against it. This is indeed, I allow, a hard and perilous contest, but the faithful ought not to faint, even when such a thing happens to them, that is, when it seems to be all over with them and no hope remains; but, on the contrary, they ought nevertheless to go on hoping, and that, indeed, as the Scripture says elsewhere, against hope, or above hope. (Rom. iv. 18.)

Let us then learn from this passage, that the faithful are not free from despair, for it enters into their souls; but that there is yet no reason why they should indulge despair; on the contrary, they ought courageously and firmly to resist it; for when the Prophet said this, he did not mean that he succumbed to this trial, as though he had embraced what had come to his mind; but he meant, that he was as it were overwhelmed for a short time. Were any one to ask, How can it be that hope and despair should reside in the same man? the answer is, that when faith is weak, that part of the soul is empty, which admits despair. Now, faith is sometimes not only enfeebled, but is also nearly stifled. This, indeed, does not happen daily, but there is no one whom God deeply exercises with temptations, who does not feel that his faith is almost extinguished. It is then no wonder, that despair then prevails; but it is for a moment. In the meantime, the remedy is, immediately to flee to God and to complain of this misery, so that he may succour and raise up those who are thus fallen. He then adds,—

19. Remembering mine affliction and my misery, the wormwood and the gall.

19. Recordari (*vel,* recordando, *alii,* recordare) afflictionis meæ et ærumnæ meæ (*alii vertunt,* humiliationem, *alii,* peccatum; *sed nomen afflictionis vel ærumnæ melius convenit*) veneni et fellis (*iterum ponitur* לענה *quod vertunt quidam,* absynthium, *sed potius est amaritudo vel venenum,* veneni *ergo* et fellis.)

The verb may be considered as an imperative; it is an infinitive mood, but it is often taken in Hebrew as an imperative. Thus, many deem it a prayer, *Remember my affliction and my trouble, the gall and the poison.* This might be admitted; but what others teach I prefer: that this verse depends on the last. For the Prophet seems here to express how he had almost fallen away from hope, so that he no longer found strength from God, even because he was overwhelmed with evils; for it is very unreasonable to think, that those who have once experienced the mercy of God should cast away hope, so as not to believe that they are to flee to God any more. What seems then by no means congruous the Prophet here in a manner excuses, and shews that it was not strange that he succumbed under extreme evils, for he had been so pressed down by afflictions and troubles, that his soul became as it were filled with poison and gall.[1]

But in the meantime, he shews by the word *remember,* how such a trial as this, when it comes, lays hold on our minds, that is, when we think too much of our evils. For the faithful ought to hold a middle course in their afflictions,

[1] The verb "remember" is rendered as an imperative by the *Targ.*, the *Vulg.*, and the *Syr.;* and it is so rendered by *Henderson.—Ed.*

lest they contract a torpor; for as hence indifference and stupidity arise, they ought to rouse themselves to a due consideration of their evils; but moderation ought to be observed, lest sorrow should swallow us up, as Paul also warns us (2 Cor. ii. 7.) They then who fix their minds too much on the remembrance of their evils, by degrees open the door to Satan, who may fill their hearts and all their thoughts with despair. The Prophet then describes here the fountain of evils, when he says, that he remembered his *affliction and trouble;* and suitable to this is what immediately follows,—

20. My soul hath *them* still in remembrance, and is humbled in me.	20. Recordando recordabitur, et humiliabitur in me (*vel,* super me) anima mea.

The Prophet seems in other words to confirm what he had said, even that the memory of afflictions overwhelmed his soul. For the soul is said to be humbled in or upon man, when he lies down under the burden of despair. It is the soul that raises man up, and as it were revives him; but when the soul is cast as it were on man, it is a most grievous thing; for it is better to lie down a dead body than to have this additional burden, which makes the case still worse. A dead body might indeed lie on the ground without strength and motion, but it may still retain its own place; but when the soul is thus cast down, it is said to press down man, though lifeless, more and more. This then is what the Prophet means. And yet he says that he was so occupied with this remembrance, that he could not thence withdraw his mind.

There is no doubt but that he also intended here to confess his own infirmity, and that of all the faithful; and the reason of this we have already explained. Then relying on this doctrine, even when all our thoughts press us down, and not only lead us to despair, but also hurry us on and cast us headlong into it, let us learn to flee even then to God and to lay before him all our complaints, and let us not be ashamed, because we see that this mode of proceeding is suggested to us by the Holy Spirit. It follows,—

21. This I recall to my mind, therefore have I hope.	21. Hoc revocabo ad cor meum, propterea sperabo.

We see here what I have already stated, that if we struggle against temptations, it will be a sure remedy to us, because our faith will at length emerge again, and gather strength, yea, it will in a manner be raised up from the lowest depths. This is what the Prophet now shews: *I will recall this,* he says, *to my heart, and therefore will I hope.* How can despair produce hope from itself? This would be contrary to nature. What then does the Prophet mean here, and what does he understand by the pronoun *this,* זאת, *zat?* Even that being oppressed with evils, he was almost lost, and was also nearly persuaded that no hope of good any more remained. As then he would recall this to mind, he says that he would then have new ground of hope, that is, when he had recourse to God; for all who devour their own sorrows, and do not look to God, kindle more and more the hidden fire, which at length suddenly turns to fury. Hence it comes that they clamour against God, as though they were doubly insane. But he who is conscious of his own infirmity, and directs his prayer to God, will at length find a ground of hope.

When therefore we recall to mind our evils, and also consider how ready we are to despair, and how apt we are to succumb under it, some hope will then arise and aid us, as the Prophet here says.[1]

It must still be observed, that we ought to take heed lest we grow torpid in our evils; for hence it happens that our minds become wholly overwhelmed. Whosoever then would profit by his evils, should consider what the Prophet says here came to his mind: for he at length came to himself, and surmounted all obstacles. We see then that God brings

[1] The pronoun "this" is by most referred to what the next verse contains; but as a clause intervenes, this can hardly be the meaning. The verses 19, 20, and 21, I render thus,—

19. Remember my affliction and my abasement,
The wormwood and the gall.
20. Remembering thou wilt remember *them*,
For bowed down within me is my soul:
21. This I recall to my mind;
Therefore will I hope.

He prays, then he expresses his confidence that God would hear his prayer; and "this" refers to the assurance he felt that God would remember his afflicted state, and on this ground he entertained hope. In the next verse he states what confirmed this hope.—*Ed.*

light out of darkness, when he restores his faithful people from despair to a good hope; yea, he makes infirmity itself to be the cause of hope. For whence is it that the unbelieving cast away hope? even because security draws them away from God; but a sense of our own infirmity draws us even close to him; thus hope, contrary to nature, and through the incomprehensible and wonderful kindness of God, arises from despair. It follows,—

22. It *is of* the Lord's mercies that we are not consumed, because his compassions fail not.	22. Clementiæ Jehovæ, quòd non sumus consumpti (*vel*, certè non sunt consumptæ,) certè non defecerunt miserationes ejus.

The first clause may be explained in two ways: The view commonly taken is, that it ought to be ascribed to God's mercy that the faithful have not been often consumed. Hence a very useful doctrine is elicited—that God succours his own people, lest they should wholly perish. But if we attend to the context, we shall see that another sense is more suitable, even that the *mercies of God were not consumed, and that his compassions had not failed.* The particle כי, *ki*, is inserted, but ought to be taken as an affirmative only, *surely the mercies of God are not consumed;*[1] and then,—*surely his compassions have not failed.* And he afterwards adds,—

23. *They are* new every morning: great *is* thy faithfulness.	23. Novæ ad singula mane; magna veritas tua.

This verse confirms what I have said, that the same truth is here repeated by the Prophet, that God's mercies were not consumed, nor had his compassions failed. How so? Because they were *new*, or renewed, every day; but he puts

[1] So the *Targ.* and all the versions, except the Vulg.; they read תמו. "The mercies of Jehovah" is the nominative case absolute,—

22. The mercies of Jehovah, verily they have no end,
For his compassions never fail.
23. Renewed (are they) in the morning;
Great is thy faithfulness.

"Renewed" refers to "mercies," *i. e.*, blessings, the fruit of mercy; and God's mercies have no end, because his compassions ever continue. "In the morning," that is, after a night of affliction. If the rendering be made literal, "in the mornings," the meaning is the same; they follow the previous nights of trouble. Blessings, being as it were suspended or withheld during the night, are again renewed in the morning.—*Ed.*

morning, and that in the plural number. I am surprised at the hour striking so soon; I hardly think that I have lectured a whole hour.

PRAYER.

Grant, Almighty God, that as there are none of us who have not continually to contend with many temptations, and as such is our infirmity, that we are ready to succumb under them, except thou helpest us,—O grant, that we may be sustained by thine invincible power, and that also, when thou wouldest humble us, we may loathe ourselves on account of our sins, and thus perseveringly contend, until, having gained the victory, we shall give thee the glory for thy perpetual aid in Christ Jesus our Lord.—Amen.

Lecture Tenth.

In the last lecture the Prophet said that the *mercies* of God are renewed daily. This must indeed be viewed according to the apprehension of men, for to God belongs no change. But the mercies of God seem to be renewed when he for a time hides his face, and again becomes reconciled to us. The Prophet mentions *morning;* and he alludes, as I think, to this passage in the Psalms—"If weeping dwells with us in the evening, yet joy will return in the morning." (Ps. xxx. 5.) He then means that God hastens to succour men in misery.

He subjoins the word *truth*, because a sense of God's mercy can never come to us except he offers it to us. Were then God to take away the promise, all the miserable would inevitably perish; for they can never lay hold on his mercy except through his word. This, then, is the reason why Scripture so often connects these two things together, even God's mercy and his faithfulness in fulfilling his promises. It now follows,—

24. The Lord *is* my portion, saith my soul; therefore will I hope in him.	24. Portio mea Jehova, dixit anima mea; ideo sperabo in eo.

The Prophet intimates in this verse that we cannot stand firm in adversities, except we be content with God alone and his favour; for as soon as we depart from him, any adversity that may happen to us will cause our faith to fail. It is then the only true foundation of patience and hope to trust in God alone; and this is the case when we are persuaded that his favour is sufficient for our perfect safety. In this sense it is that David calls God his portion. (Ps. xvi. 5.) But there is in the words an implied contrast, for most men seek their happiness apart from God. All desire to be happy, but as the thoughts of men wander here and there, there is nothing more difficult than so to fix all our hopes in God so as to disregard all other things.

This then is the doctrine which the Prophet now handles, when he says, that those alone could hope, that is, persevere in hope and patience, who have so received God as their portion as to be satisfied with him alone, and to seek nothing else besides him. But he speaks emphatically, that his *soul* had thus *said.* Even the unbelieving are ashamed to deny what we have stated, that the whole of our salvation and happiness is found in God alone. Then the unbelieving also confess that God is the fountain of all blessings, and that they ought to acquiesce in him; but with the mouth only they confess this, while they believe nothing less. This then is the reason why the Prophet ascribes what he says to his *soul,* as though he had said, that he did not boast, like hypocrites, that God was his portion, but that of this he had a thorough conviction. *My soul* has said, that is, I am fully convinced that God is *my portion; therefore will I hope in him.* We now understand the meaning of this passage.

It remains for us to make an application of this doctrine: That we may not then fail in adversities, let us bear in mind this truth, that all our thoughts will ever wander and go astray, until we are fully persuaded that God alone is sufficient for us, so that he may become alone our heritage. For all who are not satisfied with God alone, are immediately seized with impatience, whenever famine oppresses them, or sword threatens them, or any other grievous calamity. And for this reason Paul also says, "If God be for us, who can be against us? I am persuaded that neither famine, nor nakedness, nor sword, nor death, nor life, can separate me from the love of God, which is in Christ." (Rom. viii. 31, 35-39.) Then Paul lays hold of the paternal favour of God as a ground of solid confidence; for the words *in Christ* sufficiently show that those are mistaken interpreters who take this love passively, as though he had said, that the faithful would never cease to love God, though he exercised them with many afflictions. But Paul meant that the faithful ought so to fix their minds on God alone, that whatever might happen, they would not yet cease to glory in him. Why? because God is their life in death, their light in darkness, their rest in war and tumult, their abundance in penury and want. It is in the same sense our Prophet now says, when he intimates that none hope in God but those who build on his paternal favour alone, so that they seek nothing else but to have him propitious to them. It afterwards follows,—

25. The Lord *is* good unto them that wait for him, to the soul *that* seeketh him.	25. Bonus Jehova expectanti ipsum, (*vel*, speranti in eum,) animæ quærenti ipsum.

He continues the same subject: he however adds now something to it, even that God always deals mercifully with his servants, who recumb on him, and who seek him. We hence see that the last verse is confirmed, where he said that he was content with God alone, while suffering all kinds of adversity: How so? for God, he says, is *good to those who wait for him.*[1] It might have been objected and said, that adversities produce sorrow, weariness, sadness, and anguish, so that it cannot be that they retain hope who only look to God alone; and it is no doubt true that, when all confess that they hope in God, they afterwards run here and there; and the consequence is, that they fail in their adversities. As, then, this might have been objected to the Prophet, he gives indirectly this answer, that God is good to those who wait for him, as though he had said, that the confidence which recumbs on God alone cannot disappoint us, for God will at length shew his kindness to all those who hope in him. In short, the Prophet teaches us here, that the bless-

[1] There is more authority for the word for "wait" being in the singular than in the plural, as it is given in the *Syr.*—*Ed.*

ings of God, by which he exhilarates his own children, cannot be separated from his mercy or his paternal favour. Such a sentence as this, "Whatever can be expected is found in God," would be deemed frigid by many; for they might object and say, as before stated, that they were at the same time miserable. Hence the Prophet reminds us here that God's blessings flow to us from his favour as from a fountain, as though he had said, "As a perennial fountain sends forth water, so also God's goodness manifests and extends itself."

We now, then, understand the Prophet's meaning. He had indeed said, that we ought to acquiesce in God alone; but now he adds, by way of favour, regarding the infirmity of men, that God is kind and bountiful to all those who hope in him. The sum of what he states is, as I have said, that God's goodness brings forth its own fruits, and that the faithful find by experience, that nothing is better than to have all their thoughts fixed on God alone. God's goodness, then, ought to be understood, so to speak, as actual, even what is really enjoyed. As, then, God deals bountifully with all who hope in him, it follows that they cannot be disappointed, while they are satisfied with him alone, and thus patiently submit to all adversities. In short, the Prophet teaches here what the Scripture often declares, that hope maketh not ashamed. (Rom. v. 5.)

But the second clause must be noticed: for the Prophet defines what it is to hope in God, when he says that he is good to *the soul that seeks him.* Many indeed imagine hope to be I know not what—a dead speculation; and hypocrites, when God spares them, go on securely and exult, but their confidence is mere ebriety, very different from hope. We must then remember what the Prophet says here, that they alone hope in God who from the heart seek him, that is, who acknowledge how greatly they need the mercy of God, who go directly to him whenever any temptation harasses them, and who, when any danger threatens them, flee to his aid, and thus prove that they really hope in God. It now follows,—

26. *It is* good that *a*

26. Bonum et expectabit et silebit ad sa-

man should both hope and quietly wait for the salvation of the Lord.

lutem Jehovæ (*ad verbum; vertunt tamen quidam*, bonus sperabit et silebit ad salutem Jehovæ; *sed potius in neutro genere accipio vocem*, טוב, *sicut in proximo versu qui sequetur*, Bonum viro, *et cætera.*)

It is, indeed, an abrupt phrase when he says, *Good and he will wait;* for these words are without a subject; but as it is a general statement, there is no ambiguity. The Prophet means that it is *good to hope and to be silent as to the salvation of God.* Then the verbs in the future tense ought to be rendered as subjunctives, as though it was said, "It is good when any one hopes in the salvation of Jehovah, and is silent, that is, bears patiently all his troubles until God succours him."[1]

But the Prophet here reminds us, that we are by no means to require that God should always appear to us, and that his paternal favour should always shine forth on our life. This is, indeed, a condition sought for by all; for the flesh inclines us to this, and hence we shun adversities. We, then, naturally desire God's favour to be manifested to us; how? in reality, so that all things may go on prosperously, that no trouble may touch us, that we may be tormented by no anxiety, that no danger may be suspended over us, that no calamity may threaten us: these things, as I have said, we all naturally seek and desire. But in such a case faith would be extinguished, as Paul tells us in his Epistle to the Romans, "For we hope not," he says, "for what appears, but we hope for what is hidden." (Rom. viii. 24, 25.) It is necessary in this world that the faithful should, as to outward things, be miserable, at one time exposed to want, at another subject to various dangers—at one time exposed to reproaches and calumnies, at another harassed by losses:

[1] It may be thus rendered,—
Good *it is* when he hopes and waits quietly
For the salvation of Jehovah.

The ו may often be rendered *when.* This verse, the preceding, and following, begin with "good," which renders the passage very striking,—

25. Good *is* Jehovah to him who waits for him,
To the soul who seeks him:
26. Good *it is* when he hopes and waits quietly
For the salvation of Jehovah:
27. Good *it is* for man
That he bears the yoke in his youth.—*Ed.*

why so? because there would be no occasion for exercising hope, were our salvation complete. This is the very thing which the Prophet now teaches us, when he declares that it is good for us to learn in silence to wait for the salvation of God.

But to express more clearly his mind, he first says, *He will wait,* or hope. He teaches the need of patience, as also the Apostle does, in Heb. x. 36; for otherwise there can be no faith. It hence appears, that where there is no patience, there is not even a spark of faith in the heart of man; how so? because this is our happiness, to wait or to hope; and we hope for what is hidden. But in the second clause he explains himself still more clearly by saying, *and will be silent.* To be silent means often in Scripture to rest, to be still; and here it signifies no other thing than to bear the troubles allotted to us, with a calm and resigned mind. He is then said to be silent to God, who remains quiet even when afflictions supply occasion for clamouring; and hence this quietness is opposed to violent feelings; for when some trouble presses on us, we become turbulent, and are carried away by our fury, at one time we quarrel with God, at another we pour forth various complaints. The same thing also happens, when we see some danger, for we tremble, and then we seek remedies here and there, and that with great eagerness. But he who patiently bears his troubles, or who recumbs on God when dangers surround him, is said to be silent or to rest quietly; and hence the words of Isaiah, "In hope and silence;" for he there exhorts the faithful to patience, and shews where strength is, even when we trust in God, so as willingly to submit to his will, and to be ready to bear his chastisements, and then when we doubt not but that he will be ready to bring us help when we are in danger. (Isa. xxx. 15.)

We now perceive what the Prophet means when he says, that it *is good if we wait and be silent as to the salvation of God;* even because our happiness is hid, and we are also like the dead, as Paul says, and our life is hid in Christ. (Col. iii. 3.) As then it is so, we must necessarily be silent as to God's salvation, and cherish hope within, though surrounded with many miseries. It follows,—

27. *It is* good for a man that he bear the yoke in his youth.

27. Bonum viro, si tulerit jugum in pueritia sua.

This verse admits of two meanings; for the word *yoke* may be explained as signifying teaching, or the scourges of God. We, indeed, undertake or bear in two ways the yoke of God, even when we are taught to receive his doctrine, or when we are resigned when he chastises us, when we are not obstreperous, but willingly submit to his corrections. As then some take the word עול, *oul*, for the yoke of instruction, and others for the yoke of chastisement, two explanations, as I have said, are given; and both are admissible. It is indeed truly said, that it is good for man to be accustomed from his youth to God's corrections; but Jeremiah seems rather to speak of that obedience generally, which the faithful render to God when they submit to his will. It is then our true happiness when we acknowledge that we are not our own, and allow God, by his sovereign power, to rule us as he pleases. But we ought to begin with the law of God. Hence, then, it is, that we are said to bear the yoke of God, when we relinquish our own judgment, and become wise through God's word, when, with our affections surrendered and subdued, we hear what God commands us, and receive what he commands. This, then, is what Jeremiah means by bearing the yoke.

And he says, *in youth.* For they who have lived unrestrained throughout their life, can hardly bear to be brought into any order. We indeed know, that the aged are less tractable than the young; nay, whether we refer to the arts or to the liberal sciences, the youthful age is the most flexible. The aged are also much slower; and added to this is another evil, they are very obstinate, and will hardly bear to be taught the first rudiments, being imbued with a false notion, as though they must have lived long in vain. As, then, the disposition in the old is not easily changed, the Prophet says that it is good for us to be formed from childhood to bear the yoke. And this is also seen in brute animals; when a horse is allowed full liberty in the fields, and not in due time tamed, he will hardly ever bear the curb, he will be always refractory. The oxen, also, will never be brought to bear the yoke, if they be put under it in the sixth or eighth year. The same is found to be the case with men. Jeremiah, then, does not say, without reason, that it is *good* for every one to be trained from his youth in the service of God; and thus he exhorts children and youth not to wait for old age, as it is usually the case. For it has been a common evil, in all ages, for children and youth to leave the study of wisdom to the old: "Oh! it will be time enough for me to be wise, when I arrive at a middle age; but some liberty must be given to childhood and youthful days." And for this reason, Solomon exhorts all not to wait for old age, but duly to learn to fear God in childhood. So also our Prophet declares that it is good for one to bear the yoke in his childhood. It then follows,—

28. He sitteth alone, and keepeth silence, because he hath borne it upon him.	28. Sedebit seorsum (*vel*, solus) et silebit, quia tulit super se.

Here he shews the fruit of teachableness; for when God deals severely with his children, they yet do not rebel, but even then they willingly submit to his authority. For whence comes it that so much impatience rages in men, except that they know not what it is to obey God, to prepare themselves to bear the yoke? so, then, men become furious like wild beasts, never tamed, therefore the Prophet now says, "Whosoever is thus habituated to the yoke of God, will also be silent in extreme evils, and remain quiet." We now perceive what I have just said, that the fruit of docility and obedience is set forth in this verse.

But when he says that those who are thus trained to obey God *will sit apart,* he expresses most fitly the strength and character of patience. For they for the most part who wish to appear magnanimous make a great display, and think that their valour is nothing except they appear as on a theatre; they allow themselves at the same time an unbridled liberty when they are alone; for they who seem the most valorous, except God's fear and true religion prevail in their souls, rage against God and champ the bridle in adversities, though they may not make a clamour before men, for, as I have already said, they regard display. But here a very different account is given of patience, even that we are to sit alone and be silent, that is, even were no one present as a witness, whose presence might make us ashamed; were we even then to sit, and to submit with calm minds to God, and to take his yoke, we should thus prove our patience. This verse then distinguishes between the simplicity of the godly and that vain display in which they delight who seek to obtain the praise of courage, patience, and perseverance, from the world; for these also sit and speak words as from heaven, and as though they had put off the flesh. He who has lost a son will say, that he had begotten a mortal: he who is stripped of all his goods will say, "All my things I carry with me." Thus magnanimously do ungodly men speak, so that they seem to surpass in fortitude and firmness all the children of God. But when they give utterance to these swelling words, what they regard is the opinion which men may form of them. But the faithful, what do they do? *They sit apart,* that is, though they might shamelessly clamour against God, yet they are quiet and submit to his will. We now understand what is meant by *sitting apart.*

Then he says, *because he will carry it on himself.* Some take נטל, *nuthel,* in a transitive sense, "he will cast it upon him." But this is a forced rendering. It would be a simpler meaning, were we to say, *because he will carry* or raise it *on himself.* The verb נטל, *nuthel,* means not only to carry, but also elevate or raise up. When, therefore, the Prophet says, that it is an example of real patience when we carry it on ourselves, he means that we succumb not under our adversities, nor are overwhelmed by them; for it is patience when it is not grievous to us to undergo any burdens which God may lay on us; and on this account we are said to regard his yoke as not grievous—how so? because it is pleasant to us. As, then, meekness thus extenuates the heaviness of the burden, which would otherwise overwhelm us, the Prophet says that those who raise up on themselves all their troubles *sit apart.*

I do not, however, know whether this passage has been corrupted; for the expression seems not to me natural. Were we to read עלו, *olu,* his yoke, it would be more appropriate, and a reason would be given for what goes before, that the faithful sit apart and are silent before God, because they bear his yoke ; for the pronoun may be referred to God as well as to man. But this is only a conjecture.[1] It follows,—

29. He putteth his mouth in the dust, if so be there may be hope.	29. Ponet in pulvere os suum, si fortè sit spes.

He continues the same subject; for he describes to us men so subdued to obedience that they are ready to bear whatever God may lay on them. He then says that the sitting and the silence of which he spoke, so far prevailed, that the children of God, though in extreme evils, did not yet cease to persevere in their obedience. For it sometimes happens that those who have made some progress in the fear of God, give proof of their obedience and patience in some small trial; but when they are greatly tried, then breaks forth the impatience which they had previously checked. Then the Prophet teaches us here, that the children of God do not sufficiently prove their patience, when they bear with a calm mind a moderate correction, except they proceed to a higher degree of perseverance, so as to remain quiet and resigned even when the state of things appears hopeless.

By saying that the faithful *put their mouth in the dust*, he means that they lie down humbly before God and confess themselves to be as dead. The import of what is said is this: In time of extreme affliction the wise will put his mouth in the dust, while seeing things in such confusion that all his thoughts vanish away on account of the atrocity of evils; and thus he intimates that the wise would have nothing to say. To put the mouth, then, in the dust is to become mute, as though he had said, that the faithful shut their mouth, when they do not murmur against God nor abandon themselves to complaints, when they do not expostulate that injury is done them, nor allege what the unbe-

[1] It is so found in the *Syr.;* but it comes to the same thing, if the verb be taken passively, in *Niphal*,—" Because it (the yoke mentioned before) has been laid on him." *Blayney's* version is, " When it is laid on him." —*Ed.*

lieving usually do when God deals severely with them. In short, to put the mouth in the dust, means to bring no complaints, and so to check ourselves that no clamorous words proceed from our mouth. Thus another phrase is used to set forth the silence mentioned before.

And that the Prophet here speaks of extreme trials, may be easily gathered from the next clause, *If so be that there is hope;* not that the faithful doubt whether God would give them hope, for they have no doubt but that God, who shines in darkness itself by his word, would at length by the effect prove that he is not unfaithful. But the particle אולי, *auli,* as it is well known, expresses what is difficult; for when anything appears to be incredible, the Hebrews say, *If it may be.* But here, as I have said, it does not intimate a doubt; for when the mind of a godly man fluctuates or doubts, how is it that he puts his mouth in the dust? but the Prophet shews that those who are taught to obey God, persevere even in extreme trials, so that while nothing but despair appears, they yet lie down humbly before God, and patiently wait until some hope shines forth. And here hope is to be taken for the ground or occasion of hope.[1] It afterwards follows,—

30. He giveth *his* cheek to him that smiteth him: he is filled full with reproach.	30. Dabit percutienti maxillam, saturabitur opprobriis.

Here he mentions another fruit of patience, that the faithful, even when injuries are done to them by the wicked, would yet be calm and resigned. For there are many who submit to God when they perceive his hand; as, for instance, when any one is afflicted with a disease, he knows that it is a chastisement that proceeds from God; when pestilence happens, or famine, from the inclemency of the weather, the hand of God appears to them; and many then conduct

[1] To lay the mouth in the dust, is a token of entire submission. Agreeably with this, the following words may be considered as spoken by the individual,—

He will lay in the dust his mouth (and say)—
"It may be there is hope."

It is better to render the verbs here as they are, in the future tense, as all the versions do; for he describes what is usually the character of the godly under severe trials.—*Ed.*

themselves in a suitable manner: but when an enemy meets one, and when injured, he instantly says, "I have now nothing to do with God, but that wicked enemy treats me disgracefully."

It is then for this reason that the Prophet shews that the patience of the godly ought to extend to injuries of this kind; and hence he says, *He will give the cheek to the smiter, and will be filled with reproaches.*[1] There are two kinds of injuries; for the wicked either treat us with violence, or assail us with reproaches; and reproach is the bitterest of all things, and inflicts a most grievous wound on all ingenuous minds. The Prophet, then, here declares that the children of God ought meekly to suffer when they are violently assailed, and not only so, but when they are dealt with reproachfully by the wicked. This, then, he says of patience. Now follows another confirmation,—

31. For the Lord will not cast off for ever.	31. Quia non respuet (*vel,* rejiciet) in perpetuum Dominus.

It is certain that there will be no patience, except there be hope, as it has already appeared. As, then, patience cherishes hope, so hope is the foundation of patience; and hence consolation is, according to Paul, connected with patience. (Rom. xv. 4.) And this is the doctrine which the Prophet now handles,—that the faithful bear the yoke with meek and calm minds, because they believe that God will at length be propitious to them: hence also arises patience; for the faithful are persuaded that all adversities are temporary, and that there will be a happy end, because God will at length be reconciled to them, though he gives them new evidences of his wrath.[2] The rest to-morrow.

[1] That is, he will suffer himself to be filled with reproaches; he will submit to all reproaches.—*Ed.*

[2] This verse is connected with the 25th: "Good is Jehovah to him who waits for him;" and the reason is given here, "For not reject perpetually (or, for ever) will the Lord." "For," as assigning a reason, is here repeated three times, in this verse and in the two following verses; and they seem all to be reasons given for the truth contained in the 25th verse,—

31. For not reject perpetually
Will the Lord:
32. For though he afflicts, yet he will shew compassion
According to the multitude of his mercies:

PRAYER.

Grant, Almighty God, that as it is expedient for us to be daily chastised by thy hand, we may willingly submit to thee, and not doubt but that thou wilt be faithful, and not prove us with too much rigour, but that thou wilt consider our weakness, so that we may thus calmly bear all thy chastisements, until we shall at length enjoy that perfect blessedness, which is now hid to us under hope, and as it were sealed, until Christ thy Son shall reveal it at his coming.—Amen.

Lecture Eleventh.

32. But though he cause grief, yet will he have compassion according to the multitude of his mercies.	32. Quia si dolore affecerit, etiam miserebitur secundum multitudinem clementiarum suarum.

We saw in the last Lecture that the best and the only true remedy for sorrows is, when the faithful are convinced that they are chastised only by the paternal hand of God, and that the end of all their evils will be blessed. Now this they cannot of themselves assume; but God comes to their aid, and declares that he will not be angry for ever with his children. For this promise extends generally to the whole Church, "For a moment I afflicted thee, in the time of mine indignation, but with perpetual mercies will I follow thee," (Isa. liv. 7, 8:) and again, "I will visit their iniquities with a rod, yet my mercy I will not take away from them." (Ps. lxxxix. 33, 34.) When therefore the faithful feel assured that their punishment is only for a time, then they lay hold on hope, and thus receive invaluable comfort in all their evils.

Jeremiah now pursues the same subject, even that God will *shew compassion according to the multitude of his mercies, though he causes sorrow to men.* This may indeed be generally explained as to all mankind; but as we have said, God has promised this to his own Church. All miseries,

33. For he does not depress from his heart,
Nor afflict the children of men.

All these particulars explain and elucidate the truth, that God is good. "From his heart," does not mean "willingly," but at his will, that is, arbitrarily, without reason, but when constrained by man's wickedness.—*Ed.*

regarded in themselves, are tokens of the wrath and curse of God; but as all things turn out for good and for salvation to the children of God, when they embrace this truth, that God, as the Prophet Habakkuk says, remembers mercy in wrath, (Hab. iii. 2,) so they restrain themselves and do not despond, nor are they overwhelmed with despair. We now then understand the Prophet's object in saying, that though God afflicts he yet remembers mercy.

But we must at the same time bear in mind what I have before shewed, that the faithful are exposed to various evils, because it is profitable for them to be chastised by God's hand. Hence appears the necessity of this doctrine, for were we exempt from all adversities, this admonition would be superfluous. But as it cannot be but that God will smite us with his rods, not only because we deserve to be smitten, but also because it is expedient, it is necessary to flee to this consolation which is offered to us, even that God having afflicted us with grief will again shew us compassion, even *according to the multitude of his mercies.* He confirms the truth of what he alleges by a reference to the very nature of God himself. Hence, that the faithful might not debate with themselves whether God would be propitious to them, after having inflicted on them a temporary punishment, the Prophet comes to their aid, and sets before them the mercy of God, or rather mercies, in the plural number; as though he had said, that it could not be that God should deny himself, and that therefore he would be always merciful to his people; for otherwise his mercy would be obliterated, yea, that mercy which is inseparable from his eternal essence and divinity.

And hence, when God is pleased briefly to shew what he is, he sets forth his mercy and patience; for except his goodness and mercy meet us, when we come to him, dread would immediately absorb all our thoughts; but when God comes forth as if clothed and adorned with mercy, we may then entertain hope of salvation; and though conscious of evil, yet while we recumb on God's mercy, we shall never lose the hope of salvation. We now apprehend the Prophet's meaning. It follows,—

33. For he doth not afflict willingly, nor grieve the children of men.	33. Quia non affligit ex corde suo, et dolore afficit filios viri.

This is another confirmation of the same truth, that God takes no delight in the evils or miseries of men. It is indeed a strong mode of speaking which the Prophet adopts, but very suitable. God, we know, puts on, as it were, our form or manner, for he cannot be comprehended in his inconceivable glory by human minds. Hence it is that he transfers to himself what properly can only apply to men. God surely never acts unwillingly nor feignedly : how then is that suitable which Jeremiah declares,—that God does *not afflict from his heart?* But God, as already said, does here assume the character of man ; for though he afflicts us with sorrow as he pleases, yet true it is that he delights not in the miseries of men ; for if a father desires to benefit his own children, and deals kindly with them, what ought we to think of our heavenly Father? "Ye," says Christ, "who are evil, know how to do good to your children," (Matt. vii. 11 ;) what then are we to expect from the very fountain of goodness? As, then, parents are not willingly angry with their children, nor handle them roughly, there is no doubt but that God never punishes men except when he is constrained. There is, as I have said, an impropriety in the expression, but it is enough to know, that God derives no pleasure from the miseries of men, as profane men say, who utter such blasphemies as these, that we are like balls with which God plays, and that we are exposed to many evils, because God wishes to have, as it were, a pleasant and delectable spectacle in looking on the innumerable afflictions, and at length on the death of men.

That such thoughts, then, might not tempt us to unbelief, the Prophet here puts a check on us, and declares that God does *not afflict from his heart,* that is, willingly, as though he delighted in the evils of men, as a judge, who, when he ascends his throne and condemns the guilty to death, does not do this from his heart, because he wishes all to be innocent, and thus to have a reason for acquitting them ; but yet he willingly condemns the guilty, because this is his duty. So also God, when he adopts severity towards men, he indeed does so willingly, because he is the judge of the world; but he does not do so from the heart, because he wishes all to be innocent—for far away from him is all fierceness and cruelty; and as he regards men with paternal love, so also he would have them to be saved, were they not as it were by force to drive him to rigour. And this feeling he also expresses in Isaiah, "Ah! I will take consolation from mine adversaries." (Isa. i. 24.) He calls them adversaries who so often provoked him by their obstinacy; yet he was led unwillingly to punish their sins, and hence he employed a particle expressive of grief, and exclaimed *Ah!* as a father who wishes his son to be innocent, and yet is compelled to be severe with him.

But however true this doctrine may be, taken generally, there is yet no doubt but that the Prophet here addresses only the faithful; and doubtless this privilege peculiarly belongs to God's children, as it has been shewn before. It follows,—

34. To crush under his feet all the prisoners of the earth,

35. To turn aside the right of a man before the face of the most High,

36. To subvert a man in his cause, the Lord approveth not.

34. Ad conterendum sub pedibus suis omnes vinctos terræ,

35. Ad pervertendum (ad declinandum) judicium viri coram conspectu excelsi,

36. Ad pervertendum hominem in lite sua, Dominus non videt (*vel*, non vidit.)

Many interpreters think that these three verses are connected with the previous doctrine, and shew the connexion thus,—that God does not see, that is, does not know what it is to pervert the good cause of a man, and to oppress the innocent; and, doubtless, God is said not to know what iniquity is, because he abhors all evil; for what is the nature of God but the perfection of justice? It may then be truly said, that God knows not what it is to turn man aside in judgment. Others take *not to see*, as meaning, not to approve.

If we subscribe to the opinion of those who say that injustice is contrary to the nature of God, there is here an exhortation to patience; as though the Prophet had said that afflictions ought to be borne with resignation, because the Jews had fully deserved them. For the liberty taken to complain arises from this, that men imagine that they are without fault; but he who is convicted dares not thus to rise up against God; for the chief thing in humility is the acknowledgment of sin. This, then, is one meaning. But they who give this explanation, that God does not approve of those who pervert judgment, think that there is here a ground of consolation, because God would at length succour the miserable who were unjustly oppressed. And doubtless it avails not a little to encourage patience when we are persuaded that God will be an avenger, so that he will at length help us, after having for a time suffered us to be severely treated.

But these expositions seem to me to be too remote; we may give a correcter explanation by supposing a concession to be made, as though the Prophet had said, "It is indeed true that the wicked take much license, for they imagine that God is blind to all evil deeds." For this madness is often ascribed to the ungodly, that they think that they can sin with impunity, because God, as they suppose, cares not for the affairs of men. They then imagine that God is asleep, and in a manner dead, and hence they break out into all kinds of wickedness. And for this reason it was that David so vehemently rebuked them: "He who has formed the ear, will he not hear? He who has created the heaven, will he not see?" (Ps. xciv. 9.) This explanation also I cannot approve of, it being forced and not obvious.

I therefore think that the reference is to the impious words of those who complain that God is not moved by any compassion. For this thought almost lays hold on us when pressed down by adversities,—that God has forgotten us, that he is either asleep or lies down inactive. In short, there is nothing more difficult to be assured of than this truth, that God governs the world by his counsel, and that nothing happens without a design. This is indeed what almost all confess; but when a trial comes, this doctrine vanishes, and every one is carried away by some perverted and erroneous thoughts, even that all things roll round fortuitously through blind fate, that men are not the objects of God's care. Nor is there a doubt but that in Jeremiah's time words of this kind were flying about; and it appears evident from the context that those Jews were reproved who thought that their miseries were disregarded by God, and hence they clamoured; for men are necessarily carried away into a furious state of mind, when they do not believe that they have to do with God.

The Prophet, then, refers to such impious words, or if they dared not to express in language what they thought, he refers to what was believed almost by all,—that the wicked *perverted the judgment of man,* that they *turned aside a man in his cause,* that they *tore under their feet all the bound of the earth;*[1] that is, that all those things were done by the connivance of God. The plain meaning, then, is, that judgment is perverted before the face of the Most High,—that the bound of the earth, such as are helpless, are despised, trodden under foot by the wicked,—that a man in his cause is unjustly dealt with, and that all this is done *because God does not see.*[2] We now, then, perceive what the Prophet means.

[1] The order is here reversed. It is a common thing in Scripture to state first the chief thing, the chief good or evil. Here the greatest evil is mentioned first, the tearing under foot of such as were already bound, or imprisoned; then the sparing of the guilty; and thirdly, the withholding of justice to the righteous. To turn aside or divert judgment, is not to punish the guilty; and to wrong a person in his cause, is to deny his right. By "the bound," or "prisoners of the earth," or land, *Blayney* understands persons imprisoned for debt, who were obliged to work as slaves until they satisfied their creditors. See Matt. xviii. 30-34. Cruelty to such is referred to in Isa. lviii. 3.—*Ed.*

[2] The *Targ.* and the versions differ as to the import of this clause. The verb *to see,* has been taken to mean three things,—to know, to approve, and to regard or to notice. The *Vulgate* takes the first, our version the second, and *Calvin* the third. The context seems to favour the last meaning, especially the following verses.

There is a difficulty as to the antecedent to the pronoun "his," before "feet." It seems to refer to "man" in the last verse; for the words are, "the sons (or children) of man," not of "men." The verb ראה, when followed by ל, means to look on, at, or simply to see. Ps. lxiv. 5. Then the literal rendering of the passage would be as follows,—

On the tearing under his feet
  Of all the bound of the land,—
On the diverting of a man's judgment,
  In the presence of the most High,—
On the wronging of a person in his cause
  The Lord doth not look.

Or if the "on" be dropped, the last line may be,

  The Lord doth not see.

This is manifestly the saying of unbelieving men, or of those weak in faith, as proved by the next verse, when rightly rendered.—*Ed.*

But whence came such madness? even because the Jews, as I have said, would not humble themselves under the mighty hand of God; for hypocrisy had so blinded them, that they proudly clamoured against God, thinking that they were chastised with unjust severity. As then, they thus flattered themselves in their sins, this expostulation arose which the Prophet mentions, that man's judgment was perverted, that the innocent failed in a good cause, that the miserable were trodden under foot; and whence all this? because God did not see, or did not regard these things. Now follows the reproof of this delirious impiety,—

37. Who *is* he *that* saith, and it cometh to pass, *when* the Lord commandeth *it* not?

38. Out of the mouth of the most High proceedeth not evil and good?

37. Quis iste, dixit; fuit, Deus non præcepit?

38. Ex ore Excelsi non egredietur malum et bonum (*vel,* quasi non egrediatur malum et bonum ex ore Excelsi?)

The Prophet, after having mentioned the blasphemy which prevailed everywhere at that time, strongly condemns so gross a stupidity. *Who is this?* he says. He checks such madness by a sharp rebuke—for the question implies an astonishment, as though the Prophet had said, that it was like a prodigy to find men who imagined that God was content with his own leisure, and exercised no care over the world; for this was to annihilate him altogether. God is not a dead being, he is not a spectre; what then? God is the judge of the world. We hence see that it was a monstrous thing, when men entertained the notion that God is idle or forgetful, that he gives up the world to chance. This is the reason why the Prophet asks as of a thing absurd and extremely disgraceful. *Who is this?* he says; could it be that men should give themselves up to such a degree of madness? for when they said, that anything could happen without God's command, it was the same as if they denied his power; for what is God without his judgment?

The other verse may be explained in two ways; but as to the meaning, there is but little difference. It may, then, be read as a question, "Cannot good and evil proceed from the mouth of the most High?" or it may be rendered thus,

"As though good and evil should not proceed from the mouth of God." As to the substance of what is said, we see that there is no need of disputing, for the Prophet confirms what he had said, that men are to be abhorred who imagine God to be as it were dead, and thus rob him of his power and of his office as a judge. And, doubtless, except we hold this truth, no true religion can exist in us; for except all the sayings and doings of men come to an account before the tribunal of God, and also their motives and thoughts, there will be first no faith, and, secondly, there will be no integrity, and all prayer to God will be extinguished. For if we believe that God does not regard what is done in the world, who will trust in him? and who will seek help from him? besides, who will hesitate to abandon himself to cruelty, or frauds, or plunder? Extinguished, then, is every sense of religion by this impious opinion, that God spends his time leisurely in heaven, and attends not to human affairs. This is the reason why the Prophet is so indignant against those who said, that anything could be done without the command of God.

Let us now see how God commands what is wrongly and foolishly done by men. Surely he does not command the ungodly to do what is wicked, for he would thus render them excusable; for where God's authority interposes, there no blame can be. But God is said to command whatever he has decreed, according to his hidden counsel. There are, then, two kinds of commands; one belongs to doctrine, and the other to the hidden judgments of God. The command of doctrine, so to speak, is an evident approbation which acquits men; for when one obeys God, it is enough that he has God as his authority, though he were condemned by a hundred worlds. Let us, then, learn to be attentive to the commands of doctrine, by which we ought to regulate our life, for they make up the only true rule, from which it is not right to depart. But God is said to command according to his secret decrees what he does not approve, as far as men are concerned. So Shimei had a command to curse, and yet he was not exempt from blame; for it was not his purpose to obey God; nay, he thought that he had offended God no less than David. (2 Sam. xvi. 5, 6.) Then this distinction ought to be understood, that some things are commanded by God, not that men may have it as a rule of action, but when God executes his secret judgments by ways unknown to us. Thus, then, ought this passage to be understood, even that nothing is carried on without God's command, that is, without his decree, and, as they say, without his ordination.

It hence appears, that those things which seem contingent, are yet ruled by the certain providence of God, so that nothing is done at random. And what philosophers call accident, or contingent, (ἐνδεχόμενον,) is necessary as to God; for God decreed before the world was made whatever he was to do; so that there is nothing now done in the world which is not directed by his counsel. And true is that saying in the Psalms, that our God is in heaven, and doeth whatsoever he pleaseth, (Ps. cxv. 3;) but this would not be true, were not all things dependent on God's counsel. We hence see that nothing is contingent, for everything that takes place flows from the eternal and immutable counsel of God. It is indeed true, that those things which take place in this or that manner, are properly and naturally called contingencies, but what is naturally contingent, is necessary, as far as it is directed by God; nay, what is carried on by the counsel and will of men is necessary. Philosophers think that all things are contingent (ἐνδεχόμενα,) and why? because the will of man may turn either way. They, then, conclude, that whatever men do is contingent, because he who wills may change his will. These things are true, when we consider the will of man in itself, and the exercise of it; but when we raise our eyes to the secret providence of God, who turns and directs the counsels of men according to his own will, it is certain that how much soever men may change in their purposes, yet God never changes.

Let us then hold this doctrine, that nothing is done except by God's command and ordination, and, with the Holy Spirit, regard with abhorrence those profane men who imagine that God sits idly as it were on his watch-tower and takes no notice of what is done in the world, and that human affairs change at random, and that men turn and change independently on any higher power. Nothing is more diabolical than this delirious impiety; for as I have said, it extinguishes all the acts and duties of religion; for there will be no faith, no prayer, no patience, in short, no religion, except we believe and know that God exercises such care over the world, of which he is the Creator, that nothing happens except through his certain and unchangeable decree.

Now they who object and say that God is thus made the author of evils, may be easily refuted; for nothing is more preposterous than to measure the incomprehensible judgment of God by our contracted minds. The Scripture cries aloud that the judgments of God are a great deep; it exhorts us to reverence and sobriety, and Paul does not in vain exclaim that the ways of God are unsearchable. (Rom. xi. 33.) As, then, God's judgments in their height far surpass all our thoughts, we ought to beware of audacious presumption and curiosity; for the more audacious a man becomes, the farther God withdraws from him. This, then, is our wisdom, to embrace only what the Scripture teaches. Now, when it teaches us that nothing is done except through the will of God, it does not speak indiscriminately, as though God approved of murders, and thefts, and sorceries, and adulteries; what then? even that God by his just and righteous counsel so orders all things, that he still wills not iniquity and abhors all injustice. When, therefore, adulteries, and murders, and plunders are committed, God applies, as it were, a bridle to all those things, and how much soever the most wicked may indulge themselves in their vices, he still rules them; this they themselves acknowledge; but for what end does he rule them? even that he may punish sins with sins, as Paul teaches us, for he says that God gives up to a reprobate mind those who deserve such a punishment, that he gives them up to disgraceful lusts, that he blinds more and more the despisers of his word. (Rom. i. 28; 2 Thess. ii. 10.) And then God has various ways, and those innumerable and unknown to us.

Let us then learn not to subject God to our judgment, but adore his judgments, though they surpass our comprehension ; and since the cause of them is hid from us, our highest wisdom is modesty and sobriety.

Thus we see that God is not the author of evils, though nothing happens but by his nod and through his will,—for far different is his design from that of wicked men. Then absurd would it be to implicate him as an associate in the same crime, when a murderer, or a thief, or an adulterer is condemned,—and why ? because God has no participation in thefts and adulteries ; but the vices of men are in a way wonderful and incomprehensible as his judgments. In a word, as far as the heavens are from the earth, so great is the difference between the works of God and the deeds of men, for the ends, as I have said, are altogether different.[1]

The Prophet says that *from the mouth of the most High proceed good and evil.* By " mouth" he means his decree. God indeed does not always declare that he is a judge ; he has often executed punishment on the wicked, as it were, in silence ; for there were no prophets among the heathens to proclaim the judgments he brought on them. But though God does not always speak when he punishes the wickedness of men, it is yet said that *good and evil* proceed from his mouth ; because he allots to men their punishment as it seems good to him ; and then he spares others or bears with them for a time. It follows,—

[1] The construction of these two verses is variously given. The verb rendered, " It was," or, " It came to pass," if in the third person, is feminine, while it is usually and probably always masculine, when it has this meaning. It may be taken to be here in the second person. The literal rendering of the verse then would be,—

Who-he-saying (*i.e.*, Who is he who says,)
That thou art Lord, ordering not, (*i.e.*, who dost not order, or command.)

Then the following verse contains a continuation of what the objector said,—

From the mouth of the Highest
Cometh not the evil and the good.

The answer of the Prophet is in the 39th verse, in which he intimates that God orders evil as a punishment for sin.

The objector's declaration, that God as a Lord or Sovereign does not command or order events, and for this reason, because both evil and good cannot come from him, is a proof that *not to see* in verse 36, is not to regard or notice the affairs of men.—*Ed.*

39. Wherefore doth a living man complain, a man for the punishment of his sins?

39. Cur molestia se afficit homo vivens? vir super peccato suo?

Some explain the verb יתאונן, *itaunen*, by giving it the sense of lying, "Why should man lie?" others, "Why should man murmur?" But I see not what sense there can be in rendering it lying or murmuring. Others translate thus, "Why should man harden himself?" but it is a mere conjecture. Now, this verb sometimes means to weary one's self, in *Hithpael*. So in the eleventh chapter of Numbers, "The people murmured," as some render the words; but I think differently; nor is there a doubt but that Moses meant that the people were wearied, so that they in a manner pined away; and this meaning is the most suitable here. For the Prophet had before rebuked those who imagined that God, having relinquished the care of the world, led an inactive and easy life in heaven; but now, in order to rouse the minds of all, he points out the remedy for this madness, even that men should not willingly weary themselves in their sins, but acknowledge that their wickedness is shewn to them whenever any adversity comes upon them. And surely men would not be so infatuated as to exclude God from the government of the world, were they to know themselves and seriously to call to mind their own deeds and words; for God would soon exhibit to them sure and notorious examples of his judgment. Whence then comes it, that we are so dull and stupid in considering the works of God? nay, that we think that God is like a spectre or an idol? even because we rot in our sins and contract a voluntary dulness; for we champ the bit, according to the old proverb.

We now, then, perceive why the Prophet joins this sentence, *Why does a living man weary himself?*[1] *and a man*

[1] "Murmur" is the *Sept.* and the *Vulg.* The word only occurs here and in Num. xi. 1; and "complain" is the most suitable rendering in both places,—

39. Why complain should man,
Any man alive, for his sin?

That is, on account of suffering for his sin. Thus God is justified in ordaining or commanding evil as well as good, that is, the evil of punishment.—*Ed.*

in his sins? for as long as men thus remain in their own dregs, they will never acknowledge God as the judge of the world, and thus they always go astray through their own perverse imaginations. If, then, we wish to dissipate all the mists which prevent us from seeing God's providence, (that is, by the eyes of faith,) let every one be his own witness and the judge of his own life, and carefully examine himself; it will then immediately occur to us, that God is not without reason angry with us, and that we are afflicted with so many adversities, because our sins will come forth before us. We here see the cause of that madness which makes men to exclude God's providence from human affairs, even because they look not on themselves, but torment themselves without any benefit and become wearied in their sins, and do not raise up their eyes to God. The rest, connected with our subject, I must defer till to-morrow.

PRAYER.

Grant, Almighty God, that as we are at this day tossed here and there by so many troubles, and almost all things in the world are in confusion, so that wherever we turn our eyes, nothing but thick darkness meets us,—O grant that we may learn to surmount all obstacles, and to raise our eyes by faith above the world, so that we may acknowledge that governed by thy wonderful counsel is everything that seems to us to happen by chance, in order that we may seek thee, and know that help will be ready for us through thy mercy whenever we humbly seek the pardon of our sins, through Christ Jesus our Lord.—Amen.

Lecture Twelfth.

40. Let us search and try our ways, and turn again to the Lord.

40. Percontemur (scrutemur) vias nostras, et inquiramus, et convertamur ad Jehovam.

The Prophet now shews more clearly what the reproof meant which we shortly explained yesterday: he said that men act absurdly while they weary themselves in their sins; he now adds that they would do rightly if they inquired into their own life, and faithfully examined themselves.

For hence is trouble and weariness, when men feel and deplore their outward evils, but consider not the cause, that is, when they consider not that they are justly chastised by God's hand. Then the examination now mentioned is set in opposition to the torpor and weariness with which men in vain torment themselves, and in which they pine away, because they reflect not on their vices. Hence it is that they attain nothing but weariness—and that is a sorrow to death, as Paul says ; but sorrow to life proceeds from the self-examination to which the Prophet now invites and exhorts us.

He then says that the only true remedy in adversities is when men carefully examine themselves, and consider what they deserve.[1] He also mentions conversion ; for they who are really touched with the fear of God do not stop at this examination, but rise higher ; for as God calls them back to the right way, when they acknowledge that they have departed from him, they flee to his mercy, loathe themselves on account of their vices, and seek after newness of life. Thus our Prophet prescribes to us a certain order,—that we are to examine our whole life, and that, being influenced by the fear of God, we are to return to him ; for while he treats us with severity, he still kindly invites us by ever offering to sinners a free pardon. He afterwards adds,—

41. Let us lift up our heart with *our* hands unto God in the heavens.	41. Tollamus corda nostra cum manibus ad Deum in cœlis.

To conversion he joins prayer ; for we cannot be reconciled to God except he buries our sins ; nor can repentance and faith be separated. Moreover, to taste of God's mercy opens to us the door of prayer. And this ought to be carefully noticed, because the unbelieving seem at times to be very busy in seeking to return to God's favour, but they only attend to the outward change of life ; and at the same time they are not anxious about pardon, but go boldly before God, as though they were not exposed to his judgment.

And we see under the Papacy that while they make long sermons on repentance, they hardly ever make any account

[1] The words literally rendered are very expressive,—

Let us uncover our ways, and search.

The cover was first to be stripped off, and then was a search to be made as to the character of their ways.—*Ed.*

of faith, as though repentance without faith were a restoration from death to life.

Hence I said that we ought to notice the mode of teaching which our Prophet adopts: he begins with self-examination, then he requires conversion ; but he does not separate it from faith. For when he exhorts us to pray, it is the same thing as though he had set before us the judgment of God, and had also taught us that we cannot escape death except God be propitious to us. How then is pardon to be obtained? by prayer: and prayer, as it is well known, must be always founded on faith.

By telling us to *raise up our hearts to God together with our hands,* he bids us to banish all hypocrisy from our prayers. For all without a difference raise up their hands to God; and nature itself, when we are pressed down with evils, leads us to seek God. But the greater part stifle this feeling of nature. When affliction comes, it is a common thing with all to raise up their hands to heaven, though no one should bid them to do so ; but still their hearts remain fixed on the earth, and they come not to God. And the greater part of men are included in that class mentioned by Isaiah, "This people come to me with their tongue, but their heart is far away." (Isa. xxix. 13.) As, then, men deal thus formally with God, and present a naked ceremony, as though God had changed and suffered his eyes to be covered, the Prophet bids all dissimulation to cease from prayer ; *Let us raise up hands,* he says, *to God,* and also *hearts.* Joel speaks somewhat differently, when he says, "Rend your hearts and not your garments," (Joel ii. 13;) for he seems to exclude the outward rite, because men, wishing to shew that they were guilty before God, rent their garments. Joel says that this was superfluous and useless ; and doubtless the rite itself was not so very necessary. But as prayers, when they are earnest, move the hands, our Prophet refers to that practice as useful. At the same time he teaches us that the chief thing ought not to be omitted, even to raise up the *hearts* to God : *Let us,* then, he says, *raise up our hearts together with our hands to God;* and he adds, to God *who is in heaven :* for it is necessary that men should rise up above the world, and to go out of themselves, so to speak, in order to come to God.

We now then understand the meaning of the Prophet,—that those who repent from the heart ought not to go before God, as though they were not guilty before his tribunal, but that on the contrary they ought to be penitent and humble, so that they may obtain pardon. He afterwards shews that the right way of praying is, when we not only perform the outward ceremonies, but when we open our hearts and raise them up as it were to heaven itself. It is, then, the right way of praying, when the inward feeling corresponds with the external posture. It follows,—

42. We have transgressed, and have rebelled: thou hast not pardoned.	42. Nos peccavimus et rebelles fuimus; tu non pepercisti.

The faithful do not here expostulate with God, but on the contrary acknowledge that God's severity was just. That God then had dealt with them severely, they ascribe to their own sins. This is the substance of what is said.

We hence learn that an ingenuous confession ever accompanies repentance, as also Paul teaches us, (2 Cor. vii. 11.) For when a sinner is either secure or tries to cover his wickedness, and flatters himself, as we see but a few who willingly humble themselves before God, he contracts the hardness of obstinacy. For this reason the Prophet requires confession ; nay, he suggests here the words suitable to be used, when we desire to obtain pardon from God. *We have done wickedly*, he says, *and have been rebellious.* The pronoun, *we,* is here emphatical, as though the faithful had taken on themselves the blame of all the evils, which the greater part ever sought to disown.[1]

Here then the Prophet shews that there is no other way of being reconciled to God, than by confessing ourselves to be the authors of all our evils ; and he also teaches us, that it is an evidence of true repentance, when we do not allege vain pretences as it is commonly done, nor flatter ourselves, but confess that we are guilty. He now shews that guilt

[1] To give the proper emphasis to the pronoun, the version ought to be as follows,—

We, transgressed have we, and rebelled.—*Ed.*

ought by no means to be extenuated, so that our confession may be real and complete: but in this respect the world trifle with God. The most wicked are, indeed, ashamed to deny that they are sinners; but as they are forced to make some kind of confession, this they do lightly; and it seems an extorted confession, and is therefore jejune, or at least not complete. But the Prophet here shews that they who seek to be reconciled to God, ought not only in words to acknowledge and confess their guilt, but also ingenuously to open their hearts. Hence he connects perverseness with sin, as though he had said, "We have not sinned simply or in one way, but we have exasperated God himself; and by sinning in many ways and constantly, we have provoked him against us." He says, in short, that there is then an access open to us to obtain favour, when we do not murmur against God nor contend with him as though he had dealt severely with us, but when we confess that he has been hard and rigid with us, because he had a reason to be so on account of our sins and wickedness. He adds,—

43. Thou hast covered with anger, and persecuted us: thou hast slain, thou hast not pitied.	43. Obtexisti in ira, et persequutus es nos; occidisti et non pepercisti.

At the first view, this complaint may seem to proceed from a bitter heart; for here the faithful complain that they had been slain, and then that God had executed his judgment as it were in darkness, without any indulgence; and the next verse confirms the same thing. But it is a simple acknowledgment of God's righteous vengeance; for in their extreme calamities the faithful could not declare that God dealt mercifully with them, for they had been subjected to extreme rigour, as we have before seen. Had they said that they had been leniently chastised, it would have been very strange, for the temple had been burnt, the city had been demolished, the kingdom had been overthrown, the people for the most part had been driven into exile, the remainder had been scattered, the covenant of God had been in a manner abolished; for it could not have been thought otherwise according to the judgment of the flesh. Had, then, the exiles in Chaldea said that God had smitten them leniently, would not such an extenuation have appeared very strange? and had also the Prophet spoken in the same strain? For the causes of sorrow were almost innumerable: every one had been robbed of his goods; then there were many widows, many orphans; but the chief causes of sorrow were the burning of the temple and the ruin of the kingdom. No wonder, then, that the faithful set forth here their aggravated evils: but yet they seek out no other cause than their own sins.

Hence they say now, that God had *covered them over in wrath.* It is a most suitable metaphor; as though he had said, that God had executed his vengeance in thick darkness. For an object presented to the eye produces sympathy, and we are easily inclined to mercy when a sad spectacle is presented to us. Hence it is, that even the most savage enemies are sometimes softened, for they are led by their eyes to acts of humanity. The Prophet, then, in order to set forth the horrible vengeance of God, says that there had been a covering introduced, so that God had punished the wicked people in an implacable manner. But as I have said, he does not charge God with cruelty, though he says that he had *covered them over in wrath.*[1]

He then says, *Thou hast pursued us and killed us, and hast not spared.* They intimate, in short, that God had been a severe judge; but they at the same time turned to themselves and sought there the cause, even that they might not, by their own hardness, provoke God against themselves, as hypocrites are wont to do. And the consciousness of evil leads us also to repentance; for whence is it that men grow torpid in their sins, except that they flatter themselves? When, therefore, God suspends his judgments, or when he moderates them, and does not punish men as they deserve,

[1] To "cover" is the idea given to the verb by the *Sept.*, the *Vulg.*, the *Syr.*, and the *Targ.*; but *Blayney* and some others take it in the sense of fencing in, enclosing, in allusion to the practice of hunters; and the next verb, which means to pursue, to chase, favours this meaning,—

Thou hast in wrath enclosed and chased us,
Thou hast slain and not spared.

Then the same verb begins the next verse,—

Thou hast enclosed thyself in a cloud,
That prayer might not pass through.—*Ed.*

then, if there be any repentance, it is yet frigid, and soon vanishes. This, then, is the reason why God inflicts deadly strokes, because we feel not his hand except the stroke be as it were deadly. As, then, simple chastisement is not sufficient to lead us to repentance, the Prophet introduces the faithful as speaking thus, " Behold, thou *hast in wrath covered us over*, so as not to look on us," so that there might be no opportunity for mercy, that is, that they might be the judges of themselves, and conclude from the atrocity of their punishment how grievously they must have provoked the wrath of God. It follows in the same sense,—

44. Thou hast covered thyself with a cloud, that *our* prayer should not pass through.	44. Obtexisti in nube tibi, ne transiret precatio.

The Prophet confirms the same thing, but the words are different. He again repeats the word to cover; but, that the metaphor might be clearer and more fully explained, he says, *with a cloud.* He simply intimates, that a cloud interposed, that God might more unrestrainedly punish the Jews, as they had deserved. Isaiah speaks somewhat otherwise, but for the same purpose: " The hand of God," he says, " is not shortened, nor are his ears more deaf; but your sins have interposed a distance between you and God." (Isa. lix. 1, 2.) There is no doubt but that Isaiah meant the same thing as our Prophet, even that God's nature never changes; and, therefore, that when he seems to rage against his people, the cause ought to be ascribed to their sins, because God ever remains like himself. We know what is said in the Psalms, " Thou art God who hearest prayer." (Psalm lxv. 3.) God, then, is always ready to hear his people, and he also possesses power sufficient to help them; but the distance arises from our sins. And so the Prophet now says that a *cloud* interposed.

Nearly the same sentence is found in the third chapter, as we have seen; for there the Prophet said, in the name of the whole people, that they had become separated from God, but that it was a separation, not because God had changed his purpose, but because the people had, in a manner, rejected his favour. *Thou hast*, then, he says, *covered thyself with a cloud*, that is, thou hast made for thyself a covering, *that prayer may not pass through.* This seems, indeed, very strange, because God advances to meet all the miserable, and promises to hear their prayers: what, then, can this mean, that a cloud interposed that prayer might not go through to him? even that the Jews did not pray aright, and that they had closed up against themselves every access by which God could admit them. In short, the faithful do not here contend with God, as though they had been deceived by his promises, but confess that they were unworthy to pray to God, and they also acknowledge that they did not pray aright.[1] And according to this sense they say, that they were hindered, as though a cloud interposed, so that their prayer could not ascend to God. It follows,—

45. Thou hast made us *as* the offscouring and refuse in the midst of the people.	45. Quisquilias et rejectionem posuisti nos in medio populorum.

They say here that they were exposed to reproach, so as to become, as it were, the sweepings of the world. Some render סחי, *sachi,* "refuse;" some by other words; and some "filth." But the word properly means sweepings or scrapings, called by the Greeks *περιψήματα.* Paul says, that he and his associates were the offscouring (*περιψήματα*) of the world. (1 Cor. iv. 13.) He means that they were despised as offscourings or scrapings. The word is derived from sweeping. Whatever, then, is cleaned off by sweeping or scouring, that is, the filth of the house or the floor, is called סחי, *sachi.* What the Prophet had in view is not obscure; for he means that the degradation of the people was not hidden, but open to all nations, as though God had erected a theatre in Judea, and there exhibited a remarkable and an unusual example of his vengeance. To the same purpose is what he adds,—

46. All our enemies have opened their mouths against us.	46. Aperuerunt super nos os suum omnes inimici nostri.

He repeats what he had said, that the people were an offscouring, or scrapings, or sweepings, and also a refuse.

[1] There are circumstances, no doubt, according to God's word, under which God does not hear prayer: and this seems to have been an instance of this kind.—*Ed.*

The last word is, indeed, in the infinitive mood, מאוס, *maus*, but it is to be taken as a noun. They had become all this, because they had as many *enemies* as neighbours; for we know that the Jews were hated by all the neighbouring nations. They had become, then, a refuse and filth among all people, for with an open mouth they spoke furiously against them. For the *open mouth* means that they spoke insolently, and took the liberty of cursing them all, as it has been stated elsewhere. Now it was the bitterest thing to the miserable people, when they found that the reproaches and taunts of enemies were added to their calamities: for we know how grievously does reproach wound those who are already afflicted.

47. Fear and a snare is come upon us, desolation and destruction.	47. Pavor et fovea fuit nobis, destructio (*alii* vertunt, deceptio.) et contritio.

The Prophet largely dwells on the grievousness of the calamity which had happened. He compares here the anxieties into which the people had been brought, to a *pitfall* and *dread.* There is a striking alliteration in the words פחד and פחת, *pechet* and *peched.* But the meaning is, that the people had been reduced to such straits, that there was no outlet for them; as the case is with us, when we are filled with dread, and look here and there, and see nothing but pitfalls on every side; then we are at our wits' end. Such then was the state of the people, as Jeremiah shews: filled with dread, they sought refuge, but saw pitfalls on every side.

He afterwards mentions *desolation* or destruction, and *sorrow.* It is probably a mistake in Jerome's version, where the first word is rendered "prophesying." Some think that he was led astray by the letter ש, *shin*, which he seems to have read with a point on the left side; and he took the word as coming from נשא, *nusha.* But another conjecture seems more correct, that the transcribers have committed a mistake; for what I have said is most appropriate to the passage, even that the people were overwhelmed with all kinds of evils, because there was nothing to be seen but *desolation* and *sorrow*, or bruising, or breach, שבר, *shaber.* It now follows,—

48. Mine eye runneth down with rivers of water for the destruction of the daughter of my people.

48. Rivi (*hoc est*, tanquam rivi) aquarum descendit oculus meus super contritione (*vel*, afflictione, *est idem nomen* שבר) filii populi mei.

Interpreters give different explanations of the beginning of this verse: some render it thus, "My eye comes down unto rivers of waters;" others, "My eye flows down unto rivers of waters," or, "rivers of waters flow down." But as I have explained elsewhere, the Prophet rather means, that his eye came down like rivers; and to come down, or to descend, is a metaphor for flowing down; for water, as it is well known, descends when it flows. And there is a change of number when he says, "My eye descends;" there is also understood the particle of comparison, כ, *caph*.[1] The meaning is, that his eyes descended or flowed down as rivers. The last word properly signifies divisions, but he means that many streams flowed down, as though they were so many rivers.

For the bruising, or the breach, *of my people:* the Prophet speaks here in his own person, though there is no doubt but that he exhorts all others to join him in his sorrow. For the faithful would not have prayed to God with sufficient ardour, had they not been dreadfully broken and confounded; had not the calamity deeply affected them, as it ought to have done, there would have been no serious attention to prayer. This is the reason why the Prophet here mentions his own weepings, and groanings, and tears, even that he might rouse himself to prayer, and lead others also. It follows,—

49. Mine eye trickleth down, and ceaseth not, without any intermission.

49. Oculus meus defluxit, et non quievit à non intermissionibus (*hoc est*, ut non sint intermissiones, *vel*, ut nulla sit requies.)

He repeats the same in other words,—that his eyes flowed down with tears. He still retains the singular number, but this is common in Hebrew. He then says, that *his eye with-*

[1] Let the verb have a causative sense, to cause to descend, to bring down, and there will be no difficulty in the clause; so the *Sept.* and the *Vulg.*,—

Streams of water does mine eyes bring down
For the breach of the daughter of my people.—*Ed.*

out end flowed down, so that there was no rest. But it afterwards follows,—

50. Till the Lord look down, and behold from heaven.	50. Donec aspiciat et videat Jehova è cœlis.

The Prophet here makes a distinction between his weeping and that blind sorrow by which the unbelieving are affected and violently agitated: they have no regard to God. Then the Prophet says here that he not only wept, but that he also prayed and waited for God to put an end to evils. As I have already said, the unbelieving grieve abundantly in adversities, nay, they abandon themselves to sorrow; but they turn away wholly from God, and are like wild beasts. Then the Prophet points out the right way to mourn: our eyes must flow down to weariness and without rest, but at the same time we must wait until God be propitious to us. Therefore this verse connects well with the former,[1] *until Jehovah look down and see from heaven;* for otherwise tears would draw us to despair, and despair would become the cause of fury; for we see that the ungodly murmur against God.

Thus, then, ought we to weep, in order that we may at the same time cherish hope while we wait for God to look down on us and to see our miseries from heaven. The word *heaven* is not added uselessly, because men in their evils, when they seek God, are filled with terror, for they do not think that they can ascend to him: hence, then, it is, that they despond, for they imagine that God is too remote from them. The Prophet therefore anticipates here this false notion, and says that we ought nevertheless to wait until God looks down from heaven; which corresponds with what is said in the Psalms: that God is high and yet has respect to low things. (Ps. cxiii. 4-6.) Though, then, the majesty of God is elevated above all the heavens, yet this does not prevent him familiarly to regard what is low and despised in the world. At length it follows,—

[1] The connexion of this verse with the preceding will be more evident from the following version,—

49. Mine eye hath poured down, and it will not cease,
With any intermissions,
50. Until Jehovah look down
And see from heaven.

To "see" here, as in verse 36, means to regard, so as to interfere in the

51. Mine eye affecteth mine heart, because of all the daughters of my city.	51. Oculus meus dolore afficit animam meam propter omnes filias urbis meæ (*vel*, pro omnibus filiabus urbis meæ.)

He had said, that his eye flowed down, and then, that it was like a fountain, from which many streams or rivers flowed: he now adopts another mode of speaking, that his *eyes grieved his soul ;* and it is a sign of the greatest sorrow when he who weeps seeks some relief, and is at the same time overpowered by that external feeling. For many indulge in grief and inflame themselves ; then the soul of man is like a fan to rouse the burning. But when we weep and our eyes shed tears, and when the mind in a manner exhausts itself, it is a proof of the greatest grief. And this great grief Jeremiah wished to express by saying, that *his eye troubled* or grieved *his soul.*

The latter part is explained in two ways : some render thus, " Because of all the daughters of my city." But though this meaning is generally taken, I yet prefer the opinion of those who render the words thus, " More than all the daughters of my city :" for מן, *men,* denotes a comparison, as it is also a causative. He says, then, that he was given to grief more than all the young women. As the female sex, as it is well known, are more tender and softer than men, the Prophet amplifies his lamentation by this comparison, that in weeping he exceeded all the young women of the city, so that he had almost forgotten his manhood. Had he said, the daughters of the people, it might be explained as before, as referring either to the cities, or to the whole people, that is, the whole community. But when he mentions *all the daughters of his city,* I cannot otherwise take the passage but as setting forth a comparison, that is, that he could not moderate his grief, but was so seized with it as women are, and also young girls, whose hearts, as it has been already said, are still more tender.[1] The rest to-morrow.

affairs of men. " With any," &c., literally, " With no," &c. But the English language will not admit of the two negatives, though the Welsh will.—*Ed.*

[1] The versions and the *Targ.* give the first meaning, " because of the daughters of my city ;" and the last words, " of my city," seem to favour

PRAYER.

Grant, Almighty God, that as thou hast hitherto spared us, we may not grow torpid in our vices, and that since thou hast already begun to deal more severely with thy Church, we may be awakened by thy chastisements, and so humble ourselves under thy mighty hand, as yet not to doubt but that thou wilt be propitious to us, and that we may so loathe ourselves on account of our sins, as still to be fully persuaded that, provided we wait for thee, thou wilt at length be merciful to us, so as to afford us new reasons for joy and gratitude, through Christ Jesus our Lord.—Amen.

Lecture Thirteenth.

52. Mine enemies chased me sore, like a bird, without cause.	52. Venando venati sunt me tanquam passerem (*vel,* avem) inimici mei sine causa.

We shall see to the end of the chapter the various complaints, by which the Prophet deplored the miseries of his own nation, that he might at length obtain the mercy of God. He takes here the comparison of a bird or a sparrow. He says that the Chaldeans had been like fowlers, and the Jews like sparrows: and we know that there is neither prudence nor courage in birds. He, then, means that the Jews had been destitute of all help, having been exposed as a prey to their enemies, who were like fowlers.

And he seems to allude to the words of Solomon, when he says, that without a cause is the net spread for birds (Prov. i. 17;) and he means that innocent men are circumvented by the wicked, when they spread for them their snares as it were on every side, while they are like the birds, who have no prudence to avoid them.

We now, then, understand the drift of what the Prophet says: he amplifies the indignity of their calamity by this comparison,—that the Chaldeans at their pleasure plundered the miserable people, who were not able to resist them, who were indeed without any power to defend themselves.[1] It follows,—

it; for had women as a sex been intended, they would not have been thus designated.—*Ed.*

[1] The words literally are,—

Hunting hunted me like a bird
Have mine enemies without a cause.—*Ed.*

53. They have cut off my life in the dungeon, and cast a stone upon me.	53. Succiderunt (*vel potius*, constrinxerunt) in puteo vitam meam, et projecerunt lapidem super me.

He now employs other comparisons. Some improperly confine this to Jeremiah himself, as though he explained here before God the wrongs done to himself: but there is no doubt but that he undertakes the cause of the whole people; and his object was to encourage by his own example the faithful to lament their state so that they might obtain pardon from God.

He then compares himself to a man half-dead, cast into a pit, and there left for lost. Then some improperly interpret the words, "they cast stones;" for stoning was not in the mind of the Prophet; but having said that he was fast bound in a pit or dungeon, he adds that a stone was laid over him, that he might not come forth, as we know was the case with Daniel. (Dan. vi. 16, 17.) Daniel was cast into the den of lions, and then a stone was put on the mouth of the den. So also the Prophet says, that he was bound fast in the pit, and not only that, but that a stone was laid over him, that there might be no hope of coming out; and thus the pit was like a grave. Here, then, he means that he was reduced to the last extremity, because he had not only been taken by his enemies, but had also been cast into a pit. And, as it is well known, it is a metaphorical expression or a similitude. He adds,—

54. Waters flowed over mine head; *then* I said, I am cut off.	54. Inundaverunt (*ad verbum, alii*, ascenderunt) aquæ super caput meum; dixi, succisus sum.

He now adds a third comparison,—that he had been overwhelmed, as it were, with a flood of evils. This similitude occurs often in Scripture, especially in the Psalms; for when David wished to set forth his despair, he said that he was sunk in deep waters. (Ps. lxix. 15, 16.) So also in this place the Prophet complains, that *waters had flowed over his head*, so that he thought himself lost. Though, indeed, this was the saying of a man in a hopeless state, it is yet evident from the context that the Prophet was firm in the hope of God's mercy. But he speaks according to the judgment of the flesh; and we know that the faithful are as it were divided; for as they have not put off the flesh, they must necessarily be acquainted with adversities, be stormed by fear and feel anxieties; in short, when death hangs over them, they must in a manner be exposed to fear. In the meantime, faith in their hearts obtains the victory, so that they do not succumb under terrors, or cares, or anxieties.

When, therefore, the Prophet says that in his own judgment he was lost, he does not mean that his faith was so extinguished that he ceased to pray to God; for in the next verse he shews that he persevered in prayer. How, then, did he say or believe that he was lost? even, as I have already said, according to human judgment. And we often see that the faithful complain that they are forsaken, that God is asleep in heaven, that he has turned away from them. All these things are to be referred to the perception of the flesh. While, then, the faithful cast their eyes on dangers, when death comes, they not only tremble, but fear greatly and faint also. In the meantime, as I have said, they struggle by faith against all these temptations. So, then, is this passage to be understood,—that the Prophet believed that he was lost, that is, as far as he could judge by the aspect of things at that time, for no hope appeared then to the Church. But we yet see that the Prophet did not indulge himself in this despair; for he immediately adds,—

55. I called upon thy name, O Lord, out of the low dungeon.	55. Invocavi nomen tuum, Jehova, è puteo profunditatum.

We certainly see that the Prophet had an inward conflict, which also all the faithful experience, for the spirit fights against the flesh, as Paul teaches us. (Gal. v. 17.) Though, then, he on the one hand apprehended death, he yet ceased not to flee to God; for faith strengthened his mind so that he did not succumb, but on the contrary he firmly rejected the temptation presented to him. Though, then, he was, according to the flesh, persuaded as to his own ruin, he, on the other hand, called on the name of God; for the faithful do not measure the power and grace of God by their own thoughts, but give glory to God by recumbing on him even in the greatest extremities.

And this passage ought to be carefully noticed; for when

Satan cannot in any other way turn us aside from prayer, he alleges our weakness; "What meanest thou, miserable being? will God hear thee? for what canst thou do? thou tremblest, thou art anxious, nay, thou despairest; and yet thou thinkest that God will be propitious to thee." Whenever, therefore, Satan tries to shut the door against us so as to prevent us to pray, let this example of the Prophet come to our minds; for he, though he thought himself lost, did not yet cast aside the confidence he entertained as to God's help and aid. For whence arose his perseverance, except that he in a manner rebuked himself when he found himself so overwhelmed, and as it were dead. These two states of mind are seen in this short prayer of David, "My God, my God, why hast thou forsaken me?" (Ps. xxii. 1.) For when he addressed God, and called him his God, we see his rare and extraordinary faith; and when he complains that he was forsaken, we see how, through the infirmity of the flesh, he thought that it was all over with him as to his salvation. Such a conflict, then, is described here; but faith overcame and gained the victory, for the Prophet ceased not to cry to God, even from *the pit of depths*—from the pit, that is, from death itself.

And this also ought to be carefully observed; for when God bears us on his wings, or when he carries us in his bosom, it is easy to pray; but when we seem to be cast into the deepest gulfs, if we thence cry to him, it is a real and certain proof of faith and hope. As such passages often occur in the Psalms, they may be compared together; but I touch but slightly on the subject, for it is not my object to heap together all the quotations which are appropriate; it is enough to present the real meaning of the Prophet. It follows,—

56. Thou hast heard my voice; hide not thine ear at my breathing, at my cry.	56. Vocem meam audisti; ne occultes (*vel,* occludas) aurem tuam ad respirationem meam (*vertunt,* ad clamorem meum) et ad precationem meam (*sed prius nomen accipio potius pro gemitu vel clamore.*)

When the Prophet says that God *heard,* it is the same as though he said, that he had so prayed that God became a witness of his earnestness and solicitude; for many boast in high terms of their earnestness and fervour and constancy in prayer, but their boastings are all empty and vain. But the Prophet summons God as a witness of his crying, as though he had said that he was not so overwhelmed by his adversity, but that he always fled to God.

He then says, *Close not*, &c.; it is properly, "hide not;" but as this is not quite suitable to *ears*, I am disposed to give this version, *Close not thine ear to my cry.* The verb רוח *ruch*, means to dilate, to respire; hence almost all render the noun here, "breathing;" but what follows cannot admit of this sense, *to my prayer* or cry. I have no doubt but that these two words mean crying; for in groaning the spirit of man dilates itself, and the soul, compressed by grief, expands. But when we cast our cares and troubles into the bosom of God, then the spirit forcibly emerges. This, then, is what the Prophet means, when he asks God *not to close his ear to his dilation* or groaning, *and to his cry.*[1] It follows,—

57. Thou drewest near in the day *that* I called upon thee: thou saidst, Fear not.

57. Appropinquasti in die in quo clamavi ad te (*vel*, invocavi te,) dixisti, Ne timeas.

Here the Prophet tells us that he had experienced the goodness of God, because he had not suffered a repulse when he prayed. And this doctrine is especially useful to us, that is, to call to mind that we had not in time past prayed in vain. For we may hence feel assured, that as God ever continues like himself, he will be ever ready to help us whenever we implore his protection. This, then, is the reason why the Prophet declares here that he had experienced the readiness of God to hear prayer: *Thou didst come nigh*, he says, *in the day when I called on thee; thou didst say, Fear not.* And this approach or coming nigh refers to what was

[1] Materially correct, no doubt, is this explanation. We may give this version,—

My voice hast thou heard, deafen not thy ear
To my sighing, to my cry.

The verb עלם means to veil, and hence to hide. To veil the eye is, not to look at what is set before it; and to veil the ear is, to render it deaf to what is said. The Prophet says that God had heard his voice, for he had prayed; but he further asks God not to turn a deaf ear to his sighing, or sobbing, as given by the *Vulg.*, and to his cry.—*Ed.*

real or actually done, that God had stretched forth his hand and helped his servants. Since, then, they had been confirmed by such evidences, they had the privilege of ever fleeing to God. God, indeed, supplies us with reasons for hope, when he once and again aids us; and it is the same as though he testified that he will ever be the same as we have once and again found him to be.

He then adds an explanation, *Thou didst say, Fear not.* He does not mean that God had spoken; but, as I have said, he thus sets forth the fact, that he had not sought God in vain, for he had relieved him. Though God may not speak, yet when we find that our prayers are heard by him, it is the same as though he raised us up and removed from us every fear. The sum of what is said is, that God had been propitious to his servants whenever they cried to him. It now follows,—

58. O Lord, thou hast pleaded the causes of my soul; thou hast redeemed my life.	58. Disceptasti, Domine, disceptationes animæ meæ, redemisti vitam meam.

For the same purpose he now says, that God had been his judge to undertake his cause, and not only once, for he had contended for him as though he had been his perpetual advocate. The meaning is, that the Prophet (who yet speaks in the name of all the faithful) had found God a defender and a helper, not only in one instance, but whenever he had been in trouble; for he uses the plural number, and says, *Thou hast pleaded the pleadings of my soul.*

He adds, *Thou hast redeemed my life.* It is the way of God's pleading when he delivers us as it were from death. Friends do, indeed, sometimes anxiously exert themselves, interposing for our defence, but they do not always succeed. But God is such a pleader of our cause, that he is also a deliverer, for our safety is in his hand. It follows,—

59. O Lord, thou hast seen my wrong; judge thou my cause.	59. Vidisti, Jehova, oppressionem (subversionem; *alii vertunt,* iniquitatem) meam; judica judicium meum.

The word עותתי, *outti,* is rendered by some "iniquity," but in an ironical sense, as though the Prophet had said, "Thou, God, knowest whether I have offended." But the word is to be taken passively; the verb עות, *out*, means to subvert, as we have elsewhere seen, even in this chapter. Then, by *his subversion,* he means oppression, even when his adversaries unworthily trod him under their feet. And hence he asks God at the same time to *judge his judgment,* that is, to undertake his cause, and to appear as his defender, as he had formerly done; for he saw his *subversion,* that is, he saw that he was unjustly cast down and laid prostrate by the wicked. It follows,—

60. Thou hast seen all their vengeance, *and* all their imaginations against me:	60. Vidisti omnes ultiones ipsorum, omnes cogitationes eorum contra me.

This mode of speaking was often used by the saints, because God, when it pleased him to look on their miseries, was ever ready to bring them help. Nor were they words without meaning, when the faithful said, *O Lord, thou hast seen;* for they said this for their own sake, that they might shake off all unbelief. For as soon as any trial assails us, we imagine that God is turned away from us; and thus our flesh tempts us to despair. It is hence necessary that the faithful should in this respect struggle with themselves and feel assured that God has seen them. Though, then, human reason may say, that God does not see, but neglect and disregard his people, yet on the other hand, this doctrine ought to sustain them, it being certain that God does see them. This is the reason why David so often uses this mode of expression.

Thou, Jehovah, he says, *hast seen all their vengeances.* By vengeances here he means acts of violence, according to what we find in Ps. viii. 2, where God is said "to put to flight the enemy and the avenger." By the avenger there he simply means, not such as retaliate wrongs, but cruel and violent men. So also, in this place, by vengeances, he means all kinds of cruelty, as also by *thoughts* he means wicked counsels, by which the ungodly sought to oppress the miserable and the innocent. He again repeats the same thing,—

61. Thou hast heard their reproach, O Lord, *and* all their imaginations against me;	61. Audivisti probra ipsorum, Jehova, omnes cogitationes eorum contra me.

We see that this is a repetition, but for vengeances he now mentions *reproaches.* And in this way he sought again to turn God to mercy; for when he brings no aid, he seems to close his eyes and to render his ears deaf; but when he attends to our evils, he then soon brings help. The Prophet, then, having said that God *saw,* now refers to hearing: *he had heard their reproaches.* Adopting a language not strictly proper, he adds, that he had heard their *thoughts;* though he speaks not only of their secret counsels, but also of all the wicked conspiracies by which his enemies had contrived to ruin him.[1] He adds,—

62. The lips of those that rose up against me, and their device against me all the day.	62. Labia (*vel,* sermones, *aut,* linguas) insurgentium contra me, et sermones eorum contra me tota die (*vel,* quotidie.)

Instead of thoughts, he now mentions *lips,* or words. The verb הגה, *ege,* means to meditate, when no voice is uttered; but as the noun is connected here with lips, there is no doubt but that the Prophet refers to words, rather than to hidden meditations.[2] He then says, that such were the conspiracies, that they did not conceal what they had in their hearts, but publicly avowed their wicked purposes. Now this insolence must have moved God to aid his people, so unjustly oppressed.

He adds, *every day,* or daily. This circumstance also must have availed to obtain favour, so that God might the sooner aid his people. For had the ungodly made violent assaults, and soon given over, it would have been easy to persevere in so short a trial, as when a storm soon passes by; but when they went on perseveringly in their machina-

[1] There is no necessity, as some have supposed, of making לי in the former verse, and עלי in this verse, the same. The difference is occasioned by the verbs "thou hast seen," and, "thou hast heard." God had seen the thoughts or purposes effected "against" him; and he had heard the purposes formed "concerning" him. He refers first to the purposes carried into effect, and then, as it is common in the prophets, he refers to the purposes previously formed respecting him.—*Ed.*

[2] The best word is *muttering,*—

The lips of my adversaries,
And their muttering concerning me all the day.

It is עלי here, as in the previous verse, "concerning me," not "against me."—*Ed.*

tions, it was very hard to bear the trial. And hence we derive a ground of hope, supplied to us by what the Holy Spirit suggests to us here, that God will be merciful to us on seeing the pertinacity of our enemies. He then adds,—

63. Behold their sitting down, and their rising up; I *am* their music.	63. Sessionem eorum et surrectionem eorum aspice; ego canticum eorum (*vel,* pulsatio, *ut alii vertunt.*)

The Prophet repeats still the same thing, only in other words. He had spoken of the lyings in wait, and the conspiracies and the speeches of his enemies; he now adds, that nothing was hid from God. By *sitting* and *rising,* he means all the actions of life, as when David says, "Thou knowest my sitting and my rising," (Ps. cxxxix. 2;) that is, whether I rest or walk, all my actions are known to thee. By *rising,* then, the Prophet denotes here, as David did, all the movements or doings of men; and by *sitting,* he means their quiet counsels; for men either deliberate and prepare for work while they sit, or rise, and thus move and act.

He means, in short, that whether his enemies consulted silently and quietly, or attempted to do this or that, nothing was unknown to God. Now, as God takes such notice of the counsels and all the actions of men, it cannot be but that he restrains and checks the wicked; for God's knowledge is always connected with his office as a judge. We hence see how the Prophet strengthens himself, as we have lately stated, and thus gathers a reason for confidence; for the wicked counsels of his enemies and their works were not hid from God.

He adds, *I am become a song.* He again sets before God his reproach, cast upon him by the ungodly. For that indignity also availed much to lead God not to suffer his people to be unworthily treated. It now follows,—

64. Render unto them a recompense, O Lord, according to the work of their hands.	64. Repende illis mercedem, Jehova, secundum opus manuum suarum.

He adds here a conclusion; for he has hitherto been relating, as I have said, the evils which he suffered, and also the reproaches and unjust oppressions, in order that he might have God propitious to him; for this is the way of conciliating favour when we are wrongfully dealt with; for it cannot be but that God will sustain our cause. He indeed testifies that he is ready to help the miserable; it is his own peculiar work to deliver captives from prison, to illuminate the blind, to succour the miserable and the oppressed. This is the reason, then, why the Prophet now confidently asks God to *render* to his enemies *their reward, according to the work of their hands.*

Were any one to object, and say, that another rule is prescribed to us, even to pray for our enemies, even when they oppress us; the answer is this, that the faithful, when they prayed thus, did not bring any violent feelings of their own, but pure zeal, and rightly formed; for the Prophet here did not pray for evil indiscriminately on all, but on the reprobate, who were perpetually the enemies of God and of his Church. He might then with sincerity of heart have asked God to render to them their just reward. And whenever the saints broke forth thus against their enemies, and asked God to become an avenger, this principle must be ever borne in mind, that they did not indulge their own wishes, but were so guided by the Holy Spirit—that moderation was connected with that fervid zeal to which I have referred. The Prophet, then, as he speaks here of the Chaldeans, confidently asked God to destroy them, as we shall again presently see. We find also in the Psalms the same imprecations, especially on Babylon,—"Happy he who shall render to thee what thou hast brought on us, who shall dash thy children against a stone." (Ps. cxxxvii. 8, 9.) It follows,—

65. Give them sorrow of heart, thy curse unto them.	65. Des illis impedimentum cordis, (*alii*, obstinationem,) maledictionem tuam illis (*vel*, maledictio tua illis.)

He expresses what the vengeance was to be, even that God would give them up to a reprobate mind; for by מגנת־לב, *meganet-leb*, he no doubt meant the blindness of the heart, and at the same time included stupidity, as though he had said, "O Lord, so oppress them with evils, that they may become stupified." For it is an extremity of evil, when we are so overpowered as not to be as it were ourselves, and when our evils do not drive us to prayer.[1]

We now then perceive what the Prophet meant by asking God to *give* to his enemies *the impediment of heart,* even that he might take away a sound mind, and smite them with blindness and madness, as it is said elsewhere.—I run on quickly, that I may finish, lest the hour should prevent us. The last verse of this triple alphabet follows,—

66. Persecute and destroy them in anger from under the heavens of the Lord.	66. Persequere in ira et perde eos è sub cœlis Jehovæ (*quidam in vocativo casu legunt,* Jehova; *sed quia non ponitur* שמים, *sed in constructione* שמי, *ideo retineo proprietatem.*)

He first asks God to *persecute them in wrath,* that is, to be implacable to them; for persecution is, when God not only chastises the wicked for a short time, but when he adds evils to evils, and accumulates them until they perish. He then adds, and prays God to *destroy them from under the heavens of Jehovah.* This phrase is emphatical; and they extenuate the weightiness of the sentence, who thus render it, "that God himself would destroy the ungodly from the earth." For the Prophet does not without a design mention the *heavens of Jehovah,* as though he had said, that though God is hidden from us while we sojourn in the world, he yet dwells in heaven, for heaven is often called the throne of God,—"The heaven is my throne." (Is. lxvi. 1.) "O God, who dwellest in the sanctuary." (Ps. xxii. 4; lxxvii. 14.) By God's sanctuary is often meant heaven. For this reason, then, the Prophet asked here that the ungodly should be destroyed from under the *heaven of Jehovah,* that is, that their destruction might testify that he sits in heaven, and is the judge of the world, and that things are not in such a confusion, but that the ungodly must at length render an account before the celestial judge, whom they have yet long neglected. This is the end of the chapter.

[1] The word means "covering, as rendered by the *Sept.;* the *Syr.* has "sorrow," and the *Vulg.* "shield," which has no meaning. What is no doubt meant is hardness or blindness—

Give them blindness of heart:
Thy curse *be* to them.—*Ed.*

PRAYER.

Grant, Almighty God, that as at this day ungodly men and wholly reprobate so arrogantly rise up against thy Church, we may learn to flee to thee, and to hide ourselves under the shadow of thy wings, and fully to hope for thy salvation; and that however disturbed the state of things may be, we may yet never doubt but that thou wilt be propitious to us, since we have so often found thee to be our deliverer; and that we may thus persevere in confidence of thy grace and mercy, and be also roused by this incentive to pray to thee, until having gone through all our miseries, we shall at length enjoy that blessed rest which thou hast promised to us through Christ Jesus our Lord.—Amen.

CHAPTER IV.

Lecture Fourteenth.

1. How is the gold become dim! *how* is the most fine gold changed! the stones of the sanctuary are poured out in the top of every street.

1. Quomodo obscuratum est aurum! mutatum est aurum bonum! effusi sunt (*vel,* projecti) lapides sanctuarii in capite omnium platearum.

Here Jeremiah, following the order of the alphabet the fourth time,[1] deplores the ruin of the city, and the destruction of the priesthood and of the kingdom. For they are mistaken who think that the death of Josiah is here lamented; for there are here many things, which we shall see as we proceed, which do not suit that event. There is no doubt but that this mournful song refers to the destruction of the Temple and city; but when Josiah was killed, the enemy had not come to the city, and the stones of the Temple were not then cast forth into the streets and the public roads. There are also other things which we shall see, which did not then happen. It follows then that here is described the terrible vengeance of God, which we have had already to consider.

He begins by expressing his astonishment: *How obscured is the gold! and the precious gold!* for כתם, *catam,* is properly the best gold, though the word *good,* הטוב, *ethub,* is added to it. We may hence conclude that it generally de-

[1] Here, as in the two first chapters, the verses only begin alphabetically, but instead of having three or six lines, they have only two or four. —*Ed.*

notes gold only. He mentions, then, gold twice, but they are two different words in Hebrew, זהב, *zaeb*, and כתם, *catam*.[1] Now he speaks figuratively in the former part of the verse; but there is no doubt but that by the gold, and the finest gold, as it is rendered, he means the splendour of the Temple; for God had designed the Temple to be built, as it is well known, in a very magnificent manner. Hence he calls what was ornamental in the Temple gold.

He then speaks without a figure, and says, that the *stones were thrown* here and there in all directions. Some, indeed, think that these words refer to the sacred vessels, of which there was a large quantity, we know, in the Temple. But this opinion is not probable, for the Prophet does not complain that the gold was taken away, but that it was *obscured*, and *changed*. It is then, no doubt, a metaphorical expression. But he afterwards explains himself when he says that the *stones of the sanctuary were cast forth* here and there along all the streets. It was indeed a sad spectacle; for God had consecrated that temple to himself, that he might dwell in it. When therefore the stones of the sanctuary were thus disgracefully scattered, it must have grievously wounded the minds of all the godly; for they saw that God's name was thus exposed to reproaches. Nor is there a doubt but that the Chaldeans vomited forth many reproaches against God when they thus scattered the stones of the temple. It hence appears, that the Prophet did not without reason exclaim, How has this happened! for such a sight must have justly astonished all the godly, seeing as they did the degradation of the temple connected with a reproach to God himself. It follows,—

2. The precious sons of Zion, incomparable to fine gold, how are they esteemed as earthen pitchers, the work of the hands of the potter!

2. Filii Sion pretiosi (*alii vertunt*, inclytos) comparati auro (*alii vertunt*, amicti auro, *quod mihi magis placet*,) quomodo reputati sunt in lagenas testaceas (testæ, *ad verbum*) opus manuum figuli?

[1] This chapter, like the two first chapters, begins with the word איכה, "How this!" and the verbs are in the future tense, used for the present.—

How *is* this! tarnished is gold,
Changed is fine gold, the best:
Cast forth are the sacred stones
At the head of every street.—*Ed.*

The Prophet comes now to the people, though he does not include the whole people, but brings forward those who were renowned, and excelled in honour and dignity. He then says, that they were become like *earthen vessels* and the *work of the potter's hands*, which is very fitly added. Then by the *sons of Sion*, whom he calls *precious* or glorious, he means the chief men and the king's counsellors and those who were most eminent. And he seems to allude to that prophecy which we before explained: for he had said that the people were like earthen vessels; and he went into the house of the potter, that he might see what was made there. When the potter made a vessel which did not please him, he remodelled it, and then it assumed another form; then God declared that the people were in his hand and at his will, as the clay was in the hand of the potter. (Jer. xviii. 2; xix. 11.) When he now says, that the chief men were stripped of all dignity, and reduced to another form, so as to become like earthen vessels, he no doubt sets forth by this change the judgment of God, which the Jews had for a time disregarded.

And we must bear in mind the Prophet's object: he described the ruin of the Temple and city, that he might remind the people of the punishment which had at length been inflicted; for we know that the people had not only been deaf, but had also scoffed at and derided all prophecies and threatenings. As, then, they had not believed the doctrine of Jeremiah, he now shews that what he had predicted was really fulfilled, and that the people were finding to their cost that God did not trifle with them when he had so often threatened what at length happened. And hence we may conclude, that there was then a superfluous splendour in garments, for we read that they had been clad or clothed in gold; surely it was a display too sumptuous. There is, however, no wonder, for we know that Orientals are far too much given to such trumperies.

Now, if the other reading, that the *sons of Sion had been before compared to gold,*[1] be more approved, the passage must be

[1] The value, and not the appearance, is evidently meant: the "sons of Sion" were "precious," as here expressly stated. In this respect they had

extended to all their dignity and to all those gifts by which they had been favoured and had become illustrious. I have already reminded you, that the *work of the potter's hands* is here to be taken for the vessels or the earthen flagons; but it was the Prophet's object to enlarge on that reproach, which had been before incredible. It follows,—

3. Even the sea-monsters draw out the breast, they give suck to their young ones: the daughter of my people *is become* cruel, like the ostriches in the wilderness.

3. Etiam serpentes educunt mammam, lactant catulos suos; filia populi mei ad crudelem tanquam ululæ (*vel*, struthiones) in deserto.

This verse is harshly explained by many, for they think that the daughter of the people is called cruel, because she acted towards her children as serpents do to their young ones. But this meaning is not suitable, for the word בת, *beth*, is well known to be feminine. He says that the *daughter of the people had come to a savage* or cruel one, the latter word is masculine. Then the Prophet seems to mean that the whelps (such is the word) of serpents are more kindly dealt with than the Jews. Serpents are void of all humanity, yet they nourish their brood and give them the breast. Hence the Prophet by this comparison amplifies the miseries of the people, that their condition was worse than that of serpents, for the tender brood are nourished by their mothers; but the people were without any help, so that they in vain implored the protection of their mother and of others. We now see the real meaning of the Prophet.

The particle גם, *gam*, is emphatical; for had he spoken of animals, such as are careful to nourish their young, it would not have been so wonderful; but so great seems to be the savageness and barbarity of serpents, that they might be expected to cast away their brood. Now he says that *even serpents draw out the breast.* The Jews say that the breasts of serpents are covered with scales, as though they

been of the same estimate with gold; but now they were as worthless as potter's vessels: they were so esteemed and treated,—

The sons of Sion *were* precious,
Of worth equal to pure gold;
How is this! they have been deemed as earthen vessels,
The work of the hands of the potter.—*Ed.*

were hidden; but this is one of their figments. It is a common phrase, taken from a common practice; for a woman draws out the breast when she gives suck to her infant; so serpents are said to draw out the breast when they give suck to their whelps; for גורים, *gurim*, are the whelps of lions or of bears; but in this place the word is applied to serpents. *The daughter*, then, *of my people has come to the cruel one*, for the people had to do with nothing but cruelty, there being no one to bring them help or to succour them in their miseries. He, then, does not accuse the people of cruelty, that they did not nourish their children, but on the contrary he means that they were given up to cruel enemies.[1]

As the ostriches, or the owls, he says, *in the wilderness*. If we understand the ostrich to be intended, we know that bird to be very stupid; for as soon as she lays an egg, she forgets and leaves it. The comparison, then, would be suitable, were the daughter of the people said to be cruel, because she neglected her children; but the Prophet, as I think, means, on the contrary, that the Jews were so destitute of every help, as though they were banished into solitary places beyond the sight of men; for birds in solitude in vain seek the help of others. As, then, *the ostrich* or the owl has in the desert no one to bring it help, and is without its own mother, so the Prophet intimates that there was no one to stretch forth a hand to the distressed people to relieve their extreme miseries. It follows,—

4. The tongue of the sucking child cleaveth to the roof of his mouth for thirst: the young children ask bread, *and* no man breaketh *it* unto them.

4. Adhæsit lingua lactantis ad palatum ejus in siti; parvuli petierunt panem, dividens nemo illis (*hoc est,* nemo est qui illis dividat, *id est,* porrigat.)

[1] The reference here is to the conduct of mothers, called here "the daughter of my people," as it appears evident from the following verse,—

Even dragons have drawn out the breast,
They have suckled their young ones:
The daughter of my people *has been* for cruelty
Like the ostriches in the desert.

It is said that the ostrich lays her eggs and forsakes them. See Job xxxix. 15. The verb, to be, is understood, as the case often is, but it must ever be in the same tense as the verb or verbs connected with the sentence.—*Ed.*

He says that sucking children were so thirsty, that the tongue was as it were fixed to the palate; and it was a dreadful thing; for mothers would willingly pour forth their own blood to feed their infants. When, therefore, the tongue of a child clave to his mouth, it seemed to be in a manner beyond nature. Among other calamities, then, the Prophet names this, that *infants pined away with thirst*, and also that *children sought bread* in vain. He speaks not in the latter instance of sucklings, but of children three or four years old. Then he says that they *sought* or asked for *bread*, but that there was no one to give.[1]

He describes here the famine of the city, of which he had predicted, when he declared that it would be better with the slain than with the people remaining alive, for a harder conflict with famine and want would await the living. But this was not believed. Now, then, the Prophet upbraids the Jews with their former perverseness. He afterwards adds,—

5. They that did feed delicately are desolate in the streets: *they that were* brought up in scarlet embrace dunghills.

5. Qui comedebant ad delicias (*hoc est*, in deliciis, *ad verbum*, למעדנים,) perierunt in plateis; qui educati fuerant in coccino (ad coccinum,) amplexi sunt stercora.

Here he goes on farther, and says, that they had perished with famine who had been accustomed to the most delicate food. He had said generally that infants found nothing in their mothers' breasts, but pined away with thirst, and also that children died through want of bread. But he now amplifies this calamity by saying, that this not only happened to the children of the common people, but also to those who had been brought up delicately, and had been clothed in scarlet and purple.

Then he says that they *perished in the streets*, and also that they *embraced the dunghills*, because they had no place

[1] The verbs here are in the past tense, and not in the present, as in our version,—

Cleave did the tongue of the suckling
To his palate through thirst;
Children asked bread,
A breaker, none *was* to them.—*Ed.*

to lie down, or because they sought food, as famished men do, on dunghills.[1] It seems to be a hyperbolical expression; but if we consider what the Prophet has already narrated and will again repeat, it ought not to appear incredible, that those who had been accustomed to delicacies embraced dunghills; for mothers cooked their own children and devoured them as beef or mutton. There is no doubt but that the siege, of which we have before read, drove the people to acts too degrading to be spoken of, especially when they had become blinded through so great a pertinacity, and had altogether hardened themselves in their madness against God. It follows,—

6. For the punishment of the iniquity of the daughter of my people is greater than the punishment of the sin of Sodom, *that was* overthrown as in a moment, and no hands stayed on her.

6. Et major fuit pœna filiæ populi mei pœna Sodomæ (*ad verbum est,* iniquitas filiæ populi mei peccato *vel* scelere Sodomæ; *sed statim dicam cur de pœna exponam potiùs quàm de ipso scelere,*) quæ eversa fuit tanquam momento; non manserunt in ea plagæ (*alii vertunt,* et non castrametatæ sunt manus; *sed postea etiam dicam cur mihi magis placeat illa versio.*)

The Prophet says first, that the punishment of his people was heavier than that of Sodom. If any one prefers the other version, I will not contend, for it is not unsuitable; and hence also a most useful doctrine may be drawn, that we are to judge of the grievousness of our sins by the greatness of our punishment; for God never exceeds what is just when he takes vengeance on the sins of men. Then his severity shews how grievously men have sinned. Thus, Jeremiah may have reasoned from the effect to the cause, and declared that the people had been more wicked than the Sodomites. Nor is this unreasonable; for if the Jews had not fallen into that great wickedness of which the

[1] The dunghills were collections of cow-dung and other things heaped together for fuel instead of wood. They had been brought up "on scarlet," *i.e.*, on scarlet couches, they were now glad to lie down anywhere, even on dunghills, and hence they are said to have embraced them, as though they had a love for them,—

They who had fed on delicacies
  Perished in the streets;
They who had been brought up on scarlet
  Embraced the dunghills.—*Ed.*

Sodomites were guilty, yet the Prophets everywhere charged them as men who not only equalled but also surpassed the Sodomites, especially Ezekiel, (chap. xvi. 46, 47.) Isaiah also called them the people of Gomorrha, and the king's counsellors and judges, the princes of Sodom, (Isa. i. 9, 10.) This mode of speaking is then common in the Prophets, and the meaning is not unsuitable.

But as he dwells only on the grievousness of their punishment, the other explanation seems more simple; for I regard not what is plausible, but accept the true meaning. Let us then repeat the Prophet's words: *greater is the punishment of my people,* &c. The word עון, *oun,* means punishment as well as iniquity; this is certain, beyond dispute. Now חטאת, *chethat,* means also both sin and punishment. It is hence applied to expiations; the sacrifice for sin is called חטאת, *chethat.* As to the words, then, they designate punishment as well as sin, the cause of it. But the reason which follows leads me to consider punishment as intended, for he says that *Sodom was overthrown as in a moment.* Here, doubtless, we see that the sins of the Jews are not compared to the sins of the Sodomites, but their destruction only: God had overthrown Sodom, as afterwards he overthrew Jerusalem; but the ruin of Sodom was milder, for it perished in a moment—for when God had dreadfully thundered, the Sodomites and their neighbouring citizens were immediately destroyed; and we know that the shorter the punishment, the more tolerable it is. As the Prophet here compares the momentary destruction of Sodom with the prolonged ruin of the city and slaughter of the people, we see that what is spoken of is not sin, but on the contrary God's judgment.

There is yet no doubt but that the Prophet summoned the Jews to God's tribunal, that they might know that they deserved such a vengeance, and that they might perceive that they were worse than the Sodomites. For it was not the Prophet's object to expostulate with God, or to charge him with having been too rigid in destroying the city of Jerusalem. As, then, the Prophet does not charge God either with injustice or with cruelty, it is certain that punishment is what is here set forth, in order that the people might know what they deserved.[1]

But the words declare nothing more than that God's vengeance had been severer towards the Jews than towards the Sodomites. How so? it is evident from this reason, *because Sodom was consumed as in a moment;* and then it is added, *and strokes remained not on her.* The word יד, *id,* as it is well known, means hand, a place, but sometimes, metaphorically, a stroke. Interpreters vary here, but I shall not recite the opinions of all, nor is it needful. Those who seem to come nearest to the words of the Prophet, render them thus, "and hands (or forces) have not encamped against her." But this is a forced and far-fetched meaning. It would run better, "have not remained." The verb חול, *chul,* means sometimes to encamp, and sometimes to remain, to settle. Then the most appropriate meaning would be, that *strokes settled not on the Sodomites,* while the Jews pined away in their manifold evils.[2] For they did not immediately perish like the Sodomites; but when God saw them so obstinate in their wickedness, he destroyed some by famine, some by pestilence, and some by the sword; and then the city was not immediately demolished altogether, as it often happens when enemies make a slaughter and kill men, women, and children; but this people were not so destroyed. Many of them were driven into exile, and some of the common people were left to inhabit the ruined cities, for there was a dreadful desolation. The king himself, as it has before appeared, was removed to Babylon, but his eyes had previously been pulled out, and his children slain in his presence.

We hence see that the destruction of the city was like a slow consumption, and that thus strokes remained there as

[1] The early versions and the *Targ.* render the words "iniquity," and "sin;" but modern critics agree with *Calvin.* Penalty and punishment might be suitably adopted.—*Ed.*

[2] The clause might be rendered,—

And not wearied against (or, over) her were hands.

This is substantially the *Sept.* and the *Syr.* *Grotius* says that the meaning is, that Sodom was destroyed not by human means, that is, not by a siege, as Jerusalem had been.—*Ed.*

it were fixed, which did not happen to Sodom; for Sodom suddenly perished when God thundered against it; but the hand of God did not depart from the Jews, and the strokes or smitings, as I have said, were fixed on them and continued. It follows,—

7. Her Nazarites were purer than snow, they were whiter than milk, they were more ruddy in body than rubies, their polishing *was* of sapphire:

8. Their visage is blacker than a coal; they are not known in the streets: their skin cleaveth to their bones; it is withered, it is become like a stick.

7. Candidiores Nazaræi ejus nive, (*vel,* puriores,) candidiores lacte, rubicundi fuerunt corpore suo (*neque enim hoc potest accipi de ossibus*) supra lapillos preciosos, sapphirus excisio ipsorum:

8. Obtenebrata est præ caligine forma ipsorum, non agniti fuerunt in plateis; adhæsit cutis eorum ossi ipsorum, (*hoc est,* ossibus;) exaruit, fuit tanquam lignum.

Here the Prophet speaks of Nazarites, by whom we know the worship of God was honoured; for they, who were not content with the common observance of the Law, consecrated themselves to God, that by their example they might stimulate others. It was then a singular zeal in a few to consecrate themselves, so as to become Nazarites, or separated. What this custom was may be known from the sixth chapter of Numbers. For God, who has always repudiated all fictitious forms of worship, prescribed to the Nazarites what he approved in every particular. Hence Moses carefully mentioned all those things which were to be observed by the Nazarites.

As to the present passage, it is enough to say, that the Nazarites were peculiarly devoted to God's service during the time of their separation, for it was only a temporary service.

Then the Prophet brings them forward, that it might hence be evident how sad was the change, which he never could have made the Jews to believe. He says that the *Nazarites were purer than snow, and whiter than milk,* and also *ruddier than precious stones,* so that they might be compared to *sapphire;* for, by saying *sapphire* was *their cutting,* he means that they were like sapphires well polished. Now we know that the Nazarites abstained from wine and strong drink: hence abstinence might have lessened somewhat of their ruddiness. For he who is accustomed to drink wine, if he abstains for a time, is apt to grow pale; he will then lose almost all his colour, at least he will not be so ruddy; nor will there appear in his face and in his members so much vigour as when he took his ordinary support. Jeremiah, in short, teaches us that the blessing of God was conspicuous in the Nazarites, for he wonderfully supported them while they were for a time abstinents.

Now, on the contrary, he says that the *Nazarites were become withered, that their skin clave to their bones*, that, in short, they were so deformed that they could not be known, not only in obscure corners, but even in the open street, in the middle of the market-place. We hence learn that as the favour of God had before appeared as to the Nazarites, so now also his vengeance might be certainly known, because they had fallen off from their vigour, and were reduced to a degrading deformity.[1]

The Prophet at the same time shews that worship according to the law had in a manner deteriorated on account of the vices of the people; and this is the design of the whole, as I reminded you at the beginning. For there is no doubt but that he wished to rouse the Jews, that they might at length raise up their eyes to God; for they had long grown

[1] As to these two verses there is much disagreement in the early versions and the *Targ.*; that of the *Sept.* comes nearest to the original. They may be thus rendered,—

7. Clearer were her Nazarites than snow,
They were whiter than milk;
Ruddier were they in body than rubies,
Sapphire *was* their polish (or smoothness:)
8. Darker than the dusk became their appearance,
They were not known in the streets:
Cleave did their skin to their bones,
Dried up, it became like a stick.

"Rubies," rendered "pearls," by *Bochart;* "loadstones," or magnets, by *Parkhurst;* "red corals," by *Gesenius*. They were no doubt precious stones of reddish appearance. The "sapphire" is mentioned for its smoothness, as it appears from the contrast at the end of the eighth verse, where it is said that their skin had become like a dried "stick," whose rind is shrivelled. "Dusk" is rendered "soot" by the *Sept.*, and "coals" by the *Vulg.* and the *Syr.* שחור is the dusk, or the dawn: but the river Nile is also thus called on account of its muddy and dusky waters. See Jer. ii. 18. This being the case, may it not be so taken here? The character of the passage favours this, "snow," "milk," &c. Then the line would be,—

Darker than Sihor (or, the Nile) became their appearance.—*Ed.*

torpid in their vices, and had been even inflated with diabolical pride; hence was their inveterate obstinacy. As long as the Temple stood, they thought that they satisfied God by the sacrifices they offered. When the Prophet now tells them that the stones of the Temple were thrown down, it hence follows that the Temple was profaned: whence this profanation? from the wickedness of the people. The Chaldeans, indeed, thought that they brought a great reproach on God when they demolished the Temple; but, as long pollution had preceded, our Prophet now represents to the Jews their sins as in a mirror or a living form; for they had polluted the Temple before the Chaldeans. So also he shews that the worship according to the law was no longer pleasing to God, for they had mocked him with empty spectres; for it was only a vain display when there was no integrity within. The Prophet then shews to them what he could before by no means have persuaded them to believe, that God was in no way pleased with the external worship of the Jews, while they were audaciously violating the whole law. It afterwards follows,—

9. *They that be* slain with the sword are better than *they that be* slain with hunger: for these pine away, stricken through for *want of* the fruits of the field.	9. Meliores fuerunt occisi gladio quàm occisi fame; fluxerunt transfossi à fructibus agri.

The beginning of the verse is without any difficulty; for the Prophet says that it happened better to those who immediately perished by the sword than to others who had to struggle with famine, according to what he had lately said, that the punishment of Sodom was more tolerable, because it was suddenly executed. Sudden death is the easiest. And the Prophet, when complaining that the ungodly prospered, so that the faithful sometimes envied them, says that they die as it were in a moment, and are taken away from the world; but he says that the faithful are held, as it were, captive by the snares of death, and protract life in perpetual languor. For this reason the Prophet now says that the punishment of death would have been light to the Jews. And yet we know that a violent death is regarded by us with horror. For he who dies on his bed is said to yield to his fate, as he seems to pay what he owes to nature; but he who is slain by the sword is violently snatched away, and, as it were, contrary to nature. Violent death, then, is always horrible. But the comparison used by the Prophet amplifies the atrocity of their punishment, because it would have been more desirable to have been killed at once than to remain alive to struggle with famine.

And he expresses himself more clearly by saying that *they pined away, having been pierced through by the fruits of the earth.* There is here some obscurity, but by *the fruits of the earth* we are no doubt to understand all kinds of food. Some consider that "defect," or failure, is to be understood. But the Prophet speaks much more emphatically, even that all the productions of the earth took vengeance on this wicked people, by refusing the usual supply. The earth is the servant of God's bounty and kindness; for it is the same as though he with his hand extended food to us, when the earth opens its bowels; so also the productions of the earth are evidences of God's paternal love towards us. Now, when the fruits of the earth withdraw themselves from us, they are as it were the weapons to execute God's vengeance. So, then, the Prophet means that the Jews had been *pierced through by the fruits of the earth*, and *thus had pined away;* as though he had said, that they had not been pierced by the sword, but had been wounded by famine, for the productions of the earth became, as it were, swords, while yet they sustain, as we have said, the life of men.[1]

PRAYER.

Grant, Almighty God, that as thou shewest by thy Prophet that, after having long borne with thine ancient people, thy wrath at length did so far burn as to render that judgment above all others remarkable,—O grant that we may not at this day, by our obstinacy or by our sloth, provoke thy wrath, but be attentive to thy threatenings, yea, and obey thy paternal invitations, and so

[1] *Houbigant* and *Blayney* have given the following version of this clause, which has been approved by *Horsley*,—

For those (the former) departed, having been cut off
Before the fruits of the field.

That is, they had been cut off before the fruits of the field failed, which occasioned the famine. This rendering is more satisfactory than our version or that of *Calvin*.—*Ed.*

willingly devote ourselves to thy service, that as thou hast hitherto favoured us with thy blessings, so thou mayest perpetuate them, until we shall at length enjoy the fulness of all good things in thy celestial kingdom, through Christ our Lord.—Amen.

Lecture Fifteenth.

10. The hands of the pitiful women have sodden their own children: they were their meat in the destruction of the daughter of my people.

10. Manus mulierum misericordium coxerunt fœtus suos, fuerunt in alimenta ipsis in contritione filiæ populi mei.

HERE Jeremiah refers to that disgraceful and abominable deed mentioned yesterday; for it was not only a barbarity, but a beastly savageness, when mothers boiled their own children. That it was done is evident from other writers; but the Prophet is to us a sufficient witness, who had seen it with his own eyes. He then says that the mothers were *merciful*, that no one might think that they were divested of every natural feeling; but he meant thus to set forth the blindness which proceeds from God's dreadful vengeance. He does not, then, praise the mothers for their clemency, as though they felt as they ought to have done for their offspring; but he intimates that though they would have been otherwise humane, they were yet seized with unusual madness, so that they boiled their own children, even their own bowels. We now, then, perceive the meaning of the word *merciful*, as applied to the mothers by the Prophet. It is not then to be deemed as a praise to them, as though they had a maternal love for their children; but his object was to set forth that monstrous act, which would not have sufficiently touched their minds, had he not testified that the mothers of whom he speaks were not so brutal as not to have gladly given food to their children; but that they were supernaturally blinded by furious madness. It follows,—

11. The Lord hath accomplished his fury; he hath poured out his fierce anger, and hath kindled a fire in Zion, and it hath devoured the foundations thereof.

11. Complevit (*vel*, perfecit) Jehova iracundiam suam, effudit excandescentiam iræ suæ et accendit ignem in Sion, qui voravit fundamenta ejus.

He at length concludes that nothing was wanting to complete the extreme vengeance of God ; for had the Jews been chastised in an ordinary way, they would have still extenuated their sins, as we know that they were not easily led to repentance. Hence the Prophet, to shew that their offences had not been slight, but that they had been extremely wicked before God, says that the whole of God's wrath had been executed : *Jehovah has completed his wrath.* The expression is indeed harsh to Latin ears ; but the meaning is, that he had executed his extreme judgment.

He afterwards adds, *He has poured forth the indignation of his wrath.* God is indeed content with moderate punishment, provided men be awakened from their torpor; but when he pours forth his wrath, there is no hope of repentance. It is then a sign of final despair when God's vengeance overflows like a deluge. But when Jeremiah thus speaks, he does not contend with God, but rather reminds the Jews of what they deserved, as it was stated yesterday. There is, then, no doubt but that he argues, from the grievousness of their punishment, that there was no reason for the Jews to flatter themselves any longer, since God had dealt so severely with them.

He then, in other words, points out the same thing, that God had *kindled a fire which devoured* or consumed *the very foundations.* Fire is wont rather to take hold on the roofs of houses, or, when it creeps farther, it does not proceed beyond the surface. It is a very rare thing for it to penetrate into the foundations. Let us at the same time know that the Prophet speaks metaphorically of the destruction of the city, for it was such as left nothing remaining. For when some ruins remain, there is some intimation of a future restoration ; at least the minds of beholders are inclined to hope that what has fallen is to be restored ; but when the buildings are not only pulled down, but also demolished from their foundations, then the destruction seems to be without any hope of restoration. And this is what the Prophet means when he says, that the *fire had consumed,* not only what was above ground, but the *very foundations* of Jerusalem. It follows,—

12. The kings of the earth, and all the inhabitants of the world, would not have believed that the adversary and the enemy should have entered into the gates of Jerusalem.

12. Non crediderunt (*vel,* non credidissent) reges terræ, neque omnes incolæ orbis, quòd ingressus esset adversarius et inimicus in portas Jerusalem.

He confirms the same thing; for when a thing incredible happens, either we are extremely stupid, or we must be moved and affected. The Prophet, then, now says that the destruction of the city of Jerusalem had been incredible, because God had defended it by his power; it was also so fortified that no one believed that it could be taken, and the grandeur of the city was known everywhere.

He then says that Jerusalem had been taken and overthrown, which no one of the heathens, neither their kings nor their people, had thought possible. It then follows that the city had been destroyed by God's hand rather than by the power of enemies. Nebuchadnezzar had indeed brought a strong army, but the city was so well fortified that they thought that all attempts would be in vain. That the city, then, was taken and demolished, could not have been ascribed to human forces, but to a power hidden from the eyes of men. It then follows that it was God's work, and indeed singular. We now, then, understand the design of the Prophet in saying that it was not believed by kings nor people that enemies could storm Jerusalem. And in continuation he adds,—

13. For the sins of her prophets, *and* the iniquities of her priests, that have shed the blood of the just in the midst of her.

13. Propter peccatum prophetarum ejus, iniquitatem sacerdotum ejus, qui fuderunt in medio ejus sanguinem justorum.

The Prophet, as in a matter fully proved, rebukes the Jews, that he might, as it was necessary, bring down their pride. Had he at first condemned the wickedness of the prophets and the priests, no credit would have been given to his word. But after he had set before them what we have observed, and especially after he had shewn that the ruin of the city was a kind of prodigy, what he now adds must have been certainly inferred, even that the Jews had in so many ways and with such pertinacity provoked God, that it became necessary that they should be wholly destroyed, as it happened.

But he points out here the sins by which God's wrath had been kindled against the people. He then says that the fountain or the origin was in the prophets and priests. Now, we have elsewhere explained that the fault was not removed from the people when the prophets and the priests were thus condemned. Indeed, the common people readily exonerate themselves when they can plead ignorance, or say that they have been deceived by their teachers and leaders. But when Jeremiah imputes the chief part of the evils .o the prophets and priests, he does not, as I have said, devolve on them the fault of the people, but intimates that their physicians had been as it were impostors. For when the people corrupted themselves, the prophets were sent for this end, to apply a remedy to their evils, and so also were the priests: for we know that it was a duty enjoined on them to retain the people in true religion and in the worship of God. In short, Jeremiah shews that the people had been ruined, because corruption had begun with the prophets and the priests; or, which is the same thing, that the sins of the people had proved fatal, because their heads or chiefs were diseased; *because*, he says, *of the sin of the prophets, and the iniquity of the priests*, &c.

He mentions one kind of sins, that *they shed the blood of the righteous in the midst of Jerusalem.* They had no doubt led the people astray in other things, for they flattered their vices, and gave loose reins to licentiousness; but the Prophet here fixed on one particular sin, the most grievous; for they had not only, by their errors and false doctrines and flatteries, led away the people from the fear of God, but had also obstinately defended their impiety, and by force and cruelty repressed their faithful teachers, and put to death the witnesses of God; for by the *righteous* or just he no doubt means the prophets. For what Jerome and others say, that blood had been shed because false teachers draw souls to perdition, is frivolous and wholly foreign to what Jeremiah had in view; for the word *righteous* cannot be applied to those miserable men who were ensnared to their own ruin. Then Jeremiah, after having denounced the sin of the prophets and the iniquity of the priests, mentions the savage cruelty, which was as it were the summit of all their vices. Though, then, they had in various ways provoked God, yet this was their extreme wickedness, that they exercised so great a cruelty against God's servants, that they constrained as it were the Holy Spirit to be silent. For when the despisers of God went so far as to give themselves up to shed innocent blood, it was a proof of a diabolical obstinacy. We now, then, understand what the Prophet had here in view.

Now this passage teaches us, that Satan has from the beginning polluted the sanctuary of God by means even of sacred names: for the prophetic office was honourable—so also was the sacerdotal. God had established among his people the priesthood, which was as it were a living image of Christ: there was then nothing more excellent than the priesthood under the Law, if we regard the institution of God. It was also a singular blessing that God promised that his people should never be without prophets. As, then, prophets and priests were two eyes as it were in the Church, the devil turned them to every kind of profanation. This example then reminds us how much we ought to watch, lest empty titles deceive us, which are nothing but masks or spectres. When we hear the name of Church and of pastors, we ought reverently to regard the office as well as the order which has proceeded from God, provided we are not content with naked titles, but examine whether the reality also corresponds. Thus we see that the whole world has for many ages degenerated from true religion; under what pretext? even this,—that those who led astray miserable souls, boasted that they were the vicars of Christ, the successors of the apostles, so that they still arrogantly boast of these titles, and are inflated with them. But we see what happened in the time of Jeremiah.

We have had before similar passages; but this ought to be carefully noticed, for it says, that prophets and priests had destroyed the very Church of God. It was, indeed, a very grievous trial, and therefore a powerful instrument, as it were, for subverting the faith of the simple, when they saw that the very prophets and priests were the cause of ruin; but it behoved the faithful constantly to persevere in their obedience to the law. And we ought at the same time to remember what I have said, that the Prophet enhances the wickedness of the people, because the priests and the prophets themselves had been infected with impiety and contempt of God, and not only so, but they had exercised tyrannical cruelty towards the servants of God. It follows,—

14. They have wandered *as* blind *men* in the streets, they have polluted themselves with blood, so that men could not touch their garments.

14. Errarunt cæci (*subaudienda est nota similitudinis,* sicut) in plateis, polluti sunt in sanguine, quia non potuerunt quin contingerent vestes ipsorum (*ita lego, nec sine ratione, quia aliæ versiones nullo modo conveniunt, ut nunc videbimus.*)

They who simply read, that the blind had wandered, deduce this meaning, that the blind were polluted in the streets, even because there was filth everywhere. They, indeed, come near to the meaning of the Prophet, but they do not clearly explain what he intended. I regard it therefore beyond dispute, that the people are here compared to the blind, but it does not yet appear for what purpose. But my opinion is this, that the whole city was so full of defilements, that they could not avoid uncleanness; for a blind man would touch a carcase, he would touch an unclean beast, he would touch a man infected with some disease; how so? because he could not see to distinguish between a dead and a living man, between the clean and unclean. Our Prophet now compares the people to the blind, and why? because wherever they went, uncleanness met them, so that their eyes were in a manner dazzled by thick darkness. For when pestilence does not spread everywhere, we can avoid an unclean place; but when there is no corner where there is not a dead corpse or some sickness, we must pass on anyhow, having no choice to make,—and why? because uncleanness surrounds us everywhere. So, then, the Prophet says that the citizens of Jerusalem were everywhere polluted, as though they were blind.

Now follows the reason, which has not been understood by interpreters, *They were polluted,* he says, *with blood, because they could not but touch their garments.* They all give this version, "They could not touch their garments:" and as there is much obscurity and almost absurdity in this rendering, they say that the meaning is that they were to avoid to touch their garments, because the law forbade them to touch the unclean. But the Prophet meant another thing. The words are literally thus, "They could not, they will touch their garments," that is, they will inevitably touch their garments. But the particle which I have mentioned is to be understood, and the passage will read thus, *They could not but touch their garments;* and we know that the language will bear this. And as this is consistent with the subject which the Prophet handles, every one, judging rightly, will readily receive what I have stated. The meaning then is, that they *wandered as the blind, and were polluted in all the streets of the city,* because *they could not escape uncleanness,* which met them everywhere; that is, because the city, as I have said, was full of so many pollutions, that they could not turn either here or there and avoid uncleanness.[1]

[1] This clause has been variously explained. The whole passage from the 12th verse to the 16th inclusive, ought to be considered. The taking of Jerusalem is said to have been incredible, even to heathens. Then the Prophet, in verse 13, tells the cause—"the sins of the prophets and the iniquities of the priests;" and in the 14th, 15th, and 16th, he describes their shame and their punishment at the siege, when the people found out by experience that they had been deceived by them,—

13. For the sins of her prophets,
For the iniquities of her priests,
Who had shed in the midst of her
The blood of the righteous,—
14. They wandered frantic in the streets,
They were (or, had been) polluted with blood:
Inasmuch as they could not
But touch their garments,
15. "Depart ye, uncleanness," they cried to them,
"Depart, depart, touch not:"
When they fled, yea, became fugitives,
They said among the heathens,
"They shall no more dwell *there;*
16. The face of Jehovah, their portion,
Shall no more look on them;
The face of their priests they regard not,
To their elders they shew no favour."

The last five lines contain what the heathens said, when they observed that the prophets and the priests were pronounced unclean by the people, and were ordered to depart. They had shed blood, and were thus polluted, or in their frenzy they touched the slain and became thus polluted. Their retribution was just, and rendered to them by their own people, whom they had led astray: for instead of attending to the true prophets, they

As to the words, *polluted with blood,* they refer to the ceremonial law. There were indeed various kinds of pollutions, but this was the chief. He accommodates his expressions to his own age, and follows what was prescribed by the law. He, however, alludes to the sins designated by *blood.* We, in short, see that the whole of Jerusalem was so polluted with defilements, that no one could go forth without falling on some uncleanness. A confirmation follows, which also interpreters have not understood,—

15. They cried unto them, Depart ye; *it is* unclean; depart, depart, touch not: when they fled away and wandered, they said among the heathen, They shall no more sojourn *there.*

15. Discedite, pollutus, clamavit illis; discedite, discedite, ne accedatis: quia evolarunt (*aut,* festinarunt,) etiam errarunt, dixerunt in gentibus, Non adjicient ad habitandum.

The Prophet confirms the former verse, as I have said, even that no part of the city was free from filth, because they cried everywhere, " Depart, depart—unclean !" That what is said may be more evident to us, we must notice that the Prophet alludes (which also has not been perceived) to Lev. xiii. 45. For it is said there of the lepers, whose disease was incurable, that they were to go with rent garments, with a bare head, with covered lips, and cry, " Unclean, unclean," טמא טמא יקרא, *thema, thema, ikora.* God, then, would have the leprous to be driven from the assembly; and hence came into use the exclamation, Unclean, unclean, טמא, טמא, *thema, thema.* But here the Prophet says, " Depart, depart—unclean !"—סורו סורו טמא, *suru, suru, thema ;* which is substantially the same as commanded in the law. Now the Prophet speaks metaphorically when he says, that the city was infected with uncleanness, as though lepers were everywhere. We hence see how all these things agree together, " They cried, Depart ye—unclean; depart ye, depart ;" that is, no one can move a foot from his house, or go forth in public, but some uncleanness will appear to him, so that it might be rightly exclaimed, *Unclean, depart ye, depart.*

killed them, and flattered the people with falsehoods, and encouraged them in their idolatry and vices; and thus brought on the ruin of a city deemed impregnable.—*Ed.*

The Prophet, after having thus spoken, *Depart ye, come not nigh*, says, *they have fled*. It is a striking allusion to the exile of the people, as though he had said, that they were driven afar off by their defilements. As then they were removed to a distant land, he says that this happened through their own fault; how so? because they could no longer endure these defilements of their sins; they had so contaminated the holy city, that it was fœtid through their filth. As, then, the city Jerusalem was so polluted, the citizens, he says, at length fled away: and thus exile proceeded from themselves, that is, the cause of exile was their filth, because they contaminated the city. *They have fled*, he says, *and have also wandered;* that is, so great was their haste, that they kept not the right way, but turned here and there, as they usually do who hasten with trembling. For when any one travels, and his mind composed, he attends to the road that he may not go astray; but he who trembles, or is filled with fear, forgets the way, and wanders from the right course. So, then, our Prophet now says, that the Jews *fled* and also *wandered;* for he uses the particle גם, *gam, also;* they also wandered, he says, even through that trepidation by which they were smitten.

They have said among the nations, They shall not return to dwell; that is, they are scattered and driven among various nations without hope of returning.

We now see what the Prophet meant to shew, even that the Jews had no reason to complain of their exile, because they had so infected the holy city with their vices, that they were hence driven by their own filth; this is one thing: and, then, that so great was the mass of their evils, that they were seized with fear; and thus they did not keep on the right way, but turned into devious paths and met darkness; and, in the last place, he adds, as a continuation of what he had said, that there was no hope of a return.

16. The anger of the Lord hath divided them; he will no more regard them: they respected not the persons of the priests, they favoured not the elders.

16. Facies Jehovæ divisit (*vel*, dissipavit) eos; non adjiciet ad respiciendum eos; faciem sacerdotum non reveriti sunt (*vel*, honore persequuti,) et senum non fuerunt miserti.

He explains himself by saying, that they had been scattered from the face of Jehovah. He had said, that they had fled into foreign lands, and that they believed their exile to be perpetual; he now assigns the reason that God had thus banished them. But he had promised by Moses, that though they were dispersed through the four quarters of the world, he would yet be propitious to them, so as to gather them when dispersed, as it is said in the Psalms, "He will gather the dispersed of Israel." (Deut. xxx. 4; Ps. cxlvii. 2.) And we know that the time of exile had been prefixed; for the Prophet had often testified that God would at length become a deliverer to his people, so as to stretch forth again his hand, and draw them forth from Chaldea as he did from Egypt: how then does he say, that they had been scattered from the face of Jehovah, and then, that they had been so rejected, that he would not favour them hereafter with his paternal countenance? the obvious answer is this, that the Prophet here regards only the extremely dispersed state of the people. For though the promise of God as to their return was certain and clear, yet, when any one cast his eyes on the state of things at that time, he could have hoped no such thing; for the desolation, the ground of despair, was immense: no name had remained for the people, the priesthood had been extinguished, the royal dignity had been degraded, the city also and the Temple had been completely overthrown. As, then, there was nothing remaining as to the nation and the place, and also as to God's worship, how could they do otherwise than despond?

Then the Prophet, viewing the desolation, says, that nothing else could be concluded, but that the Jews would be perpetually exiles, and that all the ways were closed up, to prevent them to return to their country, and also that the eyes of God were shut, so as never to look on them. We now, then, perceive what he means by saying, that they were *scattered from the face of Jehovah*, so that he should no longer look on them. And this mode of speaking is often found in Scripture; for, on the one hand, it sets before us the wrath of God, which brings death; and then on the other, it sustains us, or when we are fallen it raises us up, by setting before us the favour of God even in death itself.

The Prophet, then, considers now no other thing than the dreadful calamity which was sufficient to sink the minds of all into the lowest abyss of despair.

He then adds, that they *respected not the face of the priests, and shewed no pity to the elders.* Some think that the reason is given why God had so severely punished the people, even because they had despised the aged and the priests ; but this is a forced view. I, then, have no doubt but that the Prophet here intimates, that the Jews had been treated reproachfully, so that there had been no account made of the aged, and no respect shewn to the priests. It is, indeed, true, that Daniel was held in great repute ; but he speaks here of the priests who had impiously despised all sound doctrine ; and he speaks of the aged who were in authority when the kingdom was yet standing. He then says that they had been, as it were, trodden under feet. He hence concludes, that all hope of restoration was taken away from the Jews, if they only considered their extreme calamity. He afterwards adds,—

17. As for us, our eyes as yet failed for our vain help: in our watching we have watched for a nation *that* could not save *us*.

17. Adhuc nobis (*hoc est*, quum adhuc staremus ; *sic interpretor ; quidam exponunt*, nobis expectantibus, *sed malè, meo judicio ;* quum *ergo* adhuc staremus,) defecerunt oculi nostri ad auxilium nostrum vanum; in expectatione nostra expectavimus (*vel,* in speculatione nostra respeximus) ad gentem quæ non servaret.

Here the Prophet charges the people with another crime, that neglecting God, and even despising his favour, they had always attached themselves to vain and false hopes. And this was a sacrilege not to be endured, because they thus robbed God of his rights : and what does he demand more than that we should depend on him, and that our minds should acquiesce in him alone ? When, therefore, salvation is expected from others rather than from God alone, he is, in a manner, reduced to nothing. The Prophet, then, accuses the Jews of this great sacrilege, that they never betook themselves to God, nor had any hope in him, but on the contrary wandered here and there for help.

As yet for us, he says, that is, while we were yet standing.[1] And this circumstance deserves to be noticed; for after the Jews had been overthrown, they at length began to know how they had been previously deceived, when they placed confidence in the Egyptians. Prosperity inebriates men, so that they take delight in their own vanities: and while we seem to ourselves to stand, or while we remain alive, God is disregarded, and we seek help here and there, and think our safety beyond all danger. The Prophet then says, that the Jews had been inebriated with false confidence, so that they disregarded God, and in the meantime fled to the Egyptians. *When*, he says, *we were standing, our eyes failed*, &c. We have before seen what this phrase means: the eyes are said to fail, when with unwearied perseverance we pursue a hope to the last, as it is said in the Psalms, "Our eyes have failed for the living God," (Ps. lxix. 3;) that is, We have persevered, and though many trials may have wearied us, yet we have been constant in our hope in God. So now the Prophet says, that the *eyes* of the people had *failed;* but he adds, *for a vain help*, or a help of vanity, by which term he designates the Egyptians: and there is an implied contrast between empty and fallacious help and the help of God, which the people rejected when they preferred the Egyptians. *Our eyes*, he says, *failed*, that is, we were unwearied in hoping vainly, for we always thought that the Egyptians would be a sufficient defence to us. This is one thing.

He afterwards adds, *In our looking out, we looked out to a nation which could not save us.* He repeats the same thing in other words. Some consider a relative to be understood, "In our expectation with which we have expected," &c.; but it seems not necessary. I, then, so connect the words of the Prophet, that the meaning is, that the Jews always turned their eyes to Egypt, as long as they stood as a state and king-

[1] The true reading is no doubt עדינו; and *Blayney* thinks that there is a ו wanting before the next verb, as it is found in other instances; 1 Kings i. 14, 22; Job i. 16, 17, 18. It is supplied in the *Sept.*, *Syr.*, and *Vulg.*

Yet we *were*, and fail did our eyes
As to our assistance;
In vain by looking out did we look out
To a nation that could not save.

The *Syr.* connect "in vain," more properly, with the third line.—*Ed.*

dom; and thus they wilfully deceived themselves, because they took delight in their own vanity. The other clause which follows has the same meaning, *In our expectation we expected a nation*, &c; and this clause is added as an explanation; for the Prophet explains how their eyes failed for a vain hope, or for a vain help, even because the people did not look to God, but only to the Egyptians.

Now the words, to look out and looking out, are not unsuitable, for they refer to those vain imaginations to which the unbelieving give heed; for God called them, but turning away from him they transferred their hope to the Egyptians. It was, then, their own looking out or speculation, when, through a foolish conceit, they imagined that safety would be secured to them by the Egyptians.

He says that they were a *nation which could not save;* and there is no doubt but that the Prophet here puts them in mind of the many warnings which had not been received by the Jews, for God had tried to call them back from that ruinous confidence, but without any success; for we know how much the Prophets laboured in this respect, but they were never believed until at length experience proved how vain was the help of Egypt, as God had testified by his servants.

PRAYER.

Grant, Almighty God, that as we are beset on every side with so many allurements, and as Satan ceases not to draw us here and there by vain flatteries,—O grant that we may recumb on thee alone, even on thy power, and, in short, on thy word, nor doubt but thou wilt be our deliverer, whatever may happen, and that we may always so seek thee in our straits, and so acquiesce in the faithfulness of thy promises, that we may calmly sustain all the assaults of afflictions, until thou at length gatherest us into that blessed rest which is prepared for us in heaven by Christ our Lord.—Amen.

Lecture Sixteenth.

18. They hunt our steps, that we cannot go in our streets: our end is near, our days are fulfilled; for our end is come.	18. Venati sunt gressus nostros ne ambularemus in compitis nostris; appropinquavit finis noster, impleti sunt dies nostri, certè venit finis noster.

Many apply this verse to the Egyptians, that they insidiously enticed the Jews to flee to them in their difficulties. It is indeed, true, that the Jews had been deceived by their false promises; and, as a harlot draws to herself young men by wicked arts, so also the Jews had been captivated by the enticements of the Egyptians. But the meaning of the Prophet seems to be different, even this,—that the Chaldeans followed the Jews as hunters, so that they observed their footsteps; and I connect together the two verses, for it immediately follows,—

19. Our persecutors are swifter than the eagles of the heaven: they pursued us upon the mountains, they laid wait for us in the wilderness.

19. Velociores fuerunt persequutores nostri aquilis cœlorum; super montes insequuti sunt nos, in deserto insidiati sunt nobis.

Here, then, the Prophet means, that the Jews were so straitened, that there was no escape for them, because their steps were observed by their enemies, and also because the Chaldeans had recourse to the greatest celerity, that they might take them.

He then, says, first, that their enemies were *like hunters*, for the Jews could not go even through the streets of their own city. We know that they were reduced to the greatest straits; but how hard the siege was is better expressed by this similitude, even that they dared not walk through the city; for there is an implied comparison, as though he had said, " We had no liberty in the very city, much less were we allowed to go out and ramble through the open fields." He, in the second place, adds what corresponds with the first clause, *Approach did our end, fulfilled were our days; surely come did our end.*[1] He concludes, that no hope remained since their enemies were thus oppressing them. He, then, infers that the end was at hand, by which he means final ruin or destruction; and he adds, that the *days were fulfilled*,

[1] He describes throughout what had taken place. Our version is not right in giving the verbs in the present tense. "For" is better than "surely" before "come."

They hunted our footsteps,
That we could not walk in our streets:
Near was our end; fulfilled were our days,
For come had our end.

Then he describes what happened when the city was taken.—*Ed.*

where he seems to compare the state of Jerusalem with the life of man; for he is said to have fulfilled his day who leaves the world—for a certain time for our sojourn has been prefixed: God, when it pleases him, calls us to himself. Hence, our time is then fulfilled, as our course is said to be finished; for, as the life of man is compared in Scripture to a race, so death is like the goal. So now, speaking of the city, the Prophet says that its *time was fulfilled*, for it was not God's will that it should remain any longer. In the third place, he says, that the *end had come.* He said before, that it was nigh, but he says now, that it had come. He, in short, shews that God, having long spared the Jews, when he saw that they made no end of sinning, at length had recourse to rigour, for they had shamefully abused his forbearance; for he had long suspended his judgment, and had often tried whether they were healable. The Prophet, then, reproves now their obstinacy, when he says that their *end* had *come*, and that their *time was fulfilled.*

He afterwards, for the same purpose, adds, that *swifter than eagles had been their persecutors* or pursuers. The Prophet, no doubt, continues the same subject. As, then, he had made the Chaldeans to be like hunters, so he says now, that in flying they exceeded the eagles. It is, indeed, a hyperbolical expression, but the Prophet could not otherwise express the incredible celerity with which the Chaldeans hastened in pursuing the Jews. Nor is there a doubt but that he indirectly derided the security of the foolish people; for we know, that whenever the prophets threatened them, this false opinion ever prevailed, that the Chaldeans would not come, because they were far away, the journey was long and difficult, there were many hinderances. The Prophet, then, now taunts them for this confidence, by which they had been deceived, when he says, that *swifter than the eagles of the heavens* were their enemies.

He mentions the ways they adopted, *Through the mountains they pursued, and laid in wait in the desert.* He means that every way of escape was closed up. For when enemies come, many hide themselves on mountains and thus escape; and others, betaking themselves to the desert, find there some hiding-places. But the Prophet says that such was the velocity of the Chaldeans, that the Jews in vain looked to the mountains or to deserts, for snares were everywhere prepared, and they were present everywhere to pursue them. Thus he confirms what he had said, that the time was fulfilled, for the Lord kept them shut up on every side.

Now, though the Prophet speaks here of the ruin of the city, yet we may gather a useful doctrine: When the hand of God is against us, we in vain look around in all directions, for there will be no safety for us on mountains, nor will solitude protect us in the desert. As, then, we see that the Jews were closed up by God's hand, so when we contend with him, we in vain turn our eyes here and there; for, however we may for a time entertain good hopes, yet God will surely at last disappoint us. It follows,—

20. The breath of our nostrils, the anointed of the Lord, was taken in their pits, of whom we said, Under his shadow we shall live among the heathen.

20. Spiritus narium nostrarum Christus Jehovæ captus est laqueis ipsorum; de quo diximus, In umbra ejus vivemus inter gentes.

This verse, as I have said elsewhere, has been ignorantly applied to Josiah, who fell in battle long before the fall of the city. The royal dignity continued after his death; he was himself buried in the grave of his fathers; and though the enemy was victorious, yet he did not come to the city. It is then absurd to apply to that king what is here properly said of Zedekiah, the last king; for though he was wholly unlike Josiah, yet he was one of David's posterity, and a type of Christ.

As it was, then, God's will that the posterity of David should represent Christ, Zedekiah is here rightly called *the Christ of Jehovah*, by which term Scripture designates all kings, and even Saul; and though his kingdom was temporary, and soon decayed, yet he is called "the Anointed of Jehovah;" and doubtless the anointing, which he received by the hand of Samuel, was not altogether in vain. But David is properly called the Anointed of Jehovah, together with his posterity. Hence he often used these words, "Look on thy Christ." (Ps. lxxxiv. 10.) And when Hannah in her song spoke of the Christ of Jehovah, she had no doubt a regard to this idea. (1 Sam. ii. 10.) And, at length, our Lord was called the Christ of the Lord, for so Simeon called him. (Luke ii. 26.)

Now, then, we perceive that this passage cannot be understood except of king Zedekiah. It ought at the same time to be added, that he is called the Christ of Jehovah, because his crown was not as yet cast down, but he still bore that diadem by which he had been adorned by God. As, then, the throne of David still remained, Zedekiah, however unworthy he was of that honour, was yet the Christ of Jehovah, as Manasseh was, and others who were wholly degenerated.

The Prophet, however, seems to ascribe to Zedekiah far more than he deserved, when he calls him *the life* of the people. But this difficulty may be easily removed; the man himself is not regarded according to his merits, but as he was called by God, and endued with that high and singular honour; for we know that what is here said extended to all the posterity of David,—"I have made him the first-begotten among all the kings of the earth." (Ps. lxxxix. 27.) For though the kings of the earth obtained not their authority, except as they were established by God's decree, yet the king from David's posterity was first-begotten among them all. In short, it was a sacerdotal, and even a sacred kingdom, because God had peculiarly dedicated that throne to himself. This peculiarity ought then to be borne in mind, that we may not look on the individual in himself.

Then the passage runs consistently, when he says, that the *Messiah*, or the anointed *of Jehovah, had been taken in snares;* for we know that he was taken; and this is consistent with history. He had fled by a hidden way into the desert, and he thought that he had escaped from the hands of his enemies; but he was soon seized, and brought to king Nebuchadnezzar. As, then, he had unexpectedly fallen into the hands of his enemies, rightly does the Prophet say metaphorically, that he was taken in their snares.

He calls him *the spirit of the nostrils* of the people, because the people without their king was like a mutilated and an imperfect body. For God made David king, and also his posterity, for this end, that the life of the people might in a manner reside in him. As far, then, as David was the head of the people, and so constituted by God, he was even their life. The same was the case with all his posterity, as long as the succession continued; for the favour of God was not extinguished until all liberty vanished, when the city was destroyed, and even the name of the people was as it were abolished.[1]

But we must observe what we have before said, that these high terms in which the posterity of David were spoken of, properly belong to Christ only; for David was not the life of the people, except as he was the type of Christ, and represented his person. Then what is said was not really found in the posterity of David, but only typically. Hence the truth, the reality, is to be sought in no other but in Christ. And we hence learn that the Church is dead, and is like a maimed body, when separated from its head. If, then, we desire to live before God, we must come to Christ, who is really the spirit or the breath of our nostrils; for as man that is dead does no longer breathe, so also we are said to be dead when separated from Christ. On the other hand, as long as there is between him and us a sacred union, though our life is hid, and we die, yet we live in him, and though we are dead to the world, yet our life is in heaven, as also Paul and Peter call us thither. (Col. iii. 3, 4; 2 Pet. iii. 16.) In short, Jeremiah means that the favour of God was as it were extinguished when the king was taken away, because the happiness of the people depended on the king, and the royal dignity was as it were a sure pledge of the grace and favour of God; hence the blessing of God ceased, when the king was taken away from the Jews.

It follows at length, *Of whom we have said, Under thy shadow we shall live among the nations.* The Prophet shews that the Jews in vain hoped for anything any more as to their restoration; for the origin of all blessing was from the king. God had bereaved them of their king; it then follows that they were in a hopeless state. But the Prophet

[1] A kingdom cannot exist without a king. Hence the king may be said to be the breath or the life of the body politic.—*Ed.*

that he might more clearly express this, says, that the people thought that they would be safe, provided the kingdom remained,—*We shall live,* they said, *even among the nations under the shadow of our king;* that is, "Though we may be driven to foreign nations, yet the king will be able to gather us, and his shadow will extend far and wide to keep us safe." So the Jews believed, but falsely, because by their defection they had cast away the yoke of Christ and of God, as it is said in Ps. ii. 3. As then they had shaken off the heavenly yoke, they in vain trusted in the shadow of an earthly king, and were wholly unworthy of the guardianship and protection of God.[1] It afterwards follows,—

21. Rejoice, and be glad, O daughter of Edom, that dwellest in the land of Uz: the cup also shall pass through unto thee; thou shalt be drunken, and shalt make thyself naked.	21. Gaude et lætare, filia Edom, quæ habitas in terra Uts (עוץ, *ad verbum;*) etiam super te transibit calix, inebriaberis et nudaberis.

The Prophet in this verse intimates that the Jews were exposed to the reproaches and taunts of all their enemies, but he immediately moderates their sorrow, by adding a consolation; and it was a sorrow that in itself must have been very bitter; for we know that nothing is harder to bear, in a state of misery, than the petulant insults of enemies; these wound us more than all other evils which we may suffer. The Prophet then intimates, that the Jews had been so reduced, that all the ungodly and malevolent were able, with impunity, to exult over them, and to taunt them with their troubles. This is done in the former clause; but as it was a prophecy, or rather a denunciation, extremely bitter, he mitigates the atrocity of the evil, when he says that their enemies would have soon in their turn to undergo punishment.

Some explain the whole verse as spoken ironically, as though the Prophet had said tauntingly,—"Go now, ye

[1] The last clause ought to be thus rendered,—

Under whose shadow, we said,
We shall live among the nations.

The *Syr.* in some measure imitates the original, but neither the *Sept.* nor the *Vulg.* The אשר is not governed by "we said." It can be rendered literally in Welsh.—*Ed.*

Idumeans, and rejoice; but your joy shall be evanescent."[1] But I rather think that he refers to the very summit of extreme misery, because the Jews had been thus exposed to the taunts of their enemies; but he afterwards adds some alleviation, because all their enemies would at length be punished. There is, in Mic. vii. 8, a similar mode of speaking, though there is no mention made there of Edom; for there the Prophet speaks generally to all those who envied the people, and were their adversaries: he compares the people, according to what was usual, to a woman; and we know that in that sex there is much more jealousy than in men; and then, when there is a grudge, they fiercely urge their pleas, that they may have an occasion to speak evil of others. Therefore the Church, after having acknowledged that she had been deservedly chastised, adds, "Rejoice not over me, mine enemy." But I have already fully explained the Prophet's meaning,—that the Church calls all her enemies an enemy, or an inimical woman, as though there had been some quarrel or jealousy between women. Hence she says, "Though I have fallen, yet rejoice thou not, my enemy; though I lie in darkness, yet the Lord will be my light: though then my enemy has rejoiced, yet my eyes shall see when she shall be trodden down." (Mic. vii. 8, 10.) The Prophet no doubt meant there to mitigate the sorrow of the godly, who saw that they were insolently taunted by all their neighbours. He then shews the necessity of a patient endurance for a time; for God would at length stretch out his hand, and render to enemies the reward of their barbarity.

But why in this place mention is made of Edom, rather than of other nations, is not evident. The Jews were, indeed, surrounded on every side with enemies, for they had as many enemies as neighbours. But the Idumeans, above others, had manifested hostility to the chosen people. And the indignity was the greater, because they had descended from the same father, for Isaac was their common father; and they derived their origin from two brothers, Esau and

[1] This is the sense that is commonly taken: *Gataker, Lowth, Scott*, and *Blayney*, regard the expression as ironical.—*Ed.*

Jacob. As, then, the Idumeans were related to the Jews, their cruelty was less tolerable; for they thus forgot their own race, and raged against their brethren and relatives. Hence it is said in Ps. cxxxvii. 7, "Remember, O Lord, the children of Edom, who said, in the day of Jerusalem, Down with it, down with it, to the very foundation." The Prophet, then, after having imprecated God's vengeance on all the ungodly, mentioned especially the Idumeans; and why? because they indulged their cruelty above all others; for they were standard-bearers, as it were, to enemies, and were like fans, by which the fire was more kindled; for this address was no doubt made to the Chaldeans, "Make bare, make bare; spare not; let not a stone remain on a stone." (Ps. cxxxvii. 7.) As, then, the Idumeans had behaved most cruelly towards their own relatives, the Prophet complains of them, and asks God to render to them what they deserved.

So now in this place our Prophet says, *Be glad and rejoice, thou daughter of Edom, who dwellest in the land of Uz.* By this clause, as I have already said, Jeremiah intimates that the Jews were exposed to the taunts of their enemies, because the Idumeans could now insult them with security. But he immediately adds, *also:* here he begins a new subject, and this is intimated by the particle גם, *gam, To thee also shall pass the cup.* He employs a common metaphor; for adversity is denoted in Scripture by the word *cup;* for God, according to his will, gives to drink to each as much as he pleases. As when a master of a family distributes drink to his children and servants; so also God, in a manner, extends his cup to every one whom he chastises; nor does he allow any one either to reject the cup offered, or to throw away the wine, but he constrains him to drink and to exhaust to the very dregs as much as he gives to each to drink. Hence it is for this reason that the Prophet says now that the *cup would pass over* to the Idumeans; for we know that, shortly after, they were subdued by the Chaldeans, with whom they had before been united. But when they had by their perfidy fallen off from their treaty, they were in their turn punished. As, then, the agreement they had made with the Chaldeans did not continue, the Prophet says, that to them also the cup would pass over.

He adds, *Thou shalt be inebriated and made naked.* God is wont thus to distinguish between his own children and aliens or the reprobate; for he indeed gives a bitter potion to his own children to drink, but it is as much as they are able to drink; but he altogether chokes others, because he constrains them, as it has been already said, to drink to the very dregs. So, then, the Prophet now compares the extreme miseries which the Idumeans suffered to drunkenness; and to the same purpose are the words which follow, *Thou shalt be made naked.* For he thus intimates, that they would be so confounded with the atrocity of their evils, as to have no care for decency, and to be dead to all shame: as a drunken man, who is overpowered by wine, disregards himself, and falls and exposes himself as Noah did; so also the Prophet says, that so great would be the calamities of Edom, that the people, exposed to every reproach, would afford occasion to all around them for taunts. As when a sot lies down in the mire, casts away his garments, and makes an exposure of himself, it is a spectacle both sad and shameful; so the Prophet says, that the Idumeans would be like the drunken, because they would lie down in their reproach. It follows,—

22. The punishment of thine iniquity is accomplished, O daughter of Zion; he will no more carry thee away into captivity: he will visit thine iniquity, O daughter of Edom; he will discover thy sins.

22. Completa est iniquitas tua, filia Sion; non adjiciet ad te in exilium trahendam; visitavit iniquitatem filiæ Edom, et discooperuit super peccatum tuum (*hoc est,* nudavit peccatum tuum.)

This verse, in my judgment, is incorrectly explained; and the Jews have toiled much, for there seems to be a kind of inconsistency, since it is certain that they were afterwards scattered into exile, not only once, but several times. Hence they interpret this place of the second dispersion by Titus, under the authority of his father Vespasian. They then say that the iniquity of the people was then completed, for after that exile no change has followed. Otherwise they do not think that this prediction of the Prophet accords with the reality or the event; for, as I have said, they have been driven into all lands. They had been, indeed, before fugitives, as Moses had declared concerning them. For we know that Jews dwelt in Greece and in Macedonia ; we know that many of the cities of Italy were full of this people, until by the edict of Claudius Cesar they were expelled from Italy ; for he thought that Italy was infected by them, and he drove them afar off, as though they were contagious. But the Jews lay hold on these refinements to no purpose ; for the Prophet simply meant to say, that such would be the punishment of the people, that it would not be necessary then to repeat it.

When, therefore, he says that *their iniquity*, or the punishment of their iniquity, *was completed*, he intimates that God had dealt so severely with them, that there was nothing short of extreme rigour : and this mode of speaking occurs elsewhere. To the same purpose is what immediately follows : The enemy, or God, which is the same, *will no more add to draw thee into exile*,—why ? for what need was there of a second exile when the whole land had been reduced to solitude ? since also the poor who had been left in the land had at length gone into Egypt, whence they were brought again into Chaldea ; but they were, at the time, fugitives from the Holy Land. Then the Prophet means, that God's judgment was, in all its parts, completed, that nothing short of extreme calamity had happened to the Jews.

It afterwards follows in the second clause, *He will visit*, which is, indeed, in the past tense, *he hath visited*, but he speaks of what was future. According to the usual manner of the prophets, in order to confirm the prediction, he speaks of the event as already past, *He has visited the iniquity of the daughter of Edom ; so that thy wickedness has been uncovered.* The meaning will be clearer if we add the particles of comparison, " As thy punishment, daughter of Sion, has been completed ; so thine iniquity, daughter of Edom, shall be visited ;" or if we render the words thus, by way of concession, " The punishment of thine iniquity, daughter of Sion, has indeed been completed ; but thy sin, daughter of Edom, shall be uncovered."[1]

[1] The word " iniquity" is used in this verse in two senses. This we

We, in short, see that the reason is explained why the Prophet, in the last verse, alleviated, with comfort, the sorrow of the people, that though the Jews were very miserable, it would yet be nothing better with Edom, when the time of visitation came. And in saying that the punishment of iniquity was completed, he refers not to their sin, but says that they had been thus chastised, as it seemed good to God to execute all his rigour towards them; and nearly the same manner of speaking is found in the fortieth chapter of Isaiah. Then the Prophet does not deny but that the Jews might at a future time become exiles; but he says that their transmigration now was complete, so that it was not necessary that Nebuchadnezzar should again denude the land of its inhabitants: this had been done, as it were, by a sudden whirlwind; for by one sweep they had been snatched away. The land, indeed, was before made desolate, but when Nebuchadnezzar took possession of the city, he only left behind the dregs of the people. And he did this on purpose that he might have there some people as tributaries. Then that transmigration was complete.

But the Prophet means not here, that God would not afterwards banish and scatter the Jews as they deserved. There is then no inconsistency, that the Jews afterwards became fugitives and wanderers through the whole world, and that yet the enemy would not again draw them into captivity, for he speaks here only of the Chaldeans: and this was said,

discover by the two verbs which are used. To complete "iniquity" can here mean no other thing than to complete the punishment due to it; and that punishment was exile, as the following words shew. But to "visit" iniquity clearly means to punish it.—

22\. Completed has been thine iniquity, daughter of Sion;
He will not again remove thee:
He has visited thine iniquity, daughter of Edom;
Having been removed for thy sins,
or,—He has removed *thee* for thy sins.

Though all the early versions and the *Targ.* agree in rendering the last verb in the sense of discovering or uncovering, yet the other meaning, which it often has, and even in the second line of this verse, is more suitable to this place. Removal or migration had been the punishment of the Jews: the same was to be the punishment of Edom. In this sense is the word rendered by *Blayney* and *Henderson*. The past time in the latter clause is evidently used for the future, according to the usual manner of the Prophets, "He will visit," &c., "he will remove, &c.—*Ed.*

because Jeremiah wished to compare the Jews with the Idumeans, and to shew, that though the Idumeans insolently exulted over them, yet their own calamity was nigh, which would wholly overwhelm them, as the case had previously been with the Jews. There is no time now to begin with the prayer of Jeremiah: I must therefore defer it till the next Lecture.

PRAYER.

Grant, Almighty God, that as thou seest that at this day the mouths not only of our enemies, but of thine also, are open to speak evil,—O grant, that no occasion may be given them, especially as their slanders are cast on thy holy name; but restrain thou their insolence, and so spare us, that though we deserve to be chastised, thou mayest yet have regard for thine own glory, and thus gather us under Christ our head, and restore thy scattered Church, until we shall at length be all gathered into that celestial kingdom, which thine only-begotten Son our Lord has procured for us by his own blood.—Amen.

CHAPTER V.

Lecture Seventeenth.

1. Remember, O Lord, what is come upon us: consider, and behold our reproach.

1. Memento (recordare,) Jehova, quid sit nobis (*hoc est*, quomodo nobiscum agatur.) aspice et vide opprobrium nostrum.

This prayer ought to be read as unconnected with the Lamentations, for the initial letters of the verses are not written according to the order of the Alphabet: yet it is a complaint rather than a prayer; for Jeremiah mentions those things which had happened to the people in their extreme calamity in order to turn God to compassion and mercy.

He says first, *Remember* what has happened to us; and then in the second part he explains himself, *Look and see our reproach.* Now the words, though brief and concise, yet contain a useful doctrine—that God is pleased to bring help to the miserable when their evils come to an account before him, especially when they are unjustly oppressed. It is, indeed, certain that nothing is unknown to God, but this mode of speaking is according to the perceptions of men ; for we think that God disregards our miseries, or we imagine that his back is turned to us when he does not immediately succour us. But as I have said, he is simply to be asked to look on our evils, for we know what he testifies of himself ; so that as he claims to himself the office of helping the miserable and the unjustly oppressed, we ought to acquiesce in this consolation, that as soon as he is pleased to look on the evils we suffer, aid is at the same time prepared for us.

There is mention especially made of *reproach*, that the indignity might move God the more : for it was for this end that he took the people under his protection, that they might be for his glory and honour, as Moses says. As, then, it was God's will that the riches of his glory should appear in that people, nothing could have been more inconsistent than that instead of glory they should have nothing but disgrace and reproach. This, then, is the reason why the Prophet makes a special mention of the *reproach* of the people. It follows,—

2. Our inheritance is turned to strangers, our houses to aliens.	2. Hæreditas nostra devoluta est ad exteros, domus nostræ ad alienos.

A catalogue of many calamities is now given by the Prophet, and as I have reminded you, for this end, that he may obtain God's favour for himself and for the whole people. It was by no means a reasonable thing, that the inheritance of the elect people should be given to aliens ; for we know that the land had been promised to Abraham four hundred years before his children possessed it ; we know that this promise had been often repeated, "This land shall be to you for an inheritance." For though God sustained all nations, yet he was pleased to take a peculiar care of his people. In short, no land has ever been given to men in so singular a way as the land of Canaan to the posterity of Abraham. As, then, this inheritance had been for so many ages possessed by the chosen people, Jeremiah does not without reason complain that it was *turned over to aliens.*

In the second clause he repeats the same thing ; but he

shews that the Jews had not only been robbed of their fields, but had been cast out of their houses, a more grievous and disgraceful thing. For it sometimes happens, that when one loses his farm, his fields, and vineyards, his house remains to him untouched; but the Prophet here amplifies the misery of his own nation, that they were not only deprived of their fields and possessions, but that they were also ejected from their own houses, and others had possession of them. For it is a sight deemed affecting even among heathens, when one unworthy of any honour succeeds in the place of another eminent in wealth and dignity. Well known are these words,—

O house of Ancus! how ruled by an unequal master![1]

As Tarquinius had succeeded and taken possession of the kingdom, the heathen poet upbraidingly said that the house of Ancus had passed over to those who were at first exiles and fugitives, but afterwards became proud and cruel tyrants. So also in this place Jeremiah says that *aliens dwelt in the houses* of the people. It follows,—

3. We are orphans and fatherless, our mothers *are* as widows.	3. Pupilli fuimus absque patre (non patre,) matres nostræ tanquam viduæ.

Here the Prophet not only speaks in the person of the whole people, but utters also the groans and complaints of each; for this could not have been suitable to the whole Church, as he speaks of fathers and mothers. We hence see that this verse does not apply to the whole body, but to individual members, though every one of the people might have said that widows and orphans were everywhere seen.

Now, this usually happens when a nation is consumed either by pestilence or by war; for in one battle all do not so fall that a whole country becomes full of orphans. But the Prophet sets forth here the orphanage and widowhood occasioned through the continued vengeance of God, for he had not ceased to afflict the people until by degrees they were exhausted. It was, indeed, a sad spectacle to see

[1] O domus Anci! quam dispari domino dominaris!

among the chosen people so many widows, and also so many children deprived of their fathers. It follows,—

4. We have drunken our water for money; our wood is sold unto us.	4. Aquas nostras pecunia bibimus, ligna nostra pretio veniunt (*non* veneunt, *nam intelligit ligna afferri, aut venire in illorum manus non sine pretio.*)

The Prophet here relates, that the people were denuded, that they laboured under the want of water and of wood. He does not say that they were only deprived of corn and wine, he does not complain that any of their luxuries were lessened; but he mentions water and wood, the common things of life; for the use of water, as it is said, is common to all; no one is so poor, if he dwells not in a land wholly dry, but that he has water enough to drink. For if there be no fountains, there are at least rivers, there are wells; nor do men perish through thirst, except in deserts and in places uninhabitable. As, then, water might be had everywhere, the Prophet here sets forth the extreme misery of the people, for water was even sold to them. In stony and high places water is sold; but this is a very rare thing. The Prophet here means that the people were not only deprived of their wealth, but reduced to such a state of want that they had no water without buying it.

At the same time he seems to express something worse when he says, *Our water we drink for money,* and our *wood is brought to us for a price.* It is not strange that wood should be bought; but the Prophet means that water was sold to the Jews which had been their own, and that they were also compelled to buy wood which had been their own. Thus the possessive pronouns are to be considered as emphatical. Then he says, "Our own waters we drink," &c.[1] He calls them the waters of the people, which by right they might have claimed as their own; and he also calls the wood the same; it was that to which the people had a

[1] To express this meaning, which is probably the true one, the words ought to be thus rendered,—

4. Our own water, for money have we drunk *it;*
Our own wood, for a price it comes *to us.*

Grotius says that in the land of Canaan the forests were free to all to get wood from. When in exile the Jews had to buy wood.—*Ed.*

legitimate right. He then says that all things had been so taken away by their enemies, that they were forced to buy, not only the wine which had been taken from their cellars, and the corn which had been taken from their granaries, but also the water and the wood.

But were any one disposed to take the words more simply, the complaint would not be unsuitable,—that the people, who before had abundance of wine and all other things, were constrained to buy everything, even water and wood. For it is a grievous change when any one, who could once cut wood of his own, and gather his own wine and corn, is not able to get even a drop of water without buying it. This is a sad change. So this passage may be understood. It follows,—

5. Our necks *are* under persecution: we labour, *and* have no rest.	5. Super colla nostra (*vel,* cervicibus nostris) persecutionem passi sumus; laboravimus, non requies nobis.

Here he says that the people were oppressed with a grievous bondage. It is, indeed, a metaphorical expression when he says, that people *suffered persecution on their necks.* Enemies may sometimes be troublesome to us, either before our face, or behind our backs, or by our sides; but when they so domineer as to ride on our necks, in this kind of insult there is extreme degradation. Hence the Prophet here complains of the servile and even disgraceful oppression of the people when he says, that the Jews *suffered persecution on their necks.*

The meaning is, that the enemies so domineered at their pleasure, that the Jews dared not to raise up their heads. They were, indeed, worthy of this reward—for we know that they had an iron neck; for when God would have them to bear his yoke, they were wholly unbending; nay, they were like untameable wild beasts. As, then, their hardness had been so great, God rendered to them a just reward for their pride and obstinacy, when their enemies laid such a burden on their necks.[1]

[1] Not one of the versions or the *Targ.*, though they all differ, gives a satisfactory rendering of this clause. Some take, "on our neck we have been pursued," as meaning, We have been closely pursued. So *Gataker.*

But the Prophet sets forth here this indignity, that he might turn God to mercy; that is, that the Chaldeans thus oppressed as they pleased the chosen people.

He adds, that they *laboured and had no rest.* He intimates by these words that there were no limits nor end to their miseries and troubles; for the phrase in Hebrew is, *We have laboured and there was no rest.* It often happens that when one is pressed down with evils for a short time, a relaxation comes. But the Prophet says that there was no end to the miseries of the people. Then to labour without rest is the same as to be pressed down with incessant afflictions, from which there is no outlet. Their obstinacy was worthy also of this reward, for they had fought against God, not for a few months or years only, but for many years. We know how long the Prophet called them without any success. Here, however, he seeks favour with God, by saying that the people were miserable without limits or end.

6. We have given the hand *to* the Egyptians, *and to* the Assyrians, to be satisfied with bread.	6. Ægyptiis dedimus manum, Assyriis, ut saturemur panibus.

He speaks here of the mendicity of the people, that they sought bread from every quarter. To give the hand, is explained in three ways: some say that it means humbly to ask; others, to make an agreement; and others, to extend it in token of misery, as he who cannot ask for help, intimates his wants by extending his hand. But the Prophet seems simply to mean that the people were so distressed by want, that they begged bread. I then take the expression, to give the hand, as meaning that they asked bread, as beggars usually do.

Others, as *Lowth* and *Henderson*, regarding על a noun, signifying a yoke, give a construction of this kind, "With the yoke on our neck we have been pursued" or persecuted, according to the words of Moses in Deut. xxviii. 48. The former seems the best,—

On our neck (closely) have we been pursued,
We laboured and had no rest.

Then comes in what they did when thus pursued by their enemies,—

To Egypt gave we the hand,
To Assyria, to be satisfied with bread.

To give the hand, in this case, was to put it forth as suppliants to ask help. This seems to refer to a time previous to their exile.—*Ed.*

He now says that they *gave* or extended *the hand* both to the *Egyptians* and to the *Assyrians*, which was a most unworthy and disgraceful thing; for the Egyptians had been their most troublesome enemies, and the Assyrians afterwards followed their example. At that time, indeed, the Egyptians pretended to be the friends of the chosen people, and made a treaty with them; but the Jews were held in contempt by them as they deserved, for they had prostituted as it were themselves like harlots. As, then, they had been despised by the Egyptians, it was a disgrace and reproach the most bitter, when they were compelled to beg bread in Egypt, and then in Assyria; for this might have been turned to the bitterest taunts.

We now, then, perceive the meaning of the Prophet; even this reward also God justly rendered to them. He had promised them a fruitful land, in which he was ready to support them to the full. How often is mention made by Moses of corn, wine, and oil; and why? in order that God might shew that that land exceeded every other in fertility. It was, then, an evidence of an extreme curse when the people were compelled to beg bread here and there, while yet the abundance of all things ought to have been sufficient to supply even aliens, "Thou shalt lend to others, but thou shalt not borrow." (Deut. xv. 6.) They then who ought to have fed others by their plenty, were so reduced that their want forced them to undergo this disgrace, to beg bread of the Egyptians and Assyrians. It follows,—

7. Our fathers have sinned, and *are* not; and we have borne their iniquities.	7. Patres nostri peccarunt, non sunt (non ipsi, *ad verbum*,) nos vero iniquitatem eorum portavimus.

The Prophet seems here to contend with God, and to utter that blasphemy mentioned by Ezekiel. For when God severely chastised the people, that proverb was commonly used by them, "Our fathers did eat a sour grape, and our teeth are blunted." (Ezek. xviii. 2.) Thus they intimated that they were unjustly and cruelly treated, because they suffered the punishment of others, when they themselves were innocent. So the Prophet seems to quarrel with God when he says that the *fathers who sinned were no more;* but as we shall presently see, the Prophet confesses also the sins of those who were yet alive. As, then, an ingenuous confession is made by the Prophet, he no doubt abstained here from that blasphemy which is so severely reproved by Ezekiel. Jeremiah had nothing farther from his purpose than to free the people from all blame, as though God had dealt cruelly with them, according to what is said by a heathen poet,—

"For the sins of the fathers thou undeservedly sufferest, O Roman!"[1]

Another says,—

"Enough already by our blood
Have we suffered for the perjuries of Laomedonian Troy."[2]

They mean that the people of their age were wholly innocent, and seek in Asia and beyond the sea the cause of evils, as though they never had a sin at Rome. But the meaning of Jeremiah was not this, but he simply intended to say that the people who had been long rebellious against God were already dead, and that it was therefore a suitable time for God to regard the miseries of their posterity. The faithful, then, do not allege here their own innocency before God, as though they were blameless; but only mention that their fathers underwent a just punishment, for that whole generation had perished. Daniel speaks more fully when he says, "We have sinned, and our fathers, and our kings." (Dan. ix. 8.) He involved in the same condemnation both the fathers and their children.

But our Prophet's object was different, even to turn God to mercy, as it has been stated; and to attain this object he says, "O Lord, thou indeed hast hitherto executed just punishment, because our fathers had very long abused thy goodness and forbearance; but now the time is come for thee to try and prove whether we are like our fathers: as, then, they have perished as they deserved, receive us now into favour." We hence see that thus no quarrel or contention is carried on with God, but only that the miserable

[1] Horace, *Od.* vi. 1,—
"Delicta majorum immeritus lues, Romane."

[2] Virgil, *Georg.*, lib. i.,—
"Satis jampridem sanguine nostro
Laomedonteæ luimus perjuria Troiæ."

exiles ask God to look on them, since their fathers who had provoked God and had experienced his dreadful vengeance, were already dead.[1]

And when he says that the *sons bore the iniquity* of the fathers, though it be a strong expression, yet its meaning is not as though God had without reason punished their children and not their fathers; for unalterable is that declaration, "The son shall not bear the iniquity of the father, nor the father the iniquity of the son; but the soul that sinneth it shall die." (Ezek. xviii. 20.) It may yet be said that children are loaded with the sins of their fathers, because God, as he declares by Moses, extends his vengeance to the third and fourth generation. (Exod. xx. 5.) And he says also in another place, "I will return into the bosom of children the iniquity of their fathers." (Jer. xxxii. 18.) God then continued his vengeance to their posterity. But yet there is no doubt but that the children who had been so severely punished, bore also the punishment of their own iniquity, for they deserved a hundred deaths. But these two things well agree together, that God returns the iniquity of the fathers into the bosom of their children, and yet that the children are chastised for their own sins.

8. Servants have ruled over us: *there is* none that doth deliver *us* out of their hand.	8. Servi dominati sunt nobis; eripiens nemo ex manibus ipsorum (*hoc est*, nemo est qui nos eripiat è manibus ipsorum.)

Another circumstance aggravated the calamity of the people, that they came under the power of servants, which is more degrading than when the rich and the eminent in wealth and power make us their servants. For it is no shame to serve a king, or at least a man who possesses some eminence; for that servitude which is not apparently degrading is deemed tolerable. But when we become the servants of servants, it is a most afflicting degradation, and most grievously wounds our minds.

It is, then, for this indignity that Jeremiah now expos-

[1] The words may be thus rendered,—

Our fathers, they sinned and are not;
We, their iniquities have we borne.

To bear iniquities, is here evidently to bear their penalty. So when Christ is said to bear our sins, the same thing is meant.—*Ed.*

tulates, and says that *servants ruled over them.* There is, indeed, no doubt but that they were driven into exile by some of the lowest; for the Chaldeans thought it right to exercise towards them every kind of cruelty. But it was yet a very mournful thing for God's children to be the slaves of servants; for they were before a sacerdotal kingdom, and God had so taken them under his protection, that their condition was better and more desirable than that of any other kingdom. As, then, they had been robbed of their liberty, and not only so, but also made subject to servants, the change was sad in the extreme.[1] Therefore the Prophet sought another occasion to plead for mercy, when he said that they were *ruled by servants.* It now follows,—

9. We gat our bread with *the peril of* our lives, because of the sword of the wilderness.	9. In anima nostra (*alii vertunt,* in periculo vitæ nostræ, *vel,* cum periculo) adduximus ad panem nostrum ob siccitatem deserti (*alii vertunt,* a facie gladii, in deserto.)

The word חרב, *chereb,* means drought as well as sword. As the Prophet is speaking of famine and the desert, I have no doubt but that dryness or drought is what the word means here; and I wonder that the word *sword* had occurred to any; they could not have regarded the context.

He then says that the people *sought bread with the soul,* that is, at the hazard of their own life. If danger be preferred, I do not object. But as he simply says, *with the soul,* he seems to express this, that for food they hazarded their own life. Food, indeed, is the support of life, for why is bread sought but for sustaining life? But the hungry so rush headlong to procure food, that they expose themselves to thousand dangers, and they also weary themselves with many labours; and this is to *seek bread with their soul,* that is, when men not only anxiously labour to procure food, but pour forth as it were their own blood, as when one undertakes a long journey to get some support, he is almost lifeless when he reaches the distant hospital. As, then, the Jews nowhere found food, the Prophet says that they sought bread with their life, that is, at the hazard of life. This is the view I prefer.

[1] See Neh. v. 15.—*Ed.*

He then adds, *For the dryness of the wilderness.* What has the sword to do with wilderness? We see that this is wholly unsuitable; there was then no reason why interpreters should pervert this word. But what he calls the dryness of the wilderness was the want by which the people were distressed, as though they were in the wilderness. This is said by way of comparison,—that on account of the dryness of the desert, that is, on account of sterility, they were under the necessity of exposing their life to death, only that they might anywhere find bread.[1]

It may also be, that the Prophet meant, that they were fugitives, and thus went in hunger through woods and forest, when they dared not to go forth into the open country lest the enemy should meet them. But what I have said is most suitable, that is, that they were so famished as though they were in a vast desert, and far away from every hospital, so that bread could nowhere be found. We now, then, perceive the meaning of the Prophet. He adds,—

10. Our skin was black like an oven, because of the terrible famine.	10. Pelles nostræ quasi clibanus nigredinem contraxerunt ob exustiones famis.

Some read, "for tremors;" literally, "from the face of tremors." Jerome renders it, "tempests:" but the word "burnings" is the most suitable; for he says that their *skins were darkened,* and he compares them to an *oven.* This metaphor often occurs in Scripture, "Though ye have been as among pots in the smoke, and deformed by blackness, yet your wings shall shine." (Ps. lxviii. 14.) God says that his people had contracted blackness, as though they had touched smoky pots, because they had been burnt as it were by many afflictions; for when we pine away in our evils, filthiness itself deforms us. But here he compares to an oven (which is the same thing) their skins or skin. He then says that the skin of every one was so wrinkled

[1] The versions and the *Targ.* render the word, "sword;" and so do *Gataker*, *Blayney*, and *Henderson*. And by "the sword of the desert" are to be understood freebooters who carried swords and made incursions from desert places.

At the risk of our life we got our bread,
On account of the sword of the desert.—*Ed.*

and darkened by blackness, that it was like an oven which is black through constant fire and smoke. The Prophet, or whoever was the author of the 119th Psalm, uses another comparison, that he was like a bottle or a bladder, contracted by the smoke, and had wrinkles together with blackness.[1]

The meaning is, that there was a degrading deformity in the people, for they were so famished that no moisture remained in them; and when moisture fails, then paleness and decay follow; and then from paleness a greater deformity and blackness, of which the Prophet now speaks. Hence I have said, that the word "burnings" is the most proper. For, if we say tempests or storms, a tempest does not certainly darken the skin; and if we render it tremors or tremblings, this would be far remote; but if we adopt the word *burnings*, the whole passage will appear consistent; and we know, that as food as it were irrigates the life of man, so famine burns it up, as Scripture speaks also elsewhere. It follows,—

11. They ravished the women in Zion, *and* the maids in the cities of Judah.	11. Mulieres in Sion afflictæ fuerunt, virgines in urbibus Jehudah.

He mentions here another kind of reproach, that women had been ravished in Jerusalem, and in other cities.[2] God had commanded chastity to be observed among his people. When, therefore, virgins and women were thus defiled, it was a thing extremely disgraceful. But the Prophet mentioned this also, in order that God might at length shew

[1] The word זלעפות, occurs in Ps. xi. 6, and in the singular number in Ps. cxix. 53. The versions and the *Targ.* render it differently in the three places, for it is not found anywhere else. In Ps. cxix. 53, it is rendered "horror" in our version, and this meaning suits the passage in Ps. xi. 6, and also this passage,—

Our skins, like an oven they became black,
Because of the horrors of famine (or, horrible famine.)

The word for "skins" is in the plural number according to several copies, and the verb requires it to be so.—*Ed.*

[2] There is here a delicate word for a disgraceful act. The words literally are,—

Women in Sion they humbled (or, were humbled,)
And virgins in the cities of Judah.

It is "humbled" by the *Sept.* and *Vulg.* "And" before "virgins," is supplied by the *Vulg.* and *Syr.*—*Ed.*

himself propitious to his people after having been entreated. (Deut. xxii. 21-24.)

And he mentioned *Sion* rather than Jerusalem,—it was indeed to state a part for the whole; but that place, we know, had been chosen by God that his name might be there worshipped. Sion, then, was a holy place above any other; it was, in a word, the earthly dwelling of God. As, then, God had there his palace, that he might dwell in the midst of his people, it was a disgraceful sight in the extreme to see women ravished there, for the temple of God was thus violated. It was not only a thing disgraceful to the people, that women were thus ravished, but it was a filthy profanation of God's worship, and therefore sacrilegious. We now see the design of the Prophet. He mentions also the cities of Judah, but with reference to the same thing. It follows,—

12. Princes are hanged up by their hand: the faces of elders were not honoured.	12. Principes manu sua fuerunt suspensi, facies senum non fuerunt in honore (non fuerunt honoratæ, *ad verbum.*)

The beginning of the verse may be explained in two ways. All render thus, "The princes have been slain by their hand," that is, of their enemies. But I wonder how it never occurred to them, that it was far more grievous, that they were slain by their own hand. I certainly do not doubt but that the Prophet says here, that some of the princes had laid violent hands on themselves. For it would be a frigid expression, that the princes were hung by the hand of enemies; but if we read, that the princes were hung by their own hand, this would be far more atrocious, as we have before seen that even women, excelling in humanity, devoured their own offspring. So he says now that princes were hung, not by enemies, for it was a common thing for the conquered to be slain by their enemies, and be also hung by way of reproach; but the Prophet, as it appears to me, meant to express something more atrocious, even that the miserable princes were constrained to lay violent hands on themselves.[1]

[1] The most obvious meaning of the words is, that princes were hung or suspended by the hand, and not by the neck. Such a punishment is not

He adds, that *the faces of the aged were not honoured;* which is also a thing not natural; for we know that some honour is always rendered to old age, and that time of life is commonly regarded with reverence. When, therefore, no respect is shewn to the aged, the greatest barbarity must necessarily prevail. It is the same, then, as though the Prophet had said that the people had been so disgracefully treated, that their enemies had not even spared the aged. We also now understand why he adds this, for it would have otherwise appeared incredible, that the princes hung themselves by their own hand. But he here intimates that there was no escape for them, except they in despair sought death for themselves, because all humanity had disappeared. It follows,—

13. They took the young men to grind, and the children fell under the wood.	13. Adolescentes ad molam sumpserunt, et pueri in ligno ceciderunt (*vel,* impegerunt.)

I cannot proceed farther now.

PRAYER.

Grant, Almighty God, that since thou hast once stretched forth thy hand to consecrate us a people to thyself,—O grant, that thy paternal favour may perpetually shine on us, and that we may, on the other hand, strive always to glorify thy name, so that having once embraced us thou mayest continue thy goodness, until we shall at length enjoy the fulness of all blessings in thy celestial kingdom, which has been obtained for us by the blood of thine only-begotten Son.—Amen.

Lecture Eighteenth.

THE Prophet now says, that *young men had been delivered to the mill,* or to the grinding-house; and we know that of all servile works this was the lowest; for as they used asses to grind, so also they used slaves. The meaning is, that the

recorded as having been then practised; but it may have been a barbarity resorted to by the Chaldeans. This seems to be the meaning conveyed by the versions and the *Targ.*,—

Princes were by their hand hung up,
The persons of the aged were not honoured.—*Ed.*

Jews were shamefully treated, and were reduced to the most abject condition. I know not how came Jerome to give this version, that they were basely used for lust; for טחן, *thechen,* means to grind or to tear. He thought that it means here something base, which could not be named, as though the enemies had shamefully abused the young men; but we may gather from the second clause of the verse that such an idea does not accord with the passage.

He then says that *young men* were compelled *to grind,* and that *boys stumbled under the wood.* He means that boys were loaded with wood, as drudges were wont to be; and it was a vile work. As, then, he said previously, that the young men were employed in grinding, so now he says that boys succumbed under the wood, because they carried burdens on their shoulders too heavy for them, which they were not able to bear. We now, then, apprehend what the Prophet means. It follows,—

14. The elders have ceased from the gate, the young men from their music.

14. Senes cessarunt è porta, adolescentes à pulsatione sua (*vel,* canticis musicis.)

Here the Prophet briefly shews that the city was reduced to ruins, so that nothing but desolation could be seen there. For when cities are inhabited, judges sit at the gate and young men exercise themselves in lawful pursuits; but he says that there were no judgments; for at that time, as it is well known, they were wont to administer justice and to hold assemblies at the gates of cities. It was then the same as though all civil order had been abolished.

Then he adds, the *young men had ceased from their own beating* or musical songs. The meaning is, that there was so great a desolation in the city, that it was no more a city. For men cannot dwell together without laws and without courts of justice. Where courts of justice are closed up, where laws are mute, where no equity is administered, there barbarity prevails, which is worse than solitude; and where there are no assemblies for legitimate amusements, life becomes brutal, for we know that man is a sociable being. By these words, then, the Prophet shews that a dreadful desolation appeared in the city after the people had gone into exile. And among the Chaldeans, and in Assyria, they had not their own judges nor any form of government, for they were dispersed and scattered, and that designedly, that they might not unite together any more; for it was the purpose of the Chaldeans to obliterate by degrees the very name of the people; and hence they were not there formed into a community. So justly does the Prophet deplore their desolation even in exile. It follows,—

15. The joy of our heart is ceased; our dance is turned into mourning.	15. Cessavit gaudium cordis nostri, versus est in luctum chorus noster (*sic enim vertunt* לאבל מחלנו.)

He pursues the same subject, but he seems more clearly to explain what he had briefly stated in the preceding verse, when he says that *all joy of the heart had ceased, and* that all the *dances were turned into mourning.*[1] We know that life is more bitter than death when men are in constant mourning; and truly where there is no hilarity, that state of life is worse than death. And this is what the Prophet now means by saying that all joy had ceased, and that all dances were converted into mourning.

16. The crown is fallen *from* our head: woe unto us, that we have sinned!	16. Cecidit corona capitis nostri; væ nunc nobis, quia peccavimus.

By the crown of the head he no doubt understands all those ornaments by which that people had been adorned. They had a kingdom and a priesthood, which were like two luminaries or two precious jewels; they had also other things by which the Lord had adorned them. As, then, they were endued with such excellent things, they are said to have borne a *crown on their head.* But a crown was not only taken for a diadem,—it was also a symbol of joy and of honour; for not only kings then wore crowns, but men were crowned at weddings and feasts, at games also, and theatres. The Prophet, in a word, complains, that though many ornaments did belong to the people, yet now

[1] The words ought rather to be thus rendered,—

Turned into mourning was our piping.

The word does not mean dancing, but playing on some fistular instrument.—*Ed.*

they were denuded of them all: *The crown*, he says, *has fallen from our head.*[1]

He then exclaims, *Woe to us now, for we have sinned!* Here he sets forth an extreme misery, and at the same time shews that all hope of restoration was taken away. He, however, mentions the cause, *because they had done wickedly.* By saying this he did not intend to exasperate their sorrow, so that they who were thus afflicted might murmur against God; but, on the contrary, his object was to humble the afflicted, so that they might perceive that they were justly punished. It is the same as though he had summoned them as guilty before the tribunal of God, and pronounced in one word that they justly suffered or sustained so grievous a punishment; for a just God is an avenger of wickedness.

We hence conclude, that when he said yesterday that the fathers who had sinned were dead, and their iniquity was borne by their children, he did not so speak as to exempt the living from all blame; for here he condemns them and includes himself in the number. But I explained yesterday the meaning of that verse; and here the Prophet ingenuously confesses that the people were justly punished, because they had by their sins provoked the wrath of God. And this doctrine ought to be carefully observed; because when we are pressed down by adversities, Satan will excite us to sorrow, and at the same time hurry us on to rage, except this doctrine comes to our minds, that we have to do with God, who is a righteous Judge. For the knowledge of our sins will tame our pride and also check all those clamorous complaints, which the unbelieving are wont to utter when they rise up against God. Our evils, then, ought to lead us to consider God's judgment and to confess our sins; and this was the end which our Prophet had in view. It follows,—

17. For this our heart is faint; for these *things* our eyes are dim.	17. Propterea debile est cor nostrum; super hoc (*id est*, propter hanc causam) obtenebrati sunt oculi nostri.

[1] The words are,—

Fallen has the crown of our head.

Then the "woe" in the next line is only declarative,—

Woe *is* now to us, because we have sinned.

The particle "now" is omitted in our version.—*Ed.*

He connects sorrow here with the acknowledgment of sin, that the people under the pressure and agony of sorrow might apply their minds so as to consider their own sins. At the same time the Prophet, no doubt, includes here all that we have already observed, as though he had said that the people were not without reason wearied with sorrow, for they had ample and manifold reasons for their grief.

For this reason, he says, that is, we do not exceed a due measure in our sorrow, for our afflictions are not ordinary, so that our grief cannot be moderate; but as we are come to an extremity, it cannot then be but our minds should be overwhelmed with sorrow. As, then, the curse of God appeared everywhere, he says that this was the cause *of the fainting heart;* and he says also, *Therefore were our eyes darkened.* This is a common metaphor, that the eyes become dim through sorrow; for the senses through sorrow are blunted. Hence it is that the sight of the eyes is injured; and David especially makes use of this mode of speaking. Our Prophet then says that *the eyes were darkened,* because their grief was, as it were, deadly. It follows,—

18. Because of the mountain of Zion, which is desolate, the foxes walk upon it.	18. Propter montem Sion qui in vastitatem redactus est, vulpes incedunt in eo.

Though he had in general included all kinds of evils, he yet mentions now the principal cause of sorrow, that *mount Sion* had lost its beauty and its excellency. For that place had been chosen by God, as though he had descended there from heaven, that he might dwell there; and we know also that its beauty is spoken of in high terms. For there the face of God shone forth, as Moses and the Prophets often speak. It was then an extremely sad change, that as God had dwelt in mount Sion, foxes should lodge there as in a deserted cave. For on mount Sion was the tabernacle or the sanctuary; and God says that it was the tabernacle of meeting, מועד, *muod,* because there he wished to hold intercourse with his people. As, then, that place included God and his Church, it was, as I have said, a dreadful and monstrous thing, that it had become so desolate, that foxes succeeded in the place of God and the faithful. It was not, then, without reason that Jeremiah, after having spoken of so many and so bitter calamities, mentioned this as the chief, that *mount Sion was reduced to desolation, so that foxes ran there hither and thither.*[1]

For as it is the principal thing, and as it were the chief of all blessings, to be counted God's people, and to have a familiar access to him, so in adversities nothing is so sad as to be deprived of God's presence. When David testified his gratitude to God, because he had been enriched by every kind of blessing, he added this, " I shall dwell in the house of God." (Ps. xxiii. 6.) For though he had spoken of wealth and riches and of the abundance of all things, yet he saw that his chief happiness was to call on God together with the faithful, and to be deemed one of his people. So, also, on the other hand, the Prophet here shews that nothing can be sadder to the godly than when God leaves his dwelling and makes it desolate, in order to terrify all who may see it.

This had been predicted to them by Jeremiah himself, as we have seen in the seventh chapter of his prophecies, " Go ye to Shiloh," he said, where the ark of the covenant had long been; though that place had been a long time the habitation of God, yet it was afterwards rejected with great disdain. Jeremiah then declared to the Jews, while they

[1] Some connect this verse with the foregoing, as a special reason why their eyes were darkened,—

17. For this become faint did our heart;
For these things darkened were our eyes,
18. *Yea*, for mount Sion, which is desolate;
Foxes have walked through it.

"This" was the "woe" which sin had brought; and "these things" were the various things which he had previously stated, but the desolation of mount Sion was the chief cause of sorrow.

Others take this verse by itself, as it is done by the *Sept.*, where על is rendered "on," and ש for אשר, is translated "because,"—

On mount Sion, because it has become desolate,
Foxes have walked in (or through) it.

If על be rendered concerning, or, as to, or, with regard to, the best construction would be the following,—

As to mount Sion, which has become desolate,
Foxes have walked in it (or, traversed it.)—*Ed.*

were yet in safety, that such would be the condition of Jerusalem; but his prophecy was not believed. He now, then, confirms, by the event, what he had predicted by God's command, when he says that mount Sion was become the den of foxes. It follows,—

19. Thou, O Lord, remainest for ever; thy throne from generation to generation.	19. Tu Jehova perpetuò sedebis, solium tuum in ætatem et ætatem (*id est*, omnibus seculis.)

The Prophet here raises up his eyes to God, and, by his example, he encourages all the godly, that they might not cease, notwithstanding their extreme calamities, to look to God, as we find in the hundred and second Psalm, where the Psalmist speaks of the destruction of the city of Jerusalem. Indeed the subject of that psalm is similar to that of this chapter; nor is there a doubt but that it was composed when the people, as it clearly appears, were in exile in Babylon. There the Psalmist, after having spoken of the ruin of the city, and calamities of the people, says, that the heavens were growing old and wasting as it were with rottenness, together with the whole world; but he afterwards adds, "But thou, O Lord, remainest perpetually." (Ps. cii. 27-29.) At the same time he speaks more clearly than Jeremiah, for he applies his doctrine to the consolation of the Church, "Children's children," he says, "shall inhabit it." Hence, from the perpetuity and immutability of God, he infers the perpetuity of the Church. This is not done by Jeremiah, though it is implied; and for this reason, no doubt, he exclaims, that *God dwells for ever*, and that *his throne remains fixed in all ages*, or through all ages.

For when we fix our eyes on present things, we must necessarily vacillate, as there is nothing permanent in the world; and when adversities bring a cloud over our eyes, then faith in a manner vanishes, at least we are troubled and stand amazed. Now the remedy is, to raise up our eyes to God, for however confounded things may be in the world, yet he remains always the same. His truth may indeed be hidden from us, yet it remains in him. In short, were the world to change and perish a hundred times, nothing could ever affect the immutability of God. There is, then, no doubt but that the Prophet wished to take courage and to raise himself up to a firm hope, when he exclaimed, "Thou, O God, remainest for ever." By the word *sitting* or remaining, he doubtless meant that the world is governed by God. We know that God has no body, but the word *sitting* is to be taken metaphorically, for He is no God except he be the judge of the world.

This, also, he expresses more clearly, when he says, that God's throne remains through all ages. The throne of God designates the government of the world. But if God be the judge of the world, then he doeth nothing, or suffereth nothing to be done, but according to his supreme wisdom and justice.[1] We hence see, that inasmuch as the state of present things, as thick darkness, took away all distinction, the Prophet raises up his eyes to God and acknowledges him as remaining the same perpetually, though things in the world continually change. Then the throne of God is set in opposition to chance or uncertain changes which ungodly men dream of; for when they see things in great confusion in the world, they say that it is the wheel of fortune, they say that all things happen through blind fate. Then the Prophet, that he might not be cast down with the unbelieving, refers to the throne of God, and strengthens himself in this doctrine of true religion,—that God nevertheless *sits on this throne*, though things are thus confounded, though all things fluctuate; yea, even though storms and tempests mingle as it were heaven and earth together, yet God sits on his throne amidst all such disturbances. However turbulent, then, all the elements may be, this derogates nothing from the righteous and perpetual judgment of God. This is the meaning of the words; and hence fruit and benefit may be easily gathered. It follows,—

20. Wherefore dost thou forget us for ever, *and* forsake us so long time?

20. Ut quid in perpetuum oblivisceris nostri, deseres nos in protractionem (*vel*, longitudinem) dierum?

[1] The words literally are,—

Thou Jehovah for ever sittest,
Thy throne *is* from generation to generation.

Sitting is the posture of a judge, and the reference here is to Jehovah, not as to his essence or existence, but as to his judicial office.—*Ed.*

He seems, indeed, here to expostulate with God; but the faithful, even when they patiently bear their evils, and submit to God's scourges, do yet familiarly deposit their complaints in his bosom, and thus unburden themselves. We see that David prayed, and no doubt by the real impulse of the Spirit, and at the same time expostulated, "Why dost thou forget me perpetually?" (Ps. xiii. 1.) Nor is there a doubt but that the Prophet took this complaint from David. Let us, then, know, that though the faithful sometimes take this liberty of expostulating with God, they yet do not put off reverence, modesty, submission, or humility. For when the Prophet thus inquired why God should for ever forget his people and forsake them, he no doubt relied on his own prophecies, which he knew had proceeded from God, and thus he deferred his hope until the end of the seventy years, for that time had been prefixed by God. But it was according to human judgment that he complained in his own person, and in that of the faithful, that the affliction was long; nor is there a doubt but that he dictated this form of prayer to the faithful, that it might be retained after his death. He, then, formed this prayer, not only according to his own feeling, and for the direction to those of his own age; but his purpose was to supply the faithful with a prayer after his own death, so that they might flee to the mercy of God.

We now, then, perceive how complaints of this kind ought to be understood, when the prophets asked, "How long?" as though they stimulated God to hasten the time; for it cannot be, when we are pressed down by many evils, but that we wish help to be accelerated; for faith does not wholly strip us of all cares and anxieties. But when we thus pray, let us remember that our times are at the will and in the hand of God, and that we ought not to hasten too much. It is, then, lawful for us on the one hand to ask God to hasten; but, on the other hand, we ought to check our impatience and wait until the suitable time comes. Both these things the Prophet no doubt joined together when he said, *Why shouldest thou perpetually forget us and forsake us?*[1]

[1] Why shouldest thou to the end forget us—
Forsake us for the length of *our* days?

We yet see that he judged according to the evils then endured; and doubtless he believed that God had not forsaken his own people nor forgotten them, as no oblivion can happen to him. But, as I have already said, the Prophet mentioned these complaints through human infirmity, not that men might indulge themselves in their own thoughts, but that they might ascend by degrees to God and overcome all these temptations. It follows,—

21. Turn thou us unto thee, O Lord, and we shall be turned; renew our days as of old.	21. Converte nos, Jehova, ad te, et convertimur: innova (*vel,* instaura) dies nostros sicuti olim (*vel,* ab initio.)

The Prophet shews, in this verse, that the remedy is in God's hand whenever he is pleased to succour his people. He, then, exalts here the power of God, as though he had said, that God is not without power, but that he can, whenever he pleases, help his people. This is not, indeed, a sufficient ground for confidence, yet it is the beginning of hope; for whence is it that despair weakens us, so that we cannot call on God? because we think that it is all over with us; and whence is this? because we impiously confine the power of God; nay, we in a manner, through our unbelief, repel his power, which would otherwise be exerted in our behalf. As, then, we thus close the door against God, when we extenuate his power, and think that our evils will prevail; it is, therefore, as I have said, the beginning of hope to believe that all the issues of death are in God's hand, and that were we a hundred times swallowed up, yet he, by stretching forth his hand to us, can become the author of salvation to us at any moment.

This is now the argument which the Prophet handles, when he says, *Turn us, O Jehovah, and we shall be turned;* that is, "If thou, O Jehovah, be pleased to gather us, salvation is already certain to us." And he does not speak

"To the end," or perpetually, and "the length of our days," are the same. The length of days, as it appears from Ps. xxiii. 6, means the extent of the present life; the phrase is there used as synonymous with all the days of one's life. Might not the Prophet here refer to the life of those then living? As to restoration after seventy years, he could have had no doubt. He seems to have pleaded for the restoration of the generation then living. —*Ed.*

here of repentance. There is, indeed, a twofold turning or conversion of men to God, and a twofold turning of God to men. There is an inward turning when God regenerates us by his own Spirit; and turning with respect to us is said to be the feeling of true religion, when, after having been alienated from him, we return to the right way and to a right mind. There is also an exterior turning as to God, that is, when he so receives men into favour, that his paternal favour becomes apparent; but the interior turning of men to God takes place when they recover life and joy.

Of this second turning, then, does the Prophet now speak, *Turn us, O Jehovah, and we shall be turned;* that is, If thou, Jehovah, lookest on us, our condition will immediately become prosperous, for in thy hand there is a sure salvation for us." As, then, the Jews were at that time like the dead, the Prophet says, that if it pleased God to gather them, they could in a moment, as they say, have been restored, as it is said also in the Psalms, "Thou takest away life, and all things change; send forth thy Spirit, and renew the face of the earth." (Ps. civ. 29, 30.) As, then, God renews the face of the earth and restores it by only looking at it, hence now the Prophet says, that the Jews, though they had been destroyed, could yet be immediately restored, if it were the will of God to receive them into favour.[1]

He adds, *Renew our days as of old.* This is an explanation of the former clause: the renewing of days was restoration to their former state. God had been for many ages the deliverer of his people; under David had been their greatest happiness; under Solomon also they had greatly flourished; but from the time when God had redeemed his people, he had given, as we know, many and constant proofs of his favour and mercy. As, then, God's goodness had, by so many evidences been made conspicuous, the Prophet now

[1] "The meaning of this sentence is," says *Grotius*, "Restore us to thy favour, that we may be restored to our ancient state." This being evidently the meaning, the rendering ought to be this,—

Restore us, O Jehovah, to thyself, that we may be restored.

And as *Calvin*, as well as *Grotius*, says, the following line is a confirmation,—

Renew our days as of old.—*Ed.*

says, *Renew our days as formerly*, that is, "Restore us to that happiness, which was formerly a testimony of thy paternal favour towards thy people." We now then perceive the meaning of the Prophet.

But it ought to be noticed, that he grounds his hope on the ancient benefits of God; for as God had formerly redeemed his people, had often helped the miserable, had poured forth on their posterity fulness of blessings, hence the Prophet encourages himself to entertain good hope, and suggests also to others the same ground of confidence. We see that this was done often by David; for whenever he mentions ancient testimonies of God's favour towards his people, he hence gathered, that God would extend the same goodness and kindness to posterity. It follows,—

22. But thou hast utterly rejected us; thou art very wroth against us.	22. Nisi (*vel*, sed, *vel*, quod si) rejiciendo rejecisti nos, excanduisti contra nos valde.

The two words כי אם, *ki am*, are differently explained: some render them, "but if," or "certainly if," and thus separate the verse into two parts, "Surely if thou hast rejected us, thou art very angry;" but this is a forced meaning, not intended, as I think, by the Prophet. And these seem to have been compelled by necessity to pervert the Prophet's words; because it appears hard simply to declare that the people had been wholly rejected by God. As, then, this harshness offended them, they contrived this comment, "If thou hast rejected us, thou art very angry." But as I have said, this exposition I do not approve of, because it is a very forced one; and the greater part of interpreters follow what I stated in the first place, for they take כי אם, *ki am*, adversatively. The two particles are often connected together, and rendered, "though," or although,—"Though thou hast rejected us:" and hence the last verse has been repeated.

For the Jews labour under this superstition, that when a book ends with a hard and severe sentence, or one containing a dreadful threatening, grating to the ears, in order to avoid the sad omen, they repeat the last verse but one. So they do at the end of Isaiah, and at the end of Malachi.

As Isaiah says, "It shall be a horror (or abomination) to all flesh;" they therefore repeat the previous verse. So in Malachi; as he says, "Lest I come and smite the earth with a curse—חרם, *cherem*," they think that as he pronounces there an anathema, it is a sort of charm that may absorb this curse, to have the previous verse repeated after it. There is, then, no doubt but that they took this passage in the same sense, "Though thou hast rejected us," &c.

If this explanation be approved, we must hold that the Prophet here exceeded due limits, as also the faithful, in their prayers, do not always so restrain themselves, but that some heat bubbles up; for we see how David, in the Psalms, too often shewed this kind of feeling; and it is hence evident, that his mind was not always sufficiently calm. We must then say, that the Prophet was impelled by a turbulent feeling when he uttered these words.

But כי אם, *ki am*, may also be rendered, "Unless," or except: and it is singular that no one has perceived this, though it be not an unsuitable meaning, "Except it may be thou rejecting hast rejected us, and hast become very angry with us," or above measure angry; for עד מאד, *od mad*, in Hebrew, means the same as above measure (*supra modum*) in Latin. Though the Prophet seems to speak doubtingly, by laying down this condition, there is yet no doubt but that he struggled against all unbelief, when he said, *Except it may be;* for he reasons from what is impossible, "Turn thou us to thee and we shall be turned, renew our days as formerly; *except it may be thou hast rejected us:*" but this was impossible. Then, as I have said, the Prophet here strengthens himself by setting up a shield against all the assaults of temptations when he says, *Except it may be thou hast rejected us.*[1]

[1] The particles, כי אם, seem to have the meaning of "except," as in Gen. xxxii. 26, "except thou bless me." But the exposition is too refined. The usual meaning of the particles is, *but in truth, for surely, when indeed.* See 1 Sam. xxi. 5; Prov. xxiii. 18; Ex. xxii. 23. They are rendered here, "for," by the *Sept.*, *Syr.*, and *Arab.;* "but," by the *Vulg.*, and "although," by the *Targ.* The version of *Blayney* and *Henderson* is, "For surely." The Prophet assigns a reason for his petition

But it cannot be that God will reject his people, and be so angry with them, as never to be reconciled. We hence see that the Prophet does not simply set down the condition, as though he said, "O God, if thou art to be perpetually angry with us, and wilt never be reconciled, it is then all over with our salvation; but if thou wilt be reconciled to us, we shall then entertain good hope." No, the Prophet did not thus keep his own mind and the minds of others in suspense, but had a sure confidence as to God's favour; for it cannot be that God will ever forsake those whom he has chosen, as Paul also shews in the eleventh chapter of the Epistle to the Romans.

As it has so seemed good to the brethren, I will begin to-morrow the explanation of Ezekiel.

PRAYER.

Grant, Almighty God, that as thou didst formerly execute judgments so severe on thy people,—O grant, that these chastisements may at this day teach us to fear thy name, and also keep us in watchfulness and humility, and that we may so strive to pursue the course of our calling, that we may find that thou art always our leader, that thy hand is stretched forth to us, that thy aid is ever ready for us, until, being at length gathered into thy celestial kingdom, we shall enjoy that eternal life, which thine only-begotten Son has obtained for us by his own blood.—Amen.

in the preceding verse; as though he had said, "I ask for restoration to thy favour and to our land, because thou hast clearly manifested thy rejection of us, and thy displeasure towards us."

For surely rejecting thou hast rejected us,
Thou hast been wroth with us exceedingly,

or, more literally,

Thou hast foamed against us exceedingly.

The first line here corresponds with the latter part of the previous verse, "Restore us to our land, and renew the ancient days,"—"Thou hast wholly rejected us." He speaks of things as they were then. Then the last line in this verse bears a relation to the first part of the preceding verse, "Restore us to thy favour,"—"Thou hast been exceedingly displeased with us." Thus, for displeasure he asked favour, and for repudiation, a restoration.—*Ed.*

PRAISE TO GOD.

A TRANSLATION

OF

CALVIN'S VERSION OF JEREMIAH.

CHAPTERS XLVIII.—LII.

CHAPTER XLVIII.

1 CONCERNING Moab:
Thus saith Jehovah of hosts, the God of Israel,—
Woe upon Nebo! for it is laid waste,
Ashamed, taken is Kiriathaim;
Ashamed is Misgab and dismayed.
2 No more shall be the boasting of Moab over Heshbon;
They have consulted an evil against her,—
"Come and let us cut her off from being a nation."
Also Madmen, thou shalt be cut off,
After thee shall go the sword.
3 The sound of a cry from Horonaim!
A waste and great destruction!
4 Distressed is Moab;
A cry have her little ones made to be heard.
5 For in the ascent to Luhith,
With weeping shall ascend weeping;
For in the descent to Horonaim,
The enemies a cry of distress shall hear:
6 Flee ye, save your lives;
And ye shall be as the juniper in the desert.

7 Therefore, because thy confidence
Was in thy works and in thy treasures,
Even thou shalt be taken:
And go forth shall Chemosh into captivity,
His priests and his princes together.
8 And come shall a waster to every city,
Nor shall a city escape;
Perish also shall the valley,
And destroyed shall be the plain,
As Jehovah hath spoken.
9 Give wings to Moab,
For flying she shall fly,

And her cities shall be a waste,
That there will be none to inhabit them.
10 Cursed is he who doeth the work of Jehovah deceitfully,
And cursed is he who restrains his sword from blood.

11 Quiet has been Moab from his childhood,
And hath settled on his dregs,
And hath not been changed from vessel to vessel,
And to captivity he hath not gone:
Therefore remained has his flavour in him,
And his odour was not changed.
12 Therefore, behold, the days are coming, saith Jehovah,
That I will send to him drivers,
Who will drive him out;
And his vessels will they empty,
And his bottles will they scatter:
13 And ashamed will be Moab of Chemosh,
As ashamed was the house of Israel of Beth-el,
The object of their confidence.

14 How say ye, "We are valiant, and men strong for war:"
15 Wasted is Moab, and from his cities they have vanished,
And his young men have descended to the slaughter,
Saith the King, Jehovah of hosts is his name.
16 Nigh is the destruction of Moab to come,
And her calamity greatly hastens.
Be ye moved for him all who are around him,
And all ye who know his name, say,—
"How has the strong staff been broken, the beautiful rod!"

17 Come down from glory, and dwell in thirst,
Thou inhabitant, the daughter of Dibon!
18 For the waster of Moab comes up against thee,
The destroyer of thy fortresses.
19 On the way stand and look,
Thou inhabitant of Aroer.
Ask the fugitive, and her who has escaped,
"Say, what hath happened?"
20 Ashamed is Moab, for he is broken.
Howl ye, and cry out,
And proclaim in Arnon that Moab is laid waste.
21 Judgment also shall come on the plain country,
On Holon, and on Jahazah, and on Mephaath,
22 And on Dibon, and on Nebo, and on Beth-diblathaim,
23 And on Kiriathaim, and on Beth-gamul, and on Beth-meon,
24 And on Kerioth, and on Bozrah,
And on all the cities of the land of Moab, far and near.
25 Cut off is the horn of Moab,
And his strength is broken, saith Jehovah.

26 Make him drunk, for against Jehovah hath he magnified himself;
And roll himself shall Moab in his own vomit;
And he also shall be a derision;
27 For has not Israel been a derision to thee?
Has he been found among thieves?
For since thou hast spoken of him, thou hast been excited.

28 Leave the cities, and dwell in the rock,
Ye inhabitants of Moab:
And they shall be as a dove,
Which makes a nest in the passages,
Beyond the mouth of the cleft.

29 Heard have we of the pride of Moab;
Very proud is his haughtiness,
And his pride, and the loftiness of his heart.
30 I know, saith Jehovah, his insolence,
And his lies are not stable, they shall not do so.
31 Therefore for Moab will I howl,
And to all Moab will I cry aloud;
I will mutter to the men of the city of potsherd.

32 With the weeping of Jazer
Will I weep for thee, vine of Sibmah:
Thy shoots have passed over the sea,
Even to the sea came Jazer:
On thy summer-fruits and on thy vintages
Has fallen a waster.
33 And taken away shall be joy and exultation,
From the fruitful field, from the land of Moab;
And the wine from the presses will I make to cease:
He will not tread with shouting, shouting,
There will not be shouting.
34 At the cry of Heshbon, to Elealeh, to Jahaz,
Will they send forth their voice,
From Zoar to Horonaim;
An heifer three years old *is Moab;*
Verily even the waters of Nimrim shall be dried up.

35 And I will cause to cease from Moab, saith Jehovah,
Him who offers on the high place,
And who burns incense to his gods.
36 Therefore my heart for Moab
Shall make a sound like pipes,
And my heart for the men of the city of potsherd
Like pipes shall make a sound;
For the treasures he had made have perished.
37 For on every head *shall be* baldness,

And to every beard, a shaving,
And on all hands, incisions, and on loins, sackcloth.
38 On all the roofs of Moab,
And in all her streets, shall be mourning altogether;
For I will break Moab like a vessel
In which there is no pleasure, saith Jehovah.
39 How Moab is broken! they will howl;
How has he turned his back! he is ashamed:
Yea, Moab is become a derision,
And a terror to all around.

40 For thus saith Jehovah,—
Behold, as an eagle will he fly,
And extend his wings over Moab:
41 Taken are the cities, the strongholds are seized,
And the heart of the men of Moab shall be in that day
As the heart of a woman in distress.
42 And broken shall Moab be, so as not to be a people,
Because against Jehovah hath he exalted himself.
43 Terror, and the pit, and the snare, *shall be* on thee,
Inhabitant of Moab, saith Jehovah:
44 He who flies from terror shall fall into the pit,
And he who ascends from the pit shall be taken in the snare;
For I will bring upon her, upon Moab,
The year of their visitation, saith Jehovah.
45 Under the shadow of Heshbon shall they stand,
Who from violence shall flee:
But fire shall go forth from Heshbon,
And a flame from the midst of Sihon;
And it shall consume the corner of Moab,
And the extremities of the sons of tumult.

46 Woe to thee, Moab!
Perished have the people of Chemosh!
For driven have been thy sons into captivity,
And thy daughters into exile.
47 But I will restore the captivity of Moab
In the latter days, saith Jehovah.
Thus far the judgment of Moab.

CHAPTER XLIX.

1 Concerning the children of Ammon:
Thus saith Jehovah,—
Hath Israel no children? hath he no heir?
Why doth their king inherit Gad,
And his people dwell in its cities?

2 Therefore, behold, the days are coming, saith Jehovah,
That I will cause to be heard the trumpet of war
At Rabbah, of the children of Ammon;
And she shall be a heap of desolation,
And her daughters shall be burned with fire,
And possess his possessors shall Israel, saith Jehovah.

3 Howl thou, Heshbon, for laid waste is Ai;
Cry aloud, ye daughters of Rabbah.
Gird on sackcloth, lament,
Run here and there by the fences;
For their king, into captivity is he gone,
And his priests and his princes with him.

4 Why gloriest thou in thy deep valleys?
Flown down has thy valley, rebellious daughter!
Who trusted in her hidden places,
Saying, Who can come to me?
5 Behold, I will bring on thee terror, saith the Lord,
Jehovah of hosts, from all around thee;
And ye shall be driven out, each one before him,
And there will be none to gather the dispersed.
6 But I will afterwards restore
The captivity of the children of Ammon, saith Jehovah.

7 Concerning Edom:
Thus saith Jehovah of hosts,—
Is there not wisdom any more in Teman?
Has counsel perished from the intelligent?
Overflowing has been their wisdom!
8 Flee, ye inhabitants of Dedan,
Who have turned *and* made deep *your* dwelling;
For the ruin of Esau will I bring on him,
At the time of his visitation.
9 If vintagers had come to thee,
Would they not have left some grapes?
If thieves in the night, would they not have destroyed
What would suffice them?
10 But I will uncover Esau,
I will disclose his hidden things,
So that he cannot be concealed:
Plundered shall be his seed,
And his brethren and his neighbours;
And he shall be no more.
11 Leave thy orphans, I will nourish them;
And thy widows, let them trust in me.
12 For thus saith Jehovah,—
Behold, those to whom it was not their judgment

To drink the cup, shall surely drink,
And shalt thou be exempted?
Thou shalt not be exempted,
For drinking thou shalt drink *it*.

13 For I have by myself sworn, saith Jehovah,
That a waste, a reproach, a desert,
And a curse, shall Bozrah become;
And all her cities shall be perpetual wastes.
14 A hearing have we heard from Jehovah,
And a messenger to the nations has been sent,—
"Be ye gathered and come against her,
And rise ye up to the battle."
15 For behold, small made I thee among the nations,
Contemptible among men:
16 Deceived thee has thy terror, the pride of thine heart;
Thou who dwellest in the fissures of rocks,
Who occupiest the heights of mountains:
Though thou raisest high, as an eagle, thy nest,
Thence will I draw thee down, saith Jehovah.
17 And Edom shall become a waste;
Every one passing by her shall be astonished,
And shall hiss on account of all her strokes.
18 As in the overthrow of Sodom and Gomorrah
And of their neighbouring cities, saith Jehovah,
Dwell there shall no man,
Nor shall a son of man abide there.

19 Behold, as a lion from the swelling of Jordan,
Will he ascend to the habitation of strength:
After having made him to rest,
I will make him flee from her;
And who is the chosen one whom I shall set over her?
For who is as I am?
And who will protest against me?
And who is the shepherd that before me will stand?
20 Therefore, hear ye the counsel of Jehovah,
Which he hath counselled against Edom,
And his thoughts which he hath thought
Against the inhabitants of Teman;
Surely draw them forth shall the least of the flock,
Surely destroyed over them shall be their dwellings.
21 At the sound of their fall, tremble shall the earth,
The cry of their voice shall at the Red Sea be heard.

22 Behold, as an eagle will he ascend and fly,
And will spread his wings over Bozrah;
And the heart of the valiant men of Edom in that day
Shall be like the heart of a sorrowful woman.

23 Concerning Damascus:
Ashamed is Hamath and Arpad;
Because they heard a bad report, they melt away,
Like a turbulent sea which cannot rest.
24 Weakened is Damascus, she turns to flight,
Terror hath laid hold on her,
Anguish and pangs have seized her,
As a woman in travail.
25 How is not forsaken the city of praise—
The city of my joy?
26 Yet fall shall her young men in her streets,
And all the men of war shall be cut off
In that day, saith Jehovah of Hosts.
27 For I will kindle a fire in the wall of Damascus,
And it shall consume the palaces of Ben-hadad.

28 Concerning Kedar, and the kingdoms of Hazor, which Nebu-
chadnezzar, the king of Babylon, had smitten:
Thus saith Jehovah,—
Arise ye, ascend against Kedar,
And destroy the children of the east.
29 Their tents and their flocks shall they take away,
And their curtains and all their vessels;
Their camels also shall they take to themselves,
And they shall cry to them, "Terror *is* on every side."
30 Flee ye, depart far away,
(Though deep have they made to dwell
The inhabitants of Hazor, saith Jehovah;)
For consulted against you hath Nebuchadnezzar,
The king of Babylon, a counsel,
And he hath purposed against you a purpose.

31 Arise ye, ascend against a secure nation,
That dwelleth in confidence, saith Jehovah;
It hath neither gates nor bars, it dwelleth alone.
32 And their camels shall became a prey,
And the abundance of their cattle a plunder;
And I will scatter them to every wind,
Even the utmost corners;
And from all the sides thereof
Will I bring their destruction, saith Jehovah.
33 And Hazor shall be the habitation of dragons,
A perpetual desolation;
Dwell there shall no man,
Nor shall a son of man abide in her.

34 The word which came to Jeremiah, the prophet, against
Elam, at the beginning of the reign of Zedekiah, the king
of Judah, saying:

35 Thus saith Jehovah of hosts,—
Behold, I will break the bow of Elam,
The chief part of their strength;
36 And I will bring against Elam four winds
From the four quarters of the heavens;
And I will scatter them to these four winds,
And there shall not be a nation
To which some fugitives from Elam shall not come.
37 For I will terrify Elam before their enemies,
And before those who seek their life;
And I will bring on them the evil
Of the indignation of my wrath, saith Jehovah;
And I will send after them the sword
Until I shall have consumed them;
38 And I will erect my throne in Elam,
And destroy thence the king and the princes, saith Jehovah.
39 But it shall be in the latter days
That I will restore the captivity of Elam, saith Jehovah.

CHAPTER L.

1 The word which Jehovah spoke concerning Babylon, con-
cerning the land of the Chaldeans, by Jeremiah the prophet:
2 Tell ye among the nations, proclaim,
Raise up also a banner, proclaim, conceal not;
Say ye, "Taken is Babylon,
Confounded is Bel, broken is Merodach,
Confounded are her images, broken are her idols."
3 For ascend against her shall a nation from the north,
Which will turn her land to a waste,
So that there will be no dweller in it, man or beast;
They have fled, they have departed.

4 In those days and at that time, saith Jehovah,
Come shall the children of Israel
And the children of Judah together;
Going and weeping they shall come,
And Jehovah their God will they seek.
5 To Sion will they ask the way, hither their faces,—
"Come ye and let us join ourselves to Jehovah,
By a perpetual covenant, not to be forgotten."
6 A lost sheep have been my people;
Their pastors have made them to wander;
On the mountains they strayed,
From mountain to hill they went,
They forgot the place of their lying down.
7 All who found them devoured them,
And their adversaries said, "We sin not,
Because they have sinned against Jehovah,

The habitation of justice,
And the hope of their fathers, *even* Jehovah."

8 Flee ye from the midst of Babylon,
And from Chaldea go forth,
And be as he-goats before the flock.
9 For, behold, I will rouse and bring against Babylon,
An assembly of great nations from the land of the north,
And they shall set in order against her ;
Thence taken will she be;
Their arrows, like those of a skilful valiant man,
They shall not return in vain.
10 And Chaldea shall be a prey,
And all who plunder her shall be satiated, saith Jehovah.
11 Surely ye rejoiced and exulted
When ye plundered mine heritage;
Ye became fat as a heifer well fed,
And neighed like strong horses.
12 Ashamed greatly shall be your mother,
Blush shall she who bare you;
Behold, the last of nations *shall she be*,
A desert, a waste, a solitude!
13 Because of the indignation of Jehovah
She shall not be inhabited,
And shall be an entire waste ;
All who pass by Babylon shall be astonished,
And shall hiss for all her strokes.

14 Set in order against Babylon around ;
All ye who bend the bow,
Shoot at her, spare not the arrows,
For against Jehovah hath she sinned.
15 Cry ye aloud against her around ;
She hath given her hand,
Fallen have her foundations,
Demolished have been her walls,
Because it is the vengeance of Jehovah ;
Vengeance take ye on her; as she has done, do to her.
16 Cut off the sower from Babylon,
And him who handles the sickle in the time of harvest :
From the face of the wasting sword
Every one shall look to his own people,
Every one to his own land shall flee.

17 A scattered flock hath Israel been,
Lions have driven him out;
The first who devoured him was the king of Assyria,
And this last hath broken his bones,
Even Nebuchadnezzar, the king of Babylon.

18 Therefore thus saith Jehovah of hosts, the God of Israel,—
Behold, I will visit the king of Babylon and his land,
As I visited the king of Assyria :
19 And I will restore Israel to his folds,
And he shall feed on Carmel and Bashan,
And on mount Ephraim and Gilead ;
And satisfied shall be his soul.
20 In those days and at that time, saith Jehovah,
Sought will be the iniquity of Israel, and there will be none ;
And the sin of Judah, and it shall not be found :
For I will pardon those whom I shall reserve.

21 On the land of the exasperating ascend,
And against the inhabitants of visitation,
Slay and destroy after them, saith Jehovah ;
And do all that I have commanded thee.
22 A sound of battle in the land and a great ruin !
23 How has the hammer of the whole earth
Been cut off and broken in pieces !
How has Babylon become a waste among the nations !
24 I set a snare for thee, therefore taken wert thou,
Babylon, though thou knewest not :
Thou wert found, and hence taken,
Because against Jehovah thou didst contend.

25 Opened hath Jehovah his treasure,
And brought forth the instruments of his wrath ;
For this is the work of the Lord, the Jehovah of hosts,
In the land of the Chaldeans.
26 Come ye against her from the extremity,
Open her repositories, tread her as heaps,
Destroy her wholly, that there may be to her no remnant.
27 Slay all her bullocks,
Let them descend to the slaughter :
Woe to them, for their day is come,
The time of their visitation.
28 The voice of those who flee and escape
From the land of Babylon !
To announce in Sion the vengeance of Jehovah our God,
The vengeance of his temple.

29 Summon against Babylon the mighty,
All who bend the bow ;
Besiege her around, that there may be no escape ;
Render to her according to her work,
According to all she has done, do ye to her ;
For against Jehovah has she acted proudly,
Against the Holy One of Israel.
30 Therefore fall shall her young men in her streets,

And all her men of war shall be destroyed
In that day, saith Jehovah.
31 Behold, I am against thee, the proud one,
Saith the Lord, the Jehovah of hosts;
For come is thy day, the time of thy visitation.
32 And stumble shall the proud and fall,
And there will be no one to raise him up;
And I will kindle a fire in his cities,
And it shall consume all round him.

33 Thus saith Jehovah of hosts,—
Oppressed have been the children of Israel
And the children of Judah together;
And all who led them captives have prevailed against them,
They have refused to let them go.
34 Their Redeemer is strong,
Jehovah of hosts is his name,
Their cause pleading he will plead,
So as to destroy the land,
And to make to tremble the inhabitants of Babylon.

35 A sword on the Chaldeans, saith Jehovah!
And on all the inhabitants of Babylon!
And on all her princes and on her wise men!
36 A sword on her diviners! and they shall become foolish;
A sword on her valiant men! and they shall be terrified;
37 A sword on her horses! and on her chariots!
And on her multitude, in the midst of her!
They shall be as women;
A sword on her treasures! and they shall be plundered;
38 A drought on her waters! and they shall be dried up:
For it is the land of carved images,
And in idols they glory.
39 Therefore dwell there shall wild birds with wild beasts,
And dwell there shall the daughters of ostriches;
And it shall not be inhabited any more for ever;
It shall not be an habitation to all generations.
40 As in God's overthrow of Sodom and Gomorrah,
And of their neighbouring cities, saith Jehovah,
Dwell there shall no man,
Nor shall a son of man abide there.

41 Behold, a people cometh from the north,
Even a great nation and many kings
Shall be roused from the sides of the earth.
42 On the bow and the shield shall they lay hold,
Cruel shall they be, and will shew no mercy;
Their voice like the sea shall roar,
And on horses shall they ride,

Prepared as a man for battle
Against thee, daughter of Babylon.
43 Heard has the king of Babylon a report of them,
And feeble became his hands;
Anxiety laid hold on him,
And anguish, like a woman in travail.

44 Behold, as a lion from the swelling of Jordan
Will he ascend to the strong habitation:
After having made him to rest,
I will make him flee from her;
And who is the chosen one whom I shall set over her?
For who is as I am?
And who will protest against me?
And who is the shepherd that before me will stand?
45 Therefore hear ye the counsel of Jehovah,
Which he hath counselled against Babylon;
And his thoughts which he has thought
Against the land of the Chaldeans:
Surely draw them forth shall the least of the flock,
Surely destroyed over them shall be their dwellings.
46 At the sound of Babylon being taken, tremble shall the earth,
And a cry among the nations shall be heard.

CHAPTER LI.

1 Thus saith Jehovah,—
Behold, I will raise a destroying wind against Babylon,
And against boasters of wisdom, my adversaries;
2 And I will send against Babylon winnowers,
And they shall winnow her and empty her land;
For they shall be against her around in the day of evil.
3 As to him who bends the bow,
And him who raises himself up in his coat of mail,—
Spare ye not her young men,
Destroy all her army.
4 And fall shall they wounded, in her land,
And pierced through in her streets.
5 For not widowed is Israel, nor Judah
By his God, by Jehovah of hosts:
But rather their land is filled with sin
On account of the Holy One of Israel.

6 Flee ye from the midst of Babylon,
And save ye, every one his life,
Lest ye perish in her iniquity;
For it is the time of Jehovah's vengeance,
A reward will he render to her.
7 A golden cup has Babylon been

In Jehovah's hand, inebriating the whole earth;
From her wine have the nations drunk,
Therefore have the nations become mad.
8 Suddenly has Babylon fallen, and is broken;
Howl ye for her, take rosin for her wound,
It may be that she can be healed!
9 We have tried to heal Babylon,
But she was not healed;
Leave her, and let us depart,
Every one to his own land;
For to the heavens has reached her judgment
And has risen up to the clouds.
10 Brought forth has Jehovah our righteousness;
Come ye and let us declare in Sion
The work of Jehovah our God.

11 Polish the arrows, prepare the shields,
Rouse will Jehovah the spirit of the kings of Media;
For as to Babylon his thought is to destroy her.
For it is Jehovah's vengeance, the vengeance of his temple.
12 On the walls of Babylon raise the standard,
Increase the watch, set the watchmen,
Set in order the ambushes:
For as Jehovah has thought, so will he do
What he hath spoken concerning the inhabitants of Babylon.
13 Thou that dwellest among great waters,
Who aboundest in treasures,
Come is thine end, the measure of thy cupidity.

14 Sworn hath Jehovah by himself,—
Surely I will fill thee with men as with locusts,
Who will shout over thee with the vintage-shouting,—
15 (*Even*) he who made the earth by his power,
Who hath constituted the world by his wisdom,
And by his knowledge extended the heavens,
16 At whose voice there is abundance of waters in the heavens,
Who raises vapours from the extremity of the earth,
Who makes the lightnings and the rain,
And brings out the wind from his treasures.
17 Infatuated is every man become by his knowledge,
Put to shame shall be every founder by the graven image,
For a lie is the molten image,
And there is no breath in them:
18 Vanity are they, the work of illusions;
At the time of their visitation they shall perish.
19 Not like these is the portion of Jacob;
For the former of all things is He,
And the rod of his inheritance is Israel;
Jehovah of hosts is his name.

20 A hammer hast thou been to me, weapons of war;
And by thee have I broken nations in pieces,
And by thee destroyed kingdoms:
21 Yea, by thee have I broken in pieces
The horses and their riders,
And by thee have I broken in pieces
The chariots and their riders,[1]
22 And by thee have I broken in pieces
Men and women,
And by thee have I broken in pieces
Old men and children,
And by thee have I broken in pieces
Young men and maidens,
23 And by thee have I broken in pieces
The shepherds and their flocks,
And by thee have I broken in pieces
The husbandmen and their yokes of oxen,
And by thee have I broken in pieces
The captains and the rulers.
24 But I will render to Babylon
And to all the inhabitants of Chaldea,
All the evils which they have done in Sion,
Before your eyes, saith Jehovah.

25 Behold, I am against thee,
O destroying mountain, saith Jehovah,
Which destroyest all the earth;
And I will extend my hand over thee,
And will roll thee down from the rocks,
And will make thee a burnt mountain:
26 And they shall not take of thee a stone for a corner,
Nor a stone for foundations;
For perpetual wastes shalt thou be, saith Jehovah.

27 Raise a banner in the land,
Sound a trumpet among the nations,
Prepare the nations against her,
Assemble against her the kingdoms of Ararat,
Of Minni and of Ashkenaz;
Set up against her a leader,
Bring forth the horse as the horrible locust;
28 Prepare against her the nations,
The kings of Media, her captains and her princes,
And all the land of its dominion.
29 And tremble shall the land and be in pain,

[1] As Calvin in his commentary puts all the following nouns in the plural number, (though in Hebrew they are all in the singular number,) to render the whole consistent, the nouns in these lines have been put also in the plural number.—*Ed.*

For confirmed as to Babylon shall be the thoughts of Jehovah,
To set the land of Babylon a waste,
So as to have no inhabitant.

30 Ceased have the valiant men of Babylon to fight,
They sat down in their fortresses;
Fail did their valour, they became women,
Burnt were her dwellings, broken her bars.
31 A runner to meet a runner ran,
And a messenger to meet a messenger,
To announce to the king of Babylon
That taken was the city at its extremity;
32 And the fords were taken,
And the pools were burnt with fire,
And the men of war were broken in pieces.

33 For thus saith Jehovah of hosts, the God of Israel,—
The daughter of Babylon *shall be* like a threshing-floor,
(*Come will*) the time of treading her;
Yet a little while and come will her harvest.

34 Devoured me, broken me in pieces,
Hath Nebuchadnezzar, the king of Babylon;
He hath set me an empty vessel,
He hath swallowed me like a dragon,
He hath filled his belly with my delicacies,
He hath cast me off.
35 My plunder and my flesh be on Babylon,
Shall the inhabitant of Sion say;
My blood be on the inhabitants of Chaldea,
Shall Jerusalem say.
36 Therefore thus saith Jehovah,—
Behold, I will plead thy cause,
And avenge thy vengeance,
For I will make dry her sea,
And will dry up her fountain:
37 And Babylon shall become heaps
An habitation of dragons,
A wonder and a hissing, without an inhabitant.
38 They will roar as lions,
They will roar as whelps of lions.
39 In their heat will I make their feasts,
And make them drunk, that they may exult
And sleep a perpetual sleep,
And not awake, saith Jehovah.
40 I will bring them as lambs to the slaughter,
As rams and he-goats.

41 How has Sheshach been taken!

And captured, the praise of the whole land!
How has Babylon become a waste among nations!
42 Come up over Babylon has the sea,
With the multitude of its waves is she covered.
43 Her cities shall be a waste,
And a land of desert, and a land of drought,
Pass through it shall no man,
And dwell in it shall no son of man.
44 And I will visit Bel in Babylon;
And I will draw what he hath swallowed out of his mouth:
And flow to him together shall nations no more:
Even the wall of Babylon hath fallen.

45 Go out from the midst of her, my people,
And save ye, every one his life,
From the indignation of Jehovah's wrath.
46 And let not faint be your heart,
And fear ye not the rumour heard in the land;
Come in one year shall a rumour,
And afterwards in another year, a rumour;
And violence *shall be* in the land,
And a ruler after a ruler.
47 Therefore, behold, the days are coming,
That I will visit the images of Babylon;
And her whole land shall be ashamed,
And all her slain, they shall fall in the midst of her.
48 And rejoice over Babylon shall heaven and earth,
And all the things that are in them;
When from the north shall come to her
Destroyers, saith Jehovah.
49 As Babylon made to fall the slain of Israel,
So for Babylon they shall fall, the slain of all the land.
50 Ye who have escaped from the sword,
Depart, stand not still;
From afar remember Jehovah,
And let Jerusalem come to your minds.

51 We are ashamed, because we have heard reproach;
Shame hath covered our faces, because strangers came
Into the sanctuaries of the house of Jehovah.
52 Therefore, behold, the days are coming, saith Jehovah,
That I will visit her graven images,
And in the whole land groan shall the wounded.

53 Though Babylon ascended into heaven,
And though in the height she fortified her strength,
From me would come to her wasters, saith Jehovah.
54 The voice of a cry from Babylon!
And a great crashing from the land of the Chaldeans!

55 For Jehovah will lay waste Babylon,
And will destroy from her the voice of boasting:
And sound shall their waves like great waters,
Sent forth shall be the sound of their voice.
56 For come to her, to Babylon, is a waster,
And taken are her valiant men,
Broken is their bow;
For the God of retributions is Jehovah,
Recompensing he will recompense.
57 And I will inebriate her princes and her wise men,
And her captains, and her rulers, and her valiant men;
And they shall sleep a perpetual sleep,
And shall not awake, saith the King,
Whose name is Jehovah of hosts.
58 Thus saith Jehovah of hosts,—
The wall of Babylon, *though* wide,
Shall *yet* surely be demolished;
And her gates, *though* high,
Shall *yet* be consumed with fire:
Thus laboured have the people for nothing,
And the nations for the fire, and wearied themselves.

59 The word which Jeremiah the prophet commanded Seraiah,
the son of Neraiah, the son of Maaseiah, when he went for
Zedekiah, the king of Judah, to Babylon, in the fourth year of
60 his reign; and Seraiah was a quiet prince: and Jeremiah wrote
in a book all the evil that should come on Babylon, even all
61 these words which had been written against Babylon; and
Jeremiah said to Seraiah,—
"When thou comest to Babylon and hast seen it, then read
62 all these words, and say,—'O Jehovah, thou hast spoken
against this place, to destroy it, so that there should be no
inhabitant in it, neither man nor beast, but that it shall be-
63 come perpetual desolations.' And it shall be, when thou hast
made an end of reading this book, that thou shalt tie a stone
64 to it, and cast it into the midst of the Euphrates, and shalt
say,—'Thus sink shall Babylon, and shall not rise from the
evil which I shall bring on her, though they may weary themselves.'"

Thus far the words of Jeremiah.

CHAPTER LII.

1 Twenty-one years old was Zedekiah when he began to reign,
and eleven years reigned he in Jerusalem; and the name of
his mother was Hamutal, the daughter of Jeremiah of Libnah.
2 And he did evil in the sight of Jehovah, according to all the
3 things which Jehoiakim had done: and on account of the

indignation of Jehovah against Jerusalem and Judah, until he
cast them away from his presence, Zedekiah rebelled against
the king of Babylon.
4 And it was in the ninth year of his reign, in the tenth month,
in the tenth of the month, that Nebuchadnezzar, the king of
Babylon, came, he and all his army, against Jerusalem, and
encamped against it, and built against it a fortress on every
5 side. And the city was besieged till the eleventh year of Ze-
6 dekiah. In the fourth month, on the ninth of the month, the
famine prevailed in the city, so that there was no bread for
7 the people of the land: and the city was broken in upon, and
all the men of war fled, and went out of the city by night, by
the way of the gate, between two walls, which were near the
king's garden; (and the Chaldeans were near the city around:)
8 and they went out by the way of the desert. And the army
of the Chaldeans pursued the king, and they took Zedekiah in
the deserts of Jericho; for all his army were scattered from
9 him. They then took the king, and brought him to the king
of Babylon in Riblah, to the land of Hamath; who pronounced
judgment upon him.
10 And the king of Babylon slew the sons of Zedekiah before
his eyes; and all the princes of Judah he also slew in Riblah:
but he blinded the eyes of Zedekiah, and bound him with
11 chains; and the king of Babylon brought him to Babylon,
and put him in prison till the day in which he died.
12 Now, in the fifth month, in the tenth day of the month,
(that year was the nineteenth year of Nebuchadnezzar, the
king of Babylon,) Nebuzar-adan, the prince of the soldiers, who
13 stood before the king of Babylon, came into Jerusalem, and
burnt the house of Jehovah and the house of the king, and all the
houses of Jerusalem, even every great house he burnt with fire:
14 and all the walls of Jerusalem around they destroyed, even the
whole army of the Chaldeans, which was with the prince of
15 the soldiers. And some of the poor of the people and the
rest of the people who had remained in the city, and the fugitives who had fled over to the king of Babylon, and the remainder of the multitude, Nebuzar-adan, the prince of the
16 soldiers, led away captive. But some of the poor of the land,
Nebuzar-adan, the prince of the soldiers, left to be vinedressers
and husbandmen.
17 And the brass pillars which were in the house of Jehovah,
and the bases, and the brazen sea which was in the house of
Jehovah, the Chaldeans broke in pieces, and carried away all
18 their brass to Babylon. The pots also, and the shovels and
the snuffers and the basons and the spoons, and all the vessels
19 of brass, with which they ministered, they took away. And
the dishes and the pans and the basons and the pots and the
candlesticks and the spoons and the bowls, some of which were
all of gold and some were all of silver, the prince of the soldiers

20 took away. The two pillars, the one sea, and the twelve
oxen of brass, which were under the bases which Solomon had
made in the house of Jehovah, there was no weight as to the
21 brass of all these vessels. As to the pillars, the height of each
pillar was eighteen cubits, and a thread of twelve cubits surrounded it, and its thickness was four fingers; it was hollow.
22 And the chapiter which was over it was brass, and the height of
one chapiter was five cubits, and net-work and pomegranates
were on the chapiter around; all these were of brass; and like
23 these were the second pillar and the pomegranates. And
there were pomegranates, ninety-six on one side; all the
pomegranates on the net-work around were one hundred.

24 The prince of the soldiers took away also Seraiah, the chief
priest, and Zephaniah, the second priest, and the three keepers
25 of the door: and from the city he took away one eunuch, who
had been set over the men of war, and seven men of those who
attended the king, who were found in the city, and a scribe,
the chief of the army, who gathered to the army the people of
26 the land, and sixty men of the people of the land, who were
found in the midst of the city. And Nebuzar-adan, the prince
of the soldiers, took them away and brought them to the king
27 of Babylon in Riblah: and the king of Babylon smote them
and slew them in Riblah, in the land of Hamath; and he
removed Judah from his own land.

28 These are the people whom Nebuchadnezzar carried away
captive: in the seventh year, three thousand and twenty-
29 three Jews; in the eighteenth of Nebuchadnezzar, he carried
away captive from Jerusalem eight hundred and thirty-two
30 souls; in the three-and-twentieth year of Nebuchadnezzar,
Nebuzar-adan, the prince of the soldiers, carried away Jews,
seven hundred and forty-five souls;—all the souls were four
thousand and six hundred.

31 And it came to pass in the thirty-seventh year of Jehoiachin, the king of Judah, in the twelfth month, on the twenty-
fifth of the month, that Evil-merodach, the king of Babylon, in
the first year of his reign, lifted up the head of Jehoiachin, the
32 king of Judah, and brought him forth from prison; and he
spake kindly to him, and set his throne above the thrones of the
33 kings, who were with him in Babylon; and he changed his
prison garments, and ate bread before him always, all the days
34 of his life. And his portion, a perpetual portion was given
him by the king of Babylon every day, until the day he died,
all the days of his life.

PRAISE TO GOD.

A TRANSLATION

OF

CALVIN'S VERSION OF THE LAMENTATIONS.

CHAPTER I.

1 How sits solitary the city
  Which abounded in people!
How is she become as a widow,
  Who was great among the nations!
She who ruled among provinces
  Is become tributary!
2 Weeping she has wept in the night,
  And her tears are on her cheeks;
She has no comforter
  Among all her lovers;
All her friends have dealt falsely with her,
  They are become her enemies.

3 Migrated hath Judah because of oppression,
  And because of much servitude;
She dwelleth among the nations,
  She finds no rest;
All who pursued her
  Have taken her between the straits.
4 The ways of Sion mourn,
  For they come not to the festivals;
All her gates are desolate,
  Her priests are sighing;
Her virgins are afflicted,
  And she is in bitterness!
5 Her adversaries have become the head,
  Her enemies have prospered;
Because Jehovah hath afflicted her
  For the greatness of her iniquities:
Her little ones have gone into exile
  Before the adversary;
6 And departed from the daughter of Sion
  Has all her glory;
Her princes have become like harts,
  Who cannot find pasture;

And they have gone without strength
Before their pursuer.
7 Remember did Jerusalem,
In the days of her affliction and want,
All her desirable things,
Which were from ancient days;
When fall did her people into the hand of the enemy,
And she had no helper:
Seen her have enemies,
They laughed at her Sabbath.

8 A sin hath Jerusalem sinned,
Therefore she is become a wanderer;
All who honoured her have despised her,
Because they have seen her nakedness;
She even groaned,
And turned backward:
9 Her shame is in her skirts;
She remembered not her end;
Therefore she came down wonderfully,
She hath no comforter:
See, Jehovah, my affliction,
For magnified himself hath the enemy.

10 His hand did the enemy stretch out
To all her desirable things;
For she saw the heathens,
When they entered her sanctuary,
Respecting whom thou hast commanded,
They shall not come to thy congregation.
11 All her people are sighing,
They are seeking bread;
They have given their desirable things
For food, to restore life:
See, Jehovah, and look,
For I am vile.

12 Is it nothing to all of you
Who pass by the way?
Look and see, if there be a sorrow
Like the sorrow that is come to me;
For afflicted me hath Jehovah,
In the day of the indignation of his wrath.
13 From on high hath he sent fire into my bones,
And it hath prevailed over them:
He hath spread his net for my feet,
He hath turned me backward;
He hath made me desolate,
Sorrowing all the day.

14 Tied is the yoke of mine iniquities by his hand,
They are twined together:
They have come up on my neck,
He hath weakened my strength:
Given me up hath the Lord,
Into the hand of my enemies,
From whom I shall not be able to rise.
15 Trodden under foot all my valiant men
Hath the Lord in the midst of me:
He hath brought on me the fixed time
To destroy my young men;
The winepress hath the Lord trodden,
As to the virgin, the daughter of Judah.

16 For this I weep; mine eye! mine eye!
Waters flow down;
For removed far from me is a comforter,
Who might revive my soul;
My children are become desolate,
For prevailed has the enemy.
17 Expand did Sion her hands,
She had no comforter;
Given a charge had Jehovah as to Jacob,
To his adversaries all around him;
Become is Jerusalem
An abomination among them.

18 Righteous is Jehovah,
For his mouth have I provoked.

Hear, I pray, all ye people,
And behold my sorrow:
My virgins and my young men,
They are gone into captivity.
19 I called to my friends,
They deceived me;
My priests and my elders,
In the city they expired,
While they were seeking food for themselves,
To revive their soul.

20 See, Jehovah, for I am distressed,
My bowels are troubled;
Overwhelmed is my heart within me,
For rebelling I have rebelled:
Without bereaves the sword,
Within it is as death,
21 They have heard that I mourn,
That I have no comforter;

All mine enemies have heard of my evil;
They rejoice that thou hast done it,
And brought the day thou hast announced:
But they shall be as I am.
22 Let all their wickedness
Come into thy presence;
And do to them as thou hast done
To me for all my sins;
For my sighings are many,
And my heart is weak.

CHAPTER II.

1 How hath the Lord clouded in his wrath
The daughter of Sion!
He hath cast down from heaven to the earth
The glory of Israel;
And hath not remembered his footstool
In the day of his wrath!
2 Destroyed hath the Lord, and spared not,
All the habitations of Jacob;
He hath demolished in his indignation
The fortresses of the daughter of Judah;
He hath cast them to the ground, he hath profaned
Her kingdom and her princes.
3 He hath broken in the indignation of his wrath
Every horn of Israel;
He hath withdrawn his right hand
From before the enemy;
And he burned like fire in Jacob,
The flame devoured all around.
4 Bent hath he his bow as an enemy,
Stand did his right hand as an adversary,
And he slew all the delights of the eye
In the tabernacle of the daughter of Sion
He hath poured forth
As fire, his wrath.

5 The Lord hath been like an enemy,
He hath destroyed Israel;
He hath destroyed all his palaces,
He hath demolished his fortresses;
He hath increased in the daughter of Judah
Mourning and lamentation:
6 And he hath removed as a garden
His tabernacle;
He hath destroyed his testimony;
Forgotten hath Jehovah in Sion
The assembly and the Sabbath;

He hath rejected, in the indignation of his wrath,
The king and the priest:
7 Abhorred hath Jehovah his altar,
He hath cast off his sanctuary;
Given up hath he into the hand of the enemy
The walls of her palaces:
A noise they made in the house of Jehovah,
As on the day of the assembly.

8 Resolve did Jehovah to destroy the wall
Of the daughter of Sion;
He extended a line,
He drew not back his hand from scattering;
Therefore mourned hath the rampart and the wall,
They have fallen together.
9 Sunk have her gates in the ground;
He hath destroyed and broken her bars;
Her king and her princes,
They are among the heathens;
There is no law, her prophets,
They find no vision from Jehovah:
10 They sit on the ground, they are silent,
The elders of the daughter of Sion;
They cast dust on their head,
They gird themselves with sackcloth;
Bend to the ground their head
Do the virgins of Jerusalem.

11 Consume with tears did mine eyes,
Troubled were my bowels;
Poured forth on the ground was my liver,
For the breach of the daughter of my people;
When the child and the suckling
Vanished away in the streets of the city.
12 To their mothers they say,—
"Where is corn and wine?"
While they vanish away, as a dying man,
In the streets of the city,
And while they pour out their souls
Into the bosom of their mothers

13 What can I testify to thee? What can I compare to thee,
O daughter of Jerusalem?
What can I liken to thee, to comfort thee,
O virgin, the daughter of Sion?
For great as the sea is thy breach,
Who can heal thee?
14 Thy prophets have seen for thee
Vanity and insipidity.

And they disclosed not thine iniquity,
  That they might reverse thy captivity;
And they saw for thee
  Prophecies of vanity and expulsions.
15 They clapped at thee their hands,
  All who passed by on the road;
They hissed and moved their head
  At the daughter of Jerusalem,—
"Is this the city of which they said,
  Perfect in beauty, the joy of all the earth?"
16 Opened at thee their mouth
  Have all thine enemies;
They hissed and gnashed the teeth,
  They said, "We shall devour her,
Surely the day which we expected
  We have found, we have seen."

17 Jehovah hath done what he had purposed;
  He hath fulfilled his word,
Which he had commanded from days of old;
  He hath overthrown and not spared;
And he hath made to rejoice over thee the enemy,
  He hath raised up the horn of thine adversaries.
18 Cry out did their heart to the Lord:
  O wall of the daughter of Sion,
Make tears to flow down
  As a river, day and night;
Give thyself no rest,
  Let not the pupil of thine eye cease.
19 Rise, cry aloud in the night,
  At the beginning of the watches;
Pour out like waters
  Thy heart before the Lord;
Raise up to him thy hands
  For the life of thy little ones,
Who faint through famine
  At the head of all the streets.

20 See, Jehovah, and look,
  To whom thou hast done this:
Should women eat their own fruit,
  Infants while nursed!
Should they be slain in the Lord's sanctuary,
  The priest and the prophet!
21 Lie on the ground in the streets
  Did boys and old men;
My virgins and my young men,
  They fell by the sword:
Thou hast killed in the day of thy wrath,
  Thou hast slaughtered and not spared.

22 Thou hast summoned, as on a festive day,
My terrors all around;
And in the day of the indignation of Jehovah,
There was none surviving or remaining;
Whom I nursed and brought up,
The enemy consumed them.

CHAPTER III.

1 I am a man who hath seen affliction
Through the rod of his indignation:
2 Me hath he led and made to go
Into darkness, and not into light.
3 Surely against me is he turned,
He turns his hand daily.
4 To grow old hath he made my flesh and my skin,
He hath broken my bones.
5 He hath builded against me,
And surrounded me with gall and trouble.
6 In darkness hath he made me to lie
As the dead for ever.
7 He hath shut me up, that I cannot go forth,
He hath made heavy my fetter.
8 Even when I cried, and cried aloud,
He shut out my prayer.
9 He hath enclosed my ways with hewn stones,
My paths hath he perverted.
10 A bear lying in wait hath he been to me,
A lion in his den.
11 My ways hath he perverted, and he hath torn me,
He hath made me a waste.
12 He hath bent his bow, and made me
As a mark for the arrow.
13 He hath made to enter into my reins
The sons of his quiver.
14 I became a derision to all my people,
Their song all the day.
15 He hath satiated me with bitterness,
He hath filled me with gall.
16 He hath broken with pebbles my teeth,
He hath covered me with dust,
17 And far removed from peace is my soul;
I have forgotten good.
18 And I said, "Perished hath my strength
And my hope from Jehovah;"
19 When I remember my affliction and my trouble,
The poison and the gall:

20 Remembering remember does my soul,
And it is humbled within me:
21 This will I recall to my mind,
Therefore will I hope.

22 The mercies of Jehovah! surely they are not consumed;
Surely failed not have his compassions;
23 Renewed are they in the morning;
Great is thy faithfulness.
24 My portion is Jehovah, said my soul,
Therefore will I hope in him.

25 Good is Jehovah to him who waits for him,
To the soul that seeks him;
26 Good it is to hope and to be silent,
As to the salvation of Jehovah;
27 Good it is for a man
To bear the yoke in his youth:
28 He will sit apart, and be silent,
For he will raise it on himself;
29 He will put in the dust his mouth,
If so be that there is hope;
30 He will give to the smiter his cheek,
He will be filled with reproaches.
31 For not cast away for ever
Will the Lord;
32 For though he causes grief, he will yet show compassion,
According to the multitude of his mercies;
33 For he does not from his heart afflict,
Nor cause grief to the children of men.

34 When one tears under his feet
All the bound of the earth,—
35 When he perverts man's judgment
Before the face of the Most High,—
36 When he turns a man aside in his cause,—
The Lord does not regard.
37 Who is this that says, "It was,
And God has not commanded?"
38 From the mouth of the Most High
Can not good and evil proceed?
39 Why should he weary himself, a living man,
And a man in his sins?

40 Let us examine our ways, and search,
And turn to Jehovah;
41 Let us lift up our hearts with our hands
To God in the heavens.
42 We have sinned, and have been rebellious,
Thou hast not spared;

43 Thou hast covered us over in wrath, and pursued us,
Thou hast slain and not spared.
44 Thou hast covered thyself with a cloud,
So that prayer cannot pass through.
45 An offscouring and a refuse hast thou made us
In the midst of the nations;
46 Opened at us their mouth
Have all our enemies;
47 Fear and the pit have come to us,
Desolation and a breach.
48 Rivers of waters mine eye brings down,
For the breach of the daughter of my people:
49 Mine eye flows down and rests not;
There will be no intermissions,
50 Until Jehovah looks down,
And beholds from heaven.
51 Mine eye grieves my soul,
Because of all the daughters of my city.
52 Hunting they have hunted me as a sparrow,
Who are mine enemies without cause;
53 They have made fast in a pit my life,
And cast a stone over me;
54 Flowed have waters over my head;
I said, I am cut off.

55 I called on thy name, Jehovah,
From the deepest pit:
56 My voice hast thou heard; close not thine ear
To my groaning, to my cry.
57 Thou didst draw nigh in the day I cried to thee,
Thou didst say, "Fear not:"
58 Thou hast, O Lord, pleaded the causes of my soul,
Thou hast redeemed my life.
59 Thou hast seen, O Jehovah, my oppression;
Defend my cause.
60 Thou hast seen all their vengeances,
All their counsels against me.
61 Thou hast heard, O Jehovah, their reproaches,
All their counsels against me,—
62 The speeches of those who rose against me,
And their words against me daily.
63 Look on their sitting down and their rising up;
I am their song.
64 Render to them their reward, O Jehovah,
According to the work of their hands.
65 Give them blindness of heart;
Thy curse *be* on them.
66 Pursue them in wrath, and destroy them
From under the heavens of Jehovah.

CHAPTER IV.

1 How obscured is the gold!
How changed is the fine gold!
Cast forth have been the stones of the sanctuary
At the head of all the streets!
2 The precious sons of Sion,
Clothed in gold,
How they are counted as earthen pitchers,
The work of the potter's hands!

3 Even serpents draw out the breast,
They suckle their young ones:
The daughter of my people was cruel,
Like the ostriches in the desert.
4 Cleave did the tongue of the suckling
To the roof of his mouth for thirst;
The little ones asked bread,
No one divided to them.
5 They who fed on delicacies
Perished in the streets;
They who had been brought up in scarlet
Embraced the dunghills:
6 And the punishment of the daughter of my people
Has been greater than the punishment of Sodom,
Which was overthrown as in a moment,
And no strokes remained on her.

7 Purer were her Nazarites than snow,
Whiter than milk;
They were ruddy in their body,
Above precious stones;
Sapphire was their polish:
8 Darker than darkness became their form,
They were not known in the streets;
Cleave did their skin to their bones,
It became dry as wood.

9 Better were the slain with the sword
Than the slain with famine:
They pined away, having been pierced through
By the fruits of the field.
10 The hands of compassionate mothers
Boiled their own offspring;
They became food for them,
At the destruction of the daughter of my people.

11 Fulfilled has Jehovah his wrath;
He poured forth the indignation of his wrath;
And he kindled a fire in Sion,
Which devoured her foundations.
12 They could not have believed, the kings of the earth,
Nor all the inhabitants of the world,
That enter would the adversary and the enemy
Into the gates of Jerusalem.
13 For the sin of her prophets,
The iniquities of her priests,
Who shed in the midst of her
The blood of the righteous,—
14 They wandered blind in the streets,
They were polluted with blood;
Because they could not
But touch their garments.
15 Depart ye, "Unclean," they cried to them,
Depart, depart, come not near:
Because they fled, and also wandered,
They said among the Gentiles,
"They shall not return to dwell;
16 The face of Jehovah hath divided them,
He will no more regard them."
The face of the priests they respected not,
And to the elders they shewed no mercy.

17 While we were yet standing, our eyes failed,
As to our vain help;
In our looking out we looked out
To a nation that could not save us.

18 They hunted our steps,
So that we could not walk in our streets;
Draw near did our end, fulfilled were our days,
Surely come did our end.
19 Swifter were our pursuers
Than the eagles of heaven;
On the mountains they followed us,
They lay in wait for us in the desert.
20 The spirit of our nostrils, the anointed of Jehovah,
Was taken in their snares;
Of whom we said, "Under his shadow
We shall live among the nations."

21 Rejoice and be glad, thou daughter of Edom,
Who dwellest in the land of Uz!
To thee also shall the cup pass over,
Thou shalt be inebriated and made naked.

22 Completed is thy punishment, O daughter of Sion,
He will no more deliver thee into exile;
He will visit thine iniquity, O daughter of Edom,
And will uncover thy sin.

CHAPTER V.

1 Remember, O Jehovah, what has come to us;
Look, and see our reproach:
2 Our heritage is turned over to foreigners,
Our houses to aliens.
3 Orphans are we become, without a father;
Our mothers are as widows.
4 Our own water, for money we drink;
Our own wood, for a price it comes to us.
5 On our necks have we suffered persecution;
We have laboured, and had no rest.
6 To the Egyptians we extended the hand,
To the Assyrians, to be satisfied with bread.

7 Our fathers sinned, and are not;
And we their iniquities have borne.
8 Servants have ruled over us;
None delivered from their hands.
9 With our life have we procured our bread,
Because of the drought of the desert.
10 Our skins are like an oven black,
Because of the burnings of famine.

11 Women in Sion have been ravished,
Virgins in the cities of Judah.
12 Princes by their own hand were hung,
The faces of elders were not honoured.
13 Young men they took to grind,
And boys under the wood fell.
14 Elders ceased from the gate,
Young men from their music.
15 Ceased has the joy of our heart,
Turned into mourning has our dance.
16 Fallen has the crown of our head;
Woe now to us, for we have sinned!
17 Therefore faint is our heart;
For this darkened are our eyes,
18 *Even* for mount Sion, which is desolate;
Foxes pass through it.

19 Thou Jehovah for ever sittest,
Thy throne is through all ages.

20 Why shouldest thou perpetually forget us,
    And forsake us for ever?
21 Turn us, Jehovah, to thee, and we shall be turned;
    Renew our days as of old;
22 Except thou hast wholly rejected us,
    And hast become very angry with us.

PRAISE TO GOD.

INDEX

OF HEBREW WORDS EXPLAINED.

Vol. Page

אבירים v. 143
אדם ii. 291
אהבים v. 305
אולי i. 263; iii. 310; iv. 327; v. 418
און i. 223
אוץ ii. 369
אזור ii. 160
אחרי ii. 200, 201
אהרית iii. 432, 433
אי, אין i. 269
איבי v. 340
איים v. 182
איכה v. 301, 303
אימים v. 181
איש ii. 291; iii. 247
אך i. 144, 175, 263, 265; ii. 120; iii. 339; iv. 190
אל ii. 6, 179; iii. 382, 451; iv. 204, 352, 577; v. 198
אלה iii. 155, 443, 448; iv. 498, 537.
אלי i. 198
אל־תעמדו i. 208
אם i. 366; iii. 86
אם לא v. 193
אמון iv. 599
אמונה i. 408, 462
אמור iii. 119
אמן iv. 234
אמת iv. 234; v. 216

Vol. Page

אנש אנוש ii. 291
אנשים iv. 549
אנשי המלחמה iv. 476
אסף i. 440; ii. 44
אף i. 239; ii. 341; iii. 302
אפי ii. 276; iv. 192
אצר v. 62
ארחה iv. 447
אריצם v. 190
ארך ii. 280
ארמון iv. 36
אשבע i. 270
אשר i. 243, 484; ii. 319; iv. 106, 200, 239; v. 196
את ii. 6; v. 287
את הדברים iii. 83
אתבש iii. 278
אתם i. 134; iii. 426

ב ii. 231, 413: iv. 107
בא ii. 148
באמת iii. 400
באר i. 322
בגד i. 169, 277
בגדה i. 170
בגדים i. 460
בדים v. 34, 178
בהו i. 236
בהלות ii. 265
בו iv. 106
בון v. 65
בור i. 322; iv. 376

Vol. Page

בחורים i. 331, 333, 493
בחן i. 355; ii. 115
ביהוה i. 278
בים דאגה v. 97
בית iv. 429
בכה iv. 92; v. 9
בלג i. 446
בלע v. 261
במה iv. 200
בן iv. 106
בנה v. 65
בנפשותיכם ii. 378
בססו ii. 141
בעל i. 178
בעלתי i. 178; iv. 129
בער ii. 39
בערלה i. 504
בצע iii. 105
בצר, בצרה ii. 298
בקבק ii. 432, 444
בראשונה i. 379
ברית ii. 89
בשו ii. 149
בת v. 458

גאון ii. 133, 164, 165
גאל iv. 79
גבים ii. 206
גבר iv. 114
גברים i. 285; iv. 476; v. 179
גדלות iv. 570
גדר גדרה v. 393
גוים i. 407, 507
גוים רבים iii. 261
גוי־שליו v. 109

Vol. Page

גזז, גזית v. 395
גזל iii. 69, 77
גור iv. 51
גורים v. 459
גיא הנם i. 412; ii. 434
גלל iv. 325
גם i. 98, 142, 289, 429, 438; ii. 197; iii. 261; iv. 57, 104, 453, 595; v. 12, 215, 458
גרע iii. 308

דאב iv. 118
דאג ii. 352
דבר ii. 202
דברים ii. 203
דור i. 134, 409
דוש v. 143
דמה i. 442
דמיתי i. 315
דמעה ii. 231
דן ii. 269
דעי i. 344
דרך i. 461
דרש iii. 420; iv. 368
דשא ii. 208
דשאה v. 143
דשן iv. 88

ה v. 325
האמרים iii. 72
האסור iv. 376
הבל ii. 40
הגה v. 35, 310, 326, 451
הגבירה iii. 415
הגידו i. 207
הגליתי iii. 421
הוא זה iv. 44, 74
החזיקו בם v. 176
החניות iv. 376
החרם אחריהם v. 159
הטוב v. 455
הידד iii. 289; v. 37, 218
היונה iv. 590

Vol. Page

הכרם i. 313
הלך i. 464; iv. 53, 543
הלכתם iii. 434
הלל v. 181
המון ii. 36; iv. 599
הנה iv. 412
הנני ii. 312; iv. 301, 513
הפגעתי ii. 272
הפנה iv. 147
הצרים עליכם iii. 64
הקימו iv. 52
הקמתי iv. 250
הראשנים ii. 87
הרכה iv. 589
הרס iv. 122
הרע iii. 286
הררי ii. 339

ואל־יתעל v. 198
ואם עמדו iii. 172
ואת־הנשארים iii. 60
וגם iii. 339; iv. 348
ויבאו iv. 510
ולא ידעו ii. 233
ולא תנור i. 199
ונדמה־שם i. 442
ונפל v. 174

זארם v. 197
זאת v. 406
זהב v. 456
זון i. 271
זוע iii. 236
זמת ii. 198
זקן i. 333
זרה ii. 262

חול v. 463
חזון iii. 170
חזק v. 175, 176
חטא ii. 237
חטאת v. 462
חיל iv. 597
חלי ii. 48
חלותי ii. 48
חלל iii. 296; iv. 61

Vol. Page

חללים v. 41
חמס v. 353
חמר v. 339
המרמרו v. 363
חמתי iv. 192
חסד i. 70
חפץ i. 327, 330
חק ii. 13
חקים ii. 13
חקר iv. 598
חרב v. 501
חרבה iii. 255; iv. 9, 529
חרון i. 239; iii. 302; v. 327
חרם iv. 149
חרס ii. 432
חרסית ii. 432
חרש ii. 432, 435
חשב v. 7
חת i. 62; iii. 72
חתת v. 117, 179

טבח iv. 430
טהר iv. 236
טובה iii. 224
טמא טמא יקרא v. 475

יאש i. 122, 403
יאתה ii. 20
יגה v. 326
יגון iv. 568
ידידות ii. 136
יזן i. 271
יחול iii. 173, 175
יחשיך ii. 180
יין iv. 590
ילד iv. 106
ינה iii. 304
יסורי ii. 363
יסר iii. 352; iv. 97
יעור i. 350
יעלה v. 10
יענה v. 182
יפה ii. 441
יצא iv. 148
ירד i. 135
ישבי v. 196
ישבען i. 270
ישיבו iv. 285

Vol. Page
ישם v. 194
ישר iii. 71
יתאונן v. 431
יתרת v. 41

כ ii. 6,178,413
כאשר i. 162; iv. 263
כבד iv. 38
כבש ii. 111
כוה i. 386
כון, כונים i. 386
כושל iv. 589
כחש i. 278
כי i. 109, 247; ii. 6, 144, 221; iii. 126, 212, 384; iv. 107, 376, 501, 598; v. 49, 88, 190, 269, 407
כי אם i. 365; iii. 81
כי מר i. 227
כי נגע i. 227
כידון i. 350
כי על־כן iii. 457
ככר iv. 382
כל iv. 240
כל־דרכי קשת v. 169
כל־היום v. 391
כלה i. 240, 275
כלי iii. 123
כלילת v. 373
כלל i. 275; v. 373
כן v. 34
כנע ii. 44
כרם ii. 143
כשל ii. 407; v. 173, 329
כתם v. 455, 456

ל ii. 37, 231; iii. 105, 137; iv. 293
לא v. 198
לאד iv. 543
לא אצתי ii. 369
לא התאויתי ii. 370
לא כן בדיו v. 35
לא יהוה לו iv. 355
לאמר i. 152
לבו הרע ii. 405
לדוד iv. 252
להם iv. 282
להרגיעו iv. 54
לטובה ii. 218
לי ii. 263
ליהוה i. 278
לך i. 69; iv. 570
לכן i. 256; iv. 32; v. 101, 276
למלכת i. 386
לנוע ii. 215
לנפשותיכם ii. 378
לענה i. 485; iii. 164
לקח iii. 202, 203

מאבם v. 165
מאום v. 440
מאין ii. 21
מבלגיתי i. 446
מבצר i. 355
מגלה iv. 325
מגן iv. 575
מגנת־לך v. 453
מדבר i. 475
מדוחים v. 372
מדוע iv. 576
מהם i. 441
מהפכת iii. 16
מוג v. 97
מוזן i. 271
מול i. 504
מוסר i. 407; ii. 384; iii. 352; iv. 198, 316
מוסרות iii. 352
מועד iv. 592; v. 331, 354
מות ii. 179
מחלמים iii. 425
מטרא v. 398
מישור iii. 71
מכאב iv. 568
מלא ii. 135
מלאת iii. 427
מלחמה i. 229
מלך iv. 543
מלכם v. 55
ממרום v. 328
מן ii. 369; v. 36, 443
מנאפים i. 459
מנחה ii. 220, 388; iv. 260, 462
מסב iii. 55
מסביב iii. 19
מעט iv. 39
מעל iii. 238
מראשון ii. 361
מרבק iv. 595
מרוד v. 314
מרום ii. 360
מרזה ii. 306
מרמה i. 304
משא iii. 205, 216
משאה iv. 447
משאת i. 314; v. 371
משגע iii. 453
משבה i. 165
משל iii. 237, 444
משם v. 140
משפט i. 254, 264; ii. 62
מתי־עד ii. 201
מתנודד iv. 96

נא iv. 600
נאנחים v. 324
נאם יהוה iii. 203
נאץ iii. 169
נבל ii. 169, 357
נבלה iii. 449
נדה v. 334
נואש ii. 403, 404
נוד ii. 259; iv. 96
נזר i. 409
נחם ii. 260;

Vol. Page
נחם iv. 489
נחשת iv. 597
נחת iii. 72
נטה ii. 35
נטל v. 416
נטש ii. 136; iii. 217
נידה v. 319
נסך ii. 39
נער i. 31
נפל iii. 64; iv. 374
נפץ v. 18, 230
נפש ii. 378; iv. 118
נצר i. 225
נצרים i. 224
נקה iii. 288; iv. 23
נקרא iii. 287
נשא i. 314, 384; iii. 216; v. 440
נשה iii. 216
נשף ii. 178
נתק ii. 126
נתש ii. 153

סבב iv. 114
סוד ii. 287
סוף v. 94
סור i. 112, 332
סורו v. 475
סורים i. 112
סורר i. 297; v. 397
סחב iv. 398; v. 194
סחי v. 439
סלחים iv. 398
סללות iv. 184, 232
סמר v. 239
ספר iv. 325
ספרים iv. 337
סריסים iii. 415; iv. 296
סרי סררים i. 356

עבד i. 107; ii. 167; iii. 367; iv. 13
עבדו iii. 260
עבים i. 244
עבר i. 107; iii. 152; iv. 282
עברתו v. 33
עד iv. 138
עדה i. 344
עול v. 414
עולם ii. 413; iii. 254; v. 79, 112
עון ii. 229; iii. 288; v. 462
עונה iii. 361
עור ii. 265
עות v. 450
עותתי v. 449
עזב ii. 136
עזה iv. 610
עזי ומעזי ii. 330
עטף v. 364
עיפה iv. 118
עיר ii. 265
על iv. 231, 352; v. 369
על דברי הבצרות ii. 203
עלה v. 20
עלו v. 416
על־כן i. 267
עלל v. 326
עמוד i. 65
עמיד i. 495
עמק iv. 615
עמרה iv. 610
ענה ii. 210; v. 397
ענן,עננים iii. 361
עצר,עצרת i. 459
עצור iv. 350
עקב i. 464
ערב iii. 271; iv. 44
ערך iv. 575
ערמים v. 166
ערער ii. 347; v. 10, 11
ערף ii. 414
עשב ii. 208
עשות iii. 105
עשק i. 319; iii. 69, 105

פאה i. 506
פגע ii. 272; iii. 380
פדה iv. 79
פוץ iii. 123, 300
פחד ,פחת v. 440
פלא iv. 170, 186
פלאים ,פלאות v. 321
פלטים iv. 539
פליטים iv. 559
פלץ v. 83
פן i. 62
פסל v. 223
פקד ii. 254
פקותם v. 42
פרם ii. 308
פרסות iv. 612
פרש i. 250; v. 333
פשה iii. 19; v. 397
פתאם i. 355

צהל ii. 198; v. 143
צור ii. 298
צח i. 215
ציים v. 182
ציץ v. 13
צל ii. 179
צלמות ii. 179
צנה iv. 575
צער iv. 39, 600
צרה i. 249
צרי i. 455; v. 207
צרף v. 223

קדקד v. 50
קדש iii. 86
קוה ii. 212
קול i. 249
קום iv. 247
קינות v. 301
קיר־הרשת v. 35
קלה ,קלל iii. 448
קנה ii. 429; iv. 224

	Vol.	Page
קסם	iii.	361
קץ קצוצים	i.	506;
	v.	111
קרא	ii.	357;
	iv.	348;
	v.	290, 341
קרע	iv.	348
קשר	i.	138
ראיתי	ii.	199
ראש	i.	441, 481;
	iii.	164;
	v.	399
ראשה	ii.	184
ראשונה	ii.	325
רבה	v.	169
רבו	iv.	598
רבים	iii.	261, 357;
	v.	169, 184
רבק	iv.	595
רגע	v.	89, 190
רדה	i.	136;
	v.	327
רדנו	i.	135
רוד	i.	135
	v.	314
רוה	iv.	88
רוח	iii.	97
רוץ	iii.	105
רכל, רכיל	i.	464, 465
רם	iv.	122
רעה	ii.	229;
	iii.	395
רעות	iv.	533
רשעים	i.	303;
	iv.	51
שאון	iii.	292;
	iv.	590
שאל	ii.	250
שאנן	iv.	605
שארית	iii.	273
שבו	iii.	246
שבר	v.	278, 440
שדד	v.	37, 280
שדדי	v.	69.
שוב	i.	165, 423;
	v.	194
שום	v.	94
שור	i.	303
שורק	i.	112, 113
שחת	iii.	86
שכל	ii.	52
	v.	141
שכם	i.	402
שכנתי	i.	369;
	v.	215
שלום	iii.	169
שליו	v.	109
שם	ii.	143
שמה	ii.	445
שמועה	ii.	53;
	v.	80
שמם	i.	91, 454;
	iii.	255;
	v.	94, 194
שממה	iv.	529
שמנו	i.	305
שמע	iv.	284;
	v.	339
שנינה	iii.	237
שער	i.	308;
	ii.	406
שערים	iii.	442
שעררת	ii.	406
שפט	iv.	36
שקד	i.	40
שקר	i.	461;
	ii.	40;
	iii.	409
שר	iii.	19
שרי	iii.	415
שרים	v.	179
שרת	iv.	262
תבל	ii.	35
תהו	i.	236
תודה	ii.	388
תוכל	i.	163
תחנונים	iv.	72
תחת	i.	432
תמיד	i.	322
תעה	iv.	501
תער	iv.	346
תעשו	iii.	81
תעתעים	v.	224
תף	ii.	441
תפש	i.	82
תפת	i.	412;
	ii.	442
תשוב	i.	198
תתו	ii.	35

INDEX

OF PASSAGES QUOTED OR EXPLAINED.

GENESIS.

Chap.	Ver.	Vol.	Page
i.	9	i.	295
	22	ii.	301
	26, 27	v.	315
iii.	6, 7	v.	315
iv.	9, 13	ii.	315
vi.	3	iv.	351
viii.	17	ii.	301
ix.	6	iv.	473
	1, 7	ii.	301
xii.	3	i.	95
	7	iv.	19
xv.	5	iv.	265
		v.	157
	13	iv.	19
xvii.	1	ii.	392
	2	ii.	430
	10	i.	205
xviii.	20, 21	ii.	210
xxii.	2	i.	413
	17	iv.	39
	18	i.	95
xxv.	3, 15	iii.	275
	13, 16	v.	103
	27	iii.	64
xxvi.	4	i.	95
		iv.	266
xxviii.	14	iv.	266
xxx.	33	v.	210
xliii.	14	iv.	492
xlvii.	9	iv.	83

EXODUS.

Chap.	Ver.	Vol.	Page
iii.	8	ii.	79
	12	iv.	561
	21	iv.	297
xi.	3	iv.	297
xiii.	5	ii.	79
xv.	7	ii.	164
xvii.	15	iii.	144
xx.	5	i.	109
		ii.	315
		v.	500
	6	iii.	93
		iv.	171
xx.	8	ii.	383
	10	ii.	381
	11	ii.	382
	12	ii.	381
	18	i.	372
	24	ii.	241
xxi.	2	iv.	281
xxxi.	13	ii.	381
xxxii.	32	iii.	393
xxxiii.	3	ii.	79
xxxiv.	7	ii.	315
	14	i.	105

LEVITICUS.

Chap.	Ver.	Vol.	Page
xiii.	45	v.	475
xix.	10	i.	325
	13	iii.	95
	16	i.	357
			465
	23, 25	iv.	61
xx.	10	i.	153
xxi.	1	ii.	309
xxii.	24	ii.	79
xxvi.	19	i.	159
		ii.	203
	30	i.	411
	34, 35	v.	316
	43	v.	316

NUMBERS.

Chap.	Ver.	Vol.	Page
xiv.	18	ii.	175
			400
			427
xviii.	21	iv.	163
xix.	11, 16	i.	415
xxi.	27	v.	51
	28	v.	49
	29	v.	12
	30	v.	7

DEUTERONOMY.

Chap.	Ver.	Vol.	Page
ii.	26	v.	7
iv.	6-8	i.	233
		v.	276
			312
	15	ii.	378
	29	iii.	233
v.	9	ii.	315
	14	ii.	381
	22, 23	i.	372
	33	iii.	181
		iv.	181
x.	12	iii.	233
xi.	32	i.	482
xii.	4, 5	iv.	200
	26	iv.	64
xiii.	3	i.	311
		iii.	373
xv.	6	v.	498
	16, 17	iv.	281
xvii.	6	iv.	527
	12	iii.	14
	16	iv.	494
xviii.	18	iii.	372
		iv.	527
		v.	122
xxii.	22	i.	153
	21-24	v.	504
xxiv.	16	iv.	172
	21	i.	325
xxvii.	15, 16	ii.	74
	26	ii.	121
		iii.	156
xxviii.	13	v.	310
	30	iv.	61
	37	iii.	236
		iv.	251
	58	iii.	156
	66, 67	iv.	418
xxix.	4	i.	211
		iii.	228
	18	i.	485
	25	iii.	407
	29	iii.	183
xxx.	1, 2, 3	iii.	439
	4	iv.	70
			206
		v.	477
	12	i.	233
		iii.	181
xxx.	12-14	v.	377
	15-19	iii.	267
			313
xxxii.	8, 9	ii.	195
	15	iii.	113
		iv.	97
	29	v.	320
	30	i.	96
	32	i.	485
		ii.	248

JOSHUA.

Chap.	Ver.	Vol.	Page
vii.	19	ii.	177
xxiii.	11	ii.	378

JUDGES.

Chap.	Ver.	Vol.	Page
iii.	15	v.	280
vi.	36-40	iv.	561
xi.	24	v.	12
xx.	32	ii.	126

RUTH.

Chap.	Ver.	Vol.	Page
i.	17	v.	79

1 SAMUEL.

Chap.	Ver.	Vol.	Page
ii.	6	ii.	414
		iii.	150
		iv.	122
	7	ii.	246
	10	v.	484
xiv.	44	v.	79
xv.	22	i.	396
			411
		ii	102
			328
		iii.	312
	35	ii.	96
xvi.	1	ii.	96
	7	i.	258

2 SAMUEL.

Chap.	Ver.	Vol.	Page
iii.	35	v.	79
vii.	12, 13	iv.	266
	14, 15	ii.	61
			236
xii.	29	v.	58
xvi.	5, 6	v.	428
xix.	31,37	iv.	476

1 KINGS.

Chap.	Ver.	Vol.	Page
ix.	7	iii.	236
xi.	7, 33	v.	12
	40	iii.	278
xii.	29-31	iv.	64
xxi.	23	iv.	358

2 KINGS.

Chap.	Ver.	Vol.	Page
ix.	11	iii.	454
	34	iv.	358
x.	15	iv.	304
xiii.	5	v.	280
xx.	12	v.	123
xxiv.	7	iv.	573
xxv.	7	iii.	120
	22	iii.	346

1 CHRONICLES.

Chap.	Ver.	Vol.	Page
v.	14	iii.	275
xx.	1, 2	v.	58

2 CHRONICLES.

Chap.	Ver.	Vol.	Page
xii.	2	iii.	278
xv.	7	iv.	92
xvi.	14	iv.	277
xxxiii.	12	ii.	256
xxxvi.	6	iii.	120
	16	iv.	268

NEHEMIAH.

Chap.	Ver.	Vol.	Page
iv.	17	iv.	20
xiii.	3	iii.	272

JOB.

Chap.	Ver.	Vol.	Page
i.	1	iii.	272
xxi.	13	ii.	303
xxxviii.	11	i.	296

PSALMS.

Chap.	Ver.	Vol.	Page
ii.	3	v.	486
	7	iii.	139
v.	5	i.	273
viii.	2	v.	450
xv.	1, 2	ii.	247
xvi.	5	v.	409
xviii.	26	iii.	209
		iv.	327
xix.	11	ii.	284
	12	v.	171
xxii.	1	v.	447
	4	v.	454
xxiii.	4	iv.	491
	6	v.	510
	6, 7	iv.	88
xxiv.	1	ii.	327
xxvi.	9	ii.	280
xxvii.	3	iv.	491
xxviii.	2	v.	382
xxx.	5	i.	174
		ii.	427
xxxii.	2	i.	425
	6	iii.	437
xxxv.	4-6	ii.	279
xxxvii.	1, 7, 8	v.	16
	6	iii.	39
xxxviii	12	iv.	404
xl.	7	iv.	325
	14, 15	iv.	404
xli.	9	iii.	36
xliv.	2	ii.	106
	3	i.	80
	23	v.	203
l.	12	i.	346
	14, 23	ii.	388
li.	15	iv.	38
lii.	8	ii.	104
lv.	22	v.	338
	23	v.	251
lviii.	6	i.	446
lix.	11	iv.	473
	12	iii.	24
lxv.	3	v.	394
lxviii.	14	v.	502
lxix.	3	v.	479
	9	ii.	114
	10	iii.	154
	12	ii.	287
	15, 16	v.	445
	22, 23	i.	486
		ii.	112
		iii.	160
			165
lxxii.	10	iii.	274
lxxiii.	2, 3	v.	73
	4	ii.	303
lxxvii.	14	v.	454
lxxviii.	67, 68	iv.	76
lxxix.	2, 3	i.	416
		ii.	304
		iv.	275
	6	ii.	65
		iii.	108
		v.	384
	9	iv.	240
lxxx.	8	iv.	220
lxxxi.	10	iv.	85
lxxxii.	6	iii.	355
lxxxiv.	6	iv.	73
		v.	128
	9, 10	v.	483
lxxxv.	5	iii.	311
lxxxvi.	5, 15	iii.	290
lxxxvii.	1	ii.	49
		iv.	150
			229
	3, 4	ii.	158
	5	iv.	150
lxxxix.	3	iv.	252
	26	iv.	76
	27	iii.	139
		v.	484
	33, 34	ii.	61
			236
		v.	420
	36-38	i.	254
			450
		iii.	83
			119
		v.	394
	37	iv.	40
			144
			460
xciv.	8	ii.	453
		iv.	46
cii.	2	v.	394
	19	i.	385
		ii.	448
		iii.	186
	26-28	iv.	144
	27-29	v.	511
ciii.	8	ii.	175
			400
			427
civ.	4	ii.	38
	6	ii.	35
	29, 30	v.	515
	31	iv.	240
cv.	15	v.	386
cvi.	4	ii.	429
cvii.	43	i.	478
cx.	4	iii.	311
cxi.	10	i.	434
			498
cxiii.	4-6	v.	442
	7	ii.	396
cxv.	1	iv.	240
	3	v.	428
	8	i.	294
cxvi.	12, 13	v.	210
	16	iv.	18
			604
cxviii.	18	ii.	61
cxix.	10-16	iii.	233
	73, 125	iv.	48
	103	ii.	284
cxx.	5	v.	103
cxxiii.	1, 2	iv.	293
cxxv.	2	iii.	71
cxxvi.	1, 4	iv.	99
	6	iv.	72
cxxix.	6	ii.	348
cxxx.	4	iv.	219
			328
cxxxii.	7	ii.	241
	11	iv.	252
	13, 14	v.	275
	14	i.	254
			334
			383
		iii.	290
			302
		iv.	356
cxxxiv.	2	v.	382
cxxxvii.	4	iv.	81
		v.	129
	7	ii.	153
		v.	79, 95
			488
	8, 9	v.	453
cxxxviii.	8	ii.	360
cxxxix.	2	v.	452
	7-12	iii.	188
cxlii.	5	iii.	301
cxliii.	5	iv.	55
cxliv.	15	iv.	48
			208
		v.	132
cxlv.	18	ii.	218
cxlvii.	2	iii.	438
		iv.	206
		v.	477
	10	i.	502

PROVERBS.

Chap.	Ver.	Vol.	Page
i.	7	i.	434
			498
	17	v.	444
vii.	23	v.	363
ix.	10	i.	434
xvi.	1	ii.	57
	14	iv.	279
xviii.	10	v.	393

ECCLESIASTES.

Chap.	Ver.	Vol.	Page
ix.	2, 3	ii.	118

ISAIAH.

Chap.	Ver.	Vol.	Page
i.	3	i.	428
	6	i.	132
	9	i.	241
		v.	183
	9, 10	v.	462
	10	iv.	151
	12-15	i.	372
	13	ii.	377
			380
	14	i.	348
	24	i.	323
			359
		ii.	100
		iv.	29
		v.	423
ii.	3.	iv.	136
		v.	373
	21	iii.	189
iii.	9	i.	104
v.	2	iii.	227
	3	iii.	129
	6	ii.	245
	1-7	iv.	569
	26	i.	55
			275
vii.	18	i.	55
viii.	12, 16	i.	253
		ii.	234
ix.	13	i	259
			480
x.	7	iv.	515
	17	v.	351
	21, 22	v.	157
	22	iii.	133
		iv.	68
	23	iv.	22
	30	i.	32
xi.	1	iv.	43
			259
	5	ii.	160
xiii.	17	i.	351
		iii.	61
xvii.	6	i.	241
xix.	1	iv.	519
xxii.	12, 13	ii.	308
		iii.	255
		iv.	359
	14	iii.	99
xxiv.	13	i.	241
xxvi.	21	iii.	221
xxviii.	10	ii.	80
	12	i.	341
xxviii.	15	i.	245
		iii.	117
	19	iv.	294
	24-26	v.	246
xxix.	13	v.	434
	14	i.	433
		ii.	418
	15	i.	376
xxx.	2	iv.	494
	15	i.	121
		ii.	215
		v.	413
	21	iv.	181
			216
	33	ii.	442
xxxi.	1	ii.	354
		iv.	494
	3	ii.	343
xxxii.	15	i.	239
xxxiii.	1	v.	148
xxxvii.	22, 23	v.	136
xxxviii.	23	v.	391
xxxix.	1	v.	123
xl.	1	v.	360
	2	ii.	326
		iv.	490
	3	iv.	54, 73
	13	iii.	182
	21	iii.	227
xlv.	7	iii.	429
		iv.	438
	9	ii.	398
	19	iv.	288
	22	ii.	17
xlvii.	13	ii.	215
xlviii.	3, 5	ii.	17
	10	ii.	63
		iv.	24
l.	1	i.	153
		ii.	162
liv.	7, 8	v.	420
	13	iv.	134
lv.	6	iii.	176
	9	iii.	431
	11	i.	50
		iv.	51
lvii.	8	ii.	432
	10	i.	123
		ii.	46
			404
lviii.	9	iii.	437
lix.	1, 2	v.	438
	12	i.	104
lx.	15	ii.	164
lxiii.	4	iv.	50
lxv.	1	ii.	283
	24	v.	394
lxvi.	1	iii.	290
		v.	454
lxvi.	3	i.	392
	24	v.	517

LAMENTATIONS.

Chap.	Ver.	Vol.	Page
iii.	37, 38	i.	55
iv.	10	iv.	422
	20	iv.	42

EZEKIEL.

Chap.	Ver.	Vol.	Page
ii.	8	ii.	284
iii.	1, 3	ii.	284
viii.	6	iv.	151
xiv.	9	iii.	26
	14	ii.	248
xvi.	46, 47	v.	462
	48	i.	171
xviii.	2, 20	iv.	172
		v.	498
	20	ii.	256
			316
		v.	500
	25	ii.	285
		iii.	208
		iv.	248
xx.	21, 25	i.	292
xxi.	26, 27	iii.	127
		iv.	15
			259
			356
xxv.	12-14	v.	64
xxix.	14, 15	iv.	602
	20	v.	232
xxxiv.	23	iv.	251
xxxvi.	22	iv.	239
	27	iv.	217
xlvii.	1-12	v.	373
xlviii.	35	iii.	144

DANIEL.

Chap.	Ver.	Vol.	Page
i.	17	ii.	8
ii.	28	iii.	355
v.	1	v.	283
vi.	16, 17	v.	445
	22	iv.	380
ix.	4, 5	ii.	209
		v.	319
	8	v.	499

HOSEA.

Chap.	Ver.	Vol.	Page
ii.	21, 22	ii.	203
	23	iv.	74
vi.	9	iv.	64
ix.	7	ii.	418
xi.	1	iv.	76
xiv.	9	ii.	285

JOEL.

Chap.	Ver.	Vol.	Page
ii.	1, 2	i.	207
			237
	13	v.	434
	15	i.	207
	28	iv.	137
	32	v.	393

AMOS.

Chap.	Ver.	Vol.	Page
i.	13	v.	56
vi.	2	iv.	426
	6	ii.	263
		iv.	89
ix.	11	iv.	259
			356

OBADIAH.

Chap.	Ver.	Vol.	Page
	8	v.	64
	16	iii.	282

JONAH.

Chap.	Ver.	Vol.	Page
i.	3	iii.	34
iii.	3	i.	37

MICAH.

Chap.	Ver.	Vol.	Page
i.	3	iii.	221
ii.	6	iii.	37
	11	i.	213
			338
		ii.	228
iii.	12	iii.	332
		iv.	354
vi.	1	ii.	436
		iv.	353
	4	i.	100
	7	i.	346
vii.	5, 6	i.	464
	8	v.	487
	19	iv.	139

HABAKKUK.

Chap.	Ver.	Vol.	Page
i.	12	ii.	77

Chap.	Ver.	Vol.	Page
i.	12	iii.	230
		iv.	208
ii.	3	i.	51
	18	v.	225
	20	ii.	101
iii.	2	iv.	107
		v.	421
	3	v.	65

HAGGAI.

Chap.	Ver.	Vol.	Page
ii.	7	v.	247

ZECHARIAH.

Chap.	Ver.	Vol.	Page
i.	3	iii.	232
ii.	8	ii.	151
		v.	146
			163
vii.	9	iv.	72
xi.	5	v.	134
	6	iv.	148
xii.	10	i.	388
xiv.	10	iv.	147

MALACHI.

Chap.	Ver.	Vol.	Page
i.	2, 3	v.	81
ii.	4, 7	i.	33
		ii.	225
		iii.	376
		iv.	194
iv.	2	iv.	136
	6	iii.	310
		v.	518

MATTHEW.

Chap.	Ver.	Vol.	Page
i.	11	iii.	92
	25	iv.	76
ii.	18	iv.	90
vi.	24	iv.	132
vii.	2	v.	148
viii.	11	iv.	127
x.	28	iii.	328
xi.	11	iv.	137
xv.	13	ii.	106
		iv.	221
	26	v.	54
xvi.	19	ii.	252
xvii.	21	ii.	220
		iv.	336
xviii.	18	ii.	252
	20	iv.	356
xix.	6	i.	44
			395
xxii.	32	ii.	77
xxiii.	2	iii.	79
	35	ii.	316
			325
xxvi.	20	ii.	283
	52	iv.	473
xxviii.	20	iv.	356

MARK.

Chap.	Ver.	Vol.	Page
ix.	29	ii.	220
x.	9	i.	44
			395
xvi.	7	iv.	479

LUKE.

Chap.	Ver.	Vol.	Page
i.	16	iii.	310
	17	v.	281
	74, 75	v.	212
ii.	26	v.	484
ix.	54	ii.	279
	55	ii.	424
			427
x.	16	i.	282
		iii.	244
	23	iv.	136
	30-35	iv.	394
xi.	51	ii.	316
			325
xii.	47	iii.	267
		v.	104
xiv.	26, 27	iv.	132
xvi.	22	iv.	127
			275
xviii.	13	i.	384
xx.	38	iii.	231
xxiii.	31	iii.	267
		v.	75
	34	ii.	250

JOHN.

Chap.	Ver.	Vol.	Page
i.	17	iv.	140
ii.	17	ii.	114
iii.	20	i.	311
iv.	22	iv.	526
	24	i.	395
x.	29	iv.	491
	35	iii.	335
xiv.	27	iv.	21
xvi.	8	i.	468
		ii.	110
	21	iv.	92
	33	iv.	21
			255
xvii.	5, 11	iii.	145

ACTS.

Chap.	Ver.	Vol.	Page
vi.	2-4	iii.	380
vii.	6	iv.	131
	22	ii.	8
viii.	26	iv.	610
xiv.	17	i.	300
		ii.	27
			245
xvi.	7	iv.	350
xvii.	11	iii.	373
	28	ii.	27
		iv.	405

ROMANS.

Chap.	Ver.	Vol.	Page
i.	21	ii.	38
	25	ii.	24
			40
	28	ii.	228
		v.	429
ii.	16	iv.	334
	20	i.	83
	27	i.	328
	29	i.	205
iii.	3, 4	iv.	145
iv.	18	iv.	263
		v.	403
v.	1	i.	342
		iv.	255
	5	v.	411
vi.	10	iii.	142
vii.	14	i.	329
viii.	7	iv.	131
	20-25	i.	389
		v.	412
	28	iii.	24
		iv.	93
			358
		v.	75
			272
	29	iv.	76
ix.	3	iii.	393
	2-5	ii.	181
	16	ii.	58
	27	iv.	69
x.	6	iii.	181
			313
	20	ii.	283
xi.	5	ii.	330
		iv.	22
	5, 7	iv.	69
	27	iv.	125
xi.	28	ii.	99
	29	v.	131
	33	v.	429
	34	iii.	182
xii.	19	iii.	42
xiii.	1	iii.	356
xv.	3	ii.	114
	4	ii.	356
		iv.	57
		v.	419
xvi.	25	iv.	384

1 CORINTHIANS.

Chap.	Ver.	Vol.	Page
i.	19	i.	433
	30	iii.	146
		iv.	255
	31	i.	498
ii.	16	iii.	182
iv.	8	i.	186
	11	ii.	49
	13	v.	439
vii.	5	ii.	220
		iv.	336
	31	iv.	229
ix.	16	i.	61
xi.	19	iii.	373
	31	iii.	370
		v.	370
xii.	12	iv.	256
xiii.	5	iv.	457
xiv.	24, 25	i.	468
	38	iii.	176
			200
	40	iii.	179

2 CORINTHIANS.

Chap.	Ver.	Vol.	Page
i.	11	iii.	43
	20	iii.	136
	23	v.	79
ii.	7	v.	405
	15, 16	i.	36
			407
		iii.	34
			200
			428
		iv.	345
	17	ii.	286
iii.	6	ii.	76
		iv.	131
			141
	13	iv.	128
	18	iv.	138
vii.	9, 10	i.	259
	11	v.	485
x.	5, 6	i.	46, 48

Chap.	Ver.	Vol.	Page
x.	5, 6	i.	283
		ii.	185
			252
			436
		iii.	199
xiii.	1	iv.	227

GALATIANS.

Chap.	Ver.	Vol.	Page
i.	8	iii.	27
	19	ii.	297
iii.	10	ii.	121
	23	iv.	82
iv.	9	iv.	102

EPHESIANS.

Chap.	Ver.	Vol.	Page
ii.	17	ii.	330
iv.	19	i	339
vi.	1	iv.	312
	2	iv.	323
	9	iv.	283

PHILIPPIANS.

Chap.	Ver.	Vol.	Page
ii.	13	iv.	212
iii.	15	iv.	487
iv.	7	iv.	255

COLOSSIANS.

Chap.	Ver.	Vol.	Page
ii.	16	ii.	381
	23	ii.	443
iii.	3, 4	v.	413
iii.	3, 4	v.	485
iv.	1	iv.	283

1 THESSALONIANS.

Chap.	Ver.	Vol.	Page
iv.	13	iv.	277
v.	3	i.	250
			449
		ii.	126
		iii.	118
		iv.	592
		v.	22
	17	ii.	219

2 THESSALONIANS.

Chap.	Ver.	Vol.	Page
i.	5	iii.	286
	6, 7	v.	171
ii.	3	iii.	279
	10-12	iii.	398
		v.	368
			429

1 TIMOTHY.

Chap.	Ver.	Vol.	Page
ii.	8	v.	382
iii.	1	ii.	371
	15	iv.	356
iv.	8	iv.	82
			254
vi.	16	iv.	405

2 TIMOTHY.

Chap.	Ver.	Vol.	Page
ii.	8	iv.	334
	9	iv.	155
ii.	19	ii.	286
iii.	16	iii.	183
iv.	2	iii.	403

TITUS.

Chap.	Ver.	Vol.	Page
i.	9	iii.	425
iii.	11	iii.	411

PHILEMON.

Chap.	Ver.	Vol.	Page
	12	iv.	283

HEBREWS.

Chap.	Ver.	Vol.	Page
i.	5	iii.	139
iv.	9	ii.	381
	12	i.	468
		ii.	110
		iv.	354
vi.	16	iv.	557
viii.	8-12	iv.	125
	13	iv.	140
x.	16	iv.	125
	36	v.	413
xi.	13	iv.	83
xii.	8	ii.	62
	11	iii.	239
		iv.	94
			101
	13-15	ii.	389
	15	i.	485

JAMES.

Chap.	Ver.	Vol.	Page
i.	17	iii.	337
ii.	13	v.	148
iii.	1	i.	38
iv.	13	ii.	57
v.	13	iv.	38
	16	ii.	217
	17	ii.	249

1 PETER.

Chap.	Ver.	Vol.	Page
ii.	9	v.	212
iv.	11	i.	42
		ii.	435
	17	i.	471
		iii.	266
			285
v.	6	ii.	393

2 PETER.

Chap.	Ver.	Vol.	Page
ii.	1	ii.	418
iii.	16	v.	485

1 JOHN.

Chap.	Ver.	Vol.	Page
iv.	1	iii.	318

JUDE.

Chap.	Ver.	Vol.	Page
	7	v.	87
			183

REVELATION.

Chap.	Ver.	Vol.	Page
xiii.	10	iv.	473

GENERAL INDEX

TO THE COMMENTARIES ON JEREMIAH AND LAMENTATIONS.

A

Abominations, renounced by the penitent, i. 197; no shame felt for by the Jews, 338; set up even in the Temple, 410; iv. 198.

Abraham, the covenant made with, iv. 126.

Abundance of peace, promised to the restored Jews, iv. 227.

Achan, adjured by Joshua, ii. 177.

Adam, fell through ambition, v. 315.

Adultery, committed by the Jews, i. 270; iii. 449.

Adulteries, the, of Jerusalem, ii. 198; the land full of, iii. 154; committed by the Prophets, iii. 161.

Adversary, an, God became to Zion, v. 350, 390.

Aged, the, more intractable than youth, v. 414.

Ahikam, saved Jeremiah, iii. 346.

Alexander the Great, wasted the East, v. 116; took Babylon and died there, iii. 258; v. 235.

Allegories, resorted to by the fanciful, iv. 117.

Almond tree, a rod of, shewn to Jeremiah, i. 49.

Altars, the, of idols, left by fathers as memorials to their children, ii. 388.

Amend, to, their ways, the Jews exhorted, i. 361.

Amendment, a blessing on, i. 365.

Ammonites, the, a prophecy concerning, and their exile, v. 54-62; their restoration, 63.

Anathoth, Jeremiah's birthplace, i. 32; the men of, threatened, ii. 116.

Ancients, the, of the people, and of the priests, taken by Jeremiah to the valley of Hinnom, ii. 433.

Animals and trees, subject to God's vengeance, i. 389; suffer God's judgments, ii. 127.

Anointed, the, of the Lord, the breath of the people's nostrils, v. 483.

Antichrist, assumes high titles, iii. 130.

Apollo, an oracle of, i. 90.

Arabia, the kings of, iii. 275.

Arabian, an, the Jews like to, i. 157.

Aristotle, a saying of, i. 90; his opinion on free-will, i. 329.

Ark, the, of the covenant, forgotten through greater things, i. 182.

Artificer, the, images the work of, ii. 25.

Ass, an, the burial of, allotted to Jehoiakim, iii. 106.

Asses, the wild, oppressed with drought, ii. 208.

Associates, men wish to be, with God in their salvation, ii. 58.

Assyria, Israel sought the aid of, i. 100, 140, 147.

Astonishment, the, of Jeremiah, at the desolated city, v. 301.

Astrology, abused by the Egyptians and Chaldeans, ii. 8; judiciary, false, 10-12; iv. 142.

Atbash, or Athbash, an old invention, iii. 278.

Augustine, his answer to the Pelagians, ii. 58; his view of the effect of prayer, 250; his view of the Spirit's work, iv. 218.

Author of evil, God is not the, v. 429.

Authority, the, of God's word, superior to that of kings and princes, ii. 172, 173.

B

Baal, the prophets prophesied by, i. 81, 84; iii. 161; incense burnt to, ii. 93, 103; iv. 186.

Baalim, what they were, i. 84, 115, 483.

Baalis, the king of the Ammonites, iv. 455.

Babylon, threatened with punishment, iii. 256; a prophecy against, v. 121-288; was taken by the Persians, v. 125; the wall of, immensely large, 234; was destroyed by degrees, during several ages, iii. 258; v. 159; was retaken after a revolt, by the craft of Zopyrus, iii. 258; v. 125, 263.

Back, shewn to the people, not the face, ii. 414; the, Israel turned, to God, iv. 195.

Backsliding, Israel so called, i. 172; iv. 111; the, invited to return, i. 177.
Backslidings, bring their own reward, i. 103; a promise to heal, 192; the, of Jerusalem, perpetual, 423; the, of Judah, many, ii. 209.
Balaam, a prophet and an impostor, iii. 397.
Balm, expected to be in Gilead, i. 455.
Baptism, without repentance, of no avail, i. 205; is nothing without the grace it signifies, 328, 508; made a cloak to join God with the devil, i. 329.
Baruch, the evidences of the field's purchase given to, iv. 160; bidden to read the roll received from Jeremiah in the Lord's house, iv. 328; accused by Johanan of influencing Jeremiah, 504; God's word to, by Jeremiah, 564.
Baskets, two, of figs, shewn to Jeremiah, iii. 219.
Bel, the god of Babylon, confounded, v. 122.
Belie, the people did, the Lord, i. 278.
Belshazzar, the last king of Babylon, iii. 356; was feasting when the city was taken, and was slain, v. 188, 255.
Beneficence, the, of God, to man, i. 302.
Ben-hadad, the palaces of, burnt, v. 102.
Beth-shemesh, the images of, broken by Nebuchadnezzar, iv. 519.
Bitter, the fruit of wickedness, i. 226.
Blessed, the man, who trusts in God, ii. 349.
Blind, and the lame, the pregnant and those in childbed, were to be restored from exile, iv. 69.
Blindness, removed only by God, iv. 103.
Bonds and yokes, sent to several kings, iii. 348.
Bones, the, of the kings of Judah, &c., i. 418; the, of Zion, a fire sent to, v. 327; the, of the people, broken, 391.
Bottle, the, filled with wine, interpreted, ii. 169; the, of the potter, broken, explained, 447.
Branch, a righteous, raised to David, iii. 136; iv. 249.
Brass and iron, the people were, i. 356.
Bread, got by the exiles, at the peril of their life, v. 501.
Bridegroom, the, the voice of, made to cease, i. 417; ii. 312.
Brothels, the Jews made their hills, i. 156.
Burden, the, of the Lord, inquired for, iii. 205; forbidden to be mentioned, 211, 215.
Burnt-offerings. *See* Offering.

C

Cage, a, full of birds, the houses of the Jews compared to, i. 304.
Cakes, made for the queen of heaven, i. 385; iv. 542, 548, 553.
Calf, a, cut in twain, in making a covenant, iv. 294.
Call, a, to ministry, from God, i. 36; inward and outward, ii. 225; a divine, proved by two things, iii. 178.
Canaan, a pledge of heaven, ii. 77.
Candle, the light of, to cease, iii. 254.
Caphtor, the country of, iv. 613.
Captives, the, in Babylon, Jeremiah's letter to, iii. 412.
Captivity, restoration from, iv. 235.
Carcases, the, of the people, a meat for birds and beasts, i. 494; ii. 304; the, of abominable things, ii. 327.
Carpenters, taken to Babylon, iii. 219, 414.
Cedar, a house ceiled with, iii. 97.
Ceremonies, papal, human inventions, i. 194.
Chaff. *See* Wheat.
Chaldeans, destined to destroy Jerusalem, i. 52; iv. 186; called watchers, or besiegers, i. 223; compared to shepherds, 316; described as terrible, 349; compared to serpents, 445; the land of, to be desolate, iii. 256; recompensed according to their deeds, 260; threatened with the sword on all they had, v. 177-179.
Chambers, large, built by Jehoiakim, iii. 97.
Chapters, the order of, not according to time, iii. 240; v. 293.
Chastisement, prayed to be in moderation, ii. 59; paternal to the elect, and punitive to the reprobate, 61.
Cheek, the, to give, to the smiter, a proof of patience, v. 418.
Cheeks, Zion's tears on her, v. 304.
Chemos, and its priests, exiled, v. 11; Moab made ashamed of, 18.
Children, the, of Jacob, confessing their own sins and those of their fathers, i. 195; ii. 237; in vain asking for corn and wine in the siege, v. 364, 459; visited for their fathers' iniquities, 498.
Chittim, the isles of, i. 87.
Church, the, fed by true pastors, i. 151; exposed to calamities, ii. 38; first

visited with evils, iii. 285; iv. 33; corrected, not destroyed, iv. 21; the enemies of, punished, 33; the two marks of, repentance and faith, v. 338.
Cicero, quoted, ii. 277, 307; iii. 157; his opinion of oratory, iv. 89.
Circumcised, the, with the uncircumcised, threatened, i. 503.
Circumcision, required, i. 204; is nothing without the inward, 328; a sign of repentance and faith, 508.
Cisterns, broken, chosen by Israel, i. 93, 94.
City, the, of Jerusalem, threatened with exile, iii. 21; threatened with pestilence, 58; threatened with ruin, 65; was to become a wonder to all, 88; was to be forgotten and forsaken, 215; was to be rebuilt, iv. 147; its perpetuity, 151; had been a provocation to God, 192; was given up to the king of Babylon, 267; became desolate for her great iniquities, v. 311; when desolate, was an object of scoffs and taunts, 372, 375, 398. *See* Jerusalem.
Cities, resorted to by the Jews, i. 441; the, of the south, closed up against the Jews, ii. 185.
Cleansing, promised to the restored captives, iv. 236.
Cloak, a, baptism made, to join God with the devil, i. 329.
Commands, the, of God, of two kinds, v. 427.
Compassions, the, of the Lord, fail not, v. 407.
Complain, to, man has no reason, when punished for his sins, v. 431.
Confession, the, of sin, required, i. 174, 177; accompanies repentance, v. 435.
Confidences, human, rejected by God, i. 150.
Coniah, his judgment, iii. 118-127.
Conspiracy, a, formed in Judea, ii. 85; formed against Jeremiah, 415.
Contingency, under God's control, v. 428.
Controversy, a, God had with all nations, iii. 292.
Conversion, what it is, iv. 103; twofold, v. 514.
Co-operation of grace, as held by the Papists, iv. 213.
Correction, unavailing as to the Jews, i. 31, 132; not received by them, 256, 260, 406; leads to repentance, iv. 97.
Covenant, the, the words of, ought to be heard, ii. 69; urged on the Jews, 79; broken by Israel and Judah, 86; pleaded by the Prophet, 242; forsaken by the Jews, iii. 88; the, of God, never fails, iv. 58; a new, made with Israel, 124; the, with Israel, as unchangeable as the course of nature, 141; an everlasting, 214; the, of God with David, never to be broken, 261; a perpetual, the restored captives joined in, v. 129.
Covetousness, all the Jews given to, i. 334, 435.
Crown, the, fallen from the head, v. 507.
Cup, the, of consolation, ii. 310; the, of God's wrath, to be given to all nations, iii. 262-277; could not be rejected, 283.
Curse, a, to all who disregarded the covenant, ii. 69, 74; the Jews were to be, iii. 235, 266; iv. 536.
Cursed, the man, who trusts in man, ii. 342.
Customs, the, of the heathens, vain, ii. 13.
Cyrus, nephew and son-in-law to Darius, v. 159, 238; his character falsely given by Xenophon, 186; collected a large army against Babylon, 218; took the city in the night, 283.

D

Damascus, a prophecy concerning, v. 96-102.
Dan, a voice from, i. 122.
Dances, used religiously, iv. 60.
Darius, the king of the Medes, succeeded by Cyrus, v. 240.
Darkness, gross, threatened to the Jews, ii. 177.
Daughter, the, of Zion, cast down from heaven to the earth, v. 343.
David, the house of, addressed, iii. 66; a promise made to kings on the throne of, 80; a righteous Branch raised to, 136; iv. 249; promised as a king to Israel, iv. 13; a successor to, never to fail, 257; the seed of, to be multiplied as the sand, 262.
Day, the, the covenant of, unbroken, so that with Israel, iv. 265.
Dead, the, not to be wept for, iii. 90.
Dearth, the, the word concerning, ii. 202.
Death, preferred to life by the miserable Jews, i. 121; the shadow of, ii. 177.

Deceit, held fast, i. 423; pervading every rank, people, priests, and prophets, 467; the, of their own hearts, the false prophets announced, ii. 226.

Deceitful, the heart is, above all things, ii. 353.

Decree, the, of God, irreversible, i. 263; perpetual as to the sea, 294.

Deeds, the, of the wicked, surpassed by the Jews, i. 305.

Den, a, of dragons, Jerusalem was doomed to be, i. 476.

Derision, a, God's word was made, iii. 30; a, the Jews became, iv. 536.

Desolation, the, of the land lamented, i. 235.

Desolations, threatened to the Jews, iii. 251, 255.

Destroyers, prepared for Jerusalem, iii. 86.

Devices, formed against Jeremiah, ii. 109.

Devil, the, erects his palace in the Church, i. 46; serves God, though unwillingly, iii. 257; foretells future things, how, 397, 398.

Devise, to, gods, a madness, ii. 335.

Diamond, a, with a point of, Judah's sin was graven, ii. 337.

Difference, the, between the believing and unbelieving in affliction, v. 318, 338; between God's servants and impostors, 370; between believers and hypocrites, 409.

Diminish, to, a word, Jeremiah was forbidden, iii. 305.

Distress, the, of the people, likened to child-bearing, iv. 8.

Diviners, dreamers, sorcerers, were not to be hearkened to, iii. 360, 364, 423.

Divorced, the, was not to return to her former husband, i. 155.

Doctrine, the, of repentance, not preached by false teachers, iv. 32.

Dung, the slain to be like, on the ground, iii. 295.

Dunghills, embraced by the delicate at the siege of Jerusalem, v. 460.

E

Ear, the uncircumcised, i. 327.

Ears, the Jews had, without hearing, i. 293.

Earth, the, those written in, who depart from God, ii. 363.

Ebedmelech, raised Jeremiah from the dungeon, iv. 393; God's favour to, 435.

Edom, a prophecy concerning, v. 64-95; the daughter of, destined to receive the cup of wrath, v. 486, 489.

Egypt, a prophecy against, iv. 572.

Egyptians, the, the aid of, sought to the neglect of God, i. 100, 140, 147; their abuse of astrology, ii. 8.

Elam, the kings of, threatened, iii. 276; a prophecy concerning, and its exile, v. 112-118; its restoration, 119.

End, a full, what it means, i. 240, 275, 285; iv. 21, 605; her last, not remembered by Jerusalem, v. 320.

Enemy, an, God became to Israel, v. 351.

Enemies, the, of Zion, prosperous, v. 309.

Ephraim, from the mount of, a cry to come to Zion, iv. 62; was God's first-born, 71; bemoaning himself, 95; a dear son, 105.

Escape, none, from God's judgment, ii. 89.

Espousals, the love of, i. 69.

Ethiopian, the, cannot change his skin, ii. 190.

Euphrates, Jeremiah hid his girdle there, ii. 160; Pharaoh-necho smitten there, iv. 572; was divided into various streams above Babylon, v. 215.

Events, in God's hands, ii. 56.

Evil, the doing of, with joy, ii. 98; those used to, cannot do good, 191.

Evil-doers, the hands of, strengthened by false prophets, iii. 161.

Evils, two, committed by God's people, i. 92.

Examples, the, of the fathers, no safe precedents, i. 400.

Exhortation to repentance, iii. 241.

Eyes, the Jews had, without seeing, i. 295; the, of God, on all our ways, ii. 324.

F

Faith, the simplicity of, i. 169; ever brings peace, 342; founded on the word, 413, 414; the confession of, necessary, ii. 32; the firmness of, 216; rises to heaven and lies low in humility, 396; sees hidden things, iv. 119; ought not to be shaken, were the whole world in confusion, 195; the mother of hope, v. 402; emerges from despair, 406.

Fallow-ground, what it means, i. 202.

Fame, the, of the Chaldeans, its effect on the people, i. 352.

Families, the, who call not on God, to be punished, ii. 64.
Fanned into exile, Judah was to be, ii. 262.
Fanners, sent to Babylon, v. 197.
Fasting, not in itself pleasing to God, i. 348; ii. 219.
Fastings, the, of the Papists, grounded on false doctrine, ii. 220.
Fat, the Jews were become, i. 305.
Fatherless, the, oppressed by the Jews, i. 305; children, to be left to God, v. 70.
Fathers, the authority of, vainly pleaded, iv. 202.
Fear, the, of God, put in the heart, iv. 214.
Fear God, the Jews did not, notwithstanding his greatness, i. 294; nor for his bounty, 298.
Fields, to be bought again in Judea, iv. 224.
Figs, baskets of, shewn to Jeremiah, iii. 219.
Fig-trees and vines destroyed by the Chaldeans, i. 287.
Fire, God's words by the Prophet made so, i. 282.
Fishers, sent to fish the people, iii. 323.
Flock, the, of Jehovah, taken captive, ii. 181, 186; the remnant of, to be gathered, iii. 128.
Footmen, the, Jeremiah was wearied in running with, ii. 130.
Footstool, the, of God, the Temple, v. 345.
Forbearance, the time of, must be accounted for, ii. 90.
Forest, the, a tree for images cut from, ii. 13; the city so called, iii. 73.
Forgiveness, the, of sins, promised in the new covenant, iv. 138.
Forsake, to, God, is bitter, i. 104; to be followed by shame, ii. 363.
Fountain, the, of living waters, i. 92; ii. 304; a, of tears, Jeremiah wished his eyes to be, i. 457.
Fourscore men, from Shechem, &c., slain by Ishmael, iv. 461.
Fowls, the, of heaven, the dead bodies to be meat for, iv. 297.
Free-will, opinion of Aristotle on, i. 329; what it is, ii. 191; as held by the Papists, iv. 46.
Friendship, the, of the heathens, called idolatry, iv. 28.

G

Gall, the water of, i. 441, 481; given to the people, v. 392.
Garden, a watered, the soul of the restored captives like to, iv. 80.
Gate, the, of the city, Jeremiah was bidden to deliver a message at, ii. 377.
Gates, the, of Jerusalem, entrance into, by enemies, incredible, v. 470.
Gedaliah, made governor of the land, iv. 449; Jeremiah committed to, 434; was slain by Ishmael, 459.
Gentiles, the, the conversion of, ii. 329, 332.
Giddiness, the spirit of, in the ungodly, ii. 92.
Gilead, the balm of, i. 455; iv. 582; the king's house compared to, iii. 84.
Girdle, the linen, hid by Jeremiah, ii. 160; a, the house of Israel compared to, ii. 167.
Glory, to, not in wisdom, might, or riches, i. 495; to, in what man ought, 496; the wicked do, in doing evil, ii. 23.
God, the only teacher of his Church, i. 34, 43; the glory of Israel, 90; the fountain of living waters, 92; ii. 364; ready to forgive returning Israel, i. 172; none like him, great in might, ii. 17; is true, living and eternal, 26; seeks to allure men by promises, 76; a righteous judge, 113; searches the heart and tries the reins, 353, 355; iii. 39; the hope of Israel, ii. 362; not a God afar off, iii. 185; hears those who seek him, 433-438; human feelings ascribed to, iv. 108; a God to his people, 133, 208; rejoices to do good to his people, 219; his faithfulness, great, v. 407; does not afflict willingly, 422.
Gods, no nations change them, i. 88; having not made the heavens, they shall perish, ii. 29; alien, the people walked after, 88; when cried to, not able to save, 91; were as many as the cities of Judah, 93; cannot be made by man, 332.
Gomorrah. *See* Sodom.
Governor, the, of the restored Jews, from themselves, iv. 42.
Grace, the, of God, not tied to ranks or titles, i. 212; surpasses all human means, v. 330.
Greatest, the least to the, knowing God, iv. 137.
Gregory the pope, his opinion of images, ii. 23.
Guide, the, of youth, God is, i. 160.

H

HAIR, the, Jerusalem bidden to cut off, i. 408.
Hananiah, a false prophet, iii. 385-400; imitated by the Papists, 401; his judgment, 407.
Hanameel, selling his field to Jeremiah, iv. 159.
Hands, the, to raise up, a posture suitable in prayer, v. 382, 433.
Hardness, the, of the people, i. 256.
Harlots, a name given to idolaters, i. 110; Judah's children assembled in troops in the houses of, 268.
Harvest, the, the weeks of, i. 298; the, had passed with the Jews, 453.
Hazor, a prophecy concerning, v. 103-112.
Head, the, the hands on, what it means, i. 149.
Healing, the people were without, ii. 236; from God alone, 365.
Heaps, Jerusalem was to be made, i. 476.
Hear, to, God's word, the Jews refused, i. 390, 400, 404, 481.
Heart, a revolting and rebellious, the Jews had, i. 297; the, tried by God, ii. 113; the, deceitful above all things, 353; the whole, what it means, iii. 232; one, promised to Israel, iv. 210.
Heath, the, the man is like to, who departs from God, ii. 343, 347.
Heathens, all the, owned one supreme Being, i. 84.
Heaven and earth, God fills, iii. 185.
Heavens, the, called to wonder at Israel's impiety, i. 91.
Help, vain, expected from Egypt, v. 478.
Heritage, his own, forsaken by God, ii. 135; the, of God, become like a lion, 137; taken away from Israel, 341.
High places, built for Baal, iv. 199.
Hilkiah found the book of the law, i. 28.
Hill, high, the people played the harlot on every, i. 107.
Hinnom, valley of, i. 411; ii. 434; iv. 199.
Hissing, a, the Jews were to become, iii. 251, 266, 442.
Holiness to the Lord, what it means, i. 72.
Hope, the, of Israel, a stranger in the land, ii. 212; none, of a change in Judah, 401, 404; regards what is future, iv. 94; and prayer, combined, v. 411; and patience, united, 413.
Horace, quoted, ii. 16; iv. 123; v. 499.
Horrible thing, a, committed in the land, i. 308; as done by the virgin of Israel, ii. 406; a, seen in the prophets of Jerusalem, iii. 161.
Horses, the Chaldean, swifter than eagles, i. 218; fed, the Jews compared to, 271.
Hosts, the, of heaven, worshipped by the Jews, i. 418.
House, a, he who builds, by unrighteousness, is accursed, iii. 94.
Houses, the, of the Jews, threatened with destruction, i. 333; ii. 450.
Humble, the, only call really on God, v. 344.
Hunters, sent to hunt the people, ii. 323.
Hurt, the, of the people, healed slightly, i. 336, 437.
Husband, God is to his people, i. 178, 324.
Husbandmen, with their flocks, dwelling again in Judea, iv. 116.
Hypocrisy, worse than apostasy, i. 170.
Hypocrites, not able to plead ignorance, i. 77; after being chastised, cast off every fear, 86; seek circuitous courses and evasions, 198; lodge vain thoughts, 220; boast to be God's people, and reject God's grace, 405; murmur against God, when chastised, 450; claim the promises without repentance and faith, 451; iii. 128; allege the examples of fathers, ii. 238; reject mercy, iii. 53.

I

IDOLATERS, brutish and foolish, ii. 22.
Illumination by the Spirit, leads to repentance, iii. 229-232.
Images, decked with silver, fastened with nails, &c., ii. 15; cannot do good or evil, 16; counted books for the ignorant by the Papists, 23; teachers of falsehood, 24; vanity and the work of errors, 40.
Imagination, the, of the evil heart, i. 183, 390, 481; ii. 85, 165; iii. 169.
Impatience, the lot of those who are not satisfied with God alone, v. 409.
Impostors, suffered to deceive those who wish to be deceived, i. 213.
Imprecations, when proper, v. 342.

Incense, burnt by the Jews to foreign gods, i. 57; burnt to Baal, ii. 93; burnt to the hosts of heaven, ii. 449.
Indignation, the, of God, none can abide, ii. 26, 28.
Ingratitude, the, of the Jews, for past mercies, i. 76.
Inheritance, the, of the Jews, given to strangers, v. 493.
Iniquities prevent blessings, i. 300.
Innocents, the blood of, found on the skirts of the Jews, i. 141.
Iron, the northern and the steel, ii. 274.
Isaiah, the character of his prophecy, i. 30.
Ishmael, treacherous to Gedaliah, iv. 449; came to Mizpah and slew him, 459; slew men from Shechem, &c., 465; saved ten for the sake of their treasures, 466; intended to carry the people to the Ammonites, 469; was overtaken by Johanan at Gibeon, and overcome, 471; fled to the Ammonites, 473.
Islands, the, change not their gods, i. 89.
Israel, though not a servant, yet spoiled, i. 95; though redeemed by God, yet served idols, 107; sent to his gods for help, 129; called apostate, 164; comparatively better than Judah, 103, 171; invited to return, 172; made to inherit the land by God, ii. 150; the hope of, God, 212, 362; the scatterer of, will gather him, iv. 77.

J

JACOB, the portion of, not like idols, ii. 42; consumed by heathens, 64; a promise of a return to, iv. 17, 602; the tents of, to be restored, 35.
Jehoiakim, woe pronounced on, for injustice, iii. 94-98; given to covetousness, 105; the death of, not to be lamented, 106; destroyed the roll read by Baruch, iv. 344; the judgment of, 352.
Jeremiah, how long he prophesied, and his parentage, i. 27-31; Anathoth his birthplace, 32; why he called himself a child, 31, 39; refused his office, 38; what he was sent to do, 42-68; condemns all ranks, 126; forbidden to pray for the people, i. 383; ii. 95, 217; sought vengeance on his enemies, ii. 113, 125, 278, 374; dealt treacherously with by his father's house, ii. 133; bidden to go to the potter's house, 391; put in prison by Pashur, iii. 13; curse his birthday, 44-51; taken prisoner and arraigned, 317-347; saved by Ahikam, 346; bidden to make bands and yokes, 347; imprisoned by Zedekiah at the siege, iv. 152; committed to Gedaliah at Mizpah, 434-448; taken by Johanan to Egypt, 508; prophesied of the taking of Egypt by Nebuchadnezzar, 511.
Jerome, his fanciful notion about Jeremiah, i. 31; his opinion on chap. xi. 15, ii. 131; mistaken as to the Lamentations, v. 299.
Jerusalem, reminded of God's dealings in the wilderness, i. 69; the promise of all nations being gathered into it, 183; found in, not one doing judgment and seeking the truth, 251; the people of, continually backsliding, 423; would have remained perpetually, had it obeyed God's voice, ii. 385; was to be destroyed for worshipping strange gods and images, 449; iii. 88; a promise to, of being rebuilt on its own heap, iv. 35.
Jews, their audacity and vain glory, i. 57-64; acknowledged God, and worshipped idols, 115; sent to their gods for aid, 130; compared to adulterous women, 139, 147; openly slew the prophets, 142; committed theft, murder, &c., and yet came to the temple, 370; refused to hear God's voice, 406; iii. 241, 249; boasted that they were wise, i. 430; made continual advances in wickedness, 461; exhorted not to go after other gods, iii. 247; threatened with exile, 251.
Jonadab the Rechabite, iv. 302.
Johanan, revealed to Gedaliah the treachery of Ishmael, iv. 455; recovered the captives from Ishmael, 475; consulted Jeremiah on the subject of going to Egypt, 477; rejected his counsel, and went there, 503, 508.
John the Baptist, above the prophets, and the least in the kingdom of heaven, iv. 137.
Jordan. *See* Swelling.
Josephus, on the siege of Jerusalem by Titus, v. 385.
Joshua adjures Achan, ii. 177.
Joy, mourning turned to, iv. 86.
Judgments, to speak, what it means,

i. 217 ; reasons for, given, ii. 313-318.
Judiciary astrology, condemned, ii. 10-12.
Just, the, the blood of, shed by the prophets and priests, v. 470.
Justice, not done by Jewish rulers, iii. 66-69 ; the foundation of, the knowledge of God, 103.

K

Kedar, i. 88 ; a prophecy concerning, v. 103-112.
Kinds, four, of evils, appointed for Judah, ii. 254.
King, the, and the queen, exhorted to humility, ii. 182 ; the, of Judah exhorted to do justice, iii. 74-80 ; a, wisdom and probity necessary for, 141.
Kingdom, a, God speaking of, to pluck up, &c., and to plant, ii. 397 ; the, of David, a type of Christ's, 335 ; iii. 76 ; the, of Christ, spiritual, iii. 143 ; the, of Christ, begins only in us here, iv. 85.
Kingdoms, Jeremiah set over, i. 42 ; into all, the Jews were to be removed, ii. 255.
Kings, princes, priests, prophets, and people, all provoked God, iv. 193.
Know, to, the Lord, our glory, i. 496 ; to, his hand, the Lord would cause Israel, ii. 334.
Knowledge, true pastors feed with, i. 181.

L

Lament, to, the miseries of the people, Jeremiah forbidden, ii. 306; the dead, the Jews would not, 308.
Lamentation, the most bitter, threatened to the people, i. 353; a, Jerusalem bidden to take up, 408 ; a, taken up by Jeremiah for the mountains, &c., 473; bidden to be taught by women to their neighbours, 491.
Lamentations, the, Calvin's Preface to, v. 299.
Land, the, polluted by idolatry, i. 150; 168; the whole, given for a prey, 230; the, devoured by the Chaldeans, 287; the, being desolate, none so wise as to know the cause, 477; the, of God, defiled by the people, ii. 327 ; the, made a perpetual hissing, 413; the, of the north, restoration from, iv. 69.
Language, strong, needed to rouse the people, i. 232; the Chaldean, not understood by the Jews, 287 ; a verse written in the Chaldean, ii. 29 ; the blasphemous, which was used by impious men, v. 423-425.
Law, the, the book of, found by Hilkiah, i. 27; the, they that handled, did not know God, 81, 83; the, of the Lord, the people boasted that they had, 430; the, of God, set before them, yet forgotten, 481; the, the forsaking of, the cause of all evils, 482; the, for not keeping, they were banished, ii. 313; the, of God, put and written in the heart, iv. 130; the, and the Gospel contrasted, 140.
Lebanon, the snow of, ii. 407; the head of, what it means, iii. 85; Jerusalem compared to, 117.
Lees, on his, Moab settled, v. 15.
Leopard, a, would watch over the cities of Judah, i. 265; the, cannot change his spots, ii. 190.
Letter, Jeremiah's, to the captives in Babylon, iii. 412, &c.
Levites, the priests, were not to fail, iv. 256.
Liberty, ought to be limited, iv. 14 ; given to servants in Jerusalem and Judea, 280 ; afterwards withdrawn, 285-290 ; proclaimed to the sword, &c., 291.
Libyans, dexterous with the shield, iv. 580.
Life, the rule of, iii. 312-315.
Linen girdle, a, Jeremiah was bidden to take, ii. 159.
Lion, like a devouring, the sword of Judah devoured the prophets, i. 131 ; the, from the thicket, was to ascend to lay waste the land, 209; a, from the forest, was to slay the people of Jerusalem, 265 ; like a, in the forest, God's heritage had become, ii. 137 ; a, God became to his people, v. 396.
Lions, young, roared on Israel, i. 94.
Live does Jehovah, what it imports, i. 255.
Lodging-place, a, Jeremiah wished for, in the wilderness, i. 458.
Lords, Israel claimed to be, i. 135.
Love, with an everlasting, God loved Israel, iv. 56.
Lovers, the, of Judah, despised him, i. 246; the, of the people, destroyed, iii. 110; the, of Israel, had forgotten him, iv. 27.
Lovingkindness, judgment, and righteousness, the Lord delights in, i. 496.

Lydians, expert with the bow, iv. 580.

M

MAGOR-MISSABIB, Pashur so called, iii. 17.
Maid, a, never forgets her ornaments, i. 138.
Majesty, the, of God, makes bold his ministers, i. 44.
Make, to, flesh our arm, a cursed thing, ii. 343.
Manasseh, his wickedness, ii. 255, 258.
Mark, a, for God's arrow, Israel was made, v. 397.
Medes, their character, v. 186; the, the coming of, against Babylon, 239.
Mediators, Platonic figment about, i. 22; ii. 95.
Medicines, healing, Israel had not, iv. 26.
Melt, to, the people, God threatened, i. 469.
Mercy, promised to aliens, ii. 154; promised to those who would learn the ways of God's people, 156.
Mercies, the, of the Lord, new every morning, v. 407; the, of God, the multitude of, 420.
Merodach, a Babylonian idol, broken, v. 122.
Micah, his prophecy referred to, iii. 331.
Mighty, the, forbidden to glory in their might, i. 495.
Millstones, the sound of, to cease, iii. 254.
Ministers, sent to pull down, as well as to build up, i. 46; ought to be courageous, 64; ought to be received as God himself, 283, 284, 405; ought to give no offence in private matters, ii. 270.
Moab, a prophecy against, and its exile, v. 5-51; its restoration, 52.
Moabites, the, and the Idumeans, evil neighbours to God's people, ii. 151.
Mockers, Jeremiah did not sit among, ii. 287.
Molech, children burnt to, iv. 199.
Monks, pretend to be true teachers, i. 309; prop up the Papacy, 310; their shameful boastings, 311; excite the feelings by exhibiting the cross, 488.
Moses and Samuel, would not be heard for the people, ii. 287.
Mountain, the, of Zion, foxes walked on, v. 509.
Mountains, the dark, to stumble on, ii. 175.
Mourning turned into joy, iv. 86.
Mourning women, called to lament the state of the people, i. 487.
Mouth, in the, of the people, God near, but far from their reins, ii. 122.

N

NATION, mighty and ancient, the Chaldean, i. 285; a, spoken against and repents, is spared, ii. 397.
Nations, the, Jeremiah a prophet to, i. 37; God the king of, ii. 19; all, made to drink of God's cup of wrath, iii. 266; God's controversy with, 292.
Native country, their, the exiles were not to see, iii. 90.
Nazarites, their habits, i. 409; changed in their appearance at the siege of Jerusalem, v. 464.
Nebo, woe on, v. 5.
Nebuchadnezzar, many lands given to, iii. 354-358; Jerusalem given to, iv. 186; gave a charge respecting Jeremiah, 422; destined to smite Egypt, 585.
Nebuzar-adan, led the people captive, iv. 429; left the poor in the land, 431; his address and offer to Jeremiah, 440; dismissed him with a reward, 445.
Needy, the, the right of, denied by the Jews, i. 305.
Neigh, the Jews did, after their neighbours' wives, i. 271; ii. 198.
Neighbour, a, no more needed to be taught, iv. 134.
Neighbours, and brethren, deceitful and slanderous, i. 463, 465; the, of the Jews, evil, ii. 150.
Net, spread by God for Zion, v. 327.
Nitre, could not cleanse the people of Israel, i. 113.
Nobles, the, of Judah, sought water in vain, ii. 204; the, of the restored Jews, from themselves, iv. 42.
No-god, a, the people swore by, i. 269.
Noph, the sins of, i. 98.
North, the, the pot's face towards, i. 51; the, evil was to come from, 53, 209, 314; ii. 53; the, from the land of, Judah and Israel were to return, i. 188.

O

OATH, the, which God had sworn to the fathers, ii. 69, 77.
Obedience to God's voice, the chief thing, i. 390, 395; ii. 69, 80.

Obey, to, God's voice, Israel refused, i, 176, 481; to, his voice, God commanded the people from the beginning, ii. 80, 82; to, the Jews refused, as to the Sabbath, ii. 383.

Offerings, burnt, not of themselves acceptable to God, i. 347; ii. 217; not commanded on coming out of Egypt, i. 391; burnt, offered to Baal, ii. 437.

Offscouring, an, the exiles made by God, v. 439.

Oracle of Apollo, i. 90.

Ordinances, the, of the moon and stars, fixed, iv. 141.

Origen and Irenæus, quoted by Papists, ii. 112.

Ornaments, maid forgets not her, i. 138.

P

PAPACY, the, supported by the Monks, i. 310; to be under, better than licentiousness, iii. 32.

Papal ceremonies, human inventions, i. 194-

Papists, the, are like the ancient impostors, i. 85; given to all sorts of devotions, 110; have their Baalim or patrons like the Jews, 115; pray to stocks and stones like the Jews, 128; set up free-will, 220; boast of an apostolical throne, 382; regard the consent of Fathers more than the word of God, 396; pretend antiquity, 398; believe their bishops, and not God's word, ii. 51; have many gods like the Jews, 94; believe in the intercession of the dead, 250; absurdly hold that the Church cannot err, 416; are all schismatics, 418; make their own devices to be oracles, iii. 168; deny any certainty to Scripture, 171; have false views of repentance, iv. 102; fight with the same weapons with idolatrous Jews, 544; swear by dead saints, v. 78.

Paramours, the Egyptians and Assyrians were, to Israel, i. 140, 141.

Pardon, only to the penitent, i. 273; not to the Jews without correction, ii. 60.

Partridge, a, not hatching, a rich man like to, ii. 357.

Pashur, the priest, put Jeremiah in prison, iii. 13, &c.; was threatened with exile, 20.

Pashur, the son of Melchiah, sent with a message to Jeremiah, iii. 51-55.

Pastor, a, Jeremiah hastened not to be, ii. 369.

Pastors, the, of Israel, transgressed against God, i. 81; the promise of, to feed the people with knowledge, 180, 181; the, of Israel, were become brutish and did not seek God, ii. 50; had destroyed God's vineyard, 141; denounced with woe for scattering the sheep, iii. 128; good, promised, 134; the bad, threatened with ruin, 298-301.

Patience, proved by extreme evils, v. 417.

Paths, the old, to be sought, i. 340; the ancient, forsaken by the Jews, ii. 411.

Peace, promised by false prophets, i. 336, 437; iii. 169; taken away from the people, ii. 306; the man of, what it means, iii. 36; obtained only through Christ, 143; the, of Babylon, to be sought by the exiles, 420.

Pelagians, the, the cavils of, ii. 58: answered by Augustine, *ib.*

Pen, a, of iron, Judah's sin written with, ii. 337.

People, the, of Judah, foolish, i. 233; the, the sorrow of, like that of a woman in travail, 249; punished for their idolatry, 290; compared to snares, 302; loved to be deceived, 308; were like reprobate silver, 360; promised a name and a glory, but would not hear, ii. 167; loved to wander, 215; justly exposed to the delusions of impostors, 228; refused to hear and receive instruction, 383; the, the daughter of, more cruel than sea-monsters and ostriches, v. 458.

Persecutors, the, of the Jews, swifter than eagles, v. 481.

Persius, quoted, ii. 275.

Persians, the, and the Medes, overthrew the monarchy of Babylon, v. 139, 145-149; the, excelled in archery, 169.

Pharaoh, made to drink of the cup of fury, iii. 269.

Pharaoh-necho, smitten by Nebuchadnezzar near the Euphrates, iv. 572.

Pharaoh-hophra, given into the hand of Nebuchadnezzar, iv. 561.

Philistines, the, God's word against, iv. 609.

Philosophers, their view of contingencies, v. 428.

Physician, a, looked for in Gilead, i. 455.
Planted, the wicked said to be, by God, ii. 122.
Platonic figment, the, about mediators, i. 22; ii. 95.
Pliny, quoted, ii. 358; v. 234, 261.
Pollution, everywhere in Jerusalem during the siege, v. 473.
Poor, the, and the rich, wholly wicked in Jerusalem, i. 162, 163.
Pope, the, his vain boasting, while neglecting God's word, i. 44, 45; foolishly exempts himself from reproofs, iii. 80; cannot err as a Pope, 159; his tyranny better than anarchy, iv. 15.
Portion, the, of God, trodden down by pastors, ii. 141; the, allotted to the people for their sins, ii. 194; the, of his people, the Lord is, v. 408.
Potter, a, the house of, Jeremiah bidden to go to, ii. 391; a, the earthen bottle of, taken by Jeremiah, ii. 429; broken bottle interpreted, 447.
Prayer, the fruit of faith, ii. 67; iv. 67; v. 322, 434; the, of the Jews, not heard, ii. 89; v. 393; offered to God and to false gods, ii. 92; an answer to, promised, iv. 226; intercepted by an intervening cloud, v. 438; to God, from the dungeon, 446.
Precious, the, to be taken from the vile, ii. 295.
Preservation, in the midst of evils, from God alone, ii. 366.
Pride, the, of Judah, ii. 164; the, of Moab, v. 31.
Priest, the, and the prophet, dealing falsely, i. 334, 435; the, and the prophet, wandering in despair through the land, ii. 233; the, the law should not perish from, 415.
Priests, against the, Jeremiah was made a brazen wall, i. 65; the, had forsaken the Lord and turned to idols, 81; the, the shame of, made fully evident, 125; the, bearing rule by means of the prophets, 308, 309; the, and the prophets, threatened to be filled with drunkenness, ii. 169, 172.
Princes, in the courts of, hardly any religion, ii. 288.
Profession, the pretence and boast of hypocrites, i. 200.
Promise, a, to those who kept the Sabbath, ii. 384, 388
Promises to the restored Jews, iv. 35-49, 53-87.
Prophet, the, and the priest, profane, iii. 157.
Prophets and priests, two eyes of the Church, blinded by Satan, v. 472.
Prophets, *the true*, ought not to fear, i. 41; bring nothing of their own, 42; had two feelings, personal and official, 228; ii. 181; iii. 33; were called watchmen, i. 340; were sent continually to the people of Israel, 400; ii. 80; iii. 241; iv. 316.
Prophets, *the false*, deceived the people, i. 213; prophesied falsehood in God's name, 308; ii. 224; iii. 189, 191; and the priests, were deceitful, i. 435; declared that there be neither sword nor famine, but peace, ii. 222; iii. 169; were threatened with the sword and famine, ii. 227; and with exile, iii. 23-25; those of Jerusalem, a horrible thing seen in, 161; were threatened with wormwood and gall, 164; forbidden to be hearkened to by the people, 166; were not sent by the Lord, 176; did not turn the people from their evil ways, 180, 183; pretended to see dreams, 189; prophesied false things, 371-380; discovered not the people's iniquities, v. 369.
Prosperity, the Jews while in, refused to hear God, iii. 112; the, of the restored captives, iv. 238.
Protection, the, of others, preferred by the Jews to that of God, i. 147.
Proud, the Jews were, ii. 175.
Prudence commended, i. 40.
Punishment, the, of the people, the cause of, ii. 189, 194; the, of the people, according to their doings, iii. 70-73; the, of the Jews, temporary, iv. 109.

Q

Queen, the, of heaven, cakes made for, i. 385; iv. 542, 548, 553.
Quintilian, quoted, ii. 106.
Quiver, the, of the Chaldeans, compared to an open sepulchre, i. 287.
Quotations, accommodated, iv. 91.

R

Rabbins, their fancy as to Jeremiah's father, i. 32; their foolish notion about the antiquity of the temple, ii. 361; their fable about Hananiah, iii. 411.

Rachel, weeping for her children, iv. 88.
Rain, withheld for sin, i. 158; the gift of God, 298; and showers, ascribed to God, ii. 244.
Ramah. *See* Rachel.
Rebuke, suffered for God's sake, ii. 282.
Rechabites, the, offered wine by Jeremiah, iv. 302; the, a promise made to, 323.
Recompense, to, sin double, what it means, ii. 325.
Redeemer, the, of Israel and Judah, strong, v. 174.
Redemption from exile, greater than that from Egypt, ii. 320, 323; iii. 147.
Refuse. *See* Offscouring.
Reins, the, tried by God, ii. 113.
Religion, the beginning of, ii. 67.
Remedy, the true, rejected by Israel, i. 100.
Remnant, the, of Israel, gleaned, i. 325; the, of the flock, gathered, iii. 128.
Repentance, the gift of God, iii. 228, 435; when true, i. 219; iii. 310; not the cause of salvation or of pardon, i. 220; iii. 235; and faith, united, iii. 336; submits to chastisements, ii. 61; requires confession, 332; halved by the Papists, iii. 229; exhortation to, 241; the, of God, what it is, 311.
Resignation, under punishment, ii. 48; silent, a proof of patience, v. 415.
Restoration, the, of the Jews from exile, a prelude to that by Christ, i. 186; iii. 227; wholly from God, iii. 229; from all nations, 437; iv. 203; to their own land, iv. 5, 17.
Restraint, necessary, in judging of God's dealings, ii. 119.
Revolters, the Jews were, i. 356.
Reward, how given, iv. 92.
Rich, the, forbidden to glory in riches, i. 495.
Righteousness, the Lord our, iii. 136; iv. 253; the, of Christ, what it is, iii. 143.
Rising up early and sending, i. 400; ii. 80; iii. 241, 312, 443; iv. 195, 316.
Roaring, ascribed to God, iii. 289.
Rod of almond-tree shewn to Jeremiah, i. 49.
Roll, the, of a book, taken by Jeremiah, iv. 324; was destroyed by Jehoiakim, 344; another, was written and had many words added, 351, 359.
Roofs, on the, the Jews burnt incense to Baal, ii. 449.
Root, the wicked had taken and grew, ii. 122.

S

Sabbath-day, on the, the people were bidden to bear no burden, ii. 377; the, commanded to be kept holy, 380.
Sabbatharians, the Jews so called by the heathens, v. 316.
Sabbaths, the, ridiculed by the heathens, v. 313; the, God caused to be forgotten in Zion, 353.
Sackcloth, the people called to put on, i. 210, 353; sign of repentance, 353, 354.
Sacrifices, not of themselves acceptable to God, i. 346; not required on coming out of Egypt, 391.
Samaria, folly seen by the prophets of, iii. 161; vines planted on the mountains of, after the restoration, iv. 61.
Sanctuary, the, a glorious high throne, ii. 360; the, the heathens not allowed to enter, v. 323; his own, God abhorred, 355; the, the priest and the prophet, slain in, 384; the, the stones of, cast into the streets, 455.
Satan, sends forth angels of light, i. 85; suggests vain comforts, 101; is an acute disputant and a sophist, ii. 329; set loose to deceive the wilfully disobedient, iii. 177; the ministers of, teach in God's name, 190; uses various means to lead men to despair, v. 321, 447.
Satisfactions, the, of the Papists, iv. 93.
Scattered, Judah threatened to be, i. 486; the pastors' flocks were to be, ii. 50; the people, as by an east wind, 413.
Sea, the, under God's command, iv. 141.
Seething-pot, seen by Jeremiah, i. 51.
Seraiah, brought the book of the prophecies concerning Babylon, to Babylon, and cast it into the Euphrates, v. 289, &c.
Servants, ruled over the Jews, v. 500.
Seventy years, the, of the captivity, iii. 255, 427.
Shallum, was not to return from exile, iii. 91.

Shame, none felt by the Jews, i. 338, 438; the self-wise threatened with, 432.
Sheba, incense from, i. 346.
Shedding, the, of the blood of the just by prophets and priests, v. 47.
Shemaiah, the Nehelamite, iii. 450-456; his punishment, 457-460.
Shepherds, after the restoration, dwelling in Judea, iv. 245.
Sheshach, the cup of wrath given to, iii. 277.
Shiloh, the fate of, threatened to the temple, i. 377; a warning to the Jews, iii. 84, 312.
Showers, withheld on account of hardened wickedness, i. 158.
Sibmah, the vine of, lamented, v. 36.
Sign, external, of itself nothing, i. 328.
Signet, a, Coniah compared to, iii. 118.
Signs, the, of heaven, not to be dreaded, ii. 6.
Sihor, the water of, i. 100.
Sin, the servants of, no servants of righteousness, i. 109.
Skirts, the, discovered, ii. 189, 197.
Slippery, the way made so to the Jews, iii. 160.
Smiths, the, taken to Babylon, iii. 219.
Snow of Lebanon, ii. 407.
Soap, could not cleanse the stains of Israel, i. 114.
Sodom, the Jews like the people of, iii. 161; the sudden ruin of, v. 461.
Sons, their, and daughters, the Jews sacrificed to Molech, i. 411; the, and daughters, in Jerusalem, given up to famine and the sword, ii. 301, 302.
Sophists, the, ascribe absolute power to God without justice, v. 192.
Sorrow, the, of Israel, incurable, iv. 31; alleviated by sympathy, v. 304; the, of Zion, greater than that of any, 325.
Soul, the weary, satiated, iv. 118.
Sow, to, among thorns, what it means, i. 202, 203.
Sowing, the, of the house of Israel, iv. 120.
Spoiler, a, brought to Judah, ii. 264.
Stealing, murder, idolatry, &c., combined with attendance at the temple, i. 370.
Stocks, in the, Jeremiah was put, iii. 13.
Stone, a, and a stock, prayed to, by Israel, i. 126, 127.
Stones and stocks, to commit adultery with, i. 158.
Stork, the, and the turtle, &c , wiser than God's people, i. 428.
Strabo, quoted, v. 234.
Strangers, false gods so called, i. 176; Judah doomed to serve, 290.
Strangers, orphans, and widows, why so often mentioned, i. 367; iii. 78.
Succession, a, of prophets, given to Israel, i. 400.
Sucklings, swooned in the streets of Jerusalem, v. 362; died in their mothers' bosom, 364; the tongue of, clave to the roof of their mouth, 459.
Summer, the, had ended, i. 453.
Sun, the supreme god of the orientals, i. 387; the, of Jerusalem, went down at mid-day, ii. 266.
Superstition and religion, how they differ, i. 395.
Superstitions, caused God to punish the Jews, i. 57; deemed by God idolatrous, 156.
Superstitious, the, know no shame, i. 163.
Swear, to, what it means, i. 200, 255; ii. 157.
Swearing, common in the land, iii. 154.
Swelling, the, of Jordan, ii. 130; v. 87.
Sword, the, sent after the people in exile, i. 487; the, and famine, and pestilence, threatened, ii. 145, 217; iii. 237; the slain with, better than the slain with famine, v. 466.
Symbols, or signs, vain, when not founded on God's word, ii. 448; iii. 352.
Sympathy alleviates sorrow, v. 304.

T

TAHAPANES, the sons of, i. 98.
Tamarisk, ii. 343, 347.
Taunt, a, the Jews were to be, iii. 235.
Teeth, the children's, set on edge, iv. 123.
Teaching, the right way of, v. 322.
Tekoa, i. 312.
Temple, the, of the Lord, the boast of the Jews, i. 361; made a den of thieves, 370; the, the Jews forbidden to enter, ii. 98; the vessels of, carried to Babylon, iii. 381.
Thoughts, the, of peace, God had towards the captives, iii. 430-435.
Threatenings, when not feared, God is denied, i. 279; the, of God, fulfilled in the destruction of Jerusalem, v. 376.
Throne, the, of God, is for ever, v. 511.

Tongue, the, of the people, deceitful, i. 471; the, to smite with, its meaning, ii. 419.
Tophet, the high place of, i. 411; threatened with ruin, 436, 444.
Torpidity, the, of the Jews, i. 315.
Treacherous, Judah so called, i. 167, 169, 170; the whole people said to be, 458.
Treacherously, those who dealt, were happy, ii. 118, 122; Jeremiah's father's house dealt, with him, ii. 133.
Treachery, the, of Israel, i. 190; the, of Israel and Judah, 277.
Treasures, the, of Judah, given for spoil, ii. 275, 339.
Tree, every green, the people played the harlot under, i. 110; a, planted by waters, the blessed man is like to, ii. 351.
Tribe, the, of Benjamin, bidden to flee from Jerusalem, i. 312.
Tribes, the ten, their exile, iv. 126.
Troy, its ruin ascribed to the cruelty of Jupiter, v. 317.
Trumperies, magnified by hypocrites, i. 363.
Turning, the, of sinners, ascribed to God, iv. 99.
Tyrus, made to drink the cup of wrath, iii. 273.

U

UNBELIEVING, the, exasperated by calamities, v. 318.
Uncircumcised in heart, were all the house of Israel, i. 504.
Uncleanness. *See* Pollution.
Understanding, Judah was without, i. 234, 293.
Union, the, of Israel and Judah, after their exile, i. 183; how to be formed, 396; falsely boasted of by Papists, iv. 65.
Urijah, what happened to, related, iii. 339.
Usury, Jeremiah neither borrowed nor lent on, ii. 269.

V

VALLEY, the, of Hinnom, i. 411; iv. 199; to the, Jeremiah bidden to go, ii. 430, 452.
Vanity, the fathers walked after, i. 74; the graven images were, ii. 40; the people burnt incense to, 407.
Vanities, the stock the doctrine of, ii. 22; the, of the Gentiles, 245.
Vengeance, prayed for by Jeremiah on his enemies, ii. 113; threatened to the Jews, 169.
Vermilion, a house painted with, iii. 97.
Vessels, the, of the temple carried to Babylon, iii. 381.
Victuals, the Jews said they had plenty of, when they worshipped idols, iv. 542.
Vile, the, to be separated from the precious, ii. 295.
Vine, Israel a choice, became degenerate, i. 111; gleaned as a, the remnant of Israel, 325.
Vines and fig-trees, destroyed by the Chaldeans, i. 287.
Virgil, quoted, iii. 323; v. 317, 499.
Virgins, ravished in the cities of Judah, v. 503.
Vision, a false, by the false prophets, ii. 224; iii. 166; none from the Lord to the prophets of Zion, iv. 358.
Visit, to, the same as to punish, i. 272, 307, 472.
Visitation, the time of, i. 438; the year of, iii. 160.
Voice, the, of mirth, &c., made to cease in Judah, i. 417; and in Jerusalem, ii. 311; iii. 254; the, of God, the Jews refused to hear, iii. 112; the, of joy, among the restored captives, iv. 241.

W

WAGES, to retain, is accursed, iii. 94.
Wailing, the voice of, heard from Zion, i. 489.
War, to sanctify, what it means, i. 317.
Watch, God did, to build Israel, iv. 121.
Water sought for in vain by the nobles, ii. 204.
Waves, the, of the sea, under God's control, i. 294.
Way, the, of Jehovah, not known by the poor, nor the rich, i. 262-264; the good, to be sought, 340; the, of the heathen, to be avoided, ii. 5, 6; the, of man not in himself, 54; the, of life and death set before the besieged Jews, iii. 62-64; the, of the Jews made slippery, 160; one, promised to Israel, iv. 210; the evil, to return from, 327, 331.

Way-marks, to be set up for the return of captives, iv. 109.
Ways, the, of Zion mourning, v. 308; our exhortation to search and try, 432.
Wayfaring man, a, the God of Israel like to, ii. 212.
Weeping, a sign of misery, not of repentance, i. 191; for mountains and the wilderness, 473; the captives would return with, iv. 71; incessant for the destruction of Jerusalem, v. 441.
Wheat, to sow, and to reap thorns, ii. 146; the, what is the chaff to? iii. 195.
Whirlwind, a, from the Lord, iii. 173: God's judgment compared to, 294; iv. 50.
Wicked, the most, deem themselves innocent, i. 144; the, the way of, prosperous, ii. 118.
Wickedness brings its own punishment, i. 103, 104; made the land to mourn, ii. 127; and iniquity, confessed, ii. 237; found in God's house, iii. 157.
Widows, oppressed by the Jews, i. 365; increased through war, 263; are to trust in God, v. 70.
Wilderness, a, God had not been to Israel, i. 135.
Wind, dry, not to fan nor to cleanse, i. 215; God's word so regarded by the Jews, 280; the, brought forth from God's treasure, ii. 37; pestilential, threatened to the Jews, iii. 115.
Wine, bottle filled with, interpreted, ii. 162; not drunk by the Rechabites, iv. 302; much, and summer-fruits, gathered by the poor left in the land, 453.
Wise, the, are those who fear God, i. 233; the, are forbidden to glory in their wisdom, 495.
Wives, the, of the Jews, and their fields, given to others, i. 333, 435.
Woman, a, in travail, the Jews compared to, i. 249, 352; ii. 188; iii. 117; a, compassing a man, iv. 111.
Women, in the siege, did eat their own children, v. 383; the pitiful, boiled their own offspring, 468; were ravished in Zion, 503.
Word, the, of God, a fire, i. 284; a reproach, 327; iii. 30; superior to that of kings and princes, ii. 172, 173; a burning fire, iii. 30; ought to be spoken faithfully, 195; a fire and a hammer, 198.
Words, lying, the Jews trusted in, i. 369; the, of God, eaten by Jeremiah, ii. 282; the, of God, perverted, iii. 211.
Workman. *See* Artificer.
Works, the, of their own hands, the Jews worshipped, i. 57; iii. 249; their own, the fruit of, given to each, ii. 356; by the, of their hands, the Jews provoked God, iv. 189.
World, the, established by wisdom, ii. 33.
Wormwood, the people fed with, i. 481; and made drunk with, v. 399.
Wrath, the, of God, not retained, i. 172, 174; the Jews called the generation of, 409; at the, of God, the earth trembles, ii. 26, 28. *See* Cup.

X

Xenophon, referred to, i. 90; iii. 258; v. 186, 255.

Y

Years, seventy, of the captivity, iii. 255.
Yoke, the, of bondage, broken by God for Israel, i. 107, 109; the, of obedience, broken by the people, 262, 265; and bonds, sent to many kings, iii. 348; the, of iron, put on many nations, iii. 405; the, of Jacob, promised to be broken, iv. 12; the, of sins, fastened to the neck of Zion, v. 328; the, to bear, in youth, good, 414.
Young, men and women, ought not to marry without their parents' consent, iii. 419.
Youth, the reproach of, iv. 104; Israel and Judah did evil from their, 189.

Z

Zeal, pure, how to be distinguished, ii. 278, 279, 375, 376; ought to be restrained, iii. 42.
Zedekiah, made king by Nebuchadnezzar, iv. 361; was taken by the Chaldeans and brought to Riblah, 425; had his eyes pulled out, and was carried in chains to Babylon, 428; as a descendant of David, was a type of Christ, v. 483-485.
Zion, the voice of wailing heard from,

i. 489 ; loathed by God, ii. 234 ; invitation to, by watchmen on mount Ephraim, iv. 62 ; weeping in the night without a comforter, v. 304, 320, 332 ; her tears on her cheeks, 304 ; deceived by her friends, 305, 336 ; afflicted for many transgressions, 309 ; confessed herself vile, 324 ; the sorrow of, greater than that of any, 325 ; confessed God to be righteous, 335 : God became an adversary to, 350, 390 ; the prophets of, said vain things, 367 ; exhorted to lament her desolations, 378-382 ; the punishment of, greater than that of Sodom, 461 ; the punishment of, completed, 489.

www.ingramcontent.com/pod-product-compliance
Lightning Source LLC
LaVergne TN
LVHW020515100826
845148LV00010B/1236

* 9 7 9 8 3 8 5 2 1 6 8 1 9 *